DICTIONARY
OF
BUSINESS
AND
MANAGEMENT

OTHER BOOKS BY JERRY M. ROSENBERG

Inside The Wall Street Journal
The Death of Privacy
Automation, Manpower, and Education
Dictionary of Banking and Finance
The Computer Prophets

Paradox 1/7/94

DICTIONARY OF BUSINESS AND MANAGEMENT

SECOND EDITION

Jerry M. Rosenberg, Ph.D.

Professor, Graduate School of Management
Chairman, Department of Business Administration
Newark College of Arts and Sciences
Rutgers University

A WILEY-INTERSCIENCE PUBLICATION

JOHN WILEY & SONS,

New York • Chicester • Brisbane • Toronto • Singapore

Library of Congress Cataloging in Publication Data:

Rosenberg, Jerry Martin.
  Dictionary of business and management.

  "A Wiley-Interscience publication."
  Includes index.
    1. Business—Dictionaries. 2. Management—
Dictionaries. I. Title.
HF1001.R79 1983   330'.03'21   82-24743
ISBN 0-471-86730-6
       0-471-83451-3 (Paperback)

Printed in the United States of America

10 9 8 7 6 5 4 3 2

To

Bess and Ben

Preface

With the accelerated growth and change in our business language over the past five years, it became clear that the time had arrived for something more ambitious than a simple revision of the original *Dictionary of Business and Management.*

The entire list of entries in the 1978 *Dictionary* was reexamined; new phrases and terms that have become part of our everyday business lexicon were inserted; obsolete terms were dropped and others updated; and new meanings for existing concepts were added. In total, approximately 2000 additional entries were required as a result of the recent explosion of terminology.

The appendixes have also been expanded to include the most current information of use to business specialists, students, and professionals.

A note of appreciation goes to Stephen Kippur, my editor at John Wiley & Sons, for his encouragement and support in urging this second edition. My wife Ellen and daughters Lauren and Elizabeth continue to be my inspiration and source of energy.

As with the first edition, I look forward to receiving comments and suggestions to assist me in the continuous upgrading of this *Dictionary.*

JERRY M. ROSENBERG, PH.D.
New York, New York
April 1983

Preface to the First Edition

The rapid expansion of organizational life has brought with it a profusion of new words and numerous reinterpretations of old ones. As a result, even unabridged dictionaries and encyclopedias do not adequately represent the terminology of business and management. Practitioners need an up-to-date guide to current word usage.

This dictionary of more than 8000 entries has been prepared with the hope that awareness of the accepted meanings of terms may enhance the process of sharing information and ideas. Though it cannot eliminate the need for the user to determine how a writer or speaker treats a word, such a dictionary shows what usages exist. It should reduce the arguments about words and assist in stabilizing terminology. Most important, it should aid people in saying and writing just what they intend with greater clarity.

A word can take on different meanings in different contexts. There may be as many meanings as there are areas of specialty. A goal of this dictionary is to be broad and to establish core definitions that represent the variety of individual meanings. My purpose is to enhance parsimony and clearness in the communication process.

Many terms are used in different ways. I have tried to unite them without bias of giving one advantage or dominance over another. Whenever possible (without creating a controversy), I have stated the connection between multiple usages.

Commonly used symbols, acronyms, and abbreviations are given. Foreign words and phrases are included only if they have become an integral part of our English vocabulary.

The dictionary includes terms from accounting, administration, advertising, banking, business, business law, collective bargaining, commodities, computers, distribution, economics, export-import, finance, government, insurance, labor relations, management, manufacturing, marketing, merchandising, operations research, organization, packaging, personnel, production, public administration, public policy, publishing, purchasing, real estate, research methodology, retailing, salesmanship, securities, shipping, statistics, stock market, systems, testing, transportation, and warehousing.

The entries offer the most recent information taken from contemporary practice. The book closes with an appendix of useful tables, a list of graduate schools of business and management, a collection of pertinent quotations, and a dating of major relevant events in the United States.

ORGANIZATION

This is a defining work rather than a compilation of facts. The line is not easy to draw, since in the final analysis meanings are based on facts. Consequently, factual information is used where necessary to make a term more easily understood.

Although the sources are not given, all terms are presented in the language of those who use them. Obviously, the level of complexity needed for a definition will vary with the user; one person's complexity is another's precise and parsimonious statement. Several meanings are sometimes given — relatively simple for the layman, more developed and technical for the specialist.

I have organized the dictionary to provide information easily and rapidly. Keeping in mind two categories of user — the experienced person who demands precise information about a particular word, and the newcomer, support member, teacher, or student who seeks general explanation — I have in most cases supplied both general and specialized entries. This combination of "umbrella" entries and specialized definitions should make this dictionary an unusually useful reference source.

FORMAT

Alphabetization. Words are presented alphabetically. Compound terms are placed where the reader is most likely to look for them. They are entered under their most distinctive component, usually nouns, which tend to be more distinctive than are adjectives. Should you fail to locate a word where you initially look for it, turn to a variant spelling, a synonym, or another differing word of the compound term.

Entries containing mutual concepts are usually grouped for comparison. They are then given in inverted order; that is, the expected order of words is reversed to allow the major word of the phrase to appear at the beginning of the term. These entries precede those that are given in the expected order. The terms are alphabetized up to the first comma and then by words following the comma, thus establishing clusters of related terms.

Headings. The currently popular term is usually given as the principal entry, with other terms cross-referenced to it. Some terms have been included for historical significance, even though they are not presently in common usage.

Cross References. The rule followed for cross references calls for going from the general to the specific. Occasionally, "see" references from the specific to the general are used to in-from the user of words related to particular entries. "See" references to presently accepted terminology are made whereever possible. "cf." suggests words to be compared with the original entry.

Synonyms. The word "synonymous" following a definition does not imply that the term is exactly equivalent to the principal entry under which it appears.

Usually the term only approximates the primary sense of the original entry.

Disciplines. Many words are given multiple definitions based on their utilization in various fields of activity. The definition with the widest application is then given first, with the remaining definitions listed by area of specialty (identified in bold face italic type). Since the areas may overlap, the reader should examine all multiple definitions of a term.

ACKNOWLEDGMENT

No dictionary can be the exclusive product of one person's effort. Even when written by one individual, such a work requires the tapping of many sources, which is especially true of this book. By the very nature of the fields included, I have had to rely on the able and extensive efforts of others.

At no time have I deliberately quoted a definition from another copyrighted source. Any apparent similarity to existing, unreleased definitions is purely accidental and the result of the limitations of language.

Much assistance has come indirectly from authors of books, journal articles, and reference materials. They are too numerous to be named here. Various organizations have aided me directly by providing informative source materials. Some government agencies and not-for-profit associations have provided a considerable amount of usable information.

On a more personal level, I thank the various individuals whom I used as a sounding board to clarify my ideas and approach; they offered valuable suggestions and encouraged me to go on with the project. Ron Brennan, of John Wiley and Sons, had the foresight to initiate this book, and with sensitivity and creativity followed it through to publication. And I thank my wife Ellen and my daughters Lauren and Elizabeth, who showed understanding and offered full support during the preparation of this book.

FEEDBACK

The definitions given here have been reviewed by business and management specialists and educators. However I am solely responsible for choosing the terms to be included. The vast range of material makes it inevitable that definitions may vary based on perspective, background, and connotation. I welcome critical comments bringing errors to my attention, to make it possible to correct them in later editions, thus evolving a greater conformity of meaning for all.

JERRY M. ROSENBERG, PH.D.
New York, New York, 1978

Contents

Fields Included

Accounting
Administration
Advertising
Banking
Business
Business Law
Collective Bargaining
Commodities
Computers
Distribution
Economics
Export-Import
Finance
Government
Insurance
Labor Relations
Management
Manufacturing
Marketing
Merchandising
Operations Research

Organization
Packaging
Personnel
Production
Public Administration
Public Policy
Publishing
Purchasing
Real Estate
Research Methodology
Retailing
Salesmanship
Securities
Shipping
Statistics
Stock Market
Systems
Testing
Transportation
Warehousing

A: the total average dollar inventory.

a.a.: always afloat; in a ship's charter, agreement that the vessel will remain afloat whether at port or at sea during the time of the charter.

AAA: See *American Accounting Association.*

AAA Farm Relief Act: See *Agricultural Adjustment Act of 1933.*

AAA tenant: a highly rated tenant whose net worth is usually in excess of $1 million.

AAR: against all risks.

ABA: See *American Bankers Association.*

abandonment

(1) *finance:* the elimination from use of a fixed asset; the total retirement of a fixed asset from service following salvage or other reclaiming of removable parts.

(2) *insurance:* a surrender of property by the owner to the insurer in order to claim a total loss when, in fact, the loss may be less than total. This is not permitted under a fire insurance policy, but under proper circumstances the principle is applicable in ocean marine business.

(3) *real estate:* giving up a facility without the intention of regaining possession at some later time.

(4) *transportation:* a request by a carrier for permission to stop service over all or part of its route or to give up ownership or control of the cargo or carrier; a refusal to accept delivery of badly damaged items.

(5) *business law:* with a patent, trademark, or copyright, the cession of rights by the owner, whereby the invention, design, or name falls into the public domain.

abandonment stage: the final stage in a product's life cycle, when the profit potential is such that management decides that the best course is to discontinue marketing it.

abatement

(1) *finance:* cancellation of part or all of an expenditure.

(2) *finance:* cancellation or reduc-

tion of an assessed tax.

(3) *transportation:* a reduction given for damages or excess charges from the amount due on the freight bill. This is an illegal practice.

(4) *business law:* a reduction or pulling down, as with nuisance.

abatement clause: in a lease, a clause releasing a tenant from any obligation to pay rent when an act of God (fire, flood, hurricane, etc.) prevents occupancy.

abatement of a nuisance: a court action to terminate acts detrimental to the public welfare.

abator: one who gains illegal possession of an estate, thus preventing the rightful heirs from obtaining possession.

abeyance

(1) *real estate:* a temporary suspension of title to property before the correct owner is determined. See also *cloud on title.*

(2) *business law:* the state of not having been settled.

ability: skill, aptitude, and other factors essential in job performance, measured by work records, performance measures, and other ratings designed to identify an employee's day-to-day handling of work.

ability test: a test of performance to reveal the level of present ability (e.g., a typing test, an automobile driving test).

ability to pay

(1) *collective bargaining:* the ability of management to meet the financial demands of a union. This capacity depends on the financial condition of the firm and often is disputed.

(2) *finance:* a criterion used to as-

certain who shall bear the cost of federal programs; the rationale for taxing individuals in the form of a progressive income tax.

ability to pay basis: in wage and salary administration, a concept in which an employer's ability to pay specific wage rates is a factor.

ab initio: "from the beginning" (Latin). For example, an individual who enters the land of another person with permission but thereafter abuses that right becomes a trespasser ab initio—that is, becomes a trespasser from the first time he walked on the property.

able-bodied labor: workers who possess the physical strength to perform a variety of manual tasks. The term excludes the very young, the very old, and those who are incapacitated, either physically or mentally.

abnormal spoilage: existing spoilage that exceeds the amount expected to occur under normal operating conditions.

above-normal loss (ANL): a loss made greater than normal by virtue of weather, delayed alarm, or other conditions not usually expected. See also *loss expectations*; cf. *consequential loss, extraordinary gain or loss, normal foreseeable loss.*

above par: the price of a stock or bond, that is higher than its face amount.

above the line: the promotional expenses associated with advertising in one of the media.

abrasion: weight loss in coins resulting from wear in circulation.

abreaction channels: ways established by management to give employees opportunities to air dissatisfactions and blow off steam (e.g., attitude surveys, counseling).

abrogation of agreement: the cancellation or setting aside of a contract or any portion of it.

absence: an employee's temporary unavailability for work that lasts for one or more days or shifts.

absence rate: the ratio of absences to available work days, determined by the total number of man-days missed divided by the total number of man-days worked over a specified time frame.

absentee: a person who is absent, usually referring to a worker who is absent for a particular work day or shift.

absenteeism: absence from work, especially when deliberate or habitual.

absenteeism, chronic: constant recurrence of absences.

absentee owner: a property owner who does not reside on his property, leaving the managment in the hands of others.

absolute address: in computers, the actual address of a location described in terms of a machine code numbering system. Synonymous with "specific address" and *machine address.*

absolute advantage: an advantage of one nation or area over another in the costs of manufacturing an item in terms of resources used.

absolute code: in computers, coding designed so that all instructions are described in basic machine language. Synonymous with "specific coding".

absolute cost barriers: barriers to entry into an industry that are not related to economies of scale. These barriers allow established firms to produce at lower cost than potential entrants, and they derive from control of sources of raw materials, patent rights, and established marketing approaches. See also *economies of scale.*

absolute error

(1) *computers:* a form of error in which the magnitude of error is determined without regard for the algebraic sign or direction.

(2) *statistics:* the amount of error expressed in the same units as the quantity holding the error.

absolute measurement: a quantitative representation of a thing or a variable, obtained by means of units or subdivisions derived from the variable itself.

absoluteness of responsibility: the concept that managers cannot avoid responsibility for the activities of their subordinates. They may delegate authority, but they cannot delegate all responsibility.

absolute scaling: transforming obtained values from observations into a scale that permits direct comparison with a set of observations on a different scale.

absolute title: a title without any conditions.

absolutism: originally applied to a doctrine or usage of infinite power by despotic governments, this term now refers to any positive or authoritarian control over any group by a person.

absorb

(1) *accounting:* to merge by transfer all or portions of an account with another account, resulting in the loss of identity of the first account.

(2) *finance:* to include pertinent

actual costs in determining a price or standard cost.

absorbed: designating a security no longer in the hands of an underwriter and now with a shareholder.

absorbent packing: using absorbing material in a package to take up liquids resulting from any leakage of the contents.

absorption account: See *adjunct account.*

absorption costing: a type of product costing that assigns fixed manufacturing overhead to the units produced as a product cost.

absorption point: the point at which the securities market rejects further offerings that are unaccompanied by price concessions.

abstinence concept: a theory according to which a postponement in the use of an item involves a cost that should be reimbursed by a payment such as interest.

abstract:
(1) *general:* a document that summarizes another document.
(2) *personnel:* a brief summary of a potential employee's background, interests, and other relevant information.

abstract of title: an attorney's prepared statement tracing the history of the ownership of real property to determine the present title. See also *encumbrance, search.*

abutting: joining or adjacent; contiguous to another property.

accelerated depreciation: depreciation at a greater than expected rate. This makes the depreciation allowance, and therefore the tax allowance, available sooner, resulting in a benefit to the owner.

accelerating premium pay: a wage incentive system under which the bonus or premium is progressively higher as the production standard is exceeded.

acceleration clause
(1) *business law:* a clause included in the body of a contract stipulating that the entire balance shall become due and payable immediately in the event of a breach of certain other conditions of the contract, such as insolvency or the debtor's failure to pay taxes on mortgaged property.
(2) *real estate:* the statement that a debt must be paid in total in the event of default of any of its covenants.

acceleration principle: exemplified by the direct relationship in which a change in sales at the consumer level results in an even greater change in the sales of goods.

acceleration time: the period that elapses between the interpretation of instructions and the time information is transferred to or from the computer tape and memory. Synonymous with *start-stop time.*

accelerator: Synonymous with *marginal propensity to invest.*

accelerator theory of business investment: a concept that investment spending is closely related to changes in consumption. An increase or decrease in consumption spending will induce a change in investment that is proportionally even greater than the change in consumption.

acceptability: an attitude toward money resulting in its acceptance as a medium of exchange in the marketplace.

acceptance:

(1) *banking:* a time draft (bill of exchange) on the face of which the drawee has written "accepted" over his signature. The date and place payable are also indicated. The person accepting the draft is known as the acceptor. A "bank acceptance" is a draft drawn on and accepted by a bank.

(2) *transportation:* the acknowledged receipt by a shipment's consignee resulting in termination of the common carrier contract.

acceptance for honor: the receipt of a draft or bill of exchange by another party when collection has been rejected by the drawee and protest for nonacceptance has been claimed. Cf. *notice of dishonor.*

acceptance house: an organization that specializes in lending funds on the security of bills of exchange or offers its name as an endorser to a bill drawn on another party.

acceptance line: the maximum limit in monies that a bank commits itself to accept for a single client.

acceptance sampling: a method of establishing whether to accept or reject a universe on the basis of the character of a sample.

acceptance supra protest: following a protest, the payment of a bill to preserve the reputation or credit of the drawer or endorser.

acceptance theory of authority: a theory suggesting that a subordinate's decision to accept a superior's order is the ultimate source of authority. See also *authority.*

acceptor: the drawee of a note for acceptance, who agrees upon signing the form, to pay a draft or bill when due.

access: the process or act of putting data into computer storage or removing data from the computer. See also *queued access method, read-only, remote access.*

accession

(1) *personnel:* the hiring of a new employee or the rehiring of a former worker.

(2) *business law:* the doctrine that the property owner is entitled to all that is added or affixed to the property.

(3) *management:* elevation to office.

accession rate: the average number of persons added to a payroll in a given period per 100 employees. See also *turnover;* cf. *termination pay.*

accessories: articles worn or carried by an individual to enhance the apparel and complete the costume.

accessory equipment: industrial goods, such as hand tools, office equipment, or forklifts, that usually do not operate directly in the production process and normally have shorter lives and are less costly than installations.

access right: the right of an owner of property or another person with owner's approval to enter, enjoy, or leave the property without obstruction. If the property abuts on a public way, this is called a direct access right. If there is other property intervening between the owned property and the public way, the right is known as an easement right. Cf. *easement.*

access time

(1) *computers:* the time interval between the instant at which data are

requested from a storage device and the moment delivery begins.

(2) *computers:* the time interval between the moment data become ready for storage and the instant storage is terminated.

accident: an unanticipated event resulting from an unknown cause or an unusual effect of a known cause, which is therefore not expected. The result is usually an injury or damage.

accidental death benefit: an amount payable in addition to the face amount of an insurance policy in the event of accidental death of the insured.

accident and health insurance: a type of coverage that pays benefits, sometimes including reimbursement for loss of income, in case of sickness, accidental injury, or accidental death. Cf. *health insurance, hospitalization insurance, medical expense insurance, medical payments insurance.*

accident insurance: insurance against loss of earning power as the result of a disabling accident only. Cf. *health insurance.*

accident prone: applied to workers who are involved in an unusually large number of accidents. These employees, though relatively few in number, account for a substantial proportion of industrial accidents.

accident severity: a measure of the amount of time lost as the result of an accident.

accommodation: historically, the lending of currency by a person who has it to another who has need of it, without collateral; more popularly, the lending of a person's honor or credit, without any consideration, to enable another to obtain borrowed money.

accommodation bill of lading: a bill of lading issued by a common carrier before receipt of items for shipment.

accommodation desk: an area in a store for providing customer services, including gift wrapping, adjustments, and refunds.

accommodation endorsement: signature or endorsement of a note or draft solely for the purpose of inducing a bank to lend money to a borrower whose personal credit is not substantial enough to warrant a loan.

accommodation line: insurance business accepted by an insurer from an agent, a broker, or the insured (assuming his or her account is otherwise satisfactory) that would be declined if considered strictly on the merits of the individual risk.

accommodation paper: a promissory note, endorsed by an individual(s), allowing the original signer of the note to receive bank credit; thus the second or other signer(s) accepts the guarantee of credit.

accommodation party: one who signs a note as maker, drawer, acceptor, or endorser without receiving value, though remaining totally liable, for the purpose of lending the creditworthiness of his or her name to another person.

accord and satisfaction: an agreement between two people, one of whom has a right of action against the other, that the latter should do or give and that the former accepts something in satisfaction of the right of action that is different from and often less than what might be enforced by law.

account

(1) *finance:* a record of all the transactions, and the date of each, affecting a particular phase of a business, expressed in debits and credits, evaluated in money, and showing the current balance, if any.

(2) *advertising:* an advertiser; the client of an advertising agency or an organization that places promotional material directly with the media.

accountability in management: the process of making top corporate leaders responsible for their actions, goals, and so on, utilizing available objective measures.

account analysis: the process of determining and explaining the profit or loss on a checking account, using systematic procedures.

accountant: an individual engaged in accounting work. Cf. *certified public accountant.*

account balance: the net debit or net credit amount in a specific account in the ledger. An excess of total debits over total credits results in a debit balance, whereas an excess of total credits over total debits results in a credit balance.

account classification: the evaluation of retail or other buyers according to existing and, in particular, potential business.

account current: the accounting for business produced by an insurance agent for each month, reported by him or her to the company no later than the tenth of the following month.

account debtor: an individual who is obligated on an account, contract right, or general intangible.

account executive

(1) *advertising:* the member of an agency who supervises the planning and preparation of advertising for clients and is responsible for contacts between the agency and the advertiser.

(2) *securities:* Synonymous with *registered representative.*

accounting: the art, science, interpretation, and organized method of recording all the transactions affecting the financial condition of a business or organization.

accounting controls: the plan of organization and the procedures and records that are concerned with safeguarding the assets and assuring the reliability of the financial records.

accounting conventions: synonymous with *accounting principles.*

accounting costs: costs usually recorded by accountants and generally limited to cash outlays for labor, materials, and equipment. Accounting costs exclude items supplied by owner-operators of businesses. See also *implicit costs.*

accounting cycle: the series of accounting activities that occur from the commencement of an accounting period to the end of that period. The cycle begins with the determination of the account balance at the beginning of the period; then the effects of transactions occurring during the period are recorded, the records are closed, and financial statements for the period are prepared.

accounting information system: a subset of the managerial information system in which the financial data derived from recorded transactions are collected, processed, and reported.

accounting principles: broad guidelines that identify the procedures to be used in specific accounting situations.

Accounting Principles Board (APB): the top private-sector regulatory body; existed from 1959 to 1973, when it was succeeded by the Financial Accounting Standards Board. See also *Financial Accounting Standards Board.*

accounting process: the means of transforming accounting data into accounting reports that can be interpreted and used in decision making; often used interchangeably with accounting cycle.

accounting profit: revenue receipts of a firm less explicit costs. See *explicit costs.*

accounting rate of return: income for a period divided by the average investment made in that period.

account in trust: an account opened by an individual to be held in trust and maintained for the benefit of another. In the absence of a legally constituted trust fund, withdrawals from the account are subject to the approval of the party establishing the account.

account number: the numeric identification given to an account in an institution or business, such numerical identification being a part of and in direct harmony with the overall system of numerical description given to the accounts that exist in that institution or business.

accounts payable: a current liability representing the amount owed by an individual or a business to a creditor for merchandise or services purchased on an open account or short-term credit.

accounts receivable: money owed a business enterprise for merchandise bought on open account.

accretion: a small but increasing addition of land by natural causes (e.g., accumulation of land resulting from changes in the water level around property).

accretion account: a record of the increase between the acquisition value and the face value of bonds purchased at a discount.

accrual system: a method of recording and apportioning expense and income for the period in which each is involved, regardless of the date of payment or collection.

accrue
(1) *economics:* to gain or profit by.
(2) *business law:* to become eligible for a right or claim.
(3) *finance:* to accumulate, grow, or add in an orderly fashion (e.g., interest accrues on invested funds).

accrued assets: interest, commission, services offered, and items of revenue neither received nor past due but earned (e.g., accrued dividends).

accrued charges: as contrasted with payment in advance, charges that, though known, are not yet due (e.g., rent payment to be made at the end of the month).

accrued depreciation: depreciation, or loss in value, that has occurred during a specified period.

accrued dividend: the customary, regular dividend considered to be earned but not declared or payable on legally issued stock or other instruments of part ownership of a legally organized business or financial institution.

accrued expenses: expenses that are recognized by a firm prior to that firm's disbursement of cash. Accrued expenses arise when a company has used goods or services provided before it has paid for them.

accrued interest payable: interest accumulated on an indebtedness (time deposits, borrowed money, etc.) but not yet paid.

accrued interest receivable: interest earned by a bank but not yet collected.

accrued liabilities: liabilities arising from expenses that have been incurred but have not yet been paid. Cf. *prepaid expenses*.

acculturation period: a period following introduction of a new procedure or policy during which workers affected by it have time to adjust.

accumulated: added on to what had previously been in existence.

accumulated depreciation: the fixed-asset valuation account offsetting the depreciation provisions.

accumulated dividend: a dividend not paid when due. The dividend is expected to be paid at a later time, but it becomes a business liability until payment.

accumulated leave: all unused leave from the previous year that remains to the credit of the employee at the beginning of the first pay period. The taking of such leave is usually subject to administrative control.

accumulated profit tax: a tax penalty directed at corporations that avoid announcing dividends in order to reduce stockholders' declarations of additional income.

accumulation

(1) *securities:* the deliberate, well-controlled assembling of blocks of stock without necessarily bidding up prices.

(2) *insurance:* the opposite of amortization: a percentage added to policy benefits as a form of reward for continuous renewal.

(3) *securities:* profits that are not distributed to stockholders as dividends but instead are transferred to a capital account.

(4) *business law:* addition of income from dividends, interest, and other sources to the principal amount of a fund and treatment of such additions as capital.

accumulator

(1) *computers:* a device in which the result of an arithmetic or logic operation is determined.

(2) *computers:* a register that stores a quantity. When a second quantity is entered, it arithmetically combines the quantities and stores the result.

ACE See *Amex Commodities Exchange.*

ACH: See *automated clearinghouse.*

achieved penetration: a marketing measure of the ratio of existing users (or buyers) to current potential users (or buyers) of a product class.

achievement: a motive that causes people to prefer tasks that involve only a moderate amount of risk and rather immediate and clear feedback on results.

achievement battery: a collection of tests designed to measure a level of skill or knowledge attained in several areas.

achievement motive: any acquired motive, impulse, drive, or attitude that consciously arouses and maintains an individual's need to strive toward a goal or standard.

achievement test: a measure of proficiency level determined by testing performance in a particular field. It is designed to determine the relative excellence of an individual's past learning. Cf. *intelligence test, mechanical aptitude test.*

acid-test ratio: a credit barometer used by lending institutions; indicates the ability of a business enterprise to meet its current obligations. The formula used to determine the ratio is

$$\frac{cash + receivables + marketable\ securities}{current\ liabilities}$$

Usually a 1:1 ratio is considered to be satisfactory.

acknowledgment

(1) *real estate:* on a document, a signature that has received certification from an authorized person.

(2) *business law:* a statement that a proper document has been submitted.

ACL: See *action-centered leadership.*

acquisition: a general term for the takeover of one company by another. See also *amalgamation, merger.*

acquisition cost

(1) *finance:* the cost to a company of securing business; primarily commissions to agents and brokers.

(2) *real estate:* monies paid in order to obtain property title.

acquisition discount: the difference between the cost and the principal balance of a mortgage.

acquittance: a document giving written evidence of the discharge of, or freedom from, a debt or financial obligation.

acre: an area measuring 43,560 square feet; an area measuring 4,840 square yards; an area measuring 160 square rods; an area measuring 1/640 square mile.

acreage quota: the amount of land that a farmer may cultivate and still participate in government price-support programs. Cf. *soil bank.*

acronym: a word formed from the first letter or letters of words in a term, title, or proper name (e.g., COBOL for common business-oriented language).

across the board

(1) *general:* applying to all, in a uniform fashion.

(2) *advertising:* a broadcast program aired every day of the week at the same time; often also applied to such broadcast activity five or more times per week.

across-the-board increase: a general pay increase equally affecting all or most of the employees covered by a contract; may be in percentage or cents per-hour.

action

(1) *securities:* the performance by a stock with respect to trading volume and price trend.

(2) *business law:* the legal demand for rights, as asked of a court.

(3) *management:* the last step in the communication process, entailing implementation of the communication.

action-centered leadership (ACL): a training approach based on the belief that leaders are made, not born. This concept of training, developed by John Adair, emphasises that a leader's basic needs are less important than his or her actions as a measure of effectiveness.

action ex contractu: an action at law to receive damages for breach of a responsibility specified in a contract. The action can arise out of contract (ex contractu) or out of tort (ex delicto). Cf. *action ex delicto.*

action ex delicto: an action at law to receive damages arising from an infraction of a civil or criminal law (e.g., receiving damages for personal injury caused by negligent use of a car). Tort or wrong is the reason for the action. Cf. *action ex contractu.*

action group: a special group created to accomplish a particular task or purpose.

action plan: the detailed steps and resources needed for implementing departmental or individual objectives.

activate: to organize or make operative a particular task, production, activity, service unit, area, department, or function.

active account

(1) *finance:* an account in which bank deposits or withdrawals are made often.

(2) *securities:* an account handled by one broker, who makes frequent purchases and sales.

active employee: an employee who is currently at work.

active investor: an investor who not only invests equity capital but also packages, builds, or manages a project.

active market: numerous transactions in securities trading.

active money: currency in circulation.

active trade balance: a balance of trade that is favorable.

activities: what individuals do to or with others or with inanimate objects, such as machines and tools.

activity

(1) *computers:* a sign that a record in a file has moved or has been referred to.

(2) *computers:* any data resulting in use or modification of the data in a master file.

(3) *computers:* an indication of the percentage of records in a file that are processed.

activity analysis: a Department of Defense management approach for subdividing tasks or functions into specific activities or actions performed in the completion of an assignment.

activity charge: a bank service charge imposed on checking account depositors for check or deposit activity, when the average balances maintained are not enough to compensate for the cost of handling the items.

activity chart: a chart used for examining an activity or process as a whole and measuring each operation or task against a time scale.

activity ratios: ratios used during ratio analysis to indicate how well an organization is selling its products in relation to its available resources.

activity scheduling: the sequential timing of work activities in an effort to maximize efficiency.

act of God: an accident or event that is the result of natural causes, without human intervention or agency, that could not have been prevented by reasonable foresight or care (e.g., floods, earthquakes, storms). See also *vis major.*

Act to Regulate Commerce of 1887: federal legislation regulating the practices, rates, and rules of firms engaged in transportation in interstate commerce; known in its current amended state as the Interstate Commerce Act. See also *Cummins Amendment.*

actual cash value: the cost of repairing or replacing damaged property with other property of like kind and quality in the same physical condition; commonly defined as replacement cost less depreciation.

actual costing: the method of allocating costs to products according to actual direct materials consumed, direct labor used, and overhead.

actual investment: expenditures on facilities and equipment, plus adjustments in inventories; includes involuntary adjustments in inventories forced on companies by unexpected shifts in demand for their products.

actual normal system: a means of determining the costs of production by examining the number of units produced, the actual direct material consumed, the actual direct labor used, and a portion of overhead, calculated on the basis of a typical schedule of production for a specified item.

actuals: merchandise and other items available for immediate purchase and subsequent sale.

actual total loss: a loss that occurs when an item is totally destroyed or destroyed sufficiently to become useless.

actual valuation: the true value of a shipment at the time of delivery to the carrier.

actual value: the price that property commands when sold on the open market.

actuarial: related to insurance mathematics and the application of statistics.

actuarial equivalent: equivalent pension rates created after equating such factors as interest, form of pension, and mortality.

actuarial reserve retirement system: a comprehensive retirement plan that provides benefits to employees when they retire, become disabled, or die. It consists of contributions made periodically to a fund plus the compounded earnings during each year of active service.

actuary: an individual, often holding a professional degree, whose primary functions include determining rates and rating systems, determining reserves against future liabilities for corporate and rate-making purposes, and designing and interpreting experience systems.

Adamson Act of 1916: federal legislation, passed at the request of President Woodrow Wilson, fixing the eight-hour day as a pay basis for railroad employees and prohibiting wage cuts because of the shorter work day. See also *Railway Labor Act of 1926.*

adaptation: a design that reflects the dominant feature of a style that inspired it but is not an exact copy.

adaptive management: management that properly relates an organization to its environment by responding to and/or challenging conditions in the environment.

adaptiveness: a criterion of effectiveness that identifies an organization's ability to respond to change due to either internal or external forces.

ad damnum clause: a clause in a plaintiff's complaint or statement that makes the demand for damages and declares the monies involved.

addback method: the practice of beginning a statement of changes in financial position with net income and then adding or deducting income statement items that do not affect working capital.

added value: the value that is attached to the cost of unprocessed resources.

added-value tax: See *value-added tax.*

addendum: "thing added" (Latin); an addition to an agreement, contract, or written statement.

additional insured: a person, other than the one identified as the insured in a policy, who is also protected, either by being listed as an additional insured or by definition, according to the terms of the policy.

additional mark-on: an increase in the retail price of merchandise above the price placed on it when it was originally accepted for sale.

add-on conference: a system that enables a third person to participate in a telephone conversation without operator assistance.

address

(1) *computers:* an identification, as represented by a name, label, or number, for a location or any other data source.

(2) *communications:* the coded representation of the final point of a message.

(3) *computers:* the operand portion of an instruction.

(4) *real estate:* the location of a structure.

address of record: the official or primary location for an individual, company, or other organization.

address register: a register in which an address is stored in a computer.

ad hoc: "for this" (Latin); refers to a specific situation, for one purpose only.

adhocracy: a postbureaucratic form of organization structured to be flexible and responsive to change. Its primary characteristic is the conditioned absence of hierarchy.

ad idem: to the same effect.

adjacencies: programs that precede or follow a specific broadcast time period.

adjective law: a set of procedural regulations used by courts to enforce the law, usually involving situations concerning evidence, procedure, and appeals. Synonymous with *remedial law.*

adjudicate: to carry out judicial authority by hearing, trying, and identifying the claims of litigants at court.

adjudication: the resolution of a dispute by a court or tribunal; specifically, the act of a court declaring a person bankrupt.

adjunct account: an account that adds to another existing account, represented by transfers from another account (e.g., the balances of related accounts are combined when preparing a financial statement). Synonymous with *absorption account.*

adjustable peg: a system permitting changes in the par rate of foreign exchange after a country has had long-run disequilibrium in its balance of payments. It also allows for short-run variations within a narrow range of a few percentage points around the par value.

adjusted gross income: the gross income of an individual minus business expenses, deductions for income-producing property, some property losses, self-employment expenses, and moving expenses; usually applied in federal income tax returns.

adjuster:

(1) *insurance:* an individual representing the insurer in discussions to reach agreement on the amount of a loss and the company's liability. An adjuster may be a salaried employee of an adjusting organization, an individual operating independently and engaged by an insurance company to adjust a particular loss, or a representative of a company.

(2) *retailing:* an individual who reviews a customer's complaint concerning service, error, or merchandise and who has the authority to offer a refund or find other acceptable remedy.

adjusting entries: entries required at the end of each accounting period to recognize on an accrual basis all revenues and expenses for the period and to report proper amounts for assests, liabilities, and owners' equity accounts.

adjustment

(1) *insurance:* the process of determining the cause and amount of a loss, the amount of indemnity the insured may recover after all proper allowances and deductions have been made, and the proportion each company (if more than one is involved) is required to pay under its contract.

(2) *accounting:* a change in an account resulting from an incorrect entry.

adjustment board: an agency designed to deal with labor-management problems; may be given authority to adjust or resolve the grievance by majority or unanimous agreement.

adjustment bond: See *bond, adjustment.*

adjustment preferred securities: preferred stock that has resulted from an adjustment of claims in a restructuring of the company.

ad litem: for purposes of a suit; for a suit's duration. See also *guardian ad litem.*

admass: high-pressure advertising and promotion in the media to increase sales, with damaging impact on the culture of the society.

administered price: the price established under situations of imbalanced competition wherein one business has some degree of control.

administration

(1) *general:* designating those who determine purpose and policy in an organization.

(2) *business law:* the management and settling of the estate of an intestate person under a commission from a proper authority.

(3) See also *public administration.*

administrative accounting: the area of the accounting process that is generally associated with management.

administrative action: any act or decision on matters of policy that is made by executives or top management. It is usually associated with discretion and judgment.

administrative analysis: a systematic investigation of the causes and possible solutions of administrative and managerial problems within the framework of the scientific method, management science, research, and creative thinking.

administrative control: management's process of influencing organizational forces, activities, or events to make certain that the goals that have been established and the assignments given are carried out according to the requirements of organizational policies, plans, or programs; a continuous job of planning, evaluating, organizing, regulating, restraining, analyzing, verifying, and synchronizing.

administrative court: a system of administrative self-regulation whereby a court or board is appointed to decide rapidly and inexpensively in cases dealing with an official whose conduct has become inconsistent with organizational objectives, procedures, or ethics.

administrative discretion: the authority, freedom, and power delegated to an executive for discerning and making independent decisions on problems within his or her areas of responsibility.

administrative expenses: expenses chargeable to the managerial and policy-making phases of a business. Cf. *cost.*

administrative finality: an administrative decision that is not open to review except when the problems touch upon constitutional power or statutory authority.

administrative man: Herbert Simon's construct of an imaginary man in administrative settings who can be thought of as practical and cautious in dealing with the influences of the formal and informal organization. He is steady and cooperative and has high ethics. He is status-conscious.

He knows where he should stand, and, because he has internalized the values of the organization, his decisions are made on a highly rational, administrative basis.

administrative manual: a set of administrative rules, regulations, policies, and procedures that have been released by a senior executive. It is intended for and used by employees of the firm.

administrative officer: a high-level staff officer in charge of personnel, budgeting, training, or other related administrative functions.

administrative organization: the overall administrative structure, usually consisting of line, staff, and auxiliary agencies or departments through which the management and control of operations and personnel are accomplished.

administrative planning: a systematic process of looking and thinking ahead to recognize and define future trends, to see the relationships between these trends and organizational objectives, and to take necessary steps to adjust to these trends in terms of the goals and general framework of the firm by feasible, efficient, and economic use of personnel, methods, funds, and other resources.

administrative policy: a statement of a rule, judgment, or decision that, by defining and outlining the objectives of a firm, can guide and regulate organizational policies and methods.

Administrative Procedure Act of 1946: a federal law that established uniform procedures for administrative and quasi-judicial agencies. The statute requires all such agencies to promulgate, publish, and adhere to rules of procedure.

administrative procedures: fundamental methods and procedures by which an organization coordinates or regulates its actions.

administrative reorganization: an effort to reform administrative policies and procedures in order to encourage greater efficiency, economy, responsibility, and control through a simplification of the administrative apparatus of a unit.

administrative unit: any line unit in the chain of command of an organization.

administrator:

(1) *business law:* a qualified individual or bank appointed by a court of law to manage and distribute the estate of a person who died intestate (without leaving a will) or who left a will that fails to name an executor.

(2) *personnel:* a key executive in a business.

administratrix: the feminine form of *administrator.*

admiralty law: laws dealing with maritime cases. In the United States, federal courts are invested with admiralty powers.

admission by investment: the addition to a partnership of a new partner who contributes more cash to the business, thus increasing the assets and the number of owners of the firm.

admission temporaire: the free entry of normally dutiable goods for the purpose of processing items for export.

admonition: an advice, warning, or reprimand given orally by a supervisor to a subordinate about his or her area of responsibility. It carries with it an implied penalty or sanction.

adoption notice: a statement by a carrier that it is lawfully accepting an obligation (usually the freight tariffs) of a predecessor.

adoption process: a five-stage procedure by which an individual makes a decision to buy a new product. The stages are awareness, interest, evaluation, trial, and adoption.

ADP

(1) *computers:* automatic data processing; used to describe equipment.

(2) *computers:* processing of information by a system of electromechanical interaction to minimize the intervention of humans. Synonymous with *integrated data processing.*

ad referendum: indicating that, even though a contract has been signed, specific issues remain to be considered.

ad valorem: according to value; rates or duty based on a percentage of the invoice value, not on weight or quantity.

ad valorem tariff: a tariff based on a percentage of the value of the goods imported.

ad valorem tax: a real estate tax determined by the value of the property. Synonymous with *land tax.*

advance

(1) *banking:* a loan.

(2) *economics:* a price increase.

(3) *finance:* a payment on account made prior to due date.

(4) *finance:* a rise in value or cost.

advance commitment: a commitment by a lender to make or buy a loan for a stated amount on a specified property within a stated period of time to a borrower whose credit will meet the lender's approval. Synonymous with *conditional advance commitment.*

advance dating: added time allowed by a vendor to pay for goods, enabling the purchaser to receive a cash discount. Such extensions usually are arranged before the goods are shipped.

advanced optical character reader (AOCR): a new generation of optical character reader capable of storing approximately 90 fonts of typewritten addresses.

advance freight: freight paid for in advance.

advancement
(1) *personnel:* a promotion.
(2) *business law:* a gift made to a child of a portion of what will ultimately be that child's share of an intestate's estate.
(3) *finance:* money paid in advance.

advance on wages: payment of earnings prior to the regular pay day.

advance refunding: in public debt refinancing, the ability of possessors of a government security that will mature soon to exchange their securities ahead of the due date for others that mature at a later time. By this process, the national debt is extended.

advantage
(1) *general:* favorable state or circumstances.
(2) *business:* superiority over a competitor.
(3) *salesmanship:* the way an item or service can assist in solving problems or fulfilling needs.

adventure
(1) *finance:* a speculative undertaking involving the sale of goods overseas at the best available price.
(2) *securities:* a security flotation by a syndicate; a joint venture.
(3) *marine insurance:* a peril.
(4) See also *venture.*

adverse action: suspension, demotion, or separation for reasons other than reduction in force.

adverse possession: acquisition of property by a person who does not have title to it or has a defective title to it.

adverse selection
(1) *general:* a ruling "against the company."
(2) *insurance:* the tendency of less desirable insurance risks to seek or continue insurance to a greater extent than others.
(3) *insurance:* the tendency of policy owners to take advantage of favorable privileges in insurance contracts, such as renewal and conversion of term life insurance policies.

advertisement (ad): a public announcement or sale offer in a public area or medium, expressed in print, by other visual means, or orally. Major locations of advertisements are in newspapers, magazines, and journals and on signs, billboards, radio, and television. Synonymous with *commercial.*

advertising: a paid form of nonpersonal presentation or promotion of goods, services, and/or ideas. It is usually paid for by an identifiable sponsor. See also *promotion.*

advertising agency: a specialized institution that aids businesses in all phases of promoting sales of a product or service. An agency usually receives a 15 percent commission on the total billings, and the client pays for direct costs on a cost-plus basis. See also *fifteen and two.*

advertising allowance: a discount in price or payment given to a store to help meet the expense of the store's advertising of a product. Such allowances are most often granted when new products are being introduced or when manufacturers are attempting to increase promotion of their products. Cf. *promotional allowance.*

advertising campaign: the planned use of varying media and advertising methods to solicit acceptance for an idea or item or to increase the sales of a product or service.

Advertising Council: begun as the War Advertising Council in 1941, a nonprofit organization of advertisers and agencies that designs and controls the distribution of public service advertising programs.

advertising credit: the mention of a store's name in the advertisement of a producer.

advertising media: various publications, devices, and structures that carry messages to intended recipients (e.g., newspapers, television, billboards). See also *media.*

advertising specialty: a low-cost item (e.g., a ballpoint pen, a key ring) on which the seller's name, address, and telephone number are printed to give visibility and to promote awareness of the seller's name and location.

advice note: a supplier's listing of items that is sent to a customer prior to an invoice, either accompanying the merchandise or preceding it,

identifying the nature and quantity of the goods but not giving prices.

advising bank: a bank that gives notification of the issuance of credit by another bank.

advocate: usually an eloquent, colorful, and authoritarian leader who has reasons for supporting particular ideas, causes, or plans and makes every effort to persuade others to accept them.

affiant: one who swears to an affidavit.

affidavit: a written, notarized, dated, and sworn statement of the facts pertaining to a financial transaction or civil event. Such a statement must show the name and address of the affiant, must be signed by that person, and must bear the signature of the attesting official (e.g., a notary public).

affiliate

(1) *business:* an organization whose management is connected by contract with that of another organization.

(2) *advertising:* a broadcast station that belongs to or carries the programs of a national network.

affiliation

(1) *general:* adoption as a member or branch.

(2) *labor relations:* the association of a local or international union with a larger group (e.g., a state, national, or international labor union federation).

affirmative action: positive steps taken by firms or other organizations to remedy imbalances in their employment of members of minority groups. See also *Federal Contract Compliance Office.*

affluent society: a term popularized

by John Kenneth Galbraith to describe a wealthy nation, most of whose citizens enjoy an abundance of material items.

affordable method: a method of setting marketing budgets based on what a firm can afford to spend.

affreightment: an agreement for chartering a carrier for the movement of goods.

AFL: See *American Federation of Labor.*

a fortiori: "by a stronger reason" (Latin). For conclusions that are made from stated and accepted facts, there are other facts that logically follow to make the conclusion even stronger.

"A" frame: a prefabricated structure made in the form of an "A" and running the length of a freight car; used for shipment of stone or similar articles set on edge.

after charge: a charge assessed against the insured in some fire insurance rating schedules for easily correctable hazards, such as faulty wiring or improper storage of flammable liquids. The purpose of such a charge is to encourage prompt correction of the hazardous conditions.

after date: used in bills of exchange and notes; the stated maturity of the instrument.

aftersight: used in a bill to determine the due date of payment, meaning "after the bill is given to the drawee for acceptance."

against the box: in a short sale of stock, when the seller actually owns the security sold short but prefers not to or cannot deliver the stock to the buyer. The result is that, through a broker, the seller borrows the stock in order to make delivery.

agate line: a unit of measurement for advertising space, that is one column wide and 1/14 inch deep.

age change: the date halfway between natural birthdays when the age of an individual changes to the next higher age for purposes of life insurance rating.

Age Discrimination in Employment Act of 1967: federal legislation that bans employers of 20 or more workers from firing or refusing to hire an individual 40 to 65 years of age simply because of age—unless age is a bona fide job qualification; forbids employment agencies to refuse to refer a job applicant because of age and to indulge in other discriminatory practices. Violators of the law face penalties. This act was amended in 1978, raising from 65 to 70 the age at which an employer can require workers to retire involuntarily.

agency agreement: a contract between a company and an agency listing all the conditions the company grants the agency upon appointment (credit terms, commission schedule, type of enterprise, etc.).

Agency for International Development (AID): an agency of the U.S. Department of State charged with coordinating overseas economic assistance.

agency shop: the result of a provision in a collective-bargaining agreement stating that nonunion employees in the bargaining unit must pay the union a sum equal to union fees and dues as a condition of continuing employment. Nonunion workers are not required to join the union, however. This is the most commonly encountered union security measure in the public sector. See also *union se-curity clauses, union shop;* cf. *Rand formula.*

agenda: a listing of activities to be carried out during a meeting.

agent

(1) *insurance:* an individual who represents insurance companies in a sales and service capacity and is wholly or partially paid on a commission basis. An agent is licensed by the state in which he or she operates, and his or her powers are limited by the terms of the agency contract and by the state laws. See also *producer.*

(2) *business law:* an individual authorized to act in behalf of another person, the principal.

(3) *marketing:* a middleman who does not take title to the goods he sells.

agent, direct: a salaried or commissioned employee of a single insurance company.

agent, exclusive: an individual representing only one insurance company, usually on a commission basis. An exclusive agent is not an employee of the insurance firm.

agent, independent: an independent business executive who represents two or more insurance companies under contract in a sales and service capacity and is paid on a commission basis.

agent de change: a member of the Paris Bourse (stock exchange).

age reduction: the lowering of insurance payments upon attainment of a specified age. This often occurs when an individual reaches his or her late sixties or early seventies. Age reduction clauses must be identified in the insurance policy.

agglomeration diseconomies: an imbalance of scale occurring when a large number of individuals live close together. See also *diseconomies of scale.*

agglomeration economies: benefits occurring when a large number of individuals live close together. See also *economies of scale.*

aggregate: any total (e.g., the gross national product; the sum of monthly sales).

aggregate corporation: an incorporated venture that has more than one stockholder.

aggregate demand

(1) *economics:* the total spending within the economy.

(2) *economics:* the total of personal consumption expenditures, business investments, and government spending. See also *aggregate real demand.*

aggregate economics: Synonymous with *macroeconomics.*

aggregate limit: See *liability limits.*

aggregate real demand: the total in real dollars, expressed in terms of a base year, that all purchasers are willing and able to spend on all goods and services. See also *aggregate demand.*

aggregate supply: the capacity of a country's total resources to produce real goods and services.

aggressive portfolio: a portfolio of stocks and bonds usually held for appreciation.

aging of receivables: an accounting check that analyzes the time interval between the date of sale and the current date; used to evaluate the adequacy of a firm's allowance for uncollectable accounts.

agio

(1) *finance:* a premium paid for the exchange of one nation's currency for that of another Cf. *disagio.*

(2) *finance:* the sum given above a nominal value, as in "the agio of exchange."

(3) *finance:* the rate of exchange among differing countries of the world.

agreed amount clause: a provision in fire insurance policies covering certain classes of property, whereby the coinsurance clause is suspended if the insured carries an amount of insurance specified by the company, usually 90 percent or more of value.

agreed valuation: the value of a shipment agreed upon in exchange for a reduced liability.

agreement: a mutual understanding between two or more persons, requiring a consideration.

agreement, collective-bargaining: a written agreement (contract) arrived at as the result of negotiation between an employer or a group of employers and a union, that sets the conditions of employment and the procedures to be used in settling disputes that may arise during the term of the contract.

agreement, sweetheart: See *sweetheart agreement.*

agreement for deed: a contract describing additional property payments and conditions. The deed will be delivered and title will pass after fulfillment of these terms.

agribusiness: the activity of farming as a major force in the economy. California has the largest agribusiness in the United States.

Agricultural Adjustment Act of 1933: federal legislation originally intended to provide emergency assistance to agriculture during Depression years; also contains "omnibus" provisions regarding farm mortgage aid and price stimulation; also referred to as *AAA Farm Relief Act.* See also *Commodity Credit Corporation.*

agricultural economics: a speciality within economics dealing with aspects of production and movement to the market of agricultural items.

Agricultural Meat Inspection Act of 1907: legislation establishing federal regulation and inspection of meat-packaging plants engaged in interstate commerce in an attempt to ensure sanitary plant conditions and meat cleanliness.

agricultural paper: notes and acceptances resulting from transactions dealing with farming and ranching, as distinguished from traditional commercial or industrial activities. See also *Federal Intermediate Credit Banks, Federal Loan Bank.*

agricultural parity: the ratio between the price index numbers for farmers' purchases and sales; reflects an attempt to simulate conditions of a period when farm income standards were about equal to other income standards within the economy. Cf. *Brannan plan.*

agricultural price assistance: any approach purporting to hold or increase the prices paid to farmers and ranchers, to stabilize their income with respect to that of others in the nation. See also *Brannan* *plan, farm surplus.*

Agriculture and Consumer Protection Act: federal legislation of 1973 under which long-standing restrictions on agricultural production were terminated. A system of target prices established guaranteed minimum prices on basic agricultural products.

AID: see *Agency for International Development.*

aided recall: a method to survey the impression made by an advertsement or other media communication whereby an interviewer presents an advertisement or other aid to memory.

air cargo: in the United States, mail, freight, or express moving by air; in other countries, freight only.

air check: a permanent record of a broadcast, program, or commercial to determine the quality of production and delivery time or date.

air container: a container used to load and carry air freight.

airedale: (slang) a high-pressure salesman who often dresses sharply, talks fast, and is aggressive in behavior. Cf. *bird dog.*

Air Express: a service jointly operated by REA Express, Inc. and scheduled airlines.

air freight: a service offered by airlines for the movement of goods.

air pocket: noticeably extreme weakness in a specific stock.

air rights: the right to use open space above a property, or, conversely, the rights to control the air space by not constructing, to ensure that light and air will not be blocked out. See also *sky lease*

air shipment: transportation by air, either within the United States or around the world.

air taxi service: uncertified air delivery service contracts between designated points, exclusively for the movement of mail.

air waybill: a shipping statement used by international air freight carriers.

a/k/a: also known as (e.g., John Doe a/k/a J. Doe).

ALGOL: algorithmic language; primarily a means of expressing computer programs by algorithms or problem-solving formulas for machine analysis. See also *general-purpose computer, linear programming, program.*

algorithm: any series of instructions or procedural steps for the solution of a problem.

alienation: the transfer of interest and property title to another person or organization. See also *involuntary alienation, voluntary alienation.*

alien company: an incorporated company formed and operating under the regulations of a foreign nation.

aliquot: a part of the whole; a subdivision or unit of an entirety.

all-commodity distribution: a method of measuring distribution based on dollar volume. A grocery product that has 90 percent all-commodity distribution would be distributed in stores doing 90 percent of the product's dollar volume.

all-commodity rate: a freight charge applying to shipments regardless of their content.

Alliance for Labor Action: formed in May 1969, when Walter Reuther, president of the United Auto Workers, outlined plan 5 for a "grand alliance" to organize office workers and workers in industries where the AFL-CIO was only slightly represented; dissolved in 1972.

Alliance for Progress: a cooperative effort begun in 1961 by 20 countries to improve the economic and social conditions in Latin America. See also *Inter-American Development Bank.*

allied lines: types or classes of insurance that are allied with property insurance. Such insurance provides protection against perils traditionally covered by fire insurance companies, such as sprinkler leakage, water damage, and earthquake damage.

all-inclusive concept: a form of income statement presentation incorporating all items of revenue and expense in the computation of net income for an accounting period. This concept makes no distinction between items that are related to the current operations of the entity and those that are unusual and infrequent.

allocation: assigning one or more items of cost or revenue to one or more segments of an organization according to benefits received, responsibilities, or other logical measure of use.

allocation models: models used in situations where several possible candidates or activities are competing for limited resources. Such models enable the user to allocate scarce resources in order to maximize some predetermined objective.

allonge: a paper affixed to a bill on which further endorsements are written.

allotment

(1) *general:* an assignment of pay for the benefit of dependents.

(2) *accounting:* the separation of anticipated revenues among specific classes of expenditures.

(3) *securities:* the part of a stock issue apportioned or assigned by an investment firm to a purchaser or subscriber.

allottee: a person, organization, or other institution to whom an allotment is due and made payable.

allowable depreciation: the amount permitted to be deducted annually as an expense, resulting in a decrease in adjusted basis.

allowance

(1) *transportation:* a deduction from the weight or value of merchandise; a reduction permitted if the carrier does not supply appropriate equipment and the shipper then produces the equipment for use.

(2) *sales:* any price reduction.

(3) *finance:* a reserve, or money set aside, for bad debts or for depreciation.

allowance method: the recording of estimated losses due to uncollectable accounts as expenses during the period in which the sales occurred. Cf. *direct write-off method.*

allowances factor: a factor multiplied by normal time to include allowances in the time standard.

allowed time: for incentive workers, the time set aside for tool care, fatigue, and personal needs. Cf. *base time.*

all-purpose computer: a computer combining the benefits previously assigned solely to general-purpose or special-purpose computers; synonymous with *general-purpose computer.*

all-risks insurance: insurance that protects the insured from direct loss arising from any fortuitous cause other than the perils or causes specifically excluded by name. Synonymous with *floater policy;* cf. *named-peril insurance.*

All-Savers Certificates: a tax break under the Economic Recovery Tax Act of 1981 to encourage savings. The law created this instrument primarily to benefit savings and loan associations rather than investors. Under the act, thrift institutions were able to offer a new, one-year Treasury note yield for a little more than 10 percent at current interest rates. Until the end of 1982, what made the new certificate attractive was that interest income up to $1,000 ($2,000 on a joint return) was exempt from federal income tax. See also *Economic Recovery Tax Act of 1981.*

all-union shop: See *union shop.*

alphameric: Synonymous with *alphanumeric.*

alphanumeric

(1) *computers:* describing characters that may be letters of the alphabet, numerals, or symbols.

(2) *computers:* pertaining to a character set that contains letters, digits, and other characters (e.g., punctuation marks). Synonymous with *alphameric.*

altered check: a check on which the date, payee, or amount has been changed or erased. A bank is responsible for paying a check only as it is originally drawn; consequently, it may refuse to pay a check that has been altered.

alternate sponsorship: two sponsors sharing a program, usually each one taking a week.

alternative budget: a budgetary approach in which budgets are set up on the basis of the level of opera-

tions: high, medium, or low.

AM: amplitude modulation; the standard radio broadcasting method in which tone modulation is governed by variations in the height of waves rather than by frequency.

amalgamation

(1) *accounting:* a combination under a single title of all or a portion of the assets and liabilities of two or more business units by either merger or consolidation. It may take the form of a merger, whereby one company absorbs another, or a consolidation, whereby the original companies form a new one.

(2) *economics:* the joining together of businesses for the mutual advantage of all.

amenity: a feature that makes a property more attractive, such as accessibility; good design; proximity to shops, schools, public transportation, and recreation facilities; beautiful scenery; pleasant and cogenial neighbors.

American Accounting Association (AAA): the national organization representing accounting educators and practitioners; serves as a forum for the expression of accounting ideas and encourages accounting research.

American agency system: an approach for selling insurance through independent agents, who are compensated on a commission basis, as opposed to the system of selling insurance through employed company repesentatives (direct agents), who write insurance for only one company. See also *agent, direct; National Association of Insurance Agents.*

American Arbitration Association: a

private, nonprofit organization formed in 1926 to encourage the use of arbitration in the settlement of disputes.

American Bankers Association (ABA): the national organization of banking formed in 1875 to "promote the general welfare and usefulness of banks and financial institutions; consists of 35 working groups, four divisions, seven commissions, and a number of councils and committees.

American Bankers Association (ABA) number: a unit in the numerical coding system originated by the American Bankers Association for easy identification of banks and to aid in sorting checks for their proper ultimate destinations. Used principally on checks, the ABA number is usually placed in the upper right-hand corner of the check, after the drawee bank's name.

American Federation of Labor (AFL): a federation of craft unions organized in 1881. Originally called the Federation of Organized Trade and Labor Unions of the United States and Canada, the name American Federation of Labor was adopted in 1886. In 1955 the AFL merged with the Congress of Industrial Organizations (CIO), which had been expelled from the AFL in 1937, to form the AFL–CIO.

American Federation of Labor–Congress of Industrial Organizations (AFL–CIO): a federation of craft and industrial unions, as well as unions of mixed structure. Created in 1955 by the merger of the AFL and the CIO, the AFL–CIO is not itself a bargaining agent; its primary functions are education, lobbying and furnishing organizational aid to constituent unions. See also *COPE.*

American Marketing Association (AMA): a national professional organization for persons engaged in the practice and teaching of marketing.

American selling price: the price charged by U.S. producers for goods; used to determine the duty to be paid on a similar item brought into the United States, rather than determining the duty on the actual cost of the item to an importer.

American Society for Personnel Administration (ASPA): the major association of professional personnel specialists and administrators.

American Stock Exchange (Amex): the second largest securities exchange in the country; called the Little Board or the Curb Exchange, from the market's origin on a street in downtown Manhattan. See also *New York Stock Exchange.*

Amex: See *American Stock Exchange.*

Amex Commodities Exchange (ACE): a commodities exchange launched by the American Stock Exchange in 1977 to offer its member firms a broader range of products. ACE functions as an independent exchange, sharing facilities and services with the American Stock Exchange by contract.

amortisement: Synonymous with *amortization.*

amortization

(1) *real estate:* the gradual reduction of a debt by means of equal periodic payments sufficient to meet current interest and to liquidate the debt at maturity. When the debt in-

volves real property, the periodic payments often include a sum sufficient to pay taxes and insurance on the property.

(2) *finance:* an attempt to liquidate a future obligation slowly by making charges against a capital account or by adding monies to cover the debt.

amortize

(1) *finance:* to discharge a debt in periodic payments until the total, including the interest, has been paid.

(2) *finance:* to write off a portion or all of the cost of an asset; to retire debt over a period of time.

amortized loan: a loan requiring periodic payments that are used to reduce the principal so that the loan will be repaid in full by a predetermined date.

amount subject: the value that may reasonably be expected to be lost in a single fire or other casuality. It depends on the protection and construction of the insured property and on the distribution or concentration of values.

Amtrak: the National Railroad Passenger Corporation, created by Congress in 1971 as a quasi-public corporation to assist passenger train service in becoming profitable. See also *Conrail.*

analog(ue) computer: a machine that performs arithmetical functions on numbers when the numbers are represented by a physical quantity. An analog computer accepts data continuously and performs operations of addition, subtraction, multiplication, division, integration, and so on. The result may be a graph, a marking on a electron tube, or a signal to be used as a control of some machine or process. Analog computers, unlike digital computers, cannot store large quantities of financial data. See also *differential analyzer, digital computer, Turing machine.*

analogies test: a test of the ability to supply or recognize a fourth term that bears the same relation to a third as a second does to the first (e.g., tire is to car as hat is to what?).

analysis: the examination and division of anything into its major parts.

analysis, multivariate: any of a number of methods or techniques used to identify, or show the effect of, many interacting variables. Cf. *MAPS.*

analysis, sequential: a procedure in which a certain set of calculations is performed after each observation and, on the basis of that calculation, it is decided whether the hypothesis is acceptable or judgment should be withheld until more data are found. Cf. *null hypothesis.*

analysis of covariance: an extension of methods used in the analysis of variance to include two or more related variables. See also *analysis of variance.*

analysis of performance. a manager's assessment of how well the organization's members, subsystems, and goals interact to function as a unit.

analysis of variance: a method for determining whether the differences found in a dependent variable, when it is exposed to the influence of one or more experimental variables, exceed what may be expected by change. See also *assignable causes.*

analyst, programmer: an individual who possesses the talent for creating a set of instructions for a computer and for analyzing problems, systems, and specific specialities as requested. The instructions are used by the computer as numerical codes for analysis of data. See also *programming.*

analytical forecasting: an internally consistent forecast of gross national product and its major components for a short period ahead.

analytical research: a form of marketing research that focuses on why consumers purchase the products they do.

analytic models: standard mathematical equations representing the relevant variables and their relationships in such a way that the condition represented can be solved for an optimal configuration for ordering, or for establishing the values of the variables, or can provide a definition of the outputs that will occur with given inputs. See, e.g., *general equilibrium system.*

anarchism
 (1) *general:* the concept that formal government is unnecessary and wrong in purpose. Elimination of government is often intended to be achieved by riot or revolt.
 (2) *business:* the elimination of ownership or private property by coercive government.

ANL: See *above-normal loss.*

annual balanced budget: the concept that total revenues and expenditures in a government's budget should be balanced, or brought into equality, each year.

annual capital cost: the cost arrived at by a technique of determining and observing the activities of a firm ex-periencing a constant yearly cash flow that can be compared with an annual capital charge.

annual earnings: the total of all monies received during a year.

annual improvement factor: a condition of a contract clause that provides for annual wage increases of stated amount as a share of increased productivity. See also *incentive pay.*

annual mortgage statement: a written report to a borrower stating the amount of taxes and interest paid on a loan during the year and the remaining principal balance.

annual percentage rate (APR): on a loan, the basic finance charges, the service charges, and the costs of extras, if any, such as compulsory insurance on the loan.

annual report: a report of financial and organizational conditions prepared by corporate management at yearly intervals. In most cases, the Securities and Exchange Commission requires an annual report for publicly held firms.

annual statement: the annual report, as of each December 31, of an insurer to the state insurance department, showing assets and liabilities, receipts and disbursements, and other information.

annual wage: a guaranteed minimum income and/or total hours during a year.

annual wage plan: an approach designed to give continuous income to workers throughout the year.

annuitant: an individual to whom an annuity is payable, usually the person who is to receive the annuity throughout his or her lifetime.

annuity

(1) *finance:* a series of equal payments at fixed intervals.

(2) *personnel:* a scheduled payment to a retired person, synonymous with *pension plan;* see also *frozen pension.*

annuity accumulation period: the time span during which an annuitant makes a deposit in his or her retirement fund before the annuity payments begin.

annuity accumulation unit: an accounting device used to determine the value of an annuitant's accumulation account before the annuity payments begin. Under a variable annuity contract, the value of an annuitant's account is determined by multiplying the number of units owned by the daily value of one unit.

annuity accumulation value: the monetary value, as of a certain date, of the number of accumulation units credited to the account of a variable annuity contract holder.

annuity commencement date: the day on which annuity payments begin, as determined by the settlement option elected by the annuitant.

annuity period: the period after retirement during which an annuitant receives payments.

antagonistic cooperation: the concept that people work jointly for mutual advantage by suppressing their aggressive and competitive feelings. Cf. *mirror principle.*

antedate: to place on a check a date prior to the current one.

anticipated balance: a savings account balance projected through the end of the interest or dividend period, assuming that no additional deposits or withdrawals occur.

anticipated interest: the amount of interest projected as earnings on savings accounts, assuming that no deposits or withdrawals occur before the end of the current interest period. This figure is updated after each deposit or withdrawal transaction.

anticipation

(1) *business:* payment of an account before the actual due date, thus permitting a discount.

(2) *accounting:* assigning or making charges against income or profit before such gain is actually realized.

(3) *business law:* a situation in which a claimed invention is known to others, regardless of whether or not the anticipating invention has been patented.

anticipatory breach: the informing of a seller by a buyer before closing of title that the buyer plans to terminate any involvement in the transaction.

Antidumping Act of 1974: legislation designed to prevent the sale of goods at a lower price than exists in the goods' country of origin. The Treasury Department determines whether imported products are being sold at "less than fair value" in this country. If it is determined that the domestic industry is harmed by the imports, extra duties can be imposed.

Anti-Injunction Act of 1932: See *Norris–La Guardia Act.*

antikickback law: See *Copeland Act of 1934.*

antiracketeering law: See Hobbs Act of 1934.

antistrikebreaker law: See *Byrnes Act of 1936.*

antitrust: describing an action of the courts taken to curb monopolistic tendencies or to limit power stemming from monopolies.

antitrust acts: See *Celler Antimerger Act, Clayton Antitrust Act of 1914, Robinson-Patman Act of 1936, Sherman Antitrust Act of 1890.*

A/P: authority to purchase or authority to pay.

apathetic groups: groups usually made up of low-skilled and low-paid members. Leadership of such groups is not clearly defined or accepted. They typically have internal disunity and friction, and they rarely engage in pressure tactics against others.

APB: See *Accounting Principles Board.*

aperture: an opening in a magnetic card or other data medium or device that permits retention of the corresponding portions of information within the computer.

apparatchicks: (slang) all office support staff members.

appeal

(1) *salesmanship:* the motivation of a sales pitch with the expectation that the potential customer will become favorably disposed toward the product or service.

(2) *business law:* the removal or attempted removal of a case from a lower to a higher court.

appeals subsystem: the deliberately instituted process whereby grievances of managers and workers can be adjudicated before an elected body of representatives. Usually, half the representatives are chosen by management and the other half by the workers.

appellant: the party who makes a motion for an appeal from one jurisdiction or court to another.

appellee: the individual or stated party in a cause against whom an appeal is made.

apple polishing: (slang) currying favor with a supervisor or executive in order to get into his or her good graces.

applicant: a person seeking employment.

application

(1) *computers:* the problem or business situation for which a computer is used.

(2) *business law:* any offer to purchase something or to enter into some form of contract.

(3) *personnel:* a formal request or form to be filled out by a candidate for employment.

applied economics: the use of economic theory to assist in solving economic problems Cf. *positive economics.*

applied overhead: under a job-order or process costing system, the overhead costs assigned to products (including work in process) on the basis of a predetermined application rate.

applied psychology

(1) *general:* the use in practical situations of the principles developed in the field of psychology. See also *human engineering;* cf. *industrial psychology.*

(2) *personnel:* an approach to securing desired conduct that deals with physical, psychological, and/or social conditions as they relate to a person's performance. Cf. *personnel psychology.*

applied research: research concerned with solving practical problems, in which researchers have specific uses for the results of their efforts in relation to organizational issues. Cf. *descriptive research, operators research, research and development.*

apportion:

(1) *budgeting:* to assign a cost factor to a person, unit, product, or order.

(2) *retail accounting:* to hold inventory and incoming material for specific production orders, unfilled requisitions, or other expected needs.

apportionment

(1) *general:* dividing a unit into proportionate parts

(2) *insurance:* determination of how much each of two or more insurance policies will contribute to the compensation for a loss sustained by a covered risk.

appraisal:

(1) *real estate:* setting a value for or evaluating a specific piece of personal or real property or the entire property of another. See also *Baltimore method, Bernard rule, cost approach to value.*

(2) *personnel:* a judgment concerning the evidence, based on a theory and limited primarily to the behavior under consideration.

appraise: to determine the cost, quality, or value of an item.

appraising: Synonymous with *valuation.*

appreciation: the increase in the value of an asset in excess of its depreciable cost that is due to economic and other conditions; the increase of present value over the listed book value.

apprentice: in the skilled trades, a learner who is under supervision in the work experience, often with relat-

ed classroom studies. Usually, completion of four to five years of apprenticeship training leads to journeyman status.

apprenticeship training: an arrangement whereby an employee enters into an agreement with an employer and a union to learn a skilled trade by work experience and technical instruction. To protect job opportunities for journeymen, unions often restrict the number of apprentices to a certain percentage of practicing journeymen.

approach: the initial contact with a prospect by a salesperson.

approach-approach conflict: a situation in which a person is drawn toward two potentially satisfying goals that are at least partially incompatible. See also *role conflict.*

approach phase: the part of a sales presentation that includes the announcement and rapid sales work of the seller, the firm, and the product to gain customer interest.

appropriated expenditures: purchases made by a government agency that are covered by appropriations. When the purchases are added to the encumbrances, the total constitutes the expenditures undertaken during the period.

appropriate unit: as decided by an examiner of the National Labor Relations Board (NLRB) after a hearing, what constitutes (who is to be included in) a unit for purposes of an NLRB representation election and, subsequently, collective bargaining.

appropriation: an authorized sum of money set aside to pay certain known or anticipated costs of a given item or service.

approved bond. See *bond, approved.*

APR: see *annual percentage rate.*

a priori: based on presuppositions, not facts.

apron track: railroad track built for the transfer of freight between a ship and a rail car.

aptitude: the capacity to acquire proficiency, given formal or informal training.

aptitude test: a set of chosen and standardized tasks used to estimate a person's future performance on other tasks that are not necessarily identical to the test tasks (e.g., the Graduate Record Examination, which purports to identify a persons potential for work at a graduate school).

arbitrage

(1) *finance:* simultaneous purchasing and selling of an identical item in different markets in order to yield profits. The result is that the price of the item becomes equal in all markets.

(2) *finance:* the purchase of foreign exchange, stocks, bonds, silver, gold, or other commodities in one market for sale in another market at a profit.

arbitrageur: an arbitrage dealer.

arbitration: a method of setting a labor-management dispute whereby an impartial third party renders a decision that is binding on both the union and the employer; most frequently applied when labor and managment disagree on the interpretation of contract language that is applicable to a grievance. The procedures are customarily specified in the collective-bargaining agreement. See also *compulsory arbitra-tion;* cf. *mediation.*

arbitrator: an individual who has been designated by disagreeing parties to make a final and binding decision on the basis of the evidence presented to him or her. Syonymous with *umpire;* see also *impartial chairman;* cf. *mediator.*

Arbitron: a technique for acquiring television program measurements immediately by means of electronic apparatus placed in multiple homes and connected to a central measurement unit.

archmonetarist: a supporter of Milton Friedman's monetary theory, which claims that changes in growth of money supply operate on the economy with such a long time lag that it is impossible for the authorities to know at any one moment what policy should be. Cf. *balanced budget exercises, compensatory fiscal policy, New Economics.*

area agreement: an agreement between labor and management that covers all or nearly all organizations and workers in a given industry or craft within a geographical area. It is signed individually by each employer involved in the agreement.

Area Redevelopment Program: a federal program under the Area Redevelopment Act of 1961 to stimulate employment and business growth in depressed locales.

area sample: a random selection of a population in which the small geographical units chosen determine which subjects are included in the selection. Cf. *purposive sample, quota sampling.*

arguendo: (Latin) referring to a case by way of argument or within an argument.

arithmetic mean: the sum of a set of items divided by the number of items.

Arkie (Arky): (slang) a poor southern farmer or southern migratory worker.

arms-length bargaining: open, sincere, purposeful across-the-table negotiations between an employer and a union of his employees. See also *good-faith bargaining;* cf. *collusion.*

array: an arrangement of single observations or times in ranked order, from the least to the most or the reverse.

arrears: monies due but unpaid; a real or contingent obligation that remains unpaid at the date of maturity; frequently used in connection with installment notes, mortgages, rents, and other obligations that are due and payable on a specified date.

arson: willful burning of property, often with the hope of collecting insurance. It is a felony.

articles of agreement: any contract between two or more people that is reduced to a written instrument.

articles of association: an instrument similar to a corporate certificate that is usually used for nonstock corporations (e.g., charitable organizations).

articles of incorporation: a document filed with an appropriate state agency by persons establishing a corporation. When it is returned, accompanied by a certificate of incorporation, the document becomes the firm's charter.

articulated car: a railroad car of two or more full-size units that can swivel about, with the portions resting on a common center truck.

artificial intelligence: the capability of a device to perform functions that are usually associated with human intelligence, including reasoning, learning, and self-improvement.

artisan's lien: a claim to take possession of property belonging to person for whom a worker has rendered unpaid service until reimbursement is made. Cf. *mechanic's lien, particular lien;* see also *quantum meruit.*

ascribed status: a status that a worker has outside the working hierarchy, usually as a result of association or professional reputation or membership. It often affects the worker's relationship with others on the job.

Ashurst-Sumners Act of 1935: a federal law forbidding the shipping in interstate commerce of prison-made goods into states that prohibit convict labor. In the absence of a state law prohibiting the sale of goods made by convict labor, the federal law requires that such goods be labeled, showing the place of manufacture.

as is: describing items that have no warranty and may be damaged or shopworn.

asked: see *bid and asked.*

asking price

(1) *real estate:* the price that is officially offered by a seller.

(2) *securities:* the price at which a stock is offered for sale.

ASPA: See *American Society for Personnel Administration.*

as per advice: words on a bill of exchange indicating that the drawee has been notified that the bill has been drawn.

assailing thieves: a term that appears in marine insurance contracts, referring to coverage of losses due to use of force or violence by thieves.

assay: a test of content, composition, and purity of metals, usually gold and silver, often carried out in an assayer's office.

assemble

(1) *general:* to put together into one unit (e.g., to assemble a car).

(2) *computers:* to evolve a single language that is acceptable by a computer from various data inputs.

assembler: a computer program that assembles.

assembling:

(1) *general:* putting together different parts of an article or machine. Cf. *fabrication.*

(2) *marketing:* the activities involved in gathering supplies or assortments of items or services to assist in sales or purchases.

assembling land: combining nearby or contiguous properties to form one tract; synonymous with *plottage.*

assembly-line production: a procedure widely used in mass production industries whereby each worker performs a single specialized task. The materials and parts are conveyed on mechanical belts and the worker performs the appropriate task as the material or equipment moves past his or her work station. See also *interchangeable parts.*

assented securities: securities whose owners agree to a change in status, usually in cases of corporate restructuring, when an assessment is made or when the amount of securities is reduced according to a logical plan.

assess: to determine the value of something or to fix its value for tax purposes.

assessed value: the official record of a tax assessed and collected; the tax-roll value assigned to property.

assessment

(1) *finance:* any levy on members of a corporation for the purpose of raising capital

(2) *labor relations:* a levy by a union on its membership for purposes other than regular dues (e.g., to meet heavy strike expenses or to replenish a depleted defense fund).

(3) *real estate:* a charge made against property for the purpose of levying a tax.

(4) *insurance:* a company charge against all policyholders to cover the amounts paid out to sustain major losses.

assessment center: a multidimensional approach to the measurement of performance and potential.

asset:

(1) *general:* anything owned by an individual or business that has commercial or exchange value. Assets may consist of specific property or claims against others, in contract to obligations due others.

(2) *insurance:* all funds, property, goods, securities, rights of action, or resources of any kind owned by an insurance company, less any items that are declared nonadmissible by state laws—mainly deferred or overdue premiums.

(3) *accounting:* all the entries on a balance sheet that indicate the entire property or resources of a person or organization.

asset approach: a method of accounting for prepaid expenses whereby these expenses are initially debited to an asset account. A year-end adjustment is required to record the asset value used up as an expense of the period and to adjust the related asset account to its proper balance. Cf. *expense approach.*

asset management: an approach that uses manipulation of a group's or organization's strengths, both tangible and intangible, in order to achieve stated objectives.

asset turnover: the ratio of sales to total assets available.

assignability: the capacity of property to be transferred from one person or organization to another.

assignable causes: nonchance factors of variation that are traceable to their source and usually are removed. See also *analysis of variance.*

assigned risk: a risk that underwriters do not wish to insure but, because of state law or regulation, must be insured. It is handled through a pool of insurers and assigned to the several companies in turn. The term is used primarily in connection with automobile and workers' compensation insurance. See also *automobile insurance plan, fair plan.*

assigned siding: a sidetrack operated by a shipment firm, used in loading and unloading rail cars.

assignee
(1) *general:* one to whom an assignment is granted.
(2) *business law:* an individual to whom property or rights have been transferred for the benefit of that individual or others.

assignment
(1) *real estate:* the transfer in writing of property title from one individual to another.
(2) *administration:* a given task.
(3) *insurance:* the transfer in writing of the legal right in a policy to an-

other party.
(4) *securities:* the transfer of stock title.

assignment, lease: the transfer of leasehold interest to another person or group.

assignment, mortgage: the transfer of a mortgage to another person or group.

assignment of wages: initiated by an employee, a designation that future wages are to be turned over to a creditor or an authorization for managment to release a specified amount to charitable institutions or to be applied to dues, etc. The agreement in writing is signed by the employee.

assignor:
(1) *general:* an individual who makes an assignment.
(2) *business law:* an individual who assigns or transfers a claim, right, or property.

assimilation: the completed distribution of new shares of securities to the public by the issue's underwriters and syndicate members.

assistance and subsidies: direct cash assistance payments (e.g., public welfare payments, veterans' bonuses, direct cash grants for tuition, scholarships, aid to nonpublic educational institutions, aid to farmers).

assistant-to: a staff assistant to a line manager, who though normally lacking line authority, often has considerable responsibility and influence.

association: a grouping of people for mutually beneficial purposes or for the furtherance of some goal; an unincorporated group, that is not formed for profit.

assumed bond: see *bond, assumed.*

assumed liability: an obligation for payment that is accepted by another person.

assumpsit

(1) *business law:* a common-law action alleging that damages have been incurred.

(2) *business law:* a common-law action to recover damages for breach of contract.

assumption: bank loan payments that are accepted by a party other than the original maker.

assumption of mortgage: acceptance of by another person property title that has an existing mortgage, with personal liability for all payments.

assumption of risk: one of the defenses by employers against claims of employees who have been injured on the job whereby management claims that the worker was aware of the hazards of the job when he or she accepted employment and therefore assumed the risks incident to the position.

assurance: a term commonly used in England. that is similar to *insurance,* but different in that it does not depend on a possibility. It involves payment of a premium at regular periods for a stated sum that becomes payable at a given time.

astray freight: freight that is destined for a particular location and owner but does not arrive.

asynchronous computer: a computer in which the performance of each operation starts as a result of a signal generated by the completion of the previous event or operation or by the availability of the parts of the computer that are required by the next event or operation. See also *sequential computer;* cf. *queued access method.*

Atkinson system: a wage incentive plan allowing for the payment of 1.3 percent on each 1 percent of production, accompanied by a 5 percent step bonus upon achievement of the task, with a base wage or a minimum when production drops below 75 percent of the task.

ATM: See *automated teller machine.*

atomistic economy: an economy characterized by the competition of small, independent manufacturers in each industry.

at or better: in placing a purchase order for securities, buying at the price specified or under; in a selling request, selling at the price given or above.

at par: a term designating a bond or share of preferred stock that is issued or selling at its face amount.

at sight: a term used in the body of negotiable instruments indicating that payment is due upon presentation or demand.

attached account: an account against which a court order has been issued, permitting disbursement of the balance only with the consent of the court. See also *frozen account.*

attached ledger: the book or ledger in which attached accounts are kept to separate them from free accounts, since court orders are required to pay out funds.

attachment: the legal proceeding following a court's action whereby a plaintiff acquires a lien on a defendant's property as security for payment of a judgment that the plaintiff can recover.

attainable standard: a guide for judging actual performance, based on efficient but not perfect productivity.

attendance: an employee's availability for being present at work or actual participation in work when so assigned.

attention directing: the function of the accountant's information-supplying task that focuses on problems in the operation of the firm or points out imperfections or inefficiencies in certain areas of the firm's operation.

attestation: the act of bearing witness to or giving authenticity to a document by signing as a witness to the signature of another.

attitude: a lasting, learned predisposition to behaving in a consistent way toward a given class of objects or persons. This condition has a direct effect on feeling and action and refers to an aspect of personality that may account for persistent and consistent behavior.

attitude survey: a method for ascertaining employees' perceptions of their firm, usually by use of questionnaires or interviews.

attorney-at-law: an individual who has a state license to practice law.

attorney-in-fact: an individual who has the written authorization of another person to carry out business for that person out of court.

attorney-of-record: the lawyer whose name is entered in the records of the court as the representative of a party in a legal action or suit.

attrition: shrinking of employee rolls through death, resignation, or retirement.

auction: a unique trading market in which there is one seller and many potential buyers. See also *Dutch auction.*

audi alteram partem: "hear the other side" (Latin); referring to the concept that a party should not suffer without an opportunity to be heard.

audience composition: the mix of people, classified by age, sex, or other characteristics, who are reached by an advertising approach.

audience flow: the gain or loss of a broadcast audience during a program or from one program to another. See also *inherited audience;* cf. *share of audience.*

audience study: a form of analysis to determine the characteristics and attitudes of listeners, viewers, or readers of advertising media. See also *Arbitron, Hooperating, Nielsen rating, Trendex, Videodex;* cf. *media analysis.*

audience turnover: the ratio between the cumulative and average audiences for a specific broadcast.

Audimeter: an electromechanical unit used by A. C. Nielsen Company to record station tuning of radio and television receivers by tapping a sample of home users. See also *Nielsen rating, share of audience;* cf. *coincidental telephone method.*

audit
(1) *finance:* periodic or continuous verification of the stated assets and liabilities of a company or other organization.
(2) *accounting:* inspection of a firm's books.
(3) *accounting:* a final statement of account.

audited net sales: the total amount of sales for a specified period, computed after returns and allowances have been deducted. These totals are circulated by the auditing department of a store and credited to the book inventory of each department.

auditor: a person who is qualified to conduct an audit. Qualification is defined by each state.

audit trail: a printed record of transaction listings created as a by-product of data-processing runs or mechanized accounting operations.

Aunt Tom: (slang) a successful businesswoman who is not interested in furthering the cause of women's liberation.

austerity plan: a government system purporting to lower temporarily the level of consumer buying to release resources for increased capital investment, to lower imports, and to aid in balancing international payments. Cf. *archmonetarist.*

autarchy
(1) *general:* unlimited sovereignty of absolute power.
(2) *economics:* economic self-sufficiency.

authentication
(1) *business law:* verification of a document as truthful, genuine, or valid.
(2) *securities:* the signing of a certificate on a bond by a trustee in order to identify it as having been issued under a specific indenture, thereby validating the bond.

authoritarian leadership: absolute leadership, whereby a person vested with authority sets the goals and sets all policy, assigns functions, prescribes procedures, directs, checks, evaluates, and corrects the work in great detail.

authoritarian personality: a person who possesses antidemocratic val-

ues, among which conventionality, intellectual rigidity, superiority feelings, anxiety, submission conservatism, and a generally manipulative approach to other people seem to dominate.

authority
(1) *administration:* describing the relationship in an organization between positions and expectations of members. It also specifies behavior necessary for company effectiveness and is a cost of organizational membership. See *chain of command.*
(2) *administration:* the power possessed by an individual for making decisions and carrying them out. see *span of control.*

authority bond: See *bond, authority.*

authority of knowledge: the right to command that is held by the person who knows the most about a situation and is therefore put in charge of its operation.

authority of situation: the right to command that is held by a person on the basis of the need for immediate action, as in a crisis in which a leader emerges.

authority to purchase: used in Far Eastern trade, a substitute for a commercial letter of credit. This instrument permits the bank to which it is directed to purchase drafts drawn on an importer rather than on a bank.

authorization: the amount of insurance coverage an underwriter will accept on a risk of a given class or on specific property. This information is provided to agents as a guide and in response to their requests in specific instances, such as large lines or special-hazard risks.

authorization card: a card signed by a

worker in a plant being organized, authorizing the union to be that person's collective-bargaining agent. See also *cross-check.*

authorized dealer: a middleman who has received a franchise to represent or sell a manufacturer's products.

authorized stock: the maximum number of all classes of securities that can be issued by a corporation.

autocratic: referring to management by one-person control, with a minimum of decision making by others in the firm. See also *Caesar management, Theory X and Theory Y;* cf. *decentralization, delegated strategy, multiple management.*

autogestion: organization and management by a committee of workers, in factories, farms, and so on.

automated clearinghouse (ACH): a computerized facility used by member depository institutions to process (i.e., combine, sort, and distribute) payment orders in machine-readable form (computer tapes or punched cards).

automated teller machine (ATM): a machine that is capable of processing a variety of transactions between a depository institution and its customers. Its functions might include accepting deposits, providing withdrawals, transferring funds between accounts, and accepting instructions to pay third parties in a transaction. An ATM may or may not be on-line to a computer system and may be located on or off the premises of a depository institution. Placement in certain locations may permit customer access seven days a week, 24 hours a day. See also *Bellevue Project, cash dispenser, debit card;* cf. *customer-*

bank communication terminal.

automatic business mail processing system: a system in which the address on a postal customer's business reply or business return envelope is translated into a series of small vertical bars printed in the lower right-hand corner of the envelopes to permit sorting through high-speed, automatic equipment.

automatic check-off: a procedure whereby an employer deducts monies from the pay of employees and turns over these monies to a union or other approved organization.

automatic coverage: insurance coverage for a stated period and limited amount to cover increasing values and interest charges.

automatic data processing: See *ADP.*

automatic fiscal stabilizers: nondiscretionary approaches that automatically cushion recession effects by helping to create a budget deficit and that curb inflation by helping to create a budget surplus.

automatic premium loan option: a life insurance clause that permits paying any premium that is in default at the end of a grace period and charging the payment against the policy as a policy loan, provided that such premium is not in excess of the policy's cash surrender value on the due date of the premium.

automatic progression: automatic pay increases at set time intervals until a maximum rate for the job is reached. Cf. *incentive pay.*

automatic selling: the retail sale of merchandise from money-operated machines that are activated by the buyer.

automatic stabilizer: a tool of economics used to compensate for shifts in the business cycle without the involvement of a government official.

automatic wage adjustment: a wage rate fluctuation determined by a formula that responds to specific changes, such as variations in the cost-of-living index or in prevailing wage rates; sometimes included as part of a collective-bargaining agreement.

automation: conversion to the use of automatic machines or devices that are designed to control various processes. The term was coined in 1935 by D. S. Harder of the Ford Motor Company and was popularized by John Diebold. Cf. *mechanization.*

automatization

(1) *general:* the use of machines as a major replacement for people.

(2) *general:* a manufacturing process with minimal human intervention.

(3) often reduced to *automation.*

automobile insurance, liability: protection for the insured against loss arising from his or her legal liability when the car of the insured injures others or damages their property.

automobile insurance, physical damage: coverage for damages to or loss of the automobile of the policyholder resulting from collision, fire, theft, and other perils.

automobile insurance plan: a program under which automobile insurance is made available to individuals who are unable to obtain such insurance in the voluntary markets. Such programs were formerly known as automobile assigned-risk plans.

autonomous change in demand: a change in planned expenditure that is not induced by a change in income.

autonomous consumption: consumption that is independent of income; the part of total consumption that is unrelated to income.

autonomous transactions: transactions among nations that arise from factors unrelated to the balance of payments as such. The primary classes are merchandise trade and services, long-term capital movements, and unilateral transfers.

autonomous work groups: various arrangements that allow employees to decide democratically how to meet their group's work objectives.

autonomy: personal control over one's own work.

auxiliary agency: a coordinative, technical part of a firm that takes care of the financial , accounting, personnel, supply, and maintenance needs of all operating units and controls these divisions.

auxiliary operation: an off-line operation performed by computer equipment that is not under the control of the central processing unit.

avail: the amount remaining following a discount or expense deduction.

availability: the broadcast time offered to an advertiser for sponsorship.

availability date: the date on which checks payable at out-of-town banks are considered to be collected and are converted into cash; determined by the geographical location of the drawee bank, in relation to time and distance from the sending bank.

available time

(1) *general:* time other than maintenance time.

(2) *computers:* time when the computer's power is turned on and the device is ready for use.

avails: the proceeds from a discounted note.

average

(1) *statistics:* a measure of central tendency.

(2) *shipping:* the loss or damage of a ship or its freight, or the amount payable by a ship's or cargo's owners to make good such loss or damage.

(3) *securities:* to buy or sell more shares, items, and so on, with the goal of receiving a better average price.

average adjustor: the person who prepares claims made under the average clause in insurance contracts.

average blanket rate: a rate for a blanket policy, determined by multiplying the rate for each location by the value at that location declared by the insured, then dividing the sum of the results by the total value.

average bond: See *bond, average.*

average clause: a clause in an insurance contract stating that, if the insurer fails to insure property for its full value and a loss ensues, the amount to be paid will be limited to a proportion of the loss—namely, the proportion of the value of the policy that is related to the value of the property.

average cost: the sum of all output costs divided by the quantity of production.

average daily balance: the average amount of money that a customer keeps on deposit; determined by adding the daily balances of an account for a given length of time and dividing the total by the number of days covered.

average demurrage agreement: a shipper's and carrier's agreement according to which the shipper is debited for the time vehicles or vessels are held for loading and unloading (beyond a specified time) and is credited for the time they are released by the shipper within a fixed time. Demurrage charges are assessed by the transportation firm, usually at the end of the month, for outstanding debits.

average due date: the average date when several payments that are coming due at different times can be paid.

average fixed costs: production costs that do not depend on the amount produced divided by the quantity produced. Average fixed costs decline as production grows.

average gross sales: the dollar amount of gross sales divided by the number of sales transactions that created the gross sales.

average haul: the average distance in miles one ton is moved, computed by dividing the number of ton-miles by the number of tons moved.

average hourly earnings: the amount of money actually received by an employee per hour of work during a pay period.

average load: the average number of tons of freight per loaded vehicle, obtained by dividing the total number of tons by the number of vehicle loads originated.

average mark-on: the mark-on obtained when the costs and retail prices of several purchases are combined.

average rate: See *composite rate.*

average revenue: the sum of revenues divided by the quantity sold; often presented as an average revenue curve, with quantity plotted on the horizontal axis and average revenue on the vertical.

averages: various ways of measuring the trend of securities prices. One of the most popular is the Dow Jones average of 30 industrial stocks listed on the New York Stock Exchange.

average straight-time hourly earnings: actual earnings per straight-time hour, excluding shift differentials and overtime pay but including incentive and merit payments.

average total cost: See *average cost.*

average variable cost: cost per unit of production of inputs such as labor, materials, and utilities, which are used in increasing amounts as production increases.

average weekly benefit: as prescribed by law, the amount payable per week to compensate for disability or death. It is usually a percentage of the average weekly wage, subject to a minimum and a maximum amount. In workers' compensation insurance, this is referred to as weekly compensation. The benefit is paid by an insurance carrier of the company.

average weekly wage: the average rate of remuneration per week, computed as prescribed by law.

averaging
(1) *federal income taxes:* a benefit allowing individuals to average taxable income for four preceding years over a five-year period.
(2) *securities:* methods used in an attempt to improve the average price paid or received for securities by buying or selling at a variable rate as prices climb or drop.

avocation: an activity that is pursued, usually with little or no financial compensation, in addition to one's regular work or occupation for the purpose of self-expression, recreation, or general satisfaction.

avoidable cost: a cost that will not continue if an ongoing operation is changed or deleted.

avoidance: administration of a reinforcement that prevents the occurrence of an undesirable behavior.

avoidance-avoidance conflict: a situation in which a person, in moving away from one undesirable path, must move toward another undesirable path. See also *role conflict.*

avoidance conflict resolution: a strategy that generally disregards causes of a conflict by allowing the conflict to continue only under controlled conditions.

avoirdupois
(1) *general:* "having weight" (French).
(2) *economics:* commodities sold by weight.

avulsion: any shift of land from one property to another that is caused by forces of nature, without change in ownership.

award
(1) *labor relations:* the final decision of an arbitrator, which is binding on both parties to the dispute.
(2) *finance:* the acceptance of a bid or the assigning of a project on the basis of a made offer.

awareness: in the marketing cycle, the recognition by a consumer that he or she has a need or problem and wishes to have it satisfied. Awareness is the first stage in the adoption process. See also *adoption process.*

axle holddown: any strap, lock, or bracket used to keep vehicle springs compressed and secured around the axle and frame.

baby bond: See *bond, baby*.

Baby Wagner Acts: state and territorial labor laws, based on the Wagner-Connery Act, that deal with representation procedures and unfair labor and management practices.

back: to finance, sponsor, or endorse (e.g., to back a plan for adding a wing to a plant).

backdating: placing on a statement a date prior to the date on which it was drawn up.

backdoor financing: a practice that enables a government agency to borrow from the U.S. Treasury rather than relying on congressional appropriations. Synonymous with *public debt transaction*.

backer: an individual who supports a project or person with money. Cf. *promoter*.

back freight: freight that is payable when delivery is not taken within a reasonable period at the discharge point. The executive in charge deals with the items at the owner's expense.

background investigation: a procedure to determine if an applicant's past work experience is related to the qualifications needed for a job.

background processing: automatic execution of lower-priority computer programs when higher-priority programs are not using system resources.

background program: a program that has a lower need than the main program and is on standby while the main program runs.

backing up: doing a second press run to print the reverse side of a page after the front has been completed.

backlog: an excess or accumulation (e.g., of orders).

back order: part of an original order that was not filled in the first shipment and is to be sent when ready, without obliging the customer to reorder.

back pay: wages due an employee because of the employer's violation of minimum wage laws, layoff or discharge in violation of a collective-bargaining agreement, or adjustment of the piece rate following settlement of a grievance.

back spread: a condition that exists when the price difference for identical items in two markets is less than the normal difference (e.g., a stock selling for $50 on a New York stock exchange and for the equivalent of $55 on the London Stock Exchange, the difference being due to shipping costs, insurance, etc.).

backstamp: to make an impression with a postmarking (canceling) device on the back of a piece of mail, indicating date of receipt/dispatch or that the item was improperly sent.

back-to-back: describing adjacent time slots for broadcast programs or commercials.

back-to-work movement: a return of strikers to their jobs before their union has declared that the strike is ended. Some back-to-work movements are induced by management in an attempt to get workers to abandon the strike. Others are brought about by the workers themselves, either as a protest against the stand of their union or because economic pressures force them to return to work.

backtracking: using seniority rights to displace junior workers when business conditions warrant layoffs. See also *bumping.*

backup system: a system that contains error detection and correction techniques. See also *slave computer.*

backwardation: a basic pricing system in commodity futures trading whereby the nearer deliveries of a commodity cost more than contracts that are due to mature many months in the future. A backwardation price pattern occurs mainly because the demand for supplies in the near future is greater than the demand for supplies at some more distant time.

backward integration: expansion activity in which facilities that provide parts, supplies, or raw materials are accumulated.

Bacon-Davis Act: legislation of March 3, 1931, and since amended, dealing with wage rates on public construction projects.

bad debt: the amount due on an open account that has been proved to be uncollectible; any uncollectible receivable.

bad debt expense: the cost of uncollectible accounts receivable. In most companies, bad debt expense is debited for the estimated uncollectible amount and allowance for uncollectible accounts is credited.

bad debt writeoff: a customer's account that is removed from the books when payment appears unlikely.

bad delivery

(1) *general:* a delivered item that does not conform to the original terms of agreement.

(2) *securities:* an improperly prepared or transferred security or certificate.

bad faith: the intent to mislead or deceive (Latin: *mala fides*). It does not include misleading by an honest, inadvertent, or uncalled-for misstatement. See also *fraud.*

bagged: (slang) discharged from one's job.

bail

(1) *noun:* a bond given by an ac-

cused person in his or her behalf for the payment of money in the event that the accused fails to appear in court on a specific day. See also *bond, penal.*

(2) *verb:* to release an arrested or imprisoned individual.

bail bond: See *bond, bail.*

bailee: a person who acts as a receiver for personal property.

bailiff: a court official who is responsible for committed prisoners during a trial or a sheriff's deputy who serves warrants or other court papers.

bailment

(1) *general:* provision of bail for an arrested person.

(2) *business law:* delivery of personal property to another person for a specific purpose.

(3) *merchandising:* shipment of items in trust from one party to another for purposes of storage, with the items to be returned when the purpose is fulfilled. Bailment fixes responsibility for safekeeping.

bailor: an individual who delivers personal property for possession to another.

bailout: use of corporate monies to provide payments to shareholders that are taxable at desirable capital gains rates. The Securities and Exchange Commission has ruled that bailout is illegal.

bait advertising: advertising exceptional prices or terms for a specified product to attract prospects to a store; potential customers find, however, that it is difficult to buy the product there as advertised.

bait and switch: an unethical approach in which a retailer advertises a product at a particularly low price with the intention of inducing people who ask for the item to purchase a more costly one. Sometimes the switch is made by the salesman telling the purchaser that the advertised item is not good or has been sold out. See also *switch selling.*

balanced budget: a budget in which forward expenditures for a set period are matched by expected revenues for the same period.

balanced budget exercises: government spending that keeps the size of the budget deficit the same by simultaneously increasing and decreasing various taxes. Cf. *archmonetarist.*

balanced economic growth: economic expansion throughout the country at approximately the same geometric rate for all items manufactured.

balanced economy: a condition of national finances in which imports and exports are equal.

balanced growth equilibrium: stable economic expansion over an extensive time period.

balance due: the total amount needed to equalize the debit and credit sum of an account; the amount owed.

balance of account: the net amount of the total debits and total credits posted to a given account. Balances are of three types: *zero balance*—indicating that total debits and total credits are equal; *debit balance*—indicating an excess of total debits over total credits; and *credit balance*—indicating an excess of total credits over debits, at a given time.

balance of payments (b.o.p.): a statement identifying all financial transactions of a country and its population with the other nations of the world. Cf. *dollar shortage.*

balance-of-payments deficit: a situation in which a nation is spending more abroad than it earns abroad.

balance of trade: the difference between a country's imports and exports over a set period.

balance sheet: an itemized statement listing the total assets and total liabilities of a business to portray its net worth at a particular moment in time.

balance theory: theory used in the study of communication to explain how people react to change, placing primary attention on the consideration of three relationships: (a) the attitude of the receiver toward the sender, (b) the attitude of the receiver toward the change, and (c) the receiver's perception of the sender's attitude toward the change.

balancing: bringing two sets of related figures into agreement.

balancing time: shifting the hours of work within a time period without altering the total number of hours worked within that period.

balespace: the volume of cargo spaces under a vessel's deck, expressed in cubic feet.

ballast: iron, stone, and other heavy materials stored in the lower portion of a vessel to increase stability by lowering the center of gravity.

ballast car: a rail car holding ballast or grading materials for construction or roadbed repairs.

balloon: a huge sack or pouch of mail.

balloon freight: light, low-density, and bulky cargo.

ballooning: price manipulation used to send prices beyond safe or real values.

balloon loan: a loan on which small payments are made during the term of the obligation.

balloon mortgage: a mortgage that allows for payments that do not completely amortize the loan at the time of termination. As a result, the final payment is larger than any single previous payment.

balloon note: a promissory note requiring only a small payment during the initial loan period, offset by larger payments before the date of maturity.

Baltimore method: a formula for appraising corner lots in which the lot is determined to be worth the total value of the inside lots on each of its sides.

band seal: a steel ring placed over the cover of a pail and crimped under the curl to form a seal.

bandwagon: a propaganda technique of appealing to the tendency of workers to identify with, conform to, and follow their own particular group or the ideas that represent the group. It makes use of the concept that it is difficult to stand alone when everybody else is doing the same thing.

bank: defined according to function, organizational setup, or relationship to one another. See *branch banking, commercial bank, correspondent bank, country bank, drive-in banking, Federal Reserve Bank, group banking, independent bank, industrial bank, insured bank, investment banking, member bank, mortgage banker, multiple banking, mutual savings bank, national bank, private bank, savings bank, state bank, trust company.*

bank accommodation: a short-term bank loan to a customer, either on the individual's own note or on the endorsement of another's note owed to him or her.

bank bill: See *bank note.*

bank call: a request for a bank's balance sheet for a specified date, made by government statement.

bank clearing

(1) *banking:* bank items sent by member banks to a local clearinghouse for collection.

(2) *finance:* the total volume of dollars on all items that are exchanged among members of a local clearinghouse.

bank credit: credit created by commercial banks through loans and discounts granted with or without collateral. The amount of credit so extended is controlled in part by the rediscount rates established by the Federal Reserve Board.

bank currency: See *bank note.*

bank debits: the sum total of all debits drawn against deposited funds of individuals, partnerships, corporations, and other legal entities during a given period. Usually, debits are reported by banks daily.

Bank Deposit Insurance Act of 1934: federal legislation to protect depositors, extended to June 1935 for bank deposit insurance originally established by the Banking Act of 1933. This act eventually led to the creation of a permanent deposit insurance program in 1935.

bank deregulation: See *Depository Institutions Deregulation Committee.*

bank draft: a check drawn by one bank against funds deposited to its account in another bank.

banker's acceptance: a bill of exchange drawn on or accepted by a bank to pay specific bills for one of its customers when the bills become due.

banker's bank: a central bank. In the United States, it is one of the 12 Federal Reserve district banks: 1st District, Boston; 2nd District, New York; 3rd District, Philadelphia; 4th District, Cleveland; 5th District, Richmond; 6th District, Atlanta; 7th District, Chicago; 8th District, St. Louis; 9th District, Minneapolis; 10th District, Kansas City; 11th District, Dallas; 12th District, San Francisco.

Banking Act of 1933: the first major piece of banking legislation during the Roosevelt administration. It led to significant changes in banking laws. See, e.g., *bank credit, branch banking, insurance.* See also *Federal Deposit Insurance Corporation.*

Banking Act of 1935: federal legislation amending the Banking Act of 1933, the Federal Reserve Act, and other banking regulations to make those laws more specific.

banking power: the strength of investing possessed by a bank, as determined by the bank's excess reserves.

bank note: a promissory note released by an authorized bank that is payable on demand to the bearer and can be used as cash. Such notes, as established by law, are redeemable as money and are considered to be full legal tender. Synonymous with *bank bill, bank currency.*

bank overdraft: an amount owed to a bank by a customer on his or her account. The bank will make a charge that is calculated on the amount overdrawn on a day-to-day basis, establishing a fixed limit that the customer may withdraw.

bank post remittance: conversion into cash or a money form of a foreign bill of exchange and subsequent mailing to the payee.

bank rate

(1) *banking:* the rate of discount established by the national bank of a country for rediscounting eligible paper.

(2) *banking:* the rate charged by the national bank of a country for advances on specified collateral to banks.

bank reconciliation: the process of systematically comparing a company's cash balance as reported by the bank and as recorded on the company's books and explaining any differences.

bank run: a series of unusually large withdrawals from a bank because of customers' fears that the bank may run out of funds.

bankrupt: a person, corporation, or other legal entity that, being unable to meet its financial obligations, has been declared by a decree of the court to be insolvent and whose property becomes liable to administration under the National Bankruptcy Act. See also *insolvent.*

bankruptcy: the conditions under which the financial position of an individual, corporation, or other legal entity is such as to cause actual or legal insolvency. Two types are (1) *involuntary bankruptcy,* whereby one or more creditors of an insolvent debtor file a petition having the debtor declared a bankrupt; and (2) *voluntary bankruptcy,* whereby the debtor files a petition claiming inability to meet debts and willingness to be declared a bankrupt. A court adjudges and declares a debtor a bankrupt.

See also *insolvency, National Bankruptcy Act of 1898.*

Bank Secrecy Act of 1970: federal legislation compelling banks to keep records of all customer transactions and to report any financial dealings involving more than $10,000 to the Department of the Treasury. The government contends that the records are the bank's business records and are not owned by the depositor.

bank service charge: a bank's fee for servicing an account, usually charged monthly.

bank statement

(1) *banking:* a statement of a customer's account periodically rendered by the bank. It shows all deposits made and all checks paid during the period, usually one month, as well as the current balance; the customer's canceled checks are enclosed.

(2) *banking:* a bank's financial statement.

Bank Wire System: a private, computerized message system administered for and by participating banks through the facilities of Western Union. The system links about 250 banks in about 75 cities. Like the Fed Wire, the Bank Wire system transmits funds and transfers information, but it also relays data concerning loan participations, bond closings, payment for securities, borrowing of federal funds, and balances in company accounts. See also *Fed Wire.*

bantam store: a community food market that remains open in the late evening or on weekends or holidays when many supermarkets are closed. Cf. *convenience goods, depot store.*

bargain

(1) *general:* an item bought at a low or advantageous price; a good buy.

(2) *sales:* to arrive at an agreement on the price of goods to be sold.

bargain basement: the below-ground-level floor of a store, where special prices are offered on merchandise. The stock often contains lower-price merchandise or items not carried on the upper levels of the store.

bargain counter

(1) *securities:* describing stocks offered for sale at prices below their intrinsic value.

(2) *retailing:* an area for the sale of discounted merchandise.

bargain hunter

(1) *general:* an individual who seeks out the store that is selling items at the lowest possible price.

(2) *securities:* a speculator or investor who waits until stocks are on the bargain counter.

bargaining agent: the formally designated agency, usually a labor union, that represents employees seeking or having a collective-bargaining agreement (contract). Its rights and obligations are defined by federal law. See, e.g., *Wagner-Connery Act.*

bargaining book: a compilation of a negotiation team's plans for collective-bargaining negotiations with labor or management.

bargaining creep: progress in collective bargaining that is slow, with minimal compromise.

bargaining rights

(1) *general:* the legal rights of workers to bargain collectively with their employers.

(2) *labor relations:* the right of a specific union to represent its members in collective bargaining.

bargaining strategy: a school of management theory that focuses on helping managers deal more effectively with the "people side" of their organization. It highlights the importance of a manager's leadership style and group dynamics.

bargaining unit: the group of employees, usually defined by the National Labor Relations Board after a hearing, that a union may seek to represent as bargaining agent on wages, hours, and working conditions. See also *collective bargaining.*

bargain store: a store that sells merchandise at a submarket price. Assortments and sizes are often limited, and the merchandise frequently is damaged or seconds. See also *seconds.*

bargain theory: the concept according to which wages are determined by demand for and supply of labor and by the relative bargaining strengths of employer and employee.

barge: a rough-lined, flat-bottomed, powerless vessel used to hold or buoy up cargoes in inland waterways. A barge is pulled by a powered boat.

Barnard's unit concept: the idea, developed by Chester Barnard, that an organization should be made up of small departments, each composed of 10 or fewer members.

barn-burner wizards: (slang) high-power salespeople who skillfully push to achieve their stated goals or sales.

barometers: business measurements used to determine the condition of a market or economy (e.g., Consumer Price Index, housing starts, gross national product, new plant expenditures).

barratry

(1) *transportation:* an intentional act by the master of a ship or its crew to the injury of the owner of the ship or cargo.

(2) *business law:* the practice of exciting and encouraging quarrels and lawsuits.

barrel: a bulging cylindrical container of greater length than breadth, having two flat ends or heads of equal diameter. A standard barrel in the United States contains $31\frac{1}{2}$ gallons.

barren money: currency that does not earn interest or other forms of income.

barriers to change: factors that interfere with employee acceptance and implementation of change.

barriers to entry: obstacles to creating a new company within a particular industry, resulting from legal or economic advantages enjoyed by existing companies.

barrister: (British) a lawyer or counsel who pleads cases in open court, as distinguished from a solicitor, who develops briefs and handles legal issues away from the court.

barter: the direct exchange of one item for another without the transfer of money.

base

(1) *general:* a reference value.

(2) *computers:* the number of usable characters in the digital positions of a numbering system.

(3) *statistics:* a number that is multiplied by itself.

(4) *economics:* metal, coin, or

bullion that is adulterated, containing inferior or less valuable metal, and has little value when compared to precious metals such as gold and silver.

base pay: the regular rate of pay for an identified time period, excluding overtime, bonuses, and other premiums. See also *basic wages*.

base period

(1) *personnel:* the period during which an employee fulfills the length-of-employment requirement in order to receive state unemployment insurance benefits.

(2) *economics:* a chosen date from the past used in measuring the price index. See also *index number*.

base rate: under an incentive system, the amount guaranteed per hour or other time period.

base stock method: inventory assessment that assumes that a minimum normal or base stock of items must be retained at all times to ensure effective continuity of activity.

base time: the established time for the normal performance of work by an average employee, excluding time allowed for rest, mechanical failures, and other delays.

basic crops: clearly identified farm items subject to government price support, including wheat, corn, cotton, rice, and peanuts.

basic decisions: long-range decisions, often involving large expenditures of funds and carrying a high degree of importance.

basic piece rate: part of a wage incentive plan allowing for payment to be made in direct proportion to the production yield.

basic rate: the manual or experience

rating from which discounts are taken or to which charges are added to compensate for the individual circumstances of the risk.

basic research: research motivated by the search for the advancement of knowledge rather than for momentary economic gain. Cf. *applied research.*

basic station: a television station included in the list of network affiliates whose time an advertiser is contracted to buy if he uses the network.

basic stock: merchandise that is in constant demand, thus requiring perpetual inventory throughout the year.

basic wages: payment received by employees for work performed, based on time or output. See also *base pay.*

basing point pricing: an approach used by an industry whose goal is for all sellers to charge identical prices. The basing point is frequently the location of a plant near the buyer. Such pricing has been declared to be price discrimination in violation of the Clayton Antitrust Act.

basis
(1) *finance:* the yield to maturity of bonds at a given price, as shown by bond tables [see Appendix H].
(2) *taxation:* in calculating capital gains or losses, the value employed as the original property cost, which may or may not be the true cost.
(3) *securities:* the difference between the cash price of a money market instrument that is hedged and a futures contract.

basis point: 1/100 of 1 percent, a minimal measure in finance and trade.

basket purchase: the purchase of a group of assets for one price; so that

the items can be recorded individually in the accounts, however, a cost is assigned to each asset.

batch processing
(1) *computers:* the technique of executing a set of computer programs such that each is completed before the next program of the set is begun.
(2) *systems:* a sequential processing procedure that uses an accumulation or set of units.
(3) *manufacturing:* the completion of one unit or batch of product as an entity before further materials are added to the processing.

batch-type production: grouping of items in batches to be processed in these batches in various stages, with completion at about the same time.

batten
(1) *packaging:* a wood strip attached to a structure to reinforce it.
(2) *economics:* to grow wealthy at another's expense.

battery of tests: a group of tests used in screening and testing (e.g., to determine qualifications for employment).

baud: a speed unit in data processing equal to one binary digit per second.

Bayes criterion: See *Laplace criterion.*

B/E: bill of exchange.

beachhead demands: demands the union makes in current negotiations that it does not expect to receive at the time but hopes to receive in future negotiations.

bearer: any person holding a negotiable instrument.

bearer bond: See *bond, bearer.*

bearer certificate: a certificate that is not filled out in the name of a particular person. Since such certificates are negotiable without endorsement, they should be kept in a safe place.

bear hug: (slang) an unnegotiated corporate takeover proposal made privately or publicly to directors. The major goal is to force a board into a quick decision.

bear market: a declining stock market.

bear position: a stance taken by a person who expects the market to fall. Consequently, he or she sells securities short, hoping that the market will move downward.

bears: speculators who anticipate that prices are going to drop. See also *hammering the market*.

beat down: (slang) to bargain in order to lower the cost of an item.

bed: the floor of a truck or trailer.

beef: See *grievance*.

beggar-my-neighbor policy: an attempt to discourage imports by increasing tariffs or using other effective means.

behavior: the acts or decisions of individuals, groups, or organizations.

behavioral decision theory: decision models that examine the influence of individual, group, and organizational factors in decision making.

behavioral researchers: investigators and scientists who use findings from psychology, sociology, anthropology, political science, and other related areas of inquiry to develop concepts and theories pertaining to people and their environment.

behavioral school: a modern school of management theory propounded by those who view management as a psychological process. Advocates of this school are particularly con-cerned with such topics as needs, drives, motivation, leadership, personality, behavior, work groups, and the management of change.

behavior modeling: a training process for helping managers to develop interpersonal skills.

behavior modification: the increase of desirable behavioral patterns or the decrease of undesirable behavior brought about by using rewards and/or punishments whose efficacy in promoting the desired change has been proved.

Bellevue Project: a banking program of study and implementation leading to the Bellevue Exchange, an automated teller facility in Bellevue, Washington, that is available to the customers of a group of cooperating thrift institutions on a shared basis.

bell-ringer: (slang) a door-to-door salesperson.

belly: an area underneath the passenger seats of an airplane where cargo is carried.

below par: at a discount; less than face amount.

below the line: not expensed but capitalized over a period of time; does not normally affect operating budgets, percentages, or line items.

belt line: a short railroad, usually one that moves within or around a city.

bench
(1) *general:* a place where a worker performs his or her tasks.
(2) *business law:* the court or the judges sitting in the court.

bench scale production: the manufacture of a small number of units before the development of normal production techniques.

"B" end: the end of a railroad freight

car on which the brake shaft is located.

beneficial interest (owner): an individual who is not the true owner of property but who enjoys all or part of the benefits to it by reason of a trust or private arrangement.

beneficiary

(1) *general:* a person who is beneficially interested in a trust or estate.

(2) *business law:* the person for whose benefit a trust, policy, will, or contract promise is made; synonymous with *cestui que trust.*

(3) *insurance:* the person(s) to whom the proceeds of a life insurance contract are payable upon the death of the insured.

benefit

(1) *general:* a gain or advantage received by an individual.

(2) *insurance:* the amount of indemnity to be regularly paid.

(3) *salesmanship:* that which fulfills a need.

benefit-cost analysis: a technique for assessing government expenditures and programs that places a dollar value on the effects. An outlay is said to be justified if benefits are greater than costs. The technique represents an attempt to apply the test of the market to nonmarket economic decisions.

benefit principle of taxation: a rationale for taxation based on the benefits received from the government by the taxpayer.

benefit year: the period of time specified by law during which an employee fulfills the employment requirements in order to qualify for unemployment compensation.

Benelux: referring to a cooperative organization involving Belgium, the Netherlands, and Luxembourg to encourage economic activity among the three nations.

benevolent-authoritative leadership style: a basic leadership style in which management acts in a condescending manner toward subordinates and decision making at the lower levels occurs only within a prescribed framework.

bequeath: to offer personal property in a will.

bequest: a gift of personal property made by a testator. See also *legacy.*

Bernard rule: a rule for appraising a corner lot. The property is first appraised as if it were an inside lot fronting on a side street; it is then taken as an inside lot on the main street. The value placed on the corner lot is the total of the two appraisals.

Better Business Bureau: a voluntary agency of business executives created to improve business practices and to define fair standards and ethics in the conduct of business activity. The movement to improve conditions began in 1921, when vigilance committees for truth in advertising first appeared in local advertising clubs.

betterment: an improvement made to property that increases its value more than would ordinary repair or maintenance work.

bevel: the sloping edge of a container (e.g., the slanting portion of the outside of the circled heading of a wooden barrel).

BFOQ: See *bona fide occupational qualification.*

bias: an attitude that may influence an individual's feelings, resulting in a leaning toward or away from a particular idea, item, or person. See also *halo effect, proactive inhibition, stereotypes.*

bid: an offering of money in exchange for property (items, goods, etc.) put up for sale. Three types are: *best bid*—not necessarily the lowest or highest but good for the organization seeking a bid; *competitive bid*—secured from a public announcement of the competition; and *sealed bid*—not disclosed until a specified time, when all other bids are revealed and compared. (This approach purports to guarantee the independence of bidders).

bid and asked: "bid" is the quotation of a prospective buyer and "asked" is the quotation of a seller for the sale of a trading unit or other specified amount of security; often referred to as a quotation or quote. The bid is the highest price anyone has offered to pay for a security at a given time.

bidding
(1) *general:* offering money as an exchange for an item or service.
(2) *personnel:* application by an employee for consideration for a job that is open in a plant or office. In most contracts, assuming that all qualifications are equal, first preference is given to the applicant with the most seniority. See also *posting.*

bidding up: raising the price bid for a security for fear of not having an order executed before an upswing begins.

Big Board: the New York Stock Exchange, Inc. Cf. *Little Board.*

big business: a business that is very large or one that controls a substantial portion of the market. Big business often holds monopolistic markets and exercises power over a large segment of the population.

Big Eight: the eight largest public accounting firms; in alphabetical order: Arthur Andersen and Co.; Coopers and Lybrand; Ernst and Ernst; Haskins and Sells; Peat, Marwick, Mitchell and Co.; Price Waterhouse and Co.; Touche Ross and Co.; and Arthur Young and Company.

Bigelow plan: a wage incentive approach providing for a step bonus between the minimum wage and the standard wage, with more than 1 percent additional salary for 1 percent additional performance.

Big Five: the five largest credit card companies: American Express, Carte Blanche, Diners Club, MasterCard (Master Charge), and Visa (BankAmericard).

Big Steel: term referring to the United States Steel Corporation. Sometimes the term is used to include the other large manufacturers of steel: Bethlehem, Republic, National, Armco, Jones Laughlin, Inland Steel, and Youngstown Sheet and Tube; but see *Little Steel.*

Big Three: the three largest automobile manufacturers in the United States: General Motors Corporation, Ford Motor Company, and Chrysler Corporation.

big ticket items: frequently refers to merchandise that is large in size and high in price (furniture, appliances, etc.).

bilateral agreement: an agreement between two persons or groups.

bilateral assistance: foreign aid provided by one country directly to another rather than channeled via an international (multilateral) agency such as the United Nations.

bilateral contract: an agreement containing promises, with each party serving as a promisor or promisee.

bilateral monopoly: a condition that exists when there is only one purchaser for an item or service and the creation of the supply is controlled by one seller.

bilge: the area between the outer bottom of a vessel and the inner bottom or cargo hold.

bill
(1) *sales:* an invoice of charges for services or a product.
(2) *business law:* the instrument of formal issuance of a complaint before a court.
(3) *business law:* a court's formal statement reporting its findings.
(4) *finance:* paper currency.

billboard
(1) *advertising:* a poster panel in outdoor advertising.
(2) *communications:* the opening routine of a broadcast program, including identification, performer credits, producers, and similar information.

bill check: a payment system in which a debtor, on receipt of an invoice or statement, authorizes the creditor to obtain payment directly from the debtor's deposit account.

bill discounted: a promissory note or bill of exchange from which a bank deducts its interest in advance.

billed escrow: the amount of escrow payment that represents a total of the regular escrow payment plus arrears or minus prepaid escrow amounts.

billed principal: the amount of principal payment that represents a total of the normal principal amount plus any arrears.

billed weight: the weight of a shipment shown on the freight bill. It is not necessarily the actual weight.

billing
(1) *advertising:* the total amount of money charged to clients by an advertising agency. This includes production costs, expenses, media costs, and other service charges.
(2) *accounting:* the process of submitting invoices or bills.

bill of adventure: a shipper's written statement that a shipment is the venture or property of another individual and that the shipper is responsible only for its delivery as consigned.

bill of credit
(1) *banking:* an individual's written request to a bank asking for the delivery of money to the bearer on the credit or account of the writer.
(2) *finance:* an instrument used as if it were a state's currency. Article I of the U.S. Constitution forbids the states to issue their own currency.

bill of exchange: instructions from one party to another party to pay a third party following completion of an assignment. See also *commercial set.*

bill of lading: a statement whereby the carrier acknowledges receipt of freight, identifies the freight, and sets forth a contract of carriage. See also *commercial set;* cf. *accommodation bill of lading, clean bill of lading, straight bill of lading, through bill of lading, waybill.*

bill of materials: a specification of the quantities of direct materials allowed for manufacturing a given quantity of output.

bill of sale

(1) *general:* a written agreement by whose terms the ownership of goods is transferred or assigned to another person.

(2) *real estate:* a formal written agreement by which one person transfers to another his or her rights, interest, and title in specified property. It is considered to be sufficient warranty of the seller's title to the property and his or her right to sell; it need not be recorded as a deed for real property.

bill of sight: a temporary entry permit authorized by a custom's official for imported items, allowing the goods to be unloaded from a carrier to permit examination by a customs agent to identify their true character.

bills payable

(1) *general:* a comprehensive term that includes the total of notes and trade acceptances that are owed by a business to trade creditors and must be paid by the business at their maturity.

(2) *banking:* the sum of money that a member bank has borrowed on its own collateral note from a Federal Reserve Bank.

bills receivable: a comprehensive term that includes the total of all notes and trade acceptances given by customers, usually in payment of merchandise, that the debtors must pay at maturity.

bimetallism: a double standard of metals used in coins. The ratio of content and weight must be specified in terms of, for example, gold and silver. Cf. *monometallism, parallel standard, real money.*

binary

(1) *general:* pertaining to a characteristic or property involving a selection, choice, or condition in which there are two possibilities.

(2) *computers:* a numbering system based on twos rather than tens that uses only the digits 0 and 1 when written. Cf. *quinary.*

binary card: a standard data-processing card on which information is punched in binary form.

binary number: a component of computer language that usually contains more than one digit. The digits allowed are 0 and 1.

binder

(1) *insurance:* a legal agreement issued either by an agent or by a company to provide temporary insurance until a policy can be written. It usually is in writing, contains a definite time limit, and clearly designates the company in which the risk is bound as well as the amount, the perils insured against, and the type of insurance. See also *cover note.*

(2) *real estate:* an initially written agreement to purchase property, with a valuable consideration given as evidence of good faith by the offerer.

(3) *business law:* any temporary agreement obligating the several parties to the contract.

bindlestiff: (slang) a migratory harvest worker.

biodegradable: the property of a substance that allows microorganisms to break it down into stable, simple compounds (e.g., water, carbon dioxide). Cf. *nondegradable pollutants.*

bird dog (slang)

(1) *administration:* to seek data to

assist in studying a firm's position and potential earnings.

(2) *sales:* an individual who is paid to obtain business for a high-power salesperson.

(3) *business law:* an individual who is paid to spread fraudulent charges.

bit

(1) *computers:* a binary digit (acronym).

(2) *computers:* a single character in a binary number.

bit grinding: (slang) the execution of data-processing instructions.

bit twiddler: (slang) an operator of data-processing equipment.

Bituminous Coal Act of 1937: a federal law regulating the sale and distribution of bituminous coal in interstate commerce and eliminating unfair competition. Rights of collective bargaining and price regulations are included. See also *Mining Enforcement and Safety Administration.*

B/L: bill of lading.

black book: a brochure prepared to describe a private securities placement. It is not for a public offering and usually excludes data found in a public prospectus and includes information not found in a public prospectus, such as projections of sales.

black box concept: a concept of the inner workings that take place between input and output. As applied to human behavior, the concept may involve, for example, the introduction of a new wage incentive payment scheme (input) and a 10 percent increase in productivity (output). The reason for the increase may be the wage plan, but it may also be something else. The black box, or the transformation process between input and output, is said to contain the answer.

black capitalism: an attempt to increase business ownership among blacks.

Black Friday: September 24, 1869—the day of a business panic resulting from an attempt by financiers to corner the gold market. A depression followed. Coincidentally, the financial panics of 1873 and 1929 also first became serious on Fridays; hence the term indicates a day of evil.

blacking: during a union action, the refusal by employees to perform any work that they conclude will hurt their cause. Cf. *sit-down strike, slowdown, soldiering.*

blackleg: (slang) an employee who continues to work during a strike. Cf. *loyal worker;* synonymous with *fink, scab.*

blacklist: a management roster of persons deemed undesirable as employees. This was declared an unfair labor practice in 1935 by the National Labor Relations Act. Blacklisted workers often were fired or not hired in new jobs when blacklisting was used for antiunion purposes.

black market: buying or selling products and commodities or engaging in exchange of foreign currencies in violation of government restrictions. Cf. *gray market.*

black money: (slang) income that is not reported for tax purposes because of its illegal origin.

blank check: a bank form that has been signed, although the amount payable or the name of the payee has been left out.

blank-check buying: the practice of a

retailer placing an open order with a supplier, with requests to be made throughout the season as needed.

blanket agreement: a collective-bargaining agreement based on an industrywide negotiation for large geographical areas within an industry, as established by the Norris–LaGuardia Act (the Anti-Injunction Act). See also *Norris–La Guardia.*

blanket bond: See *bond, blanket.*

blanket injunction: a court order issued during a strike, or to prevent a strike, so broad in its sweep that it encompasses activities that rarely occur in connection with the conditions being enjoined. The Anti-Injunction Act identifies safeguards in the release of labor dispute injunctions. See also *Norris–La Guardia Act.*

blanket mortgage: a mortgage covering all the property of a corporation and given to secure a single debt.

blanket order: a preseason order to meet expected buyer demand.

blanket policy: an insurance policy that covers several different properties, shipments, or locations under one item rather than under separate items. See also *average blanket rate;* cf. *specific insurance.*

blanking area: the white-paper area separating the outside edges of an outdoor poster and the inside of the panel moulding.

blighted area: an area in a community or neighborhood that is about to become a slum.

blind ads: help-wanted ads that do not identify the employer.

blind alley jobs: (slang) positions accepted by workers that offer little if any chance for advancement.

blind entry: a bookkeeping entry stating only the accounts and the amounts debited and credited but not giving other data or accounting factors essential to an accurate record.

blind selling: (slang) selling merchandise or services without the customer having a chance to examine the item prior to purchase.

blister packaging: a type of plastic packaging that permits visual inspection of the merchandise.

block
(1) *broadcasting:* a group of consecutive time slots, or the same time period from day to day.
(2) *computers:* a group of words or characters considered or transported as a unit, particularly with reference to input and output.
(3) *securities:* a large holding or transaction of stock; popularly considered to be 10,000 shares or more.

blockade: the act of preventing commercial exchange with a country or port, usually during war time, by physically preventing carriers from entering a specific port or nation. See also *embargo, navicert;* cf. *preclusive purchasing.*

blockbusting: an unethical real estate practice of creating fear by renting or selling units in a neighborhood to families of a religion or race different from that of the current residents, thus exploiting the prejudices and emotions of property owners so that they will sell their homes at reduced prices.

blocked accounts: in times of war, directives issued by the president of the United States to financial institutions to suspend payment of the accounts of enemy nationals or of individuals inhabiting occupied countries in the sphere of enemy influence. These funds may be released only by executive order or by license under certain conditions.

block policy: a policy covering all the inventory of the insured against most perils, including transportation. It may also cover property of others held by the insured (a) on consignment, (b) as sold but not delivered, (c) for repairs, or (d) otherwise. It usually applies both on and off the premises of the insured.

blood bath: (slang) a horrendous loss suffered by investors when the stock market declines sharply.

blotter: a book of accounts or a journal used for entering the first or a temporary list of transactions or occurrences. Cf. *daily reports*.

BLS: See *Bureau of Labor Statistics*.

blue chip: stock market term used to describe a corporation that maintains a good dividend return and has sound management and good growth potential. See also *bond, gilt-edged; seasoned issues; seasoned security*.

blue-collar computer: computer application within a factory or plant.

blue-collar workers: production and maintenance workers, as contrasted with office and professional personnel. The force of blue-collar workers is declining numerically.

bluefingers: (slang) workers from one family who attain common goals with efficiency and team spirit; for example, relatives who successfully pursue their objectives while receiving pleasure from their togetherness; synonymous with *jebble*.

blue label: a warning statement affixed to radioactive cargo.

blue law: any state or local law restricting business activity on Sunday. Blue laws have been contested as an infringement of individual and free enterprise rights.

blue sky law: term used for certain laws enacted by the various states to regulate the sale and issuance of securities, specifically, attempting to prevent fraud in their sale and disposition. Cf. *SEC*.

blurb: (slang) a brief but highly laudatory statement (e.g., a quotation from a book review) used in further promotional activities. See also *testimonial*.

b.mod.: See *behavior modification*.

board: a standing committee of high rank or importance (e.g., a board of directors).

board lot: the unit of trading for stocks on an exchange. The unit of trading in stocks on the New York Stock Exchange is 100 shares. See also *even lots*.

board of directors: people chosen by stockholders of a corporation to manage the enterprise.

Board of Governors: the seven-member governing body of the Federal Reserve System.

board of trade: business executives who operate a local commodities exchange or a chamber of commerce.

board room

(1) *securities:* formerly, a room for registered representatives and customers in a broker's office, where opening, high, low, and last prices of leading stocks were posted by hand on a board throughout the market day. Today such price displays are electronically controlled, and most

board rooms have replaced the board with the ticker and/or quotation machines.

(2) *administration:* a room set aside for use by the board of directors of a business.

board structure: the general organization, including committees and board membership, of boards of directors. See also *board of directors.*

bobtail: a small truck used for deliveries or a trailerless tractor.

bobtail statement: an abbreviated statement prepared for demand deposit accounts.

bod biz: (slang) See *sensitivity training.*

bodily injury liability insurance: protection against loss arising from the legally imposed liability of the insured for damages due to bodily injury, sickness, or disease sustained by any person or persons other than the employees of the insured.

body language: an important part of nonverbal communications that involves the transmittal of thoughts, actions, and feelings through body movements and the interpretation of those movements by other people.

bogey

(1) *labor relations:* an informal standard that employees do exceed, set up as an effort by employees to restrict output.

(2) *salesmanship:* a standard of performance, such as the volume of sales beyond which a bonus is given.

bogus: false, counterfeit, nonexistent, or fraudulent. Bogus money is counterfeit currency; a bogus check is a check written on a nonexistent account or bank.

boiler and machinery insurance: cov-

erage for loss arising from the operation of pressure, mechanical, and electrical equipment. It may cover loss suffered by the boiler or machinery itself and may include damage done to other property as well as business interruption losses.

boiler room tactic: (slang) selling of very speculative and often worthless securities through the use of high-pressure, misleading literature. See also *dynamiter.*

boll weevil: (slang) any nonunion worker. Synonymous with *scab.*

bona fide: (Latin) "in good faith"; with honest intent. Cf. *mala fides.*

bona fide occupational qualification: an employer's justified business reason for discriminating against a member of a protected class.

bona vacentia: describing property of which there is no apparent owner nor claimant (e.g., property in the hands of a liquidator after a firm has been dissolved).

bond

(1) *general:* an interest-bearing [see Appendix H] certificate of debt, usually issued in series, by which the issuer obligates itself to pay the principal amount at a specified time, usually five years or more after date of issue, and to pay interest periodically, usually semiannually. Bonds may be distinguished from promissory notes or other evidences of debt by their formal execution under seal and by the certification by a bank that their issue has been authorized by the board of directors of a corporation or other governing body. Corporate bonds are usually secured by a lien against specified property. Bonds may be issued in bearer form

or registered.

(2) *finance:* a promise under seal (i.e., closed from view by the public) to pay money.

(3) *finance:* an obligation to answer for the debt of another person.

(4) *real estate:* an instrument used as proof of a debt, usually secured by a mortgage.

bond, adjustment: an income bond issued as a result of a firm's reorganization. See also *bond, reorganization.*

bond, approved: a bond named in the legal list prepared for fiduciaries in some states. See also *legal list.*

bond, assumed: a bond of one corporation whose liability is taken on by another corporation. See also *bond, guaranteed.*

bond, authority: a bond payable from the revenues of a specific authority. Since such authorities usually have no revenue other than charges for services, their bonds ordinarily are revenue bonds.

bond, average: a bond given by an individual in receipt of freight, stating that the recipient will contribute to any standard claim.

bond, baby: a bond with a face value that usually is $100 or less.

bond, bail: a bond guaranteeing the appearance in court of the principal named in the bond.

bond, bearer: a bond payable to the holder that does not have the owner's name registered on the books of the issuing company.

bond, blanket: a form of broad-coverage protection carried by financial institutions to cover losses from robbery, burglary, or employee dishonesty.

bond, callable: a bond issue, all of part of which may be redeemed before maturity by the issuing corporation under definite conditions.

bond, called: a bond that the debtor has declared to be due and payable on a certain date prior to maturity, in accordance with the provisions of an issue to be redeemed. The bonds to be retired are usually drawn by loss.

bond, city: See *bond, municipal.*

bond, civil: a bond circulated by any government agency.

bond, classified: a debt security that receives a designation, such as "Series A" or "Series B," to differentiate it from another bond of the same debtor. The series differ in maturity date and interest.

bond, clean: a coupon-type bond that has not been changed by any endorsement or rephrasing of the original contract, such as the words "assented" or "extended."

bond, collateral: further security for a loan.

bond, collateral trust: an issue of bonds for which collateral has been pledged to guarantee repayment of the principal. This type of bond usually arises from intercompany transactions in which the parent company issues bonds for which securities of a subsidiary are the underlying collateral.

bond, combination: a bond issued by a governmental unit that is payable from the revenues of a governmental enterprise but is also backed by the full faith and credit of the governmental unit.

bond, consolidated: a debt instrument issued to replace two or more bonds issued earlier, often done to simplify a debt structure or to benefit from a lower prevailing rate of interest.

bond, continued: a debt instrument that need not be redeemed at maturity but can continue to earn interest.

bond, convertible: a bond that gives its owner the privilege of exchanging it for other securities of the issuing corporation on a preferred basis at some future date or under certain conditions.

bond, corporate: an obligation of a corporation. See also *bond, long-term corporate.*

bond, coupon: a bond with interest coupons attached. The coupons are clipped as they come due and are presented by the holder for payment of interest. See also *talon.*

bond, court: all bonds and mortgages required of litigants to enable them to pursue certain remedies of the courts.

bond, cushion: a high-interest-rate, top-quality bond that sells at a premium level above par and that usually results in a higher yield to maturity.

bond, customhouse: a bond required by the federal government in connection with the payment of duties or for producing bills of lading.

bond, debenture: a bond for which there is no specific security set aside or allocated for repayment of the principal.

bond, deferred serial: a serial bond in which the first installment does not fall due for two or more years from the date of issue.

bond, definitive: any bond that is issued in final form; used particularly to refer to permanent bonds for which temporary bonds or interim certificates were issued.

bond, depository: a bond guaranteeing payment of funds to depositors in accordance with the terms of a deposit in a bank.

bond, drawn: a bond that has been called for redemption by lot. See also *bond, called.*

bond, endorsed: a bond that has been extraneously signed, permitting it to be considered for normal delivery according to the regulations of the exchange, and that therefore must be sold.

bond, escrow: a bond that is held in escrow. See also *escrow.*

bond, estate tax: a designated government bond that is redeemable at par less accrued interest for federal estate taxes to the extent that the entire proceeds are applied to such taxes due, provided that the bond was owned by the decedent at the time of death.

bond, extended: a bond that has matured and on which the debtor has not yet paid the principal but has agreed to extend or continue to pay the principal at a later time. Upon the creditor's acceptance of the extension, the bond is stamped to show such agreement. Synonymous with "deferred bond."

bond, external: a bond issued by a country or firm for purchase outside that country, usually denominated in the currency of the purchaser.

bond, federal: the promissory note of a central government.

bond, fidelity: insurance for an employer (the insured) for loss sustained as a result of any dishonest act by an employee covered by the insurance. Blanket fidelity bonds cover groups of employees. See also *fidelity insurance.*

bond, fiduciary: a bond in behalf of a person appointed by a court to a position of trust (e.g., the executor of an estate).

bond, flower: a U.S. government bond. Until the Tax Reform Act of 1976, flower bonds sold at a substantial premium in relation to other bonds issued at similarly low interest rates because the Treasury accepted them for estate tax payments at 100 cents on the dollar, whatever their costs were at the time of purchase. This benefit is now taxable in part as a capital gain.

bond, forgery: insurance against loss due to forgery or alteration of, on, or in checks or other instruments.

bond, free: an unpledged bond; any bond that is immediately disposable.

bond, funding: a bond issued to retire outstanding floating debt and to eliminate deficits.

bond, gilt-edged: a high-grade bond issued by a company that has demonstrated its ability to earn a comfortable profit over a period of years and to pay its bondholders their interest without interruption. See also *blue chip.*

bond, government: an obligation of the U.S. government, regarded as the highest-grade issues in existence. See also *Treasury bill, Treasury note.*

bond, guaranteed: a bond on which the principal or income or both are guaranteed by another corporation or a parent company in case of default by the issuing corporation.

bond, honor: a consumer-size certificate of deposit with denominations as low as five dollars. Many banks promoted these bonds and told purchasers that they were merely honor-bound to report the interest on their tax returns. The Internal Revenue Service moved swiftly to eliminate this irregularity.

bond, improvement: any bond issued by a municipality to finance a public improvement.

bond, improvement mortgage: a bond issued for financing improvements of the debtor's business that are secured by a general mortgage.

bond, inactive: See *inactive stock (bond).*

bond, income: a type of bond on which interest is paid when and only when earned by the issuing corporation.

bond, indemnity: a bond that protects the obligee (the party for whom the applicant for bond, or the principal, has undertaken to perform specified duties) against losses resulting from the principal's failure to fulfill the obligations. Examples of miscellaneous indemnity bonds are warehouse, lost instrument, and lien.

bond, indenture: a written agreement under which bonds are issued, setting forth maturity date, interest rate, and other terms.

bond, installment: See *bond, serial.*

bond, insular: a bond issued by a unit of the United States (e.g., Alaska, New York); synonymous with "territorial bond."

bond, interchangeable: a bond in either a registered or coupon form that can be converted to the other form or its original form at the request of the holder. A service charge is often made for such a conversion.

bond, interim: a bond sometimes

used before the issuance of permanent bonds to raise funds that are needed only temporarily.

bond, intermediate: a callable bond bearing no date of maturity. The call aspect usually is not effective until some stated time period has passed.

bond, internal: a bond issued by a country that is payable in its own currency. Cf. *bond, external.*

bond, irredeemable: a bond that contains no provisions for being called or redeemed prior to maturity date.

bond, joint and several: any debt instrument by which the holder seeks payment from more than one corporation up to the full face amount of the security.

bond, joint control: a bond needed before transfer of the assets of an estate to the custody of the principal.

bond, judgment: a bond issued to fund judgments. See also *funding.*

bond, junior: a bond that is subordinate or secondary to another issue, which, in the event of liquidation, would have prior claim to the junior bond. See also *bond, senior.*

bond, legal: a bond that federal and state laws identify as an acceptable and legal investment for fiduciary institutions. See also *bond, approved.*

bond, limited tax: a bond that is secured by a tax that is limited in amount and rate.

bond, long-term corporate: a debt of industrial corporations, finance companies, utilities, and telephone companies. Maturities range from 10 to 40 years, with intermediates running from 4 to 10 years. Such bonds are rated AAA and AA for high quality. The face denomination is $1000, but new issues often are marketed above or below par to adjust to current yields. Older bonds with lower-interest coupons sell at discounts.

bond, maintenance: a bond guaranteeing against defects in workmanship or materials for a stated time after the acceptance of work.

bond, mortgage: a bond that has a mortgage on all properties of the issuing corporation as an underlying security.

bond, municipal: a bond issued by a state or a political subdivision (county, city, town, village, etc.); also, a bond issued by a state agency or authority. In general, interest paid on municipal bonds is exempt from federal income taxes and state and local taxes in the state of issue.

bond, noncallable: a bond that, under the terms of the issue, cannot be called by the obligor (the corporation) for redemption or conversion.

bond, obligation: a bond authorized by a mortgagor that is larger than the original mortgage amount. A personal obligation is created to safeguard the lender against any costs over the amount of the mortgage that may develop.

bond, open-end: a mortgage bond of an issue that has no limit on the number or quantity of bonds that can be issued under the mortgage. Often, however, some relationship is required between the number and quantity of bonds and the value of the property that has been mortgaged.

bond, optional: See *bond, callable.*

bond, overlying: a junior bond, subject to the claim of a senior underlying bond that has priority of claim.

bond, participating: a bond that, following the receipt of a fixed rate of periodic interest, also receives some of the profit held by the issuing business. A form of profit sharing, this bond is rarely used today.

bond, passive: a bond that does not carry any interest. Such bonds are often issued following a reorganization.

bond, penal: a bond given by an accused, or by another in his or her behalf, for the repayment of money in the event that the accused fails to appear in court on a specific day. See also *bond, surety.*

bond, performance: a bond supplied by one party to another, protecting the second party against loss in the event of improper performance or completion of the terms of an existing contract.

bond, permit: a bond guaranteeing that the person to whom a permit is issued or is to be issued will comply with the law or ordinance regulating the privilege for which the permit is issued.

bond, plain: any debenture. See also *certificate of indebtedness.*

bond, preference: any income or adjustment bond.

bond, premium: in the United States, a bond that is selling above its face value; in Europe, a bond that has a lottery feature. When called, as distinguished from regular maturity, a premium bond generally pays substantially more than the face amount. The term is also used for the excess of the price at which a bond is acquired or sold over its face value. The price does not include accrued interest at the date of acquisition or sale.

bond, prior-lien: a bond that holds precedence over other bonds issued by the same corporation.

bond, privileged: a convertible bond that has attached warrants.

bond, public: any bond issued by a government agency, domestic or foreign.

bond, real estate: a bond secured by a mortgage or trust conveyance of real estate.

bond, redemption: a refunding bond. See also *redemption.*

bond, refunding: a bond issued to retire a bond that is already outstanding. Refunding bonds may be sold for cash and outstanding bonds redeemed in cash, or they may be exchanged for outstanding bonds.

bond, registered: a bond in which the name of the owner is designated and the proceeds are payable only to him or her. Bonds may be registered for both principal and interest or for principal only. Interest on a bond that is registered for both principal and interest is paid to the owner by check as it becomes due. Bonds registered for principal only have coupons attached, which are detached and collected as the interest becomes due.

bond, reorganization: a debt security issued in the recapitalization of a firm that is in financial difficulty; an adjustment bond.

bond, revenue: a bond whose principal and interest are to be paid solely from earnings. Such bonds are usually issued by a municipally owned utility or other public service enterprise, the revenues and possibly the properties of which are pledged for this purpose.

Bond, Savings (U.S.): Series EE, introduced at the start of 1980, replaced the highly popular Series E bonds. These new bonds are available in face-value denominations of $50, $75, and so on, up to $10,000 and are sold at half their face value. Series EE bonds pay varying interest rates—as much as 1 percent at six-month intervals if market conditions warrant. Currently, the maturity on Series EE bonds is eight years, down from nine years, effectively boosting the rate on those bonds to 9 percent. The rate on Series HH bonds is 8.5 percent. Series HH bonds are bought at face value, pay interest semiannually, and mature in ten years.

bond, schedule: a bond listing the names and positions of employees included as principals. See also *bond, fidelity.*

bond, second-mortgage: a bond issued on property that already has an outstanding first mortgage.

bond, secured: a bond secured by the pledge of assets (plant or equipment), the title to which is transferred to bondholders in case of foreclosure.

bond, senior: a bond that has prior claim to the assets of the debtor upon liquidation. See also *bond, junior.*

bond, serial: an issue of bonds in which a certain proportion of the bonds is retired at regular intervals. Such bonds are issued when the security depreciates through use or obsolescence. These issues usually provide that the outstanding bonds shall not exceed the value of the security.

bond, sinking fund: a bond secured by the deposit of specified amounts. The issuing corporation makes these deposits to secure the principal of the bonds, and it is sometimes required that the funds be invested in other securities.

bond, special assessment: a bond payable from the proceeds of special assessments, which must be levied against the properties presumed to be benefited by the improvements or services for which the special assessment was made.

bond, special lien: a special assessment bond that acts as a lien against a particular piece or pieces of property.

bond, surety: an agreement providing for monetary compensation in the event of failure to perform specified acts within a stated period. The firm that is the surety company becomes responsible for fulfillment of a contract if the contractor defaults. See also *bond, penal.*

bond, tax-exempt: any security of a state, city, or other public authority specified under federal law, the interest on which is either wholly or partly exempt from federal income taxes. See also *bond, municipal.*

bond, temporary: similar to a definitive bond except that it has been printed rather than engraved. See also *bond, definitive.*

bond, term: bonds of the same issue that usually mature at the same time and ordinarily are to be retired from sinking funds. Sometimes a term bond has more than one maturity date (e.g., a serial issue that has postponed maturities in only a few late years of its term).

bond, territorial: See *bond, insular.*

bond, treasury: a U.S. government long-term security sold to the public that has a maturity longer than five years. See also *Treasury bill, Treasury note.*

bond, underlying: a bond that has a senior lien where subsequent claims exist.

bond, zero-coupon: a security sold at a deep discount from its face value and redeemed at the full amount at maturity.

bond discount: the difference between the face value and the sale price of a bond when it is sold below its face value.

bonded

(1) *general:* a bond posted as security that a tax or tariff will be paid on time.

(2) *warehousing:* describing goods in a government-supervised storage facility where items are stored without payment of duties or taxes until they are removed.

bond indenture: a contract between a bond issuer and a bond buyer that specifies the terms of the bond.

bonding company: an organization whose business is forming contracts of surety and providing bonds.

bond of indemnity: an indemnity agreement used in filing a claim when the claimant, unable to show the freight bill or bill of lading, is given relief from liability for any action for which a carrier otherwise would have been liable.

bond premium: the difference between the face value and the sale price of a bond when it is sold above its face value.

bond rating: appraising and rating, by a recognized financial organization (e.g., Moody's Investors Service), the worth of a bond as a sound investment. Ratings are based on the reputation of the organization, its record of interest payments, its profitability, and so on. Bonds rated AAA are the most secure, followed by AA, A, B, and so on.

bonification

(1) *general:* rendering of an advantage or benefit.

(2) *manufacturing:* said to be achieved when certain items that are made for export relieve the manufacturer of paying an excise tax on such items.

(3) *taxation:* the return or exclusion of a tax.

bonus: additional monies paid to workers to supplement their regular salary (e.g., Christmas bonus, end-of-year corporate profit bonus).

boodle: (slang) money received through corruption in public activities; also, counterfeit money.

book crowd: See *cabinet crowd.*

book depreciation: the amount that can be deducted for depreciation purposes from the cost of an asset of the property owner.

book inventory: inventory calculated by adding the units and the cost of incoming goods to previous inventory figures and subtracting the units and the cost of outgoing goods. See also *perpetual inventory.*

bookkeeper: a person who makes entries on the general ledger of a business.

bookkeeping: the art, practice, or labor involved in the systematic recording of the transactions affecting a business.

booklet certificate: a pamphlet or booklet that serves both as an explanation of a group insurance plan and as an individual certificate of coverage under the plan.

book value

(1) *general:* the value of an asset found in the company's records, not necessarily what it could bring in the open market. See also *depreciated cost.*

(2) *securities:* a value determined from a company's records by adding all assets and then deducting all debts and other liabilities, plus the liquidation price of any preferred issues. The sum arrived at is divided by the number of common shares outstanding to determine book value per common share.

Boolean algebra: a calculus named for George Boole that is similar to general algebra but features classes, propositions, on-off circuit elements, and so on; the foundation for computer theory. See also *language, symbolic.*

boom

(1) *finance:* a time when business expands and the value of commodities and securities increases.

(2) *economics:* a period of rapidly rising prices and increased demand for goods and services, usually accompanied by full employment.

boomerang: (slang) an international program to minimize the practice of goods dumping by returning such items duty free and exempt of quantity restrictions.

boom stick: (slang) a roving railroad worker.

boondoggling: a critical term used to describe government programs that are wasteful and unproductive; first used during the 1930s.

bootlegging: illegal movement of items in order to avoid payment of taxes on such items. The items themselves may or may not be prohibited by law.

boot money: (slang) money used as an additional compensation by one of the parties to a bargain.

bootstrap

(1) *general:* a technique designed to bring about a desired state by internally generated means.

(2) *computers:* a method for getting the first few instructions into memory when a routine is initially loaded.

b.o.p: See *balance of payments.*

borax: (slang) inexpensive items (e.g., furniture) that are usually poorly designed and constructed. Cf. *jerry-built.*

bordereau: a special form for transmitting information required in reinsurance transactions, such as reinsuring an entire agency's business.

borrow: to receive something from another, with the understanding that the item is to be returned.

borrower: one who borrows cash or buys something on credit.

bosshead: (slang) the head of a project (i.e., the foreman, the boss).

bot: abbreviation for "bought," as used in the securities market.

bottle: a container that has a round neck of relatively smaller diameter than the body and an opening capable of holding a closure for retention of the contents.

bottleneck: anything that holds up the normal flow of organizational communications, operations, activities, or processes.

bottom dropped out: a situation of

sharply falling prices occurring when the market is well liquidated, thus establishing a panic atmosphere.

bottom line: the figure that reflects company profitability on the income statement.

bottomry: a loan secured by a lien on a vessel. The contract of bottomry is in the nature of a mortgage. If the carrier is lost, the debt is canceled.

bottom-up approach: an approach to strategy making whereby the lower levels of the organization push ideas to the top and strategy is then made.

boulwarism: a negotiation strategy developed and used by the General Electric Company whereby the company makes its best offer to the union at the beginning of negotiations and then remains rigid in not increasing its offer unless the union can discover where management erred in its calculations to arrive at the best offer. This approach has been ruled an unfair labor practice.

bounded discretion: describing the limits imposed on a manager for making decisions that are conditioned by social norms, rules, and organizational policies.

bounded rationality: the principle that a decision maker doesn't attempt to discover optimum solutions because he has only limited time and energy for making decisions.

bounty: added payments offered by a government as an incentive for a specific industry to export certain items.

bourse: (French) a European stock exchange.

boutique: a shop or part of a store that specializes in merchandise that is new and different.

box, corrugated: a rectangular, three-dimensional shipping container, usually made of solid or corrugated fiberboard.

boxcar: an enclosed freight car that has doors on both sides and/or sometimes on the ends.

box-top offer: an offer of a premium based on return of the top of a package or other evidence of purchase.

boycott

(1) *labor relations:* collective pressure against an employer to discourage public acceptance of his products or services (cf. *picketing*). A primary boycott involves one employer and his employees only; a secondary boycott involves a third party (cf. *situs picketing*) and in many cases is forbidden by law. See also *unfair list.*

(2) *economics:* an attempt to prevent the carrying on of a business by urging people not to buy from the firm being boycotted; frequently used on the international scene for political or economic reasons; illustrated by appeals, threats, and so on, to secure redress of a grievance.

bracing: the process of supporting contents in a package to prevent damage through movement and/or to distribute the weight on all sides of the container.

bracket creep: the process by which inflation lifts wage earners into higher tax brackets.

brainstorming: a process of generating creativity and useful concepts through team or group discussions for solving problems.

brainwashing: a systematic and radical technique of indoctrinating, manipulating, and coercing a person to abandon loyalties, values, etc., and to adopt new ones.

branch

(1) *computers:* a set of instructions in a program that consists of a series of changes from the normal sequence of steps.

(2) *manufacturing:* a point in a routine at which one of two or more alternatives is selected under control of the routine.

(3) *business:* an offshoot of a major unit of operation (e.g., a branch store).

(4) *mining:* a vein from the main lode.

branch banking: any banking system in which there are few parent institutions, each having branches operating over a large geographical area. Some states have authorized the concept of branch banking under strict regulation. Federal control is maintained by the Board of Governors of the Federal Reserve System and the Office of the Comptroller of the Currency. In the United States there is no nationwide branch banking, whereas in some countries (e.g., Canada, England, France, Germany) the branch system of banking dominates.

branch house: a location away from headquarters that is maintained by a manufacturer and used almost exclusively for purposes of stocking, selling, shipping, and servicing the company's products.

branch line: a rail line that serves one or more stations beyond the point of junction with another branch line or main line.

branch organization: an overseas office set up by a parent company that is often employed in a firm's operations in other countries.

branch store: a store owned by a parent store. Usually the parent store is located in the center of the city, with branch stores located in suburban areas of the city or other cities. Cf. *regional store.*

brand: a name, sign, or symbol used to identify items or services of the seller(s) and to differentiate them from goods of competitors. A brand aids consumers in differentiating between items of different manufacturers. Cf. *trademark.*

brand awareness: realization by a buyer of the existence and availability of a branded product. See also *determinant attributes, differential advantages.*

brand franchise: the extent to which a brand has attracted a substantial and loyal following.

brand leader: an item that is considered best in its field or is marketed with that assumption.

brand loyalty: the strength of a buyer's preference for a particular brand, which suggests a refusal to purchase a substitute. Brand loyalty is usually measured in terms of repeat sales and is also reflected in purchases of other items produced by same company.

brand mark: that part of a brand identification that can be recognized but cannot be verbalized.

brand name

(1) *marketing:* a word or term that is placed on an item for identification or to be communicated orally.

(2) *business law:* a registered name used to prevent copying.

brand-name bias: a person's tendency to respond to surveys by naming widely advertised brands, often for purposes of giving a good impression, rather than naming the brands that are actually purchased.

brand recognition: the perception by buyers, when confronted with a product, that they have been exposed to that brand name previously.

brand strategy: plans and tactics relating to the use of brand names.

brand-switching model: a model that provides a manager with some idea of the behavior of consumers in terms of their loyalty and the likelihood that they will switch from one brand to another.

Brannan plan: a proposal made in 1949 by U.S. Secretary of Agriculture Charles F. Brannan to eliminate parity payments to farmers and give them direct payments instead. Cf. *price support.*

brass: (slang) term borrowed from the military to describe key executives in a business.

brassage: the charge made by a government for producing coins from bullion. See also *seignorage.*

brazen law of wages: See *iron law of wages.*

breach of contract: not fulfilling one's part in an agreement; breaking a promise to carry out one's contractual responsibility.

bread: (slang) money.

breakage

(1) *general:* an allowance for losses resulting from damage to merchandise.

(2) *finance:* the fractional cents due either party as a result of rounding percentage calculations (e.g., when the decimal is 0.5 or more, an added point is entered).

break-even model: a model that shows the basic relationships among units produced (output), dollars of sales revenue, and the levels of costs and profits for an entire firm or a product line.

break-even point: the point of activity at which a company earns zero profit. It is reached when total revenue equals total expense. See also *margin of safety.*

break-even pricing: pricing at a level that will enable a firm to break even.

breaking bulk

(1) *finance:* the practice of some middlemen to take a large, economical shipment from a manufacturer and divide it into smaller units to sell for greater profit.

(2) *transportation:* the point when cargo is first unloaded.

breaking point: in shipping, the point at which it becomes cheaper to pay a lower rate applicable to the next higher weight group rather than to pay on the actual weight at the charge applicable to the weight group in which the shipment rests.

break point: a place in a computer routine, specified by an instruction or other condition, at which the routine may be interrupted by external intervention or by a monitor routine.

break-up value: in an investment fund or an issue of a holding firm, the value of the assets available for the issue, taking all marketable securities at their market price.

breathing package: a container that permits air to enter or leave under changing conditions, including temperature changes, with or without a device to remove moisture from entering air.

Bretton Woods Agreement of 1944: articles of agreement adopted by the international monetary conference of 44 nations that met at Bretton Woods, New Hampshire, at which the International Monetary Fund and the International Bank for Reconstruction and Development were created. The fund's major responsibility is to maintain orderly currency practices in international trade, while the Bank's function is to facilitate extension of long-term investments for productive purposes. Periodic meetings are held at Bretton Woods to amend the original agreement.

bribe: a payment resulting in the payer receiving some right, benefit, or preference to which he has no legal right and which he would not have obtained except by paying the money. A bribe is a criminal offense.

broadened collision coverage: a no-fault automobile insurance term combining the coverage afforded under regular as well as limited collision policies.

broad form insurance: a term generally understood to describe the combination, at a special discount, of various real and personal property coverages and comprehensive personal liability. It is sometimes used to describe the more comprehensive of two similar coverages (e.g., ocean marine insurance as opposed to inland insurance).

broad market: describing a time of considerable volume in the buying and selling of stocks and bonds.

broad tape: (slang) the Dow Jones news ticker, displayed in brokerage houses as a large rectangular screen with lines of copy rolling upward.

broken lot: an odd lot of a stock, usually less than 100 shares.

broken time: a work schedule or shift in which an employee works for a certain length of time, then is off duty, then returns for another period of work. Synonymous with *split shift.*

broker

(1) *business:* a person who prepares contracts with third parties on behalf of a principal.

(2) *insurance:* a specialist who represents buyers of property and liability insurance and deals with either agents or companies in arranging for the coverage required by the customer. The broker is licensed by the state or states in which he or she conducts business. See also *producer;* cf. *reinsurance broker.*

(3) *real estate:* a state-licensed individual who acts as middleman in property transactions between a buyer and seller.

(4) *securities:* a member of a stock exchange firm or any exchange member who handles orders to buy and sell securities and commodities for a commission. Cf. *street broker;* see also *floor broker.*

broker's loan: a loan made to a stockbroker and secured by stock exchange collateral.

broker's market: the condition that exists when the investing public is generally inactive while brokers are trading heavily with their own accounts.

broker's ticket: a written statement of all buy and sell orders executed by a broker, giving the date, name, and amount of the security traded, the price, the customer's name, the broker's name, and so on.

brother: term used by organized workers when referring to a co-worker.

brotherhood: a union, federation, guild, or association. The term derives from the strong fraternal nature of early trade unions and their primary concept of the brotherhood of working men.

brown goods: a retailer's term for television sets and radios.

bubble: an unwise business venture in which the price has little or no relationship to the value of the asset.

bubble company: a firm that never had any true business or did not intend to be honest, or a firm created to defraud the public.

bucketing: (slang) activity of a broker who executes a customer's order for his or her own account instead of on the market, expecting to profit from a balancing transaction at a future time. This activity is forbidden by the SEC.

bucket shop (slang)

(1) *securities:* an institution engaged in securities dealings of doubtful legality.

(2) *securities:* an unlicensed, dishonest business in which customers place bets on the increase or decrease of stock prices on the regular exchange. No orders are filled, but profits and losses are based on the actual price movement on the exchange, with a commission going to the broker. The SEC has declared such businesses illegal.

buck passing: avoiding responsibility by relying strictly on established rules and policies when making a decision.

buddy system: a method of training whereby a new worker is assigned a partner to help him or her become oriented to the job and fellow workers.

budget

(1) *general:* an itemized listing, and frequently the allotment, of all estimated revenues a business anticipates receiving and a listing, and frequently the segregation, of all estimated costs and expenses that will be incurred in obtaining those revenues during a stated period of time. See also *cash budget, flexible budget.*

(2) *government:* an annual statement of the probable revenues (see estimated revenues and expenditures of a nation for the following year. See also *estimated revenues, federal budget expenditures, federal budget receipts, general control expenditures, planning-programming-budgeting, social infrastructure expenditures, zero-base budgeting.*

budget account: See *charge account.*

budget deficit: an excess of expenditures over revenues.

budgeting: the process of determining and assigning the resources required to reach objectives.

budget loan: a mortgage loan that requires a proportionate amount of tax, insurance, and assessment to be held in escrow, in addition to interest and principal payments.

budget surplus: an excess of revenues over expenditures.

budget variance: the difference between budgeted or projected costs and actual costs.

buffer

(1) *general:* a mechanism that permits the temporary excess supply of one instant to offset the temporary shortage of another instant.

(2) *computers:* a routine or storage feature used to compensate for a difference in rate of flow of data, or time of occurrence of events, during the transmission of data from one device to another.

(3) *packaging:* any material or device placed inside a container to absorb the forces of impact. Buffers are usually made of a cushioning or compressible material.

buffer stock: merchandise kept on hand to prevent a shortage resulting from an unexpected increase in demand for the items.

bug

(1) *computers:* a mistake or malfunction. Cf. *debug.*

(2) *computers:* any electrical or mechanical defect that interferes with the operation of the computer.

(3) *computers:* a design error in the computer's program that interferes with proper operation.

build-up method: a method for arriving at national forecasts for individual regions and then aggregating the regional forecasts.

built-in stabilizer: a fiscal approach that operates automatically, without the need for congressional or presidential impetus, to mitigate the worst effects of a cyclical downturn and to keep the downturn from snowballing.

bulge packaging: a technique for packaging perishable goods in a wooden box or crate whereby the receptacle is overfilled and the cover is put in place by pressure on its ends, leaving a considerable bulge at the center.

bulk cargo: cargo that consists entirely of one commodity.

bulk cargo container: a shipping container used in handling and hauling dry, fluid materials (e.g., grain).

bulk density: the weight of a unit of volume of a substance, expressed in pounds per cubic foot or other equivalent units.

bulk discount: a reduced charge for quantity or multiple purchases.

bulk freight: liquid or dry freight that is not carried in packages or individual containers.

bulkhead: a cargo-restraining separation in a vehicle.

bulk mail: second, third, and fourth class mail, including parcel post, ordinary papers, and circulars.

bulk sales: substantial quantities of a publication bought for redistribution.

bulk zoning: division of an area by the size and number of buildings, their shape, and other characteristics.

bulletin board: wall space for the display of union messages or information, made available in conformity to a contract provision.

bulling the market: speculator trading purporting to force the level of prices upward. Techniques include spreading rumors and entering price orders at levels somewhat above the prevailing price.

bullion: usually gold or silver, formed in ingots or bars, for use in coinage.

bull market: an advancing stock market.

bulls: speculators who anticipate that prices will rise.

bumping: application of seniority in the layoff of employees, ordinarily set forth in detail in the collective-bargaining agreement. A senior employee laid off from his or her own job may displace (bump) a junior employee from a lesser post. See also *backtracking, preferential rehiring, recall;* cf. *deadheading.*

bunco game: one of a variety of methods of swindling.

bundle: several pieces of mail tied or banded together and handled as a unit.

bundle of rights: the legal rights that go with property ownership: the rights to sell, lease, build, mortgage, improve, and so on.

bunkers: area where coal is stored on a vessel.

burden: a ship's carrying capacity. Cf. *tonnage.*

burdened vessel: a vessel that does not have the right of way and is required to yield to another ship.

bureaucracy

(1) *general:* concentration of authority in administrative groups.

(2) *administration:* a written statement of the procedures and regulations in an organizational structure.

(3) *government:* administration through departments and subdivisions, managed by officials following an inflexible routine.

bureaucratic theory: relating to the characteristic of an organization that maximizes stability and controllability of its members. The ideal bureaucracy is an organization that contains these two elements to a high degree.

bureaucratization: the process of organizing and maintaining an administrative hierarchy characterized by bureaucracy; also, the extension of bureaucracy and regimentation into certain areas of social life.

Bureau of Customs: an agency of the U.S. Treasury Department, established in its present form in 1927, that is responsible for collection of customs tariffs, vessel licensing and regulation, and other functions. It maintains offices in all ports of entry.

Bureau of Employment Security: an agency of the U.S. Department of Labor that is responsible for the U.S. Employment Service, which provides a nationwide job placement service and training programs and develops resolutions of manpower problems, and the Unemployment Insurance Service, which provides assistance to state agencies in unemployment insurance programs and makes information on job opportunities available to the states.

Bureau of Labor Standards: formerly the Division of Labor Standards, an agency of the U.S. Department of Labor, that is concerned with developing and establishing better working standards, primarily in the field of labor legislation.

Bureau of Labor Statistics (BLS): a research agency of the U.S. Department of Labor that compiles statistics on hours of work, average hourly earnings, employment and unemployment, consumer prices, and many other variables.

Bureau of Old Age and Survivors Insurance: a service bureau within the Bureau of Employment Security that is responsible for the administration of benefit payments to retired employees or their survivors.

Bureau of the Budget: originally part of the Treasury Department, a federal agency that was responsible for the presentation of the federal budget; now under the Executive Office of the President and called the Office of Management and Budget. See also *Office of Management and Budget.*

Bureau of the Census: an agency of the U.S. Department of Commerce that is responsible for conducting various censuses of population, housing, business, and so on. It assists other government groups in collecting pertinent data.

burglary and theft insurance: protection for loss of property due to burglary, robbery, or larceny.

business

(1) *economics:* the buying and selling of goods and services.

(2) *finance:* the activity of an individual, partnership, or organization, involving production, commerce, and/or service.

(3) *personnel:* a person's occupation or employment.

business agent: an elected or appointed representative of one or more local unions, with responsibility for negotiating contracts, administering existing contracts, and adjusting grievances. The agent is usually a full-time unionist, as contrasted with the shop steward or committeeman. The business agent may also have organizing duties. Synonymous with *walking delegate.*

business credit: the privilege of deferring payment for purchases, extended to customers by the vendors of items and services.

business cycle: any interval embracing alternating periods of economic prosperity and depression. See also *compensatory fiscal policy, contraction, expansion, inflation, recession,*

recovery, reflation; cf. *reference cycle.*

business data processing: use of automatic data processing for a wide variety of commercial operations.

business ethics: socially accepted rules of behavior that place pressure on business executives to maintain a high sense of values and to be honest and fair in their dealings with the public.

business expenses: expenses paid or incurred in the course of business that are ordinary, necessary, and reasonable in amount.

business game: a simulation that represents an actual business situation. It attempts to duplicate selected aspects of a particular situation, which are then manipulated by the participants.

business interruption insurance: coverage for loss of earnings in case the policyholder's business is shut down by fire, windstorm, explosion, or other insured peril. Cf. *extra expense insurance;* see also *boiler and machinery insurance.*

business logistics: a set of activities dealing with the control of incoming and outgoing materials. Its major function is to create "place and time utility" in goods, locating them at the right place at the right time and in the right quantity to meet consumer demand.

business manager

(1) *business:* the individual responsible for overseeing a firm, department, or other unit, to ensure smooth operations.

(2) *labor relations:* a business agent. See also *business agent.*

business transfer payments: transfers from businesses to persons that are charges against business products but for which no services are rendered currently. Major items included are corporate gifts to nonprofit institutions and allowance for consumer bad debts.

business trust: an unincorporated business organization in which title to the property is given to trustees to hold, manage, or sell. This structure is sometimes employed when a parcel of land is divided, improved, or sold. Synonymous with *Massachusetts trust, common law trust.*

bust: a severe decrease in business activity leading to high unemployment, low incomes, and low profits.

butterfly spread: the simultaneous purchase or sale of three futures contracts in the same or different markets—for example, buying 10 soybean futures contracts in January and another 10 for April delivery and at the same moment selling (going short) 20 soybean contracts for May of the same year. Borrowing power and profits may result, and any profits are held until after the tax year ends. See also *spread, straddle.*

buy
(1) *finance:* to acquire ownership of something in exchange for a monetary consideration.
(2) *economics:* the quality of a purchase (e.g., a good buy).

buy-back agreement: a provision in a sales contract stating that the seller will repurchase the property within a specified period of time, usually for the selling price, if the purchaser is transferred from the area.

buy-backs: way of convincing an employee who attempts to resign to stay in the employ of the firm. Normally, the person is bought back with an offer of an increased wage or salary.

buyer
(1) *general:* an individual who acquires goods for purposes of making a profit, usually as the result of a resale.
(2) *retailing:* an executive responsible for purchasing merchandise to be sold in a store. See also *procurement;* cf. *purchasing agent.*

buyers' market: a market characterized by low or falling prices, occurring when supply is greater than demand and buyers tend to set the prices and terms of sale.

buyers over: a situation of more buyers than sellers. Cf. *overbought.*

buyer's right to route: the purchaser's privilege to determine the route of the shipment when the seller does not pay the freight charges. If the seller goes against the buyer's wishes, the seller is liable for any loss incurred.

buying by specifications: a store submitting specific requests for delivery rather than purchasing standard merchandise available from the manufacturer.

buying committee: a group of buyers, often chain stores, who decide by committee on the items that will and will not be purchased.

buying in: a purchaser obtaining shares wherever he or she can find them when a seller does not hand over securities at the expected time. The seller becomes responsible for all added expenses.

buying off the peg: the purchase of ready-to-wear merchandise, to be taken home or delivered immediately, thus involving no adjustments or alterations.

buying on balance: a situation that occurs when a stockbroker's orders to buy exceed his or her cumulative orders to sell.

buying on margin: purchasing securities without paying the full price immediately. Margin regulations are closely controlled by the SEC. See also *margin, marginal trading, margin call.*

buying power: money available for spending and consumption, consisting of a combination of liquid assets and available credit.

buy out: to purchase all the assets, stock, and so on, of an ongoing organization; to purchase the interest in a firm that is owned by another.

buzz group (session): a small, informal group (4 to 10 people), usually chosen from a larger group, that gathers to consider and discuss informally what they have heard at a lecture or meeting, often with full participation. The discussion, which is aimed at and should ideally develop a group point of view, lasts about 20 minutes. Following the discussion, a chosen representative presents the concepts or questions that the group decided to put to the speaker(s) during the general discussion period.

buzzwords: the language of leadership; words or terms employed for quick communication with group members who are familiar with the terms. Little concern is given to comprehension by persons who are not group members.

by-bidder: a person who makes fictious bids at an auction, on behalf of the owner or seller of the items, to obtain a higher price or to encourage further bidding.

by-laws: rules accepted by board members of a firm or other organization for governance. Such rules cannot be in opposition to laws imposed by government, and they pertain only to the rights and duties of members of the stated organization.

by-product: a secondary product obtained during the course of manufacturing.

Byrnes Act of 1936: the so-called antistrikebreaker law, making it a felony to transport interstate any person who has been employed to interfere with peaceful picketing or to block organizing or collective bargaining by violence or threats of violence. Many states and municipalities have enacted restrictions on strikebreakers since 1960.

byte: a sequence of adjacent binary digits operated on as a unit and usually shorter than a computer word.

CA See *chartered accountant.*

CAA: See *Civil Aeronautics Administration.*

cabinet crowd: the section of the bond trading unit of the New York Stock Exchange that handles trading in active bonds. Synonymous with "book crowd" and "inactive crowd."

cable transfer: use of a cablegram to place funds in the hands of an individual in a foreign country. Funds are deposited with a local (i.e., domestic) bank, which cables instructions to a correspondent bank abroad to make the funds available to the payee.

caboose: a rail car, used by the crew, attached at the rear of the other rail cars.

cackler: (slang) an office worker.

CAD: See *cash against documents.*

cadastre: the official inventory of the real property in a community, used for determining taxes and its appraised value.

Cadillac effect: A licensing strategy that provides high-quality service for high-income consumers, developed because licensing often lowers the quality and quantity of consumer service.

Caesar management: demanding autocratic, power-oriented leadership. Cf. *participative-democratic leadership style.*

CAF: See *cost and freight.*

cafeteria benefit programs: programs that allow employees to select the mix of fringe benefits they receive by substituting less desired benefits for more highly desired ones.

CAI: computer-assisted instruction; an approach in learning whereby computers are utilized to motivate the student and to aid him or her in the absorption of educational facts and concepts.

calculating machine: a machine designed to make mathematical calculations in addition to straightforward addition and subtraction.

calculator: a device that performs

79

arithmetic operations based on data and instructions placed manually or on punched cards.

calendar spreading: simultaneous purchase and sale of options within the same class that have different expiration dates.

calendar year experience: experience developed on premium and loss transactions occurring during the 12 calendar months beginning January 1, irrespective of the effective dates of the policies on which these transactions took place.

call

(1) *securities:* to demand payment of an installment of the price of bonds or stocks that have been subscribed. See also *puts and calls.*

(2) *finance:* to demand payment of a loan secured by collateral because of failure by a borrower to comply with the terms of the loan.

(3) *business:* the power of a corporation to make an assessment.

(4) *business law:* an assessment for partial or total payment on shares of unpaid stock of a corporation.

(5) *computers:* the branching or transferring of control to a specified closed subroutine.

callable

(1) *finance:* that which must be paid on request, as a loan.

(2) *securites:* preferred stock that can readily be called in for payment at a stated price.

callable bond: See *bond, callable.*

callback: the technique used by a sales representative on a second or subsequent effort to induce a potential customer to buy. Cf. *user calls.*

callback pay: premium wage paid to an employee who has been asked to return to work after completing his or her regular work shift. Contract provisions usually provide for a minimum number of hours' pay, regardless of the numer of hours actually worked.

call compensation: guaranteed monies for a worker who reports for assignment and is informed that there is no work for him or her.

call credit: credit given for the price of an item when merchandise is picked up from a customer and returned to the store.

called bond: See *bond, called.*

call-in pay: guaranteed minimum payment to an employee called to work for less than a full shift, usually on a day outside his or her regular work schedule. Provisions for call-in pay are usually spelled out in collective agreements. Synonymous with *reporting pay.*

call loan: a loan payable on request. Cf. *day loan.*

call money: currency lent by banks, usually to stock brokers, for which payment can be demanded at any time.

call of more: the right to call again for the same amount of goods previously bought; used primarily in the purchase of options.

call option: giving the option buyer the right to buy 100 shares of stock at a stated price at any time before a deadline, at which point the option expires.

call pay: a sum of money guaranteed to a worker for reporting to work for only a portion of a day that he or she was not orginally scheduled to work.

call price: the price at which a callable bond is redeemable.

call purchase: the buying of commodities when the seller has some option of pricing at a later date within a given range of the existing price.

calls: an option contract that entitles the holder to buy a number of shares of the underlying security at a stated price on or before a fixed expiration date. See *puts and calls.*

call station: an area at which a pickup and delivery service is available, although there are no dock or warehouse facilities.

call transfer: relocating a call to another person inside or outside a telephone system without using an operator.

cambism (cambistry): engaging in the sale of foreign monies.

cambist
(1) *finance:* an individual who buys and sells foreign currencies.
(2) *international trade:* a handbook in which foreign currencies are converted into currency tables of the country for which the handbook is issued.

cameralism: See *kameralism.*

campaign basis: moving forward toward a goal without concern for its relationship with the total business system.

camp-on-busy: a system that allows a telephone operator to inform a person that another call is coming in while that person is using his or her phone.

can: a receptacle of 10 gallon capacity or less, made entirely or partly of lightweight sheet metal.

cancellation:
(1) *business law:* the annulment or rendering void of any instrument upon payment.
(2) *securities:* the termination of

open doors for the purchase or sale of stock.
(3) *insurance:* the termination of an insurance policy or bond before its expiration, by either the insured or the company. Almost invariably, the contract states the type of notice necessary before cancellation becomes effective.

cancellation clause: a provision giving one or both parties the right to cancel the agreement in the event of a specified occurrence.

cancellation evidence: a terminated policy or any legal notice of cancellation.

cancellation mark: See *killer bars.*

canned presentation: a prewritten and usually memorized presentation by a sales representative, spoken sentence for sentence, with little or no deviation.

canvass
(1) *general:* to count or examine.
(2) *salesmanship:* to call on prospective customers in person or by telephone to sell merchandise or services, to determine interest, or to gather information. Cf. *cold canvassing;* see also *preapproach;* synonymous with *territory screening.*

cap. a cover type of closure that fits over a container neck or opening rather than into it.

capacity
(1) *insurance:* the largest amount of insurance a company will accept on one risk.
(2) *packaging:* the volume of space within a container or other space, expressed in units.
(3) *finance:* one of the three elements of credit.
(4) *manufacturing:* the ability of a

factory to produce at a stated level.

(5) *transportation:* the amount of cargo that can be handled by a freight car, truck, or other carrier.

(6) *business law:* competency or legal authority. Cf. *non compos mentis.*

capacity, computer: the amount of information that can be stored in a computer drum or memory.

capacity costs: an alternative term for fixed costs, emphasizing that fixed costs are needed to provide operating facilities and an organization ready to produce and sell at a planned volume of activity.

capias ad respondendum: a judicial writ commencing actions at law (e.g., an order directing the sheriff to place a defendant in custody).

capital

(1) *business:* the amount invested in a venture. See also *equity, fixed capital.*

(2) *accounting:* describing a long-term debt plus owners' equity.

(3) *finance:* net assets of a firm, partnership, and the like, including the original investment, all gains and profits.

(4) *economics:* the physical plant and equipment used to produce, transport, and market the output of an economy.

capital account: an account maintained in the name of the owner or owners of a business and indicating his or their equity in that business— usually at the close of the last accounting period.

capital assets: a collective term that includes all fixed assets, consisting of furniture and fixtures, land, buildings, machinery, and so on, as differentiated from property consumed and property that yields income.

capital budget: a budget that itemizes expenditures to be used for building and for purchasing capital goods and which identifies the source of the funds required to meet the expenditures.

capital consumption: that portion of a firm's investment used in part or in its entirety in the process of production.

capital consumption allowance: sums set aside by accountants to recover the initial costs of investments in equipment, buildings, and improvements to land; usually treated as a cost of production and occasionally accumulated in a fund for replacing the asset when necessary. Synonymous with *depreciaiton.*

capital deepening: increasing the amount of capital for each worker.

capital expenditure: an expenditure to acquire an asset with an expected useful life of more than one year; also referred to as a capital investment because it is expected to yield revenue or reduce expenses.

capital flight: a large transfer of money from one nation to another as a hedge against poor economic or political conditions.

capital formation: the development or expansion of capital goods as a result of savings.

capital gain or loss

(1) *finance:* the difference (gain or loss) between the market or book value at purchase or other acquisition and the value realized from the sale or disposition of a capital asset. See also *long-term capital gain, long-term capital loss.*

(2) *real estate:* the gain or loss

from the sale of a capital asset at above or below cost or appraised value.

capital goods: items ordinarily treated as long-term investment (capitalized) because of substantial value and life (e.g., industrial machinery).

capital improvement program: a plan that coordinates capital improvements and expenses over a specified time period to assure proper timing, location, and financing.

capital intensive: characterized by the need to utilize additional capital to increase productivity or profits.

capital investments: a collective term representing the amounts invested in capital or fixed assets or in long-term securities, as contrasted with funds invested in current assets or short-term securities. Generally, capital investments include all funds invested in assets that are not expected to be returned during the normal course of business in the coming fiscal period.

capitalism

(1) *economics:* an economic system under which the means of production are owned and controlled by the private sector of the population, with a minimum of government involvement.

(2) *economics:* an economic system based on freedoms of ownership, production, exchange, acquisition, work, movement, and open competition. See also *laissez-faire.*

capitalist

(1) *general:* loosely, a wealthy person.

(2) *economics:* in Marxist terms, an individual who owns or shares in the ownership of the means of production and employs others. Cf. *mix-*

ed *capitalism, people's capitalism, private enterprise.*

(3) *business:* an individual investor in a business.

capitalization

(1) *real estate:* the method of appraising property by deducting the estimated normal expenses from the amount of income the property is expected to yield. The resulting net profit does not necessarily represent the actual property value.

(2) *securities:* the total value of all securities in a firm.

(3) *business law:* the act of converting something into capital.

(4) *accounting:* the sum of all monies invested in a firm by the owner or owners; total liabilities.

capitalize

(1) *accounting:* to classify a cost as a long-term investment item instead of a charge to current operations.

(2) *finance:* to convert into cash that which can be used in production.

(3) *securities:* to issue shares to represent an investment.

(4) *accounting:* to divide income by an interest rate to obtain principal.

capital liability: a fixed liability (e.g., a corporate bond) that is created for acquiring fixed assets or for purposes of funding.

capital loss: See *long-term capital loss.*

capital market: a place or system in which the requirements for capital of a business can be satisfied.

capital outlay: expenditures for the acquisition of or addition to fixed assets; included are amounts for replacements and major alterations but not for repair. Cf. *operating expense.*

capital rating: a rating given by a mercantile organization in appraising the net worth of a firm.

capital rationing: the process of determining which investments offer the highest returns.

capital requirement: the total monetary investment needed to create and operate a business.

capital stock: the specified amount of stock a corporation may sell, as authorized by the state granting the corporate charter. If the stock has a stated value per share, such value is known as par value. Stock without a designated value is referred to as no par value stock. See also *common stock.*

capital sum:

(1) *finance:* the original amount of an estate, fund, mortgage, bond, or other financial dealing, together with accrued sums not yet recognized as income.

(2) *insurane:* the amount specified in an accident policy for payment in the event of the loss of a limb or sight or other physical incapacity of the insured.

capital surplus: the excess of assets over liabilities plus the value given to issued capital stock, less amounts in paid-in or earned surplus.

capital turnover: the rate at which an organization's assets are converted into cash.

caption: explanatory text accompanying a drawing or photograph.

captive audience

(1) *advertising:* people exposed to commercial messages while passengers on carriers whose use of me-

dia they cannot control.

(2) *labor relations:* a work force assembled on company property and forced to listen to antiunion propaganda on company time. See also *employer interference.*

captive insurer: an organization, whose stock is generally owned by one business firm, that undertakes insurance company ownership in an attempt to obtain its business insurance at a lower cost than purchasing coverage from other insurers.

captive market: purchasers who have little latitude in choosing the vendor of a product or service (e.g., people who want to buy hotdogs at a sporting event and must buy from the stadium concessionaire).

captive shop: a manufacturing facility whose production is used solely by the company owners (e.g., an iron ore mine owned by a steel company).

car, double-sheathed: a freight boxcar that has inside car lining and outside sheathing of wood or steel.

car, flat: a freight car without top or sides. Synonymous with *platform car.*

car, gondola: an open freight car with sides and ends. Those with sides higher than 36 inches are called high-side cars; those with sides less than 36 inches are called low-side cars.

card, column: lines of a punched card that are used for punching holes, with each column representing a specific symbol in data processing. See also *terminal, remote.*

card, computer: usually, the keypunched card used in automatic data processing. Cf. *magnetic card.*

card, hopper: the portion of a card-processing machine that holds the cards to be processed and makes them available to a card-feed mechanism.

card, punch: a card that has been or will be punched with holes to represent letters, digits, or characters.

card, reproducer: a device that reproduces a punch card by punching another identical card.

career: an occupation that a person takes up, develops in, and usually pursues throughout most of his or her productive years; i.e., a profession, a business.

career path: the sequence of jobs planned for or by a person that leads to a career objective.

career planning: the process of systematically matching an individual's career aspirations with opportunities for achieving them.

career plateau: a stage in one's career from which further advancement is not expected.

career stages: distinct but interrelated steps or phases of a career.

Carey Street: British slang term for bankruptcy.

cargo: the load of a freight vehicle; merchandise being shipped.

cargo insurance: insurance covering goods being transported, as on ships, planes, trucks, or by railroad. Cf. *hull insurance.*

carload: the amount of a commodity or product that can fill a freight car, or the amount that is sufficient to be treated as a full car.

carnet: a document of international customs that permits temporary duty-free importation of specific items into certain nations. See also *admission temporaire.*

carriage charge: the charge made by a carrier of freight for carrying items from one place to another.

carrier

(1) *transportation:* an individual or organization, usually without a permit of public franchise, that is engaged in transporting products or people. Cf. *common carrier, franchise.*

(2) *insurance:* an insurance company that writes and fulfills the conditions of an insurance policy.

carrier's lien: the carrier's right to hold the shipper's property as security until the shipping obligation is paid. Cf. *general lien, seller's lien, stoppage in transit.*

carry

(1) *accounting:* to enter or post.

(2) *computers:* a condition occurring during addition when the total of two digits in the same column equals or exceeds the numbering system (e.g., when 2 is exceeded in a binary system).

(3) *finance:* to supply funds to a customer.

(4) *securities:* to hold stocks; to be long of stock. See also *long.*

(5) *securities:* the act of a broker in providing money to customers who trade by margin accounts.

carry-back: in federal income taxes, the amount of a taxpayer's business loss, subject to adjustments, that can be deducted from the net income of three preceding years. Cf. *carryover.*

carryforward

(1) *accounting:* transferring the balance of an account from one balance sheet to another.

(2) *federal income taxes:* declaring an item of expense as minimal un-

til a later time period when revenue is received.

carrying charge
(1) *general:* the continuing cost of owning or holding any property or items.
(2) *securities:* the fee charged by stockbrokers for handling margin accounts.
(3) *merchandising:* a charge added to the price of merchandise to compensate for deferred payment.

carrying costs: costs incurred by carrying an inventory, including taxes and insurance on the goods in inventory, interest on money invested in inventory and storage space, and costs incurred because of obsolescence of the inventory.

carryouts: items bought in a store that are not shipped but are taken from the store by the customer. Synonymous with *take-withs.*

carryover: in federal income taxes, the amount of a taxpayer's loss that was not absorbed as a carryback; may be deducted as taxable income of succeeding years. See also *carryback.*

carryover clause: a clause to protect a broker for a specified time, usually beyond the expiration date of the property listing.

carry the load: (slang) being depended on by others for completion of a task.

cartage: the charge for pickup and delivery of a shipment.

cartel: a group of separate business organizations that have agreed to institute approaches to altering competition by influencing prices, production, or marketing; rarely as effective as a monopoly. See also *monopoly, oligopoly;* cf. *consortium.*

carton: a type of package used in interior packing, made from a bending grade of paperboard.

case study: an attempt to examime numerous characteristics of one person or organization, usually over an extended period of time.

cash: an all-embracing term associated with any business transaction that involves the handling of currency and coins.

cash accounting: an accounting system whereby revenues are accounted for and entered only when money is received, and expenditures are accounted for only when they are actually paid.

cash against documents (CAD): a requirement that a purchaser make payment for items before receipt of the shipping papers that will give him control of the items once they are surrendered to him.

cash and carry wholesaler: a wholesaler who demands that the buyer must pay when he picks up his merchandise, without credit, or the wholesaler will not make delivery.

cash assets: assets described on a financial statement that are represented by actual cash on hand plus the total of bank deposits.

cash audit: an examination of cash transactions during a particular time period to determine whether all received cash has been documented and all other cash accounted for.

cash-basis accounting: a system of accounting in which transactions are recorded and revenues and expenses are recognized only when payments are received or made. See also *cash accounting.*

cash-basis method: a method of measuring income whereby income is defined as cash receipts less cash disbursements during an accounting period.

cash before delivery (CBD): a requirement to pay prior to delivery of goods.

cash budget

(1) *accounting:* a schedule of expected cash receipts and disbursements.

(2) *government:* the sum of cash receipts and expenditures of an agency, including those of public trust funds (e.g., social security).

cash buying: the purchase of securities or commodities outright, for immediate delivery.

cash card: a card given by a retailer or store owner to a customer to guarantee a discount for cash payment. It is a substitute for credit cards. Some merchants give cash-paying customers up to 8 percent discount.

cash discount: a percentage deduction from the selling price permitted by the seller for merchandise sold on credit, to encourage prompt payment of the invoice covering the goods or services purchased.

cash dispenser: a machine that is capable of giving out cash representing a withdrawal from a deposit account or an extension of credit. Synonymous with *automated teller machine, cashomat.*

cash dividend: declared dividends that are payable in cash; usually paid by check.

cash flow: the reported net income of a corporation, plus amounts charged off for depreciation, depletion, amortization, and extraordinary charges to

reserves, which are bookkeeping deductions and are not actually paid out in cash. Knowledge of these factors results in a better understanding of a firm's ability to pay dividends. Cf. *net cash flow.*

cash flow program: a special insurance company concept, devised for large risks, that in effect defers customer payment of part of the insurance premium.

cashier's check: a bank's own check signed by a cashier, becoming a direct obligation of the bank. Upon issue to a customer, it becomes a loan and a debit in the cashier's account. It differs from a certified check in that it is drawn against the funds of the bank itself, not against funds in a specific depositor's account. Cf. *certified check, register(ed) check;* Synonymous with *officer's check.*

cash inflows: any current or expected revenues directly associated with an investment.

cashomat: Synonymous with *cash dispenser.*

cash on delivery (COD): describing any purchase made with the expectation that the item(s) will be paid for on delivery. Cf. *franco delivery.*

cash outflows: the initial cost and other expected outlays associated with an investment.

cash over and short: an account used to record overages and shortages in petty cash.

cash position: the ratio of cash to total net assets; the net amount after the deduction of current liabilities.

cash receipts: all sums of money received by an organization.

cash refund annuity: a policy that provides an annual income at retirement for life. Provision is made that, upon death prior to full payment of the annuity, the remainder will go to the beneficiary's estate.

cash reserve
(1) *finance:* funds readily available to be converted into cash in an emergency. See also *liquid, liquid assets.*
(2) *banking:* refer to requirements that banks maintain a sufficient portion of deposits, as required by federal law.

cash sale
(1) *securities:* a transaction on the floor of an exchange that calls for delivery of the securities the same day. In "regular way" trades, the seller is to deliver on the fifth business day.
(2) *retailing:* the surrender of cash at the time of sale.

cash surrender value: the sum total of money paid by an insurance company upon cancellation of a policy. See also *surrender value.*

cash value: the amount available to the owner of a life insurance policy when the policy is surrendered to the company.

casting up: adding up a total, as "casting up an account." Synonymous with *footing.*

casualty insurance: insurance primarily concerned with the losses caused by injuries to persons and the legal liability imposed on the insured for such injury or for damage to property of others.

casual variables: independent variables that determine the results that will be attained. Examples include management decisions, business strategies, and leadership behavior.

catalog(ue): printed material that identifies items for sale. In most cases, the merchandise is described and prices are given; sometimes, a photograph or drawing accompanies an entry. See also *mail-order wholesaler.*

catastrophe
(1) *insurance* a severe loss due to extreme force, such as hurricane or fire.
(2) *insurance:* an extensive occurrence for which the insurance industry pays $1 million or more in losses.

catastrophic insurance: a form of insurance that provides benefits that begin where popular major medical coverage leaves off (e.g., coverage given following the total benefits, often after one year, of a major medical plan).

cat plant: (slang) an oil refinery.

cats and dogs (slang)
(1) *securities:* highly speculative stocks.
(2) *business:* items that do not have satisfactory sales turnover and therefore accumulate in inventory.

cause-and-effect diagram: a graphic method to aid the decision maker in identifying factors that influence a problem or goals and in determining the effects of these factors.

cause of action: intrusion on a person's legal right by a breach of contract or of a legal duty toward person or property.

caveat
(1) *business law:* "let him beware" (Latin); a warning; a notice filed by an interested party with a proper legal authority, directing others to cease or refrain from an act

until the person filing can be heard from fully.

(2) *finance:* a notice to cease payment.

caveat emptor: "let the buyer beware" (Latin). When merchandise is sold without a warranty by the vendor, the purchaser takes the risk of loss due to defects. See also *without recourse;* Cf. *caveat subscriptor.*

caveator: one who files or sends a caveat.

caveat subscriptor (venditor): "let the seller beware" (Latin). Unless the seller states no responsibility, he or she is liable to the purchaser for any alterations from the written contract. Cf. *caveat emptor.*

caveman: (slang) describing the use of obsolete or antiquated machinery or technology; most frequently used in describing the state of the art in computers.

CBCT: See *customer-bank communication terminal.*

CBD: See *cash before delivery.*

CD: See *certificate of deposit.*

CEA: See *Council of Economic Advisers.*

cease and desist order

(1) *labor relations:* directions to management or the union, usually issued by the National Labor Relations Board, to halt an unfair labor practice. See also *Landrum-Griffin Act, Taft-Hartley Act.*

(2) *business law:* a demand by court or government agency that a person or firm cease an activity.

CEC: See *Commodities Exchange Center.*

cede: to yield or grant business by agreement (e.g., a company reinsuring liability with another company

"cedes" business to that company).

ceiling price: usually during wartime, a maximum price for goods and services, established by government regulation. Cf. *floor.*

Celler Antimerger Act: an extension of the Clayton Antitrust Act, this 1950 addition prohibits a corporation from acquiring the stock or assets of another corporation if the effect would be a substantial lessening of competition or a tendency toward monopoly.

Celler-Kefauver Antimerger Act: See *Celler Antimerger Act.*

cellular vessel: a ship built for transportation of containers placed one on top of the other in vertical guide shafts.

cent: the coin of lowest worth in the United States, equal to one-hundredth of a dollar ($0.01).

center spread: a single sheet of paper that forms the two facing pages in the center of a publication, thus permitting printing across the fold.

central bank

(1) *banking:* a banker's bank.

(2) *government:* a bank that holds the main body of bank reserves of a nation and is the prime reservoir of credit (e.g., Bank of England, Bank of France).

central body: a geographical gathering of local unions for political, legislative, and other purposes. A central body, state or local, is the focal point for the common efforts of unions within its area.

central buying: a popular approach in chain stores whereby all purchasing is done through a central or main office. Shipments of merchandise, however, are usually made directly to the branch stores of the chain.

Central Certificate Service (CCS): a privately run depository through which members effect security deliveries among themselves via computerized bookkeeping entries, thereby reducing the physical movement of stock certificates.

centralization: the bringing together of operations or functions of similar types into a common grouping.

centralized administration: a system in which authority for direction, control, and management has become concentrated in the hands of a few persons or offices.

centralized purchasing: a system by which a department or unit is authorized to procure, handle, or store all supplies, materials, and equipment required by some or all of the other departments or units of a company.

central labor union: a grouping of local unions in a specific geographical area.

central person: an informal or formal leader who is strategically the closest to all or most members of the group. This person's relationship with the unit is usually emotional, but whether liked or disliked, he or she represents the group in regard to information, objectives, direction, organization, or control.

central planning: a type of economic organization whereby resources are allocated by national authorities rather than by local bureaucrats and markets.

central processing unit (CPU): a unit of a computer that incorporates the circuits controlling the interpretation and execution of instructions.

central tendency, measure of: a sta-

tistic that is calculated from a set of distinct and independent observations or measurements of a certain item or entity and is intended to typify those observations. See also *correlation; correlation coefficient; correlation, multiple; correlation, negative; correlation, positive.*

cents per cent: usual form of quoting marine rates of insurance ("20 cents per hundred dollars").

CEO: See *chief executive officer.*

certainty: a decision situation in which the decision maker knows what is going to occur; freedom from doubt.

certificate

(1) *securities:* the piece of paper that is evidence of ownership of stock in a corporation. Watermarked paper is finely engraved with delicate etchings to discourage forgery.

(2) *business law:* any written or printed document of truth that can be used as proof of a fact.

(3) *government:* a form of paper money, issued against silver or gold deposited in the U.S. Treasury.

certificate of beneficial interest: a statement of a share of a firm's business when such ownership has been deposited with a trustee. The certificate holder receives the income from and holds an interest in the firm's assets but relinquishes management control. This certificate is used when a business is operated as a trust.

certificate of deposit (CD): a negotiable, or transferable receipt payable to the depositor, for funds deposited with a bank.

certificate of deposit, demand: a negotiable or transferable receipt issued for funds deposited with a bank and payable on demand to the holder. These receipts do not bear interest and are used principally by contractors and others as a guarantee of performance of a contract or as evidence of good faith when submitting a bid. They may also be used as collateral.

certificate of deposit, time: a negotiable or transferable receipt for funds deposited with a bank, payable to the holder at some specified date (not less than 30 days after issuance) and bearing interest.

certificate of incorporation: the franchise or charter issued by a state to the original petitioners of an approved corporation. Such franchise or charter constitutes the authority granted by the state for the organization to transact business as a corporation.

certificate of indebtedness: a short-term note issued by a government agency, describing the current debt; an unsecured promissory note whereby the holder has a general creditor's recourse against general assets.

certificate of insurance: evidence that an insurance policy has been issued, showing the amount and type of insurance provided. It may be used as evidence of reinsurance between companies, and it is the document that contains specific details of property covered by master or open policies. See also *commercial set.*

certificate of necessity: a document processed by a federal agency enabling a company to charge accelerated amortization against a specified percentage of a new installation's cost that is related to war or defense.

certificate of no defense: when a mortgage is sold, the certificate signed by the borrower that identifies the mortgage indebtedness.

certificate of occupancy: a permit issued by a building department verifying that the work meets the local zoning ordinances and that the structure is ready for occupancy.

certificate of origin: a certificate declaring that goods purchased from a foreign country have indeed been produced in that country and not in another.

certificate of ownership: See *proprietorship certificate.*

certificate of release: a certificate signed by the lender indicating that a mortgage has been fully paid and all debts satisfied.

certificate of title: a title company certification that the seller possesses sound, marketable, and/or insurable title to the property. If a title company issues this certificate and a defect is identified at a later time, the title company will indemnify the holder. See also *title insurance.*

certification

(1) *labor relations:* determination by the National Labor Relations Board or an appropriate state agency that a particular union is the majority choice, and hence the exclusive bargaining agent, of all employees in a particular bargaining unit. See also *cross-check.*

(2) *banking:* an assurance by a bank that the drawer of a check has sufficient funds on deposit to cover payment on the check and that monies have been set aside to meet the incoming obligation. "Certification"

is usually stamped across the face of the check.

certified check: the check of a depositor drawn on a bank. The face of the check bears the word "accepted" or "certified," with the date and signature of a bank official or authorized clerk. The check then becomes an obligation of the bank, and regulations require that the amount of the check be immediately charged against the depositor's account. Cf. *cashier's check.*

certified mail: a mail service that provides a receipt to the sender and a record of delivery at the office of address. Certified mail is handled in the ordinary mail, and no insurance coverage is provided. Cf. *registered mail.*

certified public accountant (CPA): an accountant who has been certified by the state as having met that state's requirements of age, education, experience, and technical qualifications. Not all who practice accounting are certified.

certiorari, writ of: a directive from an appellate court to a lower court declaring that the record of a case pending in the lower court is to be forwarded to the upper court for review.

cesser clause: a statement in a charter agreement that a charterer's obligation terminates when the freight is loaded. The owner of the carrier can, however, have a lien on the freight for appropriate charges.

cession number: a number assigned by an underwriting office to identify reinsurance premium transactions.

cestui que trust: French adaptation of a Latin phrase designating the per-son for whose benefit a trust has been established. Synonymous with *beneficiary.*

CETA (Comprehensive Employment and Training Act of 1975): federal program to place disadvantaged, long-term unemployed, or inefficiently employed persons in jobs with a future; terminated by President Reagan in 1981.

ceteris paribus: in economic theory, the assumption that the values of all variables and parameters other than those being analyzed are constant.

CFTC: See *Commodity Futures Trading Commission.*

chad
(1) *computers:* the piece of material (or chip) removed when a hole or notch is formed in a storage medium, such as punched tape or punched cards.
(2) *computers:* in paper tape, a system in which the tape is completely perforated to represent binary 1.

chain banking: a form of multiple-office banking under which a minimum of three independently incorporated banks are controlled by one or more individuals. Cf. *branch banking.*

chain of command: the organizational design for the flow of communications, outlining direction toward authority, peers, and subordinates. See also *scalar chain principle.*

chain picketing: a procedure of marching around a struck company or at entrances to the owner's property so that the line of marchers forms an impenetrable column to prevent comings or goings across the picket line.

chain store: two or more stores, usually in different locations, being operated by the same organization.

chairman of the board: the highest ranking executive of a corporation. In some cases the firm's president is also the chairman of the board.

chamber of commerce: an organization of business executives created to advance the interests of its members.

chance: See *significance, statistical.*

chance cause: a random effect in connection with an event that cannot be controlled or removed.

chance difference: any difference between two measures that is attributable to forces exerted in strengths varying at random.

chance event: the probabilistic result associated with prior choices of action in a decision network. See also *Markov chain.*

change: money returned following a purchase, when a larger sum of money was given than was required (e.g., on a sale of 98¢, a $1 handout returns 2¢ in change).

change agent: a consultant, usually from outside the organization, who aids the organization in a change process.

change in amount consumed: an increase or decrease in the amount of consumption expenditures resulting from a change in personal income.

change in consumption: an increase or decrease in consumption, shown by a shift of a consumption curve to a new position.

change in demand: an increase or decrease in demand, represented by a change of a demand curve to a new position.

change in supply: a shift of the entire supply schedule to a new position.

change order: a written agreement, signed by all parties to a contract, formalizing and defining a change in the original contract.

change process: a three-step organizational process entailing the unfreezing of old ways, the introduction of new behaviors, and the refreezing of a resulting new equilibrium.

channel: in the communication process, the style of transmission. It can take the form of oral or written communication.

channel of distribution: the route a product follows from an original grower, producer, or importer to the last consumer. Often a middleman is used (e.g., automobile manufacturers sell to car dealers, who then sell to consumers).

chapel: one of the shop clubs in old trades; most commonly known among compositors in the printing unions.

character: a letter, digit, or other symbol that is used as part of the organization, control, or representation of data in a computer.

character classification of expenditures: a classification that reflects the time element involved in expenditures, chiefly the distinction between current operations and capital outlays.

charge

(1) *finance:* a demanded price.

(2) *accounting:* a cost or expense allocated to a specific account.

(3) *business law:* a judge's instruction to a jury.

(4) *sales:* to purchase for credit without making an immediate payment; usually to pay following billing.

charge account: a means of making

sales on credit to retail customers. The various types are as follows:

(a) *open (30-day) account*— an account in which the store accepts the customer's promise to pay for items bought, usually within 30 days of purchase.

(b) *revolving account*— an account in which the store sets the maximum amount of money the customer may owe at any one time. The amount is determined at the time the account is opened and is based on individual income and credit rating.

(c) *budget or flexible account*— an account in which monthly installment payments are based on the size of the customer's account balance, and interest is charged on the unpaid amount.

(d) *coupon credit plan*— an account in which the customer is given credit coupons that may be used in the store as cash. Payment for the coupons is made over a period of time, usually six months. This plan eliminates the need for a monthly billing.

charge off: to treat as a loss; to designate as an expense an amount originally recorded as an asset. Cf. *write-off.*

charges and miscellaneous revenue: nontax revenue derived chiefly from fees, assessments, and other reimbursements for current services and from rents and sales of commodities or services furnished incident to the performance of particular general government functions.

charges foward: a system whereby the purchaser pays for merchandise and shipping charges only upon receipt of the goods or, following receipt of goods, when a bill arrives.

charismatic leadership: a highly personal, emotional, and innovative leadership style that is derived from the leader's charisma rather than from official authority, selection, or election.

charter

(1) *government:* the contract between a private corporation and the state, identifying the articles of association granted to the corporation by authority of the legislative act. Powers and privileges granted are included.

(2) *transportation:* the hiring of a vehicle or other carrier.

chartered accountant (CA): in the United Kingdom, Canada, and Australia, a certified accountant.

Chartered Life Underwriter (CLU): the professional designation awarded by the American College of Life Underwriters to those who have completed the prescribed series of examinations and have satisfied the organization's experience requirement.

Chartered Property & Casualty Underwriter (CPCU): the professional designation awarded by the American Institute for Property and Liability Underwriters to those who have completed the prescribed series of examinations and have satisfied the organization's experience requirement.

charterer: an individual or organization, usually a state agency, that grants a firm the right to incorporate and transact business.

chartist: an individual who interprets stock market activity and predicts future movement, usually over a short period, through a graphic depiction of price and volume on charts. Cf. *Delphi technique, Dow theory.*

chart of accounts: a systematic listing of all accounts used by a firm.

chattel: (derived from "cattle") all property that is not real property. A structure on real property is a chattel real; movable properties (e.g., automobiles) are chattels personal. See also *replevin;* cf. *chose(s) in action, goods and services;* synonymous with *personal property.*

chattel mortgage: an instrument prepared by a debtor (the mortgagor) transferring a chattel's interest to a creditor (mortgagee) for the purposes of providing security for a debt. If the debt is not paid, the mortgagee can sell the chattel and use the monies received to satisfy the debt.

chattel paper: written evidence, of both a monetary obligation and a security interest in or lease of specific goods. When a transaction is evidenced both by a security agreement or a lease and by an instrument or a series of instruments, the group of documents taken together constitutes chattel paper.

chauvinist: See *male chauvinist.*

cheap jack: (slang) an individual who sells merchandise rapidly by unorthodox approaches, including using unoccupied stores to set up his goods.

cheap money: money that is available at relatively low rates of interest.

cheap stock: heavily discounted stock sold to an underwriter, who will attempt to find an investor.

check

(1) *general:* a process for determining accuracy.

(2) *computers:* a process for test-ing machine validity or the correctness of the results yielded by a program. Cf. *debug.*

(3) *banking:* defined by the Federal Reserve Board as follows: "A draft or order upon a bank or banking house purporting to be drawn upon a deposit of funds, for the payment of a certain sum of money to a certain person therein named, or to his order, or to bearer, and payable instantly on demand."

check authorization/verification: an inquiry process undertaken to reduce the risk of accepting a fraudulent check or a check written for an amount that exceeds the account balance. Check authorization systems may be provided and maintained by the party accepting the check, by a financial institution, or by a third party engaged in such a business. These systems may be designed to access bank records directly or may rely on secondary data sources. In some systems check approval is accompanied by a guarantee of payment.

checking account: a demand account subject to withdrawal of funds on deposit by check.

checking copy: copy of a publication delivered to an agency or advertiser to verify the inclusion of an advertisement as requested. See also *tear sheet.*

check list: a worker-evaluation approach whereby a supervisor or other person who is familiar with an employee's work checks off statements on a list that he or she believes are characteristic of the worker's performance, attitudes, and behavior on the job.

checkoff: withholding of wages by an employer for direct payment of dues and assessments to a union. The Taft-Hartley Act states that union members must give written permission for these sums to be deducted. The checkoff cannot exist for longer than one year or until the termination of the union contract, whichever date comes first. A checkoff can also be used to deduct assessments for non-union members.

check out: Synonymous with *debug*.

check trading: selling bank checks to a customer, who is expected to repay the amount of the check plus interest in installments.

cheque: chiefly British variation of "check," used in Canada and other countries where French or English is spoken.

cherry picking: buyer selection of only a few items from a vendor's line, rather than buying a complete line or classification of merchandise from any one source.

chief: (slang) a superior; the boss.

chief engineer: the head of an engineering activity; usually a staff position in a production activity.

chief executive officer (CEO): the person accountable to the board of directors for the activities and profits of the firm.

chi-square (χ^2): a means of estimating whether a given set of data differs from expected values to such a degree as to be evidence of the operation of nonchance factors. It is the sum of the quotients obtained by dividing the square of each difference between an actual and an expected frequency by the expected frequency. Cf. *least squares*.

chose(s) in action: a right to, but not possession of, funds or property. The actual possession may result from some other event. This right may be enforced by a court ruling and may cover debts, mortgages, negotiable instruments, insurance policies, and warrants.

chose(s) in possession: tangible personal property in actual possession (e.g., an automobile), as contrasted with a chose in action. Cf. *corporeal property, goods and services*.

Christmas bonus: a special payment or yearly allotment given to regular employees during the Christmas season. See also *bonus*.

chronic unemployment: as defined by the U.S. Department of Labor, unemployment lasting for a minimum of six months. See also *unemployment*; cf. *cyclical unemployment*.

chumming: artificially inflating the market's volume to attract other orders in some issues that which stock exchanges compete.

churning: the repetitive buying and selling of securities when such activity has a minimal effect on the market but generates additional commissions to a stock broker.

CID's: See *civil investigative demands*.

CIF: See *cost, insurance, and freight*.

Cincotta-Conklin Bill of 1976: a New York State law permitting state savings banks and savings and loan associations to offer checking accounts like commercial banks, but at no cost.

CIO: See *Congress of Industrial Organizations*.

circs: circulars; third-class mail consisting of printed or reproduced materials sent to several persons. Circs must be dispatched by the post office within 24 hours of receipt, but they are not given the high priority that is accorded letters, daily newspapers, and other mail that receives preferential treatment.

circuity of action: when a bill of exchange is returned to the person who has already signed it, he or she may renegotiate it, but this person has no claim against individuals who signed the bill between the time he or she initially signed it and its return to him or her.

circular flow: a process that shows the exchange between households and firms in the interaction of the flows of real sources and commodities and money income and expenditures.

circulating capital good: any capital good item in use that is consumed by a single use (e.g., gasoline used to make a car engine function).

circulation
(1) *advertising:* the number of copies of a publication that are distributed. Cf. *readership.*
(2) *finance:* the total of all currency in use at a given period. See also *velocity of circulation.*
(3) *banking:* the total value of the issued bank notes of a bank that are in use, as distinguished from those being held in the bank's reserve.

circumstantial evidence: specific facts and circumstances from which, according to usual human experience, an ordinary, intelligent person may infer that other connected facts and circumstances must necessarily exist. The latter facts and circumstances are considered to be proved by circumstantial evidence.

city bond: See *bond, municipal.*

civil action: a court proceeding or suit by one person against another for protection of a private right or the prevention of a wrong. It includes actions ex contractu, actions ex delicto, and all equity suits.

Civil Aeronautics Administration (CAA): a federal regulatory agency for interstate civil (nonmilitary) aviation; created in 1940 to regulate air carriers by means of issuing certificates of operation, licenses, and so on. It also investigates and enforces air accidents and establishes air safety standards. Cf. *Federal Aviation Administration.*

civil bond: See *bond, civil.*

civil investigative demands (CID's): in civil antitrust investigations, instruments analogous to subpoenas issued in criminal investigations; created in legislation signed by President Ford on September 30, 1976, to give the Antitrust Division of the Justice Department added investigative authority. CID's may be issued to a company, its executives, or a third party, such as a competitor, to obtain documents or to require oral testimony.

civil law: law based on statutes, as distinguished from common law; a law that examines relationships between people, as opposed to criminal law.

civil loans: loans contracted by a federal, state, or municipal agency.

Civil Rights Act of 1964, Title VII: legislation creating the federal Fair Employment Practice Law, covering all industries that affect interstate commerce. It bars discrimination by employers, unions, and employment agencies based on race, color, sex, religion, or national origin. Employers and unions may not discriminate in regard to apprenticeship, training, or retraining programs. Employers, unions, and employment agencies may not retaliate against any person opposing, making a charge, testifying, or taking part in probes or proceedings regarding any practice deemed to be unlawful under the act, or publishing or printing notices or advertisements indicating discrimination. Employment agencies are forbidden to discriminate by failing or refusing to refer applicants on the basis of race, color, religion, sex, or national origin. The law is administered by the Equal Employment Opportunity Commission, which has five members. See also *Civil Rights Act of 1968, Fair Employment Practices Committee.*

Civil Rights Act of 1968: law guaranteeing to all citizens equal treatment in matters pertaining to housing and real estate; prohibits discrimination because of race, color, religion, national origin, or sex against individuals who are trying to obtain financing for a home or property. See also *Civil Rights Act of 1964, Title VII.*

claim

(1) *business law:* a demand for payment, reimbursement, or compensation for damages or injury as identified in a contract or under law.

(2) *insurance:* a demand by an individual or a corporation to recover, under a policy of insurance, for loss that is covered by that policy.

class

(1) *insurance:* a category of em-

ployees in a schedule of group insurance, denoting the amounts of coverage for which the members of the class are eligible.

(2) *administration:* to place in ranks or divisions.

class action: a legal action in which one or more persons move against an organization on behalf of themselves as well as an aggrieved group or class of citizens deemed to be affected by the same condition. Cf. *cooptation.*

class A stock: as distinguished from class B stock, common, a stock that usually has an advantage over other stock in terms of voting rights, dividend or asset preferences, or other special dividend provisions.

classical conditioning: the learning or acquisition of a habit (stimulus response connection) through associating an unconditioned stimulus with a conditioned stimulus.

classical decision theory: a normative approach to decision making that emphasizes achieving known objectives by choosing the alternative that maximizes expected returns.

classical design theory: a collection of literature that evolved from scientific management, classical organization, and bureaucratic theory. The theory emphasizes the design of a preplanned structure for doing work and minimizes the importance of the social system. See also *structural principles, unilateral strategy;* cf. *human relations theory.*

classical economics: economic concepts from the late eighteenth century until the 1930's, emphasizing human self-interest and the operation of universal economic laws that tend automatically to guide the economy toward full-employment equilibrium if the government adheres to a policy of laissez-faire.

classical management: the first schools of management thought, including scientific management, functionalism, and bureaucracy.

classical organization theory: a collection of literature that developed from writings of managers who proposed organizational principles. These conclusions (see, e.g., *unity of command*) were intended to serve as guidelines for other managers.

classification:

(1) *merchandising:* an assortment of items, all of which are substitutable for one another to the customer.

(2) *insurance:* the underwriting or rating group into which a particular risk must be placed; pertains to type of business, location and other factors; not to be confused with class, but see *class rate.*

(3) *statistics:* any systematic method of arranging.

classification merchandising: a system of record keeping that assists inventory control and results in categorization of merchandise.

classification method: a job-evaluation method in which jobs are grouped in a number of classes or grades. See also *job evaluation.*

classified advertising: advertising identified by product or service. Cf. *display advertisement.*

classified balance sheet: a balance sheet on which assets, liabilities, and owners' equity are subdivided by age, use, and source.

classified bond: See *bond, classified.*

classified property tax: the description of properties by owners for the purpose of setting assessments with respect to market value and tax rates.

classified taxation: a tax structure in which real property is categorized by function, with differing tax rates applied to each class. In such situations, some classes are excluded from paying any tax.

class rate: a type of insurance rate applicable to risks that are so similar in character that it is unnecessary to go to the expense of differentiating among them as to varying factors of hazards.

claw-back: a British term for the retrieval of funds spent by the government on added benefits and allowances by a corresponding tax increase.

Clayton Antitrust Act of 1914: hailed by the union movement as labor's Magna Carta, in part designed to remove labor from the purview of the Sherman Antitrust Act and to limit the use of injunctions against labor by the courts. The law has not been successful in the latter respect, however, because of the interpretations of the courts. Cf. *basing point pricing, Robinson-Patman Act of 1936, Sherman Antitrust Act of 1890, tie-in sales;* see also *Celler Antimerger Act.*

clean bill of lading: a bill of lading receipted by the carrier for goods received in appropriate condition (no damages or missing items); does not bear the notation "Shippers Load and Count." Cf. *over, short, and damaged (OS&D).*

clean bond: see *bond, clean.*

clean up: (slang) to take all available

profits in a market; to make a substantial and rapid profit.

clean up fund: provided as one of the basic services of life insurance, a reserve to cover costs of last illness, burial, legal and administrative expenses, miscellaneous outstanding debts, and so on. Synonymous with *final expense fund.*

clear

(1) *computers:* to replace information in a storage device by zero.

(2) *finance:* free from encumbrance.

(3) *banking:* having passed through or having been collected by a clearinghouse. See also *clearing and settlement.*

(4) *business:* to make a profit or gain.

(5) *retailing:* to reduce inventory (e.g., clearing out merchandise).

clearance

(1) *general:* an act of clearing.

(2) *shipping:* a certificate of authority by a customs official permitting a ship to leave or enter port after having met customs requirements.

(3) *retailing:* a reduction on the price of items; a special sale.

(4) *banking:* the adjustment of debits and credits in a clearinghouse.

clearing and settlement: the process whereby checks or other records of financial or point-of-sale transactions are moved (physically or electronically) from the point at which they were originated to the organization (bank, thrift institution, or other agency) that keeps the accounts for and expects to collect from and account to the responsible payer. The settlement process completes the internal financial transactions among the possibly many parties involved in the clearing operation.

clearing corporation: a corporation whose entire capital stock is held by or for a national securities exchange or association registered under a statute of the United States, such as the Securities Exchange Act of 1934.

clearinghouse: an association of banks in a city, created to facilitate the clearing of checks, drafts, notes, or other items among the members. It also formulates policies and rules for the mutual welfare of all members. See also *Stock Clearing Corporation.*

clear time: time periods reserved by a station for the messages of an advertiser; a check by a network on the availability of time slots with station affiliates.

clear title: Synonymous with *good title, just title, marketable title.*

cleat: a piece of material, such as wood or metal, attached to a structural unit to secure, strengthen, furnish a grip, or fulfill a similar function.

client organization: a business firm that produces products and/or services and retains advertising agencies and other suppliers for special services.

CLOB: See *composite limit order book.*

clock watcher: (slang) an employee who shows little interest in his or her work.

close

(1) *general:* to finish or wind up.

(2) *finance:* to conclude a sale or agreement.

(3) *real estate:* to sign legal papers indicating that a property has formally changed ownership.

(4) *salesmanship:* to secure the

customer's written or spoken agreement to purchase the item or service being offered.

(5) *securities:* the short period before the end of the trading session when all trades are officially declared to have been confirmed "at or on the close."

(6) *accounting:* to transfer the balances of revenue and expense accounts at the end of an accounting period (e.g., close the books). See also *accounting cycle.*

closed account: an account with equal debits and credits.

closed corporation: a corporation whose shares are held by only a few people, usually in positions of management.

closed-loop control: automatic exercise of alterations in input as a system acknowledges a change in operation that would cause the system to vary from a predetermined approach.

closed mortgage: a mortgage that cannot be paid off until maturity occurs.

closed shop

(1) *computers:* pertaining to the operation of a computer facility in which most productive problem programming is performed by a group of specialists rather than by the problem originators.

(2) *labor relations:* an agreement whereby only employees who were union members in good standing before being hired could continue to work. The closed shop was outlawed by the Taft-Hartley Act. Cf. *modified union shop, open shop, union shop.*

closed stock: merchandise sold only

in sets (e.g., glassware, china.) Individual items from a set cannot be purchased, and there is no certainty that replacements will be available at a future time.

closed structure: characterizing an organization in which there are few chances to affiliate with others, employees have little flexibility to exercise individuality, and company objectives are spelled out by top management.

closed systems: sets of interacting elements operating without any exchange with the environment in which they exist.

closed trade: a transaction concluded by selling a security that has been paid for previously, or the conversion of a short sale (i.e., purchasing a security that had been sold short earlier).

closed union: a union that is deliberately made difficult to enter by the setting of high initiation fees, the limiting of admission to those who complete apprenticeship training, the observance of racial and ethnic barriers, or the use of other methods to protect existing members. The Taft-Hartley Act forbids the charging of excessive initiation dues.

close money: term applied when changes in prices between successive stock transactions are fractional or when the last bid and asked quotations hardly differ.

close out:

(1) *business:* an offer by a manufacturer or retailer to clear away his inventory.

(2) *finance:* to liquidate; to make a final disposition.

closing costs: the expenses that are

incurred by sellers and buyers in the transfer of real estate ownership (e.g., attorney's fee, title insurance, survey charge, recording deed of and mortgage). See also *Real Estate Settlement Procedures Act of 1975.*

closing date: in publishing and advertising, the last day on which advertisements can be accepted for publication in a magazine or other periodical.

closing entries: journal entries made at the end of an accounting period to close (bring to zero balance) all revenue, expense, and other temporary accounts.

closing price: the price of securities quoted at the end of the stock exchange day.

closing purchase: a transaction in which a holder liquidates his or her position by purchasing an option that has the same terms as an option previously written (sold).

closing sale: a transaction in which an investor who had previously purchased an option demonstrates intent to liquidate his or her position as a holder by selling in a closing sale transaction an option that has the same terms as the option previously purchased.

closing title: the formal exchange of money and documents when real estate is transferred from one owner to another. Synonymous with *passing title*; see also *objection to title, paper title, presumptive title, quiet title suit, title defect.*

cloud on title: any claim or existing shortcoming that interferes with the title to real property. See also *abeyance, curing title;* cf. *marketable title, perfect title.*

clout: the influence that some managers have over decisions. This influence, or "pull," is derived from the manager's location in the formal and informal systems of the organization. Clout enables the manager to deliver valued rewards to subordinates.

CLU: See *Chartered Life Underwriter.*

Club of Rome: an international volunteer organization of political, academic, and business people who are concerned about the utilization of world resources.

cluster chain: an informal communication chain in which information is passed on a selective basis.

cluster sample: a sample used when no total listing of the statistical universe is available. Groups are established and then a sample of these groups is drawn to represent the population. Cf. *quota sampling, random sample.*

coaching: a management development technique in which junior executives work closely with a senior manager, who is called a mentor or sponsor.

coalition bargaining: a form of negotiations in which several unions representing different categories of employees of a single employer attempt to coordinate their bargaining.

coalition power: the capacity to exercise a high degree of influence as a result of combining a large number of individuals, groups, and/or organizations.

COB: See *coordination of benefits.*

COBOL: common business-oriented language; a general-purpose machine language designed for commercial data utilizing a standard form. It is a language that can present any business program to any suitable computer and can also act as a means of communicating these procedures among people.

cobweb chart: a graphic display of the conditions in a market in which sales of a perishable item that needs time to be produced are confined to a brief seasonal demand, although such demand is relatively strong during that season each year.

COD: cash on delivery; terms of sale wherein the invoice is due and payable before the merchandise is released from shipment. See also *collection on delivery.*

CODASYL (Conference on Data Systems Languages): a forum for people from the private and public sectors to work together to develop common specifications for computer languages.

code
(1) *government:* a set of statutes passed by a legislative body.
(2) *computers:* the translating and writing of information in the form of abbreviations and symbols to evolve machine instructions from the statement of a problem.

codetermination: a form of industrial democracy, first popularized in West Germany, that gives employees the right to have their representatives voting on management decisions.

codicil: a written instrument that is made subsequent to the will to which it applies. The codicil modifies certain desires and bequests of the testator.

coding: See *symbolic coding.*

coefficient of cross-elasticity: the arithmetic relationship between a percentage change in the price of an item and the actual percentage change in the sales of a substitute or competitive item.

coefficient of relative effectiveness: term employed in the Soviet Union for the expected payoff or percentage rate of return on capital investment; similar to the concept of marginal efficiency of investment, used in the United States.

coemption: purchasing the entire supply of any commodity, usually for purposes of gaining a monopoly.

coercive power: influence over others based on fear; for example, a subordinate perceiving that failure to comply with directives would lead to punishment or some other negative act. Cf. *reward power.*

COG: customer-owned goods; for example, suits left at a store after purchase for alterations.

cogeneration: a process for producing heat and electricity together.

cognition: what individuals know about themselves and their surroundings. Cognition suggests a conscious process of acquiring organized information. Cf. *creativity.*

cognitive dissonance: a mental state that occurs when there is a lack of consistency or balance among an individual's various cognitions after a decision has been made. Two cognitions are in a dissonant state if they disagree with each other (e.g., when a commercial indicates that a cigarette is mild, but the consumer finds, through experience, that it is strong and irritating).

cognovit: a plea used to avoid a trial by a defendant who admits the right of the plaintiff. It is a written acknowledgment by a defendant of his or her liability in a civil suit to avoid the expense of contending.

cohesiveness: closeness and common attitudes, behaviors, and performance of group members.

coin: a piece of stamped metal authorized by a government for use as currency; specie.

coincidental telephone method: a procedure used by C. E. Hooper in the mid-1930s for ascertaining what radio programs and commercials people listened to. Respondents were called on the telephone and asked whether they were listening to radio and, if so, to name the programs. See also *Hooperating, Trendex;* cf. *Audimeter, diary method.*

coincident indicator: a measure of activity that traditionally moves in the same direction and during the same time period as total economic movement.

coin pack: a technique of roll-wrapping a cylindrical stack of disks such as coins, lozenges, or metal washers.

coinsurance
(1) *insurance:* a provision in a policy that requires that the insured carry additional insurance equal to a certain specified percentage of the value of the property. The inclusion of this provision, whether mandatory or optional, usually gives the insured lower rates than would otherwise apply. See also *replacement-cost insurance.*
(2) *insurance:* insurance held jointly with others.

coinsurer: one who shares the loss sustained under an insurance policy or policies; usually applied to an owner of property who fails to carry enough insurance to comply with the coinsurance provision and therefore inevitably suffers part of the loss himself.

COLA: See *cost of living adjustment.*

cold call: contacting a potential investment customer without prior notice in order to make a sale or arrange for an appointment.

cold canvassing: determining potential investment customers without assistance from others or from references (e.g., selecting every tenth name in the telephone directory within a given location and having a salesman call on these persons). Cf. *territory screening.*

cold storage training: an approach for training workers for advancement or for supervisory positions in advance of any specific openings. The trainee is kept in "cold storage" until such time as he is needed by the firm.

collaborative situation: the situation that occurs when there is a high-integrative and low-distributive relationship.

collaborative style: the tendency to identify underlying causes, openly share information, and search out an alternative that is considered to be mutually beneficial.

collapse
(1) *economics:* a sudden drop in business activity or business prices.
(2) *business:* failure or ruin of a specific firm.

collapsible container: a flexible container that can be folded when not in use.

collate: to combine items from two or more ordered sets into one set that has a specified order (e.g., alphabetical, numerical). See also *sequence.*

collateral: security (e.g., a house, an automobile, jewelry) left with a creditor to assure the performance of the obligator. When the obligator has performed, the creditor must return the collateral. See also *hypothecate.*

collateral bond: See *bond, collateral.*

collateral businesses: support businesses in the advertising industry, such as package design houses, sales promotion firms, premium shops, media buying services, marketing research organizations, printing companies, and so forth.

collateral loan: a loan obtained by the pledge of title to personal property. See also *hypothecated account.*

collateral trust bond: See *bond, collateral trust.*

collator: a device used to collate, merge, or match sets of punched cards, documents, or other materials.

collectible: that which can be converted into cash. Synonymous with *liquid.*

collection

(1) *general:* presentation for payment of an obligation and the payment thereof.

(2) *retailing:* an organized gathering of related items.

(2) *banking:* the gathering of money for presentation of a draft or check for payment at the bank on which it was drawn, or presentation of any item for deposit at the place at which it is payable. See also *float, value date.*

collection cycle: the activity that takes place between the extension of credit and the receipt of payment.

collection on delivery (COD): the request that the cost of merchandise and other charges be collected at the time the goods are delivered.

collection service: a system of methods and procedures used to obtain payment of past-due consumer accounts receivable.

collective bargaining: negotiations between an employer or group of employers and a labor union for a contract covering employees in a bargaining unit. First established as a legal right by the National Industrial Recovery Act of 1933 and reconstituted by the Wagner Act and other subsequent legislation, the process is regulated by the National Labor Relations Board. Executive Order 10988 extended limited collective-bargaining rights to federal employees. See also *multiemployer bargaining.*

collective negotiations: a term used in the public sector as an alternative to "collective bargaining."

collective reserve unit (CRU): an international currency or unit of money for use along with currencies in the reserves of banks around the world.

collect shipment: a shipment for which freight charges and advances are made by the delivering carrier from the consignee.

collegial approach to supervision: an approach whereby decisions are made on the basis of knowledge that individuals hold, regardless of their organizational position. Professionalism and mutual respect are the keys to this sort of relationship. Cf. *custodial approach to supervision, supportive approach to supervision.*

collision insurance: coverage for damage to the insured object caused by collision with any object, stationary or moving.

collusion

(1) *general:* a secret agreement to defraud.

(2) *labor relations:* a conspiracy between an employer and the certified representative of his or her employees to defraud the employees represented while providing the semblance of a genuine bargaining relationship.

co-load: a trailer containing cargo from two terminals and destined for one terminal.

Co. Ltd.: a closed corporation.

comaker: an individual who signs the note of another person as support for the credit of the primary maker. Synonymous with *cosigner;* see also *unsecured loan.*

combination bond: See *bond, combination.*

combination policy: an insurance policy, or more often two policies printed on one form, that provides coverage against several hazards under a single document. Sometimes affiliated fire and casualty companies offer insurance under this type of policy.

combination rate: a special rate for advertising in two or more publications owned by a single organization.

come-along: (slang) a temporary or inexperienced member of a work team.

command

(1) *general:* a formal demand or order.

(2) *computers:* an instruction or set of instructions, usually from a terminal, for the execution of a particular program.

command economy: an economic system under which an authoritarian government exercises major control over decisions concerning what and how much to produce. The government may also decide for whom to produce.

command group: a group specified by a formal organization chart as the group of subordinates who report to one particular supervisor.

commerce: trade between states and nations.

commercial: See *advertisement.*

commercial account: in general, a checking account; a bank account established for the purpose of enabling the depositor (usually a business person) to draw checks against the balance maintained. See also *checking account.*

commercial bank: an organization chartered by the comptroller of the currency and known as a national bank or chartered by the state in which it will conduct the business of banking. A commercial bank generally specializes in demand deposits and commercial loans.

commercial credit: credit extended by firms with which an organization does business.

commercial loan: a mortgage loan placed on income-producing or industrial property.

commercial multiple peril policy: a package type of insurance for commercial establishments that includes a wide range of essential coverages.

commercial paper: any notes, drafts, checks, or deposit certificates used in a business.

commercial property: property to be used for business purposes, as contrasted with residential, agricultural, or industrial functions.

commercial set: the four major documents covering a shipment—the invoice, the bill of lading, the certificate of insurance, and the bill of exchange or draft.

commercial year: a business year. Unlike the calendar year, it consists of 12 months of 30 days each, totaling 360 days.

commission

(1) *general:* the amount paid to an agent, which may be an individual, a broker, or a financial institution, for consummating a transaction involving sale or purchase of assets or services. Cf. *override.*

(2) *insurance:* compensation for agents and brokers based on a certain percentage of the premiums they produce.

commissioner of insurance: a state official charged with enforcement of the laws pertaining to insurance in his or her state; may be referred to as superintendent or director of insurance.

commission house

(1) *marketing:* an agent who negotiates the sale of merchandise that he or she handles, with control over prices and terms of sale.

(2) *securities:* a broker who purchases and sells only for customers and does not trade his or her own account.

commitment: an advance agreement by a lender to provide funds for a loan at a later time and upon certain conditions. The commitment is usually limited to a specified period of time and designates a dollar amount and yield.

committed fixed costs: costs that do not vary in total over a relevant range of activity and that management cannot readily change.

committed principle: the principle that an organization should plan for a period of time in the future sufficient to fulfill the commitments resulting from current decisions.

committee: a group that regularly meets as a body for purposes of deliberation and decision making. A committee may or may not have authority to carry out its recommendations.

committee, temporary (ad hoc): a group of people in an organization named to accomplish a specific objective. Upon completion of the task, the committee disbands. See also *adhocracy.*

committee deed: a deed employed when the property of a child or a person declared incompetent is conveyed. A court-approved committee is obtained before the transfer. See also *guardian deed.*

Commodities Exchange Center (CEC): a facility for the four major New York commodity exchanges, opened in July 1977. Each exchange retains its own autonomy, clears transactions through separate clearing units, and shares in a single computer quotation system. The CEC combines the Commodity Exchange, the New York Coffee and Sugar Exchange, the New York Mercantile Exchange, and the New York Cotton Exchange.

commodity: an item of commerce of trade. Cf. *spot market.*

commodity agreement: an agreement among producer nations to control the price and/or output of a primary product.

Commodity Credit Corporation: an

instrument of the federal government, created by the Agricultural Acjustment Act in 1933 to provide financial services to carry forward the public price-support activities with respect to certain agricultural commodities.

commodity dollar: Synonymous with *commodity theory of money.*

Commodity Exchange: formed in 1933 by the merger of the New York Hide Exchange, the National Metal Exchange, the National Raw Silk Exchange, and the New York Rubber Exchange to provide facilities for trading in futures in crude rubber, raw silk, hides, silver, copper, and tin.

Commodity Futures Trading Commission (CFTC): a federal agency established in April 1975, responsible for coordinating the commodities industry in the United States, with primary concern for detecting and prosecuting violators of the Commodity Exchange Act. See also *Tax Reform Act of 1976.*

commodity loan: a loan made to a grain producer by the Commodity Credit Corporation.

commodity theory of money: the claim that the value of money is determined by the value of the commodity of which it is composed or which it represents. Synonymous with *commodity dollar.*

common business-oriented language: See *COBOL.*

common carrier: a carrier that moves people or goods for a price and without partiality.

common cost: a cost that is common to all the segments in question and is not clearly or practically allocable except by some questionable allocation base.

common data base: a central computerized file that contains information in a form that may be used for more than one purpose.

common disaster clause: a clause added to a life insurance policy to instruct the company in paying the proceeds of policies when the insured and the named beneficiary die in the same disaster.

common laborer: Synonymous with *unskilled worker.*

common law: law that is based on precedent.

common law liability: the responsibility for injuries or damages imposed on a party, because of his or her actions, by that part of the law based on custom and usage as established by the courts—as distinguished from liability under acts passed by a legislative body, which are known as statutory law.

common law trust: Synonymous with *business trust.*

Common Market: Synonymous with *European Economic Community.*

common stock: securities that represent an ownership interest in a corporation. If the company has also issued preferred stock, both common and preferred have ownership rights. The preferred normally is limited to a fixed dividend but has prior claim on dividends and, in the event of liquidation, assets. Claims of both common and preferred stockholders are junior to claims of bondholders or other creditors of the company. Common stockholders assume the greater risk but generally exercise a greater degree of control and may gain the greater reward in the form of dividends and capital appreciation. Often synonymous with *capital stock.* See also *leverage, voting right.*

communication: an exchange of information, ideas, concepts, feelings, and so on, between two or more people.

communication, horizontal: the exchange of information among peers or among people at the same level in an organization.

communication, one-way: the process of sending a message to another person without anticipating feedback or response.

communication, two-way: the process of sending a message to another person, followed by an exchange, response, or other form of feedback.

communication, vertical: the transmission of information among individuals at various levels in an organization.

communication barriers: factors that interfere with the process of communication. The barriers include the distortion of messages due to attributes of the receiver, selective perception, semantic problems, timing, and information overload.

communication network: network formed when a small number of people exchange information in a well-defined pattern for the purpose of resolving a specific problem or issue.

communication overload: situation that occurs when employees receive more communication inputs than they can process or more than they need.

Communications Satellite Corporation: See *Comsat.*

communism: an economic system in which all goods are collectively owned and distribution of income is based on need; a theory of the ownership of all means of production and distribution by those sharing in the work and the products.

community property: property that is owned jointly by a husband and wife by fact of their marriage. State laws vary, but, in states where community property laws apply, a husband and wife are considered to share equally in all of each other's property that is acquired during the marriage and in any income received or increase in value occurring during the marriage.

community rate of return: the net value of a project to an economy, based on the expected net increase in output that the project, such as a new factory, may bring, directly or indirectly, to the area being developed.

commuter tax: any income tax levied by a town or city on people who work there but live elsewhere.

compact: an agreement mutually arrived at by two or more people, under which all those involved have both obligations and rights.

company: an association of people for purposes of carrying on a business activity.

company man: a worker who has greater loyalty to his boss than to his fellow workers.

company mission: a company's overall purpose for existing. It is a major internal factor that affects the tasks of the personnel manager.

company objective: See *company mission.*

company standardization: a management technique for developing and securing optimum utilization of resources and maximum efficiency of operations with the formal creation of the most appropriate predetermined solutions and answers to recurring problems and needs.

company store: a store owned and operated by an organization for the exclusive use of its workers and their families.

company town: a neighborhood or town whose residents are primarily employed by one corporation, which owns most of the property and homes.

company union: an employee organization, usually of a single company, that is dominated or strongly influenced by management. The National Labor Relations Act of 1935 declared such employer domination an unfair labor practice.

comparative advantage: a country's or area's advantage in the manufacture of a particular item when its social cost of production for that item is less than the social cost experienced by other countries or areas for the same item.

comparative advertising: promotional material in which competitors' products are named.

comparison shopper: an individual sent to competitors' outlets to determine goods carried and relative prices charged as part of information-gathering activity.

compensating balance: the lowest percentage of a line of credit that the customer of a bank is expected to maintain at all times.

compensating errors: two errors, one on the credit side and the other on the debit side, such that one cancels out the other.

compensation
(1) *general:* payment for any services or items. See also *executive compensation.*
(2) *business law:* the settlement of any debt by the debtor's establishment of a counterclaim against the creditor.
(3) *personnel:* an attempt to disguise an undesirable characteristic by exaggerating a desirable one.

compensation award: compensation paid to an injured party for a number of periods, either definite or indefinite, as the nature of the injury requires. Payment is sometimes made in installments.

compensation cafeteria: a compensation strategy whereby firms permit executives to design payment packages by allowing alternate payment streams and deferral periods and at the same time permit senior management to exercise preferences for payment devices. Choices include salary raises, bonuses (paid or deferred), benefits, perquisites, qualified and nonqualified stock options, deferred retirement compensation, added life insurance, and the like.

compensatory decision process: a process whereby a decision maker allows a high value on one decision criterion to offset a low value on some other criterion.

compensatory fiscal policy: an approach to reversing the direction of the business cycle when it is believed that it is becoming inflationary or deflationary. Synonymous with *countercyclical policy;* cf. *archmonetarist.*

competition
(1) *general:* any rivalry.
(2) *business:* the situation in

which a large number of manufacturers serve a large number of consumers, when no manufacturer can demand or offer a quantity sufficiently large to affect the market price. See also *monopoly, oligopoly, invisible hand;* cf. *cutthroat competition, imperfect competition, nonprice competition, unfair competition.*

competitive price: a price determined in the market by the bargaining of a number of buyers and sellers, each acting separately and without sufficient power to manipulate the market.

compile

(1) *general:* to collect, as data.

(2) *computers:* to prepare a machine language program by means of compiler. See also *compiler.*

compiler

(1) *general:* a machine that compiles.

(2) *computers:* a routine that yields a specific program for a particular problem. The compiler converts computer instructions into a code that can be acted on by the computer.

complaint: the initial paper filed in court by the plaintiff in a law suit. It is referred to as a pleading—a statement of facts on which the plaintiff rests his or her cause of action.

complementary products: items that tend to round out a line of products (e.g., shoes and shoelaces). See also *suggestive selling.*

complete audit: an examination of all financial records. See also *audit.*

completed transaction: a sale of property that has closed. In such transactions all legal and financial aspects are identified and title to the property is transferred from seller to buyer.

complex organization: any large-scale formal organization.

complex systems: high-order, multiple-loop, nonlinear feedback structures.

component: the smallest unit of a system that performs a part of the transformation or processing activity.

composite check: a listing of payments to be made from an account, sent by the owner of the account to his or her depository institution with instructions to effect the payments and debit the account for the total amount. The payments are transmitted by the depository institution to the creditors for subsequent deposit by them in their respective accounts.

composite demand: the sum of demands for an item or service, beginning with any number of needs, all of which can be fulfilled by that particular item or service.

composite inventory: data accumulation on customers, including the most pertinent information that can be obtained about them.

composite limit order book (CLOB): a central electronic repository and display that automates all orders to buy and sell securities. It could eliminate the need for any exchanges by allowing buying and selling to be done directly by brokerage offices through a central computer system.

composite rate: a special single rate based on a measure of exposure that will reasonably reflect the variations in the insurable hazards covered for a particular insured. Bases of exposure to which the composite rate is applied include payroll, sales, receipts, and contract cost. This rate is often called an average rate in property insurance.

composite supply: an indefinite number and variety of items, each of which is able to satisfy a particular need.

compound: to add interest to principal at time intervals for the purpose of establishing a new basis for subsequent interest computations. See (Appendix G).

compounded: indicating the frequency with which interest is computed and added to the principal to arrive at a new actual balance.

compound interest: interest created by the periodic addition of simple interest to principal, the new base thus established being the principal for the computation of additional interest. See (Appendix G).

compound period: the period of time for which interest is calculated.

comprehensive: a layout prepared to resemble a completed advertisement as nearly as possible.

comprehensive budgeting: a budgeting process that covers all phases of operations.

Comprehensive Employment and Training Act of 1975: See *CETA.*

comprehensive major medical insurance: a form of major medical insurance written with a low initial deductible in place of separate basic hospital, surgical, and medical benefits.

comprehensive personal liability insurance: a type of insurance that reimburses the policyholder if he or she becomes liable to pay money for damage or injury he or she has caused to others. This coverage does not include automobile liability but includes almost every activity of the insured except his or her business operations.

comprehensive planning: planning that incorporates all levels of the organization—top, middle, and lower.

comprehensive policy: describes a variety of insurance policies that provide broad protection (e.g., a comprehensive automobile liability policy, a comprehensive personal liability policy).

compressed work week: a work schedule whereby workers spend fewer days on the job but work approximately the same number of hours.

compromise

(1) *general:* any agreement between two or more persons, usually in opposition, to settle their differences on areas of controversy without resort to legal action.

(2) *labor relations:* a settlement of a union-management dispute by an adjustment of differences by both sides, rather than resorting to outside involvement by a mediator or arbitrator.

comptroller: an executive officer whose job embraces the audit functions of the business.

comptroller of the currency: a federal office created in 1863 to oversee the chartering and regulation of national banks.

compulsory arbitration: a third-party decision resulting from the order of a judicial body or, in rare instances, agreed to by the parties in a labor-management dispute. Arbitration is a common device for settling disputes that arise under existing contracts but is not considered compulsory in ordinary usage. Cf. *conciliation.*

compulsory insurance: any form of insurance that is required by law (e.g., compulsory automobile liability insurance for all owners of automobiles in Massachusetts).

compulsory retirement: separation from employment at an age specified by union contract or company policy.

compulsory staff consultation: an organizational policy that requires operating (line) managers to confer with appropriate staff personnel before taking action.

computer: a device capable of accepting information, performing a variety of actions on such data, and supplying the results of these processes. It usually consists of input and output, arithmetic, storage, communications, and control units. See also *analog(ue) computer, digital computer, first-generation computer, general-purpose computer, second-generation computer, third-generation computer.*

computer, hybrid: hardware combining analog computer speed, flexibility, and direct communication capability with digital computer memory, logic, and accuracy.

computer-assisted instruction: See *CAI.*

computer code: a machine code for a specific computer; any system of combinations of binary digits. Synonymous with *machine code.*

computerese: (slang) computer language; used to suggest that people are becoming more like machines.

computer instruction: a machine instruction for a specific computer; a set of characters that defines an op-

eration and causes the computer to operate accordingly.

computer network: a complex consisting of two or more interconnected computing units.

computer science: the range of theoretical and applied disciplines connected with the development and application of computers.

Comsat: a consortium originally formed by 18 nations in Washington in 1963 to invest in Communications Satellite Corporation (Comsat) to provide satellite relays for electronic communication in the United States. The American Telephone and Telegraph Company is the largest stockholder. Synonymous with *Intelstat.*

concealment

(1) *insurance:* the willful withholding of any material facts that, if known, would make a risk undesirable or would necessitate payment of a higher premium.

(2) *business law:* the suppression of truth to the injury or prejudice of another. Cf. *discovery practice.*

concentrated marketing: a form of marketing segmentation in which the marketer concentrates on a single segment of a larger market.

concentration in employment: a situation in which a department or employer has a higher proportion of members of a protected class than is found in the employer's labor market. See also *underutilization.*

concentration point: a place where less-than-carload shipments are united to be shipped as a carload.

concentration ratio: in a specific industry, the breakdown of total business that is handled by a specified number of the largest organizations.

concept testing: a marketing strategy whereby members of a psychological test panel conclude whether an idea is acceptable, as contrasted with market research that attempts to determine if an appropriate market exists. Cf. *market research.*

conceptual skill: the perception and ability to see the overall picture.

concession
(1) *business:* any deviation from regular terms or previous conditions.
(2) *finance:* a reduction or rebate; an allowance from the initial price or rate.
(3) *merchandising:* a right granted to a company to sell its product or services (e.g., to rent chairs at an outdoor party; to check coats and hats in a theater).

concessionaire: the holder of a concession granted by a company, government, or other authorized body.

conciliation: in collective bargaining, the process whereby the parties seek to reconcile their differences. The discussion generated is advisory and participation is not compulsory, but under the Taft-Hartley Act a union must notify the appropriate federal agency of an impending strike. Most conciliation work is conducted by the Federal Mediation and Conciliation Service. Cf. *arbitration, mediation.*

concurrent authority: two or more brokers having an open listing for property.

concurrent control: measurement of deviations from standards as they occur.

concurrent insurance: two or more insurance policies that provide the same coverage for the same property and the same interests.

concurrent staff authority: an organizational policy requiring that line managers obtain the agreement of appropriate staff personnel on specified types of issues before they take action.

condemnation
(1) *real estate:* taking of private property for public use. Under a condemnation proceeding, the property is taken with or without the consent of the owner but upon payment of just compensation. See also *confiscation, excess condemnation;* cf. *eminent domain.*
(2) *government:* the declaration by government that a structure is unsafe for use and is a menace to the safety of people.

condemnation proceedings: court action preceded by legislation to take private property for public use. It reflects the sovereign power of eminent domain.

condition: a contractual clause, implied or expressed, that has the effect of investing or divesting with rights and duties the members of the contract.

conditional advance commitment: See *advance commitment.*

conditional sales contract: a sales contract in which ownership of sold items remains with the seller until the goods are paid for in full or until other conditions are met.

conditional value: the value that will insure if a particular event occurs.

conditioning process: the process of shaping material into a usable item. No additional materials are added, but the configuration is altered (e.g., shaping sheet plastic into a tube).

condition precedent: a contract

clause stating that immediate duties and rights will vest only upon the occurrence of an event. It is not a promise; therefore its breach is not grounds for action against damages. It is the basis for a defense, however.

conditions concurrent: conditions that are mutually dependent and must be rendered by all members of the contract at the same time (e.g., delivery of merchandise and payment for the goods if the terms are cash on delivery).

conditions of certainty: conditions under which a manager has enough information to be able to closely predict the outcome of a decision. The alternatives are known and the decision can maximize the outcome desired by the manager.

conditions of risk: conditions under which a manager can develop alternatives and can estimate the probability that they will lead to the desired outcomes.

conditions of uncertainty: conditions under which the probabilities attached to the available alternatives are less well known than those for conditions of risk.

condition subsequent: a contract clause covering the occurrence of an event that divests rights and duties (e.g., a fire insurance policy clause excusing the insurer from paying the policy if combustible materials are found within 5 feet of an area where fire occurs.)

condominium: individually owned portion of a building that has other units similarly owned. The owner holds a deed and title, pays taxes independently of other owners, and can sell, lease, or otherwise dispose of the individually owned portion. Common areas, including halls, elevators, and so on, are jointly owned by all tenants. See also *lease-purchase agreement;* cf. *cooperative building.*

Conference Board: formerly National Industrial Conference Board, founded in 1916 as a clearing house for the dissemination of information, including publication of statistical materials and other industrial relations data.

conference call: conversation among several people who use telephones linked by a central switching unit.

conference method: an instructional approach that brings together individuals with common interests to discuss and attempt to solve problems.

confidence men: professional swindlers; people who cheat and defraud.

configuration management: the combination of management principles and technological applications in building high-quality products to well-defined requirements; used primarily in the defense and aerospace industry.

confidential risk report: a report, established through investigations, of the physical condition of an insurer or his property, prior to the issuance of a policy.

confirmation
(1) *purchasing:* a statement from a supplier that he or she will accept a buyer's purchase request.
(2) *business law:* an assurance of title by the conveyance of an estate or right from one to another, by which a voidable estate is made sure or valid or at times increased.
(3) *securities:* a written order or agreement to verify or confirm one

previously given verbally, in person or by telephone. Executions of orders to buy or sell securities as substantiated in writing by brokers to their customers. See also *dealer.*

confirming bank: a bank that assures either that it will honor a credit already issued by another bank or that such a credit will be honored by the issuer or by a third bank.

confiscation: the seizure of private property without compensation, usually by a government agency. Cf. *eminent domain, expropriation, nationalization.*

conformity: compliance with existing rules or customs.

confrontation conflict resolution: a strategy that focuses on the sources of conflict and attempts to resolve them through such procedures as mutual personnel exchange, use of superordinate goals, or problem solving.

conglomerate: the result of a merging of organizations that produce different items and services to secure a large economic base, to acquire sounder management, and to gain greater potential profit. See also *merger;* cf. *consortium.*

conglomerate merger: a merger of firms that produce unrelated products.

conglomeratize: to gather together varying business units into one massive corporate structure or system. See also *conglomerate.*

conglomerchant: defined by Rolli Tillman as a multiline merchandising empire under central ownership, usually combining several styles of retailing with behind-the-scenes observations of some distribution and management functions.

congloperators: (slang) presidents and board chairmen of major worldwide conglomerates; coined by the London-based publication *Economist.*

Congress of Industrial Organizations (CIO): originally organized in 1935 as a committee (Committee for Industrial Organization) within the American Federation of Labor to spur unionization of mass-production industries. Unions organized by the committee were expelled from the AFL in 1937, and the committee reorganized itself to form the Congress of Industrial Organizations in 1938.

conjunctive decision rule: a rule whereby the decision maker establishes minimally acceptable levels on each of several decision criteria. To decide in favor of an alternative, that alternative must achieve minimally acceptable levels on every criterion.

conk off: (slang) to cease work; to rest instead of work.

connecting carrier: a carrier that has a direct connection with another carrier under which freight or people are moved in a joint-line service.

Conrail: the Consolidated Rail Corporation; the government-sponsored successor to the bankrupt railroads of the northeastern and midwestern United States. See also *Amtrak.*

conscious parallel action: identical pricing behavior among competing organizations. It has been declared illegal by the courts in antitrust cases.

consensus management: a management style in which chief executives rely on various committees, groups, and task forces to reach organization-wide agreement on a particular decision.

consent decree: in a case settlement, the instrument whereby the defendant agrees to cease certain actions that caused the action to be entered.

consent election: voting by employees in a bargaining unit as to their choice of union (or no union), when management and the union or unions have agreed on the terms of the election. See also *representation election.*

consequential loss: loss occurring as a consequence of physical damage to property. Standard fire insurance and certain other policies cover only against direct loss resulting from the perils insured against. Cf. *proximate damages.*

conservative groups: groups whose members are scattered throughout an organization, usually at top rungs of the promotional and status ladders of the organization. Members are self-assured and successful, and their work involves individual operations.

conservator: a court-appointed official responsible for the protection of the interests of an estate.

consideration

(1) *insurance:* synonymous with *premium.*

(2) *business law:* a requirement of valid contracts according to which all parties must provide something of value. Cf. *forbearance, nudum pactum, quid pro quo.*

consignee: the ultimate recipient of goods.

consignment: the act of entrusting goods to a dealer for sale but retaining ownership of them until sold. The dealer pays only when and if the goods are sold. See also *on consignment.*

consignor: the originator of a shipment, a person who delivers goods to an agent.

consol: a bond that will never reach maturity; a bond in perpetuity.

console: the part of a computer used for communication between the operator or maintenance engineer and the central processing unit.

consolidate: to bring together various financial obligations under one agreement, contract, or note.

consolidated balance sheet: a balance sheet that shows the financial condition of a corporation and its subsidiaries.

consolidated bond: See *bond, consolidated.*

consolidation: a combination of two or more organizations into one to form a new entity.

consortium: a grouping of corporations to fulfill a combined objective or project that usually requires interbusiness cooperation and sharing of resources. Cf. *cartel, conglomerate.*

conspicuous consumption: the purchase and use of items and services primarily for improving an individual's social prestige rather than for the satisfaction of material needs.

conspiracy in restraint of trade: collusion; two or more competitors who conspire to restrain trade in some manner. The conspiracy may be directed at competing firms or may be aimed at customers or suppliers. See also *restraint of trade.*

constant-cost industry: industry that experiences no increase in prices or in costs of production during expansion, despite new companies entering it.

constant dollars: the actual prices of a previous year or the average of actual prices of a previous period of years.

constraints: events that reduce the range of options that are available to a problem solver.

constructive delivery: acceptance by buyer and seller that possession and ownership have been transferred from one to another, although the purchased goods may not have been delivered.

constructive mileage: an arbitrary mileage allowed to a carrier in dividing joint rates, or mileage pro rata.

constructive receipt rule: the idea that cash is considered to have been received when the taxpayer can exercise control over it, whether or not the cash has actually been received.

constructive total loss: property so badly damaged that, although not completely destroyed, its condition is such that total loss can be prevented only at an expense greater than the value of the property would be after repair; primarily found in marine insurance. Cf. *incurably depreciated, valued policy.*

consultant a specialist in any field of activity (e.g., psychological consultant, Wall Street consultant, engineering consultant), hired by an organization to recommend solutions to a problem.

consumer: any person who uses or consumes goods and services.

consumer behavior research: a technique used to determine what satisfactions people want out of life, how they use products and services

to achieve these satisfactions, how they perceive items and various brands, what forms of promotional activities will lead to successful marketing, and how to access the effects of these activities. See also *marketing concept.*

consumer convenience goods: low-priced, frequently bought consumer items.

consumer cooperative: a group of consumers who band together to gain buying power; user-owned retail outlets. Such organizations act for the benefit of their consumer owners.

consumer credit: credit extended by a bank to a borrower for the specific purpose of financing the purchase of a household appliance, alteration, or improvement, or a piece of equipment. Such credit generally is extended to individuals rather than to business executives.

Consumer Credit Protection Act of 1968: See *Truth in Lending Act of 1968.*

consumer durables: See *consumer goods.*

consumer equilibrium: a situation in which no reallocation of a person's income will improve his or her economic situation.

consumer goods: items bought and used by the final consumer for personal or household purposes.

consumerism: the organized demand that businesses increase their concern for the public in both manufacture and sale of merchandise. See also *Consumer Product Safety Act, Fair Credit Reporting Act of 1971, Federal Equal Credit Opportunity Act of 1977, Interstate Land Sales Full Disclosure Act of 1968, Occupational*

Safety and Health Act of 1970, Radiation Control for Health and Safety Act of 1968, Real Estate Settlement Procedures Act of 1975, Truth in Lending Act of 1968, Wheeler-Lea Act of 1938.

consumerist: an individual or representative who takes a leading position to protect the interests and needs of the consumer. See also *consumerism, Naderism.*

consumer market: buyers who purchase for personal needs or family consumption.

consumer package: a container that, because of its construction or design, cannot safely be transported without further packaging, usually in an outer or shipping container.

consumer panel: a group of selected people who serve over a period of time as a sample group for marketing research studies.

consumer picketing: picketing of an establishment to persuade consumers to stop shopping there or to stop buying certain products or services.

Consumer Price Index (CPI): a measurement of the cost of living, determined by the Bureau of Labor Statistics. See also *cost of living index.*

Consumer Product Safety Act (CPSA) of 1972: legislation providing for control of the processing, manufacturing, and distribution of products that may cause unreasonable risk of personal injury. Cf. *Wheeler-Lea Act of 1938.*

consumer sale disclosure statement: a form presented by a dealer giving essential details on financing charges relative to a purchase on an installment plan. This is required under the Consumer Credit Protection (Truth in Lending) Act.

consumer sovereignty: a system wherein consumers decide by their purchasing efforts which items are to be produced.

consumer's surplus: a buyer's payment that is lower than the maximum amount he or she would have been willing to pay for the quantity of the commodity that was purchased.

consumption: the utilization of goods and services for the satisfaction of human needs.

consumption function: function that describes how consumption expenditures depend on other variables.

consumption possibility frontier: the limits of the combination of consumption items that a consumer can afford, thus creating budget constraints. Cf. *optional consumption, production possibility frontier.*

container: a nonspecific term for a receptacle capable of closure.

containerization: placing pieces of freight in a reusable container so that the entire container can be shipped as a single unit. See also *unitize.*

contango

(1) *finance:* the cost factors used in calculating from a given period to a future point.

(2) *commodities:* a basic pricing system in futures trading; a form of premium or carrying charge; for example, instead of paying for the cost of warehousing silver bullion, paying insurance finance charges and other expenses (silver users prefer to pay more for a futures contract covering later delivery).

content motivation theories: theories that focus on the factors within the person that start, arouse, energize, or stop behavior.

contingency: a future event or condition that was not predictable.

contingency fund: assets set aside for use in unpredicted situations. Cf. *sinking fund.*

contingency planning: the process of developing a set of alternative plans to fit a variety of future conditions.

contingency theory of leadership: a leadership concept developed by Fred Fiedler according to which a task-oriented style is more productive when the situation is either quite uncertain or quite well defined, and a considerate style is productive under conditions of moderate certainity. Cf. *classical management.*

contingency theory of management: theory that the success of management is said to depend on such factors as the type of technology used to generate the final service or product and the degree of external environmental uncertainity that will face the company.

contingent asset: an asset that may become actual or unqualified as presently unfulfilled situations are satisfied.

contingent interest: the right to property that depends for vesting or realization on the coming of some future uncertain occurrence.

contingent liability: the liability imposed on an individual, corporation, or partnership because of accidents caused by persons (other than employees) for whose acts the first party may be held responsible under the law. See also *guaranteed debt, switch (contingent) order.*

contingent reserve: the setting aside of a certain amount of profits to meet unanticipated needs of the business or some unexpected loss, the amount of which cannot be definitely ascertained at the time of budgeting.

continued bond: See *bond, continued.*

continuity in advertising: the extended utilization of advertising; in particular, repetition of theme, layout, or commercial format.

continuous audit: an audit performed continuously or at short regular periods during the fiscal year. See also *audit.*

continuous budget: a budget that perpetually adds a month in the future as the month just ended is dropped.

continuous production: a production activity that yields a standardized product. Raw materials are continually entered into the production process.

continuous system: any manufacturing system that operates 24 hours every day.

continuum approach to leadership: a representation of styles charted on a scale that suggests that there are an infinite number of leadership approaches a manager might follow.

contra account: a separate offsetting account; i.e., allowance for uncollectible accounts and accumulated depreciation.

contraband: illegal or prohibited goods. See also *smuggling.*

contract: an agreement between two or more persons, as established by law, by which rights are acquired by one or more parties to specific acts or forbearance from acts on the part of others.

contract, breach of: failure by one party to a contract to perform his obligation.

contract bar: a rule followed by the National Labor Relations Board that the NLRB will not disturb a valid, existing contract during its term. Cf. *living document doctrine, no-strike clause, reopener clause.*

contract carrier: a transportation firm that contracts with shippers to transport their goods. The price is negotiated between the carrier and the shipper. The contract carrier cannot accept shipments from the general public.

contract clause: a clause in the Constitution of the United States (Article 1, Section 10) declaring that no state may pass laws diminishing the obligation of a contract. Although corporate franchises are accepted as contracts and protected by this clause, it cannot act as a bar to the regulatory and police powers of the state.

contracting out: subletting certain parts of an operation to subcontractors, rather than having the firm's employees perform the task.

contraction: a decline of economic activity in the business cycle; the opposite of *expansion.*

contract market: one of the 18 commodity exchanges permitted under the Commodity Exchange Act to deal in futures contracts in the commodities.

contract purchasing: a form of purchasing defined in a contract for orders and deliveries, covering a specific time period, usually one year.

contract rent: an agreed upon rent payment.

contractual channels: a channel system based on a contractual agreement between a producer and other members of the channel of distribution.

contractual liability: liability assumed by contract; an additional coverage for a specific exposure for which the basic liability policy does not provide. It may be obtained for an additional premium.

contributed capital: that portion of stockholders' equity provided by the owners of a business, usually through the purchase of stock.

contributed value: a measure of efficiency that relates value added to sales or profit.

contribution
(1) *general:* something given, such as time or money.
(2) *insurance:* an insurance carrier's payment of, or obligation to pay, all or part of a loss.
(3) *business law:* the sharing of a common loss or benefit, paid or to be paid by each of the parties involved.

contribution clause: See *coinsurance.*

contribution margin: the excess of total revenue over total variable cost.

contribution profit: sales revenue less the variable cost of producing the revenue.

contributory negligence: the negligence attributed to the person making a claim against an insured; a defense pleaded by the insured in a lawsuit.

contributory pension plan: a pension plan jointly financed by employer and workers. The employees share in the cost of the plan.

contributory retirement system: a system whereby the responsibility for developing the resources for retirement is shared by the employer and the workers.

control: to meet a situation and handle it capably, physically as well as mentally; to execute procedures in accord with plans and policies established for future policy forming and planning. See also *coordination, POSDCORB.*

control account: a summary account in the general ledger that is supported by detailed individual accounts in a subsidiary ledger.

controllable costs: costs whose amounts can be influenced by and which are the direct responsibility of a manager.

controllable marketing activities: those marketing activities over which a firm has control, such as the product itself, the product name, packaging, advertising, pricing, sales promotion, and method of distribution.

controlled company corporation): a firm whose policies are controlled by another firm that owns 51 percent or more of its voting shares. See also *Tax Reform Act of 1969;* cf. *working control.*

controlled economy: an economy that is regulated and greatly influenced by government. See also *statism*; cf. *laissez-faire.*

controller: See *comptroller.*

controlling function: all managerial activity that is undertaken to assure that operations go according to plan.

controlling interest: any ownership of a business in excess of 50 percent. A smaller percentage of shareholders

may control the firm, however, if the remainder of the stock is distributed among many owners and is not active in voting. See also *working control;* cf. *minority interest.*

control panel: the part of a computer console that contains manual controls.

control stock: securities belonging to those who have controlling interest in a company.

convenience goods: products that the public wishes to purchase with a minimum of effort or time (toothpaste, cigarettes, sodas, paper, etc.).

convenience store: a small retail outlet that carries a limited line of high-turnover convenience goods and usually operates for extended hours.

conventional loan: a mortgage loan, usually granted by a bank or loan association. The loan is based on real estate as security rather than being guaranteed by an agency of the government.

conventional rating scale: a performance appraisal form containing a list of qualities, characteristics, or traits upon which an employee is rated on a scale ranging from poor to outstanding.

conventional warehousing: warehousing in which the primary emphasis is on storage with a minimum of service.

convergence concept: a theory that capitalism and communism resulting from industrialization will gradually merge to form a new kind of society in which personal freedoms and profit motives of Western countries blend with the government controls that exist in a communistic economy.

conversion

(1) *manufacturing:* the process of changing from one type of equipment to another.

(2) *computers:* the process of changing from one method of data processing to another or from one data-processing system to another (e.g., using COBOL instead of FOR-TRAN).

(3) *insurance:* a provision whereby a more permanent form of insurance may be elected without a medical examination if the request is made within the specified time and an additional premium is paid.

(4) *business law:* the unauthorized taking of another's goods or property.

conversion costs: the combination of direct labor and factor overhead in the manufacturing process.

convertibility: ease of exchanging one currency for that of another nation or for gold. See also *soft currency.*

convertible bond: See *bond, convertible.*

convertibles: interest-paying debentures and dividend-paying preferred shares that can be exchanged for the common stock of the issuing company on a preset basis. The conversion privilege becomes valuable only if the market value of the debenture or preferred stock is below the total value of the common shares into which it can be converted.

conveyance:
(1) *general:* the act of transporting.

(2) *business law:* a written statement, called a deed, whereby ownership of property is passed from one person or organization to another.

Cf. *mesne*

conveyor: a mechanism to support and carry moving items in a fixed path. Conveyors are operated by hand, by machine, or in some cases by gravity.

cooling-off period:
(1) *labor relations:* suspension of a planned or announced strike in the hope that the dispute can be settled during the term of suspension. If the president of the United States feels that the nation's welfare or security is at stake, he can seek an injunction calling for an 80-day cooling-off period. See also *Taft-Hartley Act.*

(2) *finance:* the term for the period, usually 20 days, that must elapse before the filing of a registration for a new security and public sale, as declared by the Securities and Exchange Commission.

cooling the client out: (slang) deliberately lowering a client's expectations so that the client will be pleased with whatever settlement he or she eventually receives. This is an unethical practice.

cooperative:
(1) *retailing:* an outlet owned and run by the final consumers for purposes of buying and selling items to the members.

(2) *business law:* anything owned jointly to the same end.

cooperative advertising: advertising paid for jointly by the advertiser and its wholesalers or retailers.

cooperative building: a building in which tenants are stockholders in a corporation that owns the real estate. All are part owners of the corporation. Stockholders sign a proprietary lease with an operating organization and, in place of rent, pay a proportionate fixed rate to cover operating costs, maintenance, and so on. Cf. *condominium.*

cooperative counseling: a mutual counselor-employee relationship that establishes a cooperative exchange of ideas to help solve an employee's problems. See also *directive counseling, nondirective counseling.*

cooperative equilibrium: an oligopoly's equilibrium, derived from a decision of the businesses within the oligopoly to maximize their combined profits.

cooperative marketing: independent manufacturers, wholesalers, retailers, or any combination of them working collectively to buy and/or sell.

co-optation: a strategy employed by an organization to minimize the uncertainty that it faces (e.g., bringing community members together to discuss the ecological impact of building a new plant before the people have a chance to organize to oppose it). Cf. *class action.*

coordination: the overall management function that integrates planning, organizing, directing, and controlling into a unified total. See also *POSDCORB.*

coordination of benefits (COB): a method of integrating benefits payable under more than one group health insurance plan so that an insured's benefits from all sources do not exceed 100 percent of allowable expenses.

coordinative planning: planning done at the middle management level where the work of different units has to be coordinated.

COPE: the Committee on Political Education, a division of the AFL-CIO whose primary function is to provide support by inducing members to vote for candidates for political office who have received the endorsement of labor unions. See also *Hatch Act, Taft-Hartley Act.*

Copeland Act of 1934: the so-called antikickback law, making it illegal for an employer or his or her agent to extract a payment as a condition of continued employment. The law prohibits employers or their agents from using force, threats, or other means to secure the return of any part of a worker's wages as a condition of retaining his job. Violators are fined.

co-plan: a unified staff-line effort of communication, coordination, consultation, analysis, and control.

copy: all components to be included in a completed advertisement.

copyright: an exclusive right, guaranteed by federal statute, to reproduce, publish, and sell the matter and form of literary, musical, or artistic works. Any attempt by another person or group to deprive the copyright holder of his or her property is cause for the latter to seek damages.

Copyright Act of 1976: federal legislation revising the copyright laws for the first time in 67 years. The act extends the length of copyright protection to the duration of the creator's life plus 50 years. Previously the protection ran 28 years from the date of publication and was renewable for another 28 years. The act also sets standards for fair use and reproduction of copyrighted material and a new system of compulsory licensing for cable television and jukeboxes. It also preempts state laws governing copyrighted materials that come within the scope of the federal act.

copy strategy: a brief statement that guides the preparation of advertising copy.

copy testing: measuring the effectiveness of an advertising campaign. See also *aided recall, hidden offer, inquiry test, keying an advertisement, split run.*

core: a configuration of magnetic material placed in a spatial relationship to current-carrying conductors to concentrate a magnetic field needed in the storage of data.

core management: the key executives of an organization who are the primary decision makers.

corner the market: to purchase a security on a scale large enough to give the purchaser control over the price.

corporate bond: See *bond, corporate.*

corporate income tax: a tax imposed on the net earnings of corporations.

corporate muscle: the ability of an organization to effectively utilize its resources, both financial and human, in meeting its goals and objectives.

corporate profits tax liability: federal and state taxes levied on corporate earnings of a given year; a measurement of taxes for the year in which they are incurred, not necessarily for the year in which they are paid.

corporate state: condition represented by the power of a corporation that is out of control, insensitive to human values, and legalistic; a concept introduced by Charles A. Reich in his book *The Greening of America.*

corporation
(1) *business law:* individuals created by law as a legal entity, vested with powers and ability to contract, own, control, convey property, and discharge business within the boundaries of the powers granted. cf. *firm.*
(2) *administration:* an organization that has purposefulness, declared social benefit, derived powers, legal entity, permanence, and limited liability.

corporation de facto: a legal entity that, despite a minor failure to comply with the regulations for incorporation, thereafter has exercised corporate powers.

corporation de jure: a corporation formed by fulfilling the requirements of the law permitting the formation of the corporation.

corporatize: (slang) to establish a legal corporation as contrasted with an unincorporated system; term coined by Neil H. Jacoby.

corporeal hereditament: tangible property that can be inherited.

corporeal property: real or personal property that has form or structure (e.g., house, furniture, land, fixtures). cf. *chose(s) in possession.*

Corps of Engineers: a federal agency founded in 1824. A new judicial interpretation of an old law plus amendments to the Water Pollution Control Act give the Corps a say in construction along waterways and marshlands and in dredging operations and mine dumping.

correcting component: any part of automated machinery that performs the alteration necessary to return a process into line after deviation.

corrective control: mechanisms designed to return an individual, department, or organization to some predetermined condition.

corrective discipline: an action that follows a rule infraction and seeks to discourage further infractions so that future actions are in compliance with standards. Cf. *preventive discipline.*

corrective model of control: the process of detecting and correcting deviations from preestablished goals or standards.

correlation: a relationship or dependence reflecting the principle that two things or variables are so related that change in one is accompanied by a corresponding or parallel change in the other.

correlation coefficient: the quotient of the sum of the products of algebraic deviations of the corresponding numbers of two sets of data and the square root of the product of the sum of the squares of the deviations of each set. See also *factor analysis, matrix correlation.*

correlation, multiple: the highest possible correlation between a criterion (standard) and two or more independent variables.

correlation, negative: a correlation between two variables such that large values of one variable tend to be associated with small values of the other, and vice versa.

correlation, positive: a correlation between two variables such that large values of one variable tend to be associated with large values of the other and small values of one tend to be associated with small values of the other.

correspondent bank: a bank that is the depository for another bank. The correspondent bank accepts all deposits in the form of cash letters and collects items for its bank depositor.

corrugated: possessing a series of alternating ridges and furrows.

cosigner: Synonymous with *comaker.*

cosmopolitans: managers, scientists, and engineers who identify with professional groups outside their organization. They may have different norms and values from those stated by the organization.

cosponsoring

(1) *general:* joining together in a mutual effort or activity.

(2) *advertising:* sharing by two or more advertisers of the cost of a single broadcast program.

cost: the value given up by an entity in order to receive goods or services. Cost is the value given up to obtain an item in the volume needed, shipped to the desired location. All expenses are costs, but not all costs are expenses.

cost accounting: a branch of accounting that deals with the classification, recording, allocation, summarization, and reporting of current and prospective costs. It provides the means by which management can control manufacturing costs.

cost and freight (CAF): shipping term indicating that the seller will pay only freight charges to a location, not insurance. Cf. *cost, insurance, and freight. (CIF).*

cost approach to value: a method of estimating the value of real property by deducting depreciation from the cost of replacement and adding the value of the land to the remainder. See also *appraisal.*

cost-benefit analysis: a branch of operations research that aids in evaluating the implications of alternative courses of action. This method is primarily concerned with the selection of equipment, products, and so on, before they become available. Synonymous with *cost-effectiveness;* see also *crossover analysis.*

cost effectiveness: Synonymous with *cost-benefit analysis.*

cost inflation: inflation caused when rising costs of labor and production increase prices even though demand has not increased.

costing: Synonymous with *cost accounting.*

cost, insurance, and freight (CIF): a quoted price that includes the handling charges, insurance, and freight costs up to delivery, usually up to a port of entry. Cf. *cost and freight.*

cost of capital: the weighted-average cost of a firm's debt and equity capital; equals the rate of return that a company must earn to satisfy the demands of its owners and creditors.

cost of distribution: costs involved in the movement of goods from the producer to the consumer.

cost of goods manufactured: all direct material, labor, and overhead transferred from work in process inventory to finished goods inventory.

cost of goods sold: the purchase price of goods sold during a specified period, including transportation costs.

cost of living
(1) *government:* the average cost to an individual of providing the basics of life. See also *price control.*
(2) *economics:* the average of the retail prices of all goods and services

required for a reasonable living standard. See also *Consumer Price Index.*

cost of living adjustment (COLA): an increase or decrease of wages based on the increase or decrease in the purchasing power of money. Inflation and deflation are primary causes for a cost of living adjustment. See also *escalator clause.*

Cost of Living Council: established in 1971, a committee of government appointees responsible for administering a 90-day freeze on wages and prices.

cost of living index: popular term for the Consumer Price Index issued monthly by the U.S. Department of Labor, Bureau of Labor Statistics; a measurement of changes in prices of goods and services purchased by moderate-income families. Wages of workers whose union contracts contain an escalator clause fluctuate with the cost of living index.

cost plus pricing: the practice of adding a percentage of the cost of goods to the cost before the selling price is established.

cost pool: a group of costs that is allocated to cost objectives in some plausible way.

cost-push inflation: increases in the price level that result from firms passing on increases in costs to purchasers, especially labor costs.

cost-volume profit analysis: a method used for measuring the functional relationships between the major aspects of profits and for identifying the profit structure of an organization.

cosurety: one of a group of surety companies executing a bond. The obligation is joint and several, but common practice provides a stated limit of liability for each surety.

Council of Economic Advisers (CEA): in accordance with the Employment Act of 1946, a group of economists charged with advising the president on a variety of matters, including the preparation of the budget message to Congress. See also *Joint Economic Committee.*

Council on Wage and Price Stability (COWPS): a federal agency responsible for the monitoring of wage and price increases in the private sector; reviews government policies contributing to inflation and reports findings to Congress and the president.

counter
(1) *general:* a device for storing a number and allowing the number to be increased or decreased, as determined by instructions.
(2) *statistics:* a device used to represent the number of occurrences of an event.
(3) *retailing:* a bench or table for the display of goods.

counterclaim: a defendant's claim that the defendant is entitled to recover from the plaintiff.

countercyclical (policy): policy of leveling the ups and downs of the business cycle with budget deficits during depression and surpluses during prosperity. Synonymous with *compensatory fiscal policy.*

counterfeit: imitation or fraudulent money.

countermand: to cancel an order that has not yet been carried out.

counterpart monies: local currency equivalents of dollar assistance given to nations by the United States following World War II that are in turn used to purchase U.S. goods or services. Cf. *tied loan.*

counterpurchasing: placing an order with a manufacturer in one country with the expectation that merchandise of equal value and/or quantity will be sold in the opposite direction to the other nation.

countersignature
(1) *insurance:* the signature of a licensed agent or representative on a policy, which is necessary to validate the contract.
(2) *business law:* a signature added to a document to authenticate it. Cf. *attestation.*

countervailing power: the balancing out of the influence of one economic group with monopolistic power by the influence of another economic group with monopolistic power.

country bank: a national or state bank that is not located in a Federal Reserve city. Country banks' legal reserve requirements are usually less than those of large city banks.

country club billing: a billing system in which the account statement is accompanied by copies of original invoices. Cf. *descriptive billing.*

coupling up: the overlap of workers at the time of shift changes.

coupon:
(1) *postal service:* the part of a manifold registry bill, separated by perforations, that is used for receipt to the dispatching clerk.
(2) *securities:* the portion of a bond that is redeemable at a given date for interest payments. Cf. *talon.*
(3) *advertising:* a part of an advertisement that can be used for ordering items or redeeming premiums.

coupon bond: See *bond, coupon.*

coupon credit plan: See *charge account.*

court bond: See *bond, court.*

covenant: a contract pertaining to an undertaking, a promise, or an agreement to do or forbear from doing that which has legal validity and is legally enforceable.

coverage

(1) *advertising* the number of homes or persons exposed to a specific advertising medium in a controlled location.

(2) *insurance:* synonymous with *insurance, protection.*

(3) *finance:* the ratio of assets to specific liabilities.

covered option: an option in which the seller (or writer) owns the underlying security, as opposed to the uncovered (or naked) condition, under which the option is written against cash or other margin.

covering

(1) *securities:* buying a stock that was previously sold short.

(2) *finance:* the act of meeting one's obligation.

cover note: a document similar to a finder, usually issued by a reinsurer as evidence of reinsurance.

cow catcher: (slang) a brief announcement preceding a television or radio broadcast that features a product of the advertiser other than the ones associated with the program.

COWPS: see *Council on Wage and Price Stability.*

cow sociology: (slang) attempts by management consultants to humanize tasks performed on the job (e.g., an attempt to manipulate employees into placidity).

CPA: See *certified public accountant.*

CPCU: See *Chartered Property & Casualty Underwriter.*

CPI: See *Consumer Price Index.*

CPM: See *critical path method.*

CPU: See *central processing unit.*

craft: a manual occupation that requires extensive training, usually including apprenticeship, and a high degree of skill (e.g., carpentry, plumbing, linotype operation).

craft union: a union whose membership is limited to practitioners of a particular craft.

crash: a sudden and disastrous drop in business activity, prices, security values, and so on, as occurred in October of 1929.

crate: a rigid container consisting of slats of wood fastened together to protect the contents.

crawling peg: a foreign exchange rate that permits the par value of a country's currency to change automatically by small increments, upward or downward, if in actual daily trading on the foreign exchange markets the price in terms of other monies persists on the floor or ceiling of the established range for a given period.

cream: insurance policyholders that pay the lowest premiums, in part because they are the best risks.

creampuff sale: (slang) an easy sale of real property.

creative boutiques: advertising agencies that specialize in developing advertising and provide no other marketing services.

creative destruction: a process whereby the attraction of monopoly profits from new products motivates companies to do research and to evolve new products, which then replace products previously available and presumed to be inferior.

creativity: human activity that produces original ideas or knowledge, usually by testing combinations of data to achieve unique results. Cf. *cognition.*

credit

(1) *finance:* sales or purchases that are accompanied by a promise to pay later.

(2) *accounting:* an entry recorded on the right side of an ledger. Cf. *debit.*

(3) *banking:* funds remaining in a bank account. See also *bank credit.*

credit application: any form used to secure information relating to consumer credit. Questions often asked deal with a person's present and previous places of residence, work history, present earnings, other credit transactions, and outstanding loans. See also *trade reference.*

credit authorization/verification: an inquiry process undertaken to reduce the risk of credit fraud or of extending credit in excess of an imposed credit limit.

credit balance: See *balance of account.*

credit bureau: an agency that holds central files of data on consumers in a given trade area. These bureaus collect personal data, data on paying habits, and so on, and make impartial reports for credit granters.

credit card: a card issued by an organization that entitles the bearer to credit at its establishments (e.g., an Exxon credit card to be used at gas stations). There are single-purpose cards issued by a specific firm, multipurpose cards (e.g., American Express, Carte Blanche), and bank cards (e.g., Master Card and Visa).

credit contract: a written statement that shows how, when, and how much the purchaser will pay for goods and services.

credit instrument: a written guarantee to pay, that serves the purpose of money in consummating commercial exchanges, although actual money or bank notes are not used.

credit insurance: an insurance company guarantee to manufacturers, wholesalers, and service organizations that they will be paid for goods shipped or services rendered. It is a guarantee of the part of their working capital represented by accounts receivable.

credit investigation: an inquiry made by a lender to verify data given in a credit application or to investigate other aspects the creditor believes to be relevant to credit worthiness. See also *acid test ratio.*

credit life insurance: term life insurance, required by some lenders, that pays off a loan in the event of the borrower's death.

credit line: See *line of credit.*

creditor: one who is due money from another. Synonymous with *lender;* see also *guaranty.*

credit rating

(1) *banking:* the amount, type, and form of credit, if any, that a bank estimates can be extended to an applicant for credit.

(2) *finance:* an estimate of the credit and responsibility assigned to mercantile and other establishments by credit-investigating organizations.

credit report: a confidential report

made by an independent individual or organization that has investigated the financial standing, reputation, and record of an applicant for insurance.

credit-reporting agencies: organizations structured to supply to business and industry the information they need to reach credit, sales, financial, and general management decisions.

credit risk: the risk assumed for the possible nonpayment of credit extended.

credit sale: a sale in which the individual is given time to pay for the items purchased. There is an extra charge for this privilege.

credit terms: specification of the terms for payment of a credit obligation.

credit union: a cooperative financial organization established within and listed to a specific group of people. See also *Federal Credit Union, share drafts.*

credit worthy: receiving a favorable credit rating. An individual is thereby entitled to use the credit facilities of the organization(s) that requested the information. See also *open credit.*

creepers: (slang) people who steal property from office buildings, usually during the day.

creeping inflation: a gradual but continuing increase in the general price level, by as little as 2.5 percent a year. Cf. *flation.*

critical incident: a management-training tool whereby participants in a discussion describe major events in their experience that have caused them difficulty. See also *sensitivity training.*

critical path method (CPM): in planning and scheduling a complex series of operations, the sequence of events that are most critical as to timing; the longest path of activities in a system. CPM is based on the network analog principle and was first used in 1957 by E.I. du Pont de Nemours and Co. to improve the planning, scheduling, and coordination of its new-plant construction effort. Cf. *program evaluation and review technique (PERT).*

critical resource factor: that element in the manuacturing process that determines operating capacity by its availability.

critical size: the point at which existing practices and procedures become inadequate to maintain an organization's continuing expansion and growth.

crop hail insurance: protection for monetary loss resulting from hail damage to growing crops. Although hail is the basic peril named in these policies, a number of other perils are covered as well, depending on the crop and area.

cross check: a check by the National Labor Relations Board of union authorization cards against employer payroll to determine whether the union in fact has a majority. With the employer's consent, such cross-checking brings the union recognition and certification without a formal hearing and an election.

cross-elasticity: the impact on the demand for one product of price changes in a related product. For example, when the price of butter goes up, the price of margarine, a substitute, usually rises as well. See also *coefficient of cross-elasticity, elastic demand.*

crossover analysis: an approach to cost analysis that shows the optimum volume of activity that should be used in alternative means of manufacture.

cross-picketing: See *picketing.*

cross rates of exchange: comparisons of exchange rates between currencies that reveal whether it would be profitable to exchange the first currency for a second, the second for a third, then the third for the first.

crowding-out effect: the possibility that increased government borrowing might reduce private borrowing by raising interest rates.

CRU: See *collective reserve unit.*

crunch: an economic squeeze; a crisis created by some financial pressure.

CSS: See *Central Certificate Service.*

culling: mechanical or manual removal of letter-size mail from nonletter-size mail, such as small parcels and rolls and other oddly shaped material. At the same time, the mail may be separated into airmail, specials, small parcels, and flats.

Cummins Amendment: an amendment to the Interstate Commerce Act that affects the liability of carriers for loss of or damage to freight. See also *Interstate Commerce Act of 1877.*

cum right: the stockholder's right to acquire shares of a new issue of stock in a company in direct proportion to existing holdings. See also *rights.*

cumulative dividend: a dividend on cumulative preferred stock payable, under the terms of issue, at intervals and before any distribution is made to holders of common stock.

cumulative mark on: the difference between total delivered cost and total original retail values of merchandise handled within a stated time frame, inclusive of the accumulated inventory.

cumulative preferred (stock): a stock whose holders are entitled, if one or more dividends are omitted, to be paid on the omitted dividends before dividends are paid on the company's common stock.

cumulative quantity discount: a type of rebate given to a store when the total price of all goods purchased is identified. The objective is to encourage the dealer to give seller all his business in that line of trade.

cumulative voting: the right of each share of stock may cast as many votes for one director of the firm as there are directors who seek elected office.

curable depreciation: depreciated property that is still considered economically useful.

Curb Exchange: the name used before 1953 for the American Stock Exchange in New York City. See *American Stock Exchange.*

curing title: the removal of a claim from a title to make it marketable.

currency appreciation: increase in the relative value of a national currency under a flexible exchange rate system.

currency depreciation: decline in the relative value of a national currency under a flexible exchange rate system. See also *depreciation.*

currency leakage: a situation in which demand deposits are converted into cash and leave the banking system. See also *demand deposit.*

currency: paper money and coin.

current account:

(1) *finance:* a running account between two companies, reflecting the movement of cash, merchandise, and so on.

(2) *advertising:* customer names taken from a list and ranked in order of past business and potential activity.

current (floating) assets: the assets of a company that are reasonably expected to be realized in cash, sold, or consumed during the normal operating cycle of the business.

current budget: the budget prepared at some level of activity or operation for the following fiscal year.

current cost: what it might cost today to replace an asset or to acquire equivalent productive capacity.

current-dividend preference: the right of preferred shareholders to receive current dividends before common shareholders receive dividends.

current dollars: a term used to describe the actual prices of goods and services each year.

current earnings distribution: the present distribution of earned income, reflecting earlier discrimination in educational opportunities or employment or bad judgment. The concept is important because the distribution of earnings in the future may be expected to be different, even without further social changes or new government policies.

current exit value: what a company could sell an asset for (or remove a liability) in today's market.

current expensing: President Reagan's idea for reviving American capital spending and improving productivity allowing a business to deduct from its taxable income the cost of all capital assets, except land and buildings, in the year in which the goods are acquired.

current liabilities: money owed and payable by a company, usually within one year.

current operation expenditures: expenditures for salaries and wages, supplies, materials, and contractual services, other than capital outlays.

current ratio: the relationship between total current assets and total current liabilities. It is calculated by dividing current assets by current liabilities.

current value accounting: an accounting approach that requires the measurement of individual assets (e.g., factories, machines, and supplies) in current prices rather than in terms of the actual dollar costs at which they were acquired in earlier years.

curtesy: a husband's life interest in the property of his deceased spouse. Cf. *dower.*

cushion bond: See *bond, cushion.*

cushion checking (credit): a check overdraft plan that is also an instant loan. When a check is issued in excess of the customer's account balance or a request is made to transfer from the customer's cash reserve to his checking account, a loan is made for up to 36 months, with a modest interest charge.

cushioning: the protection of an item from physical damage by placing about its outer surfaces materials that have been designed to absorb the impact of external forces. See also *floatation.*

custodial approach to supervision: a paternalistic or "parent knows best" approach to dealing with employees. Cf. *collegial approach to supervision, supportive approach to supervision.*

customer: an individual or organization that makes a purchase.

customer-bank communication terminal (CBCT): the name given to a remote (i.e., not on bank premises) electronic device through which customers may withdraw, deposit, or transfer funds from or to their checking or savings accounts. Cf. *automated teller machine.*

customer departmentation: the grouping of jobs into subunits based on the customers to be served, a common practice in retail organizations.

customer oriented: describing the effort to comprehend the reasons, desires, and problems of the customer with the intent to use this information in fulfilling the customer's needs, and hopefully to increase sales and profits.

customer's broker (man): Synonymous with *registered representative.*

customer's ledger: a ledger that shows accounts receivable of each customer.

customhouse bond: See *bond, customhouse.*

customs: taxes imposed by a government on the import or export of items. Cf. *duty, tariff.*

customs union: an agreement by two or more trading countries to dissolve trade restrictions such as tariffs and quotas among themslves, and to develop a common external policy or trade (e.g., a trade agreement).

cutback
(1) *labor relations:* a layoff of employees caused by a reduction in available work. See also *work sharing.*
(2) *manufacturing:* reduction to a former level (e.g., in production).

cutoff date: a specific day chosen for stopping the flow of cash, goods, or other items for closing or audit reasons. Usually such a date is chosen if an inventory is scheduled when sales or purchases are to take place.

cutthroat competition: intensive competition that may lead to the bankruptcy of a major competitor, allowing the survivor to raise prices considerably. See also *rate war.*

cutting a melon: (slang) making an extra distribution of money or stock to shareholders, usually when preceded by an unusually profitable transaction (e.g., the sale of a subsidiary).

cybernetic control model: a system of control whereby deviations from standards are measured so that corrective action can be taken to bring the system back into balance.

cybernetics: a branch of learning that brings together theories and studies on communication and control in living organisms and machines; developed by Professor Norbert Wiener of MIT.

cycle billing: matching of alphabetical breakdowns to specific days to assist in customer billing. Each breakdown is a cycle and occurs on the same day every month.

cycle stock: the amount of inventory expected to be used during a particular cycle.

cyclical demand: variations in demand for a product due to such factors as war, elections, economic conditions, and sociological pressures. The cycles are typically greater than one year and less than five years.

cyclical forecast: changes in market demand that are primarily a result of general economic conditions.

cyclical inflation: periodic sudden increases in the general price level. Cf. *secular inflation.*

cyclical stocks: securities that go up and down in value with the trend of business, rising faster in periods of rapidly improving business condi-

tions and sliding very noticeably when business conditions deteriorate.

cyclical unemployment: unemployment caused by fluctuations in the economy due to downward trend in the business cycle. Cyclical unemployment involves many more jobs than seasonal, technological, or frictional unemployment. Cf. *chronic unemployment, hard-core unemployed;* see also *simultaneous inflation and unemployment.*

cyclic duty: work that is performed periodically.

daily reports: skeleton copies of insurance policies prepared for the agent and the company, consisting of the declarations page and fill-in endorsements. Cf. *policy register, scratch daily report.*

Daily Treasury Statement: a listing of transactions that clear through the U.S. Treasurer's account. For each business day it reflects cash deposits, cash withdrawals, and the status of the Treasurer's account.

damages

(1) *business law:* money awarded by the court to the plaintiff to be paid by the defendant as compensation for the plaintiff's loss.

(2) *real estate:* loss sustained by a person or his or her property.

(3) *real estate:* loss in value to remaining property when a portion of one's property is expropriated.

data

(1) *general:* a representation of facts, concepts, or instructions in a formalized manner, suitable for communication.

(2) *computers:* any representations such as characters or analog quantities to which meaning is, or might be, assigned.

(3) *statistics:* a collective mass of factual material used as basis for inference of conclusions. (The plural "data" is often incorrectly construed as singular. "Data" is the plural of "datum.")

data bank: a comprehensive collection of information on a principal subject and related areas.

data base: a collection of information specific to an operation, business, or enterprise.

data capture: the act of collecting data into a form that can be directly processed by a computer system. Some electronic funds-transfer systems are designed to capture transaction data at the precise time and place the transaction is consummated.

datamation: the flow of information by

136

way of a computer; formed from the words "data" and "automation."

data processing

(1) **computers:** the execution of a systematic sequence of operations performed on data.

(2) **computers:** any procedure used for receiving data and yielding a specific result. Synonymous with *"information processing."*

data reduction: the process of transforming large masses of data into useful, condensed, or simplified intelligence.

data sort: See *sort.*

date: the point in time, fixed by the year, month, and day, when an occurrence takes place. See also *effective date.*

date of record: the date, selected by a firm's board of directors, on which dividend-receiving shareholders are identified.

dating: a technique of extending credit beyond the time it was originally given; often used as an inducement to dealers to place orders far in advance of the coming season.

datum: the singular form of *data.*

Davis-Bacon Act of 1931: a federal law, amended in 1935, 1940, and 1964, to protect local labor wage standards and fringe benefits on government construction contracts. The act applies to all contracts of more than $2,000. Wages for these contracts are to be based on rates usually paid for the service in a particular geographic area—the going rate. The prevailing rate may be higher or lower than the union rate. See also *wage determination, Walsh-Healey Public Contracts Act of 1936.*

daylight trading: making a purchase

followed by a sale of a security on the same day, to avoid a holding position in the shares traded overnight or longer.

day loan: a one-day loan, granted for the purchase of stock, for the broker's convenience. Upon delivery, securities are pledged as collateral to secure a regular call loan.

day order: an order to buy or sell that, if not executed, expires at the end of the trading day on which it was entered.

days of grace: the reasonable length of time allowed, without suffering a loss or penalty, for postponed payment or for the presentment for payment of certain financial documents. See also *grace period.*

days sales invested in working capital: an alternative measure of the amount of working capital used in sustaining the sales of a period; computed by dividing 365 days by the working capital turnover.

deadbeat (slang)

(1) **general:** a person who tries to avoid paying for things.

(2) **finance:** a person who pays his or her entire charge every billing period, thus avoiding revolving credit charges.

deadheading

(1) **transportation:** the movement of empty vehicles or railcars to a destination point.

(2) **transportation:** the practice of providing free transportation for workers of a transportation firm.

(3) **labor relations:** bypassing seniority regulations and promoting a lower-level employee who is more capable of doing the job. Cf. *bumping.*

(4) **administration:** the moving of

workers required to report for assignments far from their homes.

dead letter: a letter deposited in the mail that is or becomes undeliverable or is unmailable and cannot be returned to the sender.

deadline

(1) *general:* the time, day, or other period on which something is due.

(2) *advertising:* the hour or day after which the advertising material will not be accepted to appear in a publication or specific broadcast time period.

dead pledge: a mortgage that is paid on time.

dead stock: merchandise that cannot be sold.

dead time: time lost by workers for lack of materials, machine breakdown, or other causes beyond their control. Cf. *down time.*

deadweight: weight of vessel or other carrier without any cargo.

deal: (slang) a large transaction involving a change in ownership.

dealer

(1) *general:* an individual or firm that divides quantity goods or services into smaller units for resale to customers.

(2) *securities:* an individual or firm in the securities business acting as a principal rather than as an agent. Typically, a dealer buys for his or her own account and sells to a customer from the dealer's inventory. The dealer's profit or loss is the difference between the price he pays and the price he receives for the same security. The dealer's confirmation must disclose to the customer that he has acted as principal. The same individual or firm may function, at different

times, both as broker and dealer.

dealer imprint: a dealer's name, address, or other identification, put on material created by an advertiser.

dealer tie-in: a manufacturer's advertisement given at a countrywide rate with a list of local dealers to be included in the ad.

deal stream: (slang) venture capitalist term for a businessman's strategy for finding capital from a venture-financing source. Traditionally, those with ideas who seek money are more numerous than those with money who look for ideas.

dear: costly, expensive, unusually high-priced.

dear money

(1) *banking:* a situation in which interest rates are high. See also *hard money.*

(2) *finance:* a situation created when loans are difficult to obtain because of the supply and demand for credit.

death benefit: See *principal sum.*

deauthorization: a procedure that permits unionized employees to vote to determine whether they desire an open shop.

debase: to reduce the quality, purity, or content or otherwise alter the accepted intrinsic value of the coinage of a realm.

debenture

(1) *finance:* a term used to define indebtedness, usually in long-term obligations, that is unsecured.

(2) *business:* corporate obligations that are sold as investments.

(3) *business law:* a voucher or certificate acknowledging that a debt is owed by the signer.

debenture bond: See *bond, deben-*

ture.

debit

(1) ***accounting:*** any amount in dollars and cents that, when posted, will increase the balance of an asset or expense account and decrease the balance of a liability account. All asset and expense accounts normally have debit balances, and all liability, capital, and income accounts normally have credit balances. Cf. *credit.*

(2) ***securities:*** the portion of the purchase price of stock, bonds, or commodities that is covered by credit extended by a broker to margin customers.

(3) ***insurance:*** a weekly premium life insurance agent's list of all the premiums he or she is required to collect.

debit balance: See *balance of account.*

debit card: a cash machine automator and a check guarantee; a recent innovation that permits bank customers to withdraw cash at any hour from any affiliated automated teller machine in the country and to make cashless purchases from funds on deposit without incurring revolving finance charges for credit.

debris removal: describing coverage for the cost incurred in removing debris of covered property resulting from damage covered property resulting from damage caused by an insured peril.

debt: money, services, or materials owed to another person as the result of a previous agreement. See also *effective debt, funded debt, gross debt, total debt.*

debt capital: funds borrowed to fi-

nance the operations of a business.

debt ceiling: as controlled by Congress, the maximum limit on the federal debt. At times Congress has raised the debt ceiling.

debtee: a creditor.

debt financing: raising money or capital by borrowing. Cf. *equity financing.*

debt limit: the maximum amount of money that a state or local government can borrow; usually set by legislation of the state involved.

debt management: managing the sale of new federal securities to repay owners of maturing securities and to cover budget deficits.

debtor: one who owes money to another.

debtor nation: a country whose citizens, companies, and government owe more to foreign creditors than foreign debtors owe them.

debt service: interest payments and capital reduction on government, industrial, or other long-term bonds.

debt to net worth ratio: all liabilities divided by net value.

debug

(1) ***computers:*** to detect, locate, and remove mistakes from a routine or malfunction of a computer. Synonymous with *troubleshoot;* see also *postmortem; postmortem dump; test, diagnostic; volume test.*

(2) ***computers:*** to test a program on a computer to determine whether it works properly.

debureaucratization: a basic approach for shifting and delegating power and authority from a central point to subordinate levels within an organization's hierarchy to promote independence, responsibility, and more rapid decision making in implementing policies and programs to serve the needs of those levels. See also *bureaucracy.*

deceased account: a bank deposit account in the name of a deceased person. Upon notification of death, the bank segregates the decedent's account and withholds release of funds until a court of law authorizes payment to the legal heirs. See also *frozen account.*

decedent: a deceased person.

deceit: conduct in business whereby one person, through fraudulent representations, misleads another person who has the right to rely on such representations as the truth or is unable to detect the fraud. See also *estoppel;* cf. *false advertising.*

decentralization:

(1) *administration:* placing the decision-making point at the lowest managerial level, involving delegation of decision-making authority. Cf. *autocratic.*

(2) *government:* the distribution of power and responsibility from a national authority to local or state governments.

(3) *economics:* the redistribution of population and business from a city to its suburban areas.

decertification: an order by the National Labor Relations Board ending the representation rights of a union, pursuant to a vote of the workers, in an NLRB election. This is done following a petition asserting that the union no longer represents the majority of the employees. See also *Taft-Hartley Act.*

decision: a court's final judgment.

decisional roles: the roles of entre-preneur, resource allocator, disturbance handler, and negotiator. A manager who takes on these roles plays a key part in the decision-making system of the organization.

decision maker: a person, usually a member of a group, who either has the authority to make a decision or the ability to influence other members of the group.

decision making: the process of resolving differing options into one opinion or course of action so that, when supported by authority, the decision becomes a policy of the organization.

decision of coordination: an operative decision concerning the integration of activities within a firm.

decision theory model: model that focuses upon certain elements in decision making that are common to all decisions and provides means to enable a decision maker to better analyze a complex situation that contains numerous alternatives and possible consequences. This theory is strongly rooted in the fields of statistics and the behavioral science.

decision to participate: according to a proposition developed by J. G. March and H. A. Simon, the decision by an individual to continue to participate in an organization so long as the inducements provided are as great as or greater than the contributions he or she is asked to make. Cf. *dissatisfiers.*

decision to produce: according to a proposition developed by March and Simon, the decision to be a productive member of an organization, depending on the alternatives available to the person, the perceived consequences of adopting a particular production approach, and the person's own objectives.

decision tree: a description of the sequence of decision choices and the possible occurrence of chance events.

deck: a collection of computer cards.

declaration

(1) *general:* the full disclosure of items, property, or income (e.g., a customs declaration).

(2) *insurance:* a statement by an applicant for insurance, usually relating to underwriting information. Sometimes, as in most casualty and property policies, this is copied into into the policy. See also *representation;* cf. *evidence of insurability.*

(3) *business law:* the first pleading in an action.

declaration date: the date on which payment of a dividend is authorized by a corporation's board of directors.

declaration of trust: a written agreement that property to which one person holds title actually belongs to another person, for whose benefit the title is maintained. See also *fiduciary.*

declaratory judgment: a court's determination on a question of law, stating the parties' rights without ordering any action.

declared value: the value of merchandise stated by the owner when the goods are delivered to the carrier.

decline stage: the period in a product's life cycle between saturation and abandonment. Since sales are dropping, costs are carefully controlled to minimize added losses.

declining balance depreciation: a depreciation method that charges larger amounts of depreciation expense in earlier years and lesser amounts later.

decoding: the application of a set of unambiguous rules that specify the way in which data may be restored to a previous representation.

decomposition method: a method of forecasting for regions whereby a national forecast is broken down or decomposed into regional forecasts based on population or some other relevant variable or variables.

deconglomeration: a form of organization whereby a corporation is split into two or more units, each with a carefully defined product or service and its own common stock, table of organization, and plan for growth. Synonymous with *pluralism.*

de-crater: a machine that unloads items from crates automatically.

decreasing costs: costs that decline as output per unit increases.

decree: a judge's conclusion in a suit in equity (e.g., an order that an agreement be put into effect immediately).

decrement: a loss in value.

dedomiciling: relocating the headquarters of an international firm to a country where there is less or no taxation of foreign income and few restrictions on foreign investment.

deductible clause: a provision making an insurance company liable only for the excess of a stated amount, to be deducted from any loss. This is used largely on risks for which many small losses may be expected, such as scratches or dents to automobile bodies. Cf. *franchise clause.*

deductible insurance: a method of coverage under which a policyholder agrees to contribute up to a specified sum per claim or per accident toward the total amount of insured loss. Insurance is written on this basis at reduced rates. Cf. *full coverage.*

deduction

(1) *general:* the logical process of drawing conclusions from a set of assertions or hypotheses.

(2) *accounting:* an item that can be subtracted from income in defining taxable income (e.g., contributions to charities, certain payments of interest, and some taxes).

deductions from gross income: amounts allowed by the Interstate Commerce Commission as deductions in arriving at gross income (e.g., rents, taxes, interest). See also *Interstate Commerce Commission, itemized deductions, Tax Reform Act of 1976.*

deductive method: an approach to scientific inquiry in which a premise that has been accepted to be true becomes the basis of additional logical reasoning. Cf. *inductive method.*

deed: a formal, written agreement of transfer by which title to an estate or other real property is transmitted from one person to another. See also *quit claim deed, warranty deed.*

deed, general warranty: a deed that carries an agreement of warranty. The seller will warrant and defend the title against all claims. This is the best possible form of deed for the buyer.

deed, quit claim: See *quit claim deed.*

deed, special warranty: a deed in which the seller warrants only claims against himself or his heirs, not against previous owners.

deed in lieu of foreclosure: a mortgagor's way of presenting title to the mortgagee to prevent foreclosure of property.

deed of release: a deed that releases property from the lien of a mortgage.

deed of surrender: an instrument by which property is identified as an estate for life or an estate for a specified number of years to a person who will receive it in reversion.

deed of trust: a deed that is placed in trust with a third party to ensure payment of the indebtedness or to ensure that other conditions of the transaction are met. Upon satisfaction of the debt, the third party transmits the deed to the purchaser, freeing the third party from future responsibilities.

deep stock: frequently used merchandise kept in large quantities and in many sizes and colors.

de facto: in actual fact (Latin); in reality; actually; existing, regardless of legal or moral consideration (e.g., de facto segregation; de facto discrimination in employment). Cf. *de jure.*

defalcation: situation that occurs when an individual in a trust or fiduciary position is unable, by his own fault, to account for funds left in his hands; often interchangeable with embezzlement or misappropriation of funds. Cf. *peculation.*

defamation: words that attribute disreputable conduct or immoral behavior to the person of whom they are spoken.

default: the failure to do that which is required by law or to perform on an obligation previously committed. The term is commonly used when some legally constituted governing body fails to pay the principal or interest on its bond or fails to meet other financial obligations on maturity.

defeasance clause: the clause of a mortgage that is intended to define the terms and conditions upon which the mortgage will be satisfied, will cease to be security for a debt, and will become void.

defeasible: able to be annulled or made void.

defend-and-hold strategy: investment and marketing efforts designed to maintain sales and profit levels for a particular service or product.

defendant: an individual sued in a court of law; the individual answering the complaint of a plaintiff.

defense fund: Synonymous with *strike fund.*

defense mechanism: any enduring structure of the psyche that enables a person to avoid awareness of or the negative effects of something that is unpleasant or anxiety arousing. Examples are withdrawal, aggression, substitution, compensation, repression, and rationalization.

defensive behavior: the behavior of an employee who is or perceives himself or herself to be blocked in attempts to satisfy his or her needs in reaching a goal and who makes use of one or more defense mechanisms.

defensive investment: an investment policy that places its major effort on reducing both the risk of (eventual) loss and the need for special knowledge, skill, and continuous attention. Cf. *speculation.*

defensive technology: technology that is concerned with toxicology, pollution control, work safety, and quality control.

deferrals: cash collected before revenue is recognized as being earned or cash disbursed before an expense is recognized as being incurred.

deferred air freight: property received for shipment by an air carrier on a space-available basis after acceptance of all other revenue traffic.

deferred annuity: an annuity contract that provides for the postponement of the start of an annuity until after a specified period or until the annuitant attains a specified age.

deferred charges: expenditures that are written off over a time period.

deferred compensation: the postponement of distribution of a portion of current earnings until a later date, usually at retirement. The object of deferred compensation is to reduce current income taxes by postponing receipt of taxable income until a time when the receiver will likely be in a lower income tax bracket.

deferred credit: a credit that has been delayed in posting for some reason (e.g., a deposit that came into a bank after business hours and is therefore entered on the books in the following day's business.

deferred expense: an asset that has been created through the payment of cash by an entity before it will obtain benefits from that payment. Basically synonymous with *prepaid expense.*

deferred income taxes: the difference between income tax expense, calculated as a function of accounting income based on generally accepted accounting principles, and current taxes payable, calculated as a function of taxable income based on the Internal Revenue Code and other tax codes.

deferred payments
(1) *real estate:* mortgage allowances for postponement of inter-

est payments; a type of installment plan.

(2) *finance:* delayed payments postponed until a future time, usually against some future period.

deferred payment sale

(1) *retailing:* buying on installment. See also *layaway plan.*

(2) *sales:* a sale that is extended beyond a customary credit period.

deferred premium file: an electronic tape file maintained by a company office and used to record and report premium payments when due.

deferred revenue: a liability that has been created through the receipt of cash by an entity before its performance of a service or the sale of goods.

deferred sale contract: a contract in which a purchaser pays the owner all or part of the sale price of a property through an obligation other than cash.

deferred serial bond: See *bond, deferred serial.*

deferred stock: stocks whose dividends are not to be paid until the expiration of a stated date or until a specified event has taken place.

deferred tax: a tax liability accrued on income that is reported but not subject to income tax until a later time period.

deferred wage increase: a future increase specified in a union contract (e.g., 10 cents the second year, 5 cents the third).

deficit

(1) *general:* the amount of obligations and expenditures affecting a given budget period that is in excess of the budget established for the period.

(2) *finance:* obligations or ex-

penditures for items that are in excess of the amount allotted for those items in a financial budget.

(3) *accounting:* the excess of liabilities over assets.

(4) *business:* outgo in excess of income for a fiscal period.

deficit financing: when government expenditures exceed revenues, making up difference by borrowing. The objective is to expand business activity and yield an improvement in general economic conditions. The deficit is covered by release of government bonds. Cf. *deficit spending.*

deficit spending: the spending of public funds raised by borrowing rather than by taxation; a fiscal activity often associated with a government that spends more than it collects from taxes and other revenues. Some fiscal policy experts point out that an increase in the deficit stimulates the economy, whereas a decrease in the deficit has the opposite effect. Cf. *deficit financing.*

deficit weight: the difference between actual shipment weight and the minimum weight when the actual is less than the minimum.

definitive bond: See *bond, definitive.*

deflation

(1) *general:* a decline in the general price level, resulting in an increase in the purchasing power of money.

(2) *economics:* the lessening of the amount of money in circulation.

deflationary gap: the amount by which demand falls short of full employment supply, thus lowering the real value of a nation's output.

defraud: to deprive an individual, by deceit, of some right; to cheat; to withhold improperly that which belongs to another.

defray: to pay; to carry an expense (e.g., a court settlement may include an amount of money to defray the legal costs of the winning party).

defunct company: a firm that has ceased to exist; a dissolved organization.

defusion conflict resolution: a strategy that attempts to buy time to resolve intergroup conflict later, when it is less emotional or less crucial.

degree of freedom (d.o.f.): a concept in organizational theory that describes a person's exemption or liberation from the control of some other person or power. Often, within a tightly controlled company where the president dominates, employees are allowed a minimal degree of freedom. Cf. *autocratic.*

degressive taxation: a type of progressive taxation whereby the rates increase as the base amount taxed increases and each addition to the tax rate is lower than the preceding one.

dehire: to discharge from a position.

de jure: by right (Latin); rightful, legitimate, just; according to law or equity; a term describing a state of affairs or a condition based on right or law, as distinguished from one that exists de facto. Cf. *de facto.*

delayed broadcast: a repeat broadcast of a program, often used to compensate for time differentials between station locations of a network.

delayed opening: the situation created when buy and sell orders accumulate prior to the opening of a stock exchange.

del credere agency: an agency, factor, or broker who attempts to guarantee to his or her principal the payment of a buyer's debt.

delectus personae: chosen or selected person (Latin), as a designated partner.

delegated strategy: an approach that precludes participation by management. Through case discussion or sensitivity training, the employees determine an organizational development program. See also *organic structure;* cf. *autocratic.*

delegation: the process by which authority is distributed downward in the organization. See also *chain of command.*

delinquency: failure to pay a debt when due.

delinquent tax: a tax that is unpaid after the date when the payment was expected.

delisting: the removal or cancellation, by the SEC, of rights previously given to a listed security. This usually occurs when a security fails to meet some of the requirements for the listing privilege.

delivered cost: the price at which goods are billed to a store, including transportation charges.

delivery
(1) *general:* the transfer of possession of an item from one person to another.
(2) *securities:* the transmission of the certificate representing shares bought on a securities exchange; delivery is usually made to the purchaser's broker on the fourth business day after the transaction. See also *good delivery, seller's seven sale, settlement day.*

delivery date

(1) *retailing:* the date by which a vendor must ship purchases to a store in order to comply with the agreed-upon terms. Failure by the store to meet this deadline is considered reason for cancellation of the order.

(2) *securities:* formally, the first day of the month during which delivery is to be made under a futures contract. Since sales are made at the seller's option, however, the seller can make delivery on any day of the month, following proper notification to the buyer.

Delphi technique: a forecasting approach whereby, at intervals, the organization polls experts who predict long-range technological and market changes that eventually will affect the organization.

deluxe items: higher priced, unique goods maintained for sale to wealthier customers.

demand

(1) *business:* the willingness and capability to purchase goods or services. See also *market demand, reciprocal demand.*

(2) *business law:* a claim or the assertion of a legal right.

(3) *finance:* a request to call for payment or for the carrying out of an obligation. See also *sight draft.*

demand curve: the graphic representation of the quantity of goods demanded in relation to price. On each point of the curve, the consumer is in equilibrium and the value of the item equals its price. See also *excess demand curve.*

demand deposit: a deposit on account in a commercial bank on which checks can be drawn and funds taken out without any advance notification. Demand deposits are the greatest part of our money supply.

demand loan: a loan that has no fixed maturity date but is payable on demand of the bank making the loan. Demand loans can be called by a bank at any time payment is desired.

demand note: a note or mortgage that can be demanded at any time for payment by the holder. See also *scrip.*

demand price: the maximum price a purchaser is willing to pay for a stated quantity of a commodity or service.

demand-pull inflation: an increase in the price level created by an abundance of money for too few commodities. The demand for items is greater than the capability to produce or supply them.

demand schedule: a table illustrating the number of units of an item that purchasers would be able and willing to buy at differing prices at a specified time period, all other variables remaining constant.

demarketing: term coined by Philip Kotler and Sidney J. Levy for the concept that part of marketing attempts to discourage customers, either individually or collectively, from desiring a good or service.

democratic leadership: a participative or group-centered leadership in that the leader in charge attempts to encourage and aid workers in achieving goals by (1) requesting maximum initiative from and participation by members in deciding on and carrying out certain policies; (2) distributing or decreasing his leadership or authority roles and establishing close relationships with members; and (3) motivating and developing, rather than ordering or criticizing. See also *distributive leadership, permissive leadership.*

demolition clause: coverage provided by an endorsement because standard fire policies exclude liability for any loss caused by the demolition of an undamaged portion of the building due to the enforcement of "ordinance or law regulating construction or repair."

demonetization

(1) *finance:* the withdrawal of specified currency from circulation.

(2) *banking:* the reduction in the number of government bonds and securities by a commercial bank, resulting in an increase in the value of deposit and paper currency, including Federal Reserve notes.

demotion: change of a worker's status to a lower classification, salary, or title.

demurrage: detention of a freight car or ship beyond the time permitted for loading or unloading, with additional charges for detention. See also *average demurrage agreement.*

demurrer: a method of procedure in a law suit whereby the defendant admits the validity of all the plaintiff's complaints but denies that the facts warrant a cause of action. Cf. *cognovit, nonsuit.*

denomination value: the face value of currencies, coins, and securities.

density: the ratio of an item's weight to its bulk or volume.

department: a major executive or administrative unit within an organization.

departmentalization: the manner in which an organization is structurally divided—for example, by function, territory, product, customer, or task.

departmentation: the organizing process of establising subunits based on some common characteristic. Jobs are thus grouped by common functions, products, territories, customers, or processes.

department manager: an executive charged with the operation of a selling department of a store. Often this individual is the buyer, but he or she may also be involved with stock and sales.

Department of Agriculture, U.S.: the federal department established in 1889 to conduct farm educational and research programs and to administer numerous federal agricultural-aid programs and other projects to aid farmers and ranchers.

Department of Commerce, U.S.: the federal department established in 1913 to promote domestic and foreign trade of the country.

Department of Energy (DOE), U.S.: the federal department established in 1977 to control oil prices and allocations, to coordinate energy research and development efforts, to set rates for oil and oil-product appliances, and to establish energy conservation standards. See also *Federal Energy Administration.*

Department of Housing and Urban Development (HUD), U.S.: the federal agency formed in 1965 to be responsible for national programs dealing with housing needs and urban renewal and development. See also *Government National Mortgage Association.*

Department of Justice, U.S.: the federal agency created in 1870 with supervisory powers over federal prosecuting agencies, representing the federal government to the courts. The department has jurisdiction over issues of antitrust and civil rights and supervises the government's activities relating to immigration.

Department of Labor, U.S.: the federal agency created in 1913 to advance workers' welfare, working conditions, and employment opportunities in general.

Department of the Treasury, U.S.: the federal agency created in 1789 to impose and collect taxes and customs duties, to enforce revenue and fiscal laws, to disburse federal funds, to manage the public debt, and to coin and print money.

Department of Transportation (DOT), U.S.: the federal agency created in 1966 to promote a coordinated national transportation policy embracing all media except water transport. See also *Federal Aviation Administration.*

department store: a retail organization that employs 25 or more people and sells merchandise in the following categories: home furnishings; apparel for men, women, and children; and home linens and dry goods.

department store banking: Synonymous with *multiple banking.*

dependency ratio: the ratio between the number of workers in a society and the number of people who are retired.

dependent: an individual who requires support from another, as distinguished from one who merely derives a benefit from the earnings of another. See also *dependents.*

dependent covenants: two or more related agreements by which the performance of one promise must take place before the performance of other promises (e.g., a buyer must pay for goods before the purchased items will be delivered).

dependent nations: nations that rely heavily on other nations for imports of essential goods.

dependents
(1) *insurance:* an insured employee's spouse and unmarried children who meet certain eligibility requirements for coverage under a life or health plan.
(2) *taxation:* relatives or nonrelatives receiving more than half of their support from a taxpayer. Under Internal Revenue law, an exemption is provided for dependents.

depersonalism: the attempt to dehumanize a situation or to remove the human factor when managing.

depletion: an accounting practice consisting of charges against earnings based on the amount of an asset taken out of the total reserves in the period for which accounting is made. A bookkeeping entry, depletion does not represent any cash outlay, nor are any funds earmarked for the purpose.

depletion allowance: as permitted by the Internal Revenue Code, a deduction from taxable income derived from a wasting asset. The basis of the allowance is either a percentage of the gross income from specified property or a per-unit-of-product condition.

deposit: an amount of funds consisting of cash and/or checks, drafts, coupons, and other credit items that may be converted into cash upon collection. The deposit is given to a bank for the purpose of establishing and maintaining a credit balance.

depositary: an individual or institution identified as one to be entrusted with something of value for safekeeping (e.g., a bank or trust company).

depositary receipt: a mechanism to allow for the trading of foreign stocks on U.S. stock exchanges when the overseas nation involved will not allow foreign ownership of the stock of domestic firms. The shares are therefore deposited with a bank in the country of corporation and an affiliated or correspondent bank in the United States issues depositary receipts for the securities. U.S. investors buy these receipts and can trade them on an appropriate American stock exchange in the same way as other stocks. The major purpose of the instrument is to officially identify ownership of the stock in the foreign country.

deposit contraction: an excess of loan repayments to commercial banks over new loans.

deposit creation multiplier: the dollars of lending generated by an independent increase of one dollar in bank deposits.

deposit currency: checks and other credit items deposited with a bank as the equivalent of cash.

deposit expansion: an excess of new commercial bank loans over loan repayments.

deposit funds: funds established to account for collection that either are held in suspense temporarily and later refunded or are paid into some other fund of the government or held by the government as banker or agent for others. Cf. *escrow.*

deposit insurance: insurance to protect the depositor against bankruptcy of a bank or a savings and loan institution. See also *Federal Deposit Insurance Corporation.*

deposition: testimony not given in open court but taken by written or oral questionings, signed and witnessed, and ultimately used like testimony in court.

depositor: an individual, partnership, business proprietorship, corporation, organization, or association in whose name funds have been placed in a bank.

depository bond: See *bond, depository.*

Depository Institutions Deregulation Committee: committee created by Congress in the spring of 1980, charged with deregulation of the bank and savings industry. It has a panel of five voting members: the Federal Reserve Board chairman, the Treasury Secretary, and the chairmen of the Federal Home Loan Bank Board, the Federal Deposit Insurance Corporation, and the National Credit Union Administration.

deposit premium: the deposit on premiums required by the company on forms of insurance subject to periodic premium adjustment.

depot store: a store carrying popular items that customers purchase because of the store's convenient location. In most cases, the customer is charged higher prices for the items than in supermarkets, discount stores, and other nondepot outlets.

depreciated cost: cost less accumulated depreciation and less other valuation accounts, having the effect of reducing the original outlay to a recoverable cost; the book value of a fixed asset.

depreciation

(1) *accounting:* normally, charges against earnings to write off the cost, less salvage value, of an asset over its estimated useful life. It is a bookkeeping entry and does not represent any cash outlay, nor are any funds earmarked for the purpose. Synonymous with *capital consumption allowance;* see also *book depreciation, declining balance depreciation.*

(2) *real estate:* a decline in the value of property.

depreciation base: the amount that the Internal Revenue Service recognizes as depreciable on a property's improvements. For depreciation purposes, the value of the land and that of the improvements must be determined separately.

depreciation charges: charges made by private business and nonprofit institutions against receipts to account for the decrease in value of capital assets as a result of wear, accidental damage, and obsolescence, plus an estimate of corresponding depreciation in owner-occupied dwellings.

depressed area: a community that is not part of the nation's economic growth pattern and has a high level of unemployment; sometimes referred to as a distressed area. See also *Area Redevelopment Program.*

depression: an economic condition in which business activity is down over a long period, prices drop, purchasing power is greatly reduced, and unemployment is high.

Depression of the 1930s: the Great Depression, a severe economic crisis that afflicted the United States and also affected worldwide business; thought to have begun with the collapse of the stock market in October 1929 and finally ended in the early 1940s, when defense spending for World War II strengthened the general economy. See also *New Deal.*

depth interview: a method, based primarily on the use of open-ended questions, to elicit from the person interviewed natural and lengthy statements about a predetermined subject. Cf. *interest inventory, interview, structured.*

dereliction: the intentional abandonment of property. Derelict property is any property forsaken or discarded in a way indicating that the owner has no further use or need of it.

derivative departments: departments formed through the subdivision of major departments (e.g., derivative production departments could include manufacturing and purchasing).

derivative deposit: a deposit that is created when a person borrows money from a bank (e.g., deposit currency). A customer is loaned a sum, not in money but by credit to his account, against which he or she may draw checks as required.

derived demand: the demand for an item that grows out of the wish to fulfill the demand for another item (e.g., when a demand for community tennis courts is filled, it leads to increased sales of supplies for the courts and tennis equipment). Cf. *suggestive selling.*

descent: the passing of property, or title to the property, by inheritance, as contrasted with request or purchase.

descriptive billing: a billing system in which an account statement is not accompanied by copies of original invoices. Instead, the statement contains sufficient detail to permit the customer to identify the nature, date, and amount of each transaction processed during the statement period. Cf. *country club billing.*

descriptive decision making: a viewpoint of decision making that emphasizes what is occurring or what has happened in reaching the decision. It describes the decision and its process.

descriptive model: a model that describes how a system works. It describes things as they are and makes no value judgments about the particular factors being studied. It may display the alternative choices available to the decision maker, but it does not select the best alternative.

descriptive research: research concerned with determining the nature of something (e.g., the morale of employees).

desired investment: investments in plant, equipment, buildings, and inventories that were deliberately undertaken, as compared with inventory changes forced on a company by a period of slow sales.

desk audit: a systematic process of interviewing and/or observing workers at their place of activity to measure and identify factors affecting the completion of stated objectives. Synonymous with *work audit.*

deskilled: describing simple tasks or jobs that, because of work simplification or other reasons, require little or no skill to perform; also said of work-

ers who perform such tasks or jobs. See also *work simplification.*

desk jockey: (slang) an office employee; a person who works at an office desk.

detail operation schedule: a production control schedule covering minor details of the items produced.

detention time: additional charges made by the carrier when there is a lack of equipment or space on a store's receiving docks to enable the carrier to unload merchandise.

determinant attributes: product characteristics that help consumers discriminate among products and that influence product preferences. See also *brand awareness.*

deterministic properties: characterizing something that does not vary (e.g., if midnight is always at 12:00 P.M., then this time is a deterministic property of midnight).

detinue: a common law action to recover property.

devaluation: an action taken by the government to reduce the value of the domestic currency in terms of gold or foreign monies.

development

(1) *general:* a gradual unfolding by virtue of which something comes to be.

(2) *administration:* a criterion of effectiveness that refers to the ability of an organization to increase its capacity to react to existing or anticipated pressures.

(3) *real estate:* a venture on a large scale.

development expense: the cost of developing products, processes, or other commercial activities to make them functional.

development loan: a short-term loan, generally up to three years, for the development of unimproved land by the installation of utilities, drainage, sewers, and roads.

deviation

(1) *statistics:* a measure of dispersion, calculated to be the difference between the particular number or item and the average, which is usually the arithmetic mean, or a set of numbers or items. See also *deviation, standard.*

(2) *insurance:* a rate or policy form differing from that published by a rating bureau.

deviation, standard (SD): the square root of the arithmetic mean of the squares of the deviations from the mean of the series.

devise: a gift, often real property, given in a last will and testament.

devisee: any person receiving title to real property in accordance with the terms of a will. See also *lucrative title.*

devisor: the donor of a gift of real property by will.

devolution: the passing of real estate title by hereditary succession.

dexterity test: a measure of speed and accuracy in performing simple manual activities.

diagnostic activities: fact finding or data collection that attempts to determine what is occurring within a unit or organization.

diagonal communication: communication that involves the flow of information across departments or people at different levels of the hierarchy. It allows for messages to be transmitted directly instead of emanating from the bottom up to the top and down again.

diagonal expansion: a process whereby a business grows by creating new items that can be produced with the equipment that is already in use, requiring few additional materials.

dialectical materialism: as employed by Karl Marx, the idea that historical change results from the opposition of conflicting elements of society and that these forces are primarily economic or materialistic.

dialectic process of change: the concept that any change introduced by management will create a new situation out of which new problems will develop.

diamond-water paradox: an argument of Adam Smith's theory that asks why there is such a high demand for diamonds and a low demand for water when water is a necessity and diamonds are a luxury.

diary method: a technique used to determine brand purchase and frequency of buying. The user makes arrangements with households to keep a continuous log of brands purchased day by day over a specified period. See also *Videodex;* cf. *aided recall.*

dicta: rules or arguments given in the written statement of a judge that have no bearing on issues involved and are not critical for their determination (singular, "dictum").

Dictionary of Occupational Titles (DOT): published by the U.S. Employment Service, a reference book that lists alphabetically and describes 20,000 jobs. It is the most complete source book of its kind. See also *occupational analysis;* cf. *Standard In-*

dustrial Classification System.

Diemer plan: a wage incentive plan providing for the regular day rates to be paid plus an increase of 0.5 percent salary for each 1 percent production above the task, with a bonus of 10 percent.

dies non: a day on which no business can be transacted (Latin).

differential advantages: selling characteristics that provide an advantage over competitors. These include price, product features, location, method of delivery, advertising skills, packaging, and brand name.

differential analyzer: an analog computer that uses interconnected integrators to solve differential equations.

differential costs: the difference in costs between an actual situation and a proposed one.

differential marginal productivity: condition that exists when the marginal product of a productive factor drops when more of the productive factor is added to the given quantities of other factors.

differential oligopoly: an industry composed of a small number of sellers manufacturing products that are only slightly different.

differential piece-rate system: an inventive wage system whereby a fixed rate is paid for all production up to standard but there is a higher rate for all pieces once the standard is crossed.

differentiated marketing: a form of market segmentation in which the marketer employs different products and/or different marketing programs to reach two or more market segments.

differentiation: the process by which subunits in an organization develop particular attributes in response to the requirements imposed by their subenvironments. The greater the differences among the subunits' attributes, the greater the differentiation.

diffusion theory: the theory that tax income is eventually distributed throughout the population by price alterations or other means whereby funds find their way to the government.

digested securities: securities owned by investors who are not expected to sell them soon. Cf. *stag.*

digit: a component of an item of data; a character position in a computer that may assume one of several values; one of the symbols 0, 1, . . ., 9 (e.g., the number 557 contains three digits but is composed of two types of characters, 5 and 7).

digital computer: a computer in which discrete representation of data is used. It performs arithmetic and logic processes on these data, with numbers expressing all quantities and variables of a problem. Cf. *analog computer.*

dilution

(1) *general:* the watering down or weakening of something.

(2) *securities:* the effect of a drop in earnings per share or book value per share caused by the potential conversion of securities or by the potential exercise of warrants or options.

dimension of planning: the five factors involved in planning: organization, subject, elements, time, and characteristics.

diminishing marginal utility law: the concept that, in a specified period, the consumption of an item while tastes stay the same can lead to increasing marginal utilities per unit of the item consumed, but a point will be reached when additional units of consumption of the item will lead to decreasing marginal utilities per unit of the item consumed.

diminishing relative values: the concept that the value to a person of item A in terms of item B declines if there is a greater consumption of item A and less of item B, resulting in a condition under which the person is no better or worse off.

diminishing returns: a condition that exists when, in successively applying equal amounts of one or two factors of production (e.g., land and capital) to the remaining factor(s), an additional application produces a smaller increase in production than the preceding application. Cf. *indifference schedule, point of ideal proportion.*

direct advertising: print advertising sent by mail to prospects, salesmen, and dealers, in contrast to advertising presented by other media. Synonymous with *direct-mail advertising.*

direct control: the process of developing better managers to make more skillful use of concepts, principles, and techniques to reduce the amount and degree of undesirable results.

direct cost: the cost of any good or service that contributes to the production of an item or service (e.g., labor, material). Cf. *indirect costs;* see also *running costs.*

direct costing: a technique for implementing the economic theory of mar-ginal analysis to assist a firm in making short-term business decisions.

direct deposit of payroll: a payroll system in which employee earnings are deposited directly to the employee's account at a depository institution.

direct expenditures: payments to employees, suppliers, contractors, beneficiaries, and other final recipients of government payment (i.e., all expenditures other than intergovernmental expenditure).

direct expense: Synonymous with *direct cost.*

direct financial compensation: the pay a person receives in the form of wages, salaries, bonuses, and commissions.

direct financing: raising capital without resorting to underwriting (e.g., by selling capital stock).

direct investments: investments in foreign corporations when the investors have a controlling interest in the overseas firm.

directive counseling: the process of listening to an employee's emotional problems, deciding with the worker what should be done, and then telling and motivating the employee to do it. See also *cooperative counseling, nondirective counseling.*

directive leadership: a style of providing direction in group activities that is leader-centered. The leader makes most decisions, is task oriented, and provides little freedom of action for subordinates.

direct labor: the cost of wages paid to workers.

direct liability: a debtor's obligation arising from money, goods, or services received by him or her from an-other.

direct-mail advertising: the use of mail for the communication of a direct advertisement. See, e.g., *envelope stuffer, self-mailer.*

direct-mail list: names and addresses of potential customers, purchased by or given without charge to an organization.

direct material: all raw material that is an integral part of the finished good and can be conveniently assigned to specific physical units.

director: any person elected by shareholders to establish company policies. The directors appoint the president, vice-presidents, and all other operating officers. Directors decide, among other matters, if and when dividends shall be paid.

directorate: a corporation's board of directors.

directory advertising: advertising that appears in printed directories (e.g., telephone books, city directories).

direct overhead: factory, selling, or other expenses related directly to a specific product and resulting in a direct cost.

direct package: a bundle of letters tied together, all addressed to the same office.

direct reduction mortgage: the use of loan payments to reduce the loan's principal directly.

direct selling: a manufacturer selling directly to the user, the retailer, or the final consumer without the intervention of a middleman.

direct tax: the burden of a tax that cannot be easily shifted or passed on to another individual by the person on whom it is levied.

direct write-off method: the recording of actual losses from uncollectible accounts as expenses during the period in which accounts receivable are determined to be uncollectible. Cf. *allowance method.*

dirty float: a situation in which exchange rates are allowed to fluctuate in the market but national monetary authorities intervene to contol the extent of the fluctuation.

dirty neck: (slang) a farmer or laborer.

disability income: a benefit provided by a specific health insurance contract that indemnifies the insured for loss of time in the event of sickness or accident. Cf. *state disability plan;* see also *temporary total disability benefits, workers' compensation.*

disagio: the charge made for exchanging depreciated foreign monies. Cf. *agio.*

disbursement: an actual payment of funds toward the full or partial settlement of an obligation.

discharge

(1) *personnel:* to fire. Synonymous with *dismiss.*

(2) *business law:* the release of one party from meeting his or her obligation under a contract because other parties to the contract have failed to meet their obligation(s).

discharge of contract: the fulfillment of a contract's obligations.

disciplinary layoff: suspension of an employee because of violation of company rules.

discipline: the state of employee self-control and orderly conduct that is present in an organization.

disclaimer: a document; or a clause in a document; that renounces or repudiates the liability of an otherwise responsible party in the event of (1) noncompliance by such other party to certain conditions described in the instrument, (2) named external conditions, or (3) losses incurred because of a discrepancy in the goods delivered and the weight or count made by the shipper.

disclosure: See *full disclosure;* see also *discovery practice.*

discontinuous market: as differentiated from continuously listed securities, the unlisted stocks and bonds that form a separate market.

discotetic: describing the chaos resulting from continous shifts and changes within an organization that fails to yield constructive results in attaining a primary objective or goal.

discount

(1) *finance:* the amount of money deducted from the face value of a note.

(2) *securities:* the amount by which a preferred stock or bond sells below its par value.

(3) *securities:* to take into account (e.g., the price of the stock has discounted the expected dividend cut).

(4) *foreign exchange:* the relationship of one currency to another. (e.g., Canadian currency may be at a discount to United States currency).

(5) *sales:* the selling of an item or service at a price below the normal list price. See also *bulk discount;* cf. *rebate.*

discounted cash flow methods: capital budgeting techniques that take into account the time value of money by comparing discounted cash flows. See also *internal rate of return, net present value.*

discounted rate of return: the rate of return that equates future cash proceeds and the initial cost of the investment.

discount house (store): a retail operation in which prices are lower than at other stores selling the same merchandise.

discounting: an institution lending money to a business with a customer's debt obligation to the firm as security on the loan.

discounting the news: the situation occurring when a stock's price or the level of a major market indicator climbs or falls in expectation of a good or bad occurrence, then barely moves when the actual development takes place and is announced.

discount period: the time between the date a note is issued or sold to a financial institution and its maturity date.

discount points: the amount of money sometimes paid by a borrower to the lender to make up the difference between the current interest rate and that allowed by a government-insured loan. The discount points paid by the borrower increase the effective loan yield to the lender. Each point is equal to 1 percent of the loan amount.

discount rate: the interest rate charged by the Federal Reserve System to its members; an interest rate used in evaluating expenditures that measures the relative value of benefits or returns obtained now, as compared with later.

discovery period: under certain insurance policies, a provision to give the insured a period of time after the cancellation of a contract in which to discover whether he or she has sustained a loss that would have been recoverable if the contract had remained in force. The period may be determined by statute.

discovery practice: disclosure by one party of facts or statements needed by the party seeking the discovery in connection with a pending cause or action. Cf. *concealment.*

discretionary account: an account in which the customer gives the broker or someone else the authority, which may be complete or within specific limits, to purchase and sell securities or commodities, including selection, timing, amount, and price to be paid or received.

discretionary costs: fixed costs arising from periodic, usually yearly, appropriation decisions that directly reflect top-management policies.

discretionary policy: monetary policy, purporting to compensate for a business cycle, that leads to a decision by a person or government.

discretionary spending power: money available to consume after necessities have been purchased. Cf. *disposable income.*

discrimination: prejudice or differentiation in the screening, hiring, promoting, discharging, and so on, of individuals based on race, religion, place of birth, or other non-job-related reasons. See also *Civil Rights Act of 1964, sex differential.*

discriminatory discharge: firing of an employee for union activity; an unfair labor practice under the Taft-Hartley Act.

diseconomies of scale: situations that occur when costs increase as a business grows in size. For all firms,

there is a point at which, as the company becomes larger, costs also increase. see also *internal economies scale, law of increasing costs, point of indifference.*

disequilibrium: a condition in which incentives to change exist; usually used in reference to markets in which either purchasers or producers, or both, have not yet adjusted prices and quantities to their satisfaction.

disestablishment: a National Labor Relations Board procedure to divest an organization of its claim to represent the employees and its status as a labor organization.

dishonored: describing a negotiable instrument offered for acceptance of payment that is turned down or cannot be obtained. See also *notice of dishonor.*

disinflation: the result of a strategy to reduce the general price level by increasing the purchasing power of money.

disintermediation: the taking of money out of interest-bearing time accounts (e.g., savings and commercial bank accounts) for reinvestment at higher rates for bonds and the like.

disinvestment: reduction of capital goods.

disk: a circular metal plate with magnetic material on both sides that is rotated continuously for reading in a computer network.

disk pack: a set of magnetic disks designed to be placed in a computer central processing unit for reading and writing.

dismiss
(1) *personnel:* to release an employee.
(2) *business law:* to dispose of a

case without a trial. See also *nolo contendere.*

dismissal pay: payment in addition to regular wages to an employee who has been dismissed. It is usually based on both wage rate and length of service. Frequently the payee has the option of taking a lump sum or deferred payments. Synonymous with *severance pay, termination pay.*

dispatch earning: a saving in shipping costs arising from rapid unloading at the point of destination.

dispatcher: an agent responsible for efficiently routing and sending merchandise to its destined location.

dispatching: the control and flow of pickups and deliveries of freight and the intercity movement of cargo.

dispenser: a device permitting distribution or serving of a product in a convenient form and quantity.

dispersion: the spread of values in a frequency distribution, as distinguished from the clustering or central tendency in the distribution. See also *probable error, variance.*

displacement: the cubic volume of a container.

display: a visual presentation of data.

display advertisement: an advertisement that uses attention-attracting features, such as illustrations, white space, or colors. Cf. *classified advertising.*

disposable income: personal income minus income taxes and other taxes paid by an individual, the balance being available for consumption or savings. See also *discretionary spending power, personal savings.*

dispossess: to put an individual out of his or her property by force.

disproduct: a damaging item, particu-

larly one that results from negligence on the part of the manufacturer.

disqualification: the inability to work or to continue in employment for physical, mental, legal, or other reasons.

dissatisfiers: a term used by F. Herzberg to describe events that do not bring about continuous worker satisfaction. The concept suggests that the continued presence of such conditions (e.g., improved working conditions, increased salary) will not bring satisfaction but that their absence can create dissatisfaction. See also *decision to participate, maintenance factors, motivator-hygiene theory, organizational climate, satisfiers.*

dissaving: a lowering of net worth, caused by spending more than one's current income.

disseisin: forcible explusion of an owner from his land; the loss of property possession by claiming ownership. See also *ejectment, right of possession, seisin.*

disseminator role: a supervisor's role involving passing along special or privileged information that subordinates would not otherwise be able to obtain.

dissolution (corporate): termination of a corporation at the expiration of its charter, by order of the attorney general of the state, by consolidation, or by action of the stockholders.

dissolution (partnership): termination of a partnership at a specified time by the wishes of the partners or by operation of law because of incapacity, death, or bankruptcy of any partner.

distant: designation of a month in the

distant future, or not near in time, when a contract has recently commenced.

distrain: to seize another's property as security for an obligation.

distress for rent: the taking of a tenant's personal property in payment of rent on real estate. See also *general lien, landlord's warrant.*

distress merchandise: goods that must be sold at reduced prices.

distress selling: selling because of necessity; occurs when securities owned on margin are sold because lowered prices have hurt equities.

distribution

(1) *marketing:* the separation of merchandise into different categories and group levels.

(2) *finance:* the division of something among several people or entities.

(3) *finance:* the division of aggregate income of a community among its members.

(4) *business law:* the apportionment by a court of the personal property of a deceased person among those entitled to receive the property according to the applicable statute of distribution.

(5) *securities:* the selling, over a time period, of a large block of stock without unduly depressing the market price. Cf. *secondary distribution.*

(6) *accounting:* the process of allocating income and expenses to the appropriate subsidiary accounts.

(7) *statistics:* See *frequency distribution.*

distribution center: a warehouse in which the emphasis is on processing and moving goods rather than on simple storage.

distribution cost analysis: when marketing an item in a particular location, the breaking down of all direct and indirect costs.

distribution shipment: a truckload of small goods that are transported at a truckload rate to a specified destination.

distributive leadership: the process of delegating leadership roles and responsibilities to or sharing them with other group members. See also *democratic leadership.*

distributive variable: the degree to which one or more goals of each of the individuals or groups in an organization are perceived as incompatible.

distributor: Synonymous with *wholesaler.*

diversification

(1) *securities:* spreading investments among different companies in different fields. Another type of diversification is offered by the securities of many individual companies whose activities cover a wide range.

(2) *securities:* the purchase of varying assets in order to minimize the risk associated with a portfolio.

(3) *manufacturing:* the manufacture or sale of unrelated products.

diversion in transit: a service of rail carriers that permits a shipper to reroute merchandise to a destination other than the original while the items are in transit.

divest: to remove a vested right.

divest-and-exit strategy: efforts designed to eliminate a product or service line by selling or discontinuing it.

divided interest: an interest in only part of a property.

dividend: a portion of a firm's net profits that has been officially declared by the board of directors for distribution to stockholders. A dividend is paid at a fixed amount for each share of stock held by the stockholders. Cf. *Irish dividend.*

dividend check: a negotiable instrument in the form of a check drawn on a depository bank of the corporation issuing the dividend. It is signed by the secretary of the corporation.

dividend payout ratio: the ratio of dividends per share of common stock to earnings per share of common stock.

dividend rate: the indicated annual rate of payment to a shareholder based on a company's latest quarterly dividend and recurring extra or special year-end dividends.

dividends in arrears: missed dividends for past years that preferred stockholders have a right to receive under their cumulative-dividend preference when dividends are declared.

dividends per share: the dollar amount of dividends paid to stockholders for each share owned of a corporation's common stock.

divisionalization: the creation of autonomous units in an organization. Responsibility for performance rests with a divisional or sectional manager, who is permitted to operate the division as if it were separate from the parent organization. See also *decentralization.*

division of labor
(1) *administration:* See *horizontal specialization, vertical specialization.*
(2) *personnel:* breaking a job down into the smallest number of operations without jeopardizing performance. See also *functional*

foremanship.

dock
(1) *transportation:* a landing area used for receiving ships between voyages.
(2) *personnel:* to deduct a part of an employees's wages (e.g., an hourly worker may be docked for coming to work late). See also *docking.*

dockage and moorage: Synonymous with *wharfage.*

docking: pay deduction for breakages, poor work, absenteeism, lateness, and similar causes.

documents
(1) *general:* anything printed or written that is relied on to record or prove something.
(2) *computers:* written evidence of transactions that represent stored information (e.g., printed paper, punch cards).

DOE: See *Department of Energy, U.S.*

d.o.f.: See *degree of freedom.*

dole: welfare payments.

dollar
(1) *government:* the monetary unit of the United States. See also *purchasing power of the dollar.*
(2) *finance:* the monetary unit of other nations, (e.g., Canada, Ethiopia, Malaya).

dollar cost averaging: a system of buying securities at regular intervals with a fixed dollar amount. The investor buys by the dollars' worth rather than by the number of shares. If each investment is of the same number of dollars, payments buy more shares when the price is low and fewer when it rises.

dollar drain (gap): the amount by which imports from the United States into a foreign country exceed the nation's exports to the United States.

dollar merchandise plan: an estimate of anticipated sales, frequently over a six-month period, integrated with inventory estimates and purchase in harmony with sales and profit goals.

dollar overhang: excess of actual over desired holdings of dollars by foreign central banks.

dollar shortage: a nation's lack of sufficient money to buy from the United States, caused by a steadily favorable balance of payments for the United States.

dolly: a low platform mounted on casters or small wheels, designed primarily for moving loads short distances. Cf. *pallet.*

domestic exchange ratio: the relative costs of producing two goods domestically. The exchange ratio is the opportunity cost of one good in terms of the other. See also *opportunity cost.*

domestics: yard goods from which sheets, linens, towels, and so on, are cut. Today the term is more popularly identified with the finished products.

domicile: a dwelling; a place of permanent residence. Cf. *legal residence.*

dominant coalition: the major top-level decision makers of an organization.

domination: achieving objectives by direct command; utilizing power or influence to impose one's will on others within the firm.

dominion: in transferring property from one person to another, the separation by the transferrer from all power over the property and the passage of such power to the transferee.

doomsday strike: a threatened strike that may occur immediately, before the beginning of contract negotiations, thus putting pressure on management.

door-to-door selling: selling of a product or service directly from the manufacturer by the manufacturer's employee to potential customers in their homes or offices. This process eliminates the middleman, with the expectation of cutting costs. See also *Green River ordinance, house-to-house salesman.*

dormant account: an account that has had little or no activity for a period of time. Synonymous with *inactive account.*

dormant partner: a partner not known to the public at large who is entitled to participate in the profits and is subject to the losses. See also *secret partner.*

DOT: See *Department of Transportation, Dictionary of Occupational Titles.*

double coincidence of wants: situation in a barter exchange when each party must possess precisely what the other wishes and must be able to trade at the exact amount and terms agreeable to both.

double counting (entry): in bookkeeping, since every transaction is entered two times, counting the same quantity twice when evolving a total; procedure used in determining the gross national product.

double-decker: two outdoor advertising panels built one above the other.

double eagle: a U.S. $20 gold piece.

double employment: holding down two jobs at the same time. Synonymous with *moonlighting.*

double entry: a method of recording

transactions that requires that an increase in one account reflect an increase or decrease in another account. The total debits of each entry must equal the total credits. See also *journalize*.

double indemnity: a provision in a life insurance policy, subject to specified conditions and exclusions, whereby double the face amount of the policy is payable if the death of the insured is the result of an accident.

double insurance: insurance purchased to insure against the same risk twice. Usually, it is impossible to obtain more than the loss suffered. If a risk is insured against twice, one firm will claim contribution from the other. See also *excess coverage clause, noncurrency;* cf. *other-insurance clause, pro rata distribution clause.*

double-page spread: an advertisement appearing on two facing pages.

double spotting: placing of two broadcast commercials back to back with no program material intervening.

double taxation: short for "double taxation of dividends." The federal government taxes corporate profits once as corporate income; the remaining profits, distributed as dividends to stockholders, are taxed again as income to the recipient stockholders.

double time: twice the regular rate of pay for overtime, Sunday work, or holiday work.

double truck: See *double-page spread.*

douceur: a bribe or gratuity (French); term dating from the eighteenth century.

dower: a right for life by a married woman in a portion of the land owned by her husband, which becomes vested upon his death. In some states, a wife owns one-third of her deceased husband's real estate. See also *tenant in dower;* cf. *curtesy.*

Dow-Jones averages: the averages of closing prices of 30 representative industrial stocks, 15 public utility stocks, 20 transportation stocks, and an average of the 65 stocks computed at the end of a trading day on the New York Stock Exchange. Cf. *NYSE Common Stock Index, Standard & Poor's 500 Stock Average.*

downer: a brief work stoppage to draw attention to a particular grievance.

downgrading: a form of demotion created by a reduction in corporate functions.

down payment

(1) *finance:* a partial payment, made at the time of purchase, to permit the buyer to take the merchandise.

(2) *real estate:* money deposited as evidence of good faith for purchasing property upon contract signing.

down periods: the shutdown of plant operations to permit cleaning, repair, and maintenance of equipment.

downstairs merger: a merger of a parent corporation into a subsidiary.

downstream: describing movement of a business activity from a higher to a lower level (e.g., a loan from a parent company to one of its subsidiaries).

downtime

(1) *administration:* a period during which a worker is idled because a machine breaks down or the flow of

materials is interrupted.

(2) *computers:* the time interval during which a device is malfunctioning. Cf. *uptime.*

downward channel: the path used by management for sending orders, directives, goals, policies, memoranda, and so on, to employees at lower levels in the organization.

downward communication: the flow of information from higher levels of an organization to lower levels. Cf. *upward communication.*

Dow theory: a theory of market analysis based on the performance of the Dow-Jones industrial and transportation stock price averages. The market is said to be in a basic upward trend if one of these averages advances above a previous important high, accompanied or followed by a similar advance in the other. When both averages dip below previous important lows, this is regarded as confirmation of a basic downward trend. The theory does not attempt to predict how long either trend will continue, although it is widely misinterpreted as a method of forecasting future action. See also *Dow-Jones averages.*

draft: an order in writing signed by one party (the drawer) requesting a second party (the drawee) to make payment in lawful money at a determinable future time to a third party (the payee).

dragline: a conveyor system for handling freight, consisting of cables pulling carts.

drawee: any party expected to pay the sum listed on a check, draft, or bill of exchange.

drawer: any party who draws a check,

draft, or bill of exchange for the payment of funds.

drawing account: a regular allowance made available to salespeople employed on a straight commission basis. The commission earned is balanced against the drawing account at various intervals.

drawings: a temporary account for recording withdrawals of cash or other assets from a partnership or proprietorship by the owner(s).

drawn bond: See *bond, drawn.*

drayage: charges made for moving freight on carts or vehicles in a terminal location or city.

drive-in banking: tellers' windows facing the outside of a bank building, or separate outside booths, for the convenience of depositors. The bank customer drives up to a teller's window.

drive theory: the psychological concept that attributes action to primary (biological) and secondary (learned) motives.

dromedary: a vehicle combining the characteristics of a truck and a truck tractor. It has a fifth wheel at the end of the body and a van body at the rear of the cab.

drop

(1) *postal service:* the lobby slot or opening into which postal customers deposit mail.

(2) *manufacturing:* to discontinue an item from production.

drop dead list: (slang) employees selected to be fired from their job.

drop-rate provision: a clause in a mortgage allowing a drop in the interest rate under certain conditions.

drop shipment: merchandise shipped directly from manufacturer to retailer.

The wholesaler receives only the invoice and then bills the retailer.

drop shipper: a wholesaler who performs most wholesaling activities except storage and handling. He sends requests to the manufacturer, who ships directly to the customer. The customer pays the drop shipper, who has already paid his bill to the manufacturer. See also *jobber.*

drum: a cylindrical shipping container having straight sides and flat or bumped ends that is used for storage and/or shipment as an outer package that may be transported unsupported, without boxing or crating.

drum, magnetic: See *magnetic drum.*

drummer: a traditional American style of salesman who calls on retailers of soft goods or meets them at buying centers.

drum storage: a form of computer storage that uses magnetic recording on a rotating cylinder. See also *storage drum.*

dry goods: specifically, fabrics made from cotton, wool, rayon, silk, and other textile materials; includes ready-to-wear clothing, bed linens, and so on.

dual banking: since some banks are chartered by the state in which they operate and others by the federal government, a system whereby each independent component cooperates with the other to offer its clientele complete banking services.

dual billing and posting: posting a customer's purchases to ledger independently from the preparation of a bill for the customer.

dual-career marriage: a marriage in which both husband and wife are pursuing professional careers.

dual distribution: sale of a product through more than one distributive system.

dual labor market: a labor market consisting of a primary labor market, in which jobs are high paying and possess adequate working conditions and job security and a second labor market, in which, jobs are scarce, pay lower wages, have poor working conditions, and claim a high turnover of employees.

dual mutual funds: funds that divide their portfolios between capital growth investments and income investments.

dual-purpose fund: Synonomous with *split investment company.*

dual savings plan: a plan whereby two separate operations are required to post a savings deposit or a withdrawal to an account.

dual supervision: a form of control whereby supervisory authority and responsibility for discharging the policies of the firm are divided between a line officer and a staff officer of similar rank, each of whom is answerable to the same manager. See also *line and staff authority.*

due care: the standard of conduct displayed by an ordinary, reasonable, prudent individual. See also *prudent man rule.*

due date: the date on which an instrument of debt becomes payable; the maturity date.

due process of law: all actions of a court taken to ensure the rights of private individuals before the law; all legal steps to protect these rights; a court order to compel compliance with its wishes (e.g., a summons issued to compel attendance in court).

dues: monthly sums paid by union members to their local. The amount of the dues is sometimes set by the international union but more often by the local.

dummy: a model indicating the size, shape, and layout of a finished printed product.

dummy invoice: a statement prepared by a retailer as a temporary replacement for a vendor's invoice if the latter is not available when the goods are to be received, marked, and put in inventory.

dump

(1) *computers:* to copy the contents of all or part of a storage device, usually from internal storage into external storage. See also *memory, postmortem, rescue dump, static dump;* cf. *search.*

(2) *securities:* to offer large blocks of stock for purposes of disposal, with little concern for price or the effect on the market. See also *profit taking.*

dumping

(1) *finance:* selling items to other countries at below cost to eliminate surplus or to hurt foreign competition.

(2) *finance:* in the United States, selling imported items at prices less than the cost of manufacture. See also *Antidumping Act of 1974, boomerang.*

dun: to press for payment of a debt; to demand repeatedly what one is owed.

Dun and Bradstreet (D&B): the oldest and largest mercantile agency in the United States, offering credit data and ratings on business concerns.

dunnage: material other than packaging employed to prevent damage to freight or to support it in shipment.

Dun's Market Identifiers: a published system that identifies firms with an absolute identification number and provides regularly updated economic information on each company (e.g., address code, number of workers, and corporate affiliation).

duopoly: an industry containing two businesses that sell the identical items. In a duopoly, both firms exercise control.

duopsony: a market situation in which only two buyers are seeking an item. Cf. *monopsony, oligopsony.*

durability

(1) *general:* the lasting quality of an item.

(2) *finance:* money that can be used over an extended period or that can be replaced at minimal cost.

durable merchandise: goods that have a relatively lengthy life (television sets, radio, etc.)

duress (personal): a threat of bodily harm, criminal prosecution, or imprisonment. An individual under duress at the time of entering into or discharging a legal obligation is unable to exercise freely his or her will with respect to the transaction. Cf. *extortion.*

duress (property): forced seizure or withholding of goods by an individual who is not entitled to possess them, and the demands made by such a person as a condition for the release of the goods.

Dutch auction: an auction sale in which the prices on items are continuously lowered until a bidder responds favorably and buys.

duty

(1) *economics:* an actual tax collected.

(2) *business law:* a legal requirement established by law or voluntarily imposed by the creation of a binding promise. A legal right accompanies every legal duty.

(3) *customs:* a tax imposed on the importation, exportation, or consumption of goods.

duty drawback: a tariff concession allowing a rebate of all or part of the duty on goods imported for processing before being reexported. See also *production sharing.*

duty free: describing items that are not affected by any customs duty. See also *free list.*

duty to bargain: the obligation, under the Taft-Hartley Act, of employers and employees to bargain in good faith.

dynamic economy: an economy of growth and change.

dynamic homeostasis: the process whereby the open system maintains equilibrium over a period of time.

dynamic models: models that identify the behavior of variables over a given period.

dynamiter: (slang) a securities broker who attempts to sell fraudulent or unregistered stocks and bonds over the telephone. Cf. *boiler room tactic.*

dysfunction: Synonymous with *malfunction.*

dysfunctional behavior: actions that are in conflict with top-management goals.

each way: trading on both the buying and selling sides of a transaction. The broker earns a commission of 3 percent each way (i.e., 3 percent for selling and another 3 percent for executing the purchase order).

eager beaver: (slang) an employee who appears overly diligent to his co-workers, especially one who attempts to impress his superiors with his desire to work hard.

eagle: a U.S. $10 gold coin, first coined in 1795. The Treasury demanded the surrender of all gold coins in 1933.

EAM: See *electrical accounting machine.*

early retirement benefits: the reduced pension received by some employees when they voluntarily leave their company prior to the mandatory retirement age.

earned income: income derived from goods and services rendered as well as pension and annuity income. See also *Tax Reform Act of 1976;* cf. *unearned income.*

earned rate: the amount an advertiser pays for media space or time actually used.

earnest money: money given by a contracting party to another at the time of the signing of a contract to bind the bargain. This sum is forfeited by the donor if he or she fails to carry out the contract.

earning power: an employee's potential capacity on his or her job to earn wages over a period of time—usually the normal span of years during which the worker is productive.

earnings: the total remuneration received by a worker for a given period as compensation for services rendered, for work performed, as a commission, as overtime, and so on. Cf. *payroll deductions, wage;* synonymous with *net income.*

earnings per share: the portion of a corporation's net income that relates to each share of the corporation's common stock that has been issued

167

and is outstanding.

earnings potential: the ability of a firm to generate positive future net cash flows from operations.

earnings report: a statement issued by a company showing its earnings or losses over a given period. The earnings report lists the income earned, the expenses, and the net result.

easement: a limited right to use someone else's property. An easement can be permanent or temporary. Usually, easements pass with the land when sold. Cf. *access right, implied easement.*

easy money: money that can be obtained at low interest rates and with relative ease as the result of sufficient supply of a bank's excess reserves.

ecclesiastical corporation: an organization owned and/or operated by a religious body.

ECOA: See *Equal Credit Opportunity Act.*

econometrics: the discipline of economics that measures economic data for the purpose of increasing knowledge and forecasting ability in that field.

economic: describing any action having to do with the evolution of goods and services that are purported to satisfy a human condition.

economic climate: the degree of market and financial risks associated with investments.

economic costs: payments to the owners of the requirements for manufacturing to convince them to supply their resources in a specified activity.

economic efficiency: synonymous with *Pareto optimality.*

economic forecasting: employing behavioral relations (equations) linking many variables in the economy to obtain short-term projections of the future.

economic goods: items produced from scarce resources.

economic growth rate: the percentage rate at which total annual output grows; an increase in real per capita income.

economic imperialism: efforts toward domination of the economies of developing nations by foreign business firms, which seek profits by controlling raw materials, labor, and markets in those nations.

economic indicators: classification of economic information to be used in business cycle analysis and forecasting.

economic lot technique: an approach that purports to describe the amount of an item that should be made or sold at one time to reduce the total costs involved.

economic profit: the residual profit after explicit and implicit costs have been paid. Synonymous with *pure profit.*

Economic Recovery Tax Act of 1981: federal legislation signed by President Reagan in August 1981, providing reductions and revisions of tax liability in various areas (e.g., estate and gift taxes, pensions, stock options, depreciation and investment tax credit). See also *All-Savers Certificates, individual retirement accounts, Keogh Plan.*

economic rent: the estimated income a property should bring in the existing rental market. The economic rent can be either above or below the amount actually received. Cf. *rack rent.*

economic royalists: term used by Franklin Roosevelt to describe people of wealth who resisted his policy of improving the economic position of the average man.

economics

(1) *general:* the branch of the social sciences concerned with the production, distribution, and consumption of goods and services.

(2) *general:* a description of events dealing with consumption, distribution, exchange, and production of goods and services. See also *labor economics, normative economics, positive economics.*

economic sanction: a form of economic pressure (e.g., boycott, embargo) used to compel another country or group of countries to comply with international agreement.

economic standard order quantity: See *EOQ model.*

economic strike: a work stoppage because of money issues and working conditions rather than unfair labor practices. It is not protected under law, and employers may hire and retain replacements unless this is interdicted by a strike settlement. See also *strike.*

economic value: the value given to an item as a function of its usefulness and its scarcity.

economies of scale: the result of production functions showing that an equal percentage increase in all inputs leads output to increase by a large percentage. See also *natural monopoly.*

economism: a Marxist term for the search for material advantage at the expense of the revolution.

economizing: choosing among alternative uses of a scarce resource, such as a factor of production, money income, time.

ecosystem: the relationship between an organization and its environment. In a successful relationship, the organization and its environment gain needed support from each other.

ECR: See *electronic cash register.*

edbiz: (slang) the commercial activity of educational research and development.

edge corporation: a foreign banking organization structured in compliance with the Federal Reserve Act.

edit

(1) *computers:* to rearrange data or information into a meaningful form.

(2) *publishing:* to prepare an author's work (e.g., a report or a manuscript) for publication.

editorial credit: identification of a specific retail operation as a source for a fashion item featured editorially (i.e., not in an advertisement) in a consumer magazine or newspaper.

EDP: See *electronic data processing. See also ADP.*

EEOC: Equal Employment Opportunity Commission. See also *Civil Rights Act of 1964.*

effective date

(1) *general:* the date on which an agreement or contract goes into effect; the starting date.

(2) *insurance:* the date on which an insurance binder or policy goes into effect and from which time protection is provided.

effective debt: the total debt of a firm, including the major value of annual leases or other payments that are equivalent to interest charges.

effective gross income: the total possible income generated by a project, less an allowance and bad debts.

effective-interest amortization: a method of systematically writing off a bond premium or discount that takes into consideration the time value of money. This results in an equal rate of amortization for each period. Cf. *straight-line interest amortization;* see also *amortization.*

effective interest rate: the actual rate of return earned or paid.

effectiveness: in the management process, the optimal organizational relationship among five determinants: production, efficiency, satisfaction, adaptiveness, and development.

effective par: for preferred stocks, the par value that would ordinarily correspond to a given dividend rate.

efficiency: the measure of production relative to input of human and other resources. See also *Taylorism;* cf. *productive efficiency, technical efficiency.*

efficiency expert: a specialist who analyzes and reports on the correct thing being done at the proper time, in the right place, by the appropriate person. Sometimes incorrectly called a time and motion study expert and/or an industrial engineer, an efficiency expert has narrower functions. See also *work simplification;* cf. *methods-time measurement, motion study.*

efficiency variance: quantity variance as applied to labor.

effort: the motivated aspect of behavior; the amount of energy expended by the individual in a given act. When effort is combined with ability, behavior will result. Level of effort is influenced by the strength of the individual's motives or needs.

effort bargain: a collective-bargaining agreement that identifies the quantity of work to be completed for a stated wage payment, not merely the number of working hours.

effort scale: a system for charting the amount of effort a buyer will expend to purchase a specified item.

EFTA: See *European Free Trade Association.*

EFTS: See *electronic funds-transfer system.*

egalitarianism: the premise that the economic stature of all members of society should be as equal as possible.

eighty-twenty principle: the concept that a business gets 80 percent of its activity from 20 percent of its product line, while spending 80 percent of its energy to get the remaining 20 percent of volume. This indicates a misdirected marketing effort.

ejectment: the legal action brought to retain possession of property and to receive damage monies from the person who illegally retained it. See also *right of possession, seisin;* cf. *landlord's warrant.*

elastic demand: demand that changes in relatively large volume as prices increase or decrease. When a small change in price results in a greater change in the quantity people buy, the demand for the item is said to be elastic. The demand for jewelry, furs, and second homes is considered to be elastic. See also *cross-elasticity.*

elasticity

(1) *banking:* the ability of a bank to meet credit and currency demands during times of expansion and to reduce the availability of credit and currency during periods of over-expansion. See also *Federal Reserve notes.*

(2) *merchandising:* the impact on the demand for an item created by changes in price, promotion, or other factors affecting demand. See also, *coefficient of cross-elasticity.*

elastic supply: supply that changes in relatively large volume with a minor change in price.

electrical accounting machines (EAM): conventional punch-card equipment, including sorters, tabulators, and collectors.

electronic cash register (ECR): a cash register in which electronic circuitry replaces electromechanical parts.

electronic data processing (EDP): data processing that is largely performed by electronic devices.

electronic funds-transfer system(s) (EFTS): a loose description of computerized systems that process financial transactions, process information about financial transactions, or effect an exchange of value between two parties. See also *Bank Wire System, Fed Wire, Hinky Dinky, paperless item processing system, preauthorized payment, prestige card, service counter terminal.*

eleemosynary: describing the classification of quasi-public corporations and organizations engaged in charitable work. Cf. *not-for-profit.*

eligibility date: the date set by the National Labor Relations Board for eligi-bility to vote in a union representation election. Usually the eligibility date is determined by the last payroll period.

eligible investment: any income-producing investment that is considered to be a sound repository for the funds of savings banks and similar institutions.

eliteness motivation: the forces that lead individuals to identify with prestigious companies.

embargo

(1) *economics:* a condition resulting in the failure to accept freight at a specified location because of some crisis at the point of destination; the prohibition against handling certain goods.

(2) *government:* an official order prohibiting the entry or departure of commercial ships at a nation's ports, especially as a wartime measure. See also *blockade, sanction.*

embezzlement: the fraudulent appropriation to a person's own use of the money or property entrusted to his or her care. See also *defalcation.*

Emergency Banking Relief Act of 1933: federal legislation returning to the president World War I powers relating to transactions in credit, currency, silver and gold, and foreign currencies, and the fixing of $10,000 fine and 10 years of imprisonment for violators. It also authorized the president to fix regulations on Federal Reserve member banks.

emergency dispute: a strike or the threat of a strike that would affect the national welfare and/or safety. Under the Taft-Hartley Act, the president is authorized to determine whether a dispute imperils the nation's well-being and, if it does, to take appropriate action, which usually involves creating a fact-finding board.

emergent leader: the leader who emerges from within the group. This person embodies the group's attitudes, values, beliefs, and opinions.

eminent domain: the inherent right of certain legally constituted governing bodies to take title to and possession of real property for the public good, with just compensation to the owner. Cf. *confiscation.*

emolument: compensation for personal services in the form of wages, commissions, awards, or other personal benefits.

emotional buying motives: subjective, irrational motivation that affects consumer purchasing.

empathy: the ability to perceive how potential customers feel and what their attitudes, needs, and expectations are.

emphyteutic lease: a perpetual lease whereby the owner of an uncultivated parcel has granted it to another in perpetuity or for a lengthy period on the condition that the leasee will improve the land.

empire building: enlarging one's status and power by increasing the number of subordinates, the amount of space and physical facilities, and the number of make-work projects.

employ: to hire or engage the services of an individual or his or her equipment.

employable: describing people in the population who are able to work and who fall within certain age limits. Cf. *hard-core unemployed.*

employee: a general term referring to all those who work for a wage or salary and perform services for an employer.

employee association: a group of workers organized to accomplish specific common interests and goals.

employee attitude survey: a systematic method of obtaining expressions of employees' thoughts and feelings. See also *attitude, morale study.*

employee handbook: a manual that explains key benefits, policies, and general information about the company.

employee orientation: a program to provide needed job-related information for new employees.

Employee Retirement Income Security Act of 1974 (ERISA): legislation signed by President Ford on Labor Day, 1974, to protect the interests of workers who participate in private pension and welfare plans and their beneficiaries. The law also allows an employee not covered by a pension plan other than Social Security to put aside, on a tax-deferred basis, a certain amount of money for retirement. See also *individual retirement account; Keogh Plan.*

employee stock ownership plans (ESOPs): programs created to give workers a feeling of participation in the management and direction of a company. Workers are encouraged to purchase stock of the company. See also *compensation, retirement, self-employed.*

employer: a person, organization, or corporation that has workers in its employ.

employer interference: unfair labor practices, including the following: barring distribution of union literature or solicitation during nonworking time; speeches to employees on company time and property before a representation election, unless the union has equal opportunity to reply; questioning of employees about union activity; closing or moving the plant, or threatening to do so; circulating an antiunion petition and inducing employees to sign under duress; across-the-board increases in wages, removal of privileges; spying; encouraging or discouraging union membership; and firing for union activity. See also *Taft-Hartley Act.*

employer petition: a formal request by an employer to the National Labor Relations Board for holding an election to determine the representative for collective bargaining. See also *representation election.*

employer rights: Synonymous with *management prerogatives.*

employer's final offer: the last terms offered by an employer in an attempt to settle a contract dispute. For national emergency disputes, the National Labor Relations Board conducts a secret-ballot vote on this offer among the employees.

employment

(1)   *general:*   the state of being employed or having work that renders payment.

(2)   *government   statistics:*   the sum of people who are employed or are presently working in paid positions. See also *labor force.*

Employment Act of 1946: a law designed to seek the federal government's promotion of full employment. Provision is also made for continuing study of economic trends and the

submission of the President's Economic Report by the Council of Economic Advisers. The act also directs the president to present an annual economic report to Congress with legislative recommendations. See also *reconversion.*

employment agency: an organization that assists firms in recruiting employees and aids individuals in their attempts to locate jobs.

employment function: the aspect of personnel work that is responsible for recruiting, selecting, and hiring new workers. It usually is found in the employment section of large personnel departments.

emulate: to imitate one system with another such that the imitating system accepts the same data, executes the same programs, and achieves the same results as the system imitated.

enclosure sale: a sale in which property placed as security for a debt is sold to pay the debt.

encode: to convert data by the use of a code or a coded character set in such a manner that reconversion to the original form is possible.

encounter group: the participants in a sensitivity training program. See also *sensitivity training.*

encroachment

(1)   *business law:*   infringement on another's property without the owner's consent.

(2)   *real estate:*   the gradual expansion of a low-value district on a higher economic level residential section.

encumbered: property to which one has title but against which a claim has been made or granted to another.

encumbrance (incumbrance)

(1) *general:* that which holds back or weighs down.

(2) *real estate:* a claim or interest in land or other property that, although it depreciates value, does not prevent transfer or sale.

(3) *finance:* the amount expected to be paid for items ordered before they are received.

end money: a special fund created in the event that the costs of a project exceed original estimates.

endorsed bond: See *bond, endorsed.*

endorsee (indorsee): the person to whom a negotiable item payable or endorsed to order is negotiated by endorsement and delivery.

endorsement (indorsement)

(1) *general:* a show of support; a verification.

(2) *banking:* a signature written on the back of an instrument. An endorsement is required on a negotiable instrument in order to transfer and pass title to another party, who becomes a *holder in due course.* The endorser, in signing the endorsement, guarantees that he or she is the lawful owner of the instrument, knows of no infirmity in the instrument, accepted it in good faith for value received, and is a holder in due course and has the legal capacity to transfer title to another party in the normal course of business.

(3) *insurance:* when circumstances require that a policy be changed (e.g., change of name, addition of property, change in coverage), a form bearing the language necessary to record the change. Cf. *scratch endorsement.*

endorser (indorser): one who en-

dorses; the person who transfers his title to an instrument to another by endorsement.

endowment

(1) *insurance:* a life term contract providing for the payment of the face amount of the policy at a specified age, at the end of a specified period, or upon the death of the insured.

(2) *economics:* a gift to an institution, usually for a specific purpose. In most cases, the gift permits the giver to declare a deduction on his taxes.

endowment insurance: life insurance on which premiums are paid for at a given period, during which the insured is covered. If the person survives beyond the end of the premium period, he or she collects the face value.

end-results principles: conduct that yields the desirable results of organizing efforts: order, stability, initiative, and esprit de corps.

Energy Research and Development Administration (ERDA): the federal agency in the Department of Energy, that is responsible for government activities in energy research and development, including demonstration of commercial feasibility and practical application of fossil, nuclear, solar, and geothermal energy and programs of energy conservation.

Energy Tax Act of 1978: federal legislation that introduced taxes and credits for purposes of reducing U.S. reliance on foreign energy supplies.

enervate: to weaken; to render powerless.

enfeoff: to give a gift of ownership to property.

engage

(1) *general:* to employ or to ar-

range for services.

(2) *business law:* to commit by word or contact.

Engels' law: an economic theory claiming that the lower a person's income is, the greater the percentage of it that is spent for food. Frederick Engels was a nineteenth-century German collaborator of Karl Marx. See also *dialectical materialism.*

engross: to purchase a sufficient quantity of a commodity to secure a monopoly for purposes of reselling at a higher price.

enjoin

(1) *general:* to command or direct.

(2) *labor relations:* a court action to prevent a union from engaging in an illegal stoppage or strike action. An employer or corporation may also be enjoined during a labor dispute. See also *injunction.*

(3) *business law:* to stop; to forbid.

enlightened self-interest: the doctrine that business actually serves its own long-run interests by helping out its community.

en route: on the way. See also *in transit.*

entail: to limit or curtail the succession to property by ordinary rules of inheritance. Cf. *primogeniture.*

enterprise: any business venture requiring risk.

entirety (estate by): the property of husband and wife passed on to the survivor upon the death of one. The estate is called "entirety" because the law looks on the husband and wife as one.

entitlement: a special tax device for restoring equity under the existing

marketing arrangements governing oil. The tax is paid by the large oil companies for excess new oil, and the government transfers the receipts to the smaller companies to offset their high payments for foreign oil.

entity: See *corporation.*

Entree: a debit card produced by Visa (formerly BankAmericard).

entrepôt trade: reexport of imports from a warehouse. When the items are not sold from bonded warehouses, and duty has been paid, the reexporter may be entitled to a refund of the duty.

entrepreneur: one who assumes the financial risk of the initiation, operation, and management of a given business or undertaking. See also *threshold companies.*

entrepreneuring: (slang) the taking of risk in the running of an organization, usually a small business enterprise.

entry

(1) *computers:* an input received from a terminal device attached to a computer.

(2) *accounting:* a recording of data in an account or account book.

entry strategies: ways of entering multinational business operations. They include exporting, licensing, franchising, foreign branch operations, joint ventures, and wholly owned subsidiaries.

envelope stuffer: direct-mail advertising placed in mailings of statements.

Environmental Protection Agency (EPA): federal agency founded in 1970 to develop and enforce standards for clean air and water, to establish standards to control pollution from pesticides, toxic substances, and noise, and to approve state pollution abatement plans. See also *Noise Control Act of 1972, Toxic Substances Control Act of 1976.*

environmental selling: displaying items for sale in a setting that simulates a buyer's home.

environmental uncertainty: the state of the external environment of an organization as defined by the degree of complexity and the degree of change.

EOM (end-of-month) dating: a policy of commencing credit terms as of the month's end. For example, 7/20 EOM means that a 7 percent cash discount is taken if the invoice is paid by the 20th of the month following the invoice date. Invoices dated after the 25th of the month are considered to be dated in the following month.

EOQ (economic order quantity) model: an inventory decision-making approach used to create a formula for determining when to order supplies and in what quantity.

ephemeralization: Buckminister Fuller's concept for increasing the rate of obsolescence of products in order to increase the rate of recycling of their elements.

equal coverage: a corporation indenture protective clause providing that, in the case of an additional issue of bonds, the subject bonds shall be entitled to the same security as that of the earlier issue.

Equal Credit Opportunity Act (ECOA): federal legislation prohibiting creditors from discriminating against credit applicants on the basis of sex or marital status. After March 1977, discrimination in credit on the basis of race, color, religion, national origin, age, and receipt of public assistance was prohibited. Compliance with the law comes under the jurisdiction of the Federal Trade Commission.

equal dignity: a reference to mortgages or other legal obligations to indicate that all have equal ranking, to prevent one from taking precedence over another. See also *parity clause;* cf. *first lien, overlying mortgage, second lien, subordinated interest, tacking, underlying mortgage.*

equal employment opportunity: giving people a fair chance to succeed without discrimination on factors unrelated to job performance, such as age, sex, race, religion, or national origin. See also *Civil Rights Act of 1964; Title VII; Equal Employment Opportunity Act of 1972.*

Equal Employment Opportunity Act of 1972: an act strengthening the role of the Equal Employment Opportunity Commission by amending the Civil Rights Act of 1964. The law empowered the EEOC to initiate court action against noncomplying organizations. See also *Civil Rights Act of 1964, Title VII.*

Equal Employment Opportunity Commission (EEOC): See *Civil Rights Act of 1964, Title VII.*

Equal Pay Act of 1963: a federal law requiring that men and women performing equal work be paid equal wages, applicable to employers and workers covered by the Fair Labor Standards Act. The act prohibits lowering pay for men to equalize rates.

equal pay for equal work: the concept, frequently written into contract language, that like work shall command like pay, regardless of sex, race, or other individual characteristics of the employees.

equation price: a price attained by the adjusting action of competition in any market at any time, or in a unit of time, such that the demand and supply become equal at that price.

equifinality: the concept that there are multiple paths to an objective.

equilibrium: any condition that, once reached, continues unless one of the variables is altered or the change of one variable is not offset by an equivalent change in another variable. Cf. *noncooperative equilibrium.*

equilibrium price

(1) *general:* the price that maximizes a firm's profitability.

(2) *manufacturing:* the price of goods determined in the market by the intersection of a supply and demand curve.

equilibrium quantity

(1) *general:* the quantity that maximizes a firm's profitability.

(2) *manufacturing:* the quantity of goods determined in the market by the intersection of a supply and demand curve.

equipment leasing: the rental of expensive equipment to save a substantial and immediate cash outlay. In most cases the leasing agreement includes a maintenance arrangement with the lessor on the leased items. See also *problem determination.*

equipment trust certificate: a type of security, generally issued by a railroad, to pay for new equipment (e.g., locomotives). Title to the equipment is held by a trustee until the notes are paid off. An equipment trust certificate is usually secured by a first claim on the equipment.

equitable conversion: permitting real property to be converted into personal property. Real property owned by a partnership is, for the purpose of the partnership, personal property, because the real property must be reduced to cash to determine a partner's interest.

equitable mortgage: a written statement making certain property security for a debt.

equitable title: the right that exists in equity to secure total ownership to property when its title is in someone else's name.

equity

(1) *business law:* the law of trusts, divorces, injunctions, and other rules of performance, enforced in courts of equity to determine fairness, right, and justice.

(2) *economics:* the value placed on the distribution of income.

(3) *real estate:* the difference between liens against property and the current market value.

(4) *securities:* the ownership interest of common and preferred stockholders in a company.

(5) *securities:* the excess of value of securities over the debit balance in a margin account. See also *margin call.*

equity capital: stockholders' or owners' investments made in an organization.

equity financing: the selling of capital stock by a corporation.

equity of redemption: a mortgagor's right to get back his or her property after it has been forfeited for nonpayment of the debt it secured. The mortgagor, by law, can pay the debt and therefore receive his property.

equity securities: any stock issue, common or preferred.

equity transaction: a transaction resulting in an increase or decrease of net worth or involving the transfer between accounts that make up the net worth.

equity turnover: the ratio that measures the relationship between sales and the common stockholders' equity. It is used to compute the rate of return on common equity.

erase: to obliterate information from a storage medium.

ERDA: See *Energy Research and Development Administration.*

ergonomics: matching of machines and people to increase efficiency by expanding production, raising output quality or quantity, minimizing training, improving working conditions, and setting a better union-management atmosphere. See also *human engineering;* cf. *methods-time measurement.*

ERISA: See *Employee Retirement In come Security Act of 1974.*

ERP: See *European Recovery Program.*

erratic fluctuations: short-term changes that are difficult to measure and predict because they tend to be unexpected.

erratic groups: groups chiefly found where jobs are nearly identical and are primarily worker controlled. There is a large amount of member interaction, centralized leadership, and an easily inflamed membership.

errors and omissions: referring to insurance coverage for liability arising out of errors or omissions in the per-

formance of professional services other than in the medical profession; applicable to such services as engineering, banking, accounting, insurance, and real estate. See also *retroactive extension;* cf. *malpractice insurance.*

escalator clause

(1) *labor relations:* a contract clause that provides for an adjustment of wages in accordance with such factors as cost of living, productivity, or material costs. Escalator clauses are designed to keep real wages reasonably stable during the term of a contract.

(2) *real estate:* a contract clause that provides for increased payments in the event of unforeseen occurrences (e.g., increased fuel or maintenance costs).

(3) *purchasing:* a clause permitting adjustments of price or profit in a purchase contract under specified conditions.

escape clause

(1) *labor relations:* in a maintenance-of-membership agreement, a provision setting a period during which union members may withdraw from membership without affecting their employment.

(2) *business law:* a contractual provision outlining the circumstances under which either party may be relieved of any obligation previously incurred or agreed to.

escheat: the reversion of property to the government when a person dies without leaving a will and has no heirs, or when the property is abandoned.

escheat law: a law pertaining to the reversion of land to the state by the failure of persons having legal title to hold the same.

escrow: a written agreement or instrument setting up for allocation funds or securities deposited by the giver or grantor to a third party (the escrow agent) for the eventual benefit of the second party (the grantee). The escrow agent holds the deposit until certain conditions have been met. The grantor can get the deposit back only if the grantee fails to comply with the terms of the contract, and the grantee cannot receive the deposit until the conditions have been met. See also *billed escrow;* cf. *deposit funds.*

escrow agreement: an arrangement whereby two parties agree to place a sum of money in the hands of a third party for conditional delivery under specified circumstances.

escrow bond: See *bond, escrow.*

ESOPs: See *employee stock ownership plans.*

esprit de corps: group spirit; an enthusiastic feeling or state of mind that workers have in being identified with each other in a group that works toward the establishment of an objective that is important to all or most group members.

essay method: a method of evaluation in which the rater simply writes a brief narrative describing the employee's performance.

establishment: a factory, or several, under the ownership of one management, located in one geographic area, and producing related goods; more recently, those in power, and the system under which such power is exercised, maintained, and extended.

estate
(1) *general:* any right, title, or other interest in real or personal property.
(2) *business law:* all assets owned by an individual at the time of his or her death. The estate includes all funds, personal effects, interests in business enterprises, titles to property (real estate and chattels), and evidence of ownership, such as stocks, bonds, and mortgages owned, and notes receivable.

estate at will: an estate of indefinite duration, allowing the lessee possession so long as both lessor and lessee mutually agree to it.

estate in reversion: the remaining portion of an estate that the grantor retains after certain interests in it have been transferred to another.

estate in severalty: an estate held by one person only. No other party has any part of it.

estate in tail: See *entail.*

estate tax: a state or federal excise tax placed on an estate, to be paid before property is transferred to heirs. This is different from an inheritance tax, which is levied against the receivers of the estate. See also *Tax Reform Act of 1976;* cf. *succession tax.*

estate tax bond: See *bond, estate tax.*

esteem needs: Maslow's fourth set of human needs, including the human desire for self-respect and respect from others.

estimate: an informed guess about the future effect on an organization of specific current conditions.

estimated cost: the expected cost of a product to be manufactured. It includes standard costs projected to future operations.

estimated revenues: the account title used in governmental accounting to set up the budgeted revenues for a period. The estimated revenues are compared against the actual revenues at the end of the period.

estoppel: a legal stoppage. When an individual who knows the truth but does not reveal it, making another person believe something to be truthful, and that other person acts to his detriment based on belief of the facts given to him, the giver of the untruthful information must reveal the full details of the situation. See also *deceit.*

et al.: and others (abbreviation of *et alii,* Latin).

ethical-moral value orientation: the tendency of an individual to respond to highly important concepts as "right."

Ethical Practices Committee: established by the AFL-CIO in 1955, a group charged with keeping the organization "free from any taint of corruption or communism."

ethics: a system of moral principles and their application to particular problems of conduct.

ethnicity: a marketing approach to attracting buyers by emphasizing the satisfactions and fulfillment of needs in acquiring ethnic goods or services.

ethod: the moral value of an organization to society—its universal appeal as a contributor to the well-being of mankind.

Eurobond: a bond released by a U.S. or other non-European company for sale in Europe.

Eurocard: a European credit card developed by the West German banking system that is accepted in most Western European countries.

Eurocheque: a credit card for purchasing goods in several Western European countries.

Eurocurrency: monies of various nations deposited in European banks that are used in the European financial market. Synonymous with *Euromoney.*

Eurodollars: European claims for U.S. dollars. These claims arise when, through the purchase of a bill of exchange or other financial transaction, a foreign bank debits the account of a U.S. bank and credits a dollar deposit account.

Euromarket (Euromart): Synonymous with *European Economic Community.*

Euromoney: Synonymous with *Eurocurrency.*

European Coal and Steel Community (ECSC): proposed in 1950 by Jean Monnet, a leader in European confederation, the pooling of resources and duty restrictions on coal, iron, and steel between France, West Germany, Italy, Belgium, the Netherlands, and Luxembourg, known as the Schuman Plan. See also *European Economic Community.*

European Common Market: Synonymous with *European Economic Community.*

European Economic Community (EEC): an agreement made in 1957 among France, Italy, West Germany, Belgium, The Netherlands, and Luxembourg (the original Inner Six nations) for the purposes of establishing common import duties and abolishing tariff barriers between borders. Denmark, Ireland, and England joined the EEC in 1973, and in 1975 many countries of Africa and the Caribbean became members, while Turkey and Greece became associate member. Synonymous with *Common Market, Euromarket (Euromart). See also European Free Trade Association.*

European Free Trade Association (EFTA): formed in 1959 by Austria, Denmark, Norway, Portugal, Sweden, Switzerland, and the United Kingdom (the original Outer Seven) to establish common regulations for tariffs and trade. Later, Iceland became a member and Finland an associate member. See also *European Economic Community.*

European Recovery Program (ERP) (Marshall Plan): a multibillion-dollar project begun in 1947 (often called the Marshall Plan after its initiator, U.S. Secretary of State George C. Marshall) designed to redevelop European industries on an aid-sharing principle after World War II. All together, 17 European countries received about $12 billion of U.S. aid. See also *counterpart monies.*

evaluation

(1) *personnel:* the judgment of a person's fitness for a job, a training project, or other new or existing programs.

(2) *marketing:* a step in the adoption process; a consumer's estimate of the value, quality, and reaction to a product or service. See also *adoption process.*

even keel: when a ship is in an upright, level position, not dipping to either side.

even lots: lots or amounts of stock shares sold in units of 100 or multi-

ples thereof. See also *board lots.*

event: an accomplishment at a particular point in time on a PERT network that consumes no time.

Everest syndrome: the tendency to research or investigate something for the sole reason that it exists, thus often leading to overemphasis on the research approach or methodology, which becomes more important than the subject of inquiry itself.

eviction: depriving an individual(s), by due process of law, of land or property possession in keeping with the judgment of a court. See also *disseisin, ejectment, writ of entry.*

evidence: the testimony of witnesses and the information presented to a court.

evidence of insurability: any statement or proof of a person's physical condition and/or other factual information affecting his acceptability for insurance. Cf. *declaration.*

ex-ante quantities: planned or intended consumption, investment, and so on, at the beginning of a time period.

exception principle: the concept that managers should permit their subordinates to make routine, recurring decisions and that only unusual or highly important problems should be referred to higher levels in the organization.

excess capacity: surplus ability to produce, especially unused factory space or staff.

excess condemnation: in condemnation proceedings, taking more land or property than is truly required for the government project in question.

excess coverage clause: a clause claiming that, in the event of a loss, a specific insurance will be considered in excess of any other insurance held against the identical risk. See also *double insurance.*

excess demand curve: graphic representation of the quantity of goods demanded less the quantity offered at each price.

excess insurance: a policy or bond covering the insured against certain hazards and applying only to loss or damage in excess of a stated amount. The risk of initial loss or damage (excluded from the excess policy or bond) may be carried by the insured himself or may be insured by another policy or bond, providing what is known as primary insurance. Cf. *service excess.*

excess loan: a bank loan made to one customer that is in excess of the maximum stated by law. Directors of banks approving such loans have been held by court decisions to be personally liable for the bank's losses.

excess materials requisitions: forms to be filled out by the production staff to secure any materials needed in excess of the standard amount allotted for output.

excess of loss reinsurance: reinsurance that indemnifies the ceding company for the excess of a stipulated sum or primary retention in the event of loss.

excess profits tax: a tax added to the normal tax placed on a business. It is usually levied on profits above what the law declares as normal during periods of wartime.

excess reserves: designating the amount of funds held in reserve in excess of the legal minimum requirements, whether the funds are on deposit in a Federal Reserve bank, in a bank approved as a depository, or in the cash reserve carried in a bank's own vaults.

excess supply curve: a graphic representation of the quantity of goods offered less the quantity asked at each price.

exchange

(1) *business:* an organization or place for carrying out business or settling accounts.

(2) *securities:* a place for trading in securities or commodities. See also *clearinghouse, foreign exchange, stock exchanges.*

(3) *finance:* the volume of monies available for use.

(4) *retailing:* to return an item to a store to substitute another item.

exchange acquisition: a method of filling an order to purchase a block of stock on the floor of an exchange. Under certain circumstances, a member broker can facilitate the purchase of a block by soliciting sell orders. All orders to sell the security are lumped together and crossed with the buy order in the regular auction market. The buyer's price may be on a net basis or on a commission basis.

exchange commercial: the last advertisement on a program when the time is used by the alternate series sponsor.

exchange current: the current rate of exchange.

exchange distribution: a method of disposing of large blocks of stock on the floor of an exchange. Under certain circumstances a member broker can facilitate the sale of a block of stock by soliciting and inducing other member brokers to solicit orders to buy. Individual buy orders are lumped together with the sell order in the regular auction market. A special commission is usually paid by the seller; ordinarily the buyer pays no commission.

exchange rate: the price of one currency in relation to that of another.

exchange relationship: the relationship between an organization and each of its members when both the individual and the organization hope to receive greater benefits from the relationship than costs.

Excise, Estate and Gift Tax Adjustment Act of 1970: federal legislation that extended excise tax rates on automobiles and telephone service until January 1972 and sped up collections of estate and gift taxes.

excise taxes: taxes levied by federal and state governments on the manufacture, sale, or consumption of commodities, or taxes levied on the right, privilege, or permission to engage in a certain business, trade, occupation, or sport.

Excise Tax Reduction Act of 1965: federal legislation that repealed excise taxes on several items and provided for systematic reductions in the tax rates on transportation equipment and communication services.

exclusion

(1) *general:* any restriction or limitation.

(2) *insurance:* a provision of an insurance policy or bond referring to hazards, circumstances, or property not covered by the policy.

exclusion allowance: the portion of an annuity payment that can be ex-

cluded from taxable income each year. This amount is determined by dividing the annuitant's investment in the contract by his life expectancy. In a tax-deferred annuity (TDA) program, the amount of annual contribution that may be excluded from taxable income by a participant is specified by law.

exclusive

(1) *merchandising:* goods obtainable from a limited number of stores or dealers.

(2) *merchandising:* sales of merchandise limited to a single retailer in a given location. See also *exclusive outlet selling.*

exclusive dealing contract: an agreement that a buyer will make all purchases of a specific item from only one seller and will refrain from carrying competing goods.

exclusive distribution: a manufacturer's protection of a dealer against the location of other dealers in the same area, often giving the right to sell an item to the exclusion of other sellers.

exclusive listing: an arrangement whereby a broker becomes the sole agent of the owner of a property, assuming the sole right to sell or rent the property within a specified time period.

exclusive outlet selling: one retailer or wholesaler in a location having exclusive control over the sale of an article or service, usually determined by contract.

exclusivity: the right acquired by an employee organization to be the sole representative of the bargaining unit.

exculpatory clause: a clause that relieves a landlord of liability for personal injury to tenants and for property damages. The clause does not necessarily protect the landlord against liability to a third party.

ex-dividend (ex div, XD): identifying the period during which the quoted price of a security excludes the payment of any declared dividend to the buyer, and the dividend reverts to the seller. Synonymous with *without dividend*.

ex dock: from the (shipping) dock.

exec: (slang) an executive.

execute

(1) *computers:* to carry out an instruction or perform a routine.

(2) *business law:* to complete or make valid, as by signing, sealing and delivering.

executed: signed, sealed, and delivered, as of contracts or other written agreements.

executive: an individual whose position calls for decision making and the use of power over employees in the daily activities of a firm.

executive committee: a formal group responsible for the direct operation and management of an organization.

executive compensation: the total monies paid to an executive, including regular salary plus additional payments (e.g., bonuses or director's fees). It does not include warrants or options to purchase stock. See also *compensation.*

executive-dominated strategy: a focus of top management on managing the portfolio of firms under its control.

executive fallout: (slang) fired managers.

Executive Order 10988: an order issued by President Kennedy in 1962 to establish the first government labor relations program by extending limited collective-bargaining rights to federal employees.

executive subsystem: the system of jobs and their definitions that is devised to accomplish work.

executive trainee: a (usually) young person who works in various units of a business to receive on-the-job training and to acquire familiarity with the entire operation. Cf. *apprentice.*

executor: a person identified in a will to administer the estate upon the death of the maker of the will (the testator) and to dispose of it according to the wishes of the testator.

executory: until all parts of a contract are performed, the state of the part not performed.

executrix: a woman identified in a will to administer the estate upon the death of the maker of the will (the testator) and to dispose of it according to the wishes of the testator.

exemplary damages: monies or fines imposed by a court (1) in punishment of the defendant, (2) to make an example of the wrongdoers, and (3) to deter others from doing the same thing.

exempt commodity: merchandise shipped in interstate commerce to which published rates do not apply.

exempt employees

(1) *personnel:* employees who are not subject to the rulings of seniority.

(2) *labor relations:* employees who are not subject to wage and overtime provisions of the Fair Labor Standards Act. Such employees may or may not be covered by a union contract. See also *Fair Labor Standards Act of 1938.*

exemption

(1) *business law:* a person who is free from a duty required by some law (e.g., one relieved from jury duty because of prejudice of the subject).

(2) *income taxes:* a token deduction from gross income allowed for the taxpayer and other family members when the taxpayer provides at least half of their support. Additional deductions are given for people who are over 65 years of age or blind. See also *Tax Reform Act of 1976.*

exercise notice: a notice issued by a clearinghouse that was formed to insure stock deliveries, obligating a customer to send the securities covered by an option against payment of the exercise price.

exercise price: the fixed price at which a stock can be purchased in a call contract or sold in a put contract. See also *puts and calls;* synonymous with *striking price.*

ex gratia payment: a payment made by an insurance company, for which it is not liable under the terms of the insurance policy.

exhaust price: the price at which a broker is forced to sell a security that was margined and subsequently dropped in price.

exhibit

(1) *general:* a display or public show.

(2) *business law:* anything presented in a court to assist in proving a set of allegations.

(3) *administration:* materials presented in a report.

Eximbank (Ex-Im Bank): See *Export-Import Bank of the United States.*

existing mortgage: a mortgage that is encumbering a property. After the property has been sold, the mortgage may or may not remain.

exit interview: See *interview, exit.*

ex officio: by right or virtue of the office held.

exogenous demand: a demand for goods determined by factors outside the present economy and including exports and government expenditures.

expanding-pie assumption: the assumption that the amount of power or any resource held by people is not fixed but rather is expanding, and that all resources can gain. Cf. *fixed-pie assumption.*

expansion

(1) *business:* extending or broadening the operation or area of a business. See also *horizontal expansion.*

(2) *economics:* a business cycle fluctuation characterized by an increase in industrial activity.

expectancy theory of motivation: based on Vroom's theory that a person's motivational level depends on his or her objectives, perceived relationship between job performance and achievement of individual objectives, and perceived ability to influence his or her performance level.

expected exit value: the nondiscounted amount of cash a company expects to realize from holding a particular asset. Cf. *present value of expected cash flow.*

expected idle capacity variance: the excess of practical capacity over the master budget sales forecast capacity, expressed in physical or dollar terms.

expected return: the profit that is anticipated from a business venture.

expected value: a weighted average

of all the conditional values of an act. Each conditional value is weighted by its probability.

expected yield: the ratio of expected return over the investment total, usually expressed annually as a percentage.

expendable fund: a fund whose assets may be applied by administrative action to general or specific purposes.

expenditure: an actual payment, or the creation of an obligation to make a future payment, for some benefit, item, or service received. If the expenditure is to acquire or improve a relatively permanent asset, it is a capital expenditure. If the amount involved is charged to an operating account, it is a revenue expenditure.

expenditure multiplier: the amount resulting from an increase in sales because of the induced spending created thereby.

expense: the cost of resources used to create revenue. Expense is the amount shown on the income statement as a deduction from revenue. Expense should not be confused with cost; all expenses are costs, but not all costs are expenses.

expense account

(1) *accounting:* an account carried in the general ledger in which all operating expenses are recorded. Expenses are deducted from gross profits, or from the total of all income accounts, to compute the net profit of the business for the period.

(2) *administration:* money advanced to an employee, usually an executive, for travel, daily costs, and other items that are accepted by the organization as justified; monies paid by an employee that are reimbursed by the employer after the expenditures have been accepted.

expense approach: a method of accounting for prepaid expenses whereby these expenses are initially debited to an expense account, even though future benefits exist. A year-end adjustment is required to record the actual expense incurred during the period and to establish a companion asset account equal to remaining future benefits. Cf. *asset approach.*

expense budget: the planned cost of the expected volume of an activity to be undertaken.

expense constant: a flat amount included in some premiums, to cover the minimum expense of an insurance transaction.

expense ratio: the percentage of a premium used to pay all operating costs.

experience

(1) *general:* events during a person's lifetime, usually pertaining to required knowledge or skill.

(2) *insurance:* the premium and loss record of an insured or of a class of coverage.

experience curves: a phenomenon in which costs of production decrease arithmetically as experience increases geometrically.

experience effect: the concept that the longer a person works at most jobs, the less each item required for completing objectives will cost.

experience rating

(1) *personnel:* the basis for an adjustment, according to an employer's unemployment or accident record, of

the rate the employer pays for unemployment insurance or worker's compensation insurance.

(2) *insurance:* a type of individual risk rating that, based on insured experience on the risk, measures the extent to which a particular risk deviates from the average of its class and reflects this deviation in the rate for the risk. See also *basic rate, line sheet, rating bureaus;* cf. *judgment rates, retrospective rating.*

experiment: an investigation that involves two elements: manipulation of some variable (independent variable) and observation of the results (dependent variables).

Experimental Negotiations Agreement: an agreement between major steel producers and the United Steelworkers Union. It included an agreement by the union not to strike at the conclusion of the contract in return for management's promise to submit unresolved issues to arbitration.

expert power: the capacity to influence based on some expertise or knowledge. It is a function of the judgment of those less powerful that the expert has ability exceeding their own.

expiration

(1) *general:* termination, cessation.

(2) *insurance:* the date on which a policy will cease to be in effect, unless previously canceled.

expire: to arrive at the termination period of an agreement, contract, or other instrument.

explicit costs: costs of a company that involve cash outlays to individuals, other businesses, or the government. Explicit costs include the purchase of resources, land, labor, and capital needed in a firm's production process and indirect business taxes.

explicit interest: the amount of money or goods paid on a loan.

exploitation theory: a theory summarized by the claim of Karl Marx that profit is the result of unpaid labor. See also *labor theory of value.*

exploitative-authoritative leadership style: a basic leadership style in which management exhibits little confidence in its subordinates. Decision making therefore, tends to be highly centralized.

exploratory forecast: a technological forecasting technique that assumes that future technological progress will continue at its present rate. This technique moves from the present to the future and considers technical factors more heavily than other variables.

export: to ship an item away from a country for sale to another country.

Export-Import Bank of the United States (Eximbank, Ex-Im Bank): an independent federal banking corporation established in 1934 to facilitate and aid in financing exports and imports and the exchange of commodities between the United States and foreign nations. It offers direct credit to borrowers outside the United States as well as export guarantees, export credit insurance, and discount loans.

exports: items produced in one country and sold to another.

export subsidies: payments made by a government to companies that export specific goods in order to encourage them to compete in foreign markets.

Export Trade Act: See *Webb-Pomerene Act of 1918.*

ex-post facto law: a law that applies retroactively (e.g., a law that would serve to convict an individual for an activity that had not been declared illegal when the person is accused of having performed it). Such laws are forbidden by Article I of the U.S. Constitution.

ex post quantities: actual or realized consumption, investment, and so on, a certain period, calculated at the end of the period.

exposure: the condition of being open to loss from a specific hazard, event, or contingency; also, funds, or the insurable values, that are so exposed to loss.

expressive performance: product performance that embodies psychological attributes, such as style and expression of self-concept.

express mail: a speedy, reliable, dependable personal mail service to meet customer needs.

express warranty: a seller's position statement concerning the quality, benefit, or value to a consumer of his or her goods, intended to convince an individual to make a purchase. The consumer has the right to expect the seller to back up these statements based on the seller's express warranty.

expropriation: the act of taking private property for public purpose, or the modification of the right to private property by a sovereignty or any entity vested with the proper legal authority (e.g., property taken under eminent domain). Cf. *confiscation.*

ex-stock dividend: without any stock dividend (e.g., when the stock dividend is held as the property of the seller). Cf. *ex-dividend.*

extend

(1) *accounting:* to multiply the unit price by the quantity of units to assertain the total cost on an invoice.

(2) *business:* to allow a period of time for the payment of a debt beyond the date originally set.

extended

(1) *business:* describing a situation in which liabilities have increased far in excess of existing assets.

(2) *business law:* describing a contractual obligation that has been prolonged beyond the originally stated date of maturity or termination.

extended bond: See *bond, extended.*

extended coverage endorsement: an endorsement extending a fire insurance policy, usually to cover loss caused by windstorm, hail, explosion (except of steam boilers), riot, civil commotion, aircraft, vehicles, and smoke.

extended term insurance: permanent plans of life insurance that provide term coverage for the face amount of the policy, in lieu of cash settlement, when premiums are discontinued for a fixed period.

extension

(1) *banking:* moving the maturity date to a later time, resulting in prolongation of the terms of a loan. See also *lockup.*

(2) *finance:* the granting of borrowing rights or the permission to buy without immediate payment.

(3) *business law:* a postponement, by agreement of the parties, of the time set for any legal procedure.

extension of mortgage: an agreement prolonging the terms of a mortgage.

external audit: an audit conducted by an outside accounting firm.

external bond: See *bond, external.*

external environment: factors from outside the organizational boundaries that affect a firm's human resources.

external forces to change: changes in the external environment that may cause organizations to change in order to adapt (e.g., technological innovation, market changes, changes in legal requirements, and/or pressure from outside groups).

externalities: external benefits or costs of activities for which no compensation is offered. Synonymous with *spillovers.*

external storage: storage facilities that are removable from a computer but hold information in a form acceptable to the machine.

external users: investors, creditors, analysts, and other groups interested in the financial affairs of a company but not involved in managing its day-to-day activities.

extinction: the decrease in undesirable behavior because of non-reinforcement.

extinguish: to wipe out, settle, or conclude, as a debt or obligation.

extortion: the taking of something of value from someone by force. Fear of exposure and threat of force are also instruments of extortion, which is sometimes aimed at inducing the victim to pay the extortioner more than is due him or her in a legitimate connection. Cf. *duress (personal).*

extra: short form of ''extra dividend'', a dividend in the form of stock or cash in addition to a company's regular or usual dividend (not to be confused with ex-dividend'').

extractive industry: a business that takes products directly from nature, especially from land or water (e.g., lumber, coal, or oil).

extractor: a device, machine, or other tool that filters, removes, or draws something through it. Synonymous with *filter.*

extra dating: adding days beyond the regulal date for invoice payment. Extensions are usually for 30- or 60-day periods.

extra expense insurance: designed for the business firm (e.g., a bank) that must continue to operate following a loss, usually at great additional expense. It should not be confused with business interruption insurance because it does not protect against interruption of business.

extraneous items: charges for gift wrapping, special mailing, and so on, that must be removed when auditing sales to arrive at true net sales totals.

extraordinary gain or loss: income or loss to an entity caused by an unusual and infrequent event that is unrelated to the ordinary activities of the entity. Cf. *above-normal loss.*

extraordinary items: special nonoperating gains and losses that are unusual in nature, infrequent in occurrence, and material in amount.

extrapolation: the estimate of an unknown value beyond the range of a series of identifiable values (e.g., projecting the world's population in A.D. 2500).

extreme job specialization: subdivision of work to the point that it results in routine, monotonous jobs. See also *specialization.*

extrinsic rewards: rewards that a person receives from sources other than the job itself. They include compensation, supervision, promotions, vacations, and friendships.

eyeball control: visual examination of inventory to determine whether there is sufficient stock on hand until requested by the wholesaler, retailer, or consumer. See also *inventory control.*

fabrication: the process of converting materials into unit, parts, or items. Cf. *assembling.*

face amount: the principal sum involved in a contract. The actual amount payable may be decreased by loans or increased by additional benefits payable under specified conditions or stated in a rider.

faced mail: mail arranged with addresses and stamps all in the same position.

face value: the principal value of an instrument, on which interest is computed for interest-bearing obligations such as notes and bonds. The legal entity issuing a note, bond, or other obligation contracts to repay the face value of the obligation at maturity. Synonymous with *par value.*

facilitating agency:

(1) *general:* an organization that services other institutions but does not take title to goods (e.g., a stock exchange).

(2) *marketing:* an agency that aids in the performance of some marketing functions but does not own the items and is not involved in buying or selling.

facsimile

(1) *general:* an exact copy or likeness.

(2) *computers:* a system for the transmission of images.

facsimile broadcasting (fax): transmission of words or pictures by radio.

fact finding

(1) *general:* investigating, collecting, and making known to a specified organization the facts regarding a specific situation.

(2) *labor relations:* investigation of a labor-management dispute by a board, usually named by a government official, that issues a report describing the points at issue and sometimes makes recommendations for a solution. Under the Taft-Hartley Act, the president must name a board of inquiry to investigate a fact-finding dispute that threatens the nation's

welfare or safety. See also *observer, public member.*

factor

(1) *general:* an individual who carries on business transactions for another. See also *factors.*

(2) *sales:* an agent for the sale of goods who is authorized to sell and receive payment for the merchandise.

factorage: the commission collected by a factor.

factor analysis: a statistical method for interpreting scores and correlations of scores from a number of tests. It searches for factors that can be multiplied to give all the correlation coefficients of a test with other tests. The most usual restriction is that the factors be as few as possible to yield all the correlations.

factor comparison method: a form of job evaluation that allocates a part of each job's wage to the key factors of the job, resulting in a relative evaluation of the job. See also *job evaluation.*

factor hours: the sum of all hours worked by one employee who is operating two or more pieces of equipment simultaneously.

factoring

(1) *banking:* a method commonly employed by an installment loan department of a bank for computing the amount of interest to be refunded or credited when a 12-month loan is being liquidated before maturity. It is also a method for accruing earned discount.

(2) *finance:* selling accounts before their due date, usually at a discount.

factor price equalization theorem: the tendency, under simplified conditions, of trade between two countries that have different factor endowments to equalize factor price ratios in the two countries.

factors

(1) *manufacturing:* ingredients needed for the production of any good or service. The primary factors are land, labor, capital, and enterprise.

(2) *finance:* limited agents who buy accounts receivable from small firms at discount. Funds are advanced upon the delivery of duplicate invoices as evidence of sale and delivery of the goods. Factors frequently perform all accounting functions in connection with the accounts receivable, in which case purchasers are notified to remit directly to factor. See also *factor.*

factor's lien: a factor's right to retain the merchandise consigned to him or her as reimbursement for all advances previously made to the consignor. Cf. *particular lien.*

factory: a production facility in which assembled workers are organized for a common business activity.

factory overhead: manufacturing costs excluding direct material and direct labor.

factory overhead incurred: manufacturing costs accumulated during a given accounting period.

factory system: the final stage in the evolution of a materially productive civilization, characterized by the introduction of power-driven machinery. Workers come to a factory—a central site where the machinery is located—rather than working at home.

fact sheet: an outline of major product data supplied to copywriters or to broadcast announcers, who use it when ad-libbing.

facultative: describes a specific transaction, one risk at a time, with the ceding and acceptance being optional on the part of the ceding company and the reinsurer (i.e., the reinsuring company may exercise its faculty to accept or reject the risk offered).

fad: a short-lived fashion, usually limited to a small portion of the population.

failsafe: See *system, fail-safe.*

failure: inability to fulfill normal business obligations; becoming insolvent or bankrupt.

Fair Credit Billing Act: an amendment to the federal Truth in Lending Act that protects charge account customers against billing errors by permitting credit card customers to use the same legal defenses against banks or other third-party credit card companies that they previously could use against merchants.

Fair Credit Reporting Act of 1971: federal legislation giving the user of credit, the buyer of insurance, or the job applicant the right to learn the contents of his or her file at any credit bureau. See also *Freedom of Information Act of 1966.*

Fair Debt Collection Practices Act: an amendment to the Consumer Practices Act, signed by President Carter, with the basic objective of eliminating abusive and bitterly unfair debt-collection practices, such as threats of financial ruin, loss of job, and loss of reputation, and late-evening telephone calls. The law became effective in March 1978.

Fair Employment Practices Committee:

a committee set up by Executive Order 8802 in 1941 to "investigate complaints of discrimination." Fair employment practices were made part of federal law by the Civil Rights Act of 1964. See also *Civil Rights Act of 1964, Title VII.*

Fair Labor Standards Act of 1938: a federal statute setting minimum hourly wages, providing for payment of time and one-half for work beyond 40 hours a week, and regulating employment of those under 18 years of age. Known as the Wage and Hour Law, it is administered by the U.S. Department of Labor. The act has been amended to include standards for computing working time and increases of the minimum wage, rules for computing overtime pay, and requirements for equal pay for equal work without regard to sex. There are more than 40 exemptions, applying to professionals, executives, and salesmen. Similar statutes have been passed by state legislatures. See also *portal-to-portal pay, wage floor.*

fair market value: a value arrived at by bargaining between informed buyers and sellers.

Fair Packaging and Labeling Act of 1966: federal legislation requiring manufacturers of many consumer items to state clearly the net quantity of contents on the principal display panel of a package.

fair plan: a facility operating under a government–insurance industry cooperative program to make fire insurance and other forms of property insurance readily available to persons who have difficulty obtaining such coverage. Cf. *assigned risk.*

fair price: the price that results in a fair return on funds invested or has a sufficient markup on goods or services sold to claim a reasonable profit.

fair rate of return: the profit that a public utility can earn to pay interest and dividends and expand facilities, as determined by federal and state law. See also *rate regulation.*

fair trade acts: laws passed by various states by which retailers are obliged to maintain specified prices on select goods. In recent years fair trade pricing has been withdrawn by a great number of retailers and manufacturers. See also *Miller-Tydings Resale Price Maintenance Act of 1937;* cf. *unfair practices acts.*

fair trade price: the retail price fixed by the manufacturer of a branded item below which the retailer is prohibited by law from making sales. Increasingly, states are removing this form of pricing. See also *price control, resale price maintenance;* cf. *list price.*

fairy money: (slang) in advertising, coupons used by a consumer, thereby reducing the cost of the item for the consumer, with the difference paid by the manufacturer.

fallback: the condition that exists when manual functions or special computer techniques are used when a system errs or when data are prematurely erased.

fallback pay: a guaranteed minimum pay level.

fall out of bed: (slang) a crash in stock prices; a sharp drop in the market.

false advertising: advertising that is misleading in a material respect, including not only false representation of the benefits or results of using the advertised commodity or its contents but also failure to reveal any potentially damaging consequences that are likely to follow from its use. Cf. *deceit.*

family allowance plan: a scheme for providing every family, rich or poor, with a certain amount of money, based exclusively on the number and age of its children. Family units above specified levels would return all or a portion of the money with their income taxes; those below specified income levels would retain the funds.

family brands: brands that appear on two or more products of a company (e.g., Hershey Company using the Hershey name for both candy bars and cocoa; Lipton Corporation using its name for both soups and tea). See also *brand awareness.*

family income rider: a special life term policy provision added to the basic policy, stating that a specified monthly income is to be paid to the beneficiary for the remainder of the income period if the insured dies before the expiration of the term.

family life cycle: the identified consumer marketing stages: single person; young married couple with no children; young married couple with children; older married couple with older, dependent children; older married couple with no children at home; and solitary survivor.

Fannie Mae: See *Federal National Mortgage Association.*

Farm Bankruptcy Act of 1933: federal legislation that allowed farmers added time to pay off their debts. The provisions of the act expired in 1949.

farm out: to subcontract.

Farm Relief Act of 1933: See *Agricultural Adjustment Act of 1933.*

farm subsidies: monies given or loaned, under stringent regulation, by the U.S. Department of Agriculture to producers of certain farm products if the market price drops below the percentage of agricultural parity or if a portion of acreage is used for pasturage or for purposes of conservation. See also *price support*; cf. *Brannan plan.*

farm surplus: farm products purchased by the U.S. government for purposes of keeping agricultural prices stable. These surpluses remain in warehouses until disposed of (e.g., through overseas sales or food distribution to needy people).

FAS: See *free alongside ship.*

FASB: See *Financial Accounting Standards Board.*

fascism: a centralized authoritative form of government with a private economy that is controlled by the government. In most cases, civil control rests with the military.

fast tracking: choosing of certain workers for rapid advancement while the remaining members of the work force are essentially bypassed.

fat budget items: merchandise approved by buyers in the hope that the goods will substantially increase sales potential.

father figure: a leader who, because of situational or emotional reasons, appears to symbolize and is regarded as a father by another.

fatigue: diminished ability to do work, either mental or physical, as a consequence of previous exertion.

favorable trade balance: the situation that exists when a nation's total value of exports is in excess of its total value of imports.

favoritism: a superior's attitude and behavior toward a particular worker, group, or ideas, based on considerations other than objectivity, professional judgment, impartiality, fairness, or equity, when making a decision among alternatives in employee relations. See also *bias, nepotism.*

fax: See *facsimile broadcasting.*

FCPA: See *Foreign Corrupt Practices Act of 1977.*

FDA: See *Food and Drug Administration.*

FDIC: See *Federal Deposit Insurance Corporation.*

FEA: See *Federal Energy Administration.*

feasibility study: an inquiry to determine what can be achieved given certain specified resources and constraints.

featherbedding: securing pay for work not done or for unnecessary work. See also *full-crew rule.*

feature

(1) *salesmanship:* the components of an item or service that yield a benefit.

(2) *securities:* the more active stocks in the general list.

Fed: (slang) the Federal Reserve System.

Federal Advisory Council: a committee of the Federal Reserve System that advises the Board of Governors on major developments and activities.

Federal Airport Act of 1946: a federal law that sets minimum wages for construction workers at airports that receive federal aid in the form of grants.

Federal Aviation Administration (FAA): in the U.S. Department of Transportation, the agency chartered "to provide for the regulation and promotion of civil aviation in such manner as to best foster its development and safety, and to provide for the safe and efficient use of the airspace by both civil and military aircraft." The FAA was established in 1959. Cf. *Civil Aeronautics Administration.*

federal bonds: See *bond, federal.*

federal budget expenditures: in the unified budget concept, expenditures of all federal agencies and trust funds. Expenditures are distinguished from net lending, and total budget outlays are the sum of expenditures and net lending. Expenditures of public enterprise funds and trust revolving funds are shown net of the receipts of such funds. See also *social infrastructure expenditures.*

federal budget receipts: in the unified budget concept, receipts, net of refunds, of all federal agencies and trust funds. Interfund and intragovernmental transactions are excluded. Proceeds of borrowing or receipts of public enterprise and revolving funds are not included.

Federal Coal Mine Safety Act of 1952: law administered by the Division of Coal Mine Inspection of the U.S. Department of the Interior to set hazard standards and to provide for enforcement of safety regulations. See also *Mining Enforcement and Safety Administration.*

Federal Communications Commission (FCC): agency established in 1934 to regulate interstate and foreign commerce in communications by both wire and radio activity. Its juris-

diction now includes radio, television, wire, cable, microwave, and satellite. The FCC consults with other government agencies on matters involving radio communications and with state regulatory commissions on telegraph and telephone matters; it also reviews applications for construction permits and relevant licenses.

Federal Contract Compliance Office (OFCC): a unit of the U.S. Labor Department, created in 1962, that is responsible for drawing up uniform sets of rules to guide the government agencies that enforce affirmative action programs. It prohibits discrimination on the basis of race or sex by employers that hold federal contracts.

Federal Corrupt Practices Act: See *Hatch Act.*

Federal Credit Union: a cooperative association organized under the Federal Credit Union Act for the purpose of accepting savings from people, making loans to them at low interest rates, and rendering other financial services to members.

Federal Crime Insurance: insurance against burglary, larceny, and robbery losses offered by the federal government when the Federal Insurance Administration has determined that such insurance is not readily available from commercial insurance companies. This Department of Housing and Urban Development program began in 1971.

federal debt limit: a limit imposed by law on the aggregate face amount of outstanding obligations issued, or guaranteed as to principal and interest, by the United States. Guaranteed obligations held by the Secretary of the Treasury are exempted.

Federal Deposit Insurance Corporation (FDIC): a government corporation that insures the deposits of all banks that are entitled to the benefits of insurance under the Federal Reserve Act. The FDIC was created through the Banking Act of 1933 and was affected by amendments of 1935. All national banks and state banks that are members of the Federal Reserve System are required by law to be members of the FDIC.

Federal Employees Compensation Act: legislation passed in 1908 to set up a program to cover certain federal employees engaged in hazardous occupations. It is the oldest form of social insurance in the United States.

Federal Energy Administration (FEA): a federal agency launched in 1973 to develop and implement federal energy policy, including allocation of resources; absorbed into the U.S. Department of Energy in 1977.

Federal Equal Credit Opportunity Act of 1977: legislation prohibiting discrimination, when responding to credit requests, on the basis of race, color, religion, national origin, sex, marital status, or age; because all or part of a person's income derives from any public assistance program; or because a person has exercised in good faith any right under the Truth in Lending Law. It gives married persons the right to have credit information included in credit reports in the name of both the wife and the husband if both use or are responsible for the account. This right was created, in part, to ensure that credit histories will be available to women who are later divorced or widowed.

federal expenditures: federal purchases of goods and services, transfer payments, grants-in-aid to state and local governments, net interest paid, and subsidies, less current surplus of government enterprises.

federal funds market: a market in which a bank needing additional reserves can borrow deposits in the Federal Reserve System from a bank with excess reserves.

federal funds rate: the interest rate on loans in the federal funds market.

Federal Hazardous Substances Labeling Act of 1960: law establishing a list of hazardous household substances subject to stringent labeling standards. As a result, the words "danger," "warning," and "caution" now appear more often in labeling.

Federal Home Bank: one of 11 regional banks established in 1932 to encourage local thrift and home financing during the depression. The banks are owned jointly by various savings and loan associations. The Federal Home Loan Bank Board serves as a management body.

Federal Housing Administration (FHA): the government agency that carries out the provisions of the National Housing Act, approved in June 1934. The FHA promotes the ownership of homes and also the renovation and remodeling of residences through government-guaranteed loans to home owners.

Federal Insurance Contributions Act (FICA): federal legislation that defines Social Security taxes and benefits. FICA deductions are made from paychecks to support this program. See also *payroll tax.*

Federal Intermediate Credit Banks: regional banks created by Congress to provide intermediate credit for ranchers and farmers by rediscounting the agricultural paper of financial institutions.

federal internal revenue collections: total federal taxes collected through the Internal Revenue Service. These monies make up 99 percent of all federal taxes (customs and a few miscellaneous taxes are excluded). See also *federal tax collections.*

Federal Loan Bank: one of 12 district banks originally established in 1916 to make available long-term mortgage loans, at equitable terms, to farmers to enable them to own their own farms. The Federal Loan Bank System is the largest holder of farm mortgages in the world.

Federal Maritime Commission: an agency created in 1936 to regulate foreign and domestic ocean commerce, mainly by overseeing agreements reached by a variety of ratemaking conferences of ship carriers.

Federal Mediation and Conciliation Service (FMCS): an independent agency created in 1947 as the successor to the U.S. Conciliation Service. Its functions include providing mediators for labor-management disputes in which interstate commerce is involved. See also *Maritime Labor Board, National Mediation Board.*

Federal National Mortgage Association (FNMA): an independent agency, originally chartered in 1938 and reconstituted in 1954, whose major function is to purchase mortgages from banks, trust companies, mortgage companies, savings and loan associations, and insurance companies to help these institutions with their distribution of funds for home mortgages; nicknamed Fannie Mae.

Federal Occupational Safety Act: federal legislation of 1970 requiring employers to provide their workers with safe and healthful working conditions.

Federal Open Market Committee (FOMC): the Federal Reserve System's most important policymaking group, with responsibility for creating policy for the system's purchase and sale of government and other securities in the open market.

Federal Power Commission (FPC): an agency established in 1930 to regulate interstate operations of private utilities in matters of issuance of securities, rates, and location of sites. In 1977 the FPC was made part of the Department of Energy.

Federal Reserve Bank: one of 12 banks created by and operating under the Federal Reserve System. Each Federal Reserve Bank has nine directors. For a list of the banks and districts, see *banker's bank.*

Federal Reserve Board: the seven-member governing body of the Federal Reserve System. The governors are appointed by the president, subject to Senate confirmation, for 14-year terms. Created in 1913 to regulate state-chartered banks that are members of the Federal Reserve System, the board has jurisdiction over bank holding companies and also sets national money and credit policy. Synonymous with *supreme court of finance.*

Federal Reserve notes: notes issued

by the Federal Reserve banks under the Federal Reserve Act when certain areas require large volumes of currency, or in seasons of the year when the public demand for currency is very heavy. When the need for currency relaxes, Federal Reserve banks retire these notes. Federal Reserve notes are issued to member banks through their respective Federal Reserve banks in denominations of $1, $5, $10, $20, $50, $100, $500, $1000, $5000, and $10,000. They answer the need for an elastic currency with full legal tender status.

Federal Reserve System: the title given to the central banking system of the United States as established by the Federal Reserve Act of 1913. The system regulates money supply, determines the legal reserve of member banks; oversees the mint, effects transfers of funds, promotes and facilitates the clearance and collection of checks, examines member banks, and discharges other functions. See also *Federal Reserve Board.*

Federals: name given to items drawn on banks in a large city in which a Federal Reserve bank is located, although the banks do not belong to the city's clearinghouse association.

Federal Savings and Loan Association: one of the associations established by the Home Owners' Loan Act of 1933, and amended in the Home Owners' Loan Act of 1934, which brought existing and newly formed mutual savings banks and building and loan associations under a federal charter.

federal tax collections: all internal revenue collections, plus customs collections and railroad unemployment insurance taxes collected by the Railroad Retirement Board, before refunds.

Federal Tort Claims Act of 1946: law that permits the United States to be sued for property or personal damages under circumstances such that, if the federal government were an individual, it would be liable. Before passage of this act, the government could be sued only with its permission.

Federal Trade Commission (FTC): an agency established in 1914 to enforce antitrust laws by seeking voluntary compliance or civil remedies. The enabling legislation, which also declared unfair methods of competition illegal, was amended by the Wheeler-Lea Act of 1930. See also *Equal Credit Opportunity Act.*

Federal Wage-Hour Act: See *Fair Labor Standards Act.*

Federal Works Program: program legislated by Congress in the early 1930s that authorized employment for idle persons and those without funds who were receiving relief. It was a major program during Franklin D. Roosevelt's administration to minimize the impact of the depression.

Fed Wire: a communications network linking Federal Reserve banks, branches, and member banks; used both to transfer funds and to transmit information. Cf. *Bank Wire System.*

fee
(1) *finance:* a remuneration for services.
(2) *real estate:* an inheritable estate in land. Cf. *fee simple estate, freehold.*

feedback
(1) *manufacturing:* the return of

part of the output of a machine, process, or system to another machine, process, or system (e.g., to the computer) as input for another phase, especially for self-correcting or control purposes.

(2) *salesmanship:* market data collected in the field from surveys, polls, and/or interviews.

(3) *administration:* a means for measuring how an organization learns by reinserting into its system information derived from its own activity, thus enabling the organization to modify its system.

feedback control: control that takes place after some unit of work has been performed.

feedforward: anticipating any errors in a process before it is carried out, with the intent to control it more accurately.

fee simple estate: an absolute fee; an estate of inheritance without limitation. This form of estate is not qualified by any other interest and passes unconditionally to the heirs upon the owner's death.

felony: any major crime (e.g., murder, arson, rape) punishable by a greater penalty than that for a misdemeanor or minor offense. In many states of the United States, felony is defined by statute as a crime punishable by imprisonment or death. See also *misdemeanor, tort.*

fence: (slang) a receiver of stolen items.

feoffment

(1) *general:* the granting of a fee.

(2) *real estate:* the granting of land by the act of taking possession. See also *enfeoff.*

FEPC: See *Fair Employment Prac-*

tices Committee.

FHA: See *Federal Housing Administration.*

fiat money: money circulated by government decree that has no precious metal backing. See also *gold exchange standard;* cf. *full-bodied money, real money.*

FICA: See *Federal Insurance Contributions Act.*

fidelity bond: see *bond, fidelity.*

fidelity insurance: coverage against loss from embezzlement or theft by employees.

fiduciary: an individual, corporation, or association, such as a bank, to which certain property is given to hold in trust, according to an applicable trust agreement. The property is to be utilized or invested for the benefit of the property owner to the best ability of the fiduciary. Administrators and executors of estates and trustees of organizations are common examples of fiduciaries. Investments of trust funds, unless specified in the trust indenture, are usually restricted by law.

fiduciary accounting

(1) *general:* maintaining property accounts in the hands of a trustee, executor, or administrator.

(2) *accounting:* estate accounting.

fiduciary bond: see *bond, fiduciary.*

Fiedler's model: a model of leadership that specifies that a group's performance is contingent on the motivation system of the leader and the degree to which the leader has control and influence in a particular situation.

field examiner: an employee of the National Labor Relations Board whose primary duties are to pass on union petitions for an election, to conduct certification elections, and to investigate unfair labor practice charges.

field experiment: the attempt of an investigator to manipulate and control variables in a natural or real setting rather than in the laboratory.

field man: a company employee who travels in a certain territory, developing new agencies and servicing agencies that already represent the company; also referred to as sales representative, special agent, state agent, inspector, or marketing representative.

field review method: a technique requiring that skilled representatives of the personnel department go into the field and gather information about employee performance in order to prepare an employee performance evaluation.

field survey: a survey of attitudes, opinions, or feelings of individuals in which data are collected at the location of a described sample.

field theory: See *Lewin model of behavior.*

field warehousing: a method for receiving collateral pledged in business loans. The warehouseman usually leases part of the borrower's facility and appoints a custodian to care for the items.

fieri facias: "that you cause it to be made" (Latin); a court order directing the sheriff to impose a tax on goods or personal property of the defendant to satisfy the judgment of a plaintiff.

FIFO (first in–first out)
(1) *business and manufacturing:*

a term relating to inventory valuations (and the balance sheet figures for inventory should be qualified accordingly) That means that the cost shown for the first shipment of an item is used for valuations. This could inflate or deflate profits.

(2) *finance:* a method of computing dividends or interest and the effect withdrawals have on earnings for the period. The FIFO method is considered to be using the oldest money on deposit for withdrawals during the interest period. It was originally designed to discourage withdrawals by exacting the maximum penalty. See also *LIFO.*

fifteen and two: the usual discount to advertising agencies permitted by most media, whereby 15 percent of the gross bill is the commission retained by the agency and 2 percent of the net bill is a cash discount given to the advertiser.

fifty-six: (slang) the days that replace Saturdays and Sundays for workers who are on the job on those days.

figurehead role: managerial duties that are symbolic in nature. As head of the organization or of a subunit, the manager represents the unit in formal matters, including ceremonies.

file
(1) *general:* any collection of informational items that are similar to one another in purpose.

(2) *administration:* a collection of related records treated as a unit.

(3) *business law:* to place a legal document on public record.

file, active: a file in which entries are made continuously.

file, master: a current, fully updated

file in which new entries are entered. Usually, the master file is the official file.

file maintenance

(1) *administration:* the activity of keeping a file up to date by adding, changing, or deleting data. See also *memo posting.*

(2) *administration:* the processing of a master file required to handle nonperiodic changes in it.

fill

(1) *business:* to supply requested goods (e.g., to fill an order).

(2) *mining:* materials used to occupy an area in the earth (e.g., creating a land fill).

filter

(1) *general:* a mask. Synonymous with *extractor.*

(2) *computers:* a device or program that separates data, signals, or material in accordance with specified criteria.

filtering: alteration of information by the sender to create an inaccurate impression.

final expense fund: Synonymous with *clean-up fund.*

final sales: the total of net sales to consumers, governments, and foreigners. Final sales exclude sales made to producers, except sales of durable plant and machinery.

finance

(1) *general:* to raise money by sale of stock, bonds, or notes.

(2) *economics:* the theory and practice of monetary credit, banking, and comprehensive promotion methods. This theory covers investment, speculation, credits, and securities.

(3) *government:* to raise money by taxation or bond issue, and to ad-

minister revenue and expenditures in a governmental organization. More recently, this activity has become known as public finance.

finance, public: a special branch of finance dealing with the provision of means of payment to meet public or government expenditures.

finance company: any institution other than a bank that makes loans to businesses or individuals. See also *sales finance company.*

financial accounting: the area of accounting concerned with periodically measuring and reporting on the financial status and operating results of organizations to interested external parties. Cf. *managerial accounting.*

Financial Accounting Standards Board (FASB): an independent accounting organization, formed in 1973, that is responsible for creating "generally accepted accounting principles." FASB is a self-regulatory organization affecting accounting firms and practitioners.

financial analysis: the use of specific techniques to study a firm's financial documents and to control the flow of funds, products, and services, both inside and outside the firm.

financial controls: the vital factors in control process: budgets, financial analysis, and breakeven analysis.

financial expense: interest expense on long-term debts.

financial intermediaries: organizations that operate in money markets to permit buyers and sellers, borrowers, and lenders to meet easily. See also *financier.*

financial markets: the money and capital markets of the economy. The money markets buy and sell short-term credit instruments. The capital markets buy and sell long-term credit and equity instruments.

financial position: the status of a company, indicated by combining the assets and liabilities as listed on a balance sheet.

financial ratios: the relationship that exist between various items appearing in balance sheets, income accounts, and occasionally other items. These ratios are used to measure and evaluate the economic condition and operating effectiveness of a firm.

financial reporting: periodic reporting on the financial position of an organization or part of one in terms of operating results, activities, and financial transactions.

financial responsibility law: a law under which a person who is a responsible party involved in an automobile accident may be required to furnish security up to certain minimum dollar limits. Each state has some form of financial responsibility law.

financial solvency: the normal business condition in which current assets are above current liabilities. Cf. *insolvency.*

financial statement: any statement made by an individual, a proprietorship, a partnership, a corporation, an organization, or an association regarding the financial status of the legal entity.

financier: an individual who earns his or her living by supplying money for other people's businesses. In most cases the financier receives a cash profit or retains a percentage of the business. See also *financial in-termediaries.*

financing transactions: movements of currency, gold, and gold equivalents used to settle a balance-of-payments deficit. See also *balance-of-payments deficit.*

finder's fee

(1) *finance:* a payment to an individual for bringing together a buyer and seller.

(2) *real estate:* a payment to someone for acquiring a potential buyer for a property. A fee is usually paid when the seller and the buyer conclude an arrangement.

fine: a penalty charged a violator by a government, court, or other authority for breaking a law or rule.

fine tuning: an effort to steer aggregate demand toward a target level through monetary and fiscal instruments.

finished-goods inventory: all items a manufacturer has made for sale to customers. Cf. *work-in-process inventory.*

fink: (slang) a person who works in a plant that is on strike; a strikebreaker.

fire fighting: (slang) a management approach to responding to problems by making small changes as needed rather than by developing a program of planned change.

fire insurance: coverage for losses caused by fire and lightning, plus resultant damage caused by smoke and water. See also *arson, casualty insurance, life insurance.*

fire sale: goods sold at reduced prices because they have been damaged or water-soiled in a fire.

firm

(1) *general:* describing full acceptance of an obligation to perform, de-

liver, or accept (e.g., a firm bid, a firm offer).

(2) *business:* any business, corporation, proprietorship, or partnership.

(3) *business law:* an unincorporated business or a partnership. Unlike a corporation, a firm is not recognized as a separate person apart from those managing it. (i.e., it is not an entity).

firm order: a definite order that cannot be canceled. It may be written or oral.

firmware: a computer's components that are neither hardware nor software (e.g., a unit for storing information used in programming the computer).

first class mail: letters, postcards, all matter wholly or partially in writing (e.g., books, magazines), and all matter sealed or otherwise closed against inspection.

first deed of trust: a deed of trust that is recorded first and is the first lien.

first-generation computer: a computer utilizing vacuum tube components. This equipment was predominantly made from 1953 to 1960.

first in–first out: See *FIFO.*

first level: the lowest-level position in an organization.

first-level outcome: a factor that brings about a second-level outcome. For example, productivity (first-level outcome) leads to promotion (second-level outcome) in many companies.

first lien: a first mortgage. Cf. *equal dignity.*

first-line management: the management level just above the workers, as represented, for example, by a plant foreman.

first mortgage: the mortgage on property that takes precedence over all other mortgages; a first lien. See also *prior lien, underlying mortgage.*

first mortgage bonds: bonds secured by a first mortgage on all or part of the property of the issuing organization.

first-party insurance: insurance indemnifying the policyholder against loss or damage to his own property (e.g., fire insurance).

firsts: the top grade of any item. Cf. *seconds.*

first wave of change: changes that occurred as a result of the agricultural revolution.

fiscal: relating to financial matters.

fiscal charges: expenses or charges that are normal for a given type of business and must be incurred in order to engage in that type of business.

fiscal drag: the tendency of a high-employment economy to be restrained from its full growth potential because it is incurring budgetary surpluses.

fiscal period: a 12-month accounting period for which business activities are reported.

fiscal policy: a planned course of action on budgetary issues.

fiscal year (FY)

(1) *business:* a corporation's accounting year. It can be any 12 consecutive months (e.g., February 1 of one year through January 31 of the next). Most companies operate on a calendar year basis.

(2) *government:* for the U.S. government, the accounting year beginning October 1. Before 1976 the

government's FY began on July 1.

fishyback service: transportation of loaded truck trailers on ships. Cf. *piggyback.*

fixed annuity: an annuity contract providing payments that remain constant throughout the annuity period. These payments do not vary with investment experience.

fixed assets: permanent assets required for the normal conduct of a business, which normally are not converted into cash during the period after they were declared fixed (e.g., furniture, land, buildings). See also *illiquid.*

fixed budget: a budget that remains the same after it is established, regardless of whether the activity level of the organization or program is higher or lower than projected.

fixed capital: capital invested, usually by stock and bond holders, as distinguished from current assets, which are partly supplied by banks.

fixed charges: business expenses that are not related to the level of operations.

fixed cost (expense): a cost (or expense), for a fixed period and range of activity that does not change in total but becomes progressively smaller per unit as the volume increases. Synonymous with *period cost;* See also *capacity costs;* cf. *direct cost.*

fixed factors of production: those productive resources that a company cannot alter in the short run (e.g., basic plant facilities).

fixed income: income that does not fluctuate with the general price level. People on fixed incomes have the most difficulty when prices are rising (e.g., retired pensioners in a period of inflation).

fixed liabilities: all liabilities that will not mature within the ensuing fiscal period (e.g., mortgages due 20 years hence, bonds outstanding).

fixed-order period model: a method for determining the number of items to be ordered at fixed time intervals up to a predetermined maximum level.

fixed-order quantity model: a method for determining the standard number of items to be ordered when the inventory reaches a predetermined level.

fixed-pie assumption: the assumption that the amount of power or any resource held by people is fixed and that one resource gains only at the expense of another. Cf. *expanding-pie assumption.*

fixed routing: calling on customers on a regular basis. Cf. *irregular routing.*

fixing the price

(1) *finance:* establishing a price on something arbitrarily rather than through the free enterprise system.

(2) *securities:* computing the price at which a commodity will be billed for rapid delivery. See also *spot market.*

fixture

(1) *leasing:* any equipment or furnishing (e.g., lamps, shelves) added to rented space to aid in business activity.

(2) *business law:* any chattel or personal property that is attached to real property permanently.

flag

(1) *computers:* a bit of data assigned to a character or word to indicate a boundary or a limit.

(2) *computers:* a character that signals the occurrence of some con-

dition, such as the end of a word. Synonymous with *mark, sentinel, tag.*

flagging an account: temporarily suspending activity on an account until it is brought up to date or for other relevant reasons. See also *rubricated account.*

flag of convenience: the national flag flown by a ship that is registered in a country other than that of its owners (e.g., to avoid taxes and high domestic wages).

flagship store: a downtown or home office store where executive, merchandising, and sales personnel are located.

Flammable Fabrics Act of 1953: federal legislation banning the sale of certain items of clothes and household furnishings that present an "unreasonable risk of death, personal injury or significant property damage" due to fire.

flap: the closing part of a fiber box, carton, or envelope.

flash sales report: an unaudited report of a previous day's sales.

flat
(1) *securities:* describes the price at which a bond is traded, including consideration for all unpaid accruals of interest. Bonds that are in default of interest or principal are traded flat. Income bonds, which pay interest only to the extent earned, are usually traded flat. Cf. *loaned flat.*
(2) *finance:* with no interest.

flatbed: a trailer that has no sidewalls.

flat cancellation: the cancellation of a policy as of what would have been its effective date, before the company has assumed liability. This requires the return in full of any paid premiums. Cf. *pro rata cancellation.*

flatcar: an open rail car without sides, ends, or tops, used for hauling heavy freight.

flation: neither inflation or deflation; a period of economic stability. Cf. *creeping inflation.*

flat lease: Synonymous with *straight lease.*

flat organization: an organizational hierarchy characterized by a wide span of control between the top executive and the first-level supervisors. It usually requires better than ordinary communications, independence, availability of sound control, and ability to delegate. Cf. *tall organization structure.*

flat pyramid structure: an organization type that reduces the layers of management, widens the span of control of managers at various levels, and is often more decentralized with regard to decision-making autonomy.

flat rate
(1) *advertising:* a standard rate for advertising space or time, with no discounts given for volume or repeat times.
(2) *finance:* a uniformly charged rate for each unit of goods and services, irrespective of quantity, frequency of purchases, and so on.
(3) *fire insurance:* the rate used when no coinsurance clause is attached to the policy (i.e., the rate from which the credit for coinsurance has not been deducted). In some states this is called the *gross rate.*

flats: pieces of first- or third-class letter mail too large to be distributed in a regular letter case and therefore distributed in a special case provided for that purpose; mail in envelopes larger than 6 x 11 inches.

fleece: (slang) to take money or property from an unknowing person (the "sheep") by unfair activity.

fleet policy: an insurance contract covering a number of automobiles. The automobiles may be specifically designated, or provision may be made for automatic coverage on a reporting basis of all automobiles owned by the insured (e.g., a taxi company). To be eligible for such coverage, all automobiles must be owned by a single insured. Cf. *open policy.*

flexible account: See *charge account.*

flexible budget: a budget, usually referring to overhead costs, that is established for a range rather than for a single level of activity. Direct materials and labor are sometimes included in the flexible budget.

flexitime: a system that allows employees to choose their own starting and finishing times within a broad range of available hours. Workers still have to work their regular number of hours.

flexyear: an employee scheduling concept that permits workers to be off the job part of the year. Employees usually work a normal work year in less than twelve months.

flier

(1) *advertising:* a handout used to promote an idea, product, or person (e.g., a political candidate).

(2) *securities:* a speculative purchase or investment, usually made by an individual who does not normally speculate or trade actively in the market.

flight of capital: the movement of cap-ital, which usually has been converted into a liquid asset, from one place to another to avoid loss or to increase gain.

flight saturation: maximum concentration of spot advertising in a relatively short period.

flip-flop

(1) *computers:* a circuit or device containing active elements capable of assuming either of two stable states at a given time.

(2) *computers:* an electronic circuit having two stable states, two input lines, and two corresponding output lines. Synonymous with *toggle.*

float

(1) *banking:* the amount of funds in the process of collection, represented by checks in the possession of one bank but drawn on other banks, either local or out of town. See also *uncollected funds.*

(2) *securities:* the portion of a new security that has not yet been bought by the public. Cf. *undigested securities.*

floatation (flotation)

(1) *packaging:* a method of interior packaging to protect a packed item from shock and vibration by wrapping it in a cushioning substance thick enough that the wrapped shape of the item conforms to the dimensions of the container.

(2) *securities:* launching an issue of securities. See also *float.*

(3) *finance:* the process of financing a business activity.

floater policy: a policy under whose terms protection follows movable property (e.g., jewelry, furs), covering it wherever it may be. See also *blan-*

ket policy; synonymous with *all-risks insurance.*

floating assets: Synonymous with *current assets.*

floating bag: a method of protective packaging in which the packaged goods are secured to a wooden base, then wrapped in a dust-proof or water-vapor-resistant bag.

floating charge: a business loan that is secured on assets rather than on a particular item. The lender has priority of repayment from the fund of assets that exist when a receiving order is made against the firm.

floating debt: any short-term obligation; usually, the portion of the public debt held in Treasury bills or other short-term obligations.

floating rates: the automatic determination of appropriate exchange rates by market forces, not by a nation's reserve holdings. Nations that do not follow these rates are pressured into line; otherwise they would see the value of their currency driven to unacceptably low levels or driven up to the point where no other nation would be able to purchase its goods.

flood insurance: coverage against loss resulting from the flood peril, widely available at low cost under a program developed jointly in 1968 by the private insurance industry and the federal government.

floor
(1) *securities:* the huge trading area where stocks and bonds are bought and sold on an exchange. See also *pit.*
(1) *government:* as distinguished from ceiling, the minimum level determined by regulation, law or contract for wages, prices, and so on.

floor broker: a member of a stock exchange who executes orders on the floor of the exchange to buy or sell listed securities.

floor limit: the largest amount for which a merchant may accept non-cash payment (check or credit card) without obtaining an authorization. A *zero floor limit* calls for authorization for every transaction, and this is becoming more feasible as the time and cost of obtaining authorization decline.

floorwalker: a person who moves about a store through various selling departments and assists customers in ways not handled by sales personnel.

floppy disk: a recent advance in computer technology, a thin disk that stores information, serving as a magnetic memory for typewriters and word-processing devices.

flotation: See *floatation.*

flotsam: items subject to salvage that are found floating on waters as a result of a wreck or natural disaster.

flow chart
(1) *administration:* a graphical representation for the definition, analysis, or solution of a problem, in which symbols are used to represent operations, data, flow, equipment, and other variables.
(2) *operations research:* a system analysis tool that displays a graphical picture of a procedure. May be general or detailed. see *methods study, systems flow chart.*

flower bond: See *bond, flower.*

flow of work: the way in which organizational activities or processes are being completed.

flow process chart: a graphic approach used for the classification and analysis of organizational activities in terms of the various individual operations, transfers, inspection points, and storages, so as to make these activities as feasible, economical, and efficient as possible.

flow-through: Synonymous with *pass-through.*

fluctuating unemployment: unemployment caused by temporary, often voluntary economic adjustments (e.g., when people voluntarily shift jobs, or when people are laid off during certain months of the year in seasonal industries).

fluctuation: the ups and downs of prices. See, e.g., *erratic fluctuations, seasonal fluctuations; see also hedging, yo-yo stocks.*

fluid savings: savings that have been neither spent nor invested.

flush production: the sizable production yielded by new oil wells during the first cycle of their life. The flush stage is followed by the settled production at a much slower rate.

fly-by-night activity: figuratively, an unsound operation; literally, one that is expected to move under cover of darkness to avoid paying creditors.

flying spot scanner: in optical character recognition, a device employing a moving spot of light to scan a sample space, with the intensity of the transmitted or reflected light being sensed by a photoelectric transducer. See also *Luhn scanner;* cf. *optical scanner.*

flying squadron: supervisors who rotate assignments to increase their overall understanding and skills among several departments. Synonymous with *job rotation.*

FMCS: See *Federal Mediation and Conciliation Service.*

FNMA: See *Federal National Mortgage Association.*

FOB; freight (free) on board: a term identifying the point from which a store is to pay transportation on incoming shipments. When the terms are FOB shipping point, the store must pay all charges from the vendor's shipping point. When the terms are FOB store, the vendor must pay all charges up to the store's receiving dock. Cf. *free alongside ship.*

focused market unit: a market-oriented division that services potential customers regardless of their location.

follow-up control: a management approach of checking whether assigned work has been completed in accordance with instructions or training given previously to an employee or a group of workers.

FOMC: See *Federal Open Market Committee.*

font: any source or point of origin.

Food and Drug Administration (FDA): an agency established in 1930 by federal legislation (now part of the Department of Health and Human Services) to develop standards and conduct research with respect to reliability and safety of drugs. It evaluates new drug applications and claims for drugs, conducts clinical studies on the safety of drugs, operates an adverse drug reaction reporting program, maintains a nationwide network of poison control centers, and advises the Justice Department on the results of its research. See also *Food, Drug, and Cosmetic Act of 1938.*

Food, Drug, and Cosmetic Act of 1938: federal legislation that strengthened food labeling requirements and extended strict requirements to advertising and labeling of cosmetics. The act requires that drug advertising and labels include "all material facts" about a drug.

football-bell structure: a theory proposed by Professors Leavitt and Whisler that by 1980 organizations would be characterized by a small group of middle managers, more innovators in the top ranks, and fewer lower-level managers. Cf. *line organization.*

footing: adding a column of figures. Synonymous with *casting up.*

forbidden combination: a combination of bits or other representations that is not valid according to some criteria.

forced billing: a means used to secure payments for freight delivery when no bill can be found.

forced choice: an employee evaluation method whereby several statements are given to a supervisor or other rater who, without knowing the weighted value of these statements, checks the statements that are the most or least characteristic of the person(s) being rated.

forced choice performance report: a rating method featuring a series of statements about an employee, arranged in blocks of two or more, from which the rater must choose the statements that are most or least descriptive of the person being rated.

forced sale: the sale or loss of property when one does not wish to dispose of it, as in bankruptcy. See also *involuntary alienation;* synonymous with *judicial sale.*

forced-sale value: See *liquidation value.*

forced saving: the situation that occurs when consumers are prevented from spending a portion of their income on consumption.

force-field theory: the concept that behavior or activity is the sum of numerous forces exerted in the field of the environment.

forcing style: the tendency to use coercive and reward power to dominate another person by suppressing differences and requiring the adoption of one's own position.

forebearance: surrendering the right to enforce a valid claim in return for a promise. This consideration binds a promise.

forecasting: projecting events of the future utilizing current data. See also *Delphi technique, Gantt chart, nominal group technique;* cf. *predictive research, technological forecasting.*

foreclosure: a legal process whereby a mortgagor of a property is deprived of his or her interest therein, usually by means of a court-administered sale of the property. Cf. *mother hubbard clause;* see also *deed in lieu of foreclosure, equity of redemption, referee's foreclosure deed; shortcut foreclosure.*

foreground: a program of high priority that is used immediately, or when and where needed, but still allows less critical programs to be worked on as background tasks during the time the priority programs are not being worked on (in the foreground).

Foreign Corrupt Practices Act (FCPA) of 1977: legislation that requires all companies registered with the Securities and Exchange Commission to keep accurate accounting records and to maintain an adequate system of internal control.

foreign exchange (F/X): instruments used for international payments (i.e., currency, checks, drafts, and bills of exchange).

foreign exchange rate: the price of one currency in terms of another.

foreign income: income earned by Americans from work performed in another country. Under the Tax Reform Act of 1976, the amount of annual income that can be excluded from taxable income by Americans working abroad was reduced from $20,000 (in some cases from $25,000) to $15,000. Foreign employees of U.S. charitable organizations are able to exclude $20,000 each year.

foreign investment: the purchase of assets from abroad.

foreign trade multiplier: the concept that fluctuations in exports and/or imports may lead to significant variations in national income.

foreman: a member of the management team responsible for implementing the policies and procedures in his or her department, directing the workers assigned to the department. See also *functional foremanship;* synonymous with *gang boss, straw boss.*

forfaiting: the purchase, without recourse, of receivables from the export sales of items.

forfeit: a thing lost to its owner by way of penalty for some default or offense.

forfeiture: the automatic loss of cash, property, or rights as punishment for failure to comply with legal provisions and as compensation for the resulting losses or damages.

forgery: false writing or alteration of an instrument to injure another person or with fraudulent intent to deceive (e.g., signing another person's name on a check to obtain money from a bank).

forgery bond: See *bond, forgery.*

formal communication: any communication that follows an organization's prescribed lines of authority.

formalization: attainment of a firm's objectives through uniform procedures that are established and legitimated by top management.

formal organization: the established organizational structure used to achieve goals and objectives.

form analysis: the method and practice of examining and analyzing organizational forms, charts, documents, and other records to discover the most appropriate way of facilitating procedures.

format

(1) *general:* an arrangement of data.

(2) *statistics:* a predetermined arrangement of characters, page numbers, lines, and so on.

formula investing: an investment technique. One formula calls for shifting funds from common shares to preferred shares or bonds as the market average rises above a certain predetermined point and returning funds to common share investments as the market average declines.

FORTRAN: acronym for "formula translation system," a language primarily used to express computer programs by arithmetic formulas. See also *language, general-purpose.*

forum shopping: (slang) looking for a court with favorable precedents or a friendly jury or judge. This is unethical practice.

forward, integration: See *integration, forward.*

forward exchange: a foreign bill of exchange purchased or sold at a stated price that is payable on a given date.

forwarding:

(1) *accounting:* carrying information from one page to another in an account or journal.

(2) *postal service:* sending of mail from a previously valid address to a current one.

forward market: the claim to sell or purchase securities, foreign currencies, and so on, at a fixed price at a given future date. This market deals in futures.

forward prices: a proposal for minimizing price uncertainty and encouraging greater stability in farming by utilizing the price system as an adjustment mechanism.

forward stock: stock that is brought into the selling department. See also *inventory;* cf. *reserve requisition control.*

foul bill of lading: a bill of lading identifying shortage or damage that existed at the time of shipment.

fourth-class mail: merchandise, printed matter, mailable live animals, and all other matter not included in first-, second-, or third-class mail.

fourth market: the buying and selling of unlisted securities directly between investors.

fox messages: (slang) a standard message used for evaluating tele-

typewriter circuits and machines because it includes all the alphanumerics on a teletypewriter, in addition to function characters (i.e., space, figures, letters shift).

FPC: See *Federal Power Commission.*

fractional currency: any currency that is smaller than a standard money unit (e.g., any U.S. coin worth less than $1).

fractional packaging: a consumer package, usually a folding carton, containing two or more smaller packages wrapped in a protective material so that unused portions are protected from deterioration after the package has been opened.

fragmented (fractional) bargaining: part of the collective-bargaining negotiation dealing with a set of grievances of a particular group that is looked on as a smaller but critical aspect of the total bargaining activity.

frame

(1) *computers:* an area extending across the width of a magnetic or paper tape perpendicular to its movement.

(2) *computers:* a box containing a major portion of a computer. Synonymous with *main frame.*

franchise

(1) *government:* a privilege granted by a government to utilize public property or to create a monopoly.

(2) *manufacturing:* a privilege granted to a dealer for distribution of a manufacturer's product. Cf. *refusal to sell.*

(3) *business law:* a certificate of incorporation.

franchise clause: a provision that payment shall not be made unless the loss or damage equals or exceeds a specified amount, known as the franchise. Cf. *deductible clause.*

franchised dealer: a retail dealer who, under terms of a franchise agreement, carries a supplier's products.

franchiser: an individual or company that licenses others to sell its products or services.

franchise store: an independently owned store that sells branded items produced by a franchise holder. The store pays the franchiser a percentage of sales for the use of the name.

franchise tax: the tax levied on a corporation for conducting business under its corporate name.

franco delivery: the full delivery of items to a consignee with all charges paid (e.g., a prepaid delivery).

franked mail: material mailed under the franking privilege. See also *franking.*

franking: authorization to send material by way of the U.S. Postal Service without charge. This privilege is granted to officials of the government and to departments and agencies, as designated in Part 137 of the Postal Service Manual, and to such others as may be specifically authorized by Congress.

fraud: intentional misrepresentation of the truth in order to deceive another person. Aspects of fraud include the false representation of fact intentionally made, with the intent that the deceived person act thereon; knowledge that the statement would deceive; and knowledge that the person deceived acted, leading to his injury. See also *bad faith, deceit, lapping, scienter, voidable contract.*

fraudulent conveyance: conveyance of property entered into by a debtor with the objective of defrauding creditors.

free alongside ship (FAS): shipping terms whereby an exporter pays all charges involved up to the moment of delivery. Cf. *FOB, free overside.*

free and open market: a market in which supply and demand are freely expressed in terms of price as contrasted to a controlled market, in which supply, demand, and price may all be regulated.

free astray: freight that is miscarried or delivered to the wrong location, then is billed and forwarded to the correct location without additional charge.

free bond: see *bond, free.*

freedom of contract: the right of persons engaged in producing goods and services to enter into agreements resulting in production. These agreements must be within the law and cannot be planned to damage individuals or society. Article I, Section 10, of the U.S. Constitution forbids the states to pass any "law impairing the obligation of contracts." See also *contract clause.*

Freedom of Information Act (FOIA) of 1966: federal legislation, amended in 1974 and 1976, establishing the principle that the public has the right—with certain exceptions—to information collected and kept by federal government agencies. Its aim is to make government records and decision making more accessible to public scrutiny by preventing agencies from arbitrarily withholding information. See also *Fair Credit Reporting Act of 1971.*

freedom shares: U.S. savings notes

sold from 1967 through the mid-1970s.

free economies: economies that operate on the basis of supply and demand, with price acting as the control mechanism. There is no central authority to allocate resources, as in a planned economy.

free enterprise: the condition under which a firm or individual is able to function competitively without excessive government restrictions.

free goods: items that are so abundant that it is not profitable to attempt to charge for them (e.g., sunlight).

free goods offer: merchandise received by a buyer at no cost for having purchased some unit of goods. Cf. *giveaway*.

freehold: the holding of a piece of land, an office, and so on, for life, or with the right to pass it on through inheritance.

free list: a statement prepared by a customs department of items that are not liable to the payment of duties.

free market: describes the unrestricted movement of items in and out of the market, unhampered by tariffs or other trade barriers.

free matter: matter sent through the mail free of postage (e.g., tax forms sent out by IRS). See also *franked mail, franking*.

free (freight) on board: See *FOB*.

free overside: in export price quotations, the seller paying all costs and accepting full responsibility for the goods until they have been safely unloaded at the place of importation in a foreign country. Thereafter, the buyer will pay all costs such as customs duty.

free port: a port where no duties are paid on either imports or exports.

free-rein leadership: a style of providing direction in group activities whereby subordinates are permitted to function with a high degree of independence. The leader's role is primarily to provide support resources, not to direct subordinates.

free reserves: a Federal Reserve Bank term describing the margin by which excess reserves exceed the bank's borrowings.

free ride: a situation in which an investor buys and sells in a short period, usually less than five days. The purchaser does not put up any money but still takes a profit.

free rider: a union term for an employee who fails to join the union that has negotiated a contract governing his wages and working conditions and is legally bound to protect his interests in the workplace. Cf. *Rand formula*.

free speech: the right of employers to express opinions on unionism, provided that no threats are implied or made explicit against employees who support the union.

free trade: trade among countries in the absence of policy restrictions that may interfere with its flow.

freeze
(1) *general:* to fix prices at present levels, as with a price freeze. A freeze rarely takes place except during national crises or wartime.
(2) *government:* government seizure or impounding of property, goods, and so on. This action demands an executive order or the passage of a law, usually during emergencies.

freight: all merchandise, goods, products, or commodities shipped by rail, air, road, or water, other than baggage, express mail, or regular mail.

freight absorption: a seller not charging a customer for freight out.

freight allowed: an agreement whereby a store pays the transportation charges on incoming goods but is permitted to charge back all or part of that cost to the vendor.

freight forwarder: an organization that consolidates the less-than-carload or less-than-truckload shipments of manufacturers into carload or truckload shipments.

freight inward: freight paid on shipments received.

freight outward: freight paid by a seller on outgoing customer shipments.

frequency

(1) *advertising:* the number of times an advertisement is delivered within a set time period.

(2) *statistics:* the number of cases in a class or other subdivision of a group.

frequency curve: a curve representing the frequency with which the values of a variable are obtained or observed when the number is infinite and the variation is subject to chance or the laws of probability. The curve is bell shaped, with the highest number of cases in the middle and a dropping off at both extremes. See also *kurtosis, ogive.*

frequency discount: a reduction in advertising rates based on the number of insertions or broadcasts used in a given time period.

frequency distribution: the categorization of statistical information according to size or magnitude, with the number of items (frequency) applicable to each interval. Cf. *dispersion.*

frictional unemployment: time lost in changing jobs, rather than as a result of lack of job opportunities. Cf. *cyclical unemployment.*

Friedmanite: an individual who upholds the monetary theories of Milton Friedman, who advocated direct control of money supply by governments in lieu of tax manipulations, government projects, and so on. Cf. *neo-Keynesian.*

friendship group: a group that evolves because of some common characteristics, such as age, political sentiment, or background.

fringe benefits: nonwage benefits (paid vacations, pensions, health and welfare provisions, life insurance, etc.) whose cost is borne in whole or in part by the employer.

fringes: (slang) fringe benefits.

fringe time: time slots when there are relatively few people in the audience to receive an advertisement.

frog: a device of rail sections designed and built to allow the wheels on one rail of track to cross another rail of intersecting track.

front money: a sum that includes funds needed to pay for land; permanent financing; legal engineering, and architectural fees; title insurance; and other closing costs not included in a construction loan.

front office: popular description for the offices of the major executives within a company.

frozen

(1) *general:* not easily available.

(2) *finance:* incapable of conversion to cash. Cf. *liquid.*

frozen account: an account on which payments have been suspended until a court order or legal process makes the account again available for withdrawal. The account of a deceased person is frozen pending the distribution by a court order grant to the new lawful owners of the account. Where a dispute has arisen regarding the true ownership of an account, it is frozen to preserve the existing assets until legal action can determine the lawful owners of the asset. See also *deceased account, sequestered account*, cf. *blocked accounts*.

frozen asset: any asset that cannot be used by its owner because of pending or ongoing legal action. The owner cannot use the asset or dispose of it until the process of the law has been completed and a decision has been passed down from the courts.

frozen pension: a pension that is paid up in full; the pension given when an employee leaves a company.

FTC: See *Federal Trade Commission.*

full-bodied money: gold; currency that is worth its face value as a commodity. Cf. *fiat money.*

full-cost pricing: the practice that includes all appropriate manufacturing costs in determining inventory.

full covenant and warranty deed: a deed in which the seller guarantees to the buyer (1) lawful possession; (2) quiet enjoyment, free of molestation, disturbance, or claims; (3) clear title; (4) further assurance that the seller will execute any additional assurance of the property's title; and (5) a warranty of the title forever.

full coverage: any form of insurance coverage that provides for payments of losses in full, subject to the limit of the policy, without application of a deductible. Cf. *ordinary life.*

full-crew rule: a regulation stating the minimum number of workers required for a given operation. It was originally designed as a safety precaution for both workers and the public. See also *featherbedding.*

full disclosure: as described by the Securities Exchange Act of 1934, the requirements that every company that has securities listed on an exchange must register with the SEC and file annual and other reports disclosing financial and other data for the information of the investing public. Management must also disclose basic financial information used in stockholder's meetings.

full employment: the condition existing when all people capable of working are working to the limit of their capability, when there are more jobs to be filled than there are people looking for jobs, and when employers can obtain additional labor only by raising real wage rates.

Full Employment Act: See *Employment Act of 1946.*

full faith and credit debt: a municipality's debt that is a direct obligation of the municipality.

full liability: liability that is not shared with others.

full lot: usually, 100 shares of stock traded on the New York Stock Exchange. Synonymous with *board lot, round lot;* cf. *odd-lot orders.*

full-service bank: a commercial bank that is capable of meeting the total financial needs of the banking public. Because the charters of some financial institutions limit their activities, this term draws attention to the advantages enjoyed by customers of a commercial bank. Cf. *Hinky Dinky,* *multiple banking, one-stop banking.*

full-service wholesaler: a wholesaler who provides the full line of services, including taking the merchandise title, retaining a sales force, and making credit available to consumers.

full showing

(1) *transportation:* the advertising message used on public transportation carriers.

(2) *advertising:* a 100 percent (full) display of outdoor advertising.

fully allocated costs: the accountant's definition of production costs, including a proportional share of overhead, depreciation, insurance, and so on, usually for a multiproduct firm whose distribution of these costs is somewhat arbitrary.

fully vested: describing an employee covered by a pension plan who has rights to all the benefits bought with the employer's contributions to the plan, even when the worker is not employed by that employer at retirement.

function

(1) *administration:* a special purpose or characteristic action.

(2) *computers:* the relation of one item from a set to all other items from another set.

functional authority: a management style that permits staff experts to make decisions and take actions that are normally reserved for line managers.

functional costing: classifying costs by allocating them to the various functions performed (warehousing, delivery, billing, etc.).

functional departmentation: grouping jobs into subunits based on the primary functions of the

organization, such as engineering, production, and marketing. Cf. *geographical departmentation, matrix departmentation, process departmentation, product departmentation.*

functional discount: a deduction taken to effect different prices for different customers (e.g., retailers get 40 percent off the list price, wholesalers 40 to 50 percent off). Cf. *price discrimination.*

functional distribution: the payment of wages, rent, interest, and profit to the factors of production according to their respective contributions.

functional foremanship: the application of division of labor at the foreman level. It involves splitting the task of the foreman into an arbitrary number of subtasks (usually eight) and assigning each subtask to an employee.

functional income distribution: payment of wages, rents, interests, and profits to manufacturers in return for supplying their labor, land, capital, and management talents.

functionalism: the ability to perform a task; the division of work to ensure that tasks are performed (production, marketing, etc.) See also *division of labor.*

functionalization: building or separating units of a firm according to their respective functions.

functional manager: a manager who is responsible for a specialized area of operations, such as accounting, personnel, finance, marketing, or production.

functional obsolescence: obsolescence created by structural defects that reduce a property's value and/or market ability. See also *weakest link* *theory;* cf. *planned obsolescence, product development.*

functional organization: a term originated by F. W. Taylor that currently refers to a type of organization in which the direction and management of work is divided according to specialized functions or duties, rather than pure line or staff areas of specialization.

functional status: status derived from one's profession or type of work. See also *status.*

function table: two or more sets of data so arranged that an entry in one set selects one or more entries in the remaining sets (e.g., a tabulation of the values of a variable, a dictionary).

fund

(1) *business:* an asset of an organization that is set aside for a particular purpose; not to be confused with *general fund.* See also *sinking fund.*

(2) *finance:* cash, securities, or other assets placed in the hands of a trustee or administrator to be expanded as defined by a formal agreement.

(3) *accounting:* current assests less current liabilities.

fundamental disequilibrium: a situation of chronic balance-of-payments problems brought on by an unrealistic, protected foreign exchange rate.

funded debt

(1) *general:* the condition that exists when the method of paying off a debt and its interest is determined for specific periods.

(2) *finance:* usually, interest-bearing bonds or debentures of a company; may include long-term bank loans, but does not include short loans or preferred or common stock.

funded retirement plan: a plan whereby the employer sets aside sufficient monies to meet the future payout requirements of the firm's retirement plan.

funding: the gathering together of outstanding debts of a business, leading to a reissuing of new bonds or obligations for the purpose of paying off debts.

funding bond: See *bond, funding.*

fungible: describes goods or securities for which any unit is the equal of any other like unit (e.g., wheat, corn).

funny money: convertible preferred stocks, convertible bonds, options, and warrants that appear to have characteristics of common stock equity but which did not reduce reported earnings per share before 1969.

furlough: a leave of absence from work or other duties, usually requested by an employee to meet some special problem.

Fur Products Labeling Act of 1951: federal legislation protecting the public against false labeling and advertising of furs.

fusion process: a type of socialization process whereby the goals and interests of an employee become somewhat similar to those of the organization in which he or she works. See also *goal congruence.*

future estate

(1) *general:* an estate developed for the purpose of possession, to be taken at an identified later date or upon occurrence of a future event.

(2) *business law:* Synonymous with "nonpossessory estate."

futures

(1) *finance:* foreign currencies

bought or sold based on a rate that is quoted as of some future date.

(2) *securities:* contracts for the sale and delivery of commodites at some future time, made with the expectation that no commodity will be received immediately. See also *gray market, hedging, Tax Reform Act of 1976.*

futures contract: a contract under which the seller promises to sell the purchaser a given amount of foreign currency at a stated price some time in the future, regardless of the actual market price of the currency at that future date. A futures contract thereby protects a business person against an increase in the price of foreign currency between the time he or she places an order for a shipment of foreign goods and the future delivery date.

future shock: a term coined by Alvin Toffler to describe people's problems in dealing with rapid changes in society.

future sum: the money that a borrower agrees to repay for an obligation. It is the interest or discount plus service or other charges, added to the total amount borrowed.

future worth: equivalent value at a future date on the time value of money.

futuriasis: a manager's preoccupation with the future, with little regard to common sense or the reality of daily living.

F/X: See *foreign exchange;* see also (Appendix J.)

FY: See *fiscal year.*

GAAP: generally accepted accounting principles. See also *Financial Accounting Standards Board.*

gage (gauge): a device used for inspection, usually in relation to the dimensions of an item.

gain: any benefit, profit, or advantage, as opposed to a loss.

gain on disposal: sale of a noncurrent asset for more than book value.

gain sharing: an incentive system whereby wage increments given to employees for increased output become progressively smaller as output increases.

galloping inflation: the rapid and unlimited rise of prices; swiftly increasing inflation that, if not controlled and minimized, could lead to a major crisis in the economy. Synonymous with *hyperinflation, runaway inflation.*

game plan: any strategy designed to achieve organizational goals. See also *game theory.*

game theory: a mathematical process used for choosing an optimum strategy when faced by an opponent who has a strategy of his own.

gang boss: Synonymous with *foreman.*

gangplank principle: developed by Henri Fayol, a principle holding that individuals at the same hierarchical level should be allowed to communicate directly, provided that they have permission from their supervisors to do so and that they tell their supervisors afterward what they have agreed to. The purpose of the principle is to cut red tape while maintaining hierarchical integrity.

gang punch: to punch all or part of the information from one punched card into succeeding cards.

gantry crane: a spanning carriage on tracks from which a hoisting tackle depends, for use in moving heavy cargo.

Gantt chart: a means designed by H. L. Gantt to measure graphically the relationship between actual and anticipated production records. Cf. *milestone scheduling.*

GAO: See *General Accounting Office.*

garbage: unwanted and meaningless information in computer memory or on tape. See also *GIGO;* cf. *junk.*

garnishee: a debtor of a defendant who possesses money or property that a third party (a plaintiff) wishes to acquire to satisfy a debt due him or her by the defendant; an individual upon whom a garnishment is served.

garnishment: a writ from a court directing an employer to withhold all or part of the money due an employee in wages and to pay such funds to the court or to the plaintiff in the action (the person to whom the employee is indebted) until a given debt is liquidated. Cf. *offset.*

gate: the total receipts received from admission to an establishment (e.g., a sports arena).

gateway: a place where freight is interchanged or interlined between carriers or where a carrier joins two operating authorities for the provision of through service.

GATT: See *General Agreement on Tariffs and Trade.*

GAW: See *Guaranteed Annual Wage.*

gazumping: (slang) an unethical practice whereby a salesman raises his price just before the deal is about to be completed, often using inflation as the reason.

General Accounting Office (GAO): an independent, nonpolitical agency established in 1921 that audits and reviews federal financial transactions and examines the expenditures of appropriations by federal units. The GAO is directly responsible to Congress.

general advertising: national or non-local newspaper advertising.

General Agreement on Tariffs and Trade (GATT): a 1947 arrangement among 23 nations to make numerous mutual tariff concessions. Additional countries have since joined GATT. See also *Kennedy round.*

general average: a contribution by all the parties in a sea adventure to make good a loss sustained by one of their number because of voluntarily sacrifices of part of the ship or cargo to save the remaining part and the lives of those on board from an impending peril.

general control expenditures: expenditures (for personnel administration and other general administration) of the legislative and judicial branches of the government, the office of the chief executive, auxiliary agencies, and staff services.

general equilibrium analysis: an economic inquiry in which the interaction of all markets is considered.

general equilibrium system: a model that attempts to define all relevant market interactions. See also *analytic models.*

general expenditures: total expenditures less utility, sales of alcoholic beverages, and insurance trust expenditures when used in reference to state or local governments separately. When combined for state-local totals, these items become direct general expenditures, to avoid duplicating intergovernmental payments. Cf. *general revenue.*

general fund: money that can be utilized (i.e., money that has not already been authorized for a particular project).

general journal: an accounting record into which journal entries are made.

general ledger: the most important bank record, reflecting every transaction that takes place in the bank during the business day, posted from various departmental subsidiary records. See also *suspense account.*

general lien: a lien against an individual but not his real property. It gives the right to seize personal property until a debt has been paid. The asset involved does not have to be that which created the debt. See also *distress for rent, seller's lien, vendor's lien;* cf. *particular lien.*

general macroeconomic equilibrium: a condition in which aggregate demand equals aggregate supply and the demand for money equals its supply.

general manager: a manager who is responsible for more than one specialized area, such as a company or plant. People from various functions report to this type of manager.

general mortgage: mortgage covering all properties of a debtor and not restricted to one parcel.

general mortgage bond: bond that is secured by a blanket mortgage on the company's property but may be outranked by one or more other mortgages.

general partner: partner who, along with others, is liable for the partnership debts.

general property tax: tax on the assessed value of property, computed as a percentage of the total value.

general-purpose computer: a computer designed to handle a wide variety of problems (e.g., sorting or a file-processing activity).

general revenue: total revenue less utility, sales of alcoholic beverages, and insurance trust revenue when used in reference to state or local governments separately. When combined for state-local totals, it refers only to taxes and charges and miscellaneous revenue, to avoid duplicating intergovernmental revenue. Cf. *general expenditures.*

general sales tax: a tax on most items, collected at the time of purchase. In many states purchases of food and medicine are excluded from this tax.

general store: a small retailing operation, not departmentalized, often found in country areas, where a wide variety of items can be bought, including food, clothing, and supplies.

general strike: See *strike.*

general warranty deed: a warranty by a seller of property that he has the title that he purports to convey.

generic brands: unadvertised, plain label grocery items that often sell for 30 to 40 percent less than advertised brands.

generic product: a basic product type.

gentlemen's agreement: an unsigned, unsecured contract based on the faith of the involved parties that each will perform.

geographical departmentation: grouping jobs into subunits based on geographical areas or territories. Cf. *functional departmentation, matrix departmentation, process departmentation, product departmentation.*

geographical differential: the variation in wage rates for identical work between areas or regions of the country.

Giffen good: See *inferior goods.*

gift causa mortis: a gift made in the anticipation of death, to avoid inheritance taxes. Cf. *gift inter vivos.*

gift certificate: a certificate that has an identified cash value, to be used in purchasing goods or services from the issuing store or business.

gift deed: a deed whereby property is transferred to another party without monetary compensation.

gift inter vivos: a gift of property given during the donor's life to another living person. Cf. *gift causa mortis.*

gift tax: a graduated, progressive tax imposed by some state governments and the federal government. This tax is paid by the donor, or the individual making the gift, not the donee, the recipient of the gift.

gig: (slang) any job, especially a dull or temporary one, often taken while waiting for a more desirable job.

GIGO: (garbage in, garbage out): the concept that the results produced from unreliable or useless data are equally unreliable or useless.

gilt-edged bond: See *bond, gilt-edged.*

gimmick: any clever idea or device.

Ginnie Mae: See *Government National Mortgage Association.*

gin out: (slang) to produce, implement, or execute a strategy.

giro: developed in the banking system of Germany, a payment system in which a bank depositor instructs his bank to transfer funds from his account directly to creditor accounts and to advise the creditors of the transfer.

giveaway
(1) *finance:* a premium available without charge. Cf. *free goods offer.*

(2) *media:* the award of prizes to studio contestants, radio listeners, or television viewers.

give-up: a member of a stock exchange on the floor acting for a second member by executing an order for him with a third member. See also *two-dollar brokers.*

glass insurance: protection for loss or damage to glass and its appurtenances by any cause except fire and war.

glut: to oversupply.

GNMA: See *Government National Mortgage Association.*

gnome: a banker or money expert who conducts business in the international finance market.

GNP: See *gross national product.*

goal: an objective or something specific to be achieved.

goal congruence: sharing of the same goals by top managers and their subordinates.

goal-directed behavior: behavior that consists of responses whose objectively observable characteristics can be correctly interpreted only as if they were intended for, or directed toward, attainment of a goal.

goal displacement: the situation that exists when employees view the performance measures used in the control system as more important than the organizational goals upon which they are based.

goal orientation: the focus of attention and decision making among members of a subunit in an organization in achieving objectives.

goal setting: establishing steps to meet the objectives of an individual or firm.

goal succession: the change in goals

as a result of conscious effort by management to shift the course of the organization's activities.

godown: in the Far East, a commercial storage warehouse.

go-go fund: (slang) an investment purporting to yield sizable earnings in a short time period, resulting in risky, speculative market activity.

going ahead: a broker deciding to make a trade for his own account rather than filling all his customer's orders first. A dishonest broker might go ahead (i.e., transact his own business first).

going-concern assumption: the idea that an accounting entity will have a continuing existence for the foreseeable future.

going down the tube: (slang) describing the failure of a new venture.

going matrix: an organizational restructuring whereby a shift is made to a matrix form that is market-oriented, with technical units along one axis, project departments along another, and appropriate staffing at the required nodes to do the needed tasks.

going public: a firm's shares becoming available on a major exchange, as distinguished from being held by a few shareholders.

going rate: See *Davis-Bacon Act of 1931.*

goldbricking: (slang) giving the appearance of working; also applied to actions of workers or unions (e.g., limiting output, loafing on the job).

gold bullion standard: a monetary standard according to which (1) the national unit of currency is defined in terms of a stated gold weight, (2) gold is retained by the government in bars rather than coin, (3) there is no circu-

lation of gold within the economy, and (4) gold is made available for purposes of industry and for international transactions of banks and treasuries.

gold certificates: receipts that the Treasury gives to the Fed, verifying the gold deposits that the Fed makes at Fort Knox, Tennessee.

gold clause: a contract term defining a money debt in terms of a U.S. dollar of a specified weight and quality of gold.

golden circle: a marketing term for a group of brands in a particular product field, all of which are equally acceptable to consumers.

gold exchange standard: an international monetary agreement according to which money consists of fiat national currencies that can be converted into gold at fixed price ratios.

gold points: the range within which the foreign exchange rates of gold-standard countries will differ. Gold points are equal to the par rate of exchange plus and minus the cost of transporting gold. The cost of insurance is included.

gold standard: a monetary agreement according to which all national currencies are backed 100 percent by gold and the gold is utilized for payments of foreign activity. Cf. *limping standard.*

gondola rail car: an open car with sides and ends, used for hauling gravel, sand, steel, and so on.

good delivery: basic qualifications that must be met before a security sold on an exchange may be delivered. The security must be in proper form to comply with the contract of sale and to transfer title to the purchaser.

good-faith bargaining: the requirement that both parties to a labor dispute meet and confer at reasonable times, with their minds open to persuasion and with a view to reaching agreement on new contractual terms. A requirement to reach agreement on any specific proposal is not implied. See *duty to bargain.*

good money: if two kinds of money of equal nominal value are in circulation, the one preferred by the general public because of metal content. People will tend to hoard the good money and spend the bad money, driving the good money out of circulation. See also *Gresham's law.*

goods and services
(1) *economics:* the result of industrial work, equaling the gross national product for one year.
(2) *business law:* any movable personal property, excluding livestock and excluding intangible property such as leases. Cf. *chattel, chose(s) in action, chose(s) in possession.*

goods on approval: items obtained when a potential buyer requests and receives from a seller the right to examine them for a stated time period before deciding whether to purchase them.

good 'til canceled order (GIC): an order to buy or sell that remains in effect until it is either executed or canceled. Cf. *orders good until a specified time, resting order;* synonymous with *open order.*

good title: Synonymous with *just title.*

goodwill: the intangible possession that enables a business to continue to earn a profit in excess of the nor-

mal or basic rate of profit earned by other businesses of similar type.

goon: (slang) a person hired to create a disturbance during a labor dispute or to induce nonstrikers to join the job action.

Gordon technique: a free-association creativity technique in which only the group leader knows the exact nature of the problem under discussion. Group members are given only a general idea of the problem to be solved.

Gosplan: the state planning commission of the Soviet Union, responsible for general economic planning.

gossip: Synonymous with *scuttlebutt.*

gossip chain: an informal communication chain in which one person passes information along to the rest.

go-stop: Synonymous with *stopgo.*

gouge: (slang) to acquire an excessive profit by either overcharging or defrauding.

government bond: See *bond, government.*

government deposits: funds of the U.S. government and its agencies, which are required to be placed in depositories designated by the Secretary of the Treasury.

government expenditures: gross expenditure amounts without deduction of any related receipts.

government insurance: protection up to $10,000 provided by the U.S. government to individuals who have served or are serving in the armed forces, to cover additional war hazards.

government markets: federal, state, and local government groups and agencies that are the target of marketing activity.

government monopoly: a monopoly owned and controlled by either a local, state, or federal government (e.g., the U.S. Postal System, water supply systems).

Government National Mortgage Association (GNMA): an agency of the U.S. Department of Housing and Urban Development whose primary function, in the area of government-approved special housing programs, is offering permanent financing for low-rent housing. Its nickname is "Ginnie Mae."

government revenue: all money received by a government other than from issue of debt, liquidation of investments, and agency and private trust transactions. It includes tax collections, charges and miscellaneous revenue, intergovernmental revenue, utility, sales of alcoholic beverages, and insurance trust revenue for all funds and agencies of a government. Revenue is net of refunds and other correcting acts.

government saving: tax receipts less government expenditures.

graceful degradation: (slang) in computer industries, the attainment of acceptable levels of reduced service.

grace period
(1) *insurance:* in most contracts, a provision that the policy will remain in force if premiums are paid at any time within a period (the grace period) varying from 28 to 31 days following the premium due date.
(2) *real estate:* the period when a mortgage payment becomes past due but before it goes into default.

graded tax: a form of local taxation; an attempt to place an increasingly heavy burden on land values and at the same time a lessening burden on land improvements. The primary objective is to dissuade owners from keeping their land unimproved—specifically, to encourage building on the property.

grade labeling: as authorized by government agencies, the labeling of certain consumer items as specified by standards (e.g., the grading of meat). See also *Federal Trade Commission; Food and Drug Administration; Food, Drug, and Cosmetic Act.*

grades (grading): the classification of major commodities into well-defined grades; the standardization of quality differences of staple commodities for purposes of identification during trading periods.

graduated payment mortgage: a type of mortgage that provides lower initial monthly payments than a standard mortgage. Mortgage payments and the outstanding principal increase gradually during the early years for a certain period, such as five years. After that period, payment is fixed at a somewhat higher level than the standard mortgage for the rest of the loan's term. Interest is fixed on the government-insured version.

graduated securities: stocks that have moved from one exchange to another (e.g., from the American Stock Exchange to the New York Stock Exchange).

graduated tax: a progressive tax whereby the rate of tax per unit of the tax base increases as the number of units increases.

graduated wage: wages that are adjusted on the basis of length of service with the organization or are coupled with performance standards.

graft: financial or other gain achieved through the abuse of a person's position or influence.

Graicunas's formula: a mathematical formula that shows geometrically how the addition of subordinates increases the complexity of managing.

grandfather clause: any condition that ties existing rights or privileges to previous or remote conditions or acts; more popularly used, when a new regulation goes into effect, to exempt people who are already engaged in the activity being regulated.

grand mean: the average of a set of averages.

granger

(1) *general:* a member of a grange—a farmers' association established for the purpose of promoting the interests of agriculture and for doing away with middlemen in getting produce more directly from farmer to consumer.

(2) *transportation:* a railroad that carries large amounts of grain.

grant: a clause in a deed reflecting the transfer of title to real property.

grantee: an individual to whom a grant is made; a person named in a deed to receive title to property.

granter: a person who offers credit.

grantor: an individual who makes a grant; a person who executes a deed giving up title to property.

grants-in-aid: payments made by one government unit to another for specified purposes. They represent federal support for a state or locally administered program or state support for a local program. See also

subvention; cf. *revenue sharing.*

grapevine: an informal communication network in an organization that bypasses the formal channels of communication. Synonymous with "rumor".

graphic display program: a computer program designed to display information, in graphic or alphameric form, on the face of a display tube similar to a television picture tube.

grass-roots method: a sales forecasting method that relies on input from salespeople in the field.

gratuitous coinage: a government policy of producing coins from metal without cost to the owner of the metal.

gratuity: a gift or donation.

graveyard shift: Synonymous with *midnight shift.*

gravure: the printing process that transfers an image to paper by means of the ink retained in plate depressions.

gray knight: an opportunistic second bidder in a company takeover that is not sought by the target who attempts to take advantage of the problems between the target and the initial bidder. Cf. *white knight.*

gray market: sources of supply from which scarce items are bought for quick delivery at a premium well above the usual market price. Individuals engaged in this legal activity speculate on future demands. Cf. *black market.*

grease-monkey: (slang) a worker who spends most of his time lubricating machinery.

Great Leap Forward: rural collectivization and industrialization as developed in the People's Republic of

China by Mao Tse-tung from 1958 to 1961.

Great Society: a series of programs of social welfare developed by President Lyndon B. Johnson. See also *Civil Rights Act of 1964, Title VII.*

green hands: workers who are new to a job and inexperienced in performing their tasks.

greenlining: a response of community citizens who withdraw their accounts from lending institutions that they believe practice redlining. See also *redlining.*

green power: the power of money.

Green River ordinance: a municipal law regulating house-to-house selling.

greige goods: unfinished fabric as it comes from the loom before bleaching, dyeing, printing, or the application of particular finishes.

Gresham's law: the concept that bad money drives away good money. This refers to the way in which people protect themselves from loss by spending money of questionable value and holding onto money of known better value. Cf. *quantity theory;* see also *good money.*

grid analysis: an analytical creativity technique that consists of first defining a problem, then listing every conceivable theoretical solution, and finally evaluating each of the suggestions.

grid technique: See *managerial grid, repertory grid.*

grievance: a complaint handled formally through contractually fixed procedures. If unsettled, a grievance may lead to the arbitration process. Synonymous with *gripe.*

grievance machinery: procedures identified in a collective-bargaining agreement to resolve problems that develop in interpretation and/or application of the contract.

Griggs v. Duke Power Company: a U.S. Supreme Court case holding that any employment criterion that disproportionately discriminates against a protected class requires the employer to demonstrate that the criterion is valid.

gripe: Synonymous with *grievance.*

gross
(1) *general:* coarse; common.
(2) *merchandising:* twelve dozen.
(3) *finance:* a total amount before any deductions have been made.

gross debt: all long-term credit obligations incurred and outstanding, whether backed by a government's full faith and credit or non-guaranteed, and all interest-bearing, short-term credit obligations.

gross earnings: the total income of a business, usually segregated according to types in financial income statements.

gross income: revenues before any expenses have been deducted.

gross investment: the total value of real productive assets produced in one year.

gross lease: a lease according to which the landlord will pay for all repairs, taxes, and other expenses incurred.

gross line: the amount of insurance a company has on a risk, including the amount it has reinsured. Net lines plus reinsurance equals gross line.

gross margin
(1) *sales:* the amount, determined by subtracting cost of goods sold

from net sales, that covers operating and financial expenses and provides net income. Synonymous with *gross profit.*

(2) *retailing:* the dollar difference between net sales and the net cost of goods sold during a stated time frame. Gross margin percentage is calculated by dividing net sales into this figure.

gross national debt: the total indebtedness of the federal government, including debts owed by one agency to another.

gross national disproduct: the total of all social costs or reductions in benefits to the community that result from producing the gross national product (e.g., pollution of rivers is part of the gross national disproduct).

gross national expenditure: the full amount spent by the four sectors of the economy (household, government, business, and foreign) on the nation's output of goods and services. It is equal to the gross national product.

gross national income: Synonymous with *gross national product.*

gross national product (GNP): the total retail market value of all items and services produced in a country during a specified period, usually one year. Distribution is presented in terms of consumer and government purchases, gross private national and foreign investments, and exports.

gross negligence: the lack of minimal or ordinary care.

gross private domestic investment: purchases of newly produced capital goods plus the value of the change in the volume of inventories held by business. Purchases include all new private dwellings, whether leased to tenants or owner occupied.

gross profit: Synonymous with *gross margin.*

gross rate: See *flat rate.*

gross revenue: total revenues received from selling goods or performing services; a revenue before any deductions have been made for returns, allowances, or discounts. Synonymous with *gross sales.*

gross sales: total sales over a specified period, before customer returns and allowances have been deducted.

gross savings: the sum of capital consumption (depreciation) and personal and corporate savings.

ground rent: rent for possession and use of land. A lease for ground rent runs 49 years or longer. Cf. *mixed estate.*

groupage: a service that consolidates small shipments into containers for movement.

group appraisal: evaluation of an employee by several managers who know the employee.

group banking: a form of banking enterprise whereby several existing banks form a holding company. The holding company supervises and coordinates the operations of all banks in the group. A majority of the capital stock of each bank in the group is owned by the holding company.

group bonus: a method of wage payment based on the performance of a team on the job. The bonus is an incentive for work completed beyond the average.

group coalition: two or more individuals who band together to maintain or increase their outcomes (such as money, free time) relative to another person or group.

group cohesiveness: the attraction of individuals to a group in terms of the desirability of group membership to the members; team spirit that permeates a group.

group composition: the relative homogeneity or heterogeneity of a group, based on the individual characteristics of the members.

group decision: a decision reached jointly by members of a group. Interactions among people affect the group decision process. In addition, group decision making allows for the possibility of conflict among goals to be considered.

group development: a series of stages that most groups go through over time (orientation, internal problem solving, growth and productivity, and evaluation and control).

group discount

(1) *broadcasting:* a special discount for the use of a group of broadcasting stations simultaneously.

(2) *merchandising:* a special discount for the purchase of large quantities of an item or service (e.g., group discounts on air fares).

group dynamics: the study of techniques and procedures for altering the structure and/or behavior of a social group. It emphasizes eliciting from members some behavior that will bring about a desired change in group structure or behavior without attempting to modify the behavior of individuals. See also *structural intervention.*

group enrollment card: a document signed by an individual who is eligible for group insurance as notice of his wish to participate in the group plan. In contributory insurance, this card also provides an employer with authorization to deduct contributions from an employee's pay.

group health insurance: a means for insuring a group of people (e.g., the employees of a firm) against the costs of ill health under one policy.

group incentive plan: a plan under which pay is based on total or group output. Added compensation is given to individual employees when the team to which the individual belongs produces in excess of preestablished levels or standards.

grouping: in computers, a mass of information having common characteristics that are arranged into related clusters.

group insurance: any insurance plan under which a number of employees and their dependents are covered by a single policy, issued to the employer or to an association with which the employees are affiliated, with individual certificates given to each insured person. See also *noncontributory.*

group norms: standards of behavior established by a group that describe the acceptable behavior of members.

group selling: the presentation for sale of goods or services to two or more people simultaneously.

groupthink: emphasis on group cohesiveness and individual concurrence with group beliefs in problem solving and data collection, resulting in a deterioration of the group's ability to function effectively.

grow-and-penetrate strategy: active investment and marketing efforts designed to increase the size and sales of a firm.

growth-share matrix: a display matrix showing market growth on the vertical axis and relative market share on the horizontal axis, used in analyzing the cash flow and investment requirements of a firm's products.

growth stage: the second phase in a product's life cycle, characterized by a rise in sales and profit and the appearance of competitors in the market.

growth stock: stock of a corporation whose existing and projected earnings are sufficiently positive to indicate an appreciable and constant increase in the stock's market value over an extended time period, the rate of increase being larger than those of most corporate stocks.

guarantee: a written statement assuring that something is of stated quantity, quality, content, or benefit, or that it will perform as advertised for a stated period. In some cases all or part of the purchaser's money will be refunded if the item fails to meet the terms of a guarantee. See also *guaranty.*

Guaranteed Annual Wage (GAW): a plan whereby an employer agrees to provide his employees a specified minimum of employment or income for a year. Unions argue that GAW plans add to income and employment stability. Management argues that GAW does not take into account the fluctuations in demand for goods and thus is a poor business practice. See also *makeup pay;* cf. *Halsey premium plan.*

guaranteed bond: See *bond, guaranteed.*

guaranteed debt: obligations of certain semipublic and public corporations that are guaranteed by the federal government as contingent liabilities.

guaranteed income: a term applied to proposals that the government ensure, as a matter of right, that everyone has a minimal income, even those who are unable or unwilling to work.

guaranteed letters of credit: travelers' letters of credit or commercial letters of credit, whereby the party requesting the credit issuance does not pay the bank in cash for the equivalent amount of the credit upon its issuance. The bank substitutes its own credit for people or firms, to encourage more domestic and foreign trade.

guaranteed rate: a minimum wage rate guaranteed to an employee who receives incentive pay.

guaranteed stock: usually, preferred stock on which dividends are guaranteed by another company under much the same circumstances as a bond is guaranteed.

guaranteed working week: the result of a labor-management agreement whereby workers will be paid for a full working week even when there is insufficient work for the employees during that week.

guarantees: federal credit aid whereby the federal government pledges its financial liability for loans made by private or state or local government institutions.

guarantor: one who makes a guaranty; an individual who, by contract, is prepared to answer for the debt, default, and miscarriage of another. See also *guaranty.*

guaranty: a contract, agreement, or

undertaking involving three parties. The first party (the guarantor) agrees to see that the performance of a second party (the guarantee) is fulfilled according to the terms of the contract, agreement, or undertaking. The third party is the creditor, or the party to benefit by the performance.

guardian: an individual chosen by a court to oversee the property rights and person of minors, persons adjudged to be insane, and other incompetents.

guardian ad litem: a particular guardian who is chosen for the single purpose of carrying on litigation and preserving a ward's interests but who has no control or power over property.

guardian deed: a deed to convey the property of an infant or incompetent. See also *committee deed*.

guest worker: a foreign worker who is allowed to enter a country for purposes of employment but cannot bring his or her family.

guiding principles: principles drawn up by various underwriting organizations to deal with situations in which the coverage provided by one type of insurance policy overlaps that provided by another, resulting in disputes between companies as to how a loss should be apportioned. Use of these principles minimizes the disputes, thus securing payment to the insured.

guild: an organization of skilled craftsmen established to provide services for and fulfill the needs of its membership.

gunslinger: (slang) a high-performance, high-risk fund that takes a capital role, or the manager of such a fund.

gypsy: an independent operator (e.g., trucker, cab driver) who drives his or her own vehicle and acquires cargo (or passengers) wherever possible.

habeas corpus: a writ ordering an official who has custody of a person alleged to be unlawfully detained to return the individual before a court to determine whether the imprisonment was legal.

habendum clause: a deed or mortgage clause that defines the extent of the property being transferred. It reads: "To have and to hold the premises herein granted unto the party of the second part [i.e., the grantee] his heirs and the assigns forever."

Hackman - Oldham job - enrichment model: a model that focuses on certain job characteristics that lead to critical psychological states for the worker. These states affect personal and work outcomes, which are moderated by employee growth-need strengths.

haggling: Synonymous with *higgling.*

half-stock: common or preferred stock that has a par value of $50.

halfwrapping: the process of wrapping a paper box so that the paper covers only the top or bottom and part of the ends or sides of the lid or base.

hallmark: an impression made on gold and silverware, introduced in the beginning of the fourteenth century in England, to identify the quality of the metal used.

halo effect: a bias whereby one favorable characteristic influences an overall judgment of an individual. Ratings of employees are sometimes inaccurate because of the frequency with which a single or general impression tends to permeate the rater's application of evaluation criteria. See also *interview bias;* cf. *point method rating.*

Halsey premium plan: an incentive wage plan that provides for a guaranteed wage in addition to an extra bonus for performance in excess of the norm.

hame: (slang) any undesirable position; a job that fails to utilize one's talents.

hammering the market: the persistent selling of securities by speculators operating on the short side who believe that prices are inflated and that liquidation is imminent. When the market is primarily affected by the bears, these individuals are said to be hammering the market.

handbill

(1) *advertising:* a form of direct advertising, usually a single sheet or a small pamphlet, distributed by hand.

(2) *finance:* paper currency.

hand-to-mouth purchasing: purchasing that satisfies needs of the moment only, neglecting long-range requirements of the individual or entity.

hard cash: metallic currency, as distinguished from paper money.

hard chance: a difficult situation.

hard copy

(1) *general:* a record that can be read by the human eye.

(2) *computers:* a document produced at the same time that information is converted into machine language (e.g., printed reports, summaries).

hard-core unemployed: a group within the labor-age population that is able and willing to work but remains unemployed. Cf. *unemployable.*

hard goods: major appliances, including refrigerators, dryers, washing machines, and air conditioners.

hardhat: (slang) a construction worker.

hard loan: a foreign loan that must be paid in hard money.

hard money (currency)

(1) *finance:* currency of a nation that has stability in that country and abroad.

(2) *finance:* coins, in contrast to paper currency or soft money.

(3) *finance:* a situation in which interest rates are high and loans are difficult to arrange. Synonymous with *dear money.*

hard sell: a dynamic, determined, and insistent approach to sales. Cf. *soft sell.*

hardware

(1) *general:* mechanical equipment used for conducting an activity.

(2) *computers:* the electrical, electronic, and mechanical equipment used for processing data, consisting of racks, tubes, transistors, wires, and so on. Cf. *firm ware, software.*

Harter Act: legislation that protects a ship's owner against claims for damage resulting from the behavior of the vessel's crew, provided that the ship left port in a seaworthy condition, properly manned and equipped.

harvest strategy: investment and marketing efforts designed to draw excess cash and profits generated by a particular product or service line for use elsewhere.

hash total: a summation of fields that is used for checking purposes and has no other useful meaning.

Hatch Act: the Federal Corrupt Practices Act. Section 313 of this law was amended by Section 304 of the Taft-Hartley Act to make it unlawful (1) for banks and corporations authorized by Congress to make a contribution or expenditure in connection with election to any political office or activity; and (2) for any corporation or labor organization to make a contribution or expenditure in connection with any election or political activity.

hatchways: openings in a vessel's deck permitting access to the cargo holds.

Hawthorne effect: the tendency of people who are being observed to react differently than they would otherwise. See also *Hawthorne studies.*

Hawthorne studies: a series of performance studies undertaken at the Chicago Hawthorne Plant of Western Electric between 1924 and 1933. These investigations showed the importance of the social system of an organization and became the foundation of human relations theory. See also *Hawthorne effect.*

Haymarket Square riot: the riot that took place during a mass meeting in Chicago on May 4, 1886, when a bomb was thrown at the police for attempting to break up the meeting, which involved speeches on labor unionism and the eight-hour work day. Seven policemen and four others were killed, and about one hundred people were injured. Eight radicals were tried and found guilty; four were executed, one committed suicide, and the other three were pardoned by the governor of Illinois.

Hazardous Substances Labeling Act of 1960: See *Federal Hazardous Labeling Act of 1960.*

head

(1) *computers:* a device that reads, writes, records, or erases data on a storage medium. See also *magnetic drum.*

(2) *administration:* the foremost person in an organization (president,

chief, etc.).

headboard: the front end wall of a container.

head-end business: the transportation of property (mail, express, baggage, milk, etc.) behind the locomotive of a passenger train.

headhunter: (slang) an individual or agency involved in finding managers and executives for a client organization. A flat fee or commission is paid to the headhunter.

head-on position: an outdoor advertising location that faces the flow of traffic, rather than being placed on an angle or parallel to the traffic.

head tax: a tax imposed on immigrant aliens on their entry to the United States.

health insurance: insurance that provides indemnity for loss of time and for medical expenses due to sickness. Cf. *accident insurance, hospitalization insurance, substandard health insurance.*

hearing: a process whereby an accused employee formally presents evidence and testimony before an examiner or an offical representing a board, in response to charges that have been preferred against him or her.

heavy hauler: a trucking firm that transports heavy and/or large items, therefore requiring special equipment for loading, unloading, and shipping.

heavy industry: the industries engaged in producing basic products, such as metals, or in manufacturing machinery and other equipment.

heavy market: a declining securities and commodities market created when the supply of bids for buying shares exceeds the demand for them, resulting in a price drop.

hedge fund: a partnership of people who pool their resources for purposes of investment. Cf. *investment company.*

hedging: a type of economic insurance used by dealers in commodities and securities, manufacturers, and other producers to prevent loss due to price fluctuations. Hedging consists of counterbalancing a present sale or purchase with a purchase or sale of a similar or different commodity, usually for delivery at some future date. The desired result is that the profit or loss on a current sale or purchase be offset by the loss or profit on the future purchase or sale.

hedging clause: a caution to customers attached to circulars, brochures, advertisements, and so on; a protective statement of warning for securities customers that customarily reads: "The information furnished herein has been obtained from sources believed to be reliable, but its accuracy is not guaranteed."

heirs: people who receive(d) the title to property upon the death of an ancestor or other testator.

hereditament: property that can be inherited.

hesiflation: a term suggested by former Secretary of the Treasury Henry H. Fowler for a reduced growth pattern in the economy combined with strong inflationary pressures. Cf. *stagflation.*

heuristic

(1) *general:* describing any method used to assist a person in discovering or learning something for himself or herself.

(2) *personnel:* describing a procedure or methodology designed to outline a program that will obtain desired results as an improvement over current procedures and is satisfactory in relation to the limits of time, cost, manpower, and the limited use of the result.

heuristic program: a set of computer instructions simulating the behavior of human operators in approaching similar problems.

hexadecimal: pertaining to a number system with a base of 16.

hiccup: (slang) a short-lived drop in the stock market.

hidden amenities: desirable aspects of property that are provided but not always noticed on first inspection.

hidden assets: assets of a firm that are not easily identifiable by examining the balance sheet.

hidden clause: in a contract, any obscure provision that stipulates requirements that may be against the buyer's interests.

hidden offer: a special offer buried in the copy of an advertisement as a test of readership.

hidden persuader: a term popularized by Vance Packard in 1957 in connection with the motivational and manipulative techniques used by ad agencies in their campaign programs. See also *motivational research.*

hidden tax: a tax included in the price of goods and services that is not easily identifiable by the payer of the tax.

hierarchy: positions ranked in relative importance within a firm by degree of authority. See also *chain of command, vertical strain.*

hierarchy of effects models: models

of advertising communications that conceptualize communications as proceeding through a succession of stages from awareness to purchase.

hierarchy of needs: the theoretical model developed by Abraham Maslow, detailing the sequence of accomplishment necessary for personal fulfillment. When physiological needs have been satisfied, the individual directs his attention in turn to needs for security, belonging, esteem, and self-actualization.

hierarchy of objectives: the interrelationship of objectives within an organization. Short-term objectives are related to intermediate-range objectives, which are in turn related to long-range objectives.

higgling: the procedure whereby, when the buyer offers a low price and the seller asks a high price, a third price is arrived at through bargaining to satisfy both parties. Synonymous with *haggling*.

high finance
(1) *general:* utilizing another's funds in a speculative fashion, which may result in a loss to the funds' owner.
(2) *finance:* borrowing to the maximum of one's credit.
(3) *finance:* extremely complicated transactions.

high grade: describing an item of superior quality (e.g., high grade stock or steak).

hightime: extra pay for a worker who is employed in places high above ground or deep below ground.

highway trust fund: a trust fund through which the expanded program of federal highway aid is financed. Appropriations based on certain highway user tax collections are made to the fund, and federal payments to states for highways are made from it.

Hinky Dinky: the name of a Nebraska supermarket chain whose employees operate in-store terminals provided by First Federal Savings and Loan of Lincoln, Nebraska, to permit First Federal customers to make deposits and withdrawals in the store. This service is significant because (1) it enables off-premises access to accounts maintained at a depository institution, and (2) the accounts bear interest. See also *service counter terminal.*

hir: a new pronoun recently coined by the American Management Associations to indicate the third-person singular of either sex. National acceptance is urged for "he," "she," "him," and "her" to yield to the sexless "hir."

hiring hall: a union-operated place where out-of-work members apply for jobs (in an industry for which the hiring is done through the union). There are legal restrictions on how such hiring is conducted. In many hiring halls the workers are assigned in strict order of their registration for jobs. Cf. *oligopsony, shapeup.*

historical cost: the principle requiring that all information on financial statements be presented in terms of the item's original cost to the entity. The dollar is assumed to be stable from one time period to another.

hit
(1) *computers:* a successful comparison of two items of data.
(2) *business:* a success (e.g., a hit item of clothing).

hi-tech: contraction of "high technology."

hit the bricks: (slang) to go on strike.

hoarding: collecting for the sake of accumulating; a planned effort by persons to accumulate items beyond normal need (e.g., purchasing dozens of cartons of cigarettes in anticipation of a price hike). Cf. *stockpiling.*

Hobbs Act of 1934: the so-called antiracketeering law, making it a felony to interfere with commerce by robbery or extortion, by conspiracy, or by threat of violence.

holdback: the portion of a loan commitment that is not funded until some additional requirement is met.

holdback pay: monies due an employee for services rendered but not yet paid to him or her.

holder in due course: a person who has taken an instrument under the following conditions: (1) that it is complete and regular upon its face; (2) that he or she became a holder of it before it was overdue and without notice that it had been previously dishonored, if such was the fact; (3) that the holder took it in good faith and for value; and (4) that, at the time it was negotiated to him, the holder had no notice of any infirmity in the instrument or defect in the title of the person negotiating it. See also *endorsement.*

holder of record: stockholders who own shares as of a specific date, to whom dividends are declared payable.

hold-harmless agreement: a contractual agreement in which the liability of one person for damages is assumed by another.

holding company: a corporation that owns the securities of another, in most cases with voting control. See also *group banking;* synonymous with *parent company, proprietary company.*

holding power: the ability of a product, program, or entity to retain an audience over time.

hold out: (slang) to refuse to work unless one is treated better or receives an increase in wages.

holdover tenant: one who fails to leave the premises after the term of a lease has expired but continues to pay rent. Cf. *tenancy at will.*

hold track: a railroad track where cars are sitting awaiting disposition instructions.

holiday pay: wages for holidays not worked; the premium rate established for work performed on holidays. Most union contracts specify holidays and establish premium rates.

Hollerith cards: the punched cards developed by Dr. Herman Hollerith in 1889 while working for the U.S. Bureau of the Census.

Home Owners' Loan Act of 1933: federal legislation establishing the Home Owners' Loan Corporation with $200 million from the Reconstruction Finance Corporation. The corporation was authorized to release up to $2 billion in bonds to exchange for mortgages. See also *Federal Savings and Loan Association.*

homeowners policy: a package type of insurance for the homeowner. Its provisions range from fire and extended coverage, theft, and personal liability to all-risk coverages.

homestead: land on which a family

lives, which they consider to be home.

honcho: (slang) a boss, senior executive, or headman.

honor: to pay or to accept a draft that complies with the terms of credit.

honor bond: See *bond, honor.*

hooking: the process of trapping a worker in order to have him spy on the union or his fellow workers. Synonymous with *roping;* see also *stoolpigeon.*

Hooperating: Hooper rating—the percentage of individuals who are listening to radio stations, ascertained by using the telephone coincidental method of data gathering. These data are supplied by C. E. Hooper, Inc. See also *share of audience;* cf. *Nielsen rating.*

hoosier: (slang) an inexperienced or incompetent employee.

hopper car: a rail car with a sloping floor that can release a portion of the entire load by gravity through its hopper doors.

horizontal channel: the flow of information across lines of communication. It can be classified as either a formal or an informal channel.

horizontal expansion: expansion of a business by absorbing facilities or buildings to handle an increased volume of business in which the firm is already engaged.

horizontal integration: See *integration, horizontal.*

horizontal merger: a combination formed when two or more businesses producing the same goods or services merge.

horizontal mobility: See *labor mobility.*

horizontal price fixing: an agreement on prices among competitors at similar levels of distribution.

horizontal promotion: a form of advancement of an employee whereby there is no change in the worker's job classification (e.g., promotion from junior to senior clerk, since the change involves no departure from the clerical classification). In horizontal promotion, pay may or may not be affected.

horizontal publication: a business publication edited for employees in similar job classifications in different industries (e.g., *Journal of Marketing, New Engineer).*

horizontal specialization: factors in the division of labor that involve specialties (e.g., marketing, production). Cf. *vertical specialization.*

hornblowing: (slang) bragging about one's talents; advertising that is presented in an aggressive fashion.

hospitalization insurance: insurance that provides indemnity for hospital, nursing, surgical, and miscellaneous medical expenses resulting from bodily injury or illness. Cf. *accident and health insurance;* see also *major medical expense insurance, medical expense insurance.*

host computer

(1) *computers:* the primary or controlling computer in a multiple-computer operation.

(2) *computers:* a computer used to prepare programs for use on another computer or in another data-processing system.

hot cargo: goods made or shipped by nonunion labor. Many unions refuse to handle such products, especially when they are produced or shipped by a struck company. See also

Ashurst-Sumners Act of 1935, unfair goods.

hot cargo provisions: contract provisions that allow workers to refuse to work with or handle unfair goods. The Landrum-Griffin Act of 1959 outlawed such provisions, except for those affecting suppliers or subcontractors in construction work and jobbers in the garment industry. See also *unfair goods.*

hot issue: (slang) a security that is drawing considerable public interest and for which demand causes the issue to jump to an immediate premium, usually several points.

hot items: (slang) any goods that show quick salability.

hot mail: (slang) preferential mail (e.g., airmail, first class, newspapers, magazines, and special delivery).

hot money: (slang) money that is received through means that are either illegal or of questionable legality.

hot-stove rule: the concept that disciplinary action should have the same characteristics as the penalty a person receives from touching a hot stove; that is, the discipline should be given with warning and should be immediate, consistent, and impersonal.

hourly rated workers: employees whose pay is figured on hours actually worked during a week. Cf. *Guaranteed Annual Wage, guaranteed rate.*

house agency: an advertising agency that has only one client.

House and Home Finance Agency: an agency created in 1977 to be responsible for major housing programs and activities of the federal government.

household saving: household disposable income less existing household consumption.

housekeeping
(1) *computers:* operations in a routine that do not directly contribute to the solution of the problem at hand but are made necessary by the method of operation of the computer. Cf. *maintenance.*
(2) *insurance:* the general care, cleanliness, and maintenance of an insured property. The standard of housekeeping is a primary consideration of underwriters and inspectors, since poor housekeeping is a major cause of fires and accidents.

house of issue: an investment banking firm engaged in underwriting and distribution of security issues.

House of Labor: the American Federation of Labor–Congress of Industrial Organizations.

house organ: a publication (newspaper, magazine) issued periodically by a company to its employees to keep them informed about the company, its personnel, and pertinent activities.

house-to-house salesman: a sales representative who visits homes in an attempt to make direct sales. See also *door-to-door selling.*

HR-10: See *Keogh Plan.*

huckster: a peddler or petty retailer who will attempt to sell anything profit making.

HUD: See *Department of Housing and Urban Development, U.S.*

hull insurance: an ocean, river marine, or aviation insurance contract covering loss of or damage to the ship or plane itself, but not the cargo.

human capital stock: the value of future labor earnings.

human engineering: an applied science of psychology and engineering concerned with the design of equipment and the arrangement of the physical conditions of work in relation to human sensory capacities, psychomotor abilities, learning, body functions, safety, and satisfactions. See also *ergonomics;* cf. *industrial psychology.*

human factors engineering: a process that applies information about human characteristics and behavior to the design of things people use, to the way they are used, and to the environment in which people live and work. See also *human engineering.*

human relations theory: a theory that stresses the importance of individuals in determining the future of an organization. It is a systematic, developing body of knowledge that is devoted to explaining the behavior of industrial man. See also *Hawthorne studies, multiple management, organic structure;* cf. *classical design theory, unilateral strategy.*

human resource accounting: the reporting of and emphasis on the relevance of skilled and loyal employees in a firm's earning picture.

human resource planning: estimating the size and makeup of the future work force.

human resources information system: a collection of data organized in a logical, reliable, and valid manner and used to make decisions in human resource planning.

human resources philosophy: a philosophy that holds that individuals not only want to be treated well but also want to be able to contribute creatively to organizational solutions to problems.

Hume's species flow mechanism: the process whereby economies operating on the gold standard suffer inflation if exports exceed imports (and deflation if imports exceed exports). The economy's competitiveness in international trade is altered as a result, and exports and imports ultimately are forced into balance.

hundred showing: See *one hundred showing.*

hurdle rate: the minimum rate of return that an investment must provide in order to be acceptable.

hush money: (slang) money given to assure the silence of the receiver; a bribe.

hybrid computer: a computer for data processing that uses both analog and digital representations of data. See also *system, hybrid.*

hygiene factors: Synonymous with *dissatisfiers, maintenance factors.*

hype: (slang) an activity that attempts to encourage consumer interest and sales (e.g., advertising).

hyperinflation: Synonymous with *galloping inflation.*

hypothecate: to promise and place property to secure a loan. The identified property is said to be hypothecated.

hypothecated account: an account that is pledged or assigned as collateral for a loan. Savings accounts and trust accounts are usually selected for purposes of hypothecation.

hypothecation
(1) *banking:* an agreement or contract that permits a bank or a creditor to utilize the collateral pledged to secure a loan in case the loan is unpaid at maturity. See also *respondentia.*

(2) *securities:* the pledging of securities as collateral (e.g., to secure the debit balance in a margin account).

hypothesis

(1) *general:* a tentative statement of an apparent relationship among facts that can be observed and therefore measured.

(2) *general:* a theory imagined or assumed to account for what is not understood; a model for testing.

I

IBRD: See *International Bank for Reconstruction and Development.*

ICC: See *Interstate Commerce Commission.*

iceberg company: a firm of which two-thirds is below the break-even point. See *break-even point.*

iceberg principle: the concept that 10 percent of required data are apparent and the other 90 percent are not seen.

ICFTU: See *International Confederation of Free Trade Unions.*

ideal capacity: the absolute maximum number of units that could be produced in a given operating situation, with no allowance for work stoppages or repairs. Cf. *peak capacity.*

idem sonans: describing a legal document in which absolute accuracy in the spelling of names is not demanded. (e.g., "Eliot" or "Elliott" would be acceptable as designation of a person named Elliott).

identifier:

(1) *general:* a symbol whose purpose is to identify, indicate, or name a body of data.

(2) *computers:* a key.

identity of task: the degree to which a job allows for completion of a whole or identifiable piece of work.

idle money

(1) *finance:* uninvested available funds.

(2) *banking:* inactive bank deposits. See also *unclaimed balances.*

idle time

(1) *administration:* time when an employee is unable to work because of machine malfunction or other factors not within the control of the worker. Usually the worker receives compensation during idle time.

(2) *computers:* the part of available time during which a computer is not in use.

IDP (integrated data processing)

(1) *systems:* data processing that is carried out, organized, and directed according to a systems approach.

(2) *computers:* a collection of

data-processing techniques built around a common language, in which duplication of clerical operations is minimized. Synonymous with *automatic data processing.*

ignorantia juris neminem excusat: "ignorance of the law is not excuse" (Latin); the principle according to which a person can be cited for parking illegally even if he says he did not see the "No Parking" sign.

illegal: describing behavior that is contrary to the basic principles of law. An illegal act is forbidden by law, whereas an unlawful act, though not forbidden by law, is not given the protection of the law.

illegal operation: the process resulting when a computer either cannot perform an instruction performs it with incorrect and irrelevant results. This shortcoming is often caused by built-in computer limitations.

illegal strike: a strike in violation of a contract, one that is not properly voted by the union membership or not authorized by established union or legal procedures, or one in violation of a court injunction. See also *snap strike, strike.*

illiquid
(1) *finance:* not easily convertible into cash; the opposite of liquid. Illiquid assets can be converted into cash, but usually at a major loss in value. Fixed assets are illiquid assets.
(2) *business law:* not established by any documentary evidence.

illth: consumer items that are harmful to people who consume them and to the general welfare.

illusory: appearing false. If that which seems to be a promise is found not to be a promise, it is said to be illusory.

ILO: See *International Labor Organization.*

image
(1) *marketing:* a buyer's mental picture of himself or herself; how an individual sees a product.
(2) *merchandising:* the feelings of customers toward a store.
(3) *computers:* duplication of data contained in a punch card.

image building: a public relations approach to advancing, upgrading, or generally improving the customer's attitude toward an item, service, organization, or person.

IMF: See *International Monetary Fund.*

immediate objectives: objectives that the organization can accomplish now without obtaining more resources or doing additional research.

immediate supervisor: a member of management who is placed directly over and is responsible for the activities of a worker, position, area, or function. See also *foreman, supervisor.*

immovable: describing real property that cannot be moved (e.g., land, trees, structures).

immunity: that which confers the ability to escape from the legal duties or penalties imposed on others. See, e.g., *indemnity.*

impact: the way in which an advertisement or a medium affects the audience receiving it. See also *motivational research.*

impact lag: the period between the time a stabilization decision is first implemented and the time its effect is felt on the economy.

impact of a tax: the placement of legal

responsibility for paying a tax, in contrast to the incidence of a tax, which is concerned with the extent to which the tax is passed on to others through price changes. See also *tax incidence.*

impairment

(1) *finance:* the amount by which stated capital is reduced by dividends and other distributions and by losses.

(2) *accounting:* the total, where liabilities exceed assets by reason of losses.

impartial chairman: an arbitrator jointly employed by union and management to decide (i.e., settle) or arbitrate disputes arising out of interpretation of a contract; chairman of a fact-finding board. See also *fact finding.*

impasse: the point in negotiations at which one party has determined that no further progress in reaching agreement can be made. In public negotiations, impasses often require a third party, such as a mediator.

imperfect competition: circumstances under which prices are usually altered by one or more competitors. This occurs because of unusual conditions in the market or advantages secured by some buyers or sellers.

impersonal, aggressive management: management that strives forcefully to achieve various goals but treats its employees in a rather cold or distant fashion. Cf. *paternal, agressive company.*

impersonal, passive management: management that rather apathetically pursues various tasks and treats its employees in a rather cold or distant fashion. Cf. *paternal, passive company.*

impersonality: the idea that all employees are subject to the same rules and regulations and are thus saved from the personal whims of the manager.

implementation: planning and/or putting an idea, schedule, method, or proposal into actual practice.

implicit costs: costs originating within the business that are the responsibility of the owner (e.g., time, money).

implicit tax: a government policy or activity that indirectly imposes costs or reduces purchasing power. Inflation is an example.

implied easement: infringement on property that has been left unchallenged over a period of time. The infringement is apparent from continued and lengthy use.

import: to receive goods and services from abroad; an imported item.

import duty: any tax on imported items.

import quota: a protective ruling establishing limits on the quantity of a particular product that can be imported.

import substitution: reducing imports through local manufacture of the item. Import substitutions is a common policy in developing nations, where foreign exchange is very scarce and where importers have developed the local market.

imposition: a demand or tax (e.g., bridge tolls, tariffs) on items property, and so on made by a taxing authority.

impost: a tax, usually an import duty.

impound: to seize or hold; to place in protective custody by order of a court (e.g., impounded property, impounded records).

imprest (petty cash) fund: a fund of a designated amount out of which payments for expenses of small amounts are made. This system is commonly employed in businesses.

imprint: the identification printed on a container during the process of manufacture. It may give the brand, container capacity, material quality, freight classification, and similar data.

improved value: the market value of a property after appreciation.

improvement mortgage bond: See *bond, improvement mortgage.*

impulse merchandise: items susceptible to spontaneous rather than purposeful purchasing. These goods benefit from display in store locations that have a considerable flow of customers.

impulse purchase: unpremediated buying of merchandise.

imputed: describing a value that is estimated when no cash payment is made to establish that value.

imputed cost: a cost that is not specified but is implied to exist by the policies of the organization (e.g., interest that would have been earned on cash spent to purchase inventories).

imputed negligence: negligence not attributed to a person directly but resulting from the negligence of another who participates with him and with whose fault he is chargeable.

inactive account: an account that has little or no movement. The balance may be stationary, neither deposits nor withdrawals having been posted to the account for a period of time. Cf. *idle money;* synonymous with *dormant account.*

inactive stock (bond): an issue traded on an exchange or in the over-the-counter market for which there is a relatively low volume of transactions. Volume may be a few hundred shares a week or even less. See also *cabinet crowd.*

inalienable: not able to be sold or transferred. Synonymous with *non assignable.*

in-and-out: purchase and sale of the same security within a short period—a day, a week, or a month. An in-and-out trader is generally more interested in day-to-day price fluctuations than in dividends or long-term growth.

in-basket training: a training method in which the participant is given a number of business papers that would typically come across a manager's desk. The participant is required to establish priorities and act on the information contained in these papers.

in bond: describing items shipped by a producer several months before a store's usual selling season. The items are held in bond in the store's warehouse until the selling season.

incentive: a motivational force that stimulates people to greater activity or increased efficiency.

incentive pay: a wage system based on the productivity of a worker above a specified level. It may take the form of a piece rate, a rate for performance above a fixed standard, or a rate arrived at by some other agreed-upon method. See also *accelerating premium pay, Atkinson system, base rate, basic piece rate, Diemer plan, differential piece-rate system, gain* *sharing, group bonus, group incentive plan, Halsey premium plan, Lincoln incentive management plan, piece rate (wage), push money, Rucker plan, Scanlon plan, task and bonus system, zero defects;* cf. *Guaranteed Annual Wage, speed-up, step-up.*

incentive plan: a reward scheme that attempts to tie pay directly to job performance (e.g., a piece rate, a sales commission).

incentive raise: a salary increment given after the completion of a specified, usually probationary, period.

incestuous share dealing: companies' buying and selling of one another's company securities for purposes of creating a tax or other financial advantage.

inchoate: newly begun or incomplete.

inchoate interest: a future interest in real estate.

incidence of taxation: See *tax incidence.*

income: money or its equivalent that is earned or accrued, arising from the sale of goods or services. See also *gross income, net income, profit, revenue.*

income account: an account in the general ledger of a bank. Expenses are listed under the assets, and the total expenses are usually deducted from the income accounts total to show the net profit to date as a portion of the undivided profits accounts.

income and expense statement: a summary of incomes and costs of operation over a specified time period Synonymous with *profit and loss statement.*

income approach to value: a proce-

dure for property appraisal in which the value on the net amount of income produced by the property is used. This value is determined by subtracting the total income of the property from expenses to determine net profit.

income averaging: See *averaging.*

income bond: See *bond, income.*

income distribution: the way in which personal income is dispensed throughout the various socioeconomic levels in a nation.

income effect: the change in the quantity of an item demanded because a person's purchasing power has been altered.

income of unincorporated enterprises: income of businesses not organized as corporations; a mixture of return to labor or capital.

income property: property, usually commercial, industrial, or residential, that is owned or purchased for an expected financial return.

income segmentation: dividing markets or customers on the basis of their earnings.

income statement

(1) *general:* the profit and loss statement of a given concern for a particular period of time.

(2) *accounting:* a copy of the income cash ledger for a particular trust account.

income summary: a clearing account used to close all revenues and expenses at the end of the accounting period. The balance of the income summary account before it is closed represents the operating results (income or loss) of a given accounting period.

income tax: a tax on annual earnings

and profits of a person, corporation, or other organization. Traditionally, there are federal, state, and city taxes, although not all states and not all cities tax income.

Income Velocity of Money: the average number of times each year that a dollar is spent on purchasing the economy's annual flow of final goods and/or services—its gross national product.

incontestable clause: a clause stating that after a certain period, an insurance policy may not be disputed except for nonpayment of the premiums.

inconvertible money: irredeemable funds; circulating money that cannot be converted into the standard. United States money has been inconvertible since 1933 because it is not redeemable in gold. See also *fiat money;* Synonymous with "irredeemable money."

incorporation: the procedure for obtaining a state charter to form a corporation.

incorporeal: of no material substance; existing with no physical properties (e.g., rights, privileges).

incorporeal property: intangible personal property (i.e., without body), including property rights, mortgages, and leases. See also *chose(s) in action.*

increasing-cost industry: an industry that experiences increases in resource prices or in manufacturing costs as it expands when new firms enter it.

increment: a salary increase within a pay grade. It is usually based on seniority and performance.

incremental: describing additional investment required for a project or additional cash flows resulting from a project.

incremental influence: the influence of a leader over and above the influence base bestowed on him or her because of position in the organization.

incrementalism: a decision-making approach whereby executives begin with a current situation, consider a limited number of changes in that situation based on a small number of alternatives, and test those changes by instituting them one at a time.

increment tax: a tax on the increased value of a property, levied or assessed on the basis of its appreciation.

incumbent: a worker who is legally authorized and is now occupying an office or position.

incumbrance: See *encumbrance.*

incurably depreciated: describing damaged property that is beyond rehabilitation or property that is uneconomical to repair. Cf. *constructive total loss.*

incurred losses: loss transactions occurring within a fixed period, usually a year. For example, calendar-year incurred losses are customarily computed in accordance with the following formula: losses paid during the period, plus outstanding losses at the end of the period, less outstanding losses at the beginning of the period.

indebtedness: a debt that is owed; any form of liability.

indefinite tenure: an unspecified period of time a worker may, upon satisfactory performance, expect to serve under his or her current employers without fear of arbitrary dismissal.

indemnify: to compensate for actual loss sustained. Many insurance policies and all bonds promise to indemnify the insureds. Under such a contract, there can be no recovery until the insured has actually suffered a loss, at which time he or she is entitled to be compensated for the damage that has occurred (i.e., to be restored to the same financial position enjoyed before the loss).

indemnity
(1) *securities:* an option to buy or sell a specific quantity of a stock at a stated price within a given time period.
(2) *finance:* a guarantee against losses.
(3) *finance:* payment for damage.
(4) *business law:* an act of legislation that grants exemption from prosecution to certain people.
(5) *insurance:* a bond that protects the insured against losses from others failing to fulfill their obligations. See also *bond, indemnity.*

indemnity bond: See *bond, indemnity.*

indent: the request from a purchaser to an importer to import specific items at a stated price. The importer has a given time period in which to accept or refuse the offer.

indenture
(1) *finance:* a written agreement under which debentures are issued, setting forth maturity date, interest rate, and other terms.
(2) *business law:* an agreement binding one person to work with or without pay for another for a stated period (e.g., apprenticeship). Such agreements are obsolete.
(3) *business law:* See *trust inden-*ture.

indenture bond: See *bond, indenture.*

independent:
(1) *personnel:* an individual whose behavior is self-determined.
(2) *administration:* an organization that does not belong to an association of companies or chains.

independent audit: an audit performed by an auditor who is independent of the organization whose accounts are being audited. See also *audit.*

independent bank: a bank that operates in one locality. The directors and officers are generally local to the community.

independent store: a retail operation that is controlled by individual ownership or management, not by outside management.

independent union: a union that is not affiliated with the AFL–CIO.

index
(1) *general:* an ordered reference list of the contents of a file or document, together with keys or reference notations for identification or location of those contents.
(2) *statistics:* a symbol or number used to identify a particular quantity in an array of similar quantities.
(3) *administration:* a statistical yardstick expressed in terms of percentages of a base year or years. For example, the Federal Reserve Board's index of industrial production is based on 1967 as 100. In April 1973 the index stood at 121.7, which meant that industrial production during that month was about 22 percent higher than it was in the base period.

indexing: an increasingly popular form of investing whereby investments are weighted in line with one of the major stock indices (e.g., Standard & Poor's 500 Stock Average).

index number: a measurement of relative change arrived at by employing statistical procedures. See also *base period.*

Index of National Enervation and Related Trends (INERT): a U.S. Department of Commerce measure of the rate of increase of the figure for the gross national product.

index register: a register containing a quantity that may be used to automatically modify addresses under direction of the control section of the computer.

indicator: a device that registers a condition in a computer.

indicia: imprinted designations used on mail pieces to denote payment of postage. See also *permit mail.*

indictment: the statement of a prosecuting attorney reflecting a grand jury's conclusion that it has reason to believe the accused to be guilty as charged. It names the offense with which the accused is charged, thus allowing preparation for a defense.

indifference schedule: a table illustrating all combinations of two commodities that are equally satisfactory or that yield the same total utility to a recipient at a specified time.

indirect business tax and nontax liability: all tax liabilities incurred by business, except for corporate income and social insurance taxes, plus general government nontax revenues from business. Nontax liabilities consist mainly of certain charges for government products and services, fines and penalties, donations, and special assessments by state and local governments.

indirect control: a management technique that traces the cause of an unsatisfactory result to the responsible person so that incorrect activities or practices can be corrected.

indirect costs: costs not usually identifiable with or incurred as the result of the manufacture of goods or services but applicable to a productive activity generally. Included are costs from manufacturing operations (wages, maintenance, overhead, etc.). See also *reapportionment, running costs.*

indirect damage: a consequential loss.

indirect financial compensation: all financial rewards, such as insurance plans, that are not included as direct pay.

indirect labor costs: wages of non-production employees, such as maintenance crews, inspectors, timekeepers, tool crib attendants, and sweepers. See also *tandem increase.*

indirect liability: the liability of a party who endorses the note of a maker for a bank or guarantees a note as guarantor for a maker.

indirect material costs: the costs of materials that are included as manufacturing overhead and assigned to products on some reasonable allocation basis.

indirect production: producing an item needed for the manufacture of major goods or services (e.g., producing a machine designed specifically to produce a given consumer product.

indirect taxes: taxes applied to goods, which can be readily shifted to other individuals.

individual brand: a name applied to one product only (e.g., Crest, Tide).

individual characteristics: the interests, values, attitudes, and needs that workers bring to the job.

individualism

(1) *personnel:* conducting one's affairs in one's own way.

(2) *economics:* the principle behind laissez-faire doctrine; the concept that individual economic freedom should not be restricted by governmental regulation.

individual proprietorship: Synonymous with *proprietorship.*

individual retirement accounts (IRAs): originally, individual pension accounts available to anyone who was not covered at work by a qualified pension plan. Effective January 1, 1982, all wage earners, including those who are already in company pension plans are able to make tax-deductible contributions to IRAs. See also *Economic Recovery Tax Act of 1981, Employee Retirement Income Security Act of 1974, Keogh Plan.*

individual-role conflict: conflict between individual capacity or interest and job requirements.

indivisibility: the claim that certain production factors cannot be divided into smaller components (e.g., unlike a pulley system, which can function at reduced efficiency if one or more wheelchain elements are omitted, an automobile that is divided into a set of wheels, an engine, and so on, cannot perform a function of lesser efficiency).

indoctrination: an attempt to inculcate the values, goals, policies, or procedures of a firm in the minds of new workers; an approach to helping workers understand how objectives and procedures relate to their responsibilities to the organization and to their co-workers.

indorsee: See *endorsee.*

indorsement: See *endorsement.*

indorser: See *endorser.*

induced consumption: additional consumer buying caused by new capital formation.

induced investment: new capital formation caused by an upturn in consumer buying.

inducement: an added consideration to convince an individual or firm to make an agreement.

induction: a formal process of introducing and training new employees on their job, position, or office.

inductive method: a form of reasoning that approaches a problem from the particular and arrives at a generalization, emphasizing data gathered by observing the empirical world. Cf. *deductive method.*

inductive statistics: making predictions, forecasts, and broad statements about a larger set of information, based on data collected from a smaller set of information.

industrial advertising: advertising goods or services for use in the manufacture or distribution of other goods and services.

industrial bank: a financial instutition originally organized to extend loans to employees. The bank derives its funds through a form of worker savings. Most industrial banks have now been merged into commercial banks. Cf. *labor banks.*

industrial classification: analysis and

synthesis of the factors pertinent to a business into a logical and systematic hierarchy, in which like things are combined in terms of their similarity then categorized according to their essential differences.

industrial coding: assigning identifying symbols to the permanent characteristics of items classified singly or in logical groupings, to ensure that characteristics contain the same identification.

industrial concentration: a factor reflecting the extent to which a large proportion of an industry's sales are produced by a few companies.

industrial data processing: data processing for industrial purposes.

industrial distributor: a full-service wholesaler representing industrial manufacturers and selling to industrial buyers.

industrial dynamics: a concept developed by Jay Forrester of MIT in 1957, to be used in investigating the behavior of industrial systems to demonstrate how policies, decisions, structure, and delays are interrelated to influence growth and stability.

industrial engineering: the applications within engineering dealing with the design, improvement, and installation of integrated systems of workers, materials, and equipment. It draws on specialized knowledge and skill in the mathematical, physical, and social sciences, together with the principles and methods of engineering.

industrial insurance: life insurance on an individual in an amount under $1000, with premiums payable weekly to an agent who calls at the insured's home to collect. See also

debit; synonymous with "weekly premium insurance."

industrialist: an individual who owns, controls, or plays a crucial role in the operation of an industrial organization.

industrial psychology: the branch of applied psychology concerned with the behavior and motivation of individual workers. Activities include testing, selection, training, and other aspects of individual and/or group interactions on the job.

industrial relations: any activity, event, or interaction between employer and employee. It commences with the job interview and lasts throughout the working lifetime of an employee. The most popular usage of the term limits it to union-management relations.

industrial revolution: the mid-eighteenth century movement of English manufacturing to a factory system (in which products are produced in a centralized location) from a cottage system (in which production was contracted to family living/work units).

industrial sociology: a field of specialization that investigates the multiple psychological and social energies or forces that are derived from and influence the various social, organizational, and work relationships, effectiveness, morale, or conflict.

industrial standardization: the orderly and systematic formulation, acception, usage, and revision of the given requirements to be achieved in order to attain a goal.

industrial union: a union whose members are employed in a particular industry, embracing various skilled and unskilled occupations. The union relies for its bargaining strength on the breadth of its membership rather than on the prestige associated with particular skills that they possess. Synonymous with *vertical union.*

Industrial Workers of the World (IWW): formed in 1905 and known as the "Wobblies," competed with existing unions, especially the AFL. The IWW felt that labor and management must by their natures be in continuous conflict and that collective bargaining was a futile exercise. Its primary goal was to eliminate the capitalist system and replace it with a society designed and controlled by workers.

industry

(1) *general:* trade, business, production, or manufacture.

(2) *government:* as determined by the Standard Industrial Classification System (SIC) of the U.S. Bureau of the Census, any commercial activity identified by this listing.

industrywide agreement: Synonymous with *joint agreement.*

inelastic demand (inelasticity): the condition that exists when a price increase leads to a higher total sales revenue, or a price decrease leads to a lower sales revenue. A perfectly inelastic demand occurs when the demand for an item does not change with changes in price. Cf. *priced out of the market.*

inelastic supply: a condition in which the quantity of an item produced does not alter, or changes minimally, with a price change.

inequities: rates or conditions substantially out of line with those paid or existing for comparable work in a plant, locality, or industry.

INERT: See *Index of National Enervation and Related Trends.*

infant industry argument: a dispute in support of import restrictions, claiming that specific new domestic firms have not reached their ultimate level of technical superiority and consequently required temporary protection from products from abroad.

inferior goods: any items for which demand decreases as income increases.

infirmity: in the creation or transfer of title, any known act or visible omission in detail that would invalidate the instrument.

inflation: an increase in the price level, creating a decrease in the purchasing power of the monetary unit. Cf. *deflation, flation, hesiflation, galloping inflation, overheating, prime interest (rate), simultaneous inflation and unemployment, speculation, stagflation.*

inflation, runaway: Synonymous with *galloping inflation.*

inflation accounting: the bookkeeping practice that shows the impact of inflation on corporate assets and profits.

inflationary bias: the tendency toward a persistent upward trend in the price level.

inflationary gap: the amount by which government and private spending exceeds the amount needed to maintain a stable price level and full employment.

inflationary spiral: the situation in a time of rising prices when employees demand higher wages, which in turn increases costs, leading sellers and producers then to demand still higher prices. See also *Phillips curve, stabilization policy, wage stabilization*; cf. *Pigou effect concept.*

inflation guard endorsement: an endorsement that, when added to a policy providing coverage against direct physical loss to buildings, automatically increases the amount of insurance applicable to building items at the end of each period of three months after the policy inception date.

influencer: any person who, though not directly involved in a purchase, affects the buying decision of another person.

inflump: See *simultaneous inflation and unemployment.*

informal communication channels: communication patterns that exist outside or in addition to management-approved formal channels.

informal groups: natural (i.e., unorganized) groups of employees in the work situation.

informal investigation: the method of seeking information through conversation, observation, and the subsequent analysis of data.

informal leader: a leader whose power and authority over a group is derived from his acceptance by the group, rather than from his office, position, status, or rank in the formal chain of command in the formal organization. Cf. *father figure.*

informal organization: a rather complicated and nebulous network of communication and interaction patterns of workers, supervisors, groups, or cliques within the formal organizational structure. Such a phenomenon usually arises spontaneously in order (1) to augment, interpret, speed up, or change the formal communication system (or the lack of it); (2) to regulate the flow, extent, manner, and enforcement of formal authority; (3) to humanize the formal organization by trying to maintain a feeling of individuality among the members, while providing some security, unity, integrity, and feelings of belonging; and (4) to meet related psychological and social needs to such an extent as to give the impression of being *the* organization. Cf. *formal organization.*

informatics: Synonymous with *information science.*

information

(1) *general:* the meaning that a person assigns to data by means of the conventions used in their representation.

(2) *computers:* the collection of data, numbers, characters, and so on, that is processed or produced by a computer.

information aggregation: the amount of detail with which information is maintained in a data bank. The higher the degree of aggregation, the more complex the data tend to be and the longer it usually takes for them to be added to the data bank.

informational roles: the roles of monitor, disseminator, and company spokesperson.

information costs: costs, including time, expended in securing data.

information-need-product: See *INP.*

information overload: a condition in which too much information flows through communication channels, leading people to ignore potentially crucial pieces of information.

information processing: Synonymous with *data processing.*

information recency: a factor that depends on the lapse of time between the occurrence of an event and the inclusion of data recording that event in the management information system. See also *management information system.*

information retrieval

(1) *general:* the methods and procedures for recovering specific information from stored data.

(2) *general:* a technique for cataloguing data related to one field so that such data can be called for quickly at any time.

(3) *computers:* a branch of computer science relating to the methods for storing and searching quantities of information.

information science: the study of how data are processed and transmitted through digital processing equipment. Synonymous with *informatics.*

information system: an organized method of providing past, present, and projected information related to internal operations and external intelligence.

infraction: the act of violating organizational policies, rules, or regulations.

infrastructure: the basic structure of a nation's economy, including transportation, communications, and other public services on which the economic activity relies.

infringement

(1) *manufacturing:* production of a machine that yields the same results by the same action as a patented machine. This is a patent infringement.

(2) *merchandising:* reproduction of a registered trademark and its use on merchandise to mislead the public into believing that the items bearing the reproduced trademark are the product of the true owner of the trademark. This is a trademark infringement.

(3) *real estate:* encroaching on someone else's property (i.e., trespassing). Cf. *intrusion.*

ingress: the ability to enter property or land.

inherit: to acquire the property of a person who dies intestate. See also *devolution.*

inheritance: the act of inheriting; any possession coming as a gift; any characteristic passed on by heredity. See also *Tax Reform Act of 1976.*

inheritance audience: the segment of a broadcast audience that stays tuned to a succeeding program.

inheritance taxes: taxes levied by the states on property received by inheritance or by succession; a tax on inherited property. Cf. *estate tax, succession tax.*

in-house advertising agencies: advertising agencies that are owned and controlled by client organizations.

initial mark-on: the difference between the retail value of goods and the delivered cost when they are first priced and placed on display.

initiating structures: a leader's behavior in delineating the relationship between leader and work group and the leader's work toward establishing well-defined patterns of organization, channels of communication, and procedural methods.

injunction: a court order advising that if a party does commit the enjoined-against act, there will be a penalty. A temporary restraining order is issued for a limited time. A permanent injunction is issued after a full hearing. In 1932 the Norris–LaGuardia (Anti-Injunction) Act forbade the federal courts to issue injunctions unless certain conditions were fulfilled first. See also *blanket injunction.*

injunction pendente lite: a court remedy before the hearing on the merits of a suit, for the express purpose of preventing any act whereby the conditions in the conflict might be substantially altered. See also *lis pendens.*

in kind: referring to the replacement of lost or damaged property with material or property of a similar description and quality. Cf. *kind.*

inland marine insurance: insurance developed originally by marine underwriters to cover goods while in transit by other than ocean vessels. It now covers any goods in transit (except transoceanic) and also includes numerous floater policies. Cf. *ocean marine insurance.*

innocent purchaser: an individual who, in good faith, does not expect any hidden property defects to appear when he has gained title to real property.

innovation: a new concept or approach in the production cycle, frequently involving the use of inventions in a practical task. The innovation theory developed by Joseph Schumpeter suggests that waves of innovation are followed by lulls, which mean depression.

innovation-dominated strategy: a focus of key managers on the creation and/or implementation of new technologies, products, or services.

INP: information-need-product; a traditional method of selling in which the sales presentation is made step by step.

in personam: a legal judgment that binds the defendant to a personal liability. Cf. *in rem.*

in-progress inventory: goods that are partially completed but will require additional labor and materials to become finished goods.

input
(1) *general:* the insertion of data into a device or process.
(2) *computers:* describing the routines with direct input or the devices from which such information is available to the computer.
(3) *computers:* information transferred from auxiliary or external storage into the internal storage of a computer.

input block: a segment of a computer's internal storage reserved for receiving and/or processing input data.

input data
(1) *general:* data to be processed.
(2) *computers:* any data on which one or more of the basic processing functions (coding, sorting, summarizing, reporting, etc.) are to be performed. Synonymous with *input.*

input/output (I/O): a general term for equipment used to communicate with a computer.

inquiry: a request for information from computer storage (e.g., a request for the number of available hotel rooms).

inquiry test: a technique for testing advertisements by noting the number of inquiries from listeners, viewers, or publication readers.

in rem: a legal judgment that binds, affects, or determines the status of property. Cf. *in personam.*

insertion order: written instructions for an advertisement to be placed in a particular issue of a publication at a stated rate.

inside-outside approach: a strategy approach whereby managers look first at the organization and then at the environment. Cf. *outside-inside approach.*

insider: an individual who, because of his or her employment position, has special information dealing with the financial status of a firm before that information is released to the public or to stockholders. See also *smart money.*

inside union: Synonymous with *company union.*

insolvency: the inability to pay one's debts as they mature. Even though the total assets of a business might exceed its total liabilities by a wide margin, the business is said to be insolvent if the assets are such that they cannot be readily converted into cash to meet the current obligations of the business as they mature.

insolvent: an individual who has ceased to pay his or her debts or is unable to pay such debts as demanded by creditors. See also *bankrupt, bankruptcy.*

inspection: the process of examining units or goods to determine acceptability against a standard and to accumulate information about product quality.

inspirational strategy: the use of imitation, intuition, feelings, or creativity.

installation

(1) *general:* any place of operation; a place where machinery is to be installed.

(2) *computers:* a specific computing system—the work it does and the people who manage it, operate it, apply it to problems, service it, and utilize the results it produces.

installation time: the time spent in installing and testing hardware, software, or both, until they are accepted.

installment account: See *charge account.*

installment bond: See *bond, installment.*

installment buying: acquiring goods or services with no down payment or a small down payment, to be followed by payments at regular intervals.

installment credit: a form of consumer credit involving regular payments, permitting the seller to reacquire the purchased item if the buyer fails to meet the payment schedule.

installment loan: Synonymous with *personal loan.*

instant (inst.): a business term designating the present month (e.g., on the 10th inst.) Cf. *proximo.*

instant vesting: the right of employees to change employers within a given industry or area without losing pension rights. See also *multiemployer pension plans.*

institution: an organization (e.g., bank, insurance company, investment company pension fund) that holds substantial investment assets, often for others.

institutional advertising: an attempt to sell the image of a firm—its quality, services, role in community activities, merchandise, and so on—rather than specific items. Goodwill and position are foremost in the development of institutional advertising.

institutional decisions: decisions that involve long-term planning and policy formulation aimed at assuring the organization's survival as a productive part of the economy and the society.

institutional investor: a company that has substantial funds invested in securities (e.g., a bank, a labor union, a college).

institutional level: the upper level of an organization, concerned with relating the overall organization to its environment.

institutional managers: top-level managers whose concern is surveying the environment and developing cooperative and competitive strategies that will ensure the organization's survival. Such managers tend to adopt philosophical viewpoints.

institutional operation: a factory or group of plants under one management that performs all processes of production, including preparation for sale.

in stock: describing merchandise on hand, available for shipment or sale.

instruction

(1) *computers:* a set of characters that, as a unit, causes a computer to perform one of its operations. Cf. *pseudo-instruction.*

(2) *computers:* a statement that specifies an operation and the values or locations of its operands. See also *run book.*

instrument: any written document that gives formal expression to a legal agreement or act.

instrumental conditioning: See *oper-*

ant conditioning.

instrumentalities: agencies of the federal government whose obligations are not the direct obligation of the federal government.

instrumentality: the relationship between first- and second-level outcomes.

instrumental leadership: a style characterized by managers who plan, organize, control, and coordinate the activities of subordinates to reach departmental or group goals.

instrumental performance: the performance of the physical product per se.

insufficient funds: a term used when a depositor's balance is inadequate for the bank to pay a check that has been presented. A service charge is often placed on the customer when the balance is not sufficient to pay the check.

insufficient-reason criterion: the assumption, when a manager is operating under conditions of uncertainty, that there is an equal probability that each of the possible states of nature or competitive actions might occur.

insular bond: See bond, insular.

insulation: the separation of materials by means of nonconductors to prevent the transfer of heat, electricity, sound, or other forms of energy.

insurable interest (life version): the monetary interest of the beneficiary of a life insurance contract in the continued life of the person insured. Insurable interest exists only to the extent that the beneficiary will suffer financial loss as the result of the death of an insured.

insurable interest (property and liabili-

ty version): any interest in or relation to property of such nature that the occurrence of an event insured against would cause financial loss to the insured.

insurable title: a form of title that may have objections but on which a title-insuring company is willing to issue its policy of title insurance.

insurance

(1) *general:* a method whereby those concerned about some form of hazard contribute to a common fund, usually in an insurance company, out of which losses sustained by the contributors are paid. See also *self-insurance.*

(2) *business law:* a contractual relationship that exists when one party (the insurer), for a consideration (the premium), agrees to reimburse another party (the insured) for loss to a specified subject (the risk) caused by designated contingencies (hazards or perils), or to pay on behalf of the insured all reasonable sums for which he may be liable to a third party (the claimant).

insurance company: an organization chartered under state or provincial laws to act as an insurer. In the United States, insurance companies are usually classified as fire and marine, life, casualty, and surety companies and may write only the kinds of insurance for which they are specifically authorized by their charters.

insurance coverage: the total amount of insurance that is carried.

insurance management

(1) *general:* in relation to the exposure of assets to risks, the function that examines the impact of the trans-

ferral of risk, or self-insurance of the risk, and the resulting effects of that transfer or self-insurance.

(2) *insurance:* the liaison between buyers of insurance for business needs and the sellers of this coverage.

insurance of title: insurance showing who owns a specific interest in a designated property and showing as exceptions to the insured interest the defects, liens, and encumbrances that exist against that insured interest.

insurance policy: broadly, the entire written contract of insurance. More specifically, it is the basic written or printed document, as well as the coverage forms and endorsement added to it.

insurance premium: See *premium.*

insurance trust: an instrument composed wholly or partially of life insurance policy contracts.

insurance trust expenditures: cash payments to beneficiaries of contributory social insurance programs (employee retirement funds, unemployment compensation, sickness insurance, etc.), excluding cost of administration, intergovernmental expenditures for social insurance, and noncontributory payments to former employees.

insurance trust revenue: revenue from contributions required of employers and employees for financial social insurance programs operated by state and local governments, plus earnings on assets held for such systems.

insured: the person(s) protected under an insurance contract.

insured bank: a bank that is a member

of the Federal Deposit Insurance Corporation.

insured mail: a service whereby postal customers who have paid a special fee may obtain payment for mail that has been lost, rifled, or damaged.

insurer: the party to the insurance contract who promises to indemnify losses or provide service.

insuring clause: part of an insurance policy or bond that recites the agreement of the insurer to protect the insured against some form of loss or damage. This is the core of the contract of insurance.

intangible asset: an asset that has no substance or physical body. It is incorporeal. The most widely known types of intangible assets are goodwill and patent rights. These assets are purchased, sometimes for very substantial outlays of capital. Their value to the purchaser lies in the use he or she can make of them, although they cannot be seen. See also *chose(s) in action.*

intangible rewards: feelings that derive from recognition, applause, and so on, and have no monetary value. Synonymous with *psychic income.*

intangible tax: a state tax levied on all deposits in a bank (stocks, bonds, notes, etc.), excluding certain exempted items. The tax is against the individual accounts.

integrated commercial: a broadcast commercial that appears or is heard as part of the program's entertainment.

integrated data processing: See *IDP.*

integration: centralization of authority in the hands of a top administrator or executive.

integration, forward: the expansion of the area of operation of a business to include activity near the ultimate user (e.g., a manufacturer building a retail outlet).

integration, horizontal: the absorption by one firm of other firms functioning on the same level of production; the attempt to dominate a market at a specific production stage by monopolizing resources at that stage.

integration, vertical: the absorption by one firm of other firms involved in all stages of manufacture, from raw materials to sales of the finished goods.

integrationist model: particularly in public administration, a model defining federal administration as a closed hierarchical system, with the president at the top, surrounded by a staff of loyal subordinates who are committed to his programs.

integrative growth: expansion of a firm's operation by acquiring the assets of suppliers, customers, or competitors.

integrative variable: the degree to which one or more goals of different individuals or groups are perceived as compatible.

integrator: a worker who is neither line nor staff but has informal power to bring together the efforts of overlapping working units.

intelligence: the ability to acquire knowledge or to learn from life's experiences.

intelligence quotient (IQ): a measure of a person's rate of development up to the age at which he is tested, computed by dividing the test score by the chronological age.

intelligence test: a series of tasks producing a score believed by the makers of the test to be indicative of the intelligence of the person attaining that score.

intelstat: See *Comsat.*

intensive distribution: placement of an item in all available outlets.

interaction

(1) *computers:* the technique of repeating a group of computer instructions.

(2) *salesmanship:* the impact or relationship that exists between a salesperson and his or her potential customer.

interaction analysis: a technique developed by R. F. Bales whereby, through observations of groups working on solving a problem, a profile of human relationship develops that is measurable. See also *managerial grid.*

interaction requirements: the variety of individuals, frequency, and quality necessary in intergroup activities.

inter alia: "among other things" (Latin).

Inter-American Development Bank: a bank established in 1959 to encourage economic development of the 21 member nations in Latin America. Twenty representatives from Latin American countries and the United States initiated this effort. See also *Alliance for Progress.*

interchangeable bond: See *bond, interchangeable.*

interchangeable parts: the basis of the entire concept of mass production—the ability to interchange any part of a machine with an identical part in any similar piece of equipment. See also *assembly-line pro-*

duction.

interchange track: a track on which cargo is moved from one railroad to another.

intercorporate stockholding: an unlawful condition whereby a corporation holds stock in other corporations, thus interfering with competition (e.g., restraint of trade).

interdepartmental conflict: a form of conflict that arises between two or more departments because of conflicting interests, limited resources, communication problems, and/or differing perceptions.

interdependence: the degree to which two or more groups are dependent on one another for inputs or outputs.

interest

(1) *finance:* the price paid for the borrowed use of a commodity, usually money. See also *money rates;* Cf. *pure interest.*

(2) *marketing:* following the awareness stage in the adoption process, the consumer's curiosity in pursuing the value of a product or service.

interest coverage: the frequency with which interest charges are earned, found by dividing the sum of the fixed charges into the earnings available for such charges, either before or after deducting income taxes.

interest group: a group that forms because of some special topic of concern. Usually, when the interest declines or the goal has been reached, the group disbands.

interest inventory: a questionnaire concerning the activities a person likes or in which he or she has an interest. Cf. *depth interview; interview, unstructured; Q-sort.*

interest rate: the ratio of the payment for the use of financial capital to the amount borrowed.

interface: a common boundary between automatic data processing systems or between parts of a single system.

intergovernmental expenditures: payment to other governments as fiscal aid or as reimbursements for the performance of services for the paying government. Synonymous with *revenue sharing.* cf. *direct expenditures.*

intergovernmental revenue: revenue received from other governments as fiscal aid, shared taxes, and reimbursements for services performed. Synonymous with *shared revenue.*

intergroup conflict: a form of conflict that exists between groups because of such issues as limited resources, communication problems, or different perceptions of their members. Cf. *intragroup conflict.*

interim: temporary; usually said of a position that is set up to provide for replacement of the incumbent in an existing position who is or will be absent from his position. See also *incumbent.*

interim bond: See *bond, interim.*

interim receiver: a court-appointed individual who is asked to protect a debtor's property until an official receiver is appointed.

interindustry competition: the competition that develops between companies in different industries.

interleave: a procedure for combining parts of one computer program with another program to enable both to be executed simultaneously. See also *time sharing.*

interline: describing the transfer of equipment carrying freight from one carrier to another. See also *gateway.*

interlocking directorate: the condition in which one or more members of the board of directors of one business are also members of the board of directors of other corporations.

interlocutory decree: an intermediate decree issued before a final court degree that does not resolve the matter but settles some portion of it.

Intermarket Trading System (ITS): an electronic network designed to link the nation's six major securities exchanges (New York, Midwest, Philadelphia, Boston, Pacific and American). This national system began operations on April 17, 1978.

intermediate bond: See *bond, intermediate.*

intermediate carrier: a transportation line over which a shipment moves in interline, without touching the origin or destination point.

intermediate goods: items transformed by production into other items.

intermediate-range planning: the setting of subobjectives and substrategies that are in accord with the long-run objectives and strategies of an overall plan.

intermediate report: a report by the National Labor Relations Board trial examiner, after a hearing on charges of unfair labor practices, on the examiner's findings and recommendations. If either party objects to the report, the entire matter goes to the NLRB for a decision, which may be appealed in the courts.

intermediate-term credit: credit that is extended for a period of from 3 to 10 years.

intermediation: the process by which savers place funds in a financial institution, enabling the institution, acting as an intermediary, to place those funds in housing loans and other investments. See also *disintermediation.*

intermittent process: any process designed to produce a variety of items (e.g., a job-order machine shop).

intermodalist: (slang) a freight forwarder.

intermodal shipment: freight shifted from one carrier to another (e.g., from a truck to a railroad).

internal audit: a business audit carried out by the firm itself on a continuous basis. Cf. *look back.*

internal bond: See *bond, internal.*

internal check: coordinated methods and measures adopted by an organization to check the accuracy and validity of data and to safeguard assets.

internal controls: methods and measures employed to promote efficiency, to encourage acceptance of managerial procedures and policies, to check the validity of management data, and to protect assets.

internal economies scale: factors that bring about increases or decreases to an organization's long-run average costs or scale of operations resulting from size adjustments with the company as a product unit. They occur primarily because of physical economies or diseconomies. See also *diseconomies of scale.*

internal forecast: a forecast relating to a firm's output and its internal operations.

internal memory: the internal parts of a data-processing machine that are capable of retaining data.

internal rate of return: an interest rate that, if paid on the costs of a project, would ensure that costs were equal to benefits. Synonymous with "rate of return."

Internal Revenue Code of 1954: a complete revision of the Internal Revenue Code of 1939, including provisions for dividend credit and exclusion, retirement income credit, and accelerated depreciation. Changes in tax laws since 1954 have been enacted as amendments to this code.

Internal Revenue Service (IRS): the federal agency empowered by Congress to administer the rules and regulations of the Department of the Treasury, which includes the collection of federal income and other taxes. It is divided into 9 regions with 64 districts and is also responsible for the investigation and prevention of tax frauds.

internal users: the managers of a company who are responsible for making the day-to-day decisions that lead the organization to its profit and service goals.

International Bank for Reconstruction and Development (IBRD): the World Bank, proposed at Bretton Woods in July 1944 and commencing operation in June 1946. After phasing out activities of reconstruction, its primary efforts are to provide loans for economic development. See also *International Monetary Fund.*

International Confederation of Free Trade Unions (ICFTU): a federation of labor groups in the free nations of the world. ICFTU was formed in 1949 after its predecessor, the World Federation of Trade Unions, fell under unbreakable Communist control. It comprises unions in more than 100 countries, and its headquarters is in Brussels. The United States affiliates of ICFTU are the AFL–CIO and the United Mine Workers of America.

international corporation: a corporation with business interests in different countries. It often focuses on the import or export of goods and services.

International Labor Organization (ILO): a tripartite body of representatives from labor, management, and government, initially organized as an agency of the League of Nations in 1919, now continued under United Nations auspices. The ILO disseminates labor information and sets minimum international labor standards, called "conventions," which are offered to member nations for adoption.

International Labor Review: the official monthly magazine of the ILO, describing working conditions and presenting statistical data of member countries.

International Monetary Fund (IMF): an organization established to restore orderly exchange practices following World War II. IMF was formed and became operational on March 1, 1947. Member nations can borrow foreign currencies from the fund under specified conditions. Membership in the IMF is a prerequisite to membership in the International Bank for Reconstruction and Development. See also *Bretton Woods Agreement of 1944, special drawing rights.*

international payments mechanism: the organization of markets whereby the monies of different nations are exchanged. See also *swap.*

international representative: an agent of a national or international union, who may be primarily an organizer, an administrator, or an all-around troubleshooter.

international reserves: a means of payment generally acceptable in settlement of balances among countries (e.g., gold, dollars, pounds, SDRs).

internship: an extensive period of training during which selected employees are given a complete introduction to their jobs and an opportunity to apply the theories and methods they learned earlier at school.

interpersonal conflict: disagreements over policies, practices, or plans, and emotional issues involving negative feelings between two or more individuals.

interpersonal orientation: a focus that allows an observer to determine whether a person is more concerned with achieving good social relations or with accomplishing a task. There are various techniques (e.g., the managerial grid) for measuring whether the employee is more oriented toward people or toward tasks. See also *managerial grid.*

interpleader: an individual who has an obligation to pay for services or goods but does not know which of two or more claimants should receive his obligation. He or she brings a suit requiring the claimants to litigate between themselves.

interpreter
(1) *computers:* a computer program that translates and executes

each source language statement before translating and executing the next one.

(2) *computers:* a device that prints on a punched card the data already punched in the card.

interrole conflict: role pressures associated with membership in one group or organization that are in conflict with those stemming from membership in other groups or organizations.

interrupt

(1) *computers:* to stop a process in such a way that it can be resumed without destroying work already done.

(2) *systems:* a break in the normal flow of a system or routine, permitting the flow to be restarted from that point at a later time.

(3) *operations research:* to stop a current control sequence.

interselling: assigning sales personnel so that each is able to work in two or more related departments rather than being limited to one.

intersender conflict: a conflict between a person's roles (e.g., one's role as manager and one's role as parent).

interstate carrier: a common carrier whose business extends beyond the boundaries of one state.

interstate commerce: commerce that involves more than one state, including transportation of goods and services across the boundaries.

Interstate Commerce Act of 1887: federal legislation regulating the practices, rates, and rules of transportation carriers engaged in handling interstate shipments or in moving people across state lines for a fee. See also *Cummins Amendment.*

Interstate Commerce Commission (ICC): a federal agency established to enforce the Interstate Commerce Act and other related acts affecting common carriers engaged in interstate commerce.

Interstate Land Sales Full Disclosure Act of 1968: federal legislation requiring all large land sales promoters to furnish prospective buyers with a detailed and accurate report on the land and to spell out buyers' rights in the transaction.

interstate traffic: cargo moved from one state to another.

interstore transfer forms: forms containing data from a list of items to be shipped from the central warehouse to a branch store, or from one branch store to another.

interval reinforcement: a schedule of rewards that ties reinforcements to time. Such a schedule can be fixed or variable.

intervention

(1) *labor relations:* entry by a union or unions in a representation election ordered by the National Labor Relation Board, in competition with the union or unions that originally had sought the election.

(2) *administration:* the process by which either outsiders or insiders assume the role of altering a program within an organization.

interview: a conversation designed to yield information for purposes of research or assistance in guidance, counseling, or treatment. See also *interview, structured; interview, unstructured.*

interview, exit: a conference with an

employee before termination of his relationship with the organization to determine reasons for leaving, future plans, and general attitudes toward the job and the company.

interview, structured: an interview in which the asking of definite questions closely controls the subjects discussed. Cf. *interest inventory.*

interview, unstructured: an interview in which the interviewer does not determine the format or subject to be discussed, thus leaving the interviewee in major control of the conversation. Cf. *depth interview.*

interviewer bias: influence resulting from the presence of personal prejudice in the individual conducting the interview. See also *halo effect.*

intestate: not having a valid will. When a person dies intestate, his or her estate is presented for settlement to administrators. See also *escheat.*

in the black: (slang) describing a business that is functioning with a profit.

in-the-money: (slang) a call option in which the striking price is below the market price of the underlying stock.

in the red: (slang) describing a business that is functioning with a loss.

in toto: "in the entire amount" (Latin).

intragroup conflict: conflict that emerges or develops between members within a group. When intragroup conflict reaches a significant level, members tend to become dissatisfied with the interpersonal interactions in the group. Cf. *intergroup conflict.*

in transit: describing items that have left the consignor's location and are en route to the destination.

intrasender role conflict: inconsisten-

cy between one person's various expectations regarding another's behavior. A manager, for example, may expect both rapid work and a high quality level that is impossible at a rapid pace.

intrastate carrier: a common carrier whose business is conducted entirely within the boundaries of a state.

intrastate commerce: commerce conducted solely within a state's geographic borders.

intrastate traffic: cargo that is shipped only within one state.

intrastore transfer: the purchase of goods from one selling department for use by another selling department.

intrinsic rewards: rewards associated with the job itself, such as the opportunity to perform meaningful work, to complete cycles of work, to see finished products, to experience variety, to carry out highly visible cycles of activity, and to receive feedback on work results.

intrinsic value: the market value of the material in something (e.g., the value of the metal in a gold tooth filling).

introjection: lack of objectivity, describing the tendency of an interviewee to analyze everything in an interview in a personal way, either negatively or positively.

intrusion: forcefully taking possession of another's real property.

intuitive pricing: the practice of establishing price based on the intuition of the responsible party.

inventive research: research and development activity that emphasizes the application of existing technology.

inventory: the name given to an asset

of a business. Inventories are of two general types, direct and indirect. (*a*) Direct inventory in an industrial concern consists of raw materials, work in process, and finished goods. Direct inventories represent various stages of fabrication; in commercial and retail businesses, they are inventories purchased for resale. (*b*) Indirect inventories, in general, are all supplies used to carry on the business and not purchased for resale. Indirect inventories are usually considered deferred assets. Cf. *book inventory, perpetual inventory, work-in-process inventory*.

inventory, composite: See *book inventory, composite inventory*.

inventory, real-time processing: any system or technique that provides information desired to make an up-to-date decision.

inventory change: the amount of increase or decrease in business inventories during a specified period.

inventory control

(1) *merchandising:* the control of merchandise on hand by accounting and physical methods. See also *EOQ model;* cf. *eyeball control*.

(2) *government:* an approach used in emergencies to regulate inventories for the purpose of increasing utilization of items and preventing hoarding.

inventory cutoff: the determination of which inventory items are to be included in the year-end inventory balance.

inventory model: a type of production control model that answers two questions relating to inventory management: "How much?" and "When?" An inventory model tells the manager when goods should be reordered

and what quantity should be purchased.

inventory shortage (shrinkage): inventory reduced by theft, internal or external fraud, waste, sabotage, or careless operation.

inventory turnover: the number of times, on the average, that inventory is replaced during a period. It is calculated by dividing cost of goods sold by average inventory.

inventory valuation adjustment: in contrast to corporate profits and income of unincorporated enterprises, which include inventory profit or loss in customary business accounting, the accounting for current output in the national income accounts, which includes only the value of the change in volume in inventories.

inverse demand pattern: the situation that exists when price and volume vary at the same time and more is sold at a high price than at a lower one.

invested capital: the amount of capital contributed to a company by its owners.

investment: the use of money for the purpose of making more money, to gain income or to increase capital, or both.

investment banker: the middleman between the corporation that is issuing new securities and the public. The usual practice is for one or more investment bankers to buy a new issue of stock or bonds outright from a corporation. The group forms a syndicate to sell the securities to individuals and institutions. The investment banker is the underwriter of the issue.

investment banking: the financing of the capital requirements of an enterprise, rather than the current working capital requirements of a business.

investment center: an organizational unit in which a manager has responsibility for costs, revenues, and investments. Cf. *cost center, profit center.*

investment club: a voluntary grouping of people who pool their monies to build up an investment portfolio, which members hope will give them a better return per individual than each could have expected separately.

investment company: a company or trust that uses its capital to invest in other companies. There are two principal types: the closed-end type and the open-end or mutual fund. Shares in closed-end investment companies are readily transferable in the open market and are bought and sold like other shares. Capitalization of these companies remains the same unless action is taken to change, which is seldom. Open-end funds sell their own new shares to investors, stand ready to buy back their old shares, and are not listed. Open-end funds are so called because their capitalization is not fixed; more shares are issued as people want them. See also *reinvestment privilege;* cf. *hedge fund, monthly investment plan, no-load funds, regulated investment company, split investment company.*

Investment Company Act of 1940: federal legislation requiring the registration and regulation of investment companies with the SEC.

investment counsel: a person whose principal business consists of acting as investment adviser. A substantial part of the person's business con-

sists of rendering investment services.

investment decisions: decisions that commit present funds in exchange for potential future funds. These decisions are controlled through a capital budget.

investment portfolio: the list of securities owned by a bank, an individual, or a business enterprise.

investment property: real estate acquired for profit.

investment schedule: a table of the amount of gross investment that would be undertaken at alternative rates of GNP.

investor: an individual whose principal concerns in the purchase of a security are regular dividend income, safety of the original investment, and, if possible, capital appreciation. See also *long position;* cf. *speculator.*

invisible hand: a term first used by Adam Smith to describe the ability of the perfectly competitive market to bring about the greatest benefit for all, even when all merchants selfishly maximize their own profits.

invoice: an instrument prepared by a seller of goods or services and rendered to the buyer. The instrument usually lists all items making up the bill for the convenience of the buyer; to prevent disagreements, the amount is stated on the instrument.

involuntary alienation: forced sale of real estate.

involuntary bankruptcy: See *bankruptcy.*

involuntary conversion: a transaction in which an asset is destroyed or is taken by a government agency through condemnation proceedings.

involuntary investment: the involuntary increase or decrease in business inventory as a result of either an excess of household saving over intended investment or an excess of intended investment over savings.

involuntary lien: a lien on property that is demanded without the consent of the owner (e.g., construction of sewers and sidewalks near an owner's property, property tax increases). Synonymous with *lien in invitum.*

involuntary unemployment: the situation that exists when people who wish to work are unable to locate opportunities at going wage rates for the related skills and experiences they have to offer.

iota: a minute amount of any item.

IOU: an informal written agreement acknowledging a cash debt ("I owe you").

IQ: See *intelligence quotient.*

IRA: See *individual retirement accounts.*

Irish dividend: a trade term for an assessment imposed on a security, rather than a dividend.

iron law of wages: the concept that wages tend to equal what the employee needs to maintain a subsistence level of living; synonymous with *brazen law of wages, subsistence law of wages.*

irredeemable bond: See *bond, irredeemable.*

irredeemable money: Synonymous with *inconvertible money.*

irregular routing: a sales call pattern in which the sales representative determines the frequency of calls to be made. Cf. *fixed routing.*

irregulars: items having defects that may affect appearance but not wear.

irreparable harm: injury or damage that is so constant and universal that no fair or reasonable redress can be achieved in court. Therefore, the plaintiff seeks resolution by injunction.

irrevocable trust: a trust that cannot be set aside by its originator.

I-S curve: a graphical presentation of combinations of interest rates and levels of national income for which aggregate supply and aggregate demand are equal; named for the notion that investment, *I*, should absorb savings, *S.*

island display: merchandise shown in a store's aisle or open space.

island position: the placement of newspaper advertising copy that is surrounded by editorial matter or page margin.

isoquant: a locus of points describing the various combinations of inputs needed to produce a given amount of production.

issue: any of a company's securities, or the act of distributing such securities.

issued stock: authorized stock originally issued to stockholders, which may or may not still be outstanding.

item

(1) *general:* one member of a group.

(2) *statistics:* a collection of related characters treated as a unit.

(3) *personnel:* the smallest unit of test material to be addressed by the person being tested.

item analysis: the determination of item difficulty, reliability, and other item characteristics of interest to test constructors or users. See also *item validity.*

itemized appropriation: a restriction of an appropriation to be made only for and in the amounts listed; a step-by-step listing of all pertinent funds set aside to pay a specific cost.

itemized deductions: a listing of allowed expenses that are subtracted in arriving at taxable income. See also *Tax Reform Act of 1976.*

item validity: the extent to which an item of a test, survey, poll, or other predictive device measures what it is supposed to measure. See also *item analysis.*

iteration: the process of repeating a sequence of logical steps for purposes of improving or refining.

itinerant worker: a worker who is not a permanent member of a community and finds work by moving from opportunity to opportunity.

IWW: See *Industrial Workers of the World.*

jackknife: describing the behavior of a moving tractor that turns sideways to its semitrailer and is dragged out of control.

jam auction (pitch): (slang) a store that sells inexpensive jewelry, souvenirs, and the like.

jawboning: (slang) pressured urging by an influential individual to submit to specific rules and regulations. Cf. *moral suasion.*

jebble: (slang) Synonymous with *bluefingers.*

jerry-built: constructed cheaply, flimsily, and often temporarily.

jetsam: anything that is tossed overboard to lighten a vessel's weight.

jettison: to throw overboard part of the cargo or any article on board a ship, or to cut away masts, spars, rigging, sails, or other furniture for the purpose of lightening or relieving the ship in case of necessity or emergency.

jingle: a musical commerical.

JIT: See *job instruction training.*

JMT: See *job methods training.*

job
(1) *general:* a specific group of tasks prescribed as a unit of work.
(2) *computer:* a unit of work done by the computer.
(3) *merchandising:* to purchase or sell merchandise in quantity, not in selected categories.

job action: an employee protest that falls short of a strike (e.g., a slowdown).

job analysis: a systematic study of the specific tasks, conditions, rate of pay, and so on, required for a particular job; usually includes a statement of the personal qualities needed to perform a given job. See also *time and motion study.*

job batch: a succession of job definitions placed in sequence to form a batch. Each job batch is placed on an input device in the computer and processed with a minimum of delay between one job or job step and another.

jobber: a middleman who handles

merchandise in odd or job lots. Some jobbers take possession of the title to the goods, which they resell to another jobber, to a retailer, or directly to the consumer. Others have a buying agreement with the manufacturer to drop-ship the merchandise on orders obtained by the jobber. See also *rack jobber.*

job bidding: See *bidding.*

job characteristics model: a model that helps explain how jobs can be redesigned so that they become more motivational.

job classification: evaluation of job content and required skills, for the purpose of setting up wage brackets for each classification. See also *point method rating.*

job cluster: a group of similar jobs in a company.

job content: the duties, functions, and responsibilities for a given job classification.

job control statement: a statement in a computer job that is used to identify the job or to describe its requirements to the operating system.

job cycle: the time it takes an employee to complete every task in his or her job before repeating the cycle.

job definition: the statement of the task requirements of a job. There is a job definition for each job in a company.

job depth: the amount of control an employee can exert to alter or influence his or her job and the surrounding environment.

job description: a statement, usually in writing, of the responsibilities, approaches, conditions, and other relevant factors built into a job.

job design: the process of task de-

lineation necessary to meet various personal, work, organizational and environmental parameters.

job dilution: the division of the tasks of a job into levels of skill. The tasks needing greater skill are performed by skilled employees, and the remaining tasks are carried out by relatively unskilled employees who have a lower level of training.

job dynamics: the situational factors surrounding the tasks in a job that must be considered to define the job adequately.

job enlargement: a procedure for increasing the scope and responsibilities of a job to increase employee satisfaction. Cf. *loose jobs (rate).*

job enrichment: an approach of F. Herzberg that attempts to improve task efficiency and satisfaction by means of building into people's jobs greater scope for personal achievement and recognition, more challenging and responsible work, and greater opportunity for advancement and growth. See also *dissatisfiers, O-E-C syndrome, organic structure, satisfiers.*

job environment: all the physical, psychological, and social factors, situations, events, or relationships that surround and affect a firm and its workers.

job evaluation: a systematic rating of job content on such factors as skill, responsibility, and experience. The evaluation is primarily used to minimize wage inequities.

job factors: categories of common job characteristics used in job evaluation.

job families: groups of different jobs that require similar skills.

job grading: a form of job evaluation that assigns jobs to predetermined job classifications according to the job's relative worth to the organization. Synonymous with *job classification.*

jobholder reports: reports given to workers about a company's economic performance.

job hopper: an individual who changes jobs frequently.

job identification section: the section of a job description that contains the job title and a job number or code. See also *job description.*

job instruction training (JIT): a program of training workers within industry based on a specific outline of procedures, including rules for getting ready to instruct and rules on how to train.

job lot

(1) *merchandising:* a miscellaneous grouping of items of various styles, sizes, colors, and so on, bought at a reduced price by a store or an individual middleman.

(2) *business:* a form of contract that has a smaller unit of trading than is featured in the regular contract.

job management: a general term that collectively describes the functions of job scheduling and computer command processing.

job methods training (JMT): a training approach designed to teach management the techniques of methods improvement through the recommended steps of (1) breaking down the job, (2) questioning every detail, (3) developing and improving the methods, and (4) applying the improved methods.

job order: an order authorizing the production of a specified quantity of goods or specifying services to be rendered and dispatching personnel to perform them.

job-order costing: a method of product costing whereby each job, product, or batch of products is costed separately. Cf. *process costing.*

job-oriented terminal: a computer terminal designed for a particular application.

job performance standards: work requirements that are expected from an employee on a particular job.

job placement: assignment of a person to a job.

job posting: See *posting.*

job pricing: the placement of a dollar value on the worth of a job.

job processing: reading job control statements and data from an input stream, initiating job steps defined in the statements, and writing system output messages.

job progression ladder: a particular career path in which some jobs have prerequisites.

job range: the number of operations a job occupant performs to complete his or her work.

job ranking: a form of job evaluation that subjectively ranks jobs according to their overall worth to the company. See also *job evaluation.*

job rate: the lowest or minimum rate paid to a qualified or experienced employee for a specific task or job.

job relations training (JRT): a type of human relations training program designed to teach management (1) some of the general knowledge that is required to deal with workers as individuals and (2) some basic techniques for dealing with individual problems through the recommended steps of getting the facts, evaluating and making decisions, taking the necessary steps toward solution of the problem, and checking the results.

job rotation: a personnel practice that involves moving an employee from one work station to another to increase overall performance by promoting a greater understanding of multiple tasks in the organization.

job satisfaction: the positive or negative aspects of an employee's attitude toward his or her job or some part of it.

job scope: the relative complexity of an assigned task as reflected by its cycle time.

job security: a means of protecting a worker's job, usually described in a union contract, and often invoked when new methods or machines are introduced.

job sharing: a scheduling innovation that permits two or more employees to do the same job by working different hours, days, or even weeks. The total hours worked by job sharers are usually equivalent to the hours worked by one full-time worker.

job specification (specs): a carefully written description of a specific job, with duties and opportunities described. It identifies the requirements of the job and the desired qualifications needed for a worker to perform effectively. See also *job standardization*.

job stabilization: a process of creating and/or maintaining continuous job opportunities.

job standardization: the use of clearly defined work procedures and re-

quirements to be met to reduce individual variations in a specific work task. Cf. *job classification*.

job step
(1) *computers:* the execution of a computer program that is explicitly identified by a job control statement.
(2) *production:* a unit of work associated with one processing program or one catalogued procedure and related data. A job consists of one or more job steps.

job stress: an individual's internal frustration and anxiety regarding certain job- or organization-related situations.

job support task: a task that reads and interprets job definitions or converts job input and output data from one input/output medium to another.

job ticket: a card with instructions that accompanies a printing assignment through all departments. The progress of the work is noted on the card.

jockey: (slang) an investor who has sufficient equity gains financial control over the major decisions needed to conduct day-to-day business.

Johari window: a model illustrating the communication between any two people ("Joe and Harry").

John Family: (slang) a person who has steady work, a home, and a relatively secure life.

joint account: an account owned by two or more people, subject to deposit or withdrawal by the signatures of any of the joint owners. In banks, any account owned by two or more parties is referred to as a joint account, regardless of whether all parties or any one of the parties may sign checks.

joint adventure: two persons entering

into a single business for their mutual benefit (e.g., a partnership).

joint agreement: a statement covering salary and working conditions, agreed to and signed by employers and union representatives within an industry. Synonymous with *industry-wide agreement.*

joint and several account: an account in which, when two or more persons desire to deposit in a jointly owned account, and the account is drawn against by either check or withdrawal order, the signature of any one of the owners will be honored.

joint and several bond: See *bond, joint and several.*

joint contract: a contract whereby two or more people who make a promise to another person are joint obligors to the contract and to the other party identified.

joint control bond: See *bond, joint control.*

joint cost

(1) *accounting:* a cost that is common to all the segments in question and that can be assigned to the segments only by arbitrary allocation.

(2) *production:* the costs of two or more items that must be manufactured together.

joint demand: demand for two or more items that are usually used together because of necessity or consumer preference.

Joint Economic Committee: a committee created under the Employment Act of 1946, as the congressional counterpart to the president's Council of Economic Advisers, to gather appropriate data on economic matters, to make recommendations, and so on.

joint life insurance: insurance on two or more persons, the benefits of which are payable on the first death.

jointly and severally: a term frequently encountered in loan transactions when several persons sign a note for a loan. When the term is used, each person is legally obligated to become individually liable for the payment of the note; the group involved also must become liable.

joint ownership: the interest in property of two or more people.

joint production costs: the costs of two or more produced goods that are made by a single process and are not identifiable as individual products up to a certain stage of production, known as the split-off point.

joint profit maximization: collusion by firms in an oligopolistic industry, which enables them to obtain the maximum (monopoly) profit.

joint stock company: an association that is neither a partnership nor a corporation but has some of the characteristics of each.

joint study committee: a committee that includes representatives from management and unions who meet away from the bargaining table to study some topic of mutual interest in hopes of finding a solution that is mutually satisfactory.

joint tenancy: two or more people holding equal ownership of property. Upon the death of one of the parties, the decedent's interest automatically passes on to the surviving owner(s). See also *undivided right.*

joint tortfeasors: two people who commit an injury with a common intent.

joint venture: a commercial undertaking by two or more people, differing from a partnership in that it relates to the disposition of a single lot of goods or the termination of a specific project.

joint will: a single will of two or more individuals.

journal: a record of original entry. This record may be written in ink at the time a transaction is made or may be created in original printing or carbonized as the posting of the entry is made by machine. Cf. *ledger.*

journal entry: a method of directly recording on a profit and loss statement a transaction that did not necessarily have the direct approval of management, such as rent, monthly assessments, leases, or taxes, and/or reclassifying charges from one account or location to another.

journalize: to record a transaction in an entity's records using the double-entry system. Debits, credits, and any necessary explanations are recorded in the journal.

journeyman: a craftsman who has completed an apprenticeship and is entitled to the highest minimum rate established for the job classification.

JRT: See *job relations training.*

judgment: a debt or other obligation, as determined by the decision or decree of a court.

judgment bond: See *bond, judgment.*

judgment creditor: an individual who has proved a debt in court or has won an action for the recovery of a debt.

judgment debt: any debt contested in a suit at law and proved to be valid.

judgment debtor: an individual who has been ordered by the court to make a payment to another.

judgment in personam: a judgment against a person, directing a specific defendant to do or not to do something.

judgment in rem: a judgment against a thing (e.g., a bank account, personal property), as contrasted with a judgment against an individual. See also *lien.*

judgment note: a note authorizing a creditor to enter a judgment against a debtor in case of nonpayment, without the need for court action.

judgment rates: rates established by the judgment of an underwriter, utilizing his or her professional skills and experience, without the application of a formal set of rules or a schedule.

judgment strategy: the use of personal beliefs and experiences for choosing among alternatives and deciding how the selected alternative should be implemented.

judicial review

(1) *labor relations:* an action brought before a court to determine the legality of decisions issued by a labor relations board. The review is concerned only with whether the decision is in violation of a statute; the merits of the case are not at issue.

(2) *business law:* a legal examination of a situation that is ordered, sanctioned, prescribed, or enforced by a judge or court (e.g., a judicial proceeding).

judicial sale: a sale of real or personal property ordered by a legal body or court. Synonymous with *forced sale.*

juice man: (slang) a loaner of money at exorbitant interest rates. Synonymous with *loan shark.*

jumble display: a collection of items tossed together in a container or on a table counter.

jump: in computers, a departure from

the normal sequence of executing instructions. Synonymous with *branch*.

junior board: a group of lower-level managers who meet periodically to discuss various issues and to provide ideas and suggestions that may be valuable to upper-level management in identifying and solving problems.

junior bond: See *bond, junior*.

junior issue: an issue whose claim for dividends or interest, or for principal value, comes following that of another issue, called a senior issue.

junior mortgage: a second or third mortgage that is subordinated to a prior mortgage. Cf. *equal dignity*.

junk: a computer description of a garbled or otherwise unintelligible sequence of signals or other data. Cf. *garbage*.

jurisdiction
(1) *government:* authority given by the Constitution to the courts to try cases and determine causes. Different courts get different cases, depending on the nature of the offense, the amount of the claim involved, and other factors.
(2) *labor relations:* the area of work or the group of employees for which a union claims the right to bargain collectively.

jurisdictional dispute: a conflict between rival unions over which should maintain control over a given job or activity and be recognized as the collective-bargaining agent. See also *intervention*.

jurisdictional strike: a walkout by one union because of a dispute with another union over representation rights or performance of certain jobs. Jurisdictional strikes are unfair labor practices according to the Taft-Hartley Act.

jury of executive opinion: a forecasting approach utilizing the opinions of senior executives.

justification
(1) *computers:* the act of adjusting, arranging, or shifting digits to the left or right to fit a prescribed pattern.
(2) *advertising and publishing:* the arrangement of type in lines of uniform length by proper spacing.

justified price: a fair market price that an informed buyer will give for property.

justify
(1) *computers:* to adjust the printing positions of computer characters on a page so that the lines have desired length and both the left and right margins are regular.
(2) *computers:* to shift the contents of a register so that the most or least significant digit is at some specified position in the register.

just title: a title that will be supported against all claims and is considered to be a proper title. Synonymous with *clear title, good title*.

kameralism: a concept of mercantilism concerned with the production of wealth by the state and how the wealth is used; sometimes spelled *cameralism*.

KD: knocked down; applied to sales or shipments of equipment that are to be assembled by the receiver.

keelage: the charges paid by a ship entering or remaining in certain ports.

Kennedy round: during President Kennedy's administration, a 1964 series of world tariff negotiations to reduce tariffs; the sixth round of tariff reductions under the auspices of GATT.

kentledge goods: weighty goods, placed low in a ship to increase stability.

Keogh plan (HR 110): a form of tax-qualified retirement plan established by a nonincorporated business or self-employed individual. Investment contributions and appreciation are generally tax deferred until actually received in the form of benefits. See also *Economic Recovery Tax Act of 1981, individual retirement accounts.*

Kerr-Smith Tobacco Control Act of 1934: federal legislation, amended in 1935, that provided for processing taxes in the tobacco industry to finance a quota system for growers, including penalties for marketing beyond individual quotas.

key

(1) *general:* crucial, essential (e.g., a key decision).

(2) *computers:* one or more characters in an item of data that are used to identify it or control its use.

(3) *administration:* a crucial, important member of an organization.

keyboard: a device for encoding data by key depression, which causes the generation of the selected code element.

keyboard entry: a technique whereby access into the contents of a computer's storage may be initiated at a keyboard.

key driven: pertaining to any device for translating information into machine-sensible form that requires an operator to depress a key for each character.

keyed advertising: See *keying an advertisement.*

key industry: an industry that, because of a unique characteristic, holds major importance in the country's economy (e.g., steel, automobiles).

keying an advertisement: placing a code or letter in a coupon or in the advertiser's address so that the specific advertisement producing an inquiry can be noted.

key jobs: positions that are common in a firm and its labor market.

Keynesian economics: developed by the British economist John Maynard Keynes, a system showing that national income and employment are dependent on real investments and consumer spending. See also *consumption, liquidity preference, liquidity trap, New Economics, paradox of thrift, savings and investment theory;* cf. *Friedmanite, quantity theory.*

key personnel: workers who are regarded as essential in the performance of organizational objectives or functions.

keypunch: a keyboard device that punches holes in a card to represent data.

key question: a question of major importance asked of an interviewee by an interviewer or of a respondent by a written questionnaire, to be used in making a determination or evaluation.

key result area: an aspect of a company's operations that has direct bearing on profitability.

key subordinates: workers who are crucial to a manager's success in a particular job.

key word

(1) *general:* a significant or informative word in a title or document that describes the content of the document.

(2) *statistics:* a symbol that identifies a parameter.

(3) *operations research:* a part of a command operand that consists of a specific character string.

kickback

(1) *labor relations:* the racketeering practice of forcing employees, as a condition of employment, to return a part of the wages established by law or by union contract to the employer. This practice is outlawed in federally financed employment. See also *Copeland Act of 1934.*

(2) *government:* an illegal rebate given secretly by a seller for granting an order or contract (e.g., payoff).

kicked upstairs: (slang) describing removal of an individual from a lower position, where his or her performance is not considered acceptable, by promotion to a higher position. See also *Peter Principle.*

killer bars: the parallel lines extending to the right of the circular postmark that mark out (cancel) the stamp so it cannot be reused.

killing: (slang) an unusually profitable trade.

Kimball tags: prepunched tags affixed to goods, containing size and style data that are utilized in speeding inventory control.

kind: when used in "distribution in kind," the distribution of the property itself, not its cash value. Cf. *in kind.*

kite (kiting)

(1) *banking:* writing a check in an amount sufficient to overdraw the account, but making up this deficiency by depositing another check, also in excess of deposits, but issued on some other bank. This unorthodox procedure is considered to be evidence of fraudulent intent (e.g., mailing the rent check when your account has insufficient funds, but counting on receiving and depositing some money before the landlord has a chance to present the check for collection). See also *forgery.*

(2) *finance:* a term sometimes used for an accommodation bill.

kiting stocks: manipulation of stock prices to unprecedented high levels.

klupper: (slang) a slow, inefficient employee.

Knights of Labor: the Noble Order of the Knights of Labor, a labor organization founded in Philadelphia in 1869. It reached its membership peak in the 1880s and failed by the end of the century.

knocked down price

(1) *real estate:* a lowered or reduced price.

(2) *retailing:* a seller's asking price that has been lowered for purposes of making the sale. Cf. *upset price.*

knocker: (slang) a door-to-door salesman.

knock off: (slang) to cease working for a break, for lunch period, or at the end of a working day.

kurtosis: a measure of the concentration or clustering of cases around the mode of a frequency curve. A high concentration will result in a peak, and a low concentration results in a flatness. See also *skewness.*

label

(1) *general:* an identification record.

(2) *computers:* one or more characters used to identify a statement or an item of data in a computer program; found on a punched card.

(3) *assembler programming:* a name entry.

(4) *systems:* a string of alphameric data placed at any location for informational and instructional purposes.

(5) *labor relations:* a marking on an item showing that the merchandise was produced by union labor.

labeling acts: See *Fair Packaging and Labeling Act of 1966, Federal Hazardous Substances Labeling Act of 1960, Flammable Fabrics Act of 1953, Pure Food and Drug Act of 1906.*

labor

(1) *general:* the human effort expended for the purpose of acquiring money or other compensation.

(2) *economics:* the effort of people applied to the production and marketing of goods and services toward an economic goal, resulting in the payment of money or another form of compensation.

labor agreement: an accord reached after collective bargaining.

laboratory training: See *sensitivity training.*

labor-augmenting technical change: a technical change that has the same effect on output as if the number of laborers had been increased. Cf. *labor-saving equipment, resource-augmenting technical change.*

labor banks: banks whose stock is owned by labor unions and their membership. Cf. *industrial bank.*

Labor Day: a national holiday in all states and territories of the United States. The first Labor Day parade was held in New York on September 5, 1882. In 1894, Congress passed a law making the first Monday after the first Tuesday in September a federal holiday. Labor Day honors the efforts and interests of all employed people.

Labor Department, U.S.: See *Department of Labor, U.S.*

labor dispute: as defined by the National Labor Relations Act, any controversy concerning terms, tenure, or conditions of employment, or concerning the association or representation of persons in negotiating, fixing, maintaining, changing, or seeking to arrange conditions of employment, regardless of whether the disputants stand in the relations of employer or employees. See also *emergency dispute.*

labor economics: a specialty in the field of economics concerned primarily with the relationship between the worker and his or her job. Areas covered include supply of labor, hours and wages, conditions of work, and other forces relating to the general economic welfare of the worker.

labor flux: Synonymous with *labor turnover; see turnover.*

labor force: as defined by the U.S. Bureau of the Census, people over 14 years of age who are gainfully employed, looking for work, or absent from work (e.g., because of illness or vacation).

labor grade: a job or job group in a rate structure, usually set through job classifications and evaluations or by agreement with a union.

labor intensive: describing the use of additional manpower to increase output or earnings. See also *labor pool.*

Labor-Management Relations Act of 1947: See *Taft-Hartley Act.*

Labor-Management Reporting and Disclosure Act of 1959: See *Landrum-*

Griffin Act.

labor market analysis: the study of an employer's labor market to evaluate the present or future availability of workers.

labor mobility: the ease with which workers change positions and jobs. Horizontal mobility pertains to the way workers move from job to job at a similar skill level. Vertical mobility pertains to the way workers change jobs by moving up and sometimes down the occupational ladder.

labor monopoly: the claim that some unions—by dominance in an industry or through control of hiring procedures, control of apprenticeship rules, or other practices—have monopoly power over the supply of labor.

labor piracy: the attempt to attract workers away from a firm by offering higher wages and other benefits.

labor pool: the established source of trained people from which prospective workers are recruited. See also *labor intensive.*

labor relations: a general term to identify all matters arising from the employer-employee relationship. See also *industrial relations.*

labor-saving equipment: any machine or mechanized equipment that reduces the need for labor by a reduction of workers or by curtailing the number of hours of potential employees. In the 1960s automation was considered to be a technological breakthrough that would result in displacement of workers. cf. *automation labor-augmenting technical change, redeployment, technological unemployment.*

labor skate: semihumorous name for

a full-time union employee. Synonymous with *pie-card*.

labor theory of value: a theory expounded by Karl Marx to describe the exploitation of workers in a capitalist system. Marx claimed that the exchange value of any product was measured by the amount of labor required for its manufacture. Since labor was not only the measure but also the source of all value, every product could be identified as relating directly to the human effort or the quantity of labor involved in production. See also *proletariat*.

labor turnover: See *turnover*.

laches: as used in equity, undue delay in asserting an individual's rights or in doing what should have been done as stated by the law but was not done. Such failure to assert a right gives an equitable defense to another person.

lading: the cargo in a vehicle or ship.

lag: the delay between two computer events.

lag indicators: a series of economic indicators that often follow changes in the economic cycle.

laissez-faire

(1) *management:* a term used to describe a leadership style of minimal involvement. Synonymous with *loose-rein supervision*.

(2) *economics:* a policy of the classic capitalistic model, suggesting that government should not interfere with the economy. See also *individualism;* cf. *controlled economy, statism*.

lamb: an inexperienced speculator.

lame duck

(1) *securities:* a speculator whose venture has failed.

(2) *securities:* a member of a stock exchange who is unable to meet his or her debts.

(3) *administration:* an individual who is going out of office shortly and is thus thought to be ineffectual or helpless.

land certificate: a legal document indicating proof of ownership of land or property, containing a description of the property and the owner's name and address.

land freeze: a government limit on the sale or transfer of land.

land grant: a donation of public land by a government agency to be used for the benefit of the public. Railroads and state universities profited from land grants.

landlord: the owner of leased property; the lessor.

landlord's warrant: to obtain overdue rental payments, a landlord's court-approved warrant that permits him or her to take possession of the lessee's personal property in the leased premises until the debt is paid. Should the debt remain, the landlord can sell the personal property at public auction. See also *distress for rent*; cf. *ejectment, reentry*.

land office business: (slang) a booming or rushing business.

land patent: a government document that provides proof of title to land. Cf. *land warrant*.

land poor: referring to a person who owns land but, because of taxes or other obligations, is short of funds.

land revenue: any form of payment derived from ownership of land. It may take various forms (e.g., farm produce, forest rights, mineral deposits.).

Landrum-Griffin Act: the Labor-Management Reporting and Disclosure Act of 1959, a federal statute designed to rid unions of corruption and to ensure internal union democracy of one man, one vote. It contains a bill of rights, rules concerning trusteeships, a definition of the fiduciary obligations, and procedures to be followed in union elections. Hot cargo clauses are forbidden; specific types of picketing are outlawed; states are given authority over labor disputes declined by the NLRB; the noncommunist provision of the Taft-Hartley Act is eliminated and replaced with a provision that Communists cannot hold office (to qualify as a "former Communist" a person must not have been a member of the Communist party for at least five years); and convicted felons are barred from holding office within five years of their release from prison.

land tax: a tax levied on the ownership of real property. An assessed valuation determines the rate of the tax. See also *cadastre, single tax;* synonymous with *ad valorem tax, property tax.*

land trust: title to land held by a trustee in the interest of the beneficiaries of a trust.

land value tax: a governmental levy on the value of land only (i.e., not including structures or agricultural produce on it). See also *single tax.*

land warrant: a government document given as proof of ownership to anyone buying public land.

language
(1) *general:* a set of representations, conventions, and rules used to convey information.

(2) *computers:* a defined character set used to form words, symbols, and so on, and the rules for combining these into useful communications.

language, absolute
(1) *computers:* a set of signs or characters and the rules for combining them to convey instructions or information to a computer.
(2) *computers:* a language for writing instructions in a form to be used by the computer.

language, artificial: a language for the computer designed for ease of communication in a particular area of endeavor.

language, common: the result of a technique that reduces all information to a form that is intelligible to the units of a data-processing system.

language, common machine: a machine-sensible information description that is common to a related group of data-processing machines.

language, general-purpose: using English words and statements, combined programming languages that serve as the mathematical notation for procedures conveniently expressed mathematically (e.g., COBOL, FORTRAN, ALGOL).

language, program: a language that is used by programmers to write computer routines. Synonymous with *machine language.*

language, symbolic: expression of a formal logic by means of a formalized artificial language or symbolic calculus whose purpose is to avoid the ambiguities and inadequacies of natural languages. See also *Boolean algebra.*

language translator: a general computer term for any assembler, compiler, or other routine that accepts statements in one language and produces equivalent statements in another language.

Lanham Act of 1947: federal legislation governing trademarks and other symbols for identifying goods sold in interstate commerce. As amended, it allows a manufacturer to protect his brand or trademark in the United States by having it recorded on a government register in the U.S. Patent Office, and provides for the legal right to register any distinctive mark. See also *trademark.*

Laplace criterion: a basis for decision making whereby a manager applies equal probabilities to all states of nature. Synonymous with *Bayes criterion.*

lapping: theft from a customer that is covered by theft from another customer by placing false entries in account books. See also *fraud.*

lapse
(1) *insurance:* the failure of the insured to pay the cost of the premium when due or within the grace period allowed.
(2) *real estate:* the discontinuance of a right by the passage of time, as when the grace period of a mortgage ends or the date of a lease has passed.
(3) *business law:* the termination of a right through disuse or failure to meet standard obligations over a fixed time period. Cf. *laches.*

lapsing schedule: a form on which are recorded the costs of fixed assets or the total yearly additions to a group of fixed assets, together with the details of the distribution of their costs over the accounting periods succeeding their purchase.

larceny: the unlawful taking of the personal property of another without the individual's consent and with intent to deprive him or her of the ownership and use of it. This offense is defined by statute in nearly all states and provinces, but there are some differences in the definitions.

last in—first out: See *LIFO.*

last will: the will last executed by an individual. All former wills are revoked by the last one.

latent defect: a defect in goods that is not visible to the naked eye.

lateral communication: communication that takes place among departments or people on the same hierarchical level.

lateral relationships: horizontal relationships among organizational components (i.e., direct relationships among units at the same organizational level).

late tape: the situation that occurs when the ticker tape in an exchange or securities office is unable to print fast enough to keep up with the heavy trading on the trading floor.

latifundism: the holding of land in sizable estates.

lawful money: all forms of money that are endowed by federal law with legal tender status for the payment of all debts, both public and private.

law of increasing costs: the concept that the average total unit cost in a production process increases as the volume of a firm increases. See also *diseconomies of scale, marginal cost;* cf. *proportional law.*

law of triviality: as formulated by C. Northcote Parkinson, a law stating that the time spent on any agenda item will be in inverse proportion to the monetary sum involved. See also *Parkinson's laws.*

lawyer: (slang) a friend who advises another in a store regarding whether or not to purchase an item, frequently resulting in the customer's not buying the item.

layaway plan: a method of deferring payments whereby goods are retained by the store until the customer has completed payments for them.

lay days: agreed-upon days that a chartered vessel is permitted, without penalty, to remain in port for loading and unloading.

layoff: a temporary and indefinite separation from work, caused by a slack season, shortage of materials, market declines, or other factors outside the control of the worker. Layoff is to be distinguished from discharge or firing. See also *share-the-work.*

layout

(1) *computers:* the overall plan for computer card columns that form an outline of the procedure for a book or document.

(2) *advertising:* the plan or make-up of an advertisement.

L/C: See *letter of credit.*

LCL: See *less than carload lot.*

LDC: See *less-developed country.*

lead

(1) *general:* to direct and govern.

(2) *salesmanship:* the name and address of a potential customer. See also *referral leads.*

leader: a person who, at a given time and place, by his actions, modifies, directs, or controls the attitudes or behavior of others, often referred to as followers.

leader, autocratic: an individual who controls employees through domination and the power of his or her title. See also *Caesar management, Theory X and Theory Y.*

leader, democratic: an individual who controls employees through personal talents and who is open, flexible, and sensitive to the needs and feelings of all those under his or her jurisdiction. See *organic structure, Theory X and Theory Y.*

leader, merchandising: a store that promotes several items at attractive prices for the purpose of inducing customers into the store. See also *loss leader.*

leader, participative: a leader who uses various styles of leadership and who tries to get people actively involved in making decisions that will affect them. Cf. *Caesar management; leader, autocratic; leader, democratic.*

leader-member relations: a leader's feeling of being accepted by the group. It is the most important influence on a leader's effectiveness.

leader power position: the extent to which a leader has legitimate, coercive, and reward power to influence subordinates.

leadership: in a group or organization, the exercise of command and direction in a skillful and responsible fashion. See also *trait theory of leadership.*

leadership continuum: a sliding scale of leadership styles from autocratic to highly participative. A leader chooses the proper style of leadership based on forces in the leader, in subordinates, and in the situation.

leadership style: the way a manager

behaves in his or her role as leader. The two most widely discussed leadership styles are task-oriented and relationship-oriented behavior. See also *theory X and Theory Y.*

leadership substitutes: variables that reduce a leader's power to improve or retard the performance or satisfaction of subordinates.

leadership training: workshops, conferences, seminars, and other programs designed to upgrade skills and to offer information of use to those in leadership positions.

lead-in: part of the interaction that permits a sales representative to move toward a summing up or to close with a customer.

lead indicators: a series of economic indicators that often precede changes in the economic cycle.

leading from strength: a rule of strategy holding that an organization should draw on its strong points in fashioning its strategy.

leadman: an employee whose job involves some supervision, planning, and organization of tasks and materials performed by a group. A leadman usually receives additional pay.

lead time: the elapsed time between the beginning of an economic or manufacturing function and the completion of that function.

leakage: any factor or pressure that prevents new capital formation from exerting its full effect on the national income.

learning curve: a graphic representation of the measured changes at successive units of practice.

lease: a form of contract transferring the use or occupancy of land, space, structures, or equipment, in consid-

eration of a payment, usually in the form of rent. Leases can be for a short period or for as long as life. In a lease, a lessor gives the use of the property to a lessee.

leaseback: a seller who remains in possession as a tenant after completing the sale and delivering the deed. Cf. *sell and leaseback agreement.*

leased department: a department that is managed by a host store but is actually operated for the store by an outside organization, which pays the store a percentage of sales as rental.

leased fee interest: an interest of the owner in a leased property.

leasehold: an estate or interest a tenant holds for a number of years in the property he or she is leasing.

leasehold improvement: any improvement made on leased property.

leasehold insurance: insurance that protects a lessee who has subleased property to another person. Rental payments are guaranteed to be made by the holder of the sublease.

leasehold obligation: an obligation in a leasehold to pay a specified rental for a specified number of years.

leasehold value: the market value of a lease, which may increase or decrease from what was originally paid.

lease-insurance: a form of protection for a landlord against a default in rental payments on the lease's remaining time. Used primarily in commercial leasing, such coverage provides relief for the tenant in the event that financial problems prevent the making of payments.

lease obligations: net present value of all future lease payments discounted at an appropriate rate of interest.

lease-purchase agreement: an agreement providing that a portion of a tenant's rent can be applied to the price of purchase.

least-cost decision: a decision to undertake an investment with the smallest negative net present value.

least-preferred co-worker (LPC): the motivational system or behavioral preferences of a leader. High-LPC leaders are relations-oriented; low-LPC leaders are task-oriented.

least squares: a method of estimation that necessitates the choice of an estimate such that the sum of the squares of the deviations of the data from the estimate is a minimum. Cf. *chi-square.*

leave of absence: time off from work, usually without loss of seniority, granted with the assumption that the employee will be reinstated. Usually, long leaves of absence are without compensation.

leave year: the period from the beginning of the first complete pay period in the calendar year to the beginning of the first complete pay period in the following calendar year.

ledger: a record of final entry in bookkeeping. An account is established for every type of transaction, and a ledger account is posted with every transaction affecting that account. Cf. *journal.*

legacy: a gift of personal property made in a will. There are four common types of legacy:

(a) *specific legacy—* a gift of a particular piece of property, (e.g., an automobile) or an investment that has been specifically described.

(b) *demonstrative legacy—* a legacy that is payable in cash from a particular designated fund.

(c) *general legacy—* a gift of money in a certain sum.

(d) *residuary legacy—* all the remaining personal property after the payment of all obligations, charges against the estate, and all other legacies. See also *bequest.*

legal asset: any property, that can be used for payment of a debt.

legal bond: See *bond, legal.*

legal capital: the amount of contributed capital not available for dividends, as restricted by state law for the protection of creditors; usually equal to the par or stated value or the contributed amount of issued capital stock.

legal entity: any individual, proprietorship, partnership, corporation, association, or other organization that, in the eyes of the law, has the capacity to make a contract or an agreement and the abilities to assume an obligation and to discharge an indebtedness. A legal entity is a responsible being in the eyes of the law and can be sued for damages if the performance of a contract or agreement is not met.

legal interest: the maximum rate of interest permitted by state law. This rate is used in contracts in which no rate has been stated. Cf. *usury.*

legal list: a list of investments selected by various states in which certain institutions and fiduciaries, such as insurance companies and banks, may invest. Legal lists are often restricted to high-quality securities that meet certain specifications. See also *prudent man rule.*

legal monopoly: a privately owned organization that is granted an exclusive right by the government to function in a specified market under strict control and pricing by the government (e.g., public utilities).

legal reserve:

(1) *insurance:* policy reserves maintained by an insurance company to meet future claims and obligations, according to the standards established by the insurance laws of the various states. Cf. *reserve.*

(2) *banking:* part of a bank's cash assets that must be retained as protection for depositors according to a ruling from the Federal Deposit Insurance Act.

legal residence: where a person lives. The law does not require anyone to spend a majority of his or her time in a certain place for it to be categorized as a legal residence; however, federal law recognizes only one legal residence for an individual. Cf. *domicile.*

legal security: a stock or bond that can be bought by a fiduciary and retained for beneficiaries.

legal tender: any money that is recognized as being lawful for use by a debtor to pay a creditor, who must accept same in the discharge of a debt unless the contract between the parties specifically states that another type of money is to be used.

legal title: the claim of right to property that is recognized by law.

legatee: an individual to whom a legacy is given by will.

legitimate power: the power a leader has in the managerial hierarchy because of rank. For example, a department manager who is ranked higher than the foreman in the managerial hierarchy possesses more legitimate power.

lend: to give up something of person-

al value for a definite or indefinite period of time, without relinquishing ownership. See also *loan.*

lender: an individual or financial institution that makes a trade of placing an interest on the use of money, with the expectation that the money (or other item) will be returned with the interest. See also *note.*

lender of last resort: a central bank that will lend to individual banks whenever they experience large withdrawals.

lending institution: a finance company, bank, loan organization, or the like, that lends money and makes money by advancing funds to others. See also *personal finance company.*

length of load: the space occupied by containers or items from end to end of a freight car.

length of service: the period of a worker's continuous service with a particular firm. It is calculated from the date the worker is placed on the payroll to the time the length of service is computed.

leniency bias: a tendency to rate employees higher than their performance justifies.

less-developed country (LDC): a country showing (1) a poverty level of income, (2) a high rate of population increases, (3) a substantial portion of its workers employed in agriculture, (4) a low proportion of adult literacy, (5) high unemployment, and (6) a significant reliance on a few items for export. See also *underdeveloped country.*

lessee: a tenant.

lessor: a landlord.

less than carload lot (LCL): goods requiring less space when shipped than that available in a single freight car; the rate applied to such a shipment.

let

(1) *real estate:* Synonymous with *lease.*

(2) *administration:* to award or assign work to be done by or equipment to be rented from a supplier.

let out: (slang) to dismiss from employment; to fire.

letter of attorney: a document showing a power of attorney.

letter of credit (L/C): an instrument or document issued on behalf of a buyer by a bank on another bank or banks or on itself. It gives the buyer the prestige and the financial backing of the issuing bank. The acceptance by the bank of drafts drawn under the letter of credit satisfies the seller and the seller's bank in the handling of the transaction. The buyer and the accepting bank also have an agreement as to payment for the drafts as they are presented. See also *authority to purchase, guaranteed letters of credit, revolving letter of credit;* cf. *traveler's letter of credit.*

letter of indication: a bank's letter of identification given to a traveler who has bought a letter of credit.

letterpress: a printing machine in which the ink is carried on a raised or relief surface. Cf. *offset.*

letter stock: an unregistered stock, usually issued by a new, small firm to avoid the expense of formal underwriting. These securities are sold at a discount to mutual funds and to investors who specialize in speculative purchases.

level annuity: Synonymous with *level payment mortgage.*

leveling: a procedure in time and motion study used to measure and evaluate an employee's output. The output is expected to be that of an average trained worker. A stopwatch is used to measure the time needed to complete a task. See also *time and motion study;* cf. *performance appraisal.*

level of aspiration: a degree or quality of achievement or failure by which an individual or group perceives or measures its own performance.

level(s) of authority: points or layers in the organizational hierarchy.

level payment mortgage: a loan plan with periodic payments, usually monthly, whereby the payments remain the same over the term of the loan. The portion of the payment credited to interest decreases, while the portion credited to reduction of principal increases with each successive payment. Synonymous with *level annuity, static payment loan.*

level premium insurance: insurance in which the annual premium remains the same throughout the period over which premiums are paid.

leverage: the effect on the per-share earnings of the common stock of a company when large sums must be paid for bond interest, preferred stock dividends, or both, before the common stock is entitled to share in earnings. Leverage may be advantageous for the common stock when earnings are good but may work against the common stock when earnings decline.

leverage ratios: ratios used during ratio analysis that indicate the relationship between organizational funds supplied by the owners of an organization and organizational funds supplied by creditors.

leveraging: the advantage (or disadvantage) obtained from using borrowed money to finance a business when the net interest rate of the borrowed funds is less (more) than the company's earnings rate.

levy

(1) *general:* a tax assessment.

(2) *finance:* a demand made on the members of a company to contribute added working capital or to make good on a loss.

(3) *government:* to assess, declare, and receive a sum of money against a person or property for public objectives.

levy, writ of

(1) *general:* a lien placed on land or other property of a defendant.

(2) *business law:* the instrument authorizing the sheriff to take a defendant's property to satisfy a plaintiff's judgment.

Lewin model of behavior: developed by Kurt Lewin, whose field theory shows the relationships between the person and his or her environment, a model that suggests that behavior (B) is a function (f) of the personality (P) of the individual and the climate in which the person lives (E). In equation form, it is stated: $B = f(P, E)$.

liabilities

(1) *finance:* all the claims against a corporation. See also *indirect business tax* and *nontax liability.*

(2) *banking:* the funds a bank owes. The largest liability for a bank is deposits. See also *accrued liabilities, capital liability, contingent liability, current liabilities, fixed liabilities, floating debt, long-term liabilities, se-*

cured debt.

liability

(1) *insurance:* a form of coverage that pertains, for the most part, to claims arising out of the insured's claim for injuries or damage caused by ownership of property, manufacturing operations, contracting operations, sale or distribution of products, and operation of elevators and the like, as well as professional services. See also *third-party insurance.*

(2) *business law:* any obligation an individual has by virtue of law (e.g., a debt, a responsibility). See also *liabilities, vicarious liability.*

liability insurance: any form of coverage whereby the insured is protected against claims of other parties. Most liability insurance is written by casualty companies, but some forms (especially those referring to property in the care of the insured) are underwritten in connection with fire or marine business. The insured's liability for damages usually results from negligence.

liability ledger: the record of all outstanding loans made by a bank to every borrower.

liability limits: the sum or sums up to which an insurance company protects the insured on a particular policy. Bodily injury and property damage liability covered by general liability policies is subject to a limit for each occurrence. In certain forms, however, such as malpractice, product, and manufacturers' and contractors' liability, there is also an aggregate limit of liability for the total amount of all claims during the policy period. Automobile policies covering liability for bodily injury have two limits: (1) a limit of liability to any one person, and (2) subject to this personal limit, another (usually higher) limit for any single accident involving more than one person. Automobile coverage for property damage liability is written with a limit per accident. Basic limits of liability are the lowest limits that are ordinarily written and are also the limits for which the cost of units of protection and minimum premiums are computed. Cf. *umbrella liability.*

liable

(1) *general:* subject to a particular risk, expense, or penalty, which is more or less likely to occur to be incurred.

(2) *business law:* obligated by law or equity.

liaison role: the role of a manager in making contacts outside the vertical chain of command in an effort to bring information into the unit and gain favors from others. This role includes interacting in a network of contacts with peers and others in order to get that information.

liaison unit: an organizational unit that has responsibility for coordinating the activities of two or more components of an organization.

libel: a malicious statement (oral, printed, etc.) by which an individual is defamed or one made with the intent to harm the reputation and good name of a person; "the exposing of a person to public hatred, contempt, or ridicule." Cf. *slander.*

liberal return policy: the practice of a store to accept goods returned for refund or exchange with a minimum of difficulty to the customer.

library

(1) *general:* a collection of organ-ized information used for study and references.

(2) *computers:* a group of standard, proven routines that can be utilized in larger routines.

(3) *computers:* a collection of computer programs for rapid checking, reference, or use.

license: a document (e.g., a driver's license) showing that permission has been granted to engage in an activity that could not legally be done without that document; a formal government authorization to do something (e.g., to practice law).

license and permit bonds: bonds required by various municipalities or public authorities to indemnify these entities against loss in the event of violation of the regulations or ordinances under which a permit is acquired.

licensed lender: a lending group of people or organization(s) authorized by license to conduct business in the state in which residence is shown.

lien: a claim on another's property as security against payment of a debt. See also *bond, indemnity; quantum meruit.*

lien affidavit: an affidavit either stating that there are no liens against a particular property or documenting and properly describing any existing liens. See also *recordation;* cf. *no-lien affidavit.*

lien in invitum: a lien placed on property without the owner's approval. Synonymous with *involuntary lien.*

lienor: the holder of a lien. See also *voluntary conveyance or deed.*

life annuity: an insurance policy that provides an annual income for the insured, beginning at retirement and continuing for the duration of the individual's life. See also *annuity.*

life cycle hypothesis: a theory of the saving decision stating that consumers save to be able to maintain a stable level of consumption in the future. See also *marginal propensity, to consume, marginal propensity to invest, marginal propensity to save.*

life cycle theory: a leadership theory, developed by Paul Hersey and Kenneth Blanchard, that contends that appropriate leadership behavior requires varying degrees of task and relationship orientation as the maturity of the followers increases.

life estate: an estate in real or personal property that terminates when the owner dies. The future of the property (i.e., after the owner's death) is usually provided for when the life estate is prepared.

life insurance: insurance providing for payment of a stipulated sum to a designated beneficiary upon the death of the insured. Various plans of life insurance are available to fit the differing needs of many classes of insureds—for example, endowment plans, which pay back the face amount of the policy to the insured if he or she survives the specified period of the policy; or annuity contracts, under which savings are accumulated and paid back in periodic payments of guaranteed lifetime income to the annuitant if he or she survives the specified period.

life insurance trust: a trust created by an individual for the benefit of his or her heirs, the major portion of which is in the form of life insurance.

life tenant: a beneficiary who has pos-

session of certain property for the duration of his or her life; the owner of a life estate. See also *life estate.*

LIFO (last in–first out)

(1) *accounting:* in valuation of inventories, the system whereby the price shown on the last incoming shipment of a particular item is the one used for current valuations and cost.

(2) *banking:* a method of determining the effect of withdrawals on savings account dividends or interest computations. With LIFO, withdrawals are made from money that was deposited last. The withdrawal penalty under this plan is loss of interest on the last money deposited. Cf. *FIFO.*

light gold: gold coins that have been reduced in weight, either by error of the mint or as the result of usage.

light pen tracking: the process of tracing the movement of light omitted by a penlike instrument across the screen of a display device. The tracking is used to detect images on a screen or to activate a computer to alter images it has caused to be displayed.

limitations of actions (statutes of): the laws for each state that identify the definite time limit within which a law suit can be brought under law. The terms within the statutes vary by state, but the time within which a commercial case action should be brought is usually 6 years.

limited (Ltd.): See *limited company.*

limited-access land: land or property that is difficult to reach; land that is made more inaccessible (e.g., a major highway that has few entrances or exits, limiting the right of access).

limited coinage system: the U.S.

Mint's program under which the right of the individual to bring bullion for purposes of being coined is limited.

limited collision coverage: a form of collision coverage that is applicable only when the insured is not at fault in an accident.

limited company: a British business corporation. Use of the abbreviation "Ltd." indicates registration under the Companies Act and formally establishes the limited liability of stockholders.

limited function wholesaler: a wholesaler middleman who does not perform all the marketing functions.

limited liability: legal exemption of stockholders from financial liability for the debts of the firm beyond the amount they have individually invested. See also *partnership;* cf. *nonassessable stock.*

limited life: a characteristic of a single proprietorship or partnership whereby the business ceases to exist on the death of the owners.

limited line stores: smaller retail operations that carry most goods in a narrow line of items (e.g., a women's apparel shop that carries casual and formal ladies' garments, sportswear, and lingerie, but not baby clothes).

limited order: an order in which the customer has set restrictions with respect to price. See also *composite limit order book, market order, no-limit order, percentage order, stop limit order.*

limited partner: a member of a partnership who is not personally liable for incurred debts of the partnership. By law, at least one partner must be fully liable.

limited payment life: a policy provid-ing permanent protection, but with premiums payable only for a specified, limited number of years.

limited policy: a policy providing insurance against accidents of specified types, or one that is restricted in indemnity payments, in contrast to a full-coverage policy.

limited price order: an order to buy or sell a stated amount of a security at a specified price or at a better price, according to the directions within the order. Cf. *limited order.*

limited tax bond: See *bond, limited tax.*

limiting factor: anything that restricts or constrains the production or sale of a product or service.

limping standard: a modification of the gold monetary standard leading to the acceptance of certain silver coins as standard money to the extent that they are made unlimited legal tender and are not required to be redeemed in gold.

Lincoln incentive management plan: a combination profit-sharing and incentive plan, developed by J. F. Lincoln in 1934, leading to better worker performance and sizable extra payments for the employee.

line

(1) *merchandising:* the silhouette and description of any apparel style.

(2) *retailing:* items carried by a merchant. Cf. *product line.*

(3) *insurance:* a type or class of insurance or of insurance risks. See also *accommodation line, gross line;* cf. *multiple-line underwriting.*

(4) *transportation:* a system or carrier.

(5) *management:* the chain of command and business responsibility.

(6) *labor relations:* See *assembly-line production.*

line and staff authority: a part of the organization identified as those having the right to decide and to order others to perform activities (line) and those having the right to plan, recommend, advise, or assist, but not to order others to perform activities (staff).

line-and-staff organization: an organization that, because of its size or the complexity of its functions or goals, has an advisory support staff in addition to the line staff.

linear function: a relationship between two or more variables that can be represented by a straight line. The slope of the line is given by any y value divided by a corresponding x value.

linear programing (LP)

(1) *general:* a procedure for locating the maximum or minimum of a linear function of variables that are subject to linear constraints.

(2) *production:* a means for indicating how materials should be combined to produce the highest profits, given a set of materials with specified characteristics and a set of prices for the finished product. See also *transportation.*

(3) *operation research:* a mathematical technique used to optimize a business operation subject to given resources and restraints.

line authority: authority that is exerted downward (i.e., over subordinates) in an organization.

line control: the scheme of operating procedures and control signals by which a telecommunications system is controlled.

line haul: movement of cargo between cities and towns, as distinguished from pickup and delivery activities.

line item: an income or expense account on a profit and loss statement.

line layout: the assortment of machinery and tools used in manufacturing in a sequence of chronological operations to be performed. Synonymous with "production-line layout."

line manager: a high-level officer who has direct responsibility for carrying out a superiors' requests and is authorized to pass along his or her own orders to subordinates. See also *line organization, middle management.*

line of balance: a management control system for gathering, measuring, and presenting information on time, cost, and accomplishment, as measured against a given plan. It offers the progress, status, background, timing, and phasing of intraproject movements.

line of credit: an agreement between a bank and a customer whereby the bank agrees to lend the customer funds over a future period, up to an agreed maximum amount. The bank has the option to withdraw from the agreement if the financial status of the borrower changes or if the borrower fails to use the line of credit for its intended use as set forth in the agreement. The customer may borrow as much of the line as is required and pay interest on the borrowed portion only. Lines of credit are widely used by large organizations to finance future commitments and for purchasing inventory.

line of discount: the maximum credit that a bank will extend to a retailer on the basis of his or her accounts payable, which the merchant discounts with the bank.

line organization: the oldest and least complex company structure, in which top officials have total and direct authority and subordinates report to only one supervisor. Cf. *football-bell structure.*

line-out: a group of workers who carry out a complete production operation as a team.

line pricing: a pricing strategy in which all products in a multiple-product line are priced at the same level.

line printer: a computer device that prints all characters of a line as a unit.

liner

(1) *packaging:* a material separating a product in a container from the basic walls of the container.

(2) *transportation:* a luxurious passenger vessel.

line sheet: a guide prepared by an insurance company for its underwriters, setting forth the amount of liability the company is willing to assume on various classes of risks. See also *experience.*

linkage

(1) *computers:* coding that connects two separately coded routines.

(2) *economics:* the pressures an industry can exert on the rest of the economy.

linking pin: a term coined by Rensis Likert for a worker who belongs to two groups whose tasks overlap. This person is given responsibility for coordinating the activities of both groups.

Linotype: a trademarked keyboard machine that casts characters (type) and prints one line at a time.

liquid: capable of being readily con-

verted to cash. Usually the assets of an entity are considered to be most liquid when they are in cash or marketable securities. Synonymous with *collectible.*

liquid assets: assets that are easily converted into cash (e.g., government bonds). See also *flight of capital.*

liquidate

(1) *general:* to convert assets into cash.

(2) *accounting:* to discharge or pay off an indebtedness.

(3) *finance:* to settle accounts by apportioning assets and debts.

liquidated damages: the payment by all parties of an agreed-upon sum of money as damages for breaching their contract. The courts can declare the damages to be a penalty and therefore unenforceable if the amount is excessive.

liquidating dividend: the dividend declared in the closing of a firm to distribute the assets of the organization to properly qualified stockholders.

liquidation: winding up the affairs of a business by converting all assets into cash, paying off all outside creditors in the order of their preference, and distributing the remainder, if any, to the owners in proportion and in the order of preference, if any, of ownership.

liquidation value: the value of a property if the owner were forced to convert it quickly into cash, as opposed to selling it to the highest bidder after reasonable provision. Synonymous with *"forced-sale value."*

liquidator: a person who liquidates; a person who is legally in charge of liquidating a business.

liquidity

(1) *finance:* the solvency of a business, with special reference to the speed with which assets can be converted into cash without loss.

(2) *securities:* the ability of the market in a particular security to absorb a reasonable amount of buying or selling at reasonable price changes.

liquidity preference: the part of Keynesian theory; that deals with the preference of people to hold their assets in cash rather than in a less liquid form, such as an investment. See also *Keynesian economics;* cf. *marginal propensity to invest.*

liquidity ratios: ratios used during ratio analysis that indicate an organization's ability to meet upcoming financial obligations.

liquidity trap: in the liquidity preference theory of John Maynard Keynes, the concept that, at some low interest rate, the speculative desire for cash becomes infinitely elastic. Cf. *quantity theory.*

liquid ratio: the ratio of readily available current assets to current liabilities.

lis pendens: a pending suit. See also *injunction pendente lite, pendente lite.*

list

(1) *general:* an ordered set of items.

(2) *computers:* an array of items, written in a meaningful format, that designates quantities to be transmitted for input/output.

list broker: a commission agent who rents direct-mail lists to advertisers.

listed securities (stocks): any bonds or stocks that have been admitted for trading on a stock exchange and whose issues have complied in every way with the listing requirements of the exchange.

lister: a broker who sells property from a listing.

listing: a seller's offering of a property through one or more real estate brokers. The broker who successfully sells the property receives a commission. Cf. *open listing.*

list price

(1) *general:* the price of an item, subject to sale and cash discounts; any quoted price in excess of that obtained in an actual sale.

(2) *retailing:* the retail price suggested or fixed by the manufacturer rather than the retailer. Cf. *fair trade price.*

literal: describing a symbol or a quantity that is itself a piece of data rather than a reference to data.

litigant: a person engaged in a law suit.

litigation: the act of carrying on a lawsuit.

Little Board: the American Stock Exchange. Cf. *Big Board.*

Little Steel: a description used in World War II to identify all steel companies, except the U.S. Steel Corporation. See also *Big Steel.*

Little Wagner Acts: See *Baby Wagner Acts.*

livestock insurance: insurance against the death of farm animals from specified perils.

living document doctrine: part of a contract stipulating that a union may reopen wage negotiations at any time. Cf. *contract bar.*

living trust: a voluntary trust created from the assets of a living person.

Lloyds: an association of English insurance underwriters—the oldest of its kind in the world. The Corporation of Lloyds also provides a daily newspaper *(Lloyds List and Shipping Gazette),* a clasification of ships *(Lloyds Register of Shipping),* and other publications.

L-M curve: a graphical presentation of combinations of interest rates and incomes for which the demand for money equals its supply.

load:

(1) *shipping:* a package or group of packages included in a shipping unit (a carload, an airplane load, etc.).

(2) *shipping:* an item or group of items included in a single outer shipping container.

(3) *computers:* to enter data into storage or into working registers

(4) *securities:* the portion of the offering price of shares of open-end investment companies that covers sales commissions and all other costs of distribution. The load is usually incurred only on purchase; there is seldom any charge when the shares are sold. Cf. *no-load funds.*

load chart: a chart illustrating the weight of shipments loaded onto a trailer and the place in the vehicle of the larger items, harmful goods, or special shipments.

load-factor pricing: changing the price of a product at various periods to maximize the utilization of manufacturing facilities in order to minimize seasonal or time-of-day decline in demand, or to attract lower-income groups of purchasers.

load funds: mutual funds sold by sales representatives. For the shares they sell, there is a sales charge or load. Cf. *no-load funds.*

loading

(1) *finance:* the amount added to an installment agreement to cover selling and administrative overhead, interest, risk, and so on.

(2) *securities:* the amount added to the prorated market price of underlying securities to represent fees and overhead.

(3) *business:* the addition of overhead to prime cost.

(4) *insurance:* the amount added to net premiums to cover a company's operating expenses and contingencies, including the cost of securing new business, collection expenses, and general management expenses; precisely, the excess of gross premiums over net premiums.

loading charge: a premium, usually from 6 to 8 percent, charged by open-end investment funds on selling new securities, to cover selling costs.

loading of cash discounts: building up gross invoice price of goods and crediting cash discounts with the amount of the load. This is accomplished by adjusting the invoice or by altering the store's bookkeeping entry.

load point: the beginning of the recording area on a reel of magnetic tape.

load up: to buy a security or commodity to one's financial limit for purposes of speculation.

loan: a business transaction between two legal entities whereby one party (the lender) agrees to lend funds to a second party (the borrower). The funds may be lent with or without a fee, which is called interest or discount. Loans may be demand or time loans, depending on the agreement as to maturity, and they may be for short or long terms. See also *lend, lender, lending institution.*

loanable funds theory of interest: a concept that the interest rate is determined by the demand for and supply of loanable funds only, as distinguished from all money.

loan-closing payments: expenses incurred when a mortgage loan is terminated (mortgage costs, legal fees for preparing the papers, appraisal and recording fees, etc.).

loan crowd: stock exchange members who will borrow or lend securities to investors who have sold short. These individuals usually meet at a designated place in the exchange. See also *short sale.*

loaned flat: describing stock that is borrowed without an interest payment. Sometimes securities are sold short, requiring the seller to borrow them if this becomes necessary to make delivery. When he or she is able to borrow without making an interest payment for the shares, the seller is dealing in a stock that is loaned flat. See also *loan stock.*

loan fee: any charge made to the borrower in connection with a loan, particularly a new mortgage. Synonymous with *loan origination fee, premium servicing fee.*

loan interest: the amount of money paid for the use of capital or borrowed funds.

loan modification provision: a clause in a mortgage permitting the borrower to defer one or more payments in the event of financial difficulties.

loan origination fee: Synonymous with *loan fee.*

loan policy: a title insurance policy prepared by a title insurance company for a holder of a mortgage.

loan rate: the rate charged for borrowing money at a specific date for a stated period. Cf. *legal interest.*

loan shark: an unauthorized moneylender who charges excessive interest for instant cash, accepting poor credit risks, and so on; a racketeer who threatens punishment if the repayment is not on schedule. See also *usury.*

loan stock: securities that have been loaned to a broker or short seller to fulfill the terms of a short-selling contrast by delivering shares.

loan value

(1) *real estate:* the amount a lending organization will lend on property.

(2) *insurance:* the amount of money that can be borrowed on a life insurance policy.

loan-value ratio: the ratio of a property's appraised value to the amount of the mortgage loan.

lobbyist: a person or group of persons trying to affect and influence (through personal intervention) the proceedings of government agencies.

lobster shift: Synonymous with *midnight shift.*

locals: managers and professionals who have an inside-the-organization orientation. They tend to be loyal to the organizations' norms and values.

local union: also called a "local," the organization of members of an international union in a particular plant, region, or locality.

location: any place in which computer data may be stored.

lock-away: a British term for a long-term security.

locked in: describing an investor who does not sell a security because its profit would immediately become subject to the capital gains tax. See also *Tax Reform Act of 1976*.

locker stocks: a manufacturer's or wholesaler's shipment of additional inventory that is retained unopened in the store's central warehouse. When the buyer requires an item held in locker stock, payment is made to the vendor for the entire shipment.

Lockheed model: a model that identifies relevant variables for establishing spans of control, including the complexity of functions, the coordination of subordinates required, and the direction and control required by subordinates.

lockout: the phase of a labor dispute in which management refuses work to employees or closes its plant to force a settlement. The antithesis of a strike, the lockout is used to avert a threatened strike.

lockup

(1) *securities:* securities that have been withdrawn from circulation and placed in a safe deposit box as a long-term investment.

(2) *banking:* a note or obligation that has been renewed, the time of repayment having been extended beyond the original due date.

logic, computer: the sequence of steps necessary to perform a particular function.

logistics: in management, the science of planning, organizing, and arranging the most feasible combination of resources, areas, personnel and time needed to carry out established objectives, policies, and procedures.

log on: the procedure by which a computer user begins an interaction with a time-sharing system.

logo(type): two or more letters, often making a short word, that represent the name or signature of an advertiser (e.g., NBC).

lonely pay: (slang) increased wages demanded by unions to offset reduced working hours resulting from technological advances.

long: signifying ownership of stocks ("I am long 100 U.S. Steel" means that the speaker owns 100 shares); holding a sizable amount of a security or commodity in anticipation of a scarcity and price rise. See also *carry*.

longevity pay (wage): salary adjustments based on seniority or length of service.

long-form mortgage clause: a clause that provides for the assumption of responsibility for the satisfaction of the mortgage by the mortgagor when he or she takes title. The mortgagor does not simply acquire the property.

long-lived assets: resources that are held for an extended time, such as land, buildings, equipment, natural resources, and patents.

long of exchange: describing a trader in foreign currency who has bought and holds foreign bills in an amount exceeding the bills of his or her own that have been sold and remain outstanding.

long position: describing the status of a holder of securities who expects an increase in the price of his or her shares or who holds these securities for income.

long-range planning: a systematic procedure for directing and controlling future activities of a firm for periods longer than a year. It predicts the future and establishes a strategy of action and expected results.

long rate: the reduced premium rate when a policy runs longer than one year.

long run: an extensive time period that permits a firm to develop its capability to manufacture.

long-run planning capacity: the rate of activity needed to meet average sales demand over a period long enough to include seasonal and cyclical fluctuations.

long-term capital gain: the gain realized when capital assets that have been held for longer than 12 months are sold at a profit. See also *Tax Reform Act of 1976.*

long-term capital loss: the loss realized when capital assets that have been held for longer than 12 months are sold at a loss. See also *Tax Reform Act of 1976.*

long-term contract: a collective-bargaining agreement negotiated for a period longer than one year.

long-term corporate bond: See *bond, long-term corporate.*

long-term debt: liabilities that become due more than one year after the signing of the agreement. Usually, these are formal legal agreements demanding periodic payments of interest until the maturity date, at which time the principal amount is repaid.

long-term disability policies: insurance policies that pay covered workers a proportion of their wage or salary when they are disabled. Usual-

ly these policies require a six-month waiting period before they begin to pay.

long-term liabilities: debts or other obligations that will not be paid for or otherwise discharged within one year or within the normal operating cycle.

long-term operational assets: long-lived assets acquired for use in the business rather than for resale, including property, plant, and equipment; natural resources; and intangible assets.

long ton: 2240 pounds. Cf. *short ton.*

look back: the auditing of past records to locate errors that have come to the attention of a bank's auditing department. Cf. *internal audit.*

look-up: See *table look-up.*

loop: a sequence of computer instructions in which the last instruction in the series returns the machine to the first instruction in the series. See also *closed-loop control, open-loop control.*

loop computing: performance of the primary function of a loop by the instructions of the loop itself, as distinguished from loop initialization, modification, and testing, which are housekeeping operations.

loop modification: alteration of instruction addresses, counters, or data by means of instructions of a loop.

loop testing: determination of when a loop function has been completed by means of instructions of the loop.

loose jobs (rate): the situation that exists when the earnings for a worker are not in line with pay for similar positions requiring similar skills. See also *incentive pay, piece rate (wage).*

loose-rein supervision: a leadership

style based on the philosophy that the less supervision is exerted, the better it will be for the firm. Synonymous with *laissez-faire*; see also *open system*.

Lorenz curve: a graphic device for plotting the degree of inequality in the distribution of income.

loss

(1) *insurance:* any decrease in quantity, quality, or value of property. With reference to policies of indemnity, this term is often used as an expression of the amount of damage that might or might not be covered in whole or in part, depending on the cause of the loss and the coverage afforded. In its application to liability policies, loss refers to payments made on behalf of the insured.

(2) *accounting:* any item that can be listed as an expense.

(3) *finance:* the excess of the cost or depreciated cost of an asset over its price of sale.

loss constant: a flat amount included in some insurance premiums that measures the average provision for losses.

loss-control representative: an employee of an insurance company trained in the technicalities of a specific field (e.g., fire, workers' compensation, public liability, automobile fleet). The employee's main functions are to assist insureds in loss-prevention practices and to obtain rating and underwriting information. Cf. *National Fire Protection Association*.

loss draft: the insurance payment for damage to mortgaged property to cover the cost of necessary repairs.

loss expectancy: an underwriter's es-timate of damage that would result from the peril insured against. An underwriter must consider (1) "probable maximum loss expectancy," which is an estimate of damage under conditions of normally expected control and protection against the peril, and (2) "above-normal loss (ANL) expectancy," the estimate of damage that would occur if the peril were not controlled by the protection to be reasonably expected. See also *maximum foreseeable loss*.

loss information service: a listing service provided to an insurance company by the National Board of Fire Underwriters, giving the names of individuals involved in arson or fires of suspicious origin.

loss leader: a retail merchandising strategy of advertising an item at a price below cost, to attract customers to the store in the expectation that they will purchase other items at full profit margins. See also *leader, merchandising; price lining*.

loss on disposal: the result of a sale of noncurrent asset for less than the book value or unrecovered cost.

loss-payable cause: provides for payment to a party (e.g., a mortgagee or lien holder) in addition to the insured for any losses to the insured property according to the extent of that party's interest in the property at the time of the loss.

loss-prevention service: loss-control and inspection work done by insurance companies or independent organizations for the purpose of recommending the change or removal of conditions that are likely to cause loss.

loss ratio: a percentage arrived at by dividing the amount of the losses by the amount of the insurance premium. Various loss ratios are computed (e.g., earned premium to incurred losses, written premium to paid losses).

loss reserve: a part of an insurance firm's assets retained in available form to meet expected claims.

lost policy release: a statement signed by the insured releasing the insurance company from all liability resulting from a lost or mislaid contract of insurance.

lot

(1) *accounting:* any group of goods or services making up a single transaction.

(2) *real estate:* a parcel of land that has measurable boundaries.

(3) *securities:* a quantity of shares, usually 100. Cf. *block, odd-lot orders.*

loud talk: (slang) creating trouble by talking openly near a superior about co-workers' violations of regulations.

low: the lowest price paid for a purchase of securities in a specific time period.

low-baller: (slang) an executive who underestimates his expected financial situation.

lower turning point: a short period during which a downswing ends and an upswing begins. Cf. *upper turning point.*

low grade: of inferior quality, applied to merchandise, stock, and so on.

low-margin retailing: discount selling or mass merchandising.

loyal worker

(1) *general:* an employee who is faithful to his or her employer.

(2) *labor relations:* a term used by an employer to describe a worker who refuses to join fellow employees in an organizing drive, votes against the untion in a representation election, or refuses to take part in a strike. Cf. *blackleg, fink.*

LP: See *linear programming.*

lucrative title

(1) *real estate:* a title that is obtained by a person who pays less than the true market value of the property.

(2) *real estate:* title to property obtained as a gift. See also *devise, gift causa mortis, gift inter vivos.*

Luddites: nineteenth-century English workers who resisted the introduction of labor-saving equipment in the factories that employed them. A workingman named Lud is credited with destroying stocking frames in 1779. The contemporary penalty for such activity was often imprisonment or cruel punishment and sometimes death. See also *sabotage, industrial.*

lug: a box, basket, or other container used for shipping fresh produce (fruits, vegetables, etc.); usually a small, shallow, nailed wooden box.

Luhn scanner: a scanning device invented by H.P. Luhn for photoelectric scanning of punched cards as they are fed into the sorter. Cf. *flying spot scanner.*

lumpen: a Marxist term describing the degraded and contemptible section of the proletariat.

lumpiness of resources: the concept that resources are not infinitely divisible and that some waste may therefore result.

lump sum purchase: a group of assets obtained for an indicated figure, without breakdown by individual assets or classes of asset.

luxuries: comforts and beauties of life that are are excess of what is needed for normal or standard living. See also *optional consumption.*

luxury tax: a tax imposed on items that are not considered essential for daily living. In most cases, goods so taxed are expensive.

Machiavellian manager: a person of low moral and ethical values who operates with the philosophy that the end justifies the means, regardless of who gets hurt along the way.

machine: any piece of equipment used to regulate force or motion; a combination of mechanical devices and powers to carry out a task. See also *Turing machine;* cf. *hardware.*

machine, bending: in the making of paper boxes, a machine used for bending the sides and ends of the base, tray, or lid.

machine, bundling: a machine used to collate multiples of unit packages.

machine, scanning: a machine that facilitates the input of data by reading printed data and converting them into machine language. See also *flying spot scanner, Luhn scanner.*

machine address: the direct, absolute, unindexed address, expressed as such or resulting after indexing has been carried out.

machine code: an operation code that a machine is designed to recognize. Synonymous with *computer code.*

machine-hour cost: the direct and indirect cost of operating a machine for one hour.

machine instruction: an instruction that a machine can recognize and execute.

machine language: information or data expressed in a code that can be read by a computer or by peripheral equipment without interpretation.

machine-oriented language: a programming language that is more like a machine language than a human language.

machine readable: describing material that can be sensed or read by a specific device.

macroeconomics: the study of statistics (e.g., total consumption, total employment) of the economy as a whole, rather than as single economic units. Synonymous with *aggregate economics.*

macrolevel approach: a means of change that affects the entire organization. Cf. *micro-level approach.*

macromarketing: a study of the economic exchange process of a total economy. Cf. *micromarketing.*

MADCAP: a machine-oriented language for mathematical problems and set operations.

made work: employment created or work activities spread out by assigning employees activities that fulfill no productive requirement.

Madison Avenue: (slang) a grouping of communications and advertising enterprises found along Madison Avenue in New York City.

magistrate: a public officer, usually a judge, with power to issue a warrant for the arrest of a person charged with a public offense.

magnetic card: a card with a magnetic surface on which data can be stored by selective magnetization of portions of the flat surface.

magnetic core: a configuration of magnetic material that is placed in a spatial relationship to current-carrying conductors and whose magnetic properties are essential to its use.

magnetic disk: a flat circular plate with a magnetic surface on which data can be stored by selective magnetization of portions of the flat surface.

magnetic drum: a storage device in which information is recorded on the magnetizable surface of a rotating cylinder. The term usually suggests a complete system, consisting of the drum itself, reading and writing heads, and the associated selection and timing circuitry.

magnetic ink: an ink containing particles of a magnetic substance whose presence can be detected by magnetic sensors.

magnetic ink character recognition (MICR): the recognition by a computer of characters printed with magnetic ink. Cf. *optical character recognition.*

magnetic storage: designating a storage device that utilizes the magnetic properties of materials to store data.

magnetic tape

(1) *computers:* a tape with a magnetic surface on which data can be stored by selective polarization of portions of the surface.

(2) *computers:* a storage system in which information is recorded on the magnetizable surface of a strip of synthetic or steel tape. See also *Mylar.*

magnum: a glass bottle, used primarily for bottling wines, that has a capacity of two-fifths gallon.

mailgram: a low-cost message transmitted electronically by Western Union and delivered by the U.S. Postal Service. The customer is usually billed for this service on the monthly telephone bill.

mail-order advertising: advertising designed to yield orders directly from prospects by mail. Media of any form can be used to deliver the advertising message.

mail-order wholesaler: an individual who sells by mail and usually advertises goods and services in a catalog.

main frame: the major part of the computer—the arithmetic or logic unit. Synonymous with *central processing unit, frame.*

main storage: the general-purpose storage unit of a computer.

maintained mark-on: the difference between the cost for delivering goods and the price at which they are sold.

maintenance

(1) *general:* the upkeep of any form of property (land, machinery, tools, etc.).

(2) *computers:* updating of object program master files, selection of programs, and control of production procedures.

(3) *computers:* any activity intended to eliminate faults or to keep hardware or programs in satisfactory working condition, including tests, measurements, replacements, adjustments, and repairs. See also *debug;* cf. *housekeeping.*

(4) *accounting:* all expenditures made to preserve an asset's value.

(5) *business law:* support or sustenance that a person is legally bound to give to another.

(6) *business law:* interfering unlawfully in a suit between others by assisting either party (e.g., giving one party money).

maintenance bond: See *bond, maintenance.*

maintenance factors: elements of the work setting that lead to employee dissatisfaction when they are not provided adequately. Synonymous with *dissatisfiers, hygiene factors.*

maintenance mechanism: a mechanism that attempts to stop a system from changing so rapidly that it is thrown out of balance.

maintenance-of-membership: a contract provision requiring union members to retain good-standing membership during the life of the contract as a condition of employ-

ment. See also *escape clause.*

major duty: any activity or group of closely related activities of a job that is a determinant of a required qualification for employment in that position or that occupies a significant amount of the worker's time.

majority stockholders: those who own more than 50 percent of the voting stock of a corporation, thus having controlling interest. See also *working control.*

major medical expense insurance: insurance that offers protection against huge expenses resulting from a major injury or serious illness. The form of insurance usually pays from 75 to 80 percent of doctor and hospital bills after a deductible has been paid by the policy holder. See also *catastrophic insurance.*

make good

(1) *general:* to discharge an obligation or debt.

(2) *advertising:* to repeat a message without additional charge or to refund space or time charges as compensation for an error or omission of an advertisement.

make-or-buy decision: a firm's decision of whether to produce an item itself or purchase it elsewhere.

maker

(1) *general:* a manufacturer, processor, or producer of merchandise or products.

(2) *business law:* an individual, firm, or other legal entity that signs a note, check, or other negotiable form as a responsible party.

makers and shakers: (slang) those who are in power.

make the cash: to decide whether the funds on hand, following receipts and payments, balance with the record of sales and payments of obligations.

makeup pay (wages): the difference between the amount a pieceworker has actually earned and the earnings to which the worker is entitled under contract or according to a minimum.

makeup time: the part of available time used for reruns due to malfunctions or mistakes during a previous operating time.

make whole: an order to an employer to pay a worker all wages lost from the date of firing, minus what he or she may have earned elsewhere meanwhile. Used in an arbitration award or government agency ruling, the order reinstates a discharged employee.

make-work fallacy: the fallacious belief that the destruction of wealth or the uneconomic utilization of manpower is good for the general economy because it stimulates employment.

mala fides: See *bad faith.*

male chauvinist: a man who is unreasonably devoted to members of his own sex and who often belittles women or attempts to put them in an inferior position. Such a person is often referred to as a male chauvinist pig.

malfeasance: a wrongdoing; a criminal act (e.g., a public official taking graft). Cf. *misfeasance.*

malfunction
(1) *general:* usually, the failure of equipment to operate as designed. Synonymous with *dysfunction.*
(2) *computers:* the effect of a fault, in contrast to an error or mistake.

malicious: describing an improper act done purposefully, without excuse. Malice suggests a state of mind that is noncaring of the law and of other's rights.

Maloney Act: See *National Association of Securities Dealers.*

malpractice insurance: coverage afforded to a professional, such as a doctor or a lawyer, against liability claims for damages resulting from alleged improper performance of the insured's services. Cf. *errors and omissions.*

Malthusian theory: outlined by Thomas R. Malthus in 1798, the theory that population increases at a rate faster than the means of subsistence. Malthus believed that population increased by a geometric progression, whereas subsistence means increased arithmetically. Logically extended, this theory concludes that, unless population is controlled, people are destined to poverty and starvation.

managed exchange rates: aggressive efforts by a government to dictate the rate of exchange through economic policies rather than permitting market forces to determine the value of the nation's currency.

management
(1) *general:* the individual or group of individuals responsible for studying, analyzing, formulating decisions, and initiating appropriate actions for the benefit of an organization.
(2) *administration:* the functions of planning, coordinating, and directing the activities of an organization.

management access time: the time between a manager's request for certain information and receipt of the information.

management accounting: a resource of management that supplies financial information at all levels to be used in planning and administering the business.

management audit: a system for examining, analyzing, and appraising a management's overall performance. Ten categories of the audit are economic function, corporate structure, health of earnings, service to stockholders, research and development, directorate analysis, fiscal policies, production efficiency, sales vigor, and evaluation of executive performance.

management by crisis: a leadership style that attempts to deal with shortcomings and failures by waiting until things get so bad that people will accept drastic measures. It is usually destructive and fails to attain stated organizational goals.

management by exception: the practice by an executive of focusing attention primarily on significant deviations from expected results. See also *variance.*

management by objectives: See *MBO.*

management company: a firm that manages and sells the shares of open-end investment companies and claims a fee or commission.

management consulting: the service performed, for a fee, by independent and objective professionals, or by an organization, to assist managers in analyzing management problems, to recommend practical solutions, and, at times, to help in the implementation of the recommendations.

management development: leadership training for middle- or top-level personnel to upgrade their skills.

management functions: the basic activities required of managers in the performance of their jobs. The major management functions are planning and decision making, organizing for effective performance, leading and motivating, and controlling performance.

management game: a dynamic training approach utilizing a model of the business world. In most cases, this problem-solving technique attempts to examine broad business issues in a classroom setting, free of real-world consequences. See also *game theory.*

management information system (MIS): a specific data-processing system that is designed to furnish management and supervisory personnel with current information in real time. In the communication process, data are recorded and processed for operational purposes. The problems are isolated for referral to upper management for higher-level decision making, and information is fed back to top management to reflect the progress in achieving major objectives. See also *line of balance.*

management inventories: summaries of the skills and abilities of management personnel, as distinguished from skills inventories, which are used for nonmanagement employees. See also *skills inventories.*

management prerogatives: the rights believed by management to be exclusively theirs and not subject to collective bargaining. There is no accepted definition, however, of which rights should be nonbargainable. Synonymous with *employer rights*.

management process: the activities that take place in the managerial subsystem.

management process school: a modern school of management thought whose adherents believe that the way to study management is through a systematic analysis of the managerial function (i.e., planning, organizing, and controlling).

management science: the formulation of mathematical and statistical models applied to decision making and the practical application of these models through the use of digital computers.

management systems: four basic leadership styles identified by Rensis Likert: exploitive-authoritative, benevolent-authoritative, consultative-democratic, and participative-democratic.

manager: an individual responsible for the control or direction of people, a department, or an organization.

managerial accounting: the area of accounting concerned with assisting managers in decision making, specifically for planning, budgeting, and controlling costs and revenues.

managerial control: the monitoring and modification of organizational activity and resource utilization to ensure that predetermined standards are met and that plans are carried out.

managerial grid: a means of measuring a manager's leadership style in terms of concern for production and concern for task. The grid technique was developed by Robert Blake and Jane Mouton of the University of Tex-

as.

managerial performance: the extent to which a manager achieves coordinated work through the efforts of subordinates. Coordinated work results from appropriate use of relevant planning, organizing, and controlling techniques and methods.

managerial roles: the organized set of behavior that belongs to the manager's job. The three main types of managerial roles are interpersonal, informational, and decision roles.

man-catcher: (slang) an employment agency.

mandate: a court order to an authorized agency or officer to enforce a decree, judgment, or sentence to the court's satisfaction.

mandate of protest: Synonymous with *notice of dishonor*.

manifest: a statement itemizing the contents, value, point of origin, destination, and so on, of cargo that is shipped.

manipulation

(1) *general:* artful approach, often in an unfair or fraudulent fashion.

(2) *securities:* an illegal operation that involves buying or selling a security in order to create a false or misleading appearance of active trading or to raise or depress the price to induce purchase or sale by others. See also *rigged market, SEC, stock jobbing*.

manit: one man-minute of production.

man-machine manipulation: simulation with models of systems in which human beings participate.

mannerisms: peculiarities of speaking or behaving exhibited by an individual when interacting with others.

manning table: a listing of the number

of employees or the positions to be used in a machine's operation, a described task, or a unit within a firm.

manpower: all employees in an organization, from chief executive officer down.

manpower planning: a forecast of the future manpower requirements of an organization and establishment of a plan to meet these needs.

man-to-man rating: an employee evaluation technique whereby supervisors or other raters compare employees, usually two at a time, in terms of their work effectiveness; behavior and attitude on the job; potential for further development; need for additional training, guidance, or incentives; and other related factors.

manual
(1) *general:* operated by hand, without the use of tools or machinery.
(2) *communications:* a listing of information, instructions, prices, and so on, that is a handy reference book; a handbook.

manual entry: hand insertion of data for some units of a computer.

manual operation: processing of data in a system by direct hand techniques.

manual rating: Synonymous with *experience rating.*

manual skill: the ability to use one's hands efficiently in the operation of tools and machinery.

manufacture: to produce, make, or fabricate something, by hand or using equipment.

manufacturer's agent
(1) An agent (wholesale or middleman) who takes neither title to nor possession of the merchandise he or she sells. The agent represents sev-

eral noncompeting producers of goods that are purchased by one type of trade (e.g., a manufacturer's agent in women's apparel might sell dresses, blouses, belts, coats, stockings, and so on, for different manufacturers). Synonymous with *manufacturer's representative.*

manufacturer's brand: a brand name owned by the item's maker (e.g., Hershey's chocolate Kisses).

manufacturer's representative (MR): an independent sales agent for a group of manufacturers (principals) in a described sales territory. Synonymous with *manufacturer's agent.*

manufacturing: converting raw materials into a completed product by a mechanical, electrical, or chemical (i.e., not manual) process.

manufacturing costs: costs incurred in the manufacturing process to bring a product to completion, including direct-materials, direct-labor, and manufacturing overhead costs.

manufacturing inventory: a general term covering all items of inventory for a manufacturing entity. Items included are usually raw materials, work in process, and completed goods.

manufacturing management: the responsibility within management for the planning, direction, and control of production and allied services performed in a manufacturing industry.

manufacturing order: instructions for directing production.

manufacturing overhead: all expenses arising from manufacturing activities except those of labor and materials.

MAPS: (multivariate analysis, participation, and structure) a management development technique that allows members to define their task groups and choose the people most appropriate for working in them.

margin

(1) *finance:* the difference between the market value of collateral pledged to secure a loan and the face value of the loan itself. See also *remargining.*

(2) *securities:* the amount paid by the customer when he or she used a broker's credit to buy a security. Under Federal Reserve regulations, the initial margin required recent decades has ranged from 50 to 100 percent of the purchase price. See also *Regulation T.*

(3) *accounting:* the difference between the cost of sold items and the total net sales income. See also *contribution margin, profit.*

marginal: describing an existing situation characterized by the occurrence of the smallest possible increment or decrement in certain variables.

marginal analysis: analysis of economic information by examining the results of the value added when one variable is increased by a single unit of another variable. See also *direct costing.*

marginal borrower: a borrower who will reject an opportunity to borrow if the interest charge is increased.

marginal business saving rate: the proportion of an additional dollar of GNP income that goes into gross business saving.

marginal buyer: a buyer who will refuse to buy if the price is increased.

marginal cost: the increase in the to-

tal cost of production that results from manufacturing one more unit of output. See also *law of increasing costs.*

marginal cost pricing: the rule enforced by competitive markets that price should be equal to the cost of producing the final (marginal) unit.

marginal efficiency of investment: a schedule showing the expected rate of return on the last or least profitable unit of investment for alternative amount of potential investment in a given time period.

marginal land: land that will merely repay the cost of products grown on it and will not yield increased revenue.

marginal lender: a lender or investor who will refuse to lend or invest if the rate of interest is lowered.

marginal producer: a producer who is just able to meet his costs of production, with little actual profit.

marginal product: the additional product derived by increasing a given factor of production by one further unit. See also *differential marginal productivity.*

marginal productivity wage theory: the theory that, under competitive conditions, the wages of all employees will be established by the productivity, measured in money, of the last worker to be employed.

marginal profits: the increase in total profits that is obtained by producing an additional unit of output.

marginal propensity to consume (MPC): the percentage of increases in income that is spent for consumption purposes.

marginal propensity to invest (MPI): the percentage of increases in sales that is spent on investment items. Cf. *liquidity preference, oversaving, quantity theory;* synonymous with *accelerator.*

marginal propensity to save (MPS): the percentage of increases in income that individuals save. Cf. *life cycle hypothesis, multiplier principle, oversaving, quantity theory.*

marginal revenue: the added revenue a business receives from the sale of one additional unit. In the short run, under conditions of competition, this is the same as the market price.

marginal revenue product: the added revenue a business receives by the addition of one more unit of a production factor (e.g., another employee, another piece of equipment).

marginal seller: a seller who refuses to sell if the price is lowered. See also *upset price.*

marginal trading: the purchase of a security or commodity by one who borrows funds for part of the purchase price rather than paying for the entire transaction with his or her own money.

marginal utility: the increase in satisfaction one receives from adding or consuming one more unit of an item; the value of a commodity.

marginal worker: a worker the value of whose production equals his actual wage.

margin call
(1) *general:* a demand upon a customer to put up money or securities with a broker. The call is made when a purchase is made or when a customer's equity in a margin account declines below a minimum standard set by the exchange or firm.
(2) *securities:* a bank's request

for more margin from a borrower when the borrower has securities pledged as collateral for a loan, and a declining market for the securities forces the value of the securities downward. The bank is responsible for seeing that the margin requirements are maintained. When the bank requests more margin, the borrower will have to either pledge more collateral or partially pay the loan to meet the established margin requirements.

margin of profit: operating income divided by sales. Income taxes are usually excluded and depreciation is usually included in the operating expenses.

margin of safety
(1) *general:* the balance of income left after payment of fixed charges.
(2) *sales:* the amount by which sales exceeds the break-even point, thus providing a cushion against a drop in sales or other unforeseeable forces.
(3) *banking:* the difference between the total price of a bond issue and the true value of the property for which it is issued.

margin requirement: the portion of a total purchase price of securities that must be put up in cash.

marine protection and indemnity insurance: insurance against legal liability of the insured for loss, damage, or expense arising out of or incident to the ownership, operation, chartering, maintenance, use, repair, or construction of any vessel, craft, or instrumentality in use in ocean or inland waterways, including liability of the insured for personal injury or death and for loss of or damage to the property of another person. See also *assailing thieves, barratry, cargo insurance, certificate of insurance, contructive total loss, general average, hull insurance, inland marine insurance, jettison, liability insurance, loss, ocean marine insurance, particular average, seaworthiness, valued policy.*

marital deduction: provisions in federal tax laws to prevent double taxation of an estate at the time of the death of a spouse by permitting the deceased to leave up to half of his or her estate to the spouse, with this amount deductible from the taxable estate. See also *Tax Reform Act of 1976.*

Maritime Labor Board: formed by Congress in 1938, the agency responsible for mediating labor disputes between companies and organized seamen and longshoremen and for developing a general maritime labor policy. See also *Federal Mediation and Conciliation Service.*

mark
(1) *computers:* the presence of a signal. Synonymous with *flag.*
(2) *systems:* an impulse that, in a neutral circuit, causes the loop to be closed.

markdown
(1) *retailing:* a reduction of an originally established selling price.
(2) *securities:* a revaluation of stocks based on a decline in their market quotations.

markdown cancellation: the increase in the retail price of an item that has been reduced. The increase can be up to the retail price at which the item was originally placed for sale, but not higher.

market:
(1) *general:* people who possess the ability and desire to purchase, or prospects for a product or service.
(2) *business:* a geographical area that includes a significant number of potential customers.
(3) *economics:* an estimated or realized demand for an item or service.

marketability: the rapidity and ease with which a given asset can be converted into cash. Cf. *liquid.*

marketable
(1) *general:* that which can be sold.
(2) *real estate:* property that can be sold to a purchaser within a reasonable period.

marketable securities: short-term investments that can be sold readily in established markets.

marketable title: title to property that is free of defects and will be accepted by a lawyer without objection. Cf. *cloud on title, perfect title:* synonymous with *clear title, good title, just title.*

market analysis: an aspect of market research involving measurement of the extent of a market and determination of its characteristics. See also *chartist, Delphi technique, Dow theory.*

market audit: a method for studying the marketing activities and structure of a business. It is designed primarily to identify areas in which improvements are necessary to boost profits. Cf. *management audit.*

market channel: the path of the direct or indirect transfer of ownership to a product as it goes from a manufacturer to industrial or retail customers.

market demand: the total amount of an item that is wanted at a specified price at a specific time. Cf. *overall market capability, potential demand.*

market equilibrium: the balance that occurs when buyers and sellers decide to stop trading at the prevailing prices.

market failure: a condition under which markets do not allocate resources efficiently, usually because of ignorance or externalities. See also *externalities.*

market fit: the likelihood that a new item will be purchased by the same people who buy a firm's other goods. Cf. *test marketing.*

marketing: activities that accelerate the movement of goods or services from the manufacturer to the consumer, including everything connected with advertising, distribution, merchandising, product planning, promotion, publicity, research and development, sales, transportation, and warehousing of goods or services. Cf. *merchandising.*

marketing boards: agencies established to monopolize the sale of specified products, especially agricultural comodities. Marketing boards are similar to labor unions in that they organize large numbers of small producers to negotiate with a small number of purchasers.

marketing concept: a business philosophy consisting of the notions that marketing strategy should be developed based on customer needs and desires and that all marketing functions should be structured within the firm, with one person having overall responsibility. See also *consumer behavior research, marketing management, market research.*

marketing cost analysis: examination of the costs incurred from the time items are produced to final delivery and payment, with a view toward providing useful quantitative financial data for the marketing firm.

marketing-dominated strategy: a focus of key managers on managing the consumer.

marketing functions: buying, selling, shipping, warehousing, grading and standardization, financing, assuming responsibility for taking the risk, and data accumulation.

marketing information system: the entire system employed by a firm to gather, analyze, store, and disseminate relevant marketing information to those who require these data.

marketing intelligence: the part of the marketing information system that includes the procedures a company routinely uses to keep abreast of developments in the external environment.

marketing management: the planning, directing, and controlling of the total marketing operation, including formulation of marketing goals, policies, programs, and strategy, and often embracing product development, organizing and staffing to discharge plans, supervising marketing operations, and monitoring performance. See also *product manager.*

marketingmanship: the measure of skill in marketing a product or service.

marketing mix: the concept of Neil Borden that market strategy is based on the product, price, promotion, and channels in an integrated marketing program.

marketing research: the process of gathering, recording, and analyzing information pertaining to the marketing of goods and services. See also *market research.*

market off: an expression indicating that prices on the various stock exchanges were down for the day.

market order: an order to buy or sell stocks or bonds at the price prevailing when the order reaches the market. See also *limited order, no-limit order, percentage order, stop order.*

market-oriented production: production of a product or products in a foreign country that uses that product.

market out clause: a clause in underwriting statements of securities, whereby the underwriter reserves the privilege of terminating an agreement to sell securities at a stated price if unfavorable market conditions occur, rendering sale at this price unprofitable.

market outline: a summary of the relative place of a type of brand or item in the total market. See also *positioning; cf. market structure analysis.*

market penetration: the degree to which a product captures a percentage of the total market for that item. This includes the absence of competition for the item.

marketplace: a general term identifying business and trade activities.

market potential: maximum sales potential for all sellers of a product or service over a fixed period.

market power: the ability of a purchaser or seller to control price and quantity of an item.

market presence: in advertising, being present in the marketplace, having a reputation or identity with competitors or consumers.

market price

(1) *finance:* the price established in the market where buyers and sellers meet to buy and sell similar products.

(2) *finance:* a price determined by factors of supply and demand rather than by management decisions.

(3) *securities:* the last reported price at which a stock or bond sold.

market profile: data about potential customer or an analysis by individual background (sex, age, etc.) of people who make up the market for a particular item or service. See also *market segmentation, market target;* cf. *market structure analysis.*

market rate: the interest rate charged a firm in order to borrow funds.

market representative: the executive of a firm's buying office who gives his time and effort to a particular grouping of goods and makes data about it available to buyers of owned or operated stores.

market research: the part of marketing research that deals with the pattern of a market, measuring the extent and nature of the market and identifying its characteristics. Market research precedes marketing research. See also *marketing research, product planning.*

market segmentation: separating the market for an item into categories of location, personality, or other characteristics for each division. See also *market profile, zoning price.*

market share: a firm's percentage of its industry's total sales.

market skimming: an introductory pricing strategy of charging a high price in order to recover investment quickly.

market strategy: a marketing approach designed to enable a product to fulfill the objectives set for it by management.

market structure analysis: the study of competitive product offerings and buyer product preferences that account for the design features of items and the item preference characteristics of purchaser/consumer segments.

market target: the people or groups for whom an item and its program or marketing are intended. A strategy and a meaningful approach to fulfilling a stated goal must be established with respect to a market target. See also *market profile, positioning.*

market value

(1) *real estate:* the price that property will command on the open market; the price for which an owner is prepared to sell property and the amount a purchaser is willing to pay. See also *reasonable value.*

(2) *securities:* the price of a security or commodity on the daily quotation, indicating the amount required for buying or selling.

market value clause: a provision that sometimes appears in property damage insurance forms covering certain risks. It obligates the insurance company, in the event of a loss, to recognize the established market value of the destroyed and damaged property as its actual cash value as of the date of the loss and to adjust the loss accordingly.

marking: placing the correct tag on new goods, usually containing price, size, and style data. See also *Kimball tags.*

mark-on: the difference between the billed-cost price and the original retail price of an item. See also *initial mark-on.*

Markov chain: a probabilistic model of events in which the probability of an event is dependent only on the event that procedes it. Cf. *Monte Carlo method.*

mark sensing: a technique for reading marks made on a card by special pencil and automatically punching the information represented by the marks into the card.

markup

(1) *sales:* an increase, in dollars or percentage, between cost and selling price.

(2) *finance:* increasing the value of assets (i.e., securities) to show an improvement in their market value.

mask: a pattern of characters that is used to control the retention or elimination of portions of another pattern of characters. Synonymous with *filter.*

Massachusetts trust: See *business trust.*

mass appraising: appraising numerous parcels or properties at the same time.

mass communication: the delivery of quantities of identical messages at the same time by communication firms or media.

mass marketing: the approach used to sell large volumes of items to everyone. This usually requires distribution in discount stores and supermarkets.

mass picketing: See *picketing.*

mass production: the utilization of mechanization to produce a large quantity of standardized items. Synonymous with "large-scale production."

master

(1) *general:* a skilled tradesman who is certified, usually by passing an examination, to train beginners and to operate his own business.

(2) *administration:* someone who has control or dominance over others.

master agreement: a contract covering a number of companies and one or more unions, or an agreement covering several plants of a single employer. This is supplemented by local contracts covering conditions that vary among individual plants or companies.

master budget: a budget comprising all the departmental budgets.

master card: a card that contains fixed or indicative information for a group of punched cards. It is usually the first card of the group.

master file: See *file, master.*

master in chancery: an official appointed by a court to assist by taking testimony, calculating interest, projecting damage costs, determining liens, and so on, as requested by the court. Cf. *referee.*

master lease: an original lease.

master policy

(1) *insurance:* a policy issued to an insured to cover property at more than one location. If locations are in more than one state, it is customary to issue underlying policies in the respective states to meet legal requirements.

(2) *real estate:* a policy issued to

cover the interest of a lender or lessor of property that is in the possession of others.

master schedule: a schedule in production control that applies only to a completed product and its major elements.

master tariff: a tariff that controls the use of other tariffs.

matched and lost: when two bids to buy the same stock are made on the trading floors simultaneously (i.e., matched), and each bid is equal to or larger than the amount of stock offered. The bids are considered to be on an equal basis, and the two bidders then flip a coin to decide who buys the stock. This also applies to offers to sell.

material budget: a forecast of how much material will be necessary to achieve a result.

material control: the attempt to supply commodities needed in manufacturing at the lowest cost per unit consistent with required quality and with the lowest inventory investment. Cf. *quality control.*

material cost: the cost of an item that is a direct result of the cost of raw material and does not include indirect expenses such as wages and overhead.

materiality: the concept that accounting should disclose only those events important enough to have an influence on the decision maker.

material management: the material-handling functions as they relate to the physical distribution chain.

materials handling: the physical movement of materials and products within a work facility.

materials requisition form: a document used to request raw materials from the storeroom.

matrix

(1) *computers:* a logic network in the form of an array of input leads and output leads, with logic elements connected at some of their intersections.

(2) *statistics:* an enclosure that gives form to what lies in it.

matrix correlation: a table showing the correlation coefficient of every variable in a group with every other variable in the group.

matrix departmentation: using two forms of departmentation to group jobs into subunits. Functional departmentation occurs vertically and product or program departmentation horizontally. The resulting organization chart is a matrix. Cf. *functional departmentation, geographical departmentation, process departmentation, product departmentation.*

matrix organization: an organizational structure in which organization members have a dual allegiance—to a particular assignment or task and to their department.

mature economy: describing the condition of a nation's economy with a declining rate of population growth and a decrease in the proportion of national income utilized for new capital investment, accompanied by a relative increase of national income used in purchasing consumer goods. Cf. *underdeveloped country.*

maturity

(1) *finance:* the date on which a note, time draft, bill of exchange, bond, or other negotiable instrument becomes due and payable. The ma-

turity date of a note, time draft, or bill of exchange drawn for a future date is set to run a specified number of days from the date of the loan or acceptance of maturity. Presentation and request for payment of the instrument are made on the maturity date.

(2) *business law:* the completion of a contract (e.g., an insurance policy).

maturity date: the date on which a financial obligation becomes due for payment and/or the date an obligation or contract expires.

maturity stage: the beginning of the demise of a product. The product's life cycle conclusion is measured by the leveling off of demand, a decline in profit, and increasing competition. Small and financially insecure institutions tend to drop out of the market in the maturity stage.

maturity value: the money that is to be paid when a financial obligation or other contract becomes due.

maxim: a proposition of law needing no proof or argument because of its general acceptance. The mere announcement of a maxim invokes the authority understood to exist for its enforcement.

maximax criterion: a basis for decision making whereby a manager determines the greatest payoff for each possible strategy and then chooses the one that is most favorable, thus maximizing the maximum gain. Cf. *maximin criterion.*

maximin criterion: a basis for decision making whereby a manager determines the most negative payoff for each possible strategy and then chooses the one that is most favorable, thus maximizing the minimum gain. Cf. *maximax criterion.*

maximizing: decision-making behavior in which a manager selects the best alternative from all possible alternatives.

maximum foreseeable loss: the estimate of the damage that would result if the occurrence insured against were not controlled by the protection that might reasonably be expected. See also *loss expectancy;* cf. *normal foreseeable loss, probable maximum loss.*

maximum loan-to-value ratio: the highest loan-to-value ratio (loan amount as a percentage of assessed valuation) that a lender is willing to undertake.

MBO (management by objectives): a process whereby superiors and those who report to them jointly establish objectives over a specified time frame, meeting periodically to evaluate their progress in meeting these goals.

McGuire Act: See *Miller-Tydings Resale Price Maintenance Act of 1937.*

mean: any statistical measure of central tendency.

means-end chain: a hierarchy of objectives for an organization in which objectives (ends) of component units becomes the means by which the broader objective is achieved.

means-goal staircase: systematic linkage of the goals of lower-level units or individuals with those of higher-level units or individuals.

means test: an inquiry into a person's ability to support himself or herself as a criterion for receiving public assistance, unemployment relief, and so on.

measure of value: a function of money that gives the standard for identifying the results of production, using the monetary unit as the common denominator.

mechanical aptitude test: a test designed to predict how well a person can learn to perform tasks that involve understanding and manipulating mechanical devices.

mechanic's lien: the legal, enforceable claim of a person who has performed work on or provided materials for a given property. Such claims are permitted by law in certain states as a claim against the title to the property. A mechanic's lien may also grant the claimant a degree of preference in case of liquidation of an estate or business. Cf. *artisan's lien, particular lien.*

mechanistic structure: an organization in which all activities are specified and regulated so that the organization functions like a machine. See also *bureaucracy.*

mechanization: the use of machines to replace human effort. Cf. *automation.*

media: the means used by transmitters of messages to deliver them to the intended receivers in a communication system. In advertising, the term refers to newspapers, radio, television, magazines, billboards, direct mail, and other such institutions that are used to carry advertisements.

media analysis: the study and evaluation of various media approaches for promoting items and services to a wide or specific audience. See also *zero-base media planning;* cf. *audi-*

ence study.

media director: an advertising agency executive who is responsible for choosing the media to be employed and scheduling the appearance of promotional material in such media.

median: a statistical average indicating central tendency, identified by a midpoint. Half the items being averaged must fall below the midpoint and half above.

mediation: an attempt by a third party, usually a government official, to bring together the parties to an industrial dispute. The mediator has no power to force a settlement. Mediation is different from conciliation, which also brings the two groups together, in that mediation includes suggestions for a compromise solution by a third party. See also *Federal Mediation and Conciliation Service, Maritime Labor Board;* cf. *arbitration.*

mediator: a person, acting as a third party, who attempts to resolve a labor dispute. Cf. *arbitrator.*

media typewriter: an electric typewriter coupled with a recording medium, such as magnetic tape, that enables the typist to keyboard material, edit and correct it, and store the material so that it can be played back for later use. See also *word processing.*

medical expense insurance: coverage available in various forms against expenses incurred for medical treatment and care as a result of bodily injury or illness (e.g., major medical expense, surgical expense, or hospitalization insurance).

medical payments insurance: coverage available in various liability insurance policies in which the insurer agrees to reimburse the insured and others, without regard for the insured's liability, for medical or funeral expenses incurred as the result of bodily injury or death by accident under the conditions specified in the policy.

medium (plural, media): any means for transmitting a message to an intended recipient in a communication network (plural, *media*). Examples include newspapers, radio, television, magazines, billboards, and direct mail. See also *SRDS.*

medium-range planning: development of major plans that extend beyond the traditional operating period of one year. An average medium-range planning period is five years.

meet and confer negotiations: negotiations in the public sector in which the ultimate decision about the terms and conditions of employment of public employees is determined by the public employer.

megabit: a unit of information equal to one million bits or binary digits.

megabuck: (slang) a million dollars.

melon: (slang) unusually large profits that have not been dispersed to eligible persons. See also *cutting a melon.*

member bank: all national banks and any state bank that has applied successfully for membership in the Federal Reserve System.

member-bank reserves: funds that commercial banks are required to keep on deposit at regional Federal Reserve Banks. See also *reserve.*

member corporation: a securities brokerage firm, organized as a corporation, that has at least one person who is a member of a stock exchange as a director and a holder of voting stock in the corporation.

member firm: a securities brokerage firm organized as a partnership and having at least one general partner who is a member of a stock exchange.

memo posting: a systems technique whereby item records are posted to a temporary file before permanent master files are updated.

memorandum sale: the sale in a retail operation of consigned goods whose title rests with the vendor for a stated period. At the end of the period, unsold items are eligible for return to the vendor, and the sold or held goods are billed to the merchant.

memory: computer storage; a device into which a unit of information can be copied, held, and retrieved at another time. See also *random access, read-only.*

memory dump: a listing of the contents of a storage device or selected parts of it.

memory register: See *register, memory.*

memory unit: a component within automated equipment that registers what the equipment should be accomplishing at each step of the operation.

mercantile agency: an organization that supplies its subscribers with credit data on individuals and firms. In addition, some mercantile agencies gather statistical information and serve as collection depositories of past-due accounts. See also *Dun and Bradstreet.*

mercantile rate of return: the ratio, expressed in percentages, between the figure showing on the contemporary income statement and the figure appearing on the contemporary balance sheet.

mercantilism: the economic policy under which nations measure their power by the amount of precious metal they have acquired. See also *kameralism.*

merchandise
(1) *general:* purchased articles of business held for sale.
(2) *sales:* to plan or promote the sale of goods.

merchandise charge: extraneous costs (including shipping, insurance, demurrage, etc.) added to the cost of goods prior to mark-on.

merchandise control: collection and analysis of data on purchases and sales items, either by unit or by dollars.

merchandise inventory: products held by an entity for resale to customers.

merchandise manager: an executive who is responsible for supervising the purchasing, selling, and inventory control activities in a store.

merchandise mart: a building, usually large, that contains manufacturers' showrooms where retailers can examine the goods and place orders. Cf. *resident buyer.*

merchandise transfer: the transfer of goods from one accounting unit of a store to another. Merchandise can be transferred from department to department, from one branch store to another branch, or from home office to branch store.

merchandising
(1) *retailing:* all activities connected with the buying and selling of merchandise, including displays,

promotions, pricing, and buying.

(2) *manufacturing:* the activities required in the attempt to make a product interesting to buyers, (packaging, promotion, pricing arrangements, etc.). Cf. *marketing.*

merchandising the advertising: selling the advertising and sales promotion program to channel intermediaries in order to generate their enthusiasm and gain their support.

merchant: an individual who takes title to goods by buying them, for the purpose of resale.

merchant wholesaler: a middleman who receives title to merchandise purchases for resale to firms that plan to resell the goods or process them in some fashion for resale.

merge

(1) *general:* to combine two or more items into one.

(2) *computers:* to combine items from two or more similarly ordered sets into one set that is arranged in a specified order.

merger

(1) *general:* the combining of two or more entities through the direct acquisition by one of the net assets of the other. A merger differs from a consolidation in that no new entity is created by a merger, whereas in consolidation a new organization comes into being and acquires the net assets of all the combining units. See also *conglomerate;* cf. *takeover.*

(2) *economics:* any business combination. See, for example, *downstairs merger, horizontal merger.*

merit goods: items for which the government determines or heavily influences levels of consumption according to argument that individuals are not qualified to make the choices (e.g., education, drugs, automobile safety equipment).

merit increase (pay): an individual wage increase in recognition of superior performance or service, commonly specified as negotiable in a contract between union and management. Cf. *incentive pay.*

merit rating

(1) *insurance:* a system of evaluation in which the past experience of the individual risk is a factor in determining the rate. Synonymous with *experience rating.*

(2) *personnel:* periodic evaluation of workers' efficiency as a basis for pay increases and/or promotion. See also *point method rating.*

Merit System Protection Board, U.S.: created on January 1, 1979, one of the major agencies established to replace the Civil Service Commission, with responsibility for protecting the integrity of the Civil Service. See also *Office of Personnel Management, U.S.*

mesne: intermediate, intervening (e.g., mesne profits are those profits accruing between the illegal ejection of a tenant and his repossession of the property).

message

(1) *general:* any communication between persons.

(2) *computers:* an arbitrary amount of information whose beginning and end are defined or implied.

message feedback: the response of a message receiver to the message.

message sender: anyone who communicates something to someone else.

metapolicymaking: a strategy for making policy on how to make organizational policy.

meter, postage: an electrically operated device for imprinting postage on a gummed tape for application to letters and parcel post packages.

metered mail: any class of mail on which the required postage is printed by meter approved for the purpose by the U.S. Postal Service. Metered mail is entitled to all the privileges and is subject to all the conditions that apply to matter mailed with stamp affixed.

metes and bounds: real property boundary lines.

methods analysis: Synonymous with *time and motion study.*

methods study: analysis of the flow of work, particularly the utilization of materials to permit more efficient use of manpower.

methods-time measurement (MTM): the listing of basic human movements and the assignment of time values to each. MTM is used in establishing time standards for varying tasks. See also *ergonomics;* cf. *efficiency expert.*

metrocorporation: the corporation seen as having unlimited social responsibilities, with its managers holding themselves accountable to several groups in society. This view of the corporation is the opposite of the traditional one, in which managers are mainly accountable to the stockholders. Cf. *traditional corporation, well-tempered corporation.*

Mexican promotion (raise): (slang) an increase of rank or position with-

out an increase in salary.

MFN: see *most favored nation.*

MICR: See *magnetic ink character recognition.*

microcomputer: See *microprocessor.*

microeconomics: the examination of the economic behavior of individual units in the economy, such as households or corporations.

microlevel approach: a method used to respond to changes of small magnitude, such as for individuals or groups. Cf. *macrolevel approach.*

micromarketing: a study of the economic exchange process of individual firms. Cf. *macromarketing.*

micromotion study: a time or motion study in which photographs or motion pictures are taken as part of an investigation of the details of body movements needed to complete a task.

microprocessor: a tiny electronic circuit chip that contains the so-called logic elements needed for computation. When attached to memory units, input/output devices, and other hardware, the microprocessor becomes a functioning microcomputer.

microsecond (μsec): one-millionth of a second

midcareer plateau: the stage of a career at which the individual has no opportunity for further advancement.

middleman: an individual who buys merchandise with the expectation of reselling it for profit. At times a middleman may arrange for such transactions without actually having possession of the goods.

middle management

(1) *general:* management personnel who report directly to top man-

agement.

(2) *administration:* the level of management responsible for carrying out the directives of top management.

midnight shift: in an operation running on a 24-hour day, the work shift commencing at midnight and usually terminated at 8 A.M. Synonymous with *graveyard shift, lobster shift, third shift.*

migrant worker: an individual without a permanent home who shifts from one region of the country to another, taking advantage of seasonal demand for his or her services during the harvesting seasons of various types of produce.

milestone scheduling: a scheduling and controlling procedure that employs bar charts to monitor progress. In essence, it is very similar to a Gantt chart, but its use is not restricted to production activities. Cf. *Gantt chart.*

military-industrial complex: the community of interests created between armed services officials and manufacturers of weapons and defense material.

milking: (slang) management's attempt to squeeze the last remaining profits from the firm without leaving sufficient reserves for improvements or for a downturn period.

millage: the factor usually employed as the rate of taxation in computing taxes. One mill per thousand is equal to $1 of taxes per $1000 of assessed value. The assessed value multiplied by the millage rate equals the tax rate.

Miller-Tydings Resale Price Maintenance Act of 1937: federal legislation enabling manufacturers to take advantage of state fair trade laws without being prosecuted for violation of the federal antitrust laws.

millisecond (msec): one-thousandth of a second.

mill supply house: the industrial equivalent of a general line, full-service merchant wholesaler, often focusing on supplying one industry.

minimum premium: the smallest premium an insurance company may charge under the manual rules for writing a particular policy or bond for a designated period. It is calculated to allow defraying of the necessary expenses of the insurance transaction and to leave an adequate amount to contribute to the payment of losses.

minimum (charge) rate: the lowest rate a public utility company charges for a commodity or service, even though on a per unit, per hour basis the amount of the charge would be less (e.g., the minimum monthly charge for your telephone, regardless of the frequency of telephone calls made).

minimum subscription: the figure given in a firm's prospectus identifying the minimum that must be raised for the organization to become operational.

minimum wage: the lowest allowable rate, by union contract, or by federal or state law, for a given job. The term is most widely used in reference to the federal wage-hour law (Fair Labor Standards Act), which sets a minimum hourly rate for all workers to which it applies, and to supplementary state and municipal statutes. See also *union rate, wage floor;* cf. *substandard rate.*

Mining Enforcement and Safety Administration (MESA): a federal agency created in 1973 to remove mine safety from the control of the industry-dominated Bureau of Mines. MESA enforces all mine safety regulations, including air quality and equipment standards. See also *Bituminous Coal Act of 1937, Federal Coal Mine Safety Act of 1952.*

ministerial duty: a duty requiring little judgment or discretion (e.g., posting of an eviction notice by a sheriff).

minor duty: incidental or miscellaneous duty or responsibility of a position that is not a determinant of a required qualification for employment in that position and does not occupy a significant amount of the worker's time.

minority interest: the part of the net worth of a subsidiary that relates to shares not owned by the controlling company or by other members of the combined group.

minority investment: a holding of less than 50 percent of a corporation's voting stock.

minority union: a union that does not enjoy exclusive bargaining or majority status. Usually it is an organization that has been unable to obtain a majority of the workers in the appropriate unit for certification but still retains its identity as a group within the firm.

mint ratio: the ratio of the weight of one metal to another, and to their equivalent in terms of the national unit of currency, such as the dollar (e.g., x grains of silver $= x$ grains of gold $= \$1.00$).

minute book: an official record of a corporation's scheduled meetings (stockholders' gathering, board of director's meeting, etc.).

MIP: See *monthly investment plan.*

mirror principle: a human relations approach suggesting that people will respond in the same fashion as they are treated. Cf. *antagonistic cooperation, Theory X and Theory Y.*

MIS: See *management information system.*

misdemeanor: a criminal offense, less than a felony, that is not punishable by imprisonment or death.

misdirected marketing effort: See *eighty-twenty principle.*

misfeasance: illegal or improper exercise of a legal responsibility; failure to properly perform a lawful act, or performance of an action without proper notice to those involved. Cf. *nonfeasance.*

misrepresentation

(1) *insurance:* willfully misleading an insurance company with regard to information affecting the acceptance of a risk, the issuance of a policy, or the settlement of a claim. See also *declaration, warranty.*

(2) *business law:* giving a positive statement or claiming an alleged fact that is not true, thus leading to a false conclusion.

missent item: an item that has been sent in error to another bank.

missionary sales: the activity of personnel from a manufacturer who work closely with various firms and middlemen to increase the product sales.

missionary worker: a worker who is hired to break a strike using nonviolent techniques.

mission budgeting: budgeting by social function; a term used in President Carter's Office of Policy Analysis to determine how much the government spends on projects (child care, housing, etc.). Various related programs, scattered in many agencies, are examined cumulatively as single units. Cf. *performance budgeting.*

mix: See *audience composition, product mix, promotional mix.*

mixed capitalism: an economic system in which the major portion of the tools of production is owned and operated by the private sector and the market process is the principal factor in determining the allocation of resources.

mixed conflict situation: a relationship that is both highly distributive and highly integrative.

mixed costs: costs which include both fixed and variable elements within a relevant range of activity. Synonymous with *semivariable costs.*

mixed economy (system): an economic system that combines characteristics of both capitalism and socialism. Resources are allocated partly through decentralized markets and partly by means of decisions of a centralized government.

mixed estate: ground rent for 99 years that is forever renewable.

mixed property: property having characteristics of both personal and real property (e.g., house fixtures).

mixed-use property: a property under a single ownership and legal description that is used for two or more uses, such as residential plus nonresidential, commercial, or industrial.

MNC: See *multinational corporation.*

mnemonic: tending to assist human memory.

mod: modifications made in computer programs after they have been written.

mode: a statistical measure of common tendency or average that identifies the value of the variable that gives the greatest height on a graph of the frequency distribution.

model: a theory used to analyze various forms of behavior. The closer the model is to the real world, the more useful it is for analysis.

model bank: an integration of various models, including linear programming models, simulations, and queuing models, for use in describing, predicting, and possibly controlling organizational behavior.

modeling: identifying the fixed and variable components in a system, assigning them numerical or economic values, and relating them to one another in a logical fashion so that solutions to operational problems can be obtained.

models of development: economic success stories, such as postwar Japan, that are examined for clues about how to accelerate the growth of countries.

model stock: the right goods at the right time in the right quantities at the right price.

modified half-year convention: under the class life system, the practice whereby assets put into service before midyear are eligible for a full year of depreciation, and assets put into service after midyear are not eligible for depreciation until the following year.

modified union shop: one in which nonunion workers already employed need not join the union, but all new employees must join and those who are already members must remain in the union. Cf. *closed shop, open shop, union shop.*

module: a program unit that is discrete and identifiable with respect to compiling, combining, and loading.

mom and pop outlets: small stores, generally operated by members of a family with limited capital.

monetarist: a believer in the concept that a balanced economy depends on the supply of money. Cf. *archmonetarist.*

monetary base: a monetary aggregate composed of funds retained by banks and by the public, and including member-bank deposits at the various Federal Reserve banks.

monetary items: assets or liabilities that are fixed, either by nature or by contract, as to the amount of future dollars they can command in the marketplace.

monetary liability: the promise to pay a claim against a specified quantity of money, the amount of which is unaffected by inflation or deflation.

monetary policy: a policy of the Federal Reserve System that attempts to affect the terms on which credit can be obtained in private markets. Its purpose is to regulate the nation's sales level, level of employment, and prices. See also *discretionary policy, Operation Twist;* cf. *fiscal policy.*

monetary reserve: the amount of bullion held by the government or by banks as security for fiduciary or credit money in circulation. See also *reserve.*

monetary rule: a proposal that the Federal Reserve System should increase the money supply at a constant percentage rate.

monetizing a loan: the process in granting a loan whereby a borrower's note is converted into money, usually in the form of a demand deposit. See also *demand deposit.*

monetizing the debt: increasing government debt financed through purchases of government securities by commercial or Federal Reserve banks.

money: any denomination of coin or paper currency of legal tender that passes freely as a medium of exchange; anything that is accepted in exchange for other things (e.g., precious metals). Major characteristics of money include easy recognition, uniformity in quality, easy divisibility, and a relatively high value within a small area. Cf. *currency.*

money illusion: the perception that an increase in all prices and incomes by the same proportion produces an increase in consumption, although real incomes remain the same.

money income: the amount of money received for work performed.

money market (brokers): all financial organizations that handle the purchase, sale, and transfer of short-term credit instruments and notes.

money measurement concept: the idea that money, as the common medium of exchange, is the accounting unit of measurement, and that only economic activities measurable in monetary terms are included in the accounting model.

money order (postal, bank): an instrument commonly purchased for a fee by an individual who does not maintain a checking account but wishes to send money to others. The names of the purchaser and the payee are shown on the face of the money order. An advantage of the money order over checks is that presentation for payment at the original place of purchase is not required. A disadvantage is that a bank or other financial institution may charge for the service of supplying a money order.

money price: the number of money units that must be sacrificed to purchase a particular commodity.

money rates: interest rates that lenders charge their borrowers.

money supply: a general term for the total sum of currency circulating in a country. See also *price-specie flow theory.*

money wages: the number of dollars received by employees, as contrasted with what those dollars will purchase. See also *purchasing power of the dollar, real wages.*

monger: a trader or seller, often used in a derogatory fashion.

monitor
(1) *general:* an observer, human or machine, installed to record either continuous or sample data about a system.
(2) *computers:* a device that examines the condition of a system to show any change from some prescribed operational activity (e.g., a device that is able to follow a signal in a communications network).

monitor role: an informational role in which a manager continually scans the environment to collect information pertinent to the organization or unit he or she manages.

monometallism: a monetary system in which the monetary component is defined in terms of only one metal, which is accepted in unlimited quantities for producing coins. See also *real money;* cf. *bimetallism.*

monopolistic competition: a form of competition in which the product of each competitor in a particular field differs from other competitors' products in some way so that an exact duplicate cannot be obtained from another source. Most competition in the United States is monopolistic competition.

monopoly
(1) *general:* ownership of the source of a commodity or domination of its distribution. See also *competition, engross.*
(2) *economics:* exclusive dominance of the supply and price of a commodity that is acquired by a franchise or government patent. Cf. *bilateral monopoly, legal monopoly, natural monopoly, partial monopoly, perfect (pure) monopoly, strategic resource monopoly.*

monopsony: a market situation in which there is only one buyer for an item. Cf. *duopsony, oligopsony.*

monotony: a condition that results in a worker showing low interest and boredom. The reasons for monotony are job related, but other external and internal factors may play a major role in creating this condition.

Monte Carlo method: the use of statistical sampling techniques to obtain a probabilistic approximation to the solution of a mathematical or physical problem. Cf. *Markov chain.*

monthly investment plan (MIP): a pay-as-you-go method of buying odd lots of exchange-listed shares on a regular payment plan for as little as

$40 a month or every three months, and up to $1,000 per payment. Under MIP the investor buys a stock designated by a securities broker by the dollar's worth. If the price advances, he or she gets fewer shares; if it declines, more shares. The investor may discontinue purchases at any time without penalty. Cf. *investment company.*

moonlighting: holding two jobs at one time—usually a full-time job and a part-time job. Synonymous with *double employment, secondary employment.*

moot: in law, not covered, debatable, or made clear by earlier cases or decisions of the court (e.g., there is no uniform or clear-cut opinion on a moot point).

morale: the extent to which an employee's needs are met and the extent to which the person perceives that satisfaction as stemming from his or her total job situation. See also *dissatisfiers, organizational climate, satis ,ers.*

morale study: a technique for measuring the level of morale among a group of employees. Often both questionnaires and interviews are used to acquire information on which to base a judgment of the state of morale.

moral hazard: the possibility of loss being caused or aggravated by dishonesty or carelessness of the insured or his or her agents or employees. It arises from the character and circumstances of the insured, as distinguished from the inherent nature of the property covered, or its location. See also *physical hazard.*

moral suasion: in banking, Federal Reserve System pressure exerted on U.S. banking, unaccompanied by an effort to compel compliance with the suggested action. See also *jawboning.*

morning loan: banks loans made to stockholders on an unsecured basis, with the broker handling stock deliveries until reimbursement has been made.

morphological research: a form of marketing research that focuses on how decisions are made.

mortality
(1) *general:* death on a large scale; the proportion of deaths to the population of a region, city, or nation.
(2) *accounting:* the expectancy of an asset or class of assets to expire or depreciate through use or the passage of time.

mortality guarantee: a guarantee in a contract that contract owners will not be affected by losses arising if mortality experience is different from that assumed in the contract.

mortality table: an actuarial table based on a sample group of the population, giving the percentage of people who live to any given age.

mortgage
(1) *real estate:* a written conveyance of title to property, but not possession, to obtain the payment of a debt or the performance of some obligation, under the condition that the conveyance is to be void upon final payment.
(2) *finance:* property pledged as security for payment of a debt. See also *chattel mortgage;* cf. *conventional loan.*

mortgage amortization schedule: a table that shows the breakdown between interest and principal for each payment over the life of a mortgage.

mortgage banker: a banker who specializes in mortgage financing; an operator of a mortgage financing company. Mortgage financing companies are mortgagees themselves, as well as being mortgage agents for other large mortgages.

mortgage bond: See *bond, mortgage.*

mortgage broker: an individual or corporation that rarely originates loans but brings together a lender and a borrower for a fee.

mortgage clause: a provision attached to a fire or other direct damage insurance policy covering mortgaged property, stating (1) that the loss shall be payable to the mortgagee according to the amount of his or her interest, (2) that the mortgagee's right of recovery shall not be defeated by any act or neglect of the insured, and (3) that the mortgagee has other rights and privileges.

mortgage debt: an indebtedness created by a mortgage and secured by the property mortgaged. A mortgage debt is made evident by a note or bond.

mortgagee: the creditor or lender to whom a mortgage is made. The mortgagor retains possession and use of the property during the term of the mortgage (e.g., the bank is the mortgagee on your house).

mortgage insurance policy: a policy issued by a title insurance firm to a mortgage holder, resulting in a title policy.

mortgage lien: a lien in a mortgage given as security for a debt, serving as a lien on the property after the mortgage is recorded.

mortgage note: a note that offers a mortgage as proof of an indebtedness and describes the manner in which the mortgage is to be paid. This note is the actual amount of debt that the mortgage obtains, and it renders the mortgagor personally responsible for repayment.

mortgage payable: a written promise to pay a stated amount of money on or before specified future dates, secured by the pledging of certain assets as collateral.

mortgage premium: an additional bank fee charged for giving a mortgage when the legal interest rate is less than the prevailing mortgage market rate and there is a shortage of mortgage money.

mortgagor(er): a debtor or borrower who gives or makes a mortgage to a lender, on property owned by the mortgagor.

most favored nation clause: in international business treaties, a provision against tariff discrimination between two or more nations. It provides that each participant will automatically extend to other signatories all tariff reductions that are offered to nonmember nations. Cf. *open door policy;* see also *retaliatory duty.*

mother hubbard clause: a mortgage provision permitting the lender, upon default of the conditions of the mortgage, to foreclose on the overdue mortgage. Courts around the country have questioned the legality of this clause.

motion study: measurement and observation of the movements of equipment and materials as they relate to workers' motions. The objective is to increase performance, make correct performance easier, and reduce wasted time. Cf. *ergonomics, therbligs, time and motion study.*

motivation: a stimulus that differentially energizes certain responses within a person.

motivation, unconscious: a motivation (e.g., to buy) inferred from a person's pattern of behavior but of which the individual is not aware. See also *hidden persuader, packaging wants, self-concept theory, subliminal advertising;* cf. *rational buying motives.*

motivational needs: psychological forces that affect thinking and behavior (e.g., needs for self-actualization, belonging, feelings of security). A theory developed by A. Maslow details an individual's motivational needs. See also *hierarchy of needs.*

motivational research: a technique developed by E. Dichter, purporting to correlate behavior, needs, emotions, and desires with consumer activity. See also *consumer behavior research, hidden persuader.*

motivator-hygiene theory: F. Herzberg's theory that identifies conditions of a job that operate primarily to dissatisfy employees when they are not present (i.e., hygiene factors, salary, job security, etc.) and job conditions that lead to high levels of satisfaction when present (e.g., achievement, growth). Failure to meet the latter conditions is not highly dissatisfying. See also *dissatisfiers, two-factor theory.*

motor freight: merchandise that is moving through the use of motorized vehicles.

movement: an increase or decrease in the price of a specific stock.

moving average: a perpetual inventory cost-flow assumption whereby the cost of goods sold and the ending inventory are determined to be a weighted-average cost of all merchandise on hand after each purchase.

moving budgeting: a form of budgeting that involves periodic updating through time.

MPC: See *marginal propensity to consume.*

MPI: See *marginal propensity to invest.*

MPS: See *marginal propensity to save.*

MTM: See *methods-time measurement.*

muckracker: an individual who seeks to uncover business corruption or other activities that are unethical or harmful to the well-being of society.

multiallegiant worker: an employee who possesses allegiance to a variety of institutions (e.g., company, church, family, professional society).

multicompany: diverse organizations or a variety of firms under a single management.

multiemployer bargaining: the result of a collective-bargaining agreement covering more than one company in a given industry. It may be industry-wide, regional, or limited to a city or a metropolitan area. A related process is pattern bargaining, in which key terms reached in one settlement are closely followed by other settlements in similar companies. Synonymous with *multiunit bargaining.*

multiemployer pension plans: plans in which several employers pool pension contributions in a single fund, which is administered by labor and management of all companies involved. Workers can transfer between the participating firms without any loss in pension rights. See also *instant vesting, portability.*

multi-industry: the management of firms involved in different activities.

multinational corporation (MNC): a corporation that participates in international business activities; a firm that produces, markets, and finances its operations throughout various nations of the world. Cf. *production sharing.*

multipack: a container holding two or more separately packaged items.

multiple access: describing a system in which output or input can be received or released from more than one location. Cf. *queued access method, serial transfer*

multiple-address message: a message to be delivered to more than one destination.

multiple banking: the offering of all types of banking services to a bank's customers, as distinguished from specialization in a few services, as in savings and loan associations and other banking institutions. Synonymous with *department store banking;* cf. *full-service bank.*

multiple brands: several brand names used by a manufacturer on essentially the same product to open up new market segments.

multiple expansion of bank deposits: the situation that occurs when a loan made by one bank is used to finance business transactions and becomes a deposit in another bank. A portion of this loan can be used by the second bank as a required reserve, and the remainder can be loaned out for business use, so that it is eventually deposited in a third bank.

multiple-line underwriting: the issuance of fire and casualty insurance by a single company, by authority granted under multiple-line underwriting laws.

multiple-line underwriting laws: statutes granting underwriting powers that enable a single company to write both fire and casualty insurance.

multiple-location risks insurance: insurance that provides protection of property owned or controlled by one person or corporation in a number of different locations. See also *master policy.*

multiple management: a description of worker participation in a firm's management by assisting in the development and execution of policy. See also *human relations theory;* cf. *Caesar management, unilateral strategy.*

multiple packaging: including more than one item in a single container (e.g., the six-pack approach to beverage packaging).

multiple pricing: a price reduction offered if more than one unit is purchased.

multiple regression analysis: a technique for studying the relationship between independent and dependent variables with the derivation of a regression equation that is used to predict the latter from the former. See *regression, multiple.*

multiple sales: the result of selection by customers of multiple rather than single items to purchase.

multiple scenarios: a set of different assumptions used in planning.

multiplex: to carry out two or more

functions in a computer essentially simultaneously.

multiplier principle: the reciprocal of the marginal propensity to save. The multiplier is a figure that identifies the changes in investment and spending to alterations in aggregate income. See also *Keynesian economics.*

multiprocessing

(1) *computers:* using several computers to divide jobs or processes logically and to execute programs simultaneously.

(2) *systems:* loosely, parallel processing. See also *parallel computer.*

(3) *systems:* two or more processors in a system configuration.

multiprogramming: pertaining to the concurrent execution of two or more programs by a computer.

multiunit bargaining: Synonymous with *multiemployer bargaining.*

multivariate analysis, participation, and structure: See *MAPS.*

municipal bond: See *bond, municipal.*

municipal lien: a government lien against a property owner to solicit monies for the purpose of making improvements to his and neighboring properties. See also *eminent domain;* cf. *tax lien.*

municipals: a popular term for the securities of a governmental unit.

munifunds: Synonymous with *mutual funds.* see *investment company.*

muniment of title

(1) *general:* anything that protects or enforces.

(2) *real estate:* written proof that enables an owner to defend his or her title to property.

(3) *business law:* deeds and contracts that show conclusive proof of ownership. See, e.g., *warranty deed.*

Murphy's law: the theory that if something can go wrong, eventually it will.

mutual assent: agreement by all parties to a contract to the same thing. Each party must know what the other wishes.

mutual company: a corporation without capital stock (e.g., a mutual savings bank) in which the profits, after deductions, are distributed among the owner-customers in proportion to the business activity they carried out with the corporation.

mutual funds: See *investment company.*

mutual goal setting: an employee evaluation system consisting of a series of discussions between a supervisor and a subordinate in which the goals of future performance are identified and/or reviewed.

mutual rating: a relatively infrequent employee evaluation system whereby a worker is formally evaluated and rated by all or most members of the unit in which he or she works.

mutual savings bank: a banking organization without capital stock, operating under law for the mutual benefit of the depositors. The depositors are encouraged to practice thrift, and the savings of these small depositors are invested in very high grade securities and some first-class mortgages. Dividends from these investments are mutually distributed after deduction of expenses of the association and reserves for a guaranty fund for depositors. The principal idea of a mutual savings bank is to perform a social service for small depositors who cannot invest their savings at high yield. See also *mutu-*

al company.

mutual wills: a common arrangement executed pursuant to an agreement in which a husband and wife leave everything to each other.

Mylar: a Dupont trademark for a polyester film used as a base for magnetic tape.

N

N: the number of instances, of whatever sort, in the total population being studied.

n: the total number of cases or observations in a small group.

Naderism: synonym for consumerism, named for consumer advocate Ralph Nader.

named insured: person, firm, or corporation or any of its members, specifically designated by name as insured(s) in a policy, as distinguished from others who, although unnamed, are protected under some circumstances.

named-peril insurance: coverage that specifies the perils that are insured against. Cf. *all-risks insurance.*

name slug: an advertiser's signature or logotype.

nanosecond (nsec): one-billionth of a second.

Napier's bones: a technique devised by John Napier in which rods were used to aid in multiplication.

narrow market: a condition that exists when the demand for a security is so limited that small alterations in supply or demand will create major fluctuations in the market price.

NASD: See *National Association of Securities Dealers.*

NASDAQ: See *National Association of Securities Dealers Automated Quotations.*

national advertising: the advertising of a manufacturer or wholesaler, as contrasted with that of a retailer or local advertiser.

National Aeronautics and Space Administration (NASA): established by Congress in 1958, an independent agency responsible for directing the aeronautical and space programs sponsored by the government, excluding defense-related activities. NASA conducts research on problems of flight within and outside the earth's atmosphere, and develops, constructs, tests, and operates aeronautical and space vehicles; it also conducts activities required for

336

manned and unmanned exploration of space.

National Alliance of Businessmen: a coalition of business firms founded in 1968 to combat structural unemployment among the nation's hard-to-employ by reducing the barriers to their employment.

National Association of Insurance Agents (NAIA): the countrywide organization of stock fire and casualty insurance company agents whose primary purpose is the protection and advancement of the American agency system.

National Association of Manufacturers (NAM): a major organization of employers, founded in 1895 and structured with departments of trade, law, industrial relations, and publicity.

National Association of Securities Dealers (NASD): an association established in accordance with the Maloney Act of 1938, which amended the Securities Exchange Act of 1934, providing for self-regulation of the over-the-counter securities market by associations registered with the SEC. The NASD is the only association so registered. Most companies that offer variable annuities are NASD members.

National Association of Securities Dealers Automated Quotations (NASDAQ): an automated information network that provides brokers and dealers with price quotations on securities traded over the counter.

national bank: a commercial bank organized with the consent and approval of the Comptroller of the Currency and operated under the supervision of the federal government. National banks are required to be members of the Federal Reserve System and must purchase stock in the Federal Reserve Bank in their district.

National Bank Act of 1863: the act of Congress providing for the incorporation of banks under federal supervision. Such national banks are now under the supervision of the Federal Reserve System.

National Bankruptcy Act of 1898: a federal law stating the conditions under which an individual or business may declare bankruptcy and detailing the procedures for declaration. See also *reorganization.*

national brand: a brand distributed widely, through numerous outlets, in contrast to a private brand or label owned by a distributor or retailer.

national debt: the debt owed by the federal government.

National Fire Protection Association (NFPA): an organization that includes manufacturers, merchants, fire fighters, scientists, and insurance agents. It is primarily a clearinghouse for authoritative information on fire protection and prevention. Cf. *loss-control representative.*

National Highway Traffic Safety Administration: a federal agency created in 1970 to implement motor vehicle safety programs, to issue safety standards, to conduct testing programs to determine compliance with standards, to fund local and state motor vehicle and driver safety programs, and to conduct research on motor vehicle development, equipment, and safety and traffic safety.

national income: the total of the incomes received by all the people in a country over a stated period. It is equal to the gross national product minus depreciation minus sales taxes and other small items.

National Industrial Conference Board: founded in 1916, an organization that serves as a clearinghouse for the dissemination of information, publications of statistical materials, and other industrial relations data.

National Institute of Occupational Safety and Health (NIOSH): an organization created by the Occupational Safety and Health Act to conduct research and to develop additional safety and health standards.

nationalization: takeover by the government, with or without compensation, of a public or private activity. Cf. *confiscation, eminent domain.*

National Labor Relations Act of 1935: See *Wagner Act.*

National Labor Relations Board (NLRB): a five-member body created by the Wagner Act of 1935 and charged with the administration of the act. Its members and general counsel are named by the president. The board supervises representation elections to determine the choice of a bargaining agent and prepares cases arising from changes of unfair labor practices.

National Labor Union: an organization formed in Baltimore in 1866 with subsidiaries, groups of local unions, trade assemblies, national unions, farm societies, and other political groups. By 1870 the union had lost most of its national affiliates, and it became highly political.

National Mediation Board: a body set up by the Railway Labor Act of 1926 to attempt to settle disputes between rail and air carriers and their employees. It also conducts representation elections. Its three members are appointed by the President with the Senate confirmation. See also *Federal Mediation and Conciliation Service.*

National Railroad Passenger Corporation: See *Amtrak.*

National Recovery Administration (NRA): an agency created by passage of the National Industrial Recovery Act of 1933 during Franklin Roosevelt's administration. Its primary objectives were the self-government of industry through regulations of fair competition procedures for setting minimum wages and maximum working hours. The act was declared unconstitutional in 1935 by the Supreme Court in Schechter v. *U.S.*

National Stock Exchange: the third stock exchange of New York City, established in 1960.

national union: the parent organization that charters local unions.

national wealth: the combined monetary value of all the material economic products owned by all the people in a country.

nationwide marine definition: a statement of the types of insurance that may properly be written under marine or inland marine policies. Because the definition is filed as part of rating plans in many states, it has real legal significance.

natural business year: a 12-month period, usually selected to end when inventory or business activity is at a low point.

natural capital: land that is used as a factor of production.

natural financing: a real estate transaction requiring no outside financing, as is demanded in cash sales; the selling of properties that do not call for a third party.

natural monopoly

(1) *general:* a monopoly that results from natural conditions (e.g., a crop that demands special climate is subject to monopolization by a grower in the area having that climate).

(2) *economics:* among industries that experience economies of scale, the situation in which cost per unit is lowest when there is only one company in the industry.

natural resources: all materials furnished by nature (minerals, timber, water, etc.). See also *severance taxes.*

navicert: an official document released by a belligerent country authorizing specified items to be transported overseas by a neutral nation through a blockade to a named neutral port of entry.

near money: highly liquid assets (e.g., government securities) other than official currency.

need hierarchy model: See *hierarchy of needs.*

needle: a probe that may be passed through holes or notches to assist in sorting or selecting computer cards.

needle trades: apparel-producing industries.

needs assessment: diagnosis of present problems and future challenges that can be dealt with through training or development.

negative elasticity: the concept that demand moves in the same direction as price.

negative file: an authorized system file containing a simple list of ac-

counts for which credit, check cashing, and other privileges should be denied. Cf. *positive file.*

negative income tax: a proposed system to provide financial aid to individuals with incomes below a certain minimum. Rulings of the Internal Revenue Service would be followed, but the procedure would be to distribute rather than collect revenue.

negative sum game: the concept that the amount losers lose will always exceed the amount winners win.

negative verification: if a bank does not hear otherwise from a depositor, the assumption that the depositor finds no discrepancies between the statement presented and his or her records. Many banks have a legend printed on the statement form going to the depositor to the effect that, if no difference is reported within 10 days, the account will be considered correct.

negligence

(1) *business law:* failure to do that which an ordinary, reasonable, prudent person would do, or doing some act that an ordinary, prudent person would not do. Reference must be made to the situation, the circumstances, and the awareness of the parties involved. See also *contributory negligence, gross negligence, imputed negligence.*

(2) *insurance:* failure to use the degree of care that is considered to be a reasonable precaution under the given circumstances. Acts of omission or commission, or both, may constitute negligence.

negotiable

(1) *general:* anything that can be

sold or transferred to another for money or as payment of an obligation.

(2) *securities:* refering to a security whose title is transferable by delivery.

negotiable instrument: as stated in the Uniform Negotiable Instruments Act: "An instrument, to be negotiable, must conform to the following requirements: (*a*) it must be in writing and signed by the maker or drawer; (*b*) it must contain an unconditional promise or order to pay a certain sum in money; (*c*) it must be payable on demand, or at a fixed or determinable future time; (*d*) it must be payable to order or to bearer; (*e*) where the instrument is addressed to a drawee, he must be named or otherwise indicated therein with reasonable certainty."

negotiable order of withdrawal: See *NOW account.*

negotiated price: the result obtained by a purchaser who desires something different from what is available or is powerful enough to force the seller to accept prices lower than those usually charged. See also *upset price.*

negotiation

(1) *finance:* the act by which a negotiable instrument is placed in circulation by being physically passed from the original holder to another person.

(2) *labor relations:* the deliberation or discussion by representatives of labor and management to set conditions of work (e.g., wages, hours, benefits, working conditions, a mechanism for handling grievances); the bargaining that goes on between these parties. See also *collective bargaining;* cf. *arbitration, mediation.*

negotiator role: the role of a manager in discussing and bargaining with other units to obtain advantages for his or her unit.

Nenko system: the general pattern of human resource management commonly used in large-scale Japanese organizations.

neoclassical economics: an economic approach, developed between 1870 and 1918, that uses mathematics in the analysis of data and models. Neoclassicists were primarily concerned with refining the concepts of price and allocation theory, marginalism, and the theory of capital.

neo-Keynesian: a follower of concepts dealing with tax adjustment and government spending as primary forces of economic expansion. See also *Keynesian economics.*

nepotism: the practice of placing relatives in organizational positions without regard to the claims by others that better qualified people can be found (e.g., the president of the firm, without consideration of qualifications, hiring his nephew).

nested: packaged one within another.

net: that which remains after certain designated deductions have been made from the gross amount.

net assets: the property of a business, corporation, organization, or estate that remains after all obligations have been met.

net asset value: the resulting per-share value derived when investment companies compute assets daily, or even twice daily, by totaling the market value of all securities owned, then deduct all liabilities and divide by the number of shares outstanding.

net avails: the funds given to a borrower in the discounting of a note. It is equal to the face value of the note minus the discount.

net cash flow: the net cash consumed or produced in a period by an activity or product during a unit of time, including all revenue and expenses except noncash items such as depreciation.

net change: the change in the price of a security between the closing price on one day and the closing price on the following day on which the stock is traded. The net change is ordinarily the last figure on the stock price list. The notation ''+1¼'' means ''up $1.250 a share from the last sale on the previous day the stock traded.''

net cost

(1) *accounting:* the true cost of an item. The net cost is determined by subtracting all income or financial gain from the gross cost.

(2) *insurance:* the total premiums paid on a policy less any dividends, and the surrender value as of the time the net cost is determined.

net debt: the sum of fixed and existing liabilities less the sinking fund and other assets that are earmarked for payment of the liabilities.

net earnings: the figure that results when Income taxes applicable to operating earnings are deducted from the excess of gross operating income over gross operating expenses (referred to as ''operating earnings before taxes''). Synonymous with ''net operating earnings.''

net estate: the part of an estate remaining after all expenses to manage it have been taken out.

net export of goods and services: the excess of exports of goods and services (domestic output sold abroad and production abroad credited to U.S.-owned resources) over imports (U.S. purchases of foreign output, domestic production credit to foreign-owned resources, and net private cash remittances to creditors abroad).

net income: the remains from earnings and profits after all costs, expenses, and allowances for depreciation and probable loss have been deducted.

net interest: Synonymous with *pure interest.*

net investment: the actual change in value of productive assets in a given year, determined by subtracting from gross investment the value of depreciation or the value of all capital that has been consumed.

net lease: a lease stating that the landlord will incur all maintenance costs, taxes, insurance, and other expenses usually paid by the owner.

net long-term debt: total long-term debt, less cash and investment assets of sinking funds and other reserve funds specifically held for redemption of long-term debt.

net loss: the excess of expenses and losses during a specified period over revenues and gains in the same time frame.

net national product: gross national product minus capital consumption (depreciation); the market value of the net output of goods and services produced by the nation's economy.

net-net income: a term that uses the repetition of the word ''net'' to emphasize the actual profit, resulting in usable cash, after all expenses have been paid.

net present value (NPV): the difference between the present values of an investment's expected cash inflows and outflows.

net price: the price after deductions, allowances, and discounts have been made.

net profit: the excess of all revenues over all costs and expenses incurred to obtain the income in a given enterprise during a given period of time. If the total expenses exceed the income, such amount is known as net loss. Synonymous with *net revenue.*

net railway operating income: operating revenue left after deducting expenses, railway tax accruals, and land rental on leased equipment leased for less than a year.

net rate: an advertising medium's published rate, less the agency commission. See also *fifteen and two.*

net realizable value: the selling price of an item less reasonable selling costs.

net revenue: Synonymous with *net profit.*

net sales: gross sales, minus returns and allowances, over a stated period.

net tax liability: the amount of tax computed by subtracting tax credits from the gross tax liability.

net ton-miles: the number of 2000-pound tons of revenue and nonrevenue freight transported in one mile.

network

(1) *broadcasting:* a group of broadcasting stations affiliated by contract and interconnected for instant broadcast of the same program.

(2) *general:* a diagram of the se-

quence of activities that must be performed to complete a project.

network analog: the expression and solution of mathematical relationships between variables using a circuit or circuits to represent these quantities. See also *critical path method.*

net working capital: the excess of existing assets over present liabilities.

network planning: a family of planning and control techniques whereby all of the planning steps are schematically tied together through a common network.

net worth

(1) *general:* the owner's equity in a business, represented by the excess of the total assets over the total amounts owed to outside creditors at a given time.

(2) *accounting:* refering to an individual, the figure determined by deducting the amount of all personal liabilities for the total value of personal assets.

net yield: the return from an investment following subtractions for costs and losses incurred in operating the investment.

neutral tax: a tax that does not affect the allocation of resources.

never-outs: items that should never run out of stock during a season because of continuous demand.

new business venture group: a separate company unit with a mandate to develop one or more new businesses or items that fall outside the natural charter of the firm's existing activities.

New Deal: the social and economic programs of Franklin Roosevelt during the depths of the Great Depression in the 1930s. He reformed the banking system with the National Banking Act. Congress created the Agricultural Adjustment Administration, the National Recovery Administration, the Civilian Conservation Corps, the Public Works Agency, and the Tennessee Valley Authority. The Securities and Exchange Commission and the Federal Communications Commission were established in 1934 and the National Youth Administration, the Social Security system, the Works Progress Administration, and the National Labor Relations Board in 1935.

New Economics: the economic theory, initially developed by John Maynard Keynes in the 1930s, that claims that an economy may be in equilibrium at any level of employment and that appropriate government fiscal and monetary policies are required to maintain full employment and keep economic growth with minimal inflation. See also *Keynesian economics.*

new issue: a stock or bond sold by a corporation for the first time. Proceeds may be issued to retire outstanding securities of the company to finance new plant or equipment or to secure additional working capital.

New York Coffee and Sugar Exchange: founded in 1882 and originally known as the New York Coffee Exchange, the principal U.S. exchange for the trading of coffee and sugar futures contracts.

New York Curb Exchange: former name for the American Stock Exchange.

New York Mercantile Exchange: an exchange founded in 1872 as a market for cheese, butter, and eggs. Its principal commodities now include potatoes, silver coins, and platinum.

New York Stock Exchange (NYSE): the largest, most prestigious security exchange in the world, reorganized under its existing name in 1863. The New York Stock and Exchange Board in 1817 moved indoors to a second floor room at 40 Wall Street in New York City. On January 2, 1863, its name was changed to the New York Stock Exchange; on the next day, the first subsidiary, the New York Stock Exchange Building Company, was created. See also *NYSE Common Stock Index.*

nexus: a relationship used in tax laws to express a connection between a tax and the activities of the individual or group being taxed. See also *tax incidence.*

NGT: See *nominal group technique.*

NICs: newly industrializing countries (i.e., Mexico, South Korea, Brazil, Taiwan).

Nielsen Drug (Food) Index: developed by A. C. Nielsen, statements on the market change of products, by type and brand, issued through panels of experts from drugstores and other stores.

Nielsen rating: the percentage of households tuned to a stated radio or television program, as reported by the A. C. Nielsen Company. A device called an Audimeter is installed out of sight in each sample household and is electronically connected to each television set in the home. The Audimeter produces a minute-by-minute photographic record identifying the times the sets are turned on and off and the stations tuned in. See also *Audimeter;* cf. *Hooperating.*

night differential: extra, nonovertime pay for time worked between 6 P.M. and 6 A.M.

NIOSH: See *National Institute of Occupational Safety and Health.*

nixie mail: letters or packages not easily deliverable because of incorrect, illegible, or insufficient address.

NLRB: See *National Labor Relations Board.*

no-bill: (slang) an employee who is unwilling to join a union.

node: a state or an event, as represented by a point on a diagram.

no-fault automobile insurance: personal injury protection in a form of state-mandated insurance under which a person's financial losses resulting from an automobile accident (e.g., medical and hospital expenses and loss of income) are automatically paid by his or her own insurance company without regard to the identity of the party at fault. One result of this form of insurance is that the responsible party cannot be sued, at least up to a certain limit. See also *broadened collision coverage;* cf. *limited collision coverage, nonownership automobile insurance.*

noise: any disturbance tending to interfere with normal computer operation.

Noise Control Act of 1972: federal legislation to establish noise standards for items made in the United States that produce excessive sound. The act gave the Environmental Protection Agency authority to work with the Federal Aviation Agency in creating noise control standards for aircraft. The EPA administers programs on noise pollution, enforces noise pollution standards, and provides information about noise pollution litigation.

no-lien affidavit: a written document by a property owner stating that the work has been finished on an identified property and that no liens or mortgages encumber it. Cf. *lien affidavit.*

no-limit order: a request to buy or sell a security without any stipulation about price. See also *limited order, market order.*

no-load funds: mutual funds that are not sold by a salesperson. They do not involve extensive marketing schemes and contain no sales charge or load.

no-lockout agreement: a collective-bargaining clause stating that the employer will not withhold work from individuals or close down the plant to force acceptance of management's terms.

nolo contendere: "I will not contest (it)" (Latin); in a criminal case, a form of guilty plea on the basis of which a sentence may be passed. By pleading, the defendant admits to the facts of the case without admitting his or her formal guilt of a crime. The plea is most often used when a guilty plea would affect other interests (e.g., a contract, insurance).

nominal: a term used as a modifier to indicate that values are expressed in current money prices.

nominal group technique (NGT): a forecasting strategy in which seven to ten experts gather to exchange their ideas and projections.

nominal partner: an individual who lends his or her name to a business organization but is not a true partner because he or she may not have given sufficient financial backing or does not take a full share of the profit.

nominal price

(1) *finance:* an amount of money so small in relation to the item purchased that it hardly justifies use of the word "price."

(2) *securities:* an estimated price for a security or commodity that is not traded often enough to warrant setting a definite market price.

nominal yield: the rate of return stated on a security, calculated on its par or face value.

nonaccrual asset: an asset, such as a loan, that has been questioned on bank examination and is known to be a slow or doubtful (of payment) loan. A reserve is set up or applied on this type of loan, and it is excluded from the earning or accrual assets.

nonassessable stock: most securities—stock whose owners cannot be assessed in the event of failure or insolvency. Cf. *limited liability.*

nonassignable: Synonymous with *inalienable.*

noncallable bond: See *bond, noncallable.*

noncommunist affidavit: an affidavit by union officers declaring that they are not members of the Communist party. This is required if the union is to be eligible for National Labor Relations Board services.

non compos mentis: describing an individual who does not possess sufficient understanding to comprehend the nature, extent, and meaning of his or her obligations or contracts.

nonconcurrency: the situation that exists when two or more policies provide different coverages on the same risk. See also *double insurance.*

noncontributory: describing a group insurance plan under which the policyholder (employer) pays the entire cost.

noncontributory retirement system: a system in which the employer bears the entire cost of deferred compensation for the worker.

noncontrollable costs: costs assigned to a responsible center whose amounts cannot be influenced by and are only indirectly the responsibility of the manager of that center.

noncooperative equilibrium: an equilibrium that occurs when each of the participants in a market tries to improve its own well-being without consideration for the welfare of others.

noncumulative: describing a preferred stock on which unpaid dividends do not accrue. As a rule, omitted dividends are gone forever.

noncumulative quantity discount: a price reduction that is given based on the size of the individual order placed.

noncurrent: describing that which is due more than one year after the date of issuance.

noncurrent accounts: all operational asset, long-term investment, long-term liability, and owners' equity accounts; all accounts except for working capital accounts.

noncurrent liabilities: claims against the assets of an entity that will become due a year or more in the future.

nondegradable pollutants: impurities (e.g., glass, plastics, certain industrial wastes) that do not disintegrate or dissolve naturally. Cf. *biodegradable.*

nondirective counseling: a client-centered process of skillfully listening and encouraging an employee to explain bothersome problems, understand them, and determine appropriate solutions. See also *cooperative counseling, directive counseling.*

nondurable goods: items that have a relatively brief lifetime (e.g., food, clothing).

nonfeasance: failure to perform a legal duty. Cf. *malfeasance.*

nonfinancial compensation: a form of compensation—other than pay and benefits—that includes the satisfaction a person receives by performing meaningful job-related tasks.

nonforfeiture options: privileges allowed under terms of a life insurance contract after cash values have been created. Four such privileges exist: (1) surrender for full cash value; (2) loans up to the full amount of the cash value; (3) paid-up policy for the amount of insurance that cash value, as a single premium, will buy at net rates; (4) term insurance for the full face amount of the original policy for as long as the cash value will last to pay necessary premiums.

noninstallment credit: credit granted with payment to be made in a lump sum at a future date.

non-interest-bearing note: a note whose maker does not have to pay any interest.

noninvestment property: property that will not yield income.

nonmanufacturing expenses: expenditures that are not closely associated with the manufacture of products, including selling and administrative expenses.

nonmarket production: production that occurs outside the market (e.g., production regulated by custom or law rather than by prices). This is a common phenomenon in less-developed nations.

nonmember bank: a U.S. bank that is not a member of the Federal Reserve System. Such institutions are either state or private banks.

nonmerchantable title: an unmarketable title that is legally unsound because it shows property defects. See *cloud on title.*

nonmonetary items: assests or equities that are not fixed as to the amount of future dollars they can command and hence fluctuate in value according to their demand n the marketplace.

nonnegotiable title: a title that cannot be transferred by delivery or by endorsement.

nonownership automobile insurance: insurance under which an accident victim is automatically compensated for medical expenses, income losses, and so on, without regard for who created the acident or owned the car. Cf. *no-fault automobile insurance, uninsured motorist protection.*

nonperformance: the failure of a contracting party to provide goods or services according to an agreement.

nonprice competition: markets in which a seller maneuvers for influence on the basis of special aspects of the items to be sold, promotion, or marketing strategy. Most larger organizations avoid price competition by emphasizing nonprice marketing forces. Cf. *trading down, trading up.*

nonprofit corporation: See *not-for-profit.*

nonprofit marketing: the application

of marketing concepts and activities to nonprofit organizations.

nonprogrammed decision: the process of finding a solution to a problem by a creative approach rather than by using a standard routine or program.

nonrecurring charge: any cost, expense, or involuntary loss that it is thought will not be likely to occur again.

nonrenewable natural resources: natural resources that are used up in the process of production.

nonroutine decisions: decisions that deal with unstructured, nonrecurring problems that have no accepted method of resolution.

nonsuit: a court judgment against the plaintiff when he or she is unable to prove the case or fails to continue with the trial once it has commenced.

nontaxable income: income that is not liable to income tax.

nontraceable costs: costs that are not directly identified with the responsibility centers to which they are assigned.

nonverbal communication: the sharing of ideas without the use of words.

nonzero sum situation: a competitive situation in which not only the winning group benefits but the other group also wins or its position remains unchanged.

no par value stock: stock of a corporation that has designated par value.

no-passbook savings: the same as a regular passbook savings account, except that no passbook is used. Deposits and withdrawal slips are receipted by the teller, with a copy returned to the depositor for personal records. A periodic statement is rendered in place of a passbook. Withdrawals must be made by the depositor personally. Cf. *passbook.*

no protest: instructions given by one bank to another collecting bank not to object to items in case of nonpayment. The sending bank stamps on the face of the item the letters "N.P." If the item cannot be collected, the collecting bank returns the item without objecting.

no-raiding agreements (pacts): agreements between international unions not to persuade workers to leave one union and join another when the first union has established bargaining relationships. Once a union is organized, no other union will attempt to break a member away. Affiliates of the AFL–CIO have signed a general no-raiding pact. Several unions have bilateral agreements covering attempts to organize unorganized workers. See also *rival unionism.*

norm: a point of reference; a standard used for comparison.

normal foreseeable loss: the estimate of the damage that would result if the occurence insured against received the normally expected protection and control. Cf. *maximum foreseeable loss.*

normal good: an item whose consumption changes directly with money income when prices remain constant (e.g., consumer goods). Synonymous with "superior good."

normalize: to shift the information in a computer word until some character, usually the leftmost, contains a nonzero digit.

normal price: the price to which the market price tends to return following fluctuations up or down.

normal profit: the lowest price that an entrepreneur will accept as compensation for his or her activity. It is part of an organization's total economic costs, since it is a payment that must be received by the owner to keep him or her from withdrawing capital and effort that might have to be used in another way.

normal sale: a transaction that pleases both the seller and buyer of property and in which no unforeseen or abnormal situations surface.

normal time: the time needed by an average employee to complete some arbitrarily determined unit of work, performing at a normal pace under standard conditions and procedures but without allowances for work fatigue or interruptions. See also *pacers;* cf. *time standard.*

normal value: the price or a property commanded on the open market.

normative decision models: the various step-by-step procedures that prescribe how managers should make decisions to reach their goals.

normative economics: the study of economics that include the value judgments of the economist. See, e.g., *overbought, oversold;* cf. *positive economics.*

normative forecasting: a technological forecasting technique that begins with the identification of some future technological objectives and works back to the present, identifying problem areas that will have to be surmounted along the way. Although it is a technological technique, normative forecasting considers both technological and nontechnological factors.

Norris–LaGuardia Act: The Anti-Injuction Act of 1932, which limited the power of federal courts in issuing injunctions in labor disputes; modified in 1947 by the Taft-Hartley Act. The act also made yellow-dog contracts unenforceable, established a policy to protect workers' freedom of association and collective bargaining, and established that a union official cannot be held responsible for acts taken during a labor dispute unless he or she had clearly initiated the dispute. See also *yellow-dog contract.*

no sale final: an organizational policy that a sale is not final until the customer is totally pleased with the purchase made.

no-strike clause: a contract clause barring a strike during the life of an agreement. Cf. *contract bar.*

nostro account: an account maintained by a bank with a bank in a foreign country. Nostro accounts are kept in foreign currencies of the country in which the monies are held, with the equivalent dollar value listed in another column. Cf. *vostro account.*

nostro overdraft: part of a bank's statement indicating that it has sold more foreign bills of exchange than it has bought, resulting in the domestic bank's owing currencies to foreign banks in the amount of the nostro overdraft.

notarial protest certificate: Synonymous with *notice of dishonor.*

notary public: a person commissioned by a state for a stipulated period (with the privilege of renewal) to administer certain oaths and to attest and certify documents, thus authorizing him or her to take affidavits and depositions. A notary is also authorized to protest negotiable instruments for nonpayment or non-acceptance. See also *notice of dishonor.*

notation credit: a credit that specifies that any person purchasing or paying drafts drawn or demands for payment made under it must note the amount of the draft or demand on the letter or advice of credit.

note: an instrument, such as a promissory note, that is the recognized legal evidence of a debt. A note is signed by the maker (the borrower), promising to pay a certain sum of money on a specified date at a certain place of business, to a certain business, individual, or bank (the lender).

note of hand: any promissory note.

note payable: a liability, evidenced by a formal written promise to pay a specified sum at a fixed future date. Notes may be either short (one year or less) or long term.

note receivable: a promissory note collected by a business from a customer.

not-for-profit: describing the activities of an organization established with the sole goal of providing service for society rather than for the purpose of making a profit. See also *eleemosynary.*

notice of dishonor: a document prepared by a notary public when a maker or drawee has refused to pay for or accept an instrument. When a holder in due course presents an instrument for payment or acceptance by a drawee, and the maker or drawee fails to honor the instrument, the holder in due course gives it to a no-

tary public. The notary public also presents the instrument to the maker or drawee as a legal formality. If the maker or drawee again dishonors the instrument by refusing to pay for or accept it, the notary public prepares the notice of dishonor. Synonymous with *mandate of protest,* notarial *protest certificate, protest jacket; acceptance for honor.*

notice sale: removing a property from open market by declaring that it has been sold. Synonymous with *sold notice.*

novation

(1) *general:* the replacement of a new debt or obligation for an older one. See also *open-end mortgage;* cf. *renewal, standstill agreement.*

(2) *finance:* the replacement of a new creditor or debtor for a former creditor or debtor.

NOW (negotiable order of withdrawal) account: a checking account requiring no service charge or minimum balance. This is a growing trend among savings institutions.

nozzle: a round fitting fastener permanently placed at the opening of a container to facilitate filling or pouring and to permit closure.

NPV: See *net present value.*

n.s.f: not sufficient funds.

n.s.f. check: a check that is not honored by a bank because of insufficient cash in the customer's bank account. See *insufficient funds.*

Nuclear Regulatory Commission: a federal agency spun off from the Atomic Energy Commission in 1973 to inspect and enforce standards of civilian nuclear safety, which basically involves licensing atomic power plants.

nucleus

(1) *general:* the center of something (e.g., the nucleus of a national corporation is often corporate headquarters).

(2) *computers:* the portion of a control program that always remains in main storage.

nudum pactum: an empty promise; a statement for which no consideration has been given.

nuisance: any prolonged conduct (e.g., littering a street) that creates annoyance, inconvenience, and damage to an individual or property.

nuisance tax

(1) *government:* any tax the revenue from which does not justify the inconvenience to a person subject to the tax.

(2) *government:* a tax that yields a low return following deduction of the costs of handling and administration.

null

(1) *general:* referring to an absence of information, as contrasted with zero or blank for the presence of no information.

(2) *statistics:* zero.

(3) *statistics:* invalid.

null hypothesis: the logical contradictory of the hypothesis that one seeks to test. If the null hypothesis is proved false, its contradictory is thereby proved true. Essentially, the null hypothesis is that there is no difference greater than could be expected by chance.

nullification of agreement: setting aside the terms of an agreement. Cf. *repudiation.*

number, random: a digit set constructed in such a sequence that each sucessive digit is equally likely to be any of *n* digits to the base *n* of the number.

number of stock turnover: stock turnover as determined by dividing average inventory at retail into the net sales for a year.

numeric: pertaining to numerals or to representation by means of numerals. Cf. *alphanumeric.*

numerical control: programming equipment by means of coded numbers, stored on magnetic tapes or cards, according to the needs of different items.

numeric character: any allowable digit in a machine's number system.

nuncupative will: a will given orally before witnesses. It is reduced to writing at a later time.

nuplex: any nuclear-powered agricultural-industrial complex.

nursery finance: institutional loans to profitable organizations that plan to go public shortly. See also *adventure, risk capital, venture capital.*

NYSE Common Stock Index: a composite index covering price movements of all common stocks listed on the Big Board. It is based on the close of the market December 31, 1965, as 50.00 and is weighted according to the number of shares listed for each issue. The index is computed continuously and printed on the ticker tape each half-hour. Point changes in the index are converted to dollars and cents to provide a meaningful measure of changes in the average price of listed stocks. The composite index is supplemented by separate indices for four industry groups: industrials, transportation, utilities, and finances. Cf. *Dow-Jones averages.*

OA: See *operational analysis.*

O/A: open account.

OASI: See *old-age and survivors' insurance.*

objection to title: a weakness in a title for property, requiring adjustment. See *cloud on title.*

objective function: expression of the sole objective of the attempt to maximize, if profit (to minimize, if cost), made up of a linear summation of the products of the quantity of each variable and the respective unit profit (cost).

objective rationality: a decision-making condition under which a manager identifies all possible alternatives, accurately predicts the consequences of each, and selects the one that will maximize returns to the firm.

objectives: the goals or specific aims of a business.

objective value: the price an item can command in terms of other items in the market.

obligation: the legal responsibility and duty of a debtor (the obligor) to pay a debt when due, and the legal right of the creditor (the obligee) to enforce payment in the event of default.

obligation bond: See *bond, obligation.*

obligee: a creditor or promisee.

obligor: a debtor or promisor.

observational technique: a research method that entails observing consumer behavior.

observer: an employee who attends a meeting of management and union negotiators but does not participate in the discussions or in the voting. Cf. *public member.*

obsolescence: the state of being out of date and therefore of little use to society. See also *functional obsolescence, planned obsolescence, product obsolescence.*

Occam's razor: Synonymous with *parsimony, principle of.*

occupation

(1) *general:* a person's trade,

business, or vocational choice.

(2) *real estate:* taking possession, with the intent of claiming ownership.

occupational accident: an accident that occurs in the course of employment and is caused by inherent or related hazards.

occupational analysis: a descriptive approach for determining jobs that have common activities, to permit grouping them under a common occupation.

occupational disease: a pathological condition caused by or resulting from employment (e.g., chemical or radium poisoning, pneumoconiosis, the bends in tunnel boring or diving).

occupational health: a general description of all activities related to protecting and maintaining the health and safety of working people.

occupational information: information resulting from analysis of questionnaires and other materials that describe the functions and characteristics of specific occupations. See e.g., *Dictionary of Occupational Titles.*

occupational mobility: the extent to which individuals in a particular occupation move into work other than that for which they were specially trained.

Occupational Outlook Handbook: a publication of the U.S. Department of Labor that indicates future needs for various jobs. See also *Dictionary of Occupational Titles.*

Occupational Safety and Health Act of 1970: federal legislation providing for health and safety standards for individuals in the performance of their labors. The act created the Occupational Safety and Health Administra-

tion (OSHA) in the U.S. Department of Labor to set the rules and enforce the laws. OSHA also administers training and educational programs on occupational safety and health standards for employers and workers, supervises regional inspections, and issues citations to employers who do not meet federal occupational safety and health standards.

occupational test: a test of ability in a given vocation.

ocean marine insurance: coverage on vessels of all types, including liabilities connected with them, and on their cargoes. Cf. *inland marine insurance, marine protection and indemnity insurance.*

OCR: optical character recognition.

OD: See *organizational development, outside dimensions.*

odd-lot dealer: a member firm of an exchange that buys and sells odd lots of stock—1 to 9 shares in the case of stocks traded in 10-share units and 1 to 99 for 100-share units. The odd-lot dealer's customers are commission brokers acting on behalf of their customers.

odd-lot orders: purchases or sales of stock that are not in 100-share units. Cf. *full lot.*

odd pricing: pricing at odd amounts (e.g., at 99 cents instead of at a dollar). Synonymous with *psychological pricing.*

OECD: See *Organization for Economic Cooperation and Development.*

O-E-C (organizing, evaluating, and coaching) syndrome: an approach to work improvement by studying jobs through analysis of work and tasks, minimizing the damaging impact of control by others, and emphasizing the dynamics of personal growth. See also *job enrichment*.

OEEC: See *Organization for Economic Cooperation and Development*.

OFCC: See *Federal Contract Compliance Office*.

off: describing a given day on which the prices of stocks and commodities drop.

off-board: describing an over-the-counter transaction in unlisted securities or a transaction involving listed shares that was not executed on a national securities exchange.

off-brand: a brand that is not considered acceptable to a consumer.

offer

(1) *general:* to present for acceptance or refusal.

(2) *securities:* the price at which a person is ready to sell, as opposed to bid, the price at which a person is ready to buy.

offering: an issue of securities or bonds offered for sale to the public. See also *secondary offering, special offering*.

Office of Federal Contract Compliance Programs: See *Federal Contract Compliance Office*.

Office of Management and Budget (OMB): a federal agency that prepares the president's budget and develops the government's fiscal program with the Council of Economic Advisers and the Treasury Department and oversees administration of the federal budget.

Office of Personnel Management, U.S.: created on January 1, 1979, one of the major agencies established to replace the Civil Service Commission, with responsibility for managing the bureaucracy. See also *Merit System*

Protection Board, U.S.

officer's check: Synonymous with *cashier's check*.

official reserve transactions balance: the account on the balance-of-payments statement that records the total of the balance on the goods-and-services account, the balance on the unilateral-transfers account, and the balance on the capital account, plus the allocation of special drawing rights and net errors and omissions. See also *special drawing rights*.

off-line: describing equipment or other devices not under the control of the central processing unit.

off-premises clause: a policy clause providing insurance protection on personal property while it is away from the premises named in the policy. See also *floater policy*.

offset

(1) *accounting:* either of two equivalent entries on both sides of an account.

(2) *banking:* the right accruing to a bank to take possession of any balances that a guarantor or debtor may have in the bank to cover a loan in default. A depositor who has both a deposit credit balance and a loan balance is denied the right of offset in case the bank becomes insolvent and closes. Cf. *garnishment*.

(3) *printing:* a lithographic printing process in which an image is transferred to a rubber roller, which in turn places the impression on the paper. Cf. *letterpress*.

offsets to long-term debt: cash and investment assets of sinking funds, bond reserve, and other reserve funds held specifically for redemption of long-term debt, and assets of credit funds that are pledged to redeem debt incurred to finance loan activities of such funds.

off-shift differential: a premium payment for work hours other than those of a worker's regular shift. See also *midnight shift.*

off time: describing a computer that is not scheduled for use, maintenance, alteration, or repair.

ogive: a distribution curve characterized by cumulative frequencies.

OJT: See *on-the-job training.*

Okie: (slang) a migratory worker.

Okun's law: a concept developed by Arthur Okun that relates declines in the idleness rate of workers to increases in the gross national product, using data that exclude the first two quarters of every economic recovery period.

old-age and survivors' insurance (OASI): the source of retirement income and other payments made to survivors of those eligible under social security legislation.

old boy network: (slang) an arrangement whereby jobs are offered to the relatives or friends of the hiring (or other) executive.

oligopoly: an industry in which a small number of producers sell identical products. See also *cooperative equilibrium;* cf. *monopoly, differential oligopoly.*

oligopoly price: a price that develops when there is a market of numerous buyers and few sellers, thus resulting in the sellers having the greatest power.

oligopsony

(1) *finance:* control by a number of buyers who attempt to influence the demand for a specific commodity. Cf. *duopsony, monopsony.*

(2) *labor relations:* employers who have some control in obtaining labor in a particular labor market locality. Cf. *hiring hall.*

oligopsony price: a price that develops when there is a market of few' buyers and numerous sellers, thus resulting in the buyers having the greatest power.

OMB: See *Office of Management and Budget.*

ombudsman: a person outside the normal chain of command who handles complaints and grievances of an individual or a small group of individuals.

omnibus clause: in an automobile liability policy, the agreement that, by virtue of its definition of "insured," extends the protection of the policy to interests included by the definition without the necessity of naming or otherwise designating them. This type of agreement is also used in ocean marine insurance.

Omnibus Reconciliation Act of 1980: federal legislation that imposed restrictions on use of mortgage subsidy bonds and made other miscellaneous tax changes.

on account

(1) *general:* describing a payment made toward the settlement of an account.

(2) *accounting:* a purchase or sale made on open account.

on a scale: in buying or selling securities, the situation in which a customer purchases or sells equal amounts of a stock at prices that are spaced by a constant interval as the market price rises or drops.

on consignment: describing items turned over by an owner (the consignor) to someone else (the consignee) with the expectation that the items (the consignment) will be sold by the consignee. If all the items are not sold, the owner is entitled to the return of the items. Cf. *memorandum sale, purchase allowance.*

on demand: describing a bill of exchange that is payable on presentation. See also *demand note.*

one-bank holding company: a corporation that owns control of one commercial bank.

one hundred showing: a standard showing of outdoor posters. The number of panels in the poster in a 100 showing varies with market size.

one-price policy: a situation in which the price for goods is firm and cannot be negotiated.

one-stop banking: the service provided by a bank whose clients can do all their banking business at that bank. Cf. *full-service bank.*

one-time rate: the advertiser's rate paid when there is not enough space or time purchased to earn volume discounts.

on-line: pertaining to equipment or devices under control of the central processing unit.

on-line, real-time: describing a system operation in which the input data are given directly from the measuring devices and the computer results are obtained during the progress of the event.

on margin: describing securities purchased when the buyer has borrowed part of the purchase price from the broker.

on order: describing goods paid for but not yet received.

on-the-job training (OJT): use of the actual work site as the setting for instructing workers while at the same time engaging in productive work. Cf. *training, vestibule.*

on the rims: (slang) approaching the point of poverty.

OPEC: See *Organization of Petroleum Exporting Countries.*

open account: credit extended that is not supported by a note, mortgage, or other formal written evidence of indebtedness (e.g., shipments of merchandise for which a buyer is billed later).

open career: a career system that permits entrance to positions at any or all grade levels.

open charge account: See *charge account.*

open credit: credit that is allowed without immediate proof of a customer's credit-worthiness.

open door policy: a policy whereby citizens and products of foreign countries receive the same treatment as domestic citizens and products. Cf. *most favored nation clause, peril point.*

open economy: an economy that is free of trade restrictions.

open-end agreement: a union contract that has no expiration date but includes a provision that either party can give notice of a desire to terminate the agreement.

open-end bond: See *bond, open-end.*

open-end contract: an agreement whereby a supplier contracts to meet the buyer's requirements for a specific item during a stated period, whatever those requirements may be. The agreement is open-end because all the terms are left indefinite.

open-ended: pertaining to a process or system that can be cut back.

open-end funds: mutual funds in which new shares of the fund are sold whenever there is a request, with the expectation that the seller will eventually request to buy back the shares at no additional charge. See also *investment company.*

open-end investment company: an investment firm that sells and reclaims its capital stock continuously, selling it at book value, adding a sales charge, and redeeming it at a slight discount or at book value.

open-end mortgage: a mortgage that permits the borrower to reborrow money paid on the principal up to the original amount.

opening
(1) *merchandising:* the first showing of a new season's line of items by a manufacturer or an entire industry.
(2) *personnel:* an unfilled position in an organization.

opening purchase: a transaction in which an investor becomes the holder of a security.

open interest: the number of outstanding contracts in the exchange market or in a particular class or series.

open listing: a listing that makes property available to more than one broker. Cf. *listing.*

open-loop control: describing a system in which the central processing unit does not directly control a process or procedure but instead displays or prints information for the operator to assist in an action-oriented decision.

open market: a general term describing a condition of trading that is not limited to any particular area or persons.

open-market operations: operations carried out by the Federal Reserve System in which it buys or sells government bonds in the same market used by other institutional investors.

open mortgage: a mortgage that can be paid off, without penalty, at any period prior to its maturity.

open order:
(1) *merchandising:* an order made without price or delivery stipulation, or an order shipped to a market representative without specifying the vendor.
(2) *securities:* an order to buy or sell securities that has not yet been executed. Such orders may be placed at market price or at a fixed price. Synonymous with *good 'til canceled order.*

open outcry: Synonymous with *outcry market.*

open policy: a marine insurance term for a continuous, open-term contract designed to insure automatically all cargo moving at the insured's risk. Cf. *fleet policy.*

open prospectus: a brochure that aims to obtain financial backing but does not clearly identify the use to be made of the investment.

open rate: an advertising rate that is subject to discounts for volume or frequency.

open shop: an unorganized establishment or one in which union membership is not a condition of employment or continuing employment. Cf. *closed shop, modified union shop, union shop;* see also *free rider.*

open stock: replacement items or additions of goods carried in quantity and retained in a warehouse for several years.

open system: an organizational department in which autonomy, interaction, and a relaxed atmosphere are encouraged. See also *loose-rein supervision, organic structure.*

open the kimono: (slang) to reveal to prospective customers company plans regarding future products, to impress upon the buyer that the firm is ahead of its competitors in developing new or superior items.

open-to-buy (OTB): describing the quantity of goods that a store can receive in stock over a stated time without exceeding its planned inventory levels.

open trade: any transaction that has not yet been closed.

open union: a union that admits any qualified worker upon payment of an initiation fee.

operand
(1) *systems:* any quantity entering into an operation.
(2) *computers:* information entered with a command name to define the data on which a command processor operates and to control the execution of the command processor.

operant conditioning: a motivation approach that focuses on the relationship between stimulus, response, and reward.

operating budget: a quantitative expresion of a plan of action that shows how a firm will acquire and use its resources over a specified period of time.

operating cycle: the general pattern of business activity whereby cash and other resources are converted to inventory and operational assets and eventually into a product or service that can be sold and for which cash and other resources are received.

operating earnings before taxes: See *net earnings.*

operating expense
(1) *finance:* any expense incurred in the normal operation of a business. This is to be distinguished from expenditures, which are disbursements that are capitalized and depreciated over a period of years. See also *margin of profit.*
(2) *real estate:* the actual expense incurred in the maintenance of property (e.g., management, repairs, taxes, insurance). Not included as operating expenses are mortgage payments, depreciation, and interest paid out.

operating income
(1) *accounting:* income to a business produced by its earning assets and by fees for services rendered.
(2) *real estate:* rental monies obtained from the operation of a business or from property.

operating losses: losses incurred in the normal (i.e., nonnegligent) operation of a business.

operating management: the process of managing the implementation of programs and projects in each area of performance, measuring and evaluating results, and comparing results with objectives.

operating profit ratio: the ratio of a firm's operating profit to its net sales. See also *turnover ratio.*

operating statement: a statement for a store's management, providing net sales, costs, expenses, and the net operating profit or loss for a fixed period.

operation

(1) *general:* any process or action that is part of a series in work.

(2) *computers:* the act specified by a single computer instruction.

(3) *computer:* a defined action of obtaining a result from one or more operands in accordance with a rule that completely specifies the result for any permissible combination of operands.

operational analysis (OA): a form of industrial engineering that separates work into activities and designs the work flow to construct the most efficient scheduled sequence of output. Synonymous with *operations research;* cf. *MAPS.*

operational control: the influence of management on the inputs and activities in the daily performance of a firm.

operational plan: a short-range plan (less than one year) that relates to the scheduling of internal operations or processes.

operations budgeting: the setting of immediate goals for sales, production, expenses, costs, and the availability of cash.

operations management: an area that takes into account the design, operations, and control of organizational systems. It is heavily concerned with such functions as work flow, production planning, purchasing, materials requirements, inventory control, and quality control.

operations research (OR): the application of scientific methods, techniques, and tools to problems involving the operation of a system, to provide those in control of the system with optimum solutions to the problems. See also *cost-benefit analysis;* cf. *organizational analysis and planning;* synonymous with *operations analysis.*

Operation Twist (Nudge): an attempt in 1961 by the Federal Reserve and the U.S. Treasury to raise short-term interest rates relative to long-term rates to harmonize domestic and foreign objectives. Bank time deposit interest rates were increased, and funds were redirected from short- to long-term goals.

operative: a rank-and-file worker in an organization.

operative personnel: workers at the lower end of the organizational hierarchy who have no subordinates to supervise.

OPIC: See *Overseas Private Investment Corporation.*

opinion leader: a member of an organization who, because of ability, power, access to information, or prestige, can influence the attitudes, opinions, or behavior of those around him or her. See also *central person, charismatic leadership, informal leader.*

OPM

(1) *general:* operations per minute.

(2) *finance:* other people's money.

opportunity cost: a maximum alternative profit that could have been obtained if the productive good, service, or capacity had been applied to some other use.

opportunity cost of capital: the expected rate of return from employing funds effectively in the company.

optical character recognition (OCR): machine identification of printed characters through use of light-sensitive devices. See also *flying spot scanner;* cf. *magnetic ink character recognition.*

optical reader: a device that interprets handwritten or machine-printed symbols into a computing system.

optical scanner: a device that scans optically and usually generates an analog or digital signal. See also *flying spot scanner; machine, scanning.* cf. *Luhn scanner.*

optimization: combining elements in just the right balance, often to secure maximum profit.

optimum capacity: the quantity of output that permits the minimum cost per unit to be incurred.

option

(1) *real estate:* a privilege to buy, sell, receive, or deliver property, given in accordance with terms stated, with a consideration for price. This privilege may or may not be exercised at the option holder's discretion. Failure to exercise the option leads to forfeiture.

(2) *securities:* an agreement, often for a consideration, to buy or sell a security or commodity within a stipulated time in accordance with the agreement. See also *puts and calls;* cf. *covered option, straddle.*

(3) *insurance:* the right of an insured or a beneficiary to select the form of payment of the proceeds of an insurance contract.

optional bond: See *bond, callable.*

optional consumption: the buying of items and services that are not required for daily fulfillment and well-being. See also *luxuries;* cf. *con-*sumption possibility frontier.*

optional dividend: a stockholder's right to choose either a stock dividend or a cash dividend.

optional valuation date: the date on which the size of an individual's estate is computed for purposes of tax payment. It can be set at the date of death or as of six months following death, provided that the assets are not disposed of in the interim.

optionee

(1) *general:* the holder of an option.

(2) *real estate:* a prospective tenant or buyer.

optioner: a property owner; a seller or landlord.

option spreading: simultaneous purchase and sale of options within the same class. The options may be either at the same striking prices with different expiration months, or at different striking prices with the same or different expiration months. The spread is the dollar difference between the buy and sell premiums.

OR: See *operations research.*

oral will: See *nuncupative will.*

order

(1) *general:* a request to deliver, sell, receive, or purchase goods or services.

(2) *administration:* a command or decree.

(3) *finance:* identifying the one to whom payment should be made (e.g., "made to the order of . . .").

(4) *securities:* a request to buy or sell. See also *buy, day order, limited order, negotiation, open order, stop order.*

order-filling cost: a marketing cost incurred in storing, packing, shipping, biling, credit and collection, and other similar aspects of selling merchandise.

order-getting cost: a marketing cost incurred in an effort to attain a desired sales volume and mix.

ordering cost: a major cost component that is considered in inventory control decisions. Each time the firm orders items for inventory, it must formally contact the supplier, which usually involves some clerical and administrative work. Labor is also used in placing the order and putting the items in inventory. The clerical, administrative, and labor costs make up the ordering cost element in inventory control models.

orders

(1) *general:* requests made for the delivery of goods or services.

(2) *securities:* instructions to a broker to buy or sell shares.

orders good until a specified time: a market or limited price order that is to be represented in the trading crowd until a specified time, after which such order or the portion not executed is to be treated as canceled. Cf. *good 'til canceled order.*

ordinance: the legislative act of a city.

ordinary annuity: a series of equal amounts to be received or paid at the end of equally spaced time intervals.

ordinary income: in income tax filing, reportable income that does not qualify as capital gains.

ordinary interest: interest that is calculated based on 360 days to the year.

ordinary life: a type of insurance policy that continues in force throughout the policyholder's lifetime and is payable on his death or when he attains a specified age. Synonymous with *straight life, whole life.*

ordinary stock: common or equity stock.

organic structure: an organization design characterized by a decentralized hierarchy, flexible work procedures, and democratic leadership, with informal and open communications. See also *human relations theory, job enrichment;* cf. *classical design theory; organization, formal; Theory X and Theory Y.*

organization: any structured system of roles and functional relationships designed to carry out a firm's policies or, more precisely, the programs such policies inspire.

organization, formal: a highly structured organization with little flexibility in the delegation of authority and assignment of tasks and responsibilities. See also *unilateral strategy, vertical strain.*

organization, informal: a flexibly structured organization, free of rigid rules for activity and authority. Synonymous with *organic structure.*

organizational analysis and planning: the study of the objectives, the surroundings, and the human, physical, and financial assets of a business, to determine the most effective design for utilizing ideas and power generated by the firm's ultimate authority for accomplishment of its stated goals. Cf. *situational design theory, universal design theory.*

organizational change: the intentional attempt by management to improve the overall performance of individuals, groups, and the organization by altering the organization's structure, behavior, and technology.

organizational chart: a graphic presentation of the relationships and interrelationships within an organization, identifying lines of authority and responsibility. See also *span of control.*

organizational climate: a set of properties of the work environment perceived by employees and assumed to be a major factor in influencing their behavior. Cf. *dissatisfiers, morale, satisfiers.*

organizational development (OD): a planned process of reeducation and training designed by administrative personnel to facilitate adaptation to demands placed on the environment of the company. See also *multiple management, unilateral strategy.*

organizational effectiveness: the degree to which an organization attains its objectives and goals.

organizational efficiency: a measure of the amount of resources used by an organization to produce a unit of output.

organizational goal: an end or a state of affairs that an organization seeks to reach.

organizational level: the middle level of a company, concerned with coordinating and integrating work performance at the technical level.

organizational managers: middle-level managers whose goal is to coordinate the technical and institutional levels of the firm in some harmonious fashion and who tend to assume a political or mediating viewpoint.

organizational mirror: an organization development technique in which each group takes its turn at being critiqued by other groups. The goal is to improve intergroup relations.

organizational multiplier: the factor by which a primary change in a particular sector of an organization is multiplied to determine the total change in the whole organization.

organizational norm: an organization's expression of what it considers the proper way of behaving or the proper code of conduct.

organizational picketing: See *picketing.*

organizational system: a system composed of human beings, money, materials, equipment, and so on, that are related in the accomplishment of some goal or goals.

organization budget: a budget system based on establishing subsidiary budgets or cost limitations for each unit of the organization.

organization character: the product of all an organization's features, such as its people, objectives, technology, size, age, unions, policies, successes, and failures.

organization expense: direct costs of forming a new corporation (incorporation fees, taxes, legal fees, etc.).

Organization for Economic Cooperation and Development (OECD): created in 1948, an organization of 17 European nations (including the German Federal Republic), known until 1960 as the Organization for European Economic Cooperation (OEEC). Initially, OEEC developed and implemented economic recovery programs following World War II. It was enlarged to 21 members, including the United States, Canada, and Japan, with the change of its name to OECD. Headquartered in Paris, it promotes the economic growth of member nations, the expansion of world investment and trade, and the economic development of emerging countries.

Organization for European Economic Cooperation (OEEC):   See *Organization for Economic Cooperation and Development.*

Organization of Petroleum Exporting Countries (OPEC):   a group comprising 13 members, concentrated in the Middle East but also including countries in Africa, South America, and the Far East.   By virtue of their large exports, Saudi Arabia and Iran have been the most powerful influences.   See also *petrodollars.*

organization structure: the formally defined framework of an organization's task and authority relationships.   The organization structure is analogous to the biological function of the skeleton.

organized labor: union labor, collectively or with respect to individual shops.

organizer: a union employee whose primary task is to recruit nonunion workers for membership in the union.

organizing function: the managerial activity involved with creating a formal structure of tasks and authority.

orgman: shortened term for "organization man."

orientation programs: programs that familiarize new workers with their roles, the organization, its policies, and other employees.

origination fee: a charge made for initiating and processing a mortgage loan.

OS: operating system.

oscillation

(1) *systems:*   fluctuations of a system's output in excess of the allowa-

ble variations.

(2) *administration:*   inability to make a decision or resolve a conflict.

OS&D: See *over, short, amd damaged.*

OSHA: See *Occupational Safety and Health Act of 1970.*

OTC: See *over-the-counter securities.*

other-insurance clause: a provision in almost every insurance policy stating what is to be done at the time of loss in case any other contract of insurance protection includes the same property and perils.   Cf. *double insurance.*

other-shoe syndrome: a fear that once management begins to dismiss personnel, morale and job satisfaction will decline in anticipation of a further decrease in manpower.

outbid: to offer a higher price for an item than that offered by other bidders.

outcry market: commodity tradings, by private contract, that must be shouted out, as on the floor of an exchange, for the agreement to be recorded.   Synonymous with *open outcry.*

outgo: any expense or other cost in running a business.

outlaw strike: See *strike.*

outlay: any expenditure.

outlay costs: the actual cash outflows directly associated with the production and transfer of goods or services.

out-of-pocket expense: a cost incurred by an individual, often when on a business trip.   The item or service is paid for in cash or by check or charge account, and the employee expects reimbursement from the company.

out of stock: describing goods that are not in the store when requested by a customer.

out-of-the-money: a call option in which the striking price is above the market price of the underlying stock.

out-of-work benefits: payments by a union to unemployed members. Cf. *strike benefits, strike pay.*

outplace: to assist an employee who is about to be fired by sending him or her to an agency or organization that specializes in helping such people find new employment.

output

(1) *manufacturing:* the quantity yielded in any operation.

(2) *computers:* information transferred from the internal storage of a computer to output devices or external storage.

(3) *economics:* the average dollar gross domestic product produced in a stated period.

output block: a segment of the internal storage reserved for output data.

output gap: the difference between actual and potential output.

outside dimensions (OD): the outer measurements of a container, a package, or any of its parts.

outside-inside approach: a strategy approach whereby managers look first at the environment and then at the organization. Cf. *inside-outside approach.*

outside market: an over-the-counter market or a market in which unlisted securities are handled.

outsiders:

(1) *labor relations:* a term applied by employers, usually in counteracting unionization, to union organizers

from another town. As interpreted by labor, it applies to nonunion members.

(2) *securities:* the general investing public.

outstanding

(1) *business:* describing any unpaid or uncollected debt.

(2) *securities:* describing stock in the hands of stockholders, as distinguished from stock that has not yet been issued or, if issued, has not been released by the corporation. Cf. *absorbed.*

outtakes: known information that is deleted from a presentation to workers, the board of directors, or other groups.

overage

(1) *general:* items additional to those shown on a bill of lading.

(2) *government:* the situation created by a spending program that exceeds a specified budget target during a specified time period. See also *shortfall.*

overall market capability: the quantity of an item or service that is absorbed, in the general market without allowing for price or market considerations. For example, the overall market capability for television sets includes everyone who owns a television and everyone who would like to own a television but hasn't purchased one to date. Cf. *potential demand, potential market saturation.*

overall performance ratio: a measure of overall performance, including management of operations, use of assets, and management of debt and equity, computed by dividing net income by average stockholders' equity.

overapplied overhead: the excess of the amount of overhead cost applied to a product over the amount of overhead cost incurred.

overbought: reflecting an opinion about price levels of a security that has had a sharp rise or of the market as a whole after a period of vigorous buying, which some are arguing has left prices too high. See also *normative economics.*

overcapitalize

(1) *general:* to provide an excessive amount of capital to a business. See also *capitalize, watered stock.*

(2) *real estate:* to set too high a value on property.

(3) *finance:* to place too high a value on the nominal capital of a company.

overdraft: a check drawn for more than the drawee's balance on deposit with a bank. The bank can return the check (the overdraft) either to the bank from which it came or to the person who presented it for payment, marked "insufficient funds." The bank can also elect to render the customer a service and pay the check.

overdraw: to write a bank check for an amount exceeding the deposit in the bank on which the check is drawn. See also *cushion checking, kite (kiting).*

overdue: describing a payment that has not been made at the time it was due.

overextension

(1) *finance:* credit received or extended beyond the debtor's ability to pay.

(2) *securities:* the condition of a dealer in securities who becomes obligated for an amount beyond his or her borrowing power or ability to pay.

(3) *administration:* the expansion by a business concern of buildings, equipment, and so on, in excess of the company's present or prospective future needs.

overfinancing: the result of an investment that does not produce a positive cash flow after amortization or that finances a property for more than its value.

overflow

(1) *computers:* the portion of the result of an operation that exceeds the capacity of the intended unit of storage.

(2) *accounting:* the generation of a quantity beyond the capacity of the register.

overhead: a general term for costs of materals and services not directly adding to or readily identifiable with the product or service of the entity. See also *conversion costs;* cf. *direct overhead, factory overhead.*

overhead application rate: the rate at which estimated overhead costs are assigned to products throughout the year. It is calculated as total estimated overhead costs divided by a suitable allocation base, such as direct-labor hours, direct materials used, or direct-labor costs.

overheating: excessive price or money activity that some economists believe will lead to inflation.

overinsurance: insurance against property loss or damage that is in excess of the possible amount of damage or loss.

overinvestment theory: a business cycle concept stating that economic variations are a function of too much investment in the economy as business people try to measure increasing demands during an upswing, and of major cutbacks in investment during a downswing when they realize that they expanded too much during the previous prosperity.

overissue: the release of stock in excess of the authorized or ordered amount. See also *registrar, undigested securities.*

overlay

(1) *computers:* the technique of repeatedly using the same blocks of internal storage during different stages of a program.

(2) *computers:* a program segment or phase that is loaded into main storage.

(3) *advertising:* a transparent flap over art work to allow writing of instructions or corrections or to indicate color breaks.

overline: an amount of liability larger than the amount an insurance company wishes to underwrite. See also *referral risks.*

overlying bond: See *bond, overlying.*

overlying mortgage: a junior mortgage that is subject to the claim of a senior mortgage, which has a prior claim to the junior mortgage. Cf. *equal dignity.*

overmanning: using more workers in an operation than are required for an efficient activity. Cf. *featherbedding.*

overnight: (slang) any task that can be planned one day and carried out the next. It is often an unimportant event.

overnight multiple: the anticipated impact of a public offering on the holdings of insiders. It usually multiplies the value of the offering signifi-

cantly.

over on bill: additional freight described on the bill of lading.

over (or short): the difference between established sales statements and the actual audited figure. This discrepancy is often a result of errors in making change or missing sales checks.

overproduction: producing more than can be sold at any price or at a profitable price. See also *Say's law.*

overproduction theory: the idea that an excessive expansion of productive capacity occurs whenever demand increases. Cf. *underconsumption theory.*

overpunch: to add holes, usually control punches, in a card column that already contains one or more holes.

overqualification: having more skills or aptitude than are required to perform a task or hold a position.

override: a commission paid to managers that is added to their salary.

overrun: the number of pieces of printed advertising in excess of the specified quantity. A 10 percent overrun is usually acceptable at pro rata cost.

oversaving: the condition that exists when planned saving exceeds planned investment. The quantity of cash removed from income movement thus exceeds the amount returned to it, resulting in the decline of income. Cf. *marginal propensity to invest, saving.*

Overseas Private Investment Corporation (OPIC): a federal agency that insures U.S. companies against seizure of their overseas property by foreign governments, damage to property from acts of war, or conditions under which they are unable to take their profits out of the foreign country. See also *nationalization, seizure.*

over, short, and damaged (OS&D): the discrepancy between the amount and/or condition of cargo on hand and that shown on the bill. Cf. *clean bill of lading.*

oversold

(1) *general:* the situation of a manufacturer who has become obligated to deliver more than he or she is able to supply within the stated period.

(2) *securities:* referring to an opinion that a single security or a market is believed to have declined to an unreasonable level. See also *normative economics.*

oversubscribed: a situation in which, for a given issue of shares, more orders have been received than can be filled. Cf. *undigested securities.*

over-the-counter (OTC) securities: securities that are not listed or traded on any of the regular exchanges. Such securities are traded through dealers in unlisted stocks. Sales or purchases are arranged by these dealers or through a chain of them until the desired securities and prices are obtained. Members of regular stock exchanges also handle trades in unlisted securities, but not through the exchange. See also *National Association of Securities Dealers Automated Quotations, third market;* cf.

off-board; synonymous with "unlisted securities."

overtime: hours worked by an employee beyond the standard hours agreed to in the contract. Hours in excess are paid in penalty or at overtime rates, which frequently is 1.5 times the normal rate.

overtrading: the activity of a firm that, even with high profitability, cannot pay its own way for lack of working capital and thus finds itself in a liquidity crisis.

over without bill: freight without its bill of lading.

overwork: mental and physical thresholds reached after excessive hours of work or other working conditions demanded by the job.

owe: to be obliged to pay something to someone for something received. An indebtedness results.

own brand: an item bearing the name or brand of the store selling the item rather than the name of the producer.

owner: a person who possesses title to property.

owner-operator: a regular driver who owns equipment and is a subcontractor to a carrier on a long-term basis.

owner's equity: the ownership interest in the assets of an enterprise. It equals net assets. Synonymous with *stockholders' equity.*

ownership: possession of a legal title with the rights to enjoy the benefits derived from any assets accompanying or accruing from such title.

pacers: fast-working employees, identified by management, who are used to establish the pace of expected work for others. See also *normal time, time standard.*

pace setter: a speedy, skilled employee whose output in a given period sets the basis on which piecework rates are determined for other workers doing similar work.

pack
(1) *computers:* to combine several fields, usually into one computer word.
(2) *merchandising:* to add to the total cost of merchandise charges for items not included or inflated charges; to give an undeserved discount without lowering the actual price.

package
(1) *labor relations:* the total gains, including fringe benefits, that result from collective bargaining.
(2) *merchandising:* any container or wrapping in which goods are placed for shipping or carrying.

package, primary: a container (can, bottle, box, etc.) that directly holds the product for sale.

package, program: a group of logically related operational program segments.

package engineering: a discipline of scientific and engineering principles applied to solving problems of functional design, formation, filling, closing, and/or preparation for shipment of containers, regardless of the type of product enclosed.

package mortgage: a home-financing mortgage that covers appliances and other household items (e.g., air conditioners, refrigerators, dryers).

package policies: combination insurance policies in which several coverages are included in one contract.

packaging: the preparation of merchandise for shipping and marketing.

packaging, materials handling: the coordination and integration of all activities and equipment needed to package a unit and deliver it to the consumer. The cycle commences with the fabrication of a container or packaging material and includes the placement of the product in its container but not the handling of the product before delivery to the packaging line.

packaging wants: the variable addressed in the attempt to impart the subconscious feeling that an item will satisfy basic psychological wants other than the obvious needs for which it was produced.

pact: Synonymous with *agreement, collective-bargaining.*

paging: identification of a computer program and data in fixed blocks, to permit transfers between disk and core to take place in storage systems.

paid-in capital: capital contributed by stockholders and assigned to accounts other than capital stock.

paid-in surplus: excesses of a business arising from sources other than profits; the surplus from the sale of capital stock at a premium.

paid-up insurance: a policy on which no further premium payments need to be made; the insurance company will be held liable for any benefits claimed under terms of the contract.

paid-up stock: capital stock on which the initial buyer has paid, in services, goods, or funds, an amount at least equal to the par value.

painting the bus: (slang) altering the appearance of a presentation, proposal, or idea without changing any of the basics. See also *window dressing.*

pallet: a portable platform for retaining material while in storage or shipment. Cf. *dolly.*

panic: a sudden, spreading fear of the collapse of business or the nation's economy, resulting in widespread withdrawal of bank deposits, stock sales, and similar transactions. A depression may but does not always follow a panic.

paper: a loan contract.

paperboard: board made of matted or felted fibrous material that is more than 0.012 inch (12 points) thick.

paperless item processing system (PIPS): an electronic funds-transit system that is capable of performing transit functions by establishing accounting transactions by which bank funds are shifted from one ledger or subledger to another.

paper local: a local union that has a charter but no members. It cooperates with an employer to freeze out legitimate efforts to organize the workers through coercion of employees, kickbacks of union dues to the employer, and other outlawed methods. Paper locals are denounced by the AFL–CIO in its Code of Ethical Practices.

paper money: currency on which a value is printed. Unlike coins, the bills have no value in themselves but usually represent bullion held in government vaults. Cf. *fiat money.*

paper profit: an unrealized profit on a security still held. A paper profit becomes a realized profit only when the security is sold. See also *short sale.*

paper standard: a monetary system based on paper money that is not convertible into gold or any other item of intrinsic value.

paper tape, punched: plastic or paper material from 300 to 1000 feet long on which data are recorded by punching holes.

paper title: a written document that appears to convey proof of ownership but may not in fact show proper title. Cf. *cloud on title.*

paper truncation: the act terminating the flow of paper in a transaction-processing system.

papoose: (slang) a nonunion employee who works with union employees.

par: describing the exchangeable value of an instrument when it is equal to that expressed on the face of the instrument, without consideration of any premium or discount. See also *face value.*

paradox of thrift: a concept of John Maynard Keynes that any effort by society to raise its savings rate can lead to a reduction in the amount it really can save.

parallel computer: a computer having multiple arithmetic or logic units that are used to accomplish parallel operations or parallel processing.

parallel standard: a monetary standard whereby two or more metals are coined and authorized unconditionally as legal tender. Cf. *bimetallism.*

parameter
(1) *general:* a quantity to which arbitrary values may be assigned; used in subroutines and generators to specify item size, decimal point, sign position, and so on.
(2) *statistics:* a variable that is given a constant value for a specific purpose or process.
(3) *system:* a definable characteristic of an item, device, or system.

paramount title: the foremost title; a title that is superior to all others. It is often the original title, which is used to prepare later ones.

parent company: a controlling organization that owns or manages business properties. Synonymous with *proprietary company.*

parent ego state: an ego state consisting of the supervisory attitudes and behaviors that children perceive in their parents and later replicate in supervisory situations.

Pareto optimality: distribution of resources that will make at least one person better off and no one else worse off. Synonymous with *economic efficiency.*

Pareto's law: the theory of Vilfredo Pareto, Italian sociologist and economist, that income tends to become distributed in the same proportion among consumers throughout the world, regardless of differing forms of taxation.

par exchange rate: the free market price of one country's money in terms of another country's currency.

pari delicto: fault or blame that is equally shared.

par item: any item that can be collected at its par or face value upon presentation.

parity
(1) *securities:* the state or quality of being equal or equivalent; equivalence of a commodity price expressed in one currency to its price expressed in another.
(2) *securities:* equality of purchasing power established by law between different kinds of money at a given ratio.
(3) *personnel:* the equivalence established between the wage schedules of some categories of employees. It is usually used in the public sector to describe the percentage

ratio maintained between the salaries of police and firemen.

(4) *government:* a farm policy established to keep the purchasing power of a unit of farm output equal to the purchasing power of the units of production bought by a farmer in the same ratio that existed during a chosen period. See also *farm subsidies, parity ratio;* cf. *Brannan plan.*

parity clause: a mortgage clause by virtue of which all notes obtained by the mortgage have equal dignity; that is, none has priority.

parity principle: the concept that the amount of authority that rests with an individual should be equal to the employee's responsibility.

parity ratio: a measurement of the extent to which prices farmers receive for farm products are on the average higher or lower in relation to the prices they paid for goods and services from 1910-1914.

parity value for currency: the official exchange rate of a currency. When exchange rates are fixed, monetary authorities are required to purchase and sell other currencies in money markets as necessary to preserve parity. See also *parity.*

Parkinson's laws: as developed by C. Northcote Parkinson, laws stating that (1) work invariably expands to fill the time available for its completion, and (2) expenditures climb to reach income. See also *law of triviality.*

par list: a Federal Reserve System list of banks that will remit in full for items that are payable to the system.

par of exchange: the market price of money in one national currency that is exchanged at the official rate for a specific amount in another national currency or for another commodity of value (gold, silver, etc.).

parsimony, principle of: the principle of scientific thinking whereby the simpler of two hypotheses is to be preferred. Synonymous with *Occam's razor.*

partial equilibrium analysis: an inquiry that looks at only one market of an economy under the assumption that solutions in other markets will not be altered by a change in the market examined.

partial loss: a loss that does not completely destroy or render useless the insured property nor exhaust the insurance applied to it.

partial monopoly: a situation that exists when there are so few sellers of an item or service that each may alter the price and market. Cf. *perfect (pure) monopoly.*

partial payment: a payment that is not equal to the full amount owed and is not intended to constitute the full payment.

participating bond: See *bond, participating.*

participating-dividend performance: the right of preferred shareholders to receive equal distributions of dividends on a proportionate basis with common shareholders.

participating insurance: insurance or reinsurance that contributes proportionately with other insurance on the same risk.

participating preferred: describing a preferred stock that is entitled to its stated dividend and also to additional dividends on a specified basis (i.e., with respect to the plan participated in) on payment of dividends on the common stock.

participation loan: a loan having two or more banks as creditors. Laws prohibit banks from lending more than a fixed percentage of their capital and surplus to any one borrower. Thus banks invite other banks to participate in making large loans.

participative-democratic leadership style: a basic leadership style in which management has complete confidence and trust in the subordinates and in which decision making is highly decentralized.

particular average: damage or loss less than the total value; partial loss. Cf. *incurably depreciated.*

particular lien: a right to keep something valuable that belongs to another person as compensation for labor, supplies, or money spent in his or her behalf. Synonymous with *special lien;* cf. *factor's lien, general lien, mechanic's lien;* see also *voluntary conveyance or deed.*

partnership: a contractual relationship between two or more people in a joint enterprise who agree to share, not necessarily equally, in the profits and losses of the organization. Cf. *joint venture.*

part-time employees: workers who work less than a full day or full week.

party at interest: an individual or group of individuals that has a vested interest in a commercial enterprise.

par value: face value. The par value of stocks on the date of issuance is the principal.

pass: one cycle of processing a body of data.

passbook: a book record prepared by a bank for a depositor, listing date and amount of deposits, with an initial or an identifying symbol indicating the teller who received the deposit. For savings accounts, the passbook lists deposits, withdrawals, interest paid by the bank, dates of all transactions, each new balance, and the initial or identifying symbol of the teller handling each transaction. The passbook also shows the depositor's name or names and account number. Cf. *no-passbook savings.*

passed dividend: a regular or scheduled dividend that has been omitted.

passing title: the handing over of title to a new owner. Synonymous with *closing title.*

passive bond: See *bond, passive.*

passive trade balance: an unfavorable balance of trade.

passive trust: a trust whose trustee has no tasks to perform but merely retains title to the trust property.

pass-through: the tax advantage of a limited partnership, which permits income, profit, loss, and deductions to pass through the legal structure for the benefit of the individuals involved in the partnership rather than their organization. Synonymous with *flow-through.*

password

(1) *computers:* a unique string of characters that a program, computer operator, or user must supply to meet security requirements before gaining access to data.

(2) *computers:* in time sharing, a one- to eight-character symbol that the user may be required to supply for purposes of security at the time he or she logs on the system.

past-due item: any note, acceptance, or other time instrument of indebtedness that has not been paid on the due date.

patch

(1) *general:* to settle; to bring to an end (e.g., to patch up a quarrel).

(2) *computers:* to modify a routine in a rough or expedient way.

patent: a government grant to an inventor to protect the results of an invention.

patent ambiguity: an unclear statement in a written document that becomes clear upon rereading.

patent applied for: a form showing the actual application by an inventor for a U.S. patent. The inventor or, if he or she is dead, the administrator of the estate must apply for the patent. The application must contain a written description of the invention, a drawing, an oath of inventorship, and a government filing fee. See also *patent pending.*

patent monopoly: an organization that holds a monopoly after the government has conferred on it the exclusive right, by way of a patent, to manufacture, use, or sell its own innovation.

patent pending: after filing for a patent, the Patent Office's statement that a search is being conducted in the United States and other countries to determine whether the invention is in fact new and patentable under the law. Should the patent be rejected, an appeal is permitted in the patent office and, if necessary, in the federal courts. See also *patent applied for.*

paternal, aggressive company: an organization that aggressively attempts to achieve various objectives and liberally rewards good performance. Cf. *impersonal, aggressive management.*

paternal, passive company: an or-

ganization that does not aggressively pursue various objectives and treats its workers in a rather protective manner. Cf. *impersonal, passive management.*

paternalism: a term used in a negative sense to describe the "fatherly" interest of an employer in "his" workers.

path: the sequence of events and activities that should be followed over the course of a project.

path-goal theory of leadership: a leadership theory that views the leader's function as clarifying the subordinates' paths to work-goal attainment and increasing their opportunities for personal satisfaction.

patronage motives: the reasons that customers shop in a particular retail outlet.

patronize: to frequent a store; to be a regular customer.

pattern bargaining: See *multiemployer bargaining.*

patternitis: the assumption that wage settlements in an industry should follow the pattern of settlement negotiated by any one of the companies in that industry.

pauper: an individual who is totally dependent on public funds for subsistence.

pawn

(1) *finance:* the pledge to pay a debt.

(2) *administration:* an individual who is easily manipulated by another.

payback period: the period of time that passes before the incoming cash equals the outgoing cash on a specific project, order, or other effort.

pay dues: (slang) to take on menial tasks while working one's way toward a specific opportunity.

payee: the legal entity named in an instrument as the recipient of the amount shown on the instrument.

payer: the party primarily responsible for payment of an amount owed, as evidenced by a negotiable instrument.

pay grade: a number of similar jobs grouped together to simplify the job-pricing process.

payload: the real or potential revenue-producing portion of an airplane's takeoff weight (passengers, cargo, mail, etc.).

payment date: the date on which dividends are paid by a corporation to its shareholders.

payment for honor: payment of a bill by someone other than the one on whom it is drawn when the latter has defaulted, to save the reputation or credit of the original drawee.

payments deficit: the excess of the value of a nation's imports over its exports.

payments surplus: the excess of the value of a nation's exports over its imports.

payments system: an approach (involving people, machines, and procedures) used to transfer value from one party to another.

payoff
(1) *finance:* money given for an unethical or illegal service.
(2) *systems:* the result of a decision problem transformed to represent its true utility to the decision maker.

payoff table: a convenient statistical tool showing the total of the expected values of a number of expected acts in the light of the varying probabilities of the events that may take place and the changing values of each act under each of the events.

payola: (slang) a gift or other valuable item offered to people who have the potential for using their influence in the promotion or sale of a product or service.

payout plan: a projection into the future that shows funds available, funds spent, and the resulting economic profit for a proposed marketing program.

pay range: a range of minimum and maximum wage rates, with enough variance between the two to allow some significant pay differences and to reflect such concerns as seniority and/or productivity.

payroll
(1) *personnel:* the wages or salary earned by a firm's employees for a certain period of time. Various deductions for withholding tax, health benefits insurance, and so on, are identified on the employee's record affixed to the payroll check.
(2) *administration:* a list of employees receiving pay during a wage period.

payroll deductions: sums withheld from an employee's gross pay for federal and state income taxes, social security, or other governmental levies. They may include, on authorization of employees, deductions for union dues and assessments, premiums for group insurance, contributions to pension plans, and so on.

payroll tax: a tax used to finance an employer's contribution to the social security program; a tax levied on a company's payroll. See also *Federal Insurance Contributions Act.*

pay secrecy: a management policy of maintaining silence or secrecy about individual employee salaries.

p/e: See *price-earnings ratio.*

peak: an exceptionally busy period in a business.

peak capacity: the sum of employee productivity, working at the fastest speed and with no regard for efficiency. The primary consideration is output rather than quality. Cf. *ideal capacity, practical capacity, production capacity.*

peak season: the period of days or months in which an item is in greatest customer demand (e.g., charcoal for barbecuing during the summer months).

peculation: the embezzlement of funds or goods, especially public funds or goods, by an individual in whose care they have been entrusted. Cf. *defalcation.*

pecuniary exchange: any trade that uses money.

peddler: a person who travels and sells small quantities of merchandise.

peddler rail car: a car used for less-than-carload shipments from one consignor over a described route. The goods are delivered at stations along the route, directly from the rail car to the consignees.

peek-a-boo: (slang) the method of checking for the presence or absence of punched holes in identical locations on cards by setting one card on top of another.

peg (pegging): to fix or stabilize the price of something (e.g., stock, currency, commodity) by manipulating or regulating the market. For example, the government may peg the price of gold by purchasing all that is available at a stated price. See also *adjustable peg, crawling peg.*

peg point: the pay rate for a major task that becomes the base from which rates of pay for other related tasks are derived.

penal bond: See *bond, penal.*

penalty: see *liquidated damages.*

pencil pusher: (slang) an office worker.

pendente lite: pending during the progress of a suit at law. See also *lis pendens.*

penetration pricing: an approach in which the price of an item is set low in order to enter the market quickly.

penny stocks: low-priced issues, often highly speculative, that sell at less than $1 a share. This is frequently a term of disparagement, although a few penny stocks have developed into investment-caliber issues.

Pension Benefit Guaranty Corporation: See *Employee Retirement Income Security Act.*

pension plan: a method used by a firm or union to pay annuities or pensions to retired and/or disabled employees. Sections 401 and 404 of the Internal Revenue Code identify conditions enabling an organization to establish a pension plan. See also *Employee Retirement Income Security Act, trust agreement.*

peon: a common laborer or a person who performs work that is primarily unskilled.

peonage: forced labor performance in payment of a debt, as controlled by either law or contract. The Thirteenth Amendment to the U.S. Constitution prohibits slavery and involuntary servitude as such.

people plucker: (slang) an executive

recruiter. Synonymous with *head-hunter.*

people's capitalism: the full range of the income levels in the population of a community being represented in the ownership of the business.

per annum: by the year.

per capita income: total income divided by the number of individuals. Per capita income can be adjusted to reflect changes in prices or purchasing power over a stated time period to show real per capita income.

per capita output: the gross national product of a nation divided by its population. This is often used to identify a country's standard of living.

per capita tax

(1) *general:* a tax based on the result of dividing stated sums of money by a specified number of people to show the amount to be paid by each person.

(2) *labor relations:* a stated periodic payment by a union, on the basis of membership, to a parent union or to local, district, and state councils. It is also the amount paid by a national union to a federation or other affiliate body.

perceived equitable rewards: the rewards people feel they should receive as the result of their performance.

perceived risk: the hazards a customer believes to be related to the buying of a specific item (e.g., difficulty of obtaining servicing, cost of servicing, lifetime of the item, obsolescence of the item).

percentage of sales method: a method of setting a marketing budget based on a forecast of sales.

percentage order: either a market or limited price order to buy (or sell) a stated amount of a specified stock after a fixed number of shares of such stock have traded.

percentile: one of the 99 point scores that divide a ranked distribution into groups or parts, each of which contains 1/100 of the scores or persons. The points are located to coincide with the obtained score below which, in each division, 1/100 of the cases fall. Scores are numbered from 1 to 99. Cf. *quartile deviation.*

per centum: by the hundred.

perception: a process by which individuals attend to incoming stimuli and translate such stimuli into a message indicating the appropriate response.

per contra item: a balance in one account that is offset by a balance from another account.

per curiam: a full court's decision (e.g., to remand) when no opinion is given.

per diem: for each day.

perfect competition: a description for an industry or market unit consisting of a large number of purchasers and sellers, all involved in the buying and selling of a homogeneous good, with awareness of prices and volume, no discrimination in buying and selling, and a mobility of resources.

perfect (pure) monopoly: a situation in which one person or organization has total control over the manufacture and marketing of an item. See *monopoly, oligopoly.*

perfect title

(1) *business law:* a title that is not open to dispute or challenge because it is complete in every detail and has no legal defects. See also

marketable title, muniment of title, quiet title suit, warranty deed; cf. *cloud on title.*

(2) *real estate:* property displaying total right of ownership.

performance: what a person does when faced with a task.

performance appraisal: a methodical review of an employee's performance on the job to evaluate the effectiveness or adequacy of the person's work.

performance bond: See *bond, performance.*

performance budgeting: grouping of budget accounts into categories related to a specific product or service that is produced, and evolution of product-cost measurements of these activities.

performance gap: the difference between the predicted or expected level of performance and the actual level.

performance report: a comparison of actual results against those anticipated in a stated budget.

performance test: a test devised to identify the potential abilities, skill, and knowledge of workers by measuring their behavior reactions while performing actual, on-the-job activities or operations of a manual or physical nature.

peril: the cause of a loss insured against in a policy (e.g., fire, windstorm, explosion).

peril point: the greatest reduction in U.S. import duty that could be made for a stated item without creating a major hardship to domestic manufacturers or to makers of a closely related item.

period cost: Synonymous with *fixed cost.*

period expense: an expenditure that cannot be associated with or assigned to a product and so is reported as an expense in the period in which it is incurred. Cf. *product costing.*

periodic stock control: a unit control system in which stock is identified and recorded periodically and sales for intervening time slots are calculated. See *inventory control, out of stock.*

periodic tenancy: month-to-month tenancy without a written lease. Synonymous with *tenancy at will.*

period of digestion: a time immediately following the release of a new or large security offering during which sales are made primarily to regular investment customers.

peripheral equipment: any of the units of computer equipment, distinct from the central processing unit, that provide the system with outside communication. Not all systems have peripheral equipment. See also *auxiliary operation, radial transfer, spooling.*

perishable goods: items that are subject to rapid decay unless given proper storage (e.g., meat, dairy products). See also *cobweb chart.*

perjury: knowingly false testimony delivered under an oath that has been properly administered in a judicial proceeding.

perks: (slang) Synonymous with *perquisites.*

permanent accounts: Synonymous with *real accounts.*

permanent disability benefits: periodic compensation, usually weekly, for a disability that renders any employment impossible. Such compensation may be limited by a maximum time or a maximum amount. If unlimited, it may run for the lifetime of the insured.

permanent financing: a long-term mortgage that is amortized over 15, 20, or more years at a fixed rate of interest.

permanent income: a worker's average income level throughout his or her working life. Actual current income varies around this long-term expected average because of transitory changes in income due to overtime work or layoffs, for example.

permanent injunction: See *injunction.*

permissive leadership: leadership characterized by the attitude or practice of permitting or encouraging subordinates to solve or make decisions concerning work-related issues according to their own judgment. See also *democratic leadership.*

permit bond: See *bond, permit.*

permit mail: mail with printed indicia in lieu of stamps, indicating that, under the permit number shown, postage has been paid by the sender.

perpetual inventory: a book inventory identifying the stock on hand by means of a detailed record, enabling the firm to know the composition of its inventory at any point in time.

perpetual inventory control: a unit control system whereby orders, receipts, and sales are identified as they occur and inventory is computed.

perpetuity

(1) *finance:* describing removal of anything that is from the ordinary channel of commerce by limiting its capacity to be sold for a period longer than that of a life or lives in being and 21 years thereafter, plus the period of development. See also *consol, emphyteutic lease.*

(2) *real estate:* endlessness; the quality of going on forever (e.g., an estate willed in perpetuity).

perquisites: additional compensation furnished by management, usually in goods or services, over and above the general payment of wages. Synonymous with *perks.*

perseverance: the tendency to continue with an activity despite difficulties.

personal care items: hair dryers, electric shavers, toothbrushes, facial cosmetics, and the like.

personal check: a check drawn by someone as an individual (i.e., not acting as an employer or in a fiduciary capacity).

personal consumption expenditures: the funds spent by households for consumer items. Disposable personal income minus savings equals personal consumption expenditures.

personal data sheet: a questionnaire eliciting facts of any description concerning an individual.

personal distribution of income: the distribution of natural income among individuals or households.

personal finance company: a business that lends small sums of money to people, usually for personal needs, at relatively high interest rates. Most states require that these organizations be licensed.

personal income: national income less various kinds of income not actually received by individuals, nonprofit institutions, and so on (e.g., undistributed corporate profits, corporate taxes, employer contributions for social insurance), plus certain receipts that do not arise from production (i.e., transfer payments and government interest).

personal injury protection (PIP): the name usually given to no-fault automobile coverage.

personal installment loan: funds borrowed by an individual for personal needs that are repaid in regular monthly installments over a specified period.

personality rating (test): an instrument that assists in the evaluation of personality. Many of these instruments are more properly described as ratings of personal characteristics than as tests.

personal loan: a type of loan generally obtained by individual borrowers in small amounts, usually less than $1000. A personal loan is often secured for consolidating debts or paying taxes, insurance premiums, or hospital bills.

personal property: the rights, powers, and privileges an individual has in movable things, such as chattels and choses in possession.

personal saving: the difference between disposable personal income and personal consumption expenditures, including the changes in cash and deposits, security holdings, indebtedness, reserves of life insurance companies and mutual savings institutions, the net investment of unincorporated enterprises, and the acquisition of real property net of depreciation.

personal selling: a promotion method involving interpersonal communication between individuals; verbal presentation to a prospective customer for the purpose of making a sale.

personal space: the physical area surrounding an employee that is assigned to him or her for use in carrying out his or her work.

personnel: a major activity performed within organizations, which includes such functions as personnel planning, recruitment, selection, training and development, compensation, health and safety, employee and labor relations, and personnel research.

personnel administration: a well-planned, properly executed, and efficiently evaluated approach to manpower recruitment, screening, usage, and development. See also *process principles.*

personnel audit: an evaluation of the personnel activities in a company.

personnel demand analysis: a method of determining the number and type of employees required to achieve a firm's objectives. Synonymous with *workload analysis.*

personnel department: the department of an organization responsible for recruiting, hiring, testing, training, counseling, and promoting employees, as well as handling industrial relations and other functions dealing with employee activities, as stated by management.

personnel management: the study of how employers obtain, develop, utilize, evaluate, maintain, and retain the right numbers and types of workers.

personnel manager: a manager who normally acts in an advisory or staff capacity and is primarily responsible for coordinating a firm's human resources management activities.

personnel planning: the analysis of future personnel requirements for accomplishing a firm's objectives.

personnel psychology: a subdivision of applied psychology that treats an individual's psychological qualities in relation to his or her job. It deals with employment procedures, selection, placement, training, promotion, supervision, morale, and other personal aspects of job attitude and behavior.

persuasion: the act of influencing an individual or group to work for a desired objective.

PERT: See *program evaluation and review technique*.

PERT/COST: a modified PERT system that, in addition to time, deadlines, and schedules, includes all cost considerations.

Peter Principle: the dictum of Dr. Lawrence J. Peter that "in a hierarchy, every employee tends to rise to his level of incompetence."

petition in bankruptcy: the form used for declaring voluntary bankruptcy. See also *bankruptcy*.

petrodollars: huge sums of money from oil-producing nations other than the United States or Great Britain. These funds are initially converted into Eurocurrency and deposited with international banks to be used for future investment and for paying debts. These banks traditionally set limits on the sums they will accept from any one country. See also *Organization of Petroleum Exporting Countries*.

petty cash: See *imprest fund*.

phantom: (slang) an individual who is on a firm's payroll under an assumed name.

phantom freight: freight charges paid by the purchaser that were never absorbed by the seller.

phantom stock: in executive compensation programs, a number of shares of the company granted to an executive. Each share entitles the executive to the amount, if any, by which the market price of the stock at some future time exceeds the current market price.

phased retirement: a system whereby a person is gradually provided additional leisure time as he or she approaches the planned retirement age.

phase zero: the preliminary evaluation or study preceding the decision to go ahead with a project or strategy.

Phillips curve: a statistical technique whereby the relationship between inflation and unemployment is plotted in curvilinear form.

physical distribution: movement of merchandise from manufacturer to consumer.

physical hazard: characteristics of an insurance risk (e.g., material, structural, or operational).

physical inventory: inventory calculation obtained by making an actual listing of stock on hand.

physical product: the actual physical entity or service that is offered to consumers.

physical quantity budget: a budget expressed in physical units rather than dollar amounts (e.g., the number of labor hours needed for completion of a project).

picketing: publicizing the existence of a labor dispute by patrolling near the firm involved in the dispute. When large numbers of employees on strike assemble, it is called mass picketing. Organizational or recognition picketing (partially limited by the Taft-Hartley and Landrum-Griffin Acts) is an attempt by a union to force acceptance of the union by the employer or to convince unorganized workers to join the union. Cross picketing applies when there are two or more rival unions, each one claiming to represent the workers. Secondary picketing is picketing of locations that are not directly involved in the dispute. See also *chain picketing, consumer picketing, pink tea picketing, situs picketing.*

picosecond (psec): one-trillionth of a second; one-thousandth of a nanosecond.

pie-card: Synonymous with *labor skate.*

piece rate (wage): the amount of money received for each unit of output. When wages are so determined, an incentive wage system is in operation.

piece work: tasks performed for wages based on unit output. See also *pace setter.*

pig: (slang) a trailer moving on a rail car.

piggyback
(1) *transportation:* trailer trucks transported by railroad cars. Cf. *fishyback service.*
(2) *transportation:* to arrange vehicles for storage and shipment.

Pigou effect concept: the concept that a lowering of the overall price level creates higher consumption of time and services.

pilferage: taking of another's property while such goods are in transit or being stored. See also *inventory shortage.*

piloting: in inland waterways, navigation that employs bearings of landmarks, soundings, and the guidance of buoys and beacons.

pilot plant scale production: production of a modest number of units in small facilities designed to prove methods that may be used in full-scale plants.

PIMS: profit impact of marketing strategy.

pinch
(1) *general:* a bind or tight situation.
(2) *finance:* a sudden, unanticipated rise in prices. When money rates go up suddenly, it is called a money pinch.

pink slip: (slang) a discharged worker.

pink tea picketing: picketing by a small group of peaceful demonstrators.

pinochle season: (slang) in the garment industry, the off-season.

pioneering stage: the first stage in the product life cycle. Emphasis is placed on achieving a demand for sale of the item.

PIPS: See *paperless item processing system.*

pit: a circular area in the middle of the floor of a stock exchange. Steps lead down into the pit, giving greater visibility to the trading action occurring there. Synonymous with *ring;* see also *floor, open order, outcry market.*

P.I.T.I.: common abbreviation for principal, interest, taxes, and insurance, used when describing the monthly carrying charges on a mortgage.

pivotal group norm: a norm to which

every member of the group must conform.

place land: the land on both sides of railroad tracks that is owned by the railroad.

placement

(1) *personnel:* assignment of a worker to a job for which he or she is judged fitted.

(2) *securities:* negotiating for the sale of a new securities issue or arranging for a long-term loan.

placement test: a test that enables an individual to be assigned to the appropriate class or instructional level.

place utility: the additional value in having a product where it is utilized or consumed.

plain bond: See *bond, plain.*

plaintiff: the complaining party or the person who begins a legal action against another person or organization, seeking a court remedy.

planholder: a pension plan shareholder.

planned economy: a system whereby the government has a major influence in directing economic resources for deciding what to manufacture, in what quantity, and often for whom.

planned gap: the difference between a forecast and a plan; the difference between what will occur assuming that no changes are made (forecast) and a projection of what the organization wants to accomplish (plan).

planned obsolescence: an approach of consciously making an item out of fashion in the eyes of the consumer by repeatedly bringing out new models or products featuring improvements that are promoted as being superior or benefcial. There is a question of the value to the consumer of these systematic changes. The weakest-link theory claims that the least durable component in a product will determine its useful life. See also *weakest-link theory;* cf. *product obsolescence.*

planned (canned) presentation: a preplanned, organized statement in which major selling points are memorized for word-by-word presentation.

planning: an organizational activity that requires establishment of a predetermined course of action, beginning with a statement of goals. See also *organizational analysis and planning.*

planning function: all managerial activities that lead to the definition of goals and to the determination of appropriate means to achieve those goals.

planning-programming-budgeting (PPB): mainly in government accounting, a system of administration for federal agencies. Its concepts include (1) long- and short-range planning of objectives and end products, (2) realistic cost estimates, (3) a search for greater efficiency, (4) budgetary projections of outputs in terms of goods and services, and (5) reports on current and prospective outlays, designed to service management controls and to supply information on budgetary administration for all levels of government.

plant: an establishment that manufactures or distributes items and services.

plant turnover ratio: the relationship between an organization's sales income and the cost of operating its physical plant. It gives the sales volume generated for each dollar invested in physical facilities.

platform car: See *car, flat.*

play around: (slang) to go after a job or business venture with minimal interest or intent.

pledging: the offering by a borrower of his or her assets as security for the repayment of a debt. Cf. *distrain, hypothecation.*

plot: in computers and statistics, to draw or diagram.

plottage: Synonymous with *assembling land.*

plow back: to put earnings from sales back into the business operation.

plug

(1) *general:* to work hard and steadily.

(2) *packaging:* a type of closure made to be inserted into the opening of a container.

(3) *advertising:* a testimonial that is received without charge.

plugboard: a perforated board into which plugs are manually inserted to control the operation of computer equipment.

plunger: an individual speculator who takes great risks, resulting in substantial profits or losses.

plural executives: committees that have the authority to order that their recommendations be implemented.

pluralism: Synonymous with *deconglomeration.*

plus tick: Synonymous with *up tick.*

plutocracy: a form of government controlled by the wealthy.

p.m.: See *push money.*

PML: See *probable maximum loss.*

P/N: See *promissory note.*

point

(1) *securities:* in shares of stock,

a term that means $1.

(2) *real estate:* a percentage of the settlement costs in exchanging real estate.

point method rating: a system for measuring the relative value of an employee or a job by looking at particular characteristics and rating them on a scale (i.e., assigning points to them), then ranking the points as contrasted with the sums for other people or positions.

point of equilibrium: the point at which supply equals demand.

point of ideal proportion: in a production process, the point at which the most profitable relative amouts of the forces of production (land, labor, capital, and management) are used.

point of indifference: in production, the point at which the cost of an added increment of land, labor, capital, or management merely equals the money return of the additional item made because of that increase. Cf. *diminishing returns, diseconomies of scale.*

point of origin: the location at which goods are received for transportation.

point-of-purchase advertising: See *POP advertising.*

point-of-sale terminal (POST): a communication and data-capture terminal located where payment is made for goods or services.

point system: a form of job evaluation that assesses the relative importance of each job's key factors in order to arrive at the relative worth of jobs. See also *job evaluation.*

point-to-point line: a line that connects a single remote station to a computer.

policy

(1) *insurance:* a written contract of insurance.

(2) *administration:* a plan of action.

policy analysis: the application of systematic research approaches, taken from the social and behavioral sciences and based on measurements of program effectiveness, quality, cost, and impact on the design, execution, and evaluation of public policy.

policyholder: a person or company that is protected by an insurance contract. Synonymous with *the insured.*

policyholders' surplus: the sum remaining in a policy after all liabilities have been deducted from all assests. Sums such as paid-in capital and special voluntary reserves are also included in this term. This surplus is an additional financial protection for policyholders in the event of unexpected or catastrophic losses.

policy keyboard: the full range of policy considerations open to an executive who makes final policy decisions.

policy loan: funds borrowed from a life insurance organization, usually at low interest rates, using as security the cash value of the holder's policy.

policy register: a record maintained by an insurance company for noting the issuance of and thus accounting for all its policies. Cf. *daily reports.*

policy reserves: See *reserve.*

policy value: the amount of money available to the insured upon the maturity of the policy.

policy year experience: an aggregate record of all transactions on contracts becoming effective during a given 12-month period (the policy year).

political-pluralist model: an administrative model that assumes the power in both the governmental bureaucracy and Congress to be highly fragmented.

political risk: the probability of occurrence of some political event that will change the profitability of a given investment.

political strategies: the general approaches used by firms in dealing with important and powerful components in the environment.

political system: the components in a business firm's environment that can influence its decisions, its survival, or its growth.

polyspecialist: a manager who is neither a generalist nor a specialist but has knowledge in a variety of areas.

pool

(1) *finance:* an agreement between two or more companies to curtail output, divide sales areas, or in any other way avoid competition.

(2) *administration:* a combination of resources of funds, for some common purpose or benefit. See also *supplementary unemployment benefits.*

(3) *insurance:* firms joined to share business over a fixed time. See also *assigned risk.*

(4) *securities:* a combination of persons (brokers, traders) organized for the purpose of exploiting stocks. The SEC prohibits pool operations. See also *SEC.*

pooled interdependence: the relationships between units of an organization such that their separate products can be added together to form the total final product.

POP advertising: promotional material placed at the point of purchase, such as interior displays, printed material at store counters, or window displays.

pork-chopper: (slang) a full-time union employee. Cf. *rank and file.*

port

(1) *computers:* an entrance to or exit from a network.

(2) *transportation:* the left side of a ship, barge, or airplane.

(3) *shipping:* a ship's place of entry; anywhere a ship goes where federal customs officials are able to inspect cargo and levy duties.

portability

(1) *finance:* a characteristic of valuables that allows them to be carried easily (e.g., diamonds or stamps are more portable than bullion).

(2) *collective bargaining:* a characteristic of pension plans that allows an employee to carry whatever pension credits he or she has earned from one position to another or from one industry to another. See also *multiemployer pension plans.*

portable pensions: pension plans that increase the mobility of employees by allowing them to transfer earned pension credits from one employer to another.

portal-to-portal pay: pay for time traveling in getting to and from the job, so called because it was originally pay for time spent going from the mine entrance to the actual place of excavation and return. Synonymous with *travel time.*

port authority: a government commission established to administer traffic movement and loading and unloading activities around a dock or in the area of a port (e.g., Port of New York Authority, administered jointly by New York State and the State of New Jersey, is responsible for all marine traffic activity in the two states).

Porter-Lawler model: an extension of the expectancy theory that draws together individual, job, and organizational characteristics to describe the motivational process.

portfolio: holdings of securities by an individual or institution. A portfolio may contain bonds, preferred stocks, and common stocks of enterprises of various types.

portfolio investment: an ownership interest in a foreign firm without managerial involvement.

POSDCORB: the seven functions of administration: planning, organizing, staffing, directing, coordinating, reporting, and budgeting.

position

(1) *securities:* an individual's stake in the market. See also *technical position.*

(2) *personnel:* a job; an employment situation.

positional power: power that comes from one's formal position in the organization. It usually includes the right to reward and punish.

position-based influence: the ability to influence or affect the behavior of others that is based on the position a person holds in the organizational hierarchy.

position classification: a process of categorizing positions on the basis of similarity of duties, functions, responsibilities, or qualifications. See also *job classification.*

position description: an official statement setting forth the methods, procedures, activities, responsibilities, relationships, and other factors that are specifically related to a particular position.

positioning: the projection of an item as possessing a desired image, to make it attractive to a part of the market for that type of merchandise (e.g., a low-priced sports car that looks like an expensive model). See also *market target*.

positive economics: the study of economics that does not depend on the value judgments of the economist. Cf. *normative economics*.

positive file: an authorization system file that contains information about every account holder and is capable of providing a variety of data to be evaluated in responding to a request for authorization of credit, check cashing, or other privileges. See also *ratio of accounts payable to purchases*; cf. *negative file*.

positive reinforcement: the administration of positive rewards, contingent on good performance, that strengthens desired behavior in the future.

POST: See *point-of-sale terminal*.

post
(1) *accounting:* to record onto detailed subsidiary records (ledgers) amounts that were recorded in chronological records of original entry. See also *suspense account*.
(2) *computers:* to enter a unit of information on a record.

postage-due mail: mail on which additional postage is collectible on delivery to the addressee.

post audit: an audit of the financial records of an organization at some point after all the transactions have been properly recorded or have been approved for recording by the internal auditor or certified public accountants. See also *audit*.

postdated check: a check bearing a date that has not yet arrived. Such a check cannot be paid by a bank before the date shown and must be returned to the maker or to the person attempting to use it. If presented on or after the date shown, the same check will be honored if the account contains sufficient funds.

poster: an advertising medium in which promotional copy, often illustrated, is printed on large sheets of paper and pasted on boards or panels. See also *one hundred showing*.

posting
(1) *labor relations:* the practice of announcing the availability of positions, promotions, or transfers. Posting is usually guaranteed in a union contract.
(2) *accounting:* See *post*.

postmark: an impression on letters and packages showing the time, date, and post office or sectional center of origin.

postmortem
(1) *computers:* a routine that prints or writes on tape, either automatically or on demand, information concerning the contents of certain registers and storage locations at the time the routine stopped, to assist in locating a mistake in coding. See also *test, diagnostic*.
(2) *administration:* an analysis of an operation after its completion.

postmortem dump: a static dump,

used for debugging purposes, performed at the end of a machine run.

potential demand: demand that can be expected to become effective at a future date (e.g., when purchasing power is increased). Cf. *overall market capability.*

potential market saturation: the maximum number of potential users (or buyers) during a specified period.

potentially dilutive: See *dilution.*

poverty

(1) *general:* the absence of most of the comforts of life and an undersupply of the necessities.

(2) *economics:* the point at which deprivation makes the level necessary for physical efficiency impossible.

poverty index: a measure of the U.S. Department of Health and Human Services that provides a sliding scale based on family size and location to determine the minimum income required for maintaining acceptable family needs as determined by the government. See also *working poor.*

power

(1) *statistics:* the product of a number multiplied by itself one or more times.

(2) *administration:* the ability to control others in an organization, utilizing personal persuasion and other personal characteristics, various approaches for reward and punishment, position title, and level of competence and experience. See also *autocratic, Caesar management, laissez-faire, Machiavellian manager.*

power of appointment: the equivalent of total ownership of part or all of a trust, since the individual having this power can identify the ultimate recip-

ients of the trust's assets.

power of attorney: a written instrument, usually acknowledged before a public officer or witness, in which one person grants to another the rights of utilization, tenancy, transfer, or disposal of assets owned by the first person as though he himself were exercising these rights. A power of attorney has the force of law; it may be limited with respect to the assets listed in the power of attorney, or it may give full power over all assets owned. Cf. *proxy, stock power.*

power of sale: a clause included in a mortgage that gives the holder or trustee the right to seize and sell the pledged property upon default in payments or upon the occurrence of any other violation of the conditions in the mortgage. See also *shortcut foreclosure.*

power structure: the positions of influence within an organization. Positions in the power structure exist because of formal authority, informal power, or some combination of the two.

PPBS: programming, planning, and budgeting systems. See also *planning-programming-budgeting.*

PPF: See *production possibility frontier.*

practical capacity: the maximum level at which a plant or department can economically operate most efficiently. Cf. *peak capacity.*

pragmatic value orientation: an individual's tendency to respond to highly important concepts as "successful."

preapproach: the step in the sales process of finding critical data about a potential customer prior to contact.

Synonymous with *territory screening.*

preaudit: the examination of a creditor's invoices, payrolls, claims, and expected reimbursements before actual payment, or the verification of sales transactions before delivery.

preauthorized payment: a banking service that enables a debtor to request that funds be transferred from his or her deposit account to the account of a creditor.

precanceled stamps: stamps canceled by printing across the face before they are sold to large mailers, thus avoiding the need for cancellation at the time of mailing. They cannot be used on first-class matter.

precautionary demand for money: money that is held in excess of that required for day-to-day transactions, because of fear of unexpected contingencies.

precautionary motive: a rationale used by firms and consumers for retaining a portion of their assets in cash, to ensure their ability to satisfy unexpected demands easily.

preclusive purchasing

(1) *finance:* buying materials with the expectation of denying their use to a competitor.

(2) *government:* the activity of a belligerent country, aimed at preventing neutrals from selling the items purchased to an enemy. Cf. *blockade.*

predatory pricing: cutting prices with the objective of harming one's competitors. See also *rate war.*

predetermined motion times system: a listing of all movements that a person can or will perform in accomplishing a stated task, and a standard performance time for making each of the motions. See also *time and motion study.*

predictive research: the category on the level-of-outcome dimension when the outcome of a research effort is to predict the future. Cf. *forecasting.*

predictive validity: an approach to test validation that involves using a test during the selection process and then waiting until the employees have been on the job for an indefinite period before correlating test scores and job performance.

preemptive right: the privilege of a stockholder to buy a portion of a new issue of stock equal to his or her existing percentage holding.

prefabricate: to manufacture standardized components of a larger unit in a factory, thus making possible the assembling of the item elsewhere (e.g., the buyer's home) without production facilities.

preference as to assets: in the event of dissolution of a firm, before disbursement of a declared dividend, the right of stockholders holding preferred shares to claim payments before payments are made to common stockholders.

preference bond: See *bond, preference.*

preference item: a consumer's choice of a particular item even when similar items are less costly (e.g., insisting on Coca Cola, although a chain grocery store's cola-type soft drink is cheaper.)

preferences about goals: the degree of agreement or disagreement between two or more managers as to the goals that should be pursued.

preferential mail: all U.S. mail that receives special handling, including airmail, first class, newspapers, and special deliveries.

preferential rehiring: a contract provision calling for reemployment of workers after layoffs on the basis of seniority. See also *bumping*.

preferential shop: a firm in which management has agreed to hire union members so long as they are available. Cf. *union shop*.

preferred debt

(1) *finance:* a debt that takes precedence over others.

(2) *real estate:* a first mortgage.

preferred position: any advertisement position (e.g., island position) for which the advertiser pays a premium when specifically requested. Cf. *split run*.

preferred stock: corporate stock whose owners have some preference as to assets, earnings, and so on, that is not granted to the owners of common stock of the same corporation. See also *adjustment preferred securities, Class A stock, cumulative preferred effective par, guaranteed stock, privileged issue, voting right*.

Pregnancy Discrimination Act of 1978: legislation that prevents discrimination in employment against women who are pregnant and able to perform their jobs. This law amends the Civil Rights Act of 1964.

prejudice: a mental bias tending toward some preconceived judgment or opinion, thus affecting one's attitude toward work or employees. See also *bias, proactive inhibition, process intervention*.

preliminary expenses: expenses incurred in the establishment of an organization (e.g., costs for developing and circulating a prospectus).

premises

(1) *business law:* part of a deed that appears before the habendum clause and identifies the names of the parties, the consideration given, and a property description.

(2) *real estate:* a parcel of land and all improvements on it.

premium

(1) *securities:* the amount by which a preferred stock or bond may sell above its par value. In the case of a new issue of bonds or stocks, a premium is the amount the market price rises over the original selling price.

(2) *securities:* a charge sometimes made when a stock is borrowed to make delivery on a short sale.

(3) *securities:* the redemption price of a bond or preferred stock if this price is higher than face value.

(4) *insurance:* the sum paid for a policy (not to be confused with *premiums*). An earned premium is the portion of the written premium covering the part of the policy term that is included in the time period. A pure premium found by dividing losses by a hazard or contingency, is one to which no operating expenses of the firm have been added (e.g., commissions, taxes).

(5) *retailing:* an offer of merchandise, at a minimal cost or at no charge, as an inducement to the customer to purchase a given item.

(6) *finance:* the amount by which one form of funds exceeds another in buying power.

premium audit: an examination by a representative of the insurer of the insured's records, insofar as they relate to the policies or coverages under consideration. See also *audit.*

premium bond: See *bond, premium.*

premium finance: a facility that allows an insured to finance his or her payment over a specified period within the term of the policy.

premium on stock: the excess of the insurance (market) price of stock over its par or stated value.

premium pay: a wage rate higher than straight time that is payable for overtime work, work on holidays or scheduled days off, or work on evening shifts.

premiums (net written): premium income retained by insurance companies directly or through reinsurance, less payments made for business reinsured. See also *loading.*

premium servicing fee: Synonymous with *loan fee.*

prenuptial agreement: a contract made before marriage; whereby each future spouse forfeits any interest in the other's estate.

prepackaging
(1) *general:* packaging of fresh foods (meats, vegetables, cheeses) in consumer units for self-service sales.
(2) *merchandising:* to avoid repackaging by the retailer, packaging of merchandise such as chinaware and furniture by the manufacturer so that it may be sold directly to the consumer without opening.

prepaid: a term indicating that shipping charges have already been paid or are to be paid at the point of delivery. See also *franco delivery.*

prepaid expenses: payment for items not yet received; a charge deferred for a period of time until the benefit for which payment has been made

occurs (e.g., rent paid for future months). Cf. *accrued liabilities.*

prepak: Synonymous with *prepackaging.*

prepay: to pay before or in advance of receipt of goods or services.

prepayment: payment of a debt before it actually becomes due.

prepayment clause
(1) *general:* the privilege of repaying part or all of a loan in advance of date or dates stated in a contract.
(2) *real estate:* a clause in a mortgage allowing the mortgagor to pay off part or all of the unpaid debt before it becomes due without penalty. This affords a saving for the mortgagor.

prepayment penalty: a penalty placed on a mortgagor for paying the mortgage before its due date. This applies when there is no prepayment clause to offset the penalty.

preposterior evaluation: a judgment made before an event about the conditions anticipated after the event.

prerefunding: refunding in which securities eligible for conversion mature in no more than one year.

preretailing: assignment by the retailer of retail prices to goods at the time an order is made, thus allowing the determination of retail values of items on order. This practice also speeds up the checking and marking procedures when merchandise arrives.

prerogatives: the rights, powers, privileges of an individual that others do not possess (e.g., diplomatic immunity.

prescientific management: the time period from the beginning of cooperative efforts to the first attempts, in about 1880, to approach the study of management scientifically. Cf. *scientific management.*

prescriptive decision making: emphasis on what ought to happen, rather than on what is happening. It is the normative way of examining decisions, decision makers, and decision processes.

present value: the discounted value of a certain sum that is due and payable at a specified future date.

present value of expected cash flow: the net cash that a company expects to realize or pay out from holding an asset or liability, discounted by an appropriate rate of interest.

president: the highest ranking executive responsible for the policy decisions of an organization. The president reports to a board of directors.

prestige card: a plastic identification card issued by savings and loan associations to their customers to be used in electronic funds-transfer systems.

prestige pricing: increasing the price of an item to establish a quality image of the product or the seller.

presumption: an assumed fact, which can serve as evidence until facts are obtained.

presumptive title: possession of property that leads others to presume ownership, when in fact ownership may not exist. See also *reputed owner;* Cf. *cloud on title.*

pretest: a test given to determine an individual's performance in some area in advance of training, education, or some other condition that is expected to improve performance.

prevailing rate: See *Davis-Bacon Act of 1931.*

preventive discipline: action taken to encourage employees to follow the standards and rules so that infractions are prevented. Cf. *corrective discipline.*

prewrap: to wrap or package merchandise before it is placed on the floor for sale.

price: the amount of money a seller receives for goods or services at the factory or place of business. Price is not what the seller asks for the product but what is actually received.

price ceiling: a government-established maximum price.

price control
(1) *merchandising:* the result of the demand by a manufacturer that the buyer for resale not be able to determine a resale price for the goods. See also *fair trade price.*
(2) *government:* regulation of the prices of goods and services with the intent to reduce increases in the cost of living. See also *rollback, valorization.*

price cutting: offering goods or services for sale at a price below that recognized as typical or appropriate by buyers and sellers. See also *underselling.*

price discretion: reflected in the decision of a sales representative to alter the price of an item for purposes of making a sale.

price discrimination: the practice of charging different prices for the same quality and quantity of merchandise to different buyers. Should this practice result in reducing competition, it is illegal under the antitrust laws. See also *Robinson-Patman Act of 1936;* cf. *functional discount, rate discrimination.*

price out of the market: describing

items that have been made so expensive that they are no longer purchased in their usual market (e.g., vendors of $12 ice cream cones would find themselves priced out of the juvenile market). Cf. *inelastic demand.*

price-earnings (p/e) ratio: the price of a share of stock divided by earnings per share for a 12-month period. For example, a stock selling for $50 a share and earning $5 a share is said to be selling at a price-earnings ratio of 10:1.

price elasticity: reflected in a reduction in sales when the price of an item is raised.

price fixing: an agreement by competing organizations to avoid competitive pricing by charging identical prices or by changing prices at the same time. Price fixing is in violation of the Sherman Antitrust Act. Cf. *conscious parallel action, price stabilization.*

price index: a measure to illustrate the changes in the average level of prices. See also *purchasing power of the dollar, wholesale price index.*

price inelasticity: a change in price that yields a disproportionately small change in demand.

price leadership: a situation in which prices can be determined by one major manufacturer in an industry, thus influencing others to accept the prices as determined. See also *administered price.*

price level: the value of money in comparison with a specified base period.

price lining: placing several items of varying costs together and selling them all at the same price. This prac-tice is used frequently in retailing.

price loco: the price at the place where a purchase occurs.

price rigidity: a long-term lack of concern for prices of raw or produced items in relation to the inflationary aspects of a depression or recession.

price-specie flow theory: a theory stating that imports of precious metals increase the supply of funds and therefore advance the price level of items that use these metals.

price spreading: the simultaneous purchase and sale of options in the same class with the same expiration date but with different striking prices.

price stabilization: keeping prices at a stated level. This is primarily a government strategy, especially during wartime or periods of rapid inflation, but it is illegal when practiced by private companies. See also *Sherman Antitrust Act of 1890;* cf. *price fixing.*

price support: subsidy or financial aid offered to specific growers, producers, or distributors, in accordance with governmental regulations, to keep market prices from dropping below a certain minimum level. See also *farm subsidies;* cf. *Brannan plan.*

price system: the market system of resource allocation.

price takers: firms that have no market power over price. Therefore, the market dictates price for them.

primacy of planning: the principle that, at least initially, planning precedes all other managerial functions.

prima facie: "at first view" (Latin); that which appears to be true until contrary evidence is given.

primary boycott: See *boycott.*

primary data: information collected

by a researcher from the original source.

primary demand: demand for a product type.

primary deposits: cash deposits in a bank.

primary distribution: the original sale of a company's securities. Synonymous with *primary offering.*

primary insurance: insurance coverage up to a specified amount or against specific perils. See also *excess insurance.*

primary offering: Synonymous with *primary distribution.*

primary organization: an organization that claims the complete personal and emotional involvement of its members. It is characterized by personal, direct, spontaneous, face-to-face relationships.

primary reserves: a bank's legal reserves of cash and demand deposits with the Federal Reserve Bank and other banks.

prime cost: the sum of direct labor expenditures plus direct materials costs that are identified with a product. See also *loading.*

prime interest (rate): the rate of interest charged by a commercial bank for large loans made to its most credit-worthy business and industrial customers. It is the lowest interest rate charged by the bank. The prime rate level is determined by how much banks have to pay for the supply of money from which they make loans. In an inflated economy, banks pay increasingly higher rates for funds, and the prime rate rises. When inflation subsides, the prime rate usually drops. The Federal Reserve Bank's

charge for negotiable business instruments, which is publicly established, influences the rate for all other business interest payments.

prime maker: the party (or parties) signing a negotiable instrument and becoming the original party responsible for its ultimate payment. See also *liabilities.*

prime rate: See *prime interest (rate).*

primogeniture: under common law, the right of the eldest child to inherit all real property of the parent. The estate usually passes to a son, but daughters are increasingly inheriting under this right. Cf. *entail.*

principal

(1) *finance:* the face value of an instrument, which becomes the obligation of the maker or drawee to pay to a holder in due course. Interest is charged on the principal amount.

(2) *securities:* the person for whom a broker executes an order, or a dealer who is buying or selling for his or her own account.

(3) *real estate:* one of the major parties to a transaction, either the seller or purchaser.

(4) *banking:* the original amount of a deposit, loan, or other amount of money on which interest is earned or paid. See also *billed principal.*

principal sum: the amount specified under an accident policy, (e.g., the death benefit).

principle of selectivity: the principle that in any series of elements to be controlled, a small number of elements always accounts for a large portion of the results.

principles of organization: in general, the division of work, authority, responsibility and accountability, span of control, lines and units of communication and command, legitimacy, and coordination.

printer: a device that writes output data from a computer system on paper or some other medium.

printout: printed pages produced by a computer's printer.

prior deductions method: an improper method of determining bond interest or preferred dividend coverage in which the requirements of senior obligations are first deducted from earnings and the balance is applied to the requirements of the junior issue.

prioritize: to set in order of preference or priority the attributes or needs of an organization. Assignments are made from this list of priorities.

prior lien: a mortgage that ranks ahead of another mortgage.

prior-lien bond: See *bond, prior-lien.*

prior-period adjustments: adjustments made directly to retained earnings that are required to correct errors in the financial statements of prior periods.

prior preferred (stock): a preferred issue that ranks ahead of another preferred issue of the same company.

prison-made goods: See *Ashurt-Sumners Act, of 1935.*

Privacy Act of 1974: federal legislation designed to protect citizens from invasion of privacy by the federal government and permitting individuals, for the first time, to inspect information about themselves contained in federal agency files and to challenge, correct, or amend the material. Law enforcement, Central Intelligence Agency, Secret Service, and certain other government records are exempt from disclosure. The act prohibits an agency from selling or renting an individual's name or address for mailing list use. It also established a privacy protection study commission to provide Congress and the president with information about problems related to privacy in the public and private sectors, and it made it illegal for any federal, state, or local agency to deny an individual any benefit provided by law because of refusal to disclose his or her social security account number to the agency. See also *Freedom of Information Act of 1966.*

private bank: a bank chartered by the state in which it operates, subject to state laws and regulations, and subject to examinations by the state banking authorities. The principal distinction between private banks and other state banks is that a private bank may arise from a partnership, with no capital stock.

private brand: a middleman-owned brand name or trademark (e.g., Sears Roebuck owns the Kenmore brand).

private carrier: a transportation line that is not a common carrier.

private cost: the cost of a specific item to an individual.

private enterprise: an organization of production in which the business is owned and operated by people who take risks and are motivated by the wish to make a profit. See also *capitalist;* cf. *people's capitalism.*

private lender: an individual who lends money from institutional funds (insurance companies, banks, etc.).

private placement agencies: private, for-profit firms that help job seekers find employment. Cf. *search firms.*

private property: all land that is not owned by the government.

private rate of return

(1) *general:* the financial rate of return anticipated by businessmen prior to investing their monies.

(2) *finance:* the expected net profit after taxes and all costs, including depreciation, expressed as a percentage annual return on the total cost of an effort or the net worth of the stockholder owners. See also *ROI.*

private sector: the segment of the total economy composed of businesses and households but excluding government. Cf. *public sector.*

privileged bond: See *bond, privileged.*

privilege issue: a preferred stock or bond that has a conversion or participating right or that has a stock purchase warrant on it.

privity: the mutual and successive relationship of persons to the same interest.

proactive inhibition: an existing barrier resulting from a worker's previous experience; an attitude that interfers with a worker's learning of new skills or relationships.

proactive management: a management style in which decision makers anticipate problems and take affirmative steps to minimize those problems, rather than waiting until a problem occurs before taking action.

probability: the likelihood of the occurrence of an event, estimated as a ratio between the number of ways in which the event may occur and the number of ways in which alternative events may occur. See also *Markov chain; significance, statistical.*

probability chain: an informal communication chain in which information is passed on a random basis.

probability sampling: a sampling technique in which each unit of the population has an equal chance of appearing in the sample. Cf. *random sample.*

probable error: a measure of dispersion, variation, or scatter on both sides of the arithmetic mean, yielding a space that includes one-half the total number of cases. It is computed by multiplying the standard deviation by 0.6745.

probable maximum loss (PML): the maximum insurance loss that can be expected under normal circumstances. Extraordinary circumstances, such as delayed alarm or insufficient water supply, can result in a loss exceeding the PML. Cf. *maximum foreseeable loss.*

probate

(1) *general:* the right or jurisdiction of hearing and determining questions or issues in matters concerning a will.

(2) *business law:* the action or process of proving before a court of law that a document offered for official recognition as the last will and testament of a deceased person is genuine.

probationary employee: a worker whose permanent employment with a firm is contingent upon his or her performance during a trial period of specified length.

problem determination: the process of identifying a hardware, software, or system failure and ascertaining whether the user is responsible for diagnosis and repair.

problem-oriented language: See *language, general-purpose.*

problem solving: an activity resulting in suggestions or recommendations that express in concise, quantified terms the advantages and disadvantages to a firm of pursuing a possible future course of action or the advantages of various alternative operations.

procedure: a way of doing something; a written and generally flow-charted description of the processing involved in an application.

proceeds

(1) *finance:* the actual amount of funds given to a borrower, following deductions for interest charges, fees, and so on.

(2) *economics:* the funds received by a seller after deductions for the payment of commissions (e.g., proceeds from a sale).

process analysis: the study of the approaches used for producing a part or a product for purposes of yielding the lowest cost and most efficient process that will produce items of adequate quality.

process control: a monitoring method to assure that the production system is functioning properly.

process costing: a method of product costing whereby costs are accumulated by process or work centers and averaged over all products manufactured in those centers for a specified period. Cf. *job-order costing.*

process departmentation: grouping jobs into subunits based on the sequential processes involved in an organization's operations. This is common in one-product plants, such as oil refineries. Cf. *functional departmentation, geographical departmentation, matrix departmentation, product departmentation.*

process effects: the increase in consumer spending and private investment as a result of the spending on public works projects.

process inspection: inspection at intervals during or between production operations. Cf. *quality control.*

process intervention: any effort to alter the attitudes of members of an organization to promote the more successful accomplishment of goals.

processor

(1) *computers:* any device that is able to carry out operations on data.

(2) *computers:* a program that includes compiling, assembling, translating, and related functions for a specific programming language.

process principles: organizational principles, defined by Henri Fayol, that describe the desirable behavior of managers as they deal with workers. Cf. *situational theory of leadership.*

procuration: the authority given to another to sign instruments and to act on behalf of the person granting the authority.

procurement: the purchase of goods for resale to a store's customers.

produce exchange: a market for perishable agricultural products.

producer

(1) *general:* an individual who manufactures goods and services.

(2) *insurance:* the individual—either an agent or a broker—who has solicited insurance business from the buyer and is placing it with the company.

producer commodity cartel: an organization of producers of a key raw material commodity in world trade (e.g., the Organization of Petroleum Exporting Countries).

producer-controlled brands: brands owned or controlled by firms that are primarily in the manufacturing business. Synonymous with *natural brand.*

producer goods: items intended to be used and worn out in the course of producing other items in the future (e.g., ink in newspaper printing).

product: goods and services made available to consumers; the total of benefits offered.

product assortment: the brands and types of items in a product class available to consumers.

product class: a group of items that are treated as natural substitutes and/or complements by most consumers.

product costing: the assignment of manufacturing costs to products in order to determine the cost of finished goods. See also *absorption costing, variable cost.*

product departmentation: grouping jobs into subunits based on the different products or programs of the organization. Cf. *functional departmentation, geographical departmentation, matrix departmentation, process departmentation.*

product development: the generation of new ideas for new or improved goods to be added to or to replace existing items.

product differentiation: a marketing approach based on the creation and promotion of differences among similar items.

production
(1) *economics:* any form of activi-

ty that adds value to goods and services, including creation, transportation, and warehousing until used.

(2) *administration:* a criterion of effectiveness that refers to an organization's ability to provide the outputs demanded of it by the environment.

production bonus: a type of incentive system that provides workers with additional compensation when they surpass stated production goals. See also *bonus.*

production budget: a schedule of production requirements for a budget period.

production capacity: the maximum quantity of units that can be made in a stated period with available equipment. Cf. *peak capacity, scheduled production.*

production control: the planning, routing, scheduling, dispatching, and inspection of operations of a given item being manufactured. The goals are to improve efficiency, cut costs, and evolve a quality product. See also *requisition.*

production costs: factory costs plus administrative expenses.

production-dominated strategy: the focus of key decision makers on manufacturing and processing know-how.

production-efficiency-oriented production: production in a foreign country because of lower factor costs or special incentives such as lower taxes.

production fit: the compatibility of a new product with established manufacturing equipment and processes.

production function: use of the technical data that show the output of which specific input routines are capable.

production possibility frontier (PPF): the limits of the combinations of items that can be made by an entire economy. This boundary is a function of the scarcity of resources and the availability of existing technology. Cf. *consumption possibility frontier.*

production sharing: a situation in which a product is manufactured in one country, assembled in another, and marketed in a third. See also *duty drawback;* cf. *reexport.*

production workers: employees engaged directly in manufacturing or operating processes, as distinct from maintenance forces, supervisors, clerical workers, stock room attendents, and so on. See also *direct labor;* cf. *indirect labor costs.*

productive efficiency: a situation that exists when there is no possibility of increasing the yield of one item without decreasing the yield of another item.

productivity: a measurement of the efficiency of production; a ratio of output to input (e.g., 10 units per man-hour).

productivity factor: a union contract provision calling for periodic pay increases, apart from negotiations, to compensate for continued increases in man-hour output by workers.

product liability: liability imposed for damages caused by accident and arising out of goods or products manufactured, sold, handled, or distributed by the insured or by others trading under his or her name. The accident must have oc-

curred after possession of goods had been relinquished to others and away from premises owned, rented, or controlled by the insured. In the case of food products, however, the accident does not have to occur away from the premises (e.g., a restaurant).

product life cycle: the six stages of market acceptance of any goods: pioneering, growth, maturity, saturation, decline, and abandonment.

product line: the assortment of items presented by a firm, or a group of items that are closely related because they either satisfy a need, are used with each other, are sold to the same consumer, are marketed within the same outlets, or are within similar price ranges.

product manager: an executive responsible for marketing approaches, such as promotion, pricing, distribution, and establishing product characteristics. The product manager deals more with the planning aspects than with actual selling to the consumer.

product markets: markets in which firms sell the outputs that they produce.

product mix: the composite of items offered for sale by one company.

product obsolescence: the effect on items that become less attractive to the consumer because of the introduction of newly improved items that do the job less expensively or better, or perhaps both. Cf. *planned obsolescence.*

product pattern: an organizational pattern whereby jobs and activities are grouped on the basis of types of products or services.

product planning: the process leading to the identification of goals and procedures as well as the precise nature of the merchandise to be marketed. See also *marketing research.*

product portfolio: a group of products marketed by the same company.

product positioning: the way in which a product is characterized to attract consumer interest and purchase. A product may be positioned in a variety of ways, such as economical, durable, stylish, safe, convenient, and so forth.

product reliability: the probability that a product will perform a stated function under specific conditions for a specified period without failure. See *guarantee.*

product/service life cycle: the market phases for most products and services.

products market equilibrium: a situation in which aggregate demand equals aggregate supply. See also *aggregate demand, aggregate supply.*

profession: an occupation that requires an extensive period of schooling, involving numerous intellectual elements, that enables the professional person to render a service to society.

professional liability: See *malpractice insurance.*

profile analysis: a method for appraising individual uniqueness and characteristics that consists of a search for patterns of behavior displayed by an individual.

profit

(1) *marketing:* the excess of the selling price over all costs and expenses incurred in making a sale.

See also *PIMS.*

(2) *finance:* the reward to the entrepreneur for the risks assumed by him or her in the establishment, operation, and management of a given enterprise or undertaking. See also *uncertainty theory.*

(3) *accounting:* the monies remaining after a business has paid all its bills. See also *contribution profit.*

profitability: a firm's ability to earn a profit and its potential for future earnings.

profitability measures: the ratios of net profit to capital, to total assests, and to sales.

profit and loss (operating) statement (P/L): the summary listing of a firm's total revenues and expenses within a specified time period. Synonymous with *income and expense statement.*

profit budget: a budget that includes expenses and revenue budgets in a single statement.

profit center: a segment of a business that is responsible for both revenues and expenses.

profit margin: sales less all operating expenses divided by the number of sales.

profit-maximizing management: a theory of business management based solely on the objective of profit maximization.

profit objective: the profit goal of a profit-seeking organization, which is achieved by efficient use of scarce resources. See also *profit.*

profit sharing: an arrangement whereby employees share in company profits, based on company successes, according to a plan. This compensation is paid in addition to wages. There are cash plans (giving a share of profits in cash) and deferred plans (setting up a trust for payment upon retirement, death, or disability). See also *employee stock ownership plans, Lincoln incentive management plan.*

profit squeeze: profit shrinkage resulting from stable prices and increasing costs.

profits tax: a tax on business profits, excluding income taxes.

profit taking: the sale of stock that has appreciated in value since purchase, in order to realize the profit that has been made possible. This activity is often cited to explain a downturn in the market following a period of rising prices. Cf. *unloading.*

pro forma invoice: a preliminary invoice indicating the value of the items listed and informing the recipient that all have been sent. It is not a demand for money.

program

(1) *administration:* a series of actions proposed in order to achieve a certain result.

(2) *computers:* a set of instructions that tells the computer exactly how to handle a complete problem. See also *processor.*

program, linear: See *linear programming.*

program budgeting: a long-range approach to budgetary decision making that relates future expenditures to broadly defined objectives of the organization.

program evaluation and review technique (PERT): a method to facilitate planning and to give management tools for the control of specific pro-

grams. Original PERT programs were developed by the U.S. Navy. Cf. *critical path method, PERT/COST.*

programmed decisions: responses to repetitive and routine problems according to a standard procedure that has been developed by management.

programmer: a person who designs, writes, and tests computer programs. See also *analyst, programmer;* cf. *system programmer.*

program merchandising: combined efforts of a retailer and a key source to make merchandising and promotion plans for a store.

programming: the art of reducing the plan for a solution to a problem to instructions that can be fed to a computer. See also *programmer.*

progressive discipline: a system of management stressing that disciplinary action should make penalties appropriate to the violation (or accumulated violations). See also *discipline.*

progressive tax: an income tax that rises as income increases. The rate of increase varies. See also *ability to pay, degressive taxation, graduated tax;* cf. *regressive taxes.*

prohibited issue: an issue that cannot be bargained over in management-labor discussions.

prohibited risk: a line that an insurance company will not insure under any condition.

project: resources and activities used to achieve a specific set of objectives within a specified time schedule.

project authority: authority exercised by project managers over personnel assigned to them for a project. This authority, which flows horizontally, contrasts with functional authority.

projective technique: a procedure for discovering a person's characteristics of behavior by observing how the individual acts in situations that do not demand a particular response.

project organization: an organization that is created for the attainment of a particular objective and is disbanded on completion of the project.

proletariat: according to Marx, people in the wage-earning class, who are usually taken advantage of by capitalists and who, at the appropriate time, will revolt and gain social and economic control. See also *exploitation theory, labor theory of value.*

promissory note (P/N): a written promise to pay; a negotiable instrument that is evidence of a debt contracted by a borrower from a creditor (a lender of funds). If the instrument does not have all the qualities of a negotiable instrument, it cannot legally be transferred. See also *accommodation paper, note.*

promotability: the qualities of a worker that indicate inherent potential for performance of more complex and more responsible duties.

promoter: an individual who brings together those forming a business venture and those interested in backing the enterprise.

promotion

(1) *retailing:* stimulating the demand for goods by advertising, publicity, and events to attract attention and create interest among consumers.

(2) *personnel:* advancement to a position of higher rank, responsibility, or prestige. See also *horizontal promotion, vertical promotion.*

promotional allowance: payments given to a middleman by a manufacturer to pay for the middleman's promotion of goods. Cf. *advertising allowance.*

promotional fit: the compatibility of a new product with existing advertising approaches.

promotional mix: the combined promotional efforts of advertising, publicity, sales promotion, and personal selling as they attempt to communicate with customers to sell a product.

promotion from within: a policy whereby management positions are filled by people who are already employees of the organization.

proof of loss: a formal statement made by an insured to the insurance company regarding a claim that serves the company as a basis for determining its liability under the policy or bond.

property

(1) *economics:* the exclusive right or interest of a person in his or her belongings.

(2) *business law:* that which is legally owned by a person or persons and may be used and disposed of as the owner(s) sees fit.

property, intangible: property that cannot be touched (e.g., choses in action) or has no physical structure. See also *intangible asset.*

property, personal: chattels, choses in possession; everything that is owned except real estate.

property, public: real and personal property held by the government for eventual use or benefit of its population. Cf. *public domain.*

property, real: land, including that which is naturally growing on it, and any improvements made to the land, including structures.

property, tangible: property that is touchable or has a physical structure; choses in possession.

property damage liability insurance: protection against liability for damage to the property of another that is not in the care, custody, and control of the insured—as distinguished from liability for bodily injury.

property dividend: distributions to shareholders of assets other than cash or company stock.

property, plant, and equipment: tangible, long-term assets acquired for use in a business rather than for resale.

property tax: Synonymous with *land tax.*

proportional law: the relationship between factors of production and the results of production; the desirable relationship among production factors that will yield maximum returns. Cf. *law of increasing costs.*

proportional tax: a tax whose percentage rate stays constant as the tax base increases, resulting in the amount of paid tax being proportional to the tax base (e.g., property tax).

proposal: an oral or written statement or offer.

proprietary company: a nonfunctioning parent company or a nonfunctioning controlling company formed for the purpose of investing in the securities of other companies and for controlling these companies through such holdings. Synonymous with *holding company, parent company.*

proprietary lease: a lease made between an operating organization and a tenant-owner in a cooperative apartment building.

proprietor: a person who has an exclusive right or interest in property or in a business.

proprietorship: a business that is owned by one person. The individual owner has the rights to all profits from the business as well as all liabilities and losses. Synonymous with *individual proprietorship.*

proprietorship certificate: a certificate filed with a bank showing the ownership of a privately owned business enterprise.

proprietory accounts: accounts showing the actual assets and liabilities of an organization.

pro rata: "according to the rate" (Latin); in proportion to a total amount. For example, if a contract is terminated before the end of the period for which payment has been given, a pro rata return of the payment is made in proportion to the unused period of time remaining.

pro rata cancellation: the termination of an insurance contract or bond, with the premium charge being adjusted in proportion to the exact time the protection has been in force. Cf. *flat cancellation, short rate cancellation;* see also *unearned premium.*

pro rata distribution clause: a clause providing for the distribution of an insurance amount over the several locations or objects covered, in proportion to their value; or, if several policies are involved, the proportionate distribution of the liability among them. See also *double insurance.*

prorate: to redistribute a portion of a cost to a department or product in accordance with an agreed-upon formula.

prospect: a potential customer. See also *qualified prospect*.

prospecting: searching for an individual or concern that needs a product or service and possesses the ability to purchase it.

prospectus

(1) *general:* a plan for a proposed enterprise.

(2) *securities:* a written offer to sell a security. It provides information about the quality of the stock as regulated by the U.S. Securities and Exchange Commission. Cf. *open prospectus, red herring*.

(3) *real estate:* a description of property for sale or lease.

prosperity: the uppermost phase of a business cycle. Cf. *depression*.

protected groups: classes of people who are protected from employment discrimination under one or more laws. See also *concentration in employment, underutilization*.

protection

(1) *insurance:* Synonymous with *coverage*.

(2) *government:* the imposition of high (i.e., protective) tariffs on imports that are presumed to compete with domestic items, with the objective of giving the domestic manufacturer an advantage. See also *infant industry argument*.

protectionists: people who favor high tariffs and other import restrictions to enable domestic items to compete more favorably with foreign items.

protective injunction: a court order prohibiting a strike or boycott. See also *injunction*.

protective tariff: a tax on imported goods designed to give domestic manufacturers an economic shield against price competition from abroad. Cf. *revenue tariffs*.

protest jacket: Synonymous with *notice of dishonor*.

proximate cause

(1) *general:* a cause that leads to other causes; the factor responsible for any harm.

(2) *insurance:* an unbroken chain of causes and effects between the occurrence of an insured peril and damage to property or persons (e.g., fire is the proximate cause of damage done by water used to extinguish it).

proximate damages: damages that are direct, immediate, and the result of negligence or wrong, and that might have been expected. Cf. *consequential loss*.

proximo: in the following month. Cf. *instant*.

proxy: a power of attorney given by a stockholder to an individual or individuals to exercise the stockholder's rights to vote at corporate meetings.

proxy statement: printed information required by the Securities and Exchange Commission to be given to potential holders of securities traded on a national exchange, supplying minimum descriptions of the stock, timing of the proposed sale, and so on.

prudent investment-cost standard: a means of defining the value of an organization by subtracting the costs of unwise, inappropriate, or wasteful investments from the original costs of the assets.

prudent man rule: an investment standard. In some states, the law requires that a fiduciary, such as a trustee, may invest the fund's money only in a list of securities designated by the state—the so-called legal list. In other states, the trustee may invest in a security if it is one that would be bought by a prudent person of discretion and intelligence who is seeking a reasonable income and preservation of capital.

psec: abbreviation for picosecond.

pseudo-instruction: a symbolic representation of information to a compiler or interpreter; a group of characters having the same general form as a computer instruction but never executed by the computer as an actual instruction, to be used to control the conversion of an original language to a machine language.

psychic income: nonmonetary income regarded by an individual as desirable to fulfill his or her needs, wants, and psychological demands. Power, control, independence, actualization are examples of psychic income. Synonymous with *intangible rewards*.

psychological contract: the sum total of what the individual expects to get from the organization and what the organization expects to get from the individual.

psychological pricing: Synonymous with *odd pricing*.

psychological product: the physical product along with its warranties, services, and psychological overtones.

psychometric: describing any quantitative measurement of an individual's psychological traits or assets. See also *Q-sort*.

psychometrician: a person skilled in administering and interpreting mental tests.

psychometrics: the study of mental testing.

psychomotor tests: tests of the motor skills of an individual in relation to his or her concomitant sensory and motor activities (e.g., aiming a rifle at a distant target).

public administration

(1) *general:* the use of individuals in federal, state, or local government agencies and the management of such agencies. In recent years, this includes other not-for-profit organizations (hospitals, welfare agencies, etc.)

(2) *government:* the coordination of individual and group efforts to carry out public policy. It is a process encompassing innumerable skills, and it uses techniques that order the efforts of large numbers of people. See also *policy analysis*.

public assistance: government payments for medical assistance and other purposes to the aged, the blind, the permanently and totally disabled, and families with dependent children.

public bond: See *bond, public*.

public consumption monopoly: a governmental monopoly created to regulate the consumption of specific items that are considered harmful. Cf. *sumptuary laws*.

public corporation: a corporation created by and for a government agency to assist in the discharge of a public service (e.g., a port authority).

public debt transaction: See *backdoor financing*.

public domain: federally owned land. Cf. *property, public*.

public employee: usually, a worker who is employed by a federal, state, county, or municipal government.

public finance: See *finance*.

public interest

(1) *general:* a moral imperative based on the assumption that there exists some collective, overarching community or national good and that this good, the public interest, should be served.

(2) *government:* the result of group struggles; the accommodation of a multiplicity of competing interests.

publicity: any event or communication, through established media or otherwise, free or paid, solicited or not, that attracts attention to a product.

Public Law 94-455: See *Tax Reform Act of 1976.*

public member: the member of a tripartite fact-finding or other goup who is not directly connected with the union or the employer.

public policy

(1) *general:* any conduct that affects the public good.

(2) *government:* an official position in regard to a national concern or public interest that may lead to legislation and other changes in activity.

public property: See *property, public.*

public relations: any communication or activity created or performed primarily to enhance prestige or goodwill for an individual or an organization.

public responsibility: the responsibilities of individuals or groups that are presumed to reflect the broader and more pervasive needs of the entire community, state, or nation.

public revenue: income received by a government agency (taxes, tariffs, customs, etc.).

public sale: a sale of property at a public auction.

public sector: the segment of the total economy that includes all levels of government and excludes businesses and households. Cf. *private sector.*

public service advertising: advertising related not to the marketing of products but to social betterment goals (e.g., preventing forest fires, promoting traffic safety, securing blood donations). See also *Advertising Council.*

public utility: a private corporation that sells services to the public (e.g., gas and water supplies). Such organizations are government regulated and are usually given a monopoly to operate in a community. See also *fair rate of return, rate regulation, utility, utility expenditures.*

Public Utility Holding Company Act of 1935: federal legislation forbidding pyramiding of holding companies in the public utilities industry.

public welfare

(1) *general:* economic assistance given to those in the population who are near or below the poverty level of subsistence. See also *subvention.*

(2) *economics:* the welfare of the public as an entity, as contrasted with the welfare of a few.

public works: governmental projects created for the public good and paid for with public funds (e.g., construction of dams, highways, government buildings). See also *process effects, social infrastructure expenditures.*

public works and ways system: use of prison labor to work on public projects.

publisher's representative: an independent organization or person that sells advertising space for a publication.

puff: (slang) a free promotion of a product or service.

pull date: the date stamped on perishable products (e.g., bakery and dairy goods), after which the items should not be sold.

pump priming: a term used originally during the New Deal to describe a government policy of making a once-and-for-all autonomous expenditure in an effort to create a self-sustaining increase in economic activity.

punch: a perforation, as in a computer punched card or tape.

punch, multiple: two or more holes in a single column of a card, permitting representation of a larger number of different characters, with a character in each column.

punch, single column: a specific coding technique in which any of the values 0 through 11 is represented by a single punch in a card column.

punched card: a card punched with a pattern of holes to represent data.

punched tape: a tape on which a pattern of holes or cuts is used to represent data.

punt: (slang) shares that will rarely turn out to be profitable.

purchase allowance: a lowering of the price of an item when the merchandise as requested does not meet the expectations as identified on the invoice. Cf. *on consignment.*

purchase contract: an agreement between a buyer and a seller that itemizes items and services to be bought and sold, respectively.

purchase discount: a reduction in the price of an order that has been paid promptly.

purchase money: monies paid to obtain ownership of property.

purchase money mortgage: a mortgage given by the purchaser to the seller at the time the property is acquired to help finance the purchase.

purchase order: a statement permitting a vendor to deliver merchandise or materials at an agreed-upon price.

purchase price
(1) *general:* the amount for which any item is bought.
(2) *real estate:* the combination of monies and mortgages given to obtain a property.
(3) *real estate:* the amount for which a property is sold.

purchaser: a buyer; a person who obtains title to or an interest in property by the act of purchase.

purchase returns and allowances: a contra-purchases account in which the returns of or allowances for previously purchased merchandise are recorded.

purchasing agent: an individual who buys products for store maintenance and daily operation, not for resale to customers. Cf. *procurement.*

purchasing power: the value of money measured by the items it can buy. Cf. *money, wages, real value of money*

purchasing power of the dollar: a measurement of the quantity of goods and services that a dollar will buy in a specified market, compared with the amount it could buy in some base period. It is obtained by taking the reciprocal of an appropriate price index. See also *money, wage.*

pure competition: a situation in which there are many sellers and buyers of a standardized product with free entrance to the market and no collusion.

pure economic discrimination: a condition that exists when, in considering two workers with the same skills and training, an employer prefers one worker over the other on the basis of race, ethnic background, or some other criterion that is not directly related to the worker's ability to perform his or her job. Cf. *halo effect*.

Pure Food and Drug Act of 1906: federal legislation prohibiting manufacturers' mislabeling of the contents of food, liquor, and medicine containers.

pure interest: the price paid for the use of capital, not including monies for risk or all other costs incurred because of the loan. Synonymous with *net interest, true interest*.

pure market economy: a competitive economic system of numerous buyers and sellers, in which prices are determined by the free interaction of supply and demand. See also *free enterprise*.

pure monopoly: See *perfect (pure) monopoly*.

pure premium: a premium, arrived at by dividing losses by exposure, to which no loading has been added for commissions, taxes, and expenses.

pure profit: Synonymous with *economic profit*.

pure public item: an item consumed in equal amount by all people, even though the item may have different value to these people. No one can be excluded from being a consumer of a pure public item (e.g., air, water, a sidewalk).

pure risks: the dangers and hazards involved in accident, fire, health, weather, or other potential perils to people.

purposive sample: a small number of observations or subjects chosen from a larger population on the basis of some given characteristic. Cf. *area sample*.

push a pan: (slang) to perform clerical or other office work.

push money (p.m.): a commission for retail clerks who are successful in selling specified goods. This is a type of incentive system.

push-pull strategy: the balance between a firm's attempts to stimulate the demand for its products by pushing them forward through the channels through efforts aimed at the middleman and pulling the goods through the channels to the consumer through promotional efforts aimed directly at the market.

put: to place a single data record into an output file of a computer.

puts: option contracts that entitle the holder to sell a number of shares of the underlying stock at a stated price on or before a fixed expiration date. See also *puts and calls*.

puts and calls: options that give the right to buy or sell a fixed amount of certain stock at a specified price within a specified time. A put gives the holder the right to sell the stock; a call conveys the right to buy the stock. Puts are purchased by those who think a stock may go down. A put obligates the seller of the contract, commonly known as the option writer, to take delivery of the stock and to pay the specified price to the owner of the option within the time limit of the contract. The price specified in a put or call is usually close to the market price of the stock at the time the contract is made. Calls are purchased by those who think a stock may rise. A call gives the holder the right to buy the stock from the writer at the specified price within a fixed period of time. Put and call contracts may be written for 30, 60, or 90 days, or longer. Six months and ten days is the most common term. If the purchaser of a put or call does not wish to exercise the option, the price paid for the option becomes a loss. See also *spread, Tax Reform Act of 1976.*

putting-out system: the second stage in the evolution of a materially productive civilization, initially characterized by an entrepreneur's agreement to take all the output an individual (or family) can produce at a fixed price. This stage eventually progressed to the stage at which the entrepreneur provided the workers with the raw materials and paid them on a piece-rate basis for finished goods. See also *factory system.*

pyramiding: employing profits of open or unliquidated positions to add to the holder's original position. See also *Public Utility Holding Company Act of 1935.*

pyramid ratio: a tool used in the analysis of management and income to determine the relationship of profits and capital.

pyramid selling (schemes): business opportunity frauds, usually promoted through advertisements for job opportunities guaranteed to yield enormous or quick profits, requiring little education or demanding a minimal personal investment. There are government regulations against certain pyramid schemes. The pyramider induces many people to buy his products, which they are to resell at a higher price. For example, if 10 people buy 50 units each but can sell only 15 each, the pyramider is still ahead, because he has sold 500 units. See also *fraud.*

Q-sort: a personality inventory in which the individual sorts a considerable number of statements into piles that represent the degrees to which the statements apply to him or her.

qualification: any physical, mental, moral, or legal requirement, condition, or ability that a candidate must have in order to be eligible for a job, office, or position.

qualification check: a formal or informal method of verifying and recording information about the skill, knowledge, experience, character, or related factors required of a candidate for employment that cannot be accurately measured by interview or examination.

qualified endorsement: an endorsement asserting that the limits of liability of an endorser release him or her of all responsibility in the event of nonpayment or nonacceptance of an instrument. A qualified endorsement is often stated on a document as "without recourse."

qualified handicapped: handicapped people who can perform jobs with reasonable employer accommodation. See also *Rehabilitation Act of 1973.*

qualified prospect: a potential customer who is able to buy a product and has the authority to make a decision to purchase. This conclusion is often arrived at following a check on the individual's credit.

qualifying period: See *waiting period.*

qualitative factor: a factor that is significant but cannot be measured precisely and easily.

quality circles: voluntary groups of operative employees who periodically brainstorm on how to increase the firm's output.

quality control: the attempt to ensure the presence of qualitative factors in a product or standards of performance in a service. Cf. *material control, process inspection, production control.*

quality market: a market in which

quality is more important than price.

quality of estate: a designation of the form in which an estate is to be owned, including type of possession and time. No indication of property value or physical characteristics is given.

quality of work life: the state of having good supervision, good working conditions, good pay and benefits, and an interesting, challenging, and rewarding job.

quantitative factor: a factor that affects decision making and can be measured numerically.

quantitative school: a modern school of management thought consisting of theories on management as a system of mathematical models and processes. Advocates of this school are greatly concerned with decision making. This school is the genesis of scientific management.

quantity demanded: amount which would be purchased at a particular price, at a moment of time.

quantity discount: a reduction that is given for volume buying.

quantity theory: a theory stating that a special relationship exists between the quantity of money and money income and that people spend excess money holdings irrespective of the interest rate and the manner in which the new money holdings were received. Cf. *Gresham's law, liquidity trap, marginal propensity to invest, marginal propensity to save.*

quantity variance: the standard price for a given resource, multiplied by the difference between the actual quantity used and the total standard quantity allowed for the number of units produced. When

applied to labor. Synonymous with *efficiency variance.*

quantization (quantize): subdivision of the range of values of a variable into a finite number of nonoverlapping and not necessarily equal subranges or intervals, each of which is represented by an assigned value lying within the subrange.

quantum meruit: "as much as is merited" (Latin); a principle of business law providing that when a service is given without a written estimate of price, there is an implied promise by the purchaser of the service to pay for the work as much as it is worth. See also *lien.*

quarter stock: stock with a par value of $25 for each share.

quartile deviation: the variability in a frequency distribution calculated by subtracting the value of the first quarter (25 percent) from the third-quarter value and dividing by two.

quasi: as if; that which resembles.

quasi corporation: any political subdivision of an organization or group (e.g., an unincorporated town.)

quasi-public company: a privately operated corporation in which the public has a special interest (e.g., eleemosynary institutions).

quasi reorganization: a restructuring that does not lead to the formation of a new company, undertaken for purposes of absorbing a deficit, avoiding bankruptcy, and affording an opportunity to begin again.

questionnaire: a set of questions seeking objective data or subjective opinion on a given subject. The questions are intended not to test an individual's ability to answer the questions (i.e., to arrive at a score) but rather to elicit responses with respect to the subject at hand.

queue: a line or group of items or people in a bank waiting for service.

queued access method: any computer access method that automatically synchronizes the transfer of data between the program using the access method and input/output devices, thereby eliminating delays for input/output operations. See also *random access;* cf. *multiple access.*

queueing theory: See *waiting line theory.*

quick assets

(1) *general:* assets that will be converted into cash within a reasonably short time in the ordinary course of business.

(2) *finance:* assets that can be readily converted into cash without appreciable loss. See also *liquidity.*

quickie strike: See *strike.*

quick ratio: the ratio between existing liabilities and quick assets, showing a firm's ability to pay off its liabilities rapidly with available funds.

quid pro quo: "something for something" (Latin); a mutual consideration; an advantage or a concession received in return for a similar favor.

quiescing: a process of bringing a device or a system to a halt by rejecting new requests for work.

quiet title: a title from which defects have been legally removed.

quiet title suit: a legal action to remove a defect or any questionable claim against the title to property. Cf. *cloud on title.*

quinary: a system of number representation in which a decimal digit N is represented by the digit pair AB, where $N = 5A + B$, $A = 0$ or 1, and B = 0, 1, 2, 3, or 4. Cf. *binary.*

quit: to end one's employment voluntarily.

quit claim deed: a document by which one's legal right, title, interest, or claim in a specific property or in an estate held by one's self or others is forever relinquished to another. It usually contains no warranty or statement against claims that others might have in the property.

quit rent: the last rental payment made by a tenant before leaving the property.

quota

(1) *general:* the amount of production expected from the average employee in order to receive the specified base pay. See also *sales quota.*

(2) *statistics:* a proportionate share of a unique population (e.g., an import quota).

quota rule: a union regulation in a labor-management contract establishing the number of workers to be hired for a particular job within the union's jurisdiction.

quota sampling: a sampling technique in which interviewers look for specific numbers of candidates with special characteristics. All units in the population do not have known or equal chances of being chosen. Cf. *area sample, cluster sample random sample.*

quota-share reinsurance: an agreement by which the reinsurer accepts a stated percentage of a risk written by an insurance company. See also *retained risk.*

quotation (quote): the highest bid to buy and the lowest offer to sell a security in a given market at a given time. For example, if you ask a broker for a "quote" on a stock, the reply may be something like "$45\frac{1}{4}$ to $45\frac{1}{2}$." This means that $45.25 is the highest price any buyer wanted to pay at the time the quote was given on the floor of a stock exchange, and $45.50 was the lowest price any seller would take at the same time. See also *bid and asked*.

quoted price: the stated price of a security or commodity.

quote sheet: an analysis of costs used as a basis for determining selling prices.

rabble hypothesis: the belief that workers are a disorganized group of individuals, each acting out of personal interest.

rack: a term used to describe the rack department, which sorts, distributes, and proves items in the commercial operations of a bank.

racketeering: the practice of unethical and extortionate use of power or violence to obtain an advantage; any dishonest scheme for obtaining money.

rack jobber: a wholesaler who maintains stocks of convenience-type merchandise, primarily in supermarkets, drugstores, and other related retail operations.

rack rail car: a freight car that has a floor laid over sills, with racks at both ends; used for shipping pulp wood that is loaded transversely.

rack rent: an unusually high rent in an amount equal to or nearly equal to the total value of the items produced on the rented property. Cf. *economic rent.*

radial transfer: a procedure for the transfer of data between peripheral equipment and the internal memory of the machine.

Radiation Control for Health and Safety Act of 1968: federal legislation establishing performance standards and limits of radiation that may be emitted from consumer items (television sets, microwave ovens, etc.).

radiation selling: using a specific sale as a starting point for future related sales, based on the first sale as the example of need (e.g., selling the camera that will lead to sales of film and film processing services).

radix: the number system base; a quantity that defines a system of representing numbers by positional notation; the number of digit symbols required by a number system.

rag business (trade): the sentimental name given to the fashion apparel industry.

raid:

(1) *securities:* a deliberate attempt by professional traders and others to depress the market price of a stock.

(2) *labor relations:* the attempt by a union to enroll members from another union (local, regional, or national), thereby encroaching on the second union's jurisdiction. See also *no-raiding agreements, rival unionism.*

Railroad Retirement Act of 1935: a federal law setting up railroad pension payments for retired employees and their families. It is administered by the five-member Railroad Retirement Board, which also administers a companion law, the Railroad Unemployment Insurance Act of 1938.

Railroad Unemployment Insurance Act of 1938: See *Railroad Retirement Act of 1935.*

Railway Labor Act of 1926: a federal law regulating relations between the carriers and their employees, including by amendment the airline industry. The act is administered by the National Mediation Board and the National Railroad Adjustment Board; the jurisdiction of the latter is confined to railroad disputes. See also *Adamson Act of 1916.*

rainmakers: (slang) law-firm partners who bring in business, sometimes because they have held high government positions. See also *revolving door.*

raise

(1) *administration:* an increase in value or amount (e.g., wages, prices).

(2) *securities:* a fraudulent increase in the face value of a negotiable instrument.

raised check: a check on which the amount has been illegally increased.

rally: a brisk rise following a decline in the general price level of the market or of an individual stock.

RAM: random-access memory. Cf. *ROM.*

Rand formula: a system whereby an employee who does not wish to become a union member pays his or her monthly union dues but is not listed as a union participant. Cf. *union shop, free rider.*

random access: a quality of a computer's memory device allowing data to be written in or read from the memory through direct locating rather than locating through reference to other data in the memory. See also *queued access method;* cf. *sequential access storage;* synonymous with "direct access."

random demand: a change in market demand that has no pattern and cannot be forecasted.

random numbers

(1) *general:* a series of numbers obtained by chance.

(2) *statistics:* a series of numbers considered to be appropriate for satisfying certain statistical tests.

(3) *statistics:* a series of numbers occurring by chance.

random processing: the treatment of data without respect to its location in external storage and in an arbitrary sequence governed by the input against which the data are to be processed.

random sample: a limited number of observations chosen by chance from an entire aggregate of a phenomenon. In this form of sampling, every item in the population has the same chance of being chosen as any other items. See also *area sample;* cf. *probability sampling, quota sampling.*

range: a measure showing the approximate extent of total variability or dispersion, found by determining the difference between the lower limit of the lowest class interval and the upper limit of the highest class interval. See also *quantization.*

rank

(1) *computers:* to arrange in an ascending or descending series according to importance.

(2) *administration:* a title or position in an organization.

(3) *statistics:* the rating from high to low. See also *percentile.*

(4) *securities:* See *restricted shares.*

rank and file

(1) *administration:* employees of an organization who do not participate in management activities.

(2) *labor relations:* members of a union who are not full-time paid officials (e.g., members of a shop committee, officers of a local union). Cf. *pork-chopper.*

ranking: a type of performance appraisal in which the rater ranks his or her subordinates from highest to lowest, based on some criterion.

rapport: the relationship, accord, and balance between a sales representative and a potential customer.

rat: Synonymous with *scab.*

rate

(1) *general:* to categorize and rank in terms of special qualities or properties.

(2) *insurance:* the cost of a unit of insurance. Cf. *premium.*

(3) *finance:* a charge, fee, or price.

rate cutting: a unilateral wage rate reduction by an employer in the absence of changes in job content.

rate discrimination: charging different prices for almost identical services. When this action tends to lessen competition, it may be illegal under antitrust laws. Cf. *price discrimination.*

rate of basic compensation: compensation fixed by law or administrative action for the position held by a worker.

rate of exchange: the amount of funds of one nation that can be bought on a specific date for a sum of currency of another country. Rates fluctuate often because of economic, political, and other forces.

rate of inflation: the average percentage rate of increase of the price of money, weighted and stated in annual terms.

rate of interest: the charge for borrowing money.

rate of return on investment (capital): See *ROI.*

rate regulation: the determination by a commission or public service agency of the maximum (and at times the minimum) charge that public utility corporations may demand for their services. See also *fair rate of return, public utility, utility.*

rate setting: the establishment of rates by agreement between labor and management or by an employer alone.

rate variance: in accounting procedures, the difference between actual wages paid and the standard wage rate, multiplied by the total actual hours of direct labor used.

rate war: a negative form of competition in which sellers drop their prices below their costs for purposes of putting the competition out of business. See also *predatory pricing, underselling.*

ratify: to confirm or approve.

rating: a traditional method of performance appraisal in which a judge evaluates performance in terms of a value or index that is used in some standard way. It traditionally involves global rating scales.

rating, merit: See *merit rating.*

rating bureaus: organizations that develop suggested rates for a substantial proportion of the fire insurance business. Rates are based on loss and expense experience of all fire insurance companies. Individual insurers are permitted to deviate, within limits, from bureau rates. See also *experience.*

rating scale: probably the most common method of appraising employees, involving evaluation of employees according to defined job and personal factors.

ratio

(1) *statistics:* a number relationship between two things (e.g., ratio of births to deaths).

(2) *accounting:* any relationship that can be used in measuring the rating or financial position of a firm (e.g., the relationship of a company's earnings to the firm's market price for its stock).

(3) *finance:* one of the various analyses made by a money-lending or credit agency of the financial statements of an individual, company, or other business enterprise seeking credit, to determine the de-

sirability of granting the requested credit.

(4) *finance:* the relative values of silver and gold in a monetary system that is based on both. See also *bimetallism.*

ratio (acid-test): See *acid-test ratio.*

ratio analysis: analysis of financial statements through a comparison of one figure, such as net profit, to another, such as sales or total investment.

rational buying motives: all costs of money, use, labor, and profit that affect a purchaser. Cf. *motivation, unconscious.*

rationality: the process of making decisions that serve to maximize the firm's goals.

rationalization: any approach that has the potential to increase efficiency or output.

rational-legal authority: an authority structure based on law (e.g., a supervisor is obeyed because of his or her position in the organization's hierarchy).

rationing: a technique for limiting purchases or usage of an item when the demanded quantity of the item exceeds the quantity available at a specific price. This occurs most often during wartime and under extremes of natural conditions (e.g., drought).

ratio of accounts payable to purchases: a ratio, determined for the present period and compared with a similar ratio for previous periods, that indicates the trend toward or away from prompt payment of current obligations.

ratio of capital to fixed assets: a ratio that is usually determined for a number of years to ascertain whether there is a trend toward converting the investment of the owners into fixed assets, thereby indicating a possible reliance on creditors for furnishing the required working capital.

ratio of finished goods inventory to the cost of goods sold: a ratio determined by dividing the cost of goods sold by the average finished-goods inventory. The resulting figure is the number of times the investment in the finished-goods inventory has turned over during the period under consideration. The present ratio is compared with a similar ratio for several previous periods, since it portrays the stability and trend of sales or a possibly overstated or expanded inventory.

ratio of fixed assets to fixed liabilities: a ratio that indicates the margin of safety to the present mortgage and bond holders, if any. Failure of the ratio to meet the minimum requirement frequently suggests that additional funds should be raised from the owners rather than by mortgaging fixed assets.

ratio of notes payable to accounts payable: a ratio whose desirability is determined by consideration of three quantitative factors: (1) notes issued in payment of merchandise; (2) notes issued to banks and brokers; and (3) notes issued to others. If a relatively large number of the outstanding notes were issued to merchandise creditors, this might indicate that the firm is unable to take advantage of the cash discounts offered in the trade and that other lending agencies might consider the firm's credit unfavorably.

ratio of notes receivable to accounts receivable: a ratio that, if large as compared with other firms in a similar line of business, indicates that the firm with the high ratio may have a lax credit policy or may be extending credit to customers whose ability to pay promptly is dubious.

ratio of owned capital to borrowed capital: a ratio considered to be important in determining the advisability of extending additional long-term credit to an applicant. If this ratio is not considered favorable, it frequently suggests that the funds desired should be raised from the owners of the business (i.e., the applicants themselves) rather than through additional pledging of any assets.

ratio of raw materials inventory to cost of manufacture: a ratio determined by dividing the cost of goods manufactured by the average raw-materials inventory. The resulting figure is the number of times the investment in the raw-materials inventory has turned over during the period under consideration. When the present ratio is compared with a similar ratio for previous periods, it portrays the trend and steadiness of production or indicates a possibly overstated or overexpanded inventory.

ratio reinforcement: a schedule of rewards that ties reinforcement directly to acts or behavior. It can be fixed or variable.

rat race: (slang) an occupation or style of living in which personal satisfaction is considered a less important goal than competition, climbing the organizational ladder, material acquisition, and the like.

raw data: data that have not been processed or reduced. They may or may not be in machine-ready form. See also *source document.*

raw material: nonprocessed resources utilized in producing an item. The act of production results in an alteration in the form of the original material.

raw-materials inventory: the items purchased by a manufacturing firm to be used in production.

razorback: (slang) manual worker.

RBO: See *relationship by objective.*

R correlation: a technique to determine relationships; the result of how closely two tasks or functions relate.

reaction: a drop in securities prices following a sustained period of increasing prices.

reaction time: tests that measure the speed of an individual's response to a stimulus. See also *human engineering, industrial psychology;* cf. *therbligs, time and motion study.*

reactive management: a management style in which decision makers respond to problems rather than anticipating problems before they occur.

read
(1) *computers:* to acquire or interpret data from a storage device, a data medium, or any other source.
(2) *computers:* to transcribe, usually from input devices or auxiliary storage to main memory.

reader
(1) *computers:* a device that converts information in one form of storage to information in another form of storage.
(2) *computers:* a part of the scheduler that transfers an input stream into the system.

readership: the total audience of a publication. Cf. *circulation.*

read-only: a type of access to data that alllows them to be read but not modified. See also *ROM.*

ready condition: the status of a task that is to be analyzed by the central processing unit. See also *access, time sharing.*

real accounts: the accounts appearing on the balance sheet that are not closed to a zero balance at the end of each accounting period. Synonymous with *permanent accounts.*

real earnings: earnings adjusted to exclude the effects of price change.

real estate: tangible land and all physical property, including all physical substances below, upon, or attached to land. Thus houses, trees, and fences are classified as real estate; all else is personal property.

real estate bond: See *bond, real estate.*

real estate market: the purchasing and selling of real property that establishes a supply and demand situation resulting in the creation of market values and prices.

Real Estate Settlement Procedures Act of 1975: legislation that provides that certain information on the nature and cost of a residential real estate resolution be given to the homeowner in a timely manner.

real income: the sum total of the purchasing power of a nation or individual.

real interest rate: the rate at which a person earns future purchasing power on monetary assets. It equals the money rate minus the rate of inflation.

real investment: an expenditure that

establishes a new capital asset, thus creating a new capital formation.

realistic job previews (RJP):   the practice of providing realistic information to new employees to avoid creating expectations that cannot be realized.

realization (realize)

(1) *finance:* the act or process of converting into cash an asset or the total assets of an individual or business.

(2) *securities:* receiving a profit from selling a security following an increase in its price.

reallocation: allocation of the costs of operating the service departments to the various production departments in proportion to the relative benefits or services received by each production department. Synonymous with *reapportionment.*

real money: money containing one or more metals that have intrinsic value, as distinguished from representative money, such as currency issued by a realm and checks, drafts, and so on, issued by legal entities. See also *bimetallism, monometallism;* cf. *fiat money.*

real price: the price of goods and services measured by the quantity of manpower needed to earn sufficient money to purchase the goods or services.

real property: the property that is devised by will to a party known as the devisee; all fixed, permanent, immovable property, such as land and tenements.

real time

(1) *computers:* the actual time during which a physical process transpires. See also *on-line, real-time.*

(2) *systems:* referring to the performance of a computation during the same time that the related physical process transpires, allowing the results of the computation to be used in guiding the physical process. See also *simulation, real-time.*

realtor: a real estate broker affiliated with the National Association of Real Estate Boards: "A professional in real estate who subscribes to a strict Code of Ethics as a member of the local and state boards and of the National Association of Real Estate Boards."

realty: a contraction of "real property."

real value of money: the price of money measured in terms of goods. Cf. *purchasing power.*

real wages: the cost of items and services that can be purchased with money wages. It is useful for comparing changes in the standard of living by eliminating the effect of changes in the general price level. See also *money wages.*

reapportionment: allocation of the costs of operating the service departments to the various production departments in proportion to the relative benefits or services received by each production unit. Synonymous with *reallocation.*

reappraisal: term applied when property is appraised a second time.

reasonable value: a value placed on property that parallels the existing market value.

reassessment: the result of a change in the assessed value of property or a reappraisal of property.

reassignment: a change of an employee from one job, position, or office to another, without promotion or demotion, while serving continuously within the same department, unit, or organization.

rebate

(1) *finance:* unearned interest that may be returned to a borrower if the loan is paid off before the maturity date.

(2) *sales:* any deduction made from a payment or charge. In contrast to a discount, a rebate is not deducted in advance but is returned to the consumer following payment of the full amount (e.g., a GE appliance costs $24, with a rebate of $5 after the consumer has mailed in a coupon from the appliance package). Cf. *discount.*

rebating: the illegal and unethical practice of selling a policy at less than the legal rate, allowing the insured a refund of the premium, or giving him or her goods of any value, thus avoiding payment of the full legal premium.

rebuild strategy: investment and marketing efforts designed to increase or exceed sales, profits, or market share levels that were held at an earlier time.

recall

(1) *labor relations:* the return to work of laid-off workers, usually on a seniority basis. See also *bumping.*

(2) *manufacturing:* the return of a distributed product for purposes of adjustment, repair, or other necessary work.

recapitalization: altering the capital structure of a firm by increasing or decreasing its capital stock.

recapture clause: a clause in a commercial lease giving the landlord the right to terminate the lease if certain conditions are not maintained or if a specified minimum volume of business does not result.

recasting a mortgage: reconstructing an existing mortgage by increasing its amount, interest rate, or time period.

receipt: written acknowledgment of value received.

receivables: accounts receivable owned by a business. These may be pledged as collateral for a loan secured from a bank or other financial institution.

receiver: a court-appointed, neutral party named to handle property under litigation or the affairs of a bankrupt person. The receiver is required to maintain the property and its assets for the benefit of those having equity in it until a court decision as to its disposition is made. See also *bailee, interim receiver, remainderman, sequestered account.*

receivership: the state of being under the care or administration of a receiver.

receiving: the process by which a computer obtains a message from a line.

receiving apron: a statement used in the receiving department of a store that contains all pertinent data concerning an incoming shipment. The form is used to identify the shipment for purposes of accounting and control. See also *financial statement, pro forma invoice.*

recency effect: a rater bias that occurs when the rater allows recent employee performance to sway the overall evaluation of the worker's performance. Cf. *halo effect.*

recency of events error: the tendency

to make biased ratings because of the excessive influence of recent events.

recession: a phase of the business cycle that shows a downswing or contraction of the economy.

reciprocal causation: the process in which a leader influences the behavior and attitudes of subordinates while the subordinates simultaneously influence the leader's behavior and attitudes.

reciprocal demand: the situation created when one person offers what another person desires, and vice versa.

reciprocal trade agreement: an international agreement between two or more countries to establish mutual trade concessions that are expected to be of equal value.

reciprocity: the purchasing of goods by one firm from another on a preferential basis, with the expectation that the second firm will preferentially buy the goods of the first.

reclamation

(1) *general:* a business term to describe the act of obtaining useful materials from waste products. Cf. *recycling.*

(2) *banking:* a sum of money due or owing by a bank, resulting from an error in the listing of the amount of a check on a clearinghouse balance.

recognition

(1) *advertising:* acceptance of an agency by a medium. A recognized agency receives standard agency discounts.

(2) *labor relations:* an agreement by an employer to accept a given union as the collective-bargaining agent of that firm's employees.

recompense: a payment or award made to anyone to make amends for a loss or damage. See also *compensation.*

reconciliation:

(1) *accounting:* a process for determining the differences between two items of an account (e.g., a bank statement and an up-to-date checkbook) so as to bring them into agreement. See also *adjustment.*

(2) *labor relations:* bringing harmony to a labor dispute; settling a labor-management conflict.

reconditioning property: improving a property's value by repairing it or making changes to enhance it.

reconsignment: any alteration, including a route change, made in a consignment before the items have arrived at their billed destination.

reconversion: following a war, the shift of a nation's economy from war efforts to a focus on peacetime needs and goals.

reconveyance: transfer of title of property back to a former owner.

recooperage: the repair of damaged containers.

record

(1) *statistics:* a collection of related items of data, treated as a unit.

(2) *computers:* a collection of information relating to one area of activity in a data-processing system.

record, unit

(1) *computers:* a single card containing one complete record (i.e., a punched card).

(2) *computers:* a printed line containing a maximum of 120 characters, a punched card with a maximum of 72 characters, and so on.

recordation: public acknowledgment

in written form that a lien exists against a specific property that is identified in a mortgage. See also *lien affidavit.*

record date: the date on which a person must be registered as a shareholder on the stock book of a company in order to receive a declared dividend or, among other things, to vote on company affairs. Cf. *ex-dividend.*

recourse: the right to seek payment on a discounted note from the payee if the maker defaults.

recoverable error: an error condition that allows continued execution of a computer program.

recovery
(1) *economics:* the period of the business cycle that follows a depression.
(2) *insurance:* following a loss, the money received by an insurance company from a reinsurer by subrogation or from salvage.
(3) *securities:* a rise in stock prices following a period of declining prices. Synonymous with *expansion,* "upswing."

Recovery Act: See *Economic Recovery Tax Act of 1981.*

recruiting: personnel department activity involving the search for employees to meet the specific needs of an organization. In addition, the company may utilize the services of outside recruiting firms. See also *headhunter, special events recruiting.*

recruitment: the attempt to attract compatible individuals to a firm as potential employees.

recurring payoff: further income from a sound investment paid back to the investor with interest paid in addition

to the original investment; a repeated return on a single investment.

recursive: pertaining to a process in which each step makes use of the results of earlier steps.

recycling: the conversion of waste products (i.e., empty beer cans) to usable material for the purpose of reducing pollution, saving money, and/ or conserving resources. Cf. *reclamation.*

red apple: (slang) a nonunion worker, usually an individual who plays up to a boss by deciding not to join the union.

red-circle rates: wages or salaries that are inappropriate for a given job according to a job evaluation plan.

redeemable rent: payments of rent that can be recovered (e.g., with a rental agreement containing the option to buy the property). When such an option is exercised, the purchaser receives all or a portion of the rents, or the monies may be applied to the sales price.

redeemable stock: a preferred stock that can be called in at the option of the issuing company. See also *redemption price.*

redemise: to renew a lease.

redemption
(1) *finance:* the liquidation of an indebtedness on or before maturity, (e.g., the retirement of a bond issue prior to its maturity date).
(2) *real estate:* purchasing back. A debtor redeems his mortgaged property when he has paid his debt.

redemption bond: See *bond, redemption.*

redemption fund: a fund created for the purpose of retiring an obligation.

redemption price: the price (usually

par value) at which a bond may be redeemed before maturity when it is retired at the option of the issuing company; the amount a company must pay to call in certain types of preferred stock.

redeployment: reassignment and accompanying training of employees, resulting from changing technology or equipment or from business decisions requiring new skills. See also *labor-saving equipment.*

red herring: a financial prospectus with a cautionary statement on the first page, printed in red. It is informational and not intended as an offer to sell the securities described. See also *open prospectus.*

rediscount
(1) *banking:* a negotiable instrument that has been discounted by a bank and subsequently discounted a second time by a Federal Reserve Bank or another bank for the benefit of the bank that originally discounted the instrument. See also *bank credit.*
(2) *finance:* to discount for the second time.

rediscount rate: the rate set by a Federal Reserve Bank for discounting a second time monies offered by their district member banks; the interest rate charged for discounting a negotiable instrument that has already been discounted.

red label: a shipping label indicating flammable contents.

redlining: the alleged practice of certain lending institutions of making it almost impossible to obtain mortgages, improvement loans, and insurance by homeowners, apartment house landlords, and businesses in neighborhoods outlined in red on a map—usually areas that are deteriorating or considered poor investments by the lending institution. See also *greenlining.*

red one: (slang) a successful business day.

red tape: (slang) the delay caused by inefficient and/or bureaucratic routine.

reduced rate average: See *coinsurance.*

redundancy
(1) *computers:* the fraction of the gross information content of a message that can be eliminated without loss of essential information.
(2) *computers:* an extra piece of information used to assist in determining the degree of accuracy of digits or words in a computer. See also *redundancy check.*
(3) *administration:* (British usage) cause for dismissal of a worker when his or her job ceases to exist.

redundancy check: an automatic or programmed check based on the systematic insertion of components or characters used especially for checking purposes.

reefer: (slang) a refrigerated container.

reel: a mounting for a roll of computer tape.

reemployment: bringing a laid-off employee back to work. See also *recall.*

reentry: a landlord's right to reacquire leased property if terms in the lease, such as the making of rent payments, are not satisfied. A reentry clause must be inserted by the landlord in the original lease. Cf. *landlord's warrant.*

reexport: to export already imported items, without duty charges, in basically similar form to a third country. Cf. *production sharing.*

referee: when a case is pending in court, an individual assigned by the presiding officer to receive testimony from the parties and present the information to the court. When appropriate, the referee can accept foreclosed property and make a deed. See also *bankruptcy, foreclosure;* Cf. *master in chancery.*

referee's foreclosure deed: a deed made by a court official that forecloses the mortgage on a property and passes the title on to the referee.

referee's partition deed: a deed made by a referee, conveying title to property when co-owners choose to divide their interest.

reference check: a procedure used to verify the accuracy of information contained in an application form and/or to increase knowledge about the applicant.

reference cycle: the sequence of expansion and contraction in the general business activity.

reference group: a sociological unit from which an individual takes his or her behavior cues.

referendum: a vote by the rank and file to choose nominees in a national union office election, to decide on dues or assessment increases, to ratify a proposed contract, or to address other issues.

referent power: the influence exerted on a subordinate who identifies with his or her superior's style and personality. A powerful superior who is admired acquires a certain amount of power over the admirer.

referral leads: names of potential customers given to a sales representa-

tive, usually by satisfied customers.

referral risks: risks beyond the underwriting authority of an office that must be referred to a supervisory office for a decision on acceptance. See also *overline, substandard.*

refinance

(1) *real estate:* to extend existing financing or to acquire new monies, usually done when a mortgage is withdrawn so that a larger one can be placed on the property. See also *refunding mortgage.*

(2) *finance:* to revise a payment timetable and, frequently, to modify interest charges on the obligation.

refinanced loan: a loan that has had an addition to the principal balance. Such increases are usually for property improvements such as an added room. Normally, the term and/or the payment amount is also affected.

refinancing: Synonymous with *refunding.*

reflation: upon recovering from a depression or a recession, the period during which prices are returned to the level they had attained during a period of prosperity by lowering the purchasing power of money.

refundable interest: the unearned portion of interest previously charged that will be returned to the debtor (maker of a note) if the indebtedness is liquidated prior to maturity.

refund check

(1) *general:* a check or other instrument of currency that is a repayment of money for any reason. See also *rebate.*

(2) *merchandising:* a statement for a customer's purchase that is returned.

(3) *taxes:* a check from a govern-

ment tax bureau for overpayment of taxes.

refunding

(1) *securities:* replacing an older bond issue with a new issue, either before or at maturity of the older one. It is often done to change the interest rate on the debt.

(2) *finance:* the act of returning a portion of money to the giver from an amount already paid out. See also *debt.*

refunding bond: See *bond, refunding.*

refunding mortgage: refinancing a mortgage with monies derived from a new loan.

refusal to sell: the right of a seller to choose the dealers that will handle his or her merchandise. Invoking this right, which is recognized by law, a seller may refuse to deal with firms that do not meet certain standards or qualifications. Cf. *franchise.*

regeneration: restoring data previously withdrawn from storage into the computer.

regional bargaining: See *multiemployer bargaining.*

regional differential: among broad geographical subdivisions, the difference in prevailing wages for equal work.

regional store: a branch store, usually located far from the central store, that functions under the name of the parent store. In most cases a regional store operates as an autonomous unit.

register

(1) *general:* to make a permanent record of events.

(2) *computers:* a device capable of storing a specified amount of data (e.g., one word).

(3) *systems:* a unit or machine for temporarily storing information while or until it is used.

(4) *transportation:* a written document prepared by a customs official that allows a ship to engage in foreign trade.

register, control: a register that holds the identification of the instruction word to be executed next in time sequence, following the current operation.

register, memory: a register that is involved in all transfers of data and instructions, as input or output, between memory and the arithmetic and control registers.

register, shift: a register that shifts every bit stored in it one place to the left upon the application of a shift pulse. It can also be shifted to the right.

register(ed) check: a check prepared by a teller, using funds recorded and placed aside in a special register, for the convenience of a purchaser who may wish to make a payment by check but does not maintain a checking account. The check has two stubs; one is for the purchaser and the other is used by the bank for record keeping. It is actually a money order, prepared in the form of a check. The bank usually charges a small fee for each registered check sold.

registered bond: See *bond, registered.*

registered mail: mail recorded in a U.S. Post Office at the mailing point and at each successive point of transmission, to guarantee special care in delivery. Registered mail can be insured to guarantee indemnity in case of loss, fire, or damage. Cf. *cer-*

tified mail.

registered representative (trader): a current term for "customer's man"; a full-time employee of a stock exchange member organization who has met the requirements of the exchange with respect to background and knowledge of the securities business. Synonymous with *account executive, customer's broker.*

registrar: an agency, usually a trust company or a bank, charged with the responsibility for preventing the issuance of more stock than has been authorized by a company. The registrar's primary function is to authenticate the issuing of securities. See also *overissue.*

registration

(1) *securities* filing of a statement with the SEC by the issuer before a public offering may be made of new securities by a company or of outstanding securities by controlling stockholders. The securities must be registered under the Securities Act of 1933. The registration statement discloses pertinent information relating to the company's operations, securities, management, and purpose of the public offering. On security offerings involving less than $300,000, the information required is less detailed.

(2) *computers:* the accurate positioning of lines and spaces in printouts or holes punched in a card.

registry: a listing by a country of ships that fly its flag and are under the regulation of maritime law.

regression, multiple: an analysis program for determining the mathematical relationships and relative significances of boundaries for a particular problem.

regression analysis: a method for predicting the values of a quantitative variable from scores of a correlated variable.

regression equation: a formula for computing the most probable value of one variable (Y) from the known value of another variable (X).

regression line: the curve or line that depicts the relationship between two variables.

regressive supply: the situation in which, when the price of an item drops, a greater quantity of the item is offered.

regressive taxes: rates in a tax system that decrease as the base amount taxed increases (a rate of 5 percent applied to a base of $500, 4 percent applied to a base of $2000, etc.). A sales tax is a regressive tax. Cf. *progressive tax.*

regs: (slang) regulations.

regular dating: referring to terms of a sale under which the period for discount and the date on which payment is required are determined from the date of the invoice. Cf. *ROG dating.*

regulated investment company: an investment company that can avoid income tax on its ordinary income and capital gains by distributing profits as dividends and by conforming to other statutory rules.

Regulation Q: as established by the Federal Reserve Board, a formula it uses to determine the maximum interest that can be paid by commercial banks to their customers on time deposits.

regulations: means of controlling and coordinating the decision-making behavior of all employees by having them follow rules.

Regulation T: the Federal Reserve Board criterion governing the amount of credit that may be advanced by brokers and dealers to customers for the purchase of securities. See also *margin*.

Regulation U: the Federal Reserve Board criterion governing the amount of credit that may be advanced by a bank to its customers for the purchase of listed stocks.

Rehabilitation Act of 1973: legislation that prohibits discrimination against those who are handicapped but qualified to perform work. It applies to employers who receive federal monies and to federal agencies of the executive branch. See also *qualified handicapped*.

rehypothecate: to pledge a second time.

reinforcement schedule: the timing or scheduling of rewards.

reinforcement theory: a motivation approach that examines factors that energize, direct, and sustain behavior.

reinforcer (reward): a stimulus that follows an act and (1) reduces the need motivating the act and (2) strengthens the habit that led to the act in the first place.

reinstatement

(1) *insurance:* when payment of a claim reduces the principal amount of a policy by the amount of the claim, provision that is usually made for reestablishing the policy to an original amount. Depending on policy conditions, it may be done automatically, either with or without premium consideration, or at the request of the insured. See also *waiver of restoration premium*.

(2) *personnel:* restoration of a worker to a former position without loss of seniority or benefits. See also *make whole*.

reinsurance: assumption by one insurance company of all or part of a risk undertaken by another insurance company. Cf. *quota-share reinsurance, retained risk;* see also *excess of loss reinsurance*.

reinsurance broker: an organization that places (brokers) reinsurance through a reinsurance underwriter; not to be confused with a broker of insurance.

reinvestment privilege: the automatic investment of dividends from holdings in a mutual fund in additional shares of the fund, sometimes without a sales charge.

REIT: real estate investment trust.

relationship by objective (RBO): a group dynamics approach, used primarily in labor-management relations, in which an atmosphere is developed that allows all sides to speak out freely and to attempt to develop mutual goals and the means of attaining them. Mediators work largely with union committeemen and key supervisors from the shop.

relationship-motivated leadership: the leadership style shown by a leader who is motivated to form or join other groups or organizations.

relative address: a number used in the address part of a computer instruction to specify a required location.

relative income concept: the hypothesis that spending is a function of a family's relative place in the income distribution of similar family units (i.e., people who earn the same amount tend to spend the same amount of money).

release

(1) *business law:* the cancellation or resolution of a claim against another person.

(2) *insurance:* the written statement of a claim's settlement.

(3) *labor relations:* dismissal of a worker for proper cause.

release clause: a clause in a mortgage permitting payment of a part of the debt so that a proportionate part of the property can be freed.

release of mortgage: dropping a claim against property established by a mortgage.

relet: to lease property again after a lease has been terminated or broken.

relevant range: the band of activity in which budgeted sales and expense relationships will be valid.

reliability

(1) *computers:* the probability that a device will function without failure over a specified period or with a given amount of usage.

(2) *statistics:* accuracy and dependability.

(3) See also *product reliability.*

reliability engineering: a structure technique for achieving maximum product reliability through systematic gathering of management, engineering, mathematical, and statistical elements and concepts.

relocate

(1) *computers:* to move a routine from one portion of storage to another and to adjust the necessarv address references so that the routine can be executed in its new location.

(2) *administration:* to move from one geographic area to another (as

done by an organization, a group, or an individual).

remainder

(1) *real estate:* upon completion of a life estate, when the property reverts to the owner or goes to an heir and the owner does not take the property back, an estate created by the same instrument. This remainder estate begins upon termination of the temporary estate (i.e., the life estate) that preceded it. See also *reversionary interest.*

(2) *publishing:* an unsold book that has never been retailed. Remainders are often offered by the publisher to special stores for sale at reduced prices.

remainderman: an individual who receives a remainder estate.

remand: the action of an appellate court in sending a cause back to the lower court that sought the appeal, accompanied by the instructions of the higher court.

remargining: placing added margin against a loan. Remargining is one option for brokers who require additional cash or collateral when their securities have lost some of their value.

remedial law: Synonymous with *adjective law.*

remise: to give or grant back; to discharge or release. Synonymous with ''quit claim.''

remittance: funds forwarded from one person to another as payment for purchased items or services.

remonetization: the reinstatement of a coin as standard money after it has been demonetized.

remote access: communication with a data-processing facility by one or more stations that are distant from that facility. See also *terminal, remote.*

remote delivery: sending goods from a central warehouse to customers via area delivery stations located in the suburbs or by truck.

removal: separation of a worker from his or her office or position for cause.

remunerations: wages and other financial benefits received from employment.

renege: to go back on a promise; to pull out of an agreement. See also *repudiation.*

renewable natural resources: natural resources that maintain their productivity over time (e.g., waterfalls that produce power).

renewal: extending the maturity of an existing loan obligation or other document of relationship. Cf. *novation.*

renewal certificate: a certificate issued to renew an insurance policy rather than writing out a new policy. The certificate refers to the policy but does not enumerate all its items.

rent: income received from leasing real estate.

rent control: federal legislation of 1942 that fixed rents as stated in the terms of many residential leases then in effect. Rent could be raised only when the premises were leased to a different tenant. Presently, throughout the nation there are other (e.g., municipal) rent control statutes in effect.

rentier: a person living on income received from fixed investments.

rent roll: all rents receivable from an estate.

renunciation: giving up a right or claim without any reservation or without naming the person who is to assume the title.

reopener clause: a provision calling for the reopening of a current contract at a specified time for negotiations on stated subjects (e.g., wage increases, pensions, health and welfare). Cf. *zipper clause.*

reorganization: an alteration of a firm's capital structure, often resulting from a merger, that affects the rights and responsibilities of the owners. The objectives of a reorganization are to eliminate the cause of failure, settle with creditors, and allow the firm to remain in business. See also *National Bankruptcy Act of 1898*; cf. *quasi reorganization.*

reorganization bond: See *bond, reorganization.*

rep

(1) *general:* short for "representative."

(2) *advertising:* short for "representative;" the person who sells space or time for an advertising medium.

repatriation: the liquidation of overseas investments and the return of the proceeds to the country of the investor.

repeat demand: the demand created for items that are frequently requested and bought.

repertory grid: a marketing technique for ascertaining the characteristics of product similarities and differences under varied use contexts.

repetition instruction: an instruction to a computer that causes one or more instructions to be executed an indicated number of times. See also *stored program computer.*

replacement charts: graphic representations of who will replace whom in the organization when a job opening occurs. See also *replacement summaries.*

replacement-cost insurance: insurance that provides for replacement of the damaged property without deduction for depreciation. The usual replacement-cost form requires that the property actually be replaced before the insured can collect a claim under it. It is primarily available only for buildings, with a few exceptions, and is subject to a coinsurance requirement.

replacement-cost standard: the cost of replacing equipment with new equipment for tasks identical to those performed by worn or obsolete equipment. It provides a way of determining a firm's value.

replacement demand: capital goods or consumer items that are in demand because of depreciation or obsolescence.

replacement summaries: lists of likely replacements for each job and their relative strengths and weaknesses. See also *replacement charts.*

replevin: a statute remedy for recovery of the possession of a chattel. The right of possession can be tried only in such action. Cf. *seisin.*

report generation: a technique for producing complete machine reports from information that describes the input file and the format and content of the output report.

reporting form: an insurance policy designed for use when values of the insured property fluctuate during the policy term. Usually, an adequate limit of liability is set; then the insured reports the values actually on hand on a given day of each month. At the end of the year or policy term, these reported values are averaged and the premium is adjusted.

reporting pay: the minimum wage that is guaranteed under union contract when an employee who is scheduled to work arrives at the assigned place for activity and finds no work opportunity. Synonymous with *call-in pay.*

repossession: the reclaiming or taking back of items that were bought on an installment sales contract on which the buyer has fallen behind in payments.

representation: the statements made by an insured person to his or her insurance company, enabling the firm to establish a policy and set the proper risk amounts and fee charges. See also *declaration, warranty.*

representation election: a vote conducted by the National Labor Relations Board to determine whether a majority of the workers in a previously established unit want to be represented by a given union. See also *appropriate unit, cross-check, Wagner-Connery Act;* cf. *consent election, run-off election.*

representative money

(1) *finance:* paper money secured by monetary metal (i.e., gold or silver certificates) deposited in the treasury of a country.

(2) *commodities:* funds that are backed in full by a commodity.

repressive tax: a tax that discourages production. Its effect is to lower potential taxable income.

reproducible capital: productive assets that can themselves be produced (e.g., equipment and buildings).

reproducer

(1) *computers:* a device used for duplicating cards and card data or for punching cards in any format.

(2) *computers:* a device used to duplicate on one card all or part of the data contained on another card.

reprographics: all the processes, techniques, and equipment used in multiple copying or reproduction of documents.

repudiation: intentional and willful refusal to pay a debt in whole or in part. The term usually refers to the willful act of a government or a subdivision thereof. Cf. *nullification of agreement.*

repurchase agreement: an agreement between a seller and a buyer that the seller will buy back the note, security, or other property at the expiration of a stated period or upon completion of certain conditions, or both. Cf. *sell and leaseback agreement.*

reputed owner: an individual who appears to be a property owner although in fact the property belongs to another person. See also *presumptive title.*

required activities: the formally assigned tasks that a group must perform.

required interaction: the condition that occurs when a person's activity follows or is influenced by the activity of another. Such interaction can be verbal or nonverbal.

required reserves: liquid assets that state-chartered banks must hold in accordance with regulations of state banking agencies and Federal Reserve officials.

required return: the lowest return or profit needed to justify an investment.

requisition: a written demand from a department to its purchasing department to release on a specific date materials to be used in a production process or other activity of consumption within an organization. See also *excess materials requisitions.*

rerun: a repeat of a machine run, usually because of a correction, an interruption, or a false start.

res adjudicata: the principle according to which a controversy that has once been decided is deemed to be settled forever; that is, the courts will not hear claims to which the issue adjudicated applies.

resale: the selling of goods or services that have been bought by the seller from another person in essentially the same form.

resale price maintenance: a supplier's control over the selling price of his or her goods at various stages of distribution by means of contractual arrangement under fair trade laws or other means.

rescind: See *right of rescission.*

rescission: making void or annulling (e.g., rescission of a law or judgment). See also *right of rescission.*

rescue dump: recording on magnetic tape the entire contents of memory, which includes the status of the computer system at the time the dump is carried out.

research and development (R & D)

(1) *general:* applying the findings of science and technology in creating a firm's products or services.

(2) *securities:* the dollar amount spent on company-sponsored research and development for the year, as reported to the SEC. The total ex-

cludes any expenditures for research and development performed under contract for others, such as U.S. government agencies.

reseller markets: firms and individuals who buy products in order to re-sell them to others.

reservation price: the highest offered price at which a seller will continue to hold back from selling. The seller will sell, however, at any offer above the reservation price. Cf. *upset price.*

reserve
(1) *accounting:* a portion of the profits allocated to various reserve accounts to protect any depreciation in asset values. The reserves are taken from profits before any declaration of dividends by the board of directors.
(2) *insurance:* funds earmarked for specific purposes (e.g., reserves for unearned premiums, reserves for losses in process of adjustment). Cf. *legal reserve.*
(3) *banking:* assets in the form of cash maintained in a bank's own vault. See also *reserve ratio.*

reserve ratio (requirement): the relationship of the amount of money that must be held in a reserve account, as declared by the Federal Reserve Bank, to the total demand deposits of a member bank.

reserve requisition control: periodic stock count control whereby all the goods in the forward stock are considered as sold and counts are made on the reserve stock that is not on the selling floor. As forward stock diminishes, additional items are requested from the reserve. Sales are determined by adding up the requisitions made in a specified time period.

reserves: See *reserve.*

reserve stock control: a technique for earmarking appropriate stock for the maintainance of business until new merchandise is purchased.

reset to zero: (slang) to rethink a problem; to return to the first step in formulating a strategy or designing a project.

reshipper: a shipping container in which empty containers (e.g., soda bottles) that are intended to be used again are received.

resident buyer: any person or firm located in a market area who aids retailers in making market contacts and assists in their purchasing. Cf. *merchandise mart.*

residual: a fee paid to an individual for repeated transmission (e.g., on radio or television) of a performance in which he or she originally participated. Cf. *royalty.*

residual error: the difference between the expected exact result from theory and an optimum result derived from experiment.

residual income: the net income of a profit center or investment center, less the imputed interest on the net assets used by the center.

residual interest: the owners' equity in an entity's assets after deducting liabilities and any other claims that have a higher priority.

residual value: the predicted disposal value of a long-lived asset.

residuary bequest: the part of a will that gives instruction for the disposal of any portion of an estate remaining after payment of debts and other obligations.

residuary devisee: a recipient by will of any real property after all other claimants to the estate have received payment.

residuary estate: the remainder of an estate after all bequests and devises have been executed according to the will.

residuary legacy: personal property of an estate remaining after all claims to the estate have been properly disposed of.

resignation: a step taken by an employee to terminate his or her relationship with an employer. Notice is usually given, and the date on which the resignation will take effect is specified.

resource

(1) *general:* anything a country uses to produce goods and services (manpower, minerals, oil, etc.). See also *nonrenewable natural resources.*

(2) *merchandising:* a producer or wholesaler from whom a merchant buys goods for resale.

resource allocator role: the function of a manager in deciding who will get what resources in the unit. The resources can include time, money, material, equipment, people, and the unit's reputation.

resource-augmenting technical change: a technical change that has the same effect on output as if the quantity of natural resources had been increased. Cf. *labor-augmenting technical change.*

resource budget: a budget based on establishing limitations for each cost element (e.g., labor hours, materials).

resource-oriented production: production of raw materials, minerals, or components in a foreign country for shipment to a multinational corpora-

tion's home country or other component unit.

respondentia: under conditions of hypothecation, the security offered against a loan (e.g., the goods on a truck).

response time: the interval between the submission of an item of work to a computing system and the return of results. Synonymous with *turnaround time;* see also *word time.*

responsibility accounting: a system under which someone is held responsible for each activity that occurs in a particular area of a firm.

responsibility center: an organizational unit in which the manager has control over and is held accountable for costs, costs and revenues, or costs, revenues, and investments. See also *cost center, investment center, profit center.*

resting order: an order that can remain open or good until canceled when (1) an order to purchase securities is limited to a price lower than the market or (2) an order to sell is limited to a price above the market.

restitution: the enforced payment of money, or its equivalent, to its rightful owner, as established by law. Cf. *replevin.*

restoration premium: the premium charged to restore a policy or bond to its original value after payment of a loss.

rest period: a brief paid interruption of the working schedule.

restraining order: a court order in aid of a suit to maintain the status quo until all parties can be heard from. See also *injunction.*

restraint of trade: the effect of any contract, combination, or agreement (e.g., a monopoly) that impedes free competition. See also *Robinson-Patman Act of 1936, Sherman Antitrust Act of 1890.*

restricted shares: common stock released under an arrangement whereby the shares do not rank for dividends until some event has taken place—usually the attainment of a certain level of earnings.

restrictive covenants: written agreements limiting the use of property.

restrictive license: an agreement under whose terms an owner of a patented item allows a licensee to sell the patented good under certain limited conditions.

results orientation: the understanding by sales representatives that they will be judged and therefore their destiny with the organization determined by individual selling ability.

resume: a brief listing of an applicant's work experience, education, personal data, and other information relevant to the applicant's employment qualifications.

retailer: a merchant whose primary activity is to sell directly to consumers.

retailing: the activity of purchasing for resale to a customer.

retail inventory method: See *retail method of inventory.*

retail method of inventory: an accounting technique for recording all inventory inputs, including sales, purchases, markdowns, and so on, at their retail values. Purchased items are recorded at cost.

retail outlet: store that sells directly to the customer.

retail price: the price at which goods are identified for sale or are sold.

retail price maintenance: allowing a manufacturer, under protection of state law, to set retail prices for his products. This is in accord with the terms of the fair trade acts. See also *fair trade acts.*

retail salesperson: an individual who works inside a store, where customers come to him or her.

retained earnings: corporate monies retained after taxes and distribution of dividends to stockholders. Synonymous with *undistributed profits.*

retained risk: the insurance for a stated risk or property that is covered by an insurance firm on its own account after some of the coverage has been reinsured. See also *quota-share reinsurance.*

retainer: payment to cover future services and advice, submitted in advance to the individual who is expected to render the services.

retaliatory duty: a differential duty designed to penalize foreign nations for alleged discriminatory commerce activity or to force them into making trade concessions. See also *tariff war;* cf. *most favored nation clause.*

retention: the amount of liability retained by a company on a given risk. It consists of the gross line less reinsurance.

retirement
(1) *personnel:* voluntary or forced termination of employment because of age, disability, or illness. Contracts usually define the age of retirement, which facilitates establishment of a retirement allowance or pension.
(2) *finance:* the paying off of a debt prior to or at maturity.

retirement fund: monies set aside by an organization in a fund that builds up value over the year to provide income for employees who are eligible to retire and receive income from it.

retirement income: a stipulated amount of income starting at a selected retirement age. This is derived by exercising one of the settlement options available against the policy or annuity cash value. See also *individual retirement accounts.*

retirement shock: the personal adjustment problems caused by going from full-time work to full-time leisure.

retiring a bill: paying a bill of exchange on its due date or before, at a discount.

retraining: a technique for preparing employees already within an organization for new skills requirements that are created by various internal (organizational) or external (economic, social, technological, etc.) changes.

retrieval: See *information retrieval.*

retroactive extension: extending the terms (except amount) of present coverage into the period of prior insurance. This is used, for example, in errors and omissions insurance to provide coverage against prior undiscovered losses.

retroactive pay: a delayed wage payment for work done when employees were being paid at a lower rate for the same work. A new contract may provide for a wage increase for work completed before the agreement goes into effect.

retroactive restoration: a provision in a policy or bond whereby, after payment of a loss, the original amount of coverage is automatically restored to take care of prior undiscovered losses as well as future losses.

retrocession: a reinsuring organization ceding (i.e., reinsuring) a portion of a reinsurance transaction.

retrogression: a procedure in some union contracts permitting a worker who, because of accident, impairment, and sometimes incapacity due to age, has become less productive to return to a position that makes less onerous demands on the individual and still allows the person to hold a job, seniority, and rights.

retrospective rating: a form of experience rating in which the premium of the risk is adjusted after expiration of the policy in accordance with the actual losses incurred under that policy, subject to prescribed minimum and maximum limits.

return: a statement of financial and related information required by government tax agencies (e.g., a tax return). See also *yield.*

return item: a negotiable instrument, usually a check, that has been sent to one bank by another for collection and payment and is returned unpaid to the sending bank.

return on investment: See *ROI.*

return on net worth: the ratio of an organization's net profit following taxes to its net worth, providing a measure of the rate of return on a shareholders' investment.

return on stockholders' equity: a measure of performance from a stockholder's viewpoint, computed by dividing net income by average stockholders' equity.

return on total assets: the ratio of an organization's net profit following taxes to its total assets, providing a measure of the rate of return on, or productivity of, total assets.

return premium: the amount due the insured if a policy is reduced in rate, reduced in amount, or canceled, or— if it is subject to audit—if the audit yields a finding of less exposure(s) than the original estimate(s).

returns to vendor: goods sent back to the vendor by a store for various reasons (e.g., damaged merchandise, lateness of delivery). See also *vendor chargebacks;* cf. *purchase allowance.*

reusable packaging: containers that have another use subsequent to their service as merchandise containers.

revaluation (revalorization): restoration of the value of a depreciated national currency that has previously been devalued by lowering the request for or raising the supply of foreign currencies by restricting imports and promoting exports.

revenue: the grand total of all resources received from the sale of a firm's product or service during a stated period; not to be confused with *general revenue.* Cf. *gross revenue;* see also *government revenue.*

Revenue Act of 1962: federal legislation that provided an investment tax credit of 7 percent on new and used property other than buildings. See also *Revenue Act of 1964, Revenue Act of 1971, Revenue Act of 1978.*

Revenue Act of 1964: federal legislation that provided for a two-stage cut in personal income tax liabilities and corporate profits tax liabilities in 1964 and 1965. See also *Revenue Act of 1962, Revenue Act of 1971, Revenue Act of 1978.*

Revenue Act of 1971: federal legislation that accelerated by one year

scheduled increases in personal exemptions and standard deductions. It repealed excise taxes on automobiles retroactive to August 15, 1971, and on small trucks and buses to September 22, 1971. It also reinstated the 7 percent investment tax credit and incorporated depreciation range guidelines. See also *Revenue Act of 1962, Revenue Act of 1964, Revenue Act of 1978.*

Revenue Act of 1978: federal legislation that reduced taxes for individuals and businesses. It contained some elements of tax reform and extended several temporary provisions of the Tax Reduction and Simplification Act of 1977. See also *Revenue Act of 1962, Revenue Act of 1964, Revenue Act of 1971, Tax Reduction and Simplification Act of 1977.*

Revenue Adjustment Act of 1975: federal legislation that provided tax reductions for the first six months of 1976. It extended corporate rate reductions enacted in the Tax Reduction Act of 1975 and reduced individual taxes in order to maintain withholding rates that applied during the last eight months of 1975. See also *Tax Reduction Act of 1975.*

Revenue and Expenditure Control Act of 1968: federal legislation that levied a 10 percent surtax on personal income taxes, effective April 1, 1968, and on corporate taxes, effective January 1, 1968. It postponed a reduction in excise tax rates on automobiles and telephone service.

revenue bond: See *bond, revenue.*

revenue freight: a local or interline shipment from which earnings go to the carrier on the basis of tariff rates.

revenue from own sources: total revenue from taxes, charges, and miscellaneous revenue, and revenue from utilities, liquor stores (where applicable), and insurance trusts.

revenue recognition principle: the concept that revenues should be recorded when the earnings process has been substantially completed and an exchange has taken place.

revenue sharing: the return by a larger unit of government, which has greater taxing powers, of a part of its revenue to a smaller component of government. See also *highway trust fund, intergovernmental expenditures, shared revenue*; cf. *grants-in-aid*.

revenue tariffs: duties placed on imports with the goal of increasing revenues rather than protecting domestic industries.

revenue ton-mile: the movement of a ton (2000 pounds) of revenue cargo a distance of one mile.

revenue waybill: a written description showing a shipment's charges and goods.

reverse discrimination: the selection of minority persons or women for jobs or education in place of better-qualified whites or men.

reverse stock split: a reduction in the number of outstanding shares. Synonymous with *stock split down*.

reversionary interest: a claim or interest that an individual can keep to property or income that has been assigned to someone else. Cf. *estate in reversion, remainder*.

revery: a term used by Elton D. Mayo to refer generally to an individual's entire outlook on life.

revocable living trust: a trust whose income is paid to the grantor during his or her lifetime, and to the heirs following the grantor's death. It can be canceled by the person granting or initiating the trust.

revolving door: (slang) describing the actions of some Washington lawyers as they pass back and forth between government and private practice. See also *rainmakers*.

revolving fund: money that is renewed as it is used, either by additional appropriations or by income from the programs it finances. Thus the fund retains a balance at all times.

revolving letter of credit: a letter of credit issued for a specific amount that is automatically renewed for the same amount over a given period. Usually the unused renewable portion of the credit is cumulative, so long as drafts are drawn before the expiration of the credit.

revolving loan: a loan that is automatically renewed (upon maturity) without additional negotiation.

reward bases: the various methods for distributing rewards in an organization (e.g., equity, equality, power, and need). A problem arises for management when bases conflict in reward policy.

reward power: the opposite of coercive power. It exists when a subordinate perceives that compliance with the wishes of his or her superior will result in positive rewards and recognition, either monetary or psychological.

riders: in insurance, forms of special provisions that are not contained in the basic policy contract. In bonding and in personal accident insurance, such added clauses are called riders rather than endorsements. See also *family income rider;* synonymous with "clauses."

riding the air: (slang) construction workers performing their duties at considerable heights.

rif: (slang) to inform a worker that he or she will be fired.

rifle technique: the sales practice of concentrating on selling only a few items, using a carefully prepared style of presentation that will lead to a rapid decision. Cf. *shotgun approach.*

rig: any combination of truck, tractor, and semitrailer, or truck and full trailer.

rigged market: the situation that exists when purchases and sales are manipulated to distort a normal supply and demand price.

right of action: the right to enforce a claim in court.

right of curtesy: See *curtesy.*

right of dower: See *dower.*

right of possession: a right that a person has to real property even when not in physical possession of it. With this right comes the legal power to evacuate all parties from the property. See also *ejectment, seisin, writ of entry.*

right of redemption: the right to free a property from foreclosure by paying off all debts.

right of rescission: the privilege, guaranteed by the Truth in Lending Act, of canceling a contract under certain circumstances within three business days, without penalty and with full refund of all deposits that have been submitted. See also *voidable contract.*

right of survivorship: the right establishing a surviving joint owner as holder of the title to the property that was jointly owned. See also *tenancy by the entirety;* cf. *tenancy in common.*

right of way: a temporary or permanent opening or easement permitting passage over privately held land (e.g., a public road or pipeline is given a right of way).

rights: when a company that wants to raise more funds by issuing additional securities gives its stockholders the opportunity, ahead of others, to buy the new securities in proportion to the number of shares each owns, the piece of paper evidencing this privilege. Because the additional stock is usually offered to stockholders below the current market price, rights ordinarily have a market value of their own and are actively traded. In most cases they must be exercised within a relatively short period. Failure to exercise or sell rights may result in actual loss to the holder. See also *cum rights, sliding scale.*

rights of consumers: a doctrine enunciated by President John F. Kennedy, stating that consumers have the right to be safe, to be informed, to choose, and to be heard.

right-to-work laws: state laws that make it illegal for a collective agreement to contain provisions for union shops, maintenance of membership, preferential hiring, or any other clauses calling for compulsory union membership. State legislatures are empowered under the rule of the Taft-Hartley Act to pass laws that are more restrictive than the union security provisions of federal law (i.e., the Wagner-Connery Act). The courts have also granted the states authority to enforce the law. Some states have amended their constitutions to prohibit enactment of union security provisions within their states.

ring: Synonymous with *pit.*

ringing out (or up): a practice of commodity brokers and commission merchants of settling existing futures contracts by exchanging sale and purchase contracts among themselves before the instruments mature and become deliverable. For example, A has agreed to purchase in the future from C and at the same time to sell the same item to C. In the meantime, B has agreed to sell the item to C. The ring is complete and the transaction can be approved. The ringing out process permits incomplete ring participants to clear up their responsibilities and commitments.

riparian: describing an owner of property that has water flowing over it or along its border.

riparian rights: an owner's natural rights with respect to the banks of his or her waterways and use of the water and the soil under the water.

ripening cost: the cost of waiting for an investment to provide a return (e.g., the cost of waiting for land to increase in value or become suitable for development).

risk

(1) *general:* any chance of loss.

(2) *insurance:* the insured or the peril insured against.

risk capital

(1) *general:* capitalization that is not secured by a lien or mortgage.

(2) *finance:* long-term loans or capital invested in high-risk business activities.

(3) *securities:* common stock from a new enterprise.

risk decisions: decision situations in which managers do not know for certain the probability of occurrence of the state of nature or of competitive actions but have some past experience and/or data upon which they can develop probabilities. These probabilities are used with conditional values to determine expected values.

risk experience program: the procedure of keeping a listing of premiums and losses on larger risks for the underwriter's reference.

risk management: an approach of management that is concerned with the preservation of the assets and earning power of the business against risks of accidental loss.

risk propensity: a personality characteristic involving a person's like or dislike for taking chances.

risk taker: one who is willing to take chances and may aggressively seek out chancy situations that offer the possibility of significant payoffs.

risky shift phenomenon: the concept that the action of people as individuals is often radically different from their group behavior and thus that the shift away from conformity can be risky.

rival unionism: competition between two or more unions for members and recognition in a company and/or industry. See also *raid.*

RJP: See *realistic job previews.*

Robinson-Patman Act of 1936: federal legislation, amending the Clayton Antitrust Act of 1914, in which price discrimination practices are more clearly identified. Quantity discounts in excess of the cost savings realized by selling in such quantities are declared illegal, as are false brokerage deals. Promotional allowances must be made to all buyers on a proportionately equal basis, and price discrimination is acceptable if it is done to meet a proper low price of a competitor and if the price does not restrict competition.

robot: a reprogrammable, multifunctional manipulator designed to move material, parts, tools, or specialized devices through variable programmed motions for the performance of a variety of tasks.

rock bottom: (slang) the lowest level that will be entertained in a business transaction (e.g., the rock bottom price is the lowest price at which a seller will agree to sell his or her goods).

ROG dating: receipt-of-goods dating. Under this condition of sales, the date for payment and the discount period are determined from the date the buyer obtains shipment, rather than from the invoice date. This procedure is primarily employed when great shipping distances are involved.

ROI: return on investment; the amount earned in direct proportion to the capital invested. See also *private rate of return.*

role: behavior patterns expected from people in various economic, social, or other status positions.

role ambiguity: lack of clarity regarding job duties, authority, and responsibilities, resulting in uncertainty and dissatisfaction.

role analysis team building: a process designed to clarify role expecta-

tions and responsibilities of team members. This clarification can be brought about by group meeting and discussion.

role conflict: a situation in which an individual faces two or more role requirements simultaneously and the performance of one role would prevent the fulfillment of the other. See also *approach-approach conflict, approach-avoidance conflict, avoidance-avoidance conflict.*

role perception: the various opinions, attitudes, or expectations of the roles associated with a given status position in an organization.

role playing: a technique developed by Dr. J. L. Moreno that permits individuals to experience an issue or case through a trainer's dramatization, often with the participants as actors. Role playing is said to be helpful in developing self-understanding. See also *sensitivity training.*

role set: the collection of roles directly targeted to the activities of an individual.

rollback

(2) *government:* an effort to create, as the legal price, a price lower than the existing market price (i.e., to return to a price that existed earlier).

(2) *computers:* a program returned to a prior point that has been verified.

rolling stock: the physical property of a railroad that performs on rails on the railroad's own wheels (locomotives, passenger cars, etc.).

rollover: Synonymous with "refund"; see also *refunding.*

ROM: read-only memory; a form of access to data that allows data to be read but not changed. Cf. *R.A.M.*

ropes, know the: (slang) to be completely familiar with the details of task or business venture.

roping: the machinations of management spies, who bring a worker among them and offer a bribe in return for information about the activities of a union. Synonymous with *hooking.*

Rorabaugh reports: quarterly statements on spot advertising expenditures in television that are released by a private advertising consultant every three months.

roro ship: a freighter that transports loaded trucks or other vehicles that enter at one port and disembark at another.

rotating shift: changing of crews, usually done to distribute day and night work on an equal basis.

roundabout process: a process that utilizes less direct but more efficient means of production, although investment in equipment must be made to initiate the modification.

rounding error: an error, usually slight enough to be insignificant, that results from rounding off numbers (e.g., 3.2 + 1.6 is 4.8, which would be rounded off to be 5).

round lot: a unit of trading or a multiple thereof. It is usually a unit of trading of 100 shares in stocks or $1000 par value in bonds. The unit of trading in some inactive stocks is 10 shares. Cf. *odd-lot orders.*

round off: to delete the least significant digit or digits of a numeral and to adjust the part retained in accordance with some rule. See also *rounding error, zero suppression.*

round-table interview: an interview that consists of a discussion of a stated topic by several candidates for employment under the leadership of a discussor. The discussion is observed and evaluated by several executives or other officers who, although present, do not participate in any way.

round turn: the completion of an order to purchase a futures contract and later sell it, or the reverse.

routine

(1) *computers:* a set of coded computer instructions, arranged in sequence, that carry out some well-defined function.

(2) *communications:* the opening of a broadcast program. See also *billboard.*

routine decisions: decisions that deal with well-structured, recurring problems to which standard decision procedures apply.

routing: the selection of a path and steps in the operations performed on materials during the manufacturing process. Cf. *traffic.*

royalty: compensation for the use of a person's property, based on an agreed percentage of the income arising from its use (e.g., to an author on sales of his or her book, to a manufacturer for use of his machinery in another manufacturer's factory, to a composer or a performer). It is a payment reserved by the grantor of a patent, lease or similar right, whereas a residual payment is often made on properties that have not been patented or are not patentable. Cf. *residual;* see also *syndicate.*

rubricated account: any earmarked account.

Rucker plan: a group incentive program that uses day-to-day employee participation and broad coverage to determine where cost reductions can be made and to improve company profits. Productivity advances are measured in terms of money, not physical components.

rule of reason: the Supreme Court decision in 1911 that only unreasonable restraint of trade was illegal, thereby permitting companies to become as large as they wished, under the argument that the law did not outlaw mere size. This interpretation has largely been reversed since World War II.

run

(1) *general:* an action of a large number of people (e.g., a run on a bank occurs when a great many customers make massive withdrawals of funds).

(2) *computers:* automatic connection of one routine to another on the operating unit, during which manual interruptions are not normally required.

(3) *transportation:* a work assignment.

(4) *computers:* a single, continuous performance of a program or routine.

runaway: the condition in which part of a system undergoes a sudden or undesirable and often destructive increase in activity.

runaway inflation: Synonymous with *galloping inflation.*

runaway shop: a company or plant that moves its facilities to another state—among other reasons, to avoid existing state labor laws, the activities of a particular union, or a union contract that it has agreed on. See also *relocate.*

run book: all material needed to execute a computer application, including problem statements, coding, and operating instructions.

runner: a merchandising term for a best-selling item, especially one that is continually kept in stock because of its heavy sales volume. Cf. *sleeper.*

running costs: direct or indirect costs that result from keeping an operation and/or machinery functioning. These costs include wages, rent, and taxes.

running days: consecutive days, including Sundays, as distinguished from working days, which exclude Sundays.

running shoes: (slang) letting an employee know that he will be dismissed shortly.

run-off election: a procedure used by the National Labor Relations Board when no single union receives a first-poll majority in a representation election. A second election is called for, in which participants are to select between the two unions receiving the highest votes.

run on a bank: See *run.*

run sizes: the number of items manufactured at one time in a given lot.

sabotage, industrial: a deliberate attempt to slow down production by workers who believe they have a grievance against their employer. It may take the form of wasting time, making equipment unworkable, or, at an extreme, the actual destruction of machinery. See also *Luddites*.

sack: (slang) to discharge a worker.

sacrifice: to make a sale at a loss for purposes of raising cash, with the awareness that the profit will be lowered.

saddle point: a term used in game theory to identify an ideal strategy.

safe deposit box: a metal container that remains under lock and key in a section of a bank vault when the person who rents it is not handling or inspecting the jewelry, stock certificates, or other valuables it contains. The boxes are kept in small compartments, each with two separate locks. A box is rented with its compartment to a customer, not necessarily a depositor, for an annual fee.

safety factor: the ratio of the interest on a funded debt to the net income after the payment of the interest.

safety stock: a minimum inventory that provides a cushion against reasonably expected maximum demand and against variations in lead time.

sag: a minimal drop or price weakness of shares, usually resulting from a weak demand for the securities.

salary: compensation received by an employee for services rendered during a specified period. See also *wage*.

salary administration: policies and procedures created for the compensation of white-collar employees and executives.

salary compression: a wage and salary program whereby salaries for one employee group slowly move up toward those for higher-classification jobs. It often stifles enthusiasm for promotions, boosts turnover, and increases personnel costs.

salary review: the examination of an

employee's wage rate in terms of his or her performance and cost of living or other economic factors.

salary standardization: the process of integrating rates of pay with the duties and responsibilities performed by employees. The result is equal pay for equal work.

sale

(1) *finance:* the transfer of title to an item or items or the agreement to perform a service in return for cash or the expectation of cash payment.

(2) *real estate:* transfer of title, for a sum of money and conditions, for the change of ownership of property.

sales

(1) *merchandising:* final sales plus producer item sales.

(2) *marketing:* Synonymous with *net sales.*

(3) *finance:* revenue received from the sale of goods.

(4) *accounting:* the sum of the income received when goods and services are sold.

(5) See also *selling.*

sales agent: a middleman who undertakes to sell the entire output of items of a business that he or she represents.

sales allowance: a lowering of the price on an item when merchandise delivered is not exactly what was ordered by a buyer.

sales analysis: an aspect of market research involving the systematic study and comparison of sales information. See also *systems selling.*

sales anchors: concepts and statements used by sales representatives when attempting to overcome customer resistance.

sales aptitude: the capability to achieve success in the sales field, as acknowledged by a sales department and measured by means of interviews, and recommendations.

sales branch: a producer's outlet that maintains inventory and delivers to buyers from that stock.

sales budget: a budget based on forecasted sales for a coming period.

sales discount: a reduction in the sales price that is allowed if payment is received within a specified period. Synonymous with *cash discount.*

sales engineer: a person who sells products that require technical knowledge and training.

sales finance company: a financial organization that purchases installment contracts from dealers and finances dealers' inventories.

sales force: canvassers and sales representatives who contact potential purchasers of goods and attempt to persuade them that they should buy the items being sold.

sales forecast: a dollar or unit sales estimate made for a specified period in a marketing campaign.

sales forecast opportunity variance: a measure of the differential between scheduled capacity and the master budget sales forecast capacity, usually expressed in dollars.

sales journal: a book in which records of sales are entered.

sales manager: an executive responsible for planning, directing, and controlling the activities of sales personnel. Cf. *product manager.*

salesmanship: the art of selling goods or services by creating a demand or need for a particular item and realizing an actual order.

sales manual: a book describing the

product, merchandise, or service to be sold and suggesting approaches for selling to a customer.

sales mix: a combination of the various company products leading to a firm's total sales.

sales office: a facility for taking orders and handling adjustments that serves as a contact point for suppliers and customers. No inventory is maintained at the office. Cf. *merchandise mart.*

sales pitch: a strong statement aimed at persuading a potential customer to buy the salesman's product or service.

sales plan: a merchandise budget that contains a detailed projection of sales for a given period, specifying the purchases, inventory, and so on, needed to achieve this goal.

sales presentation: the total selling process of describing to a potential customer the product or service, including the attempt to place an order. See also *trial close.*

sales promotion: See *promotion.*

sales quota: a projected goal for sales of a product. Usually the quota is established as part of a marketing campaign.

sales returns and allowances: a contra-sales account in which the returns of or allowances for previously sold merchandise are recorded.

sales tax: a tax levied by a state or municipality on items at the time of their purchase. It may be a tax on the sale of an item every time it changes hands or only upon its transfer of ownership at one specific time. The sales of manufacturers are taxed when the items are considered to be completed goods; the sales of whole-salers are taxed when their goods are sold to retailers; and retail sales are taxed when the goods are purchased by consumers. See also *tax.*

sales trainee: a recently hired sales representative who is engaged in learning the basic concepts of selling. Usually the trainee receives a small salary during this period.

salvage

(1) *general:* equipment or property that is no longer used for its initial purpose.

(2) *insurance:* damaged property taken over by an insurance firm following payment of a claim; in marine insurance, the cost of saving property that is exposed to a peril. See also *recovery, salvage value.*

(3) *merchandising:* goods that are soiled beyond reclamation for purposes of sale and thus usually disposed of by other means. See *scrap value.*

salvage value

(1) *accounting:* the expected worth of a depreciable item at the end of its service life.

(2) *insurance:* the value remaining in property or goods that have been damaged by a peril. See also *salvage.*

sampling

(1) *statistics:* choosing a representative portion of a population to characterize a larger population. See also *Monte Carlo method.*

(2) *advertising:* the distribution of trial packs of a product to introduce it or to promote its use among consumers.

(3) *computers:* a random method of checking and controlling the use of data by obtaining the values of a

function for regularly or irregularly spaced discrete values.

(4) *computers:* a method of communication control in which messages are selected by a computer that chooses only those for which processing is needed.

sampling, random: See *random sample.*

sampling error: an error occurs when the sample used is not representative of the population it was designed to represent. See also *standard error.*

sanction

(1) *business law:* a penalty for the breach of a rule of law.

(2) *international business:* a coercive measure, usually undertaken by several nations, to force another country to cease violation of a treaty or an international agreement. See also *embargo.*

SARs: See *stock-appreciation rights.*

satellite processor: a processor that is under the control of another piece of processing equipment and performs subsidiary operations. Cf. *slave computer.*

satisfaction: a criterion of effectiveness that refers to an organization's ability to gratify the needs of its employees. Synonymous with *morale, voluntarism.*

satisficing: decision-making behavior in which the manager selects an alternative that is good enough, (i.e., one that will yield a satisfactory return to the organization).

satisfiers: in F. Herzberg's theory of satisfiers and dissatisfiers, the activities in a job that bring satisfaction to the worker (e.g., the work itself, the quality of supervision). See also *job enrichment;* cf. *dissatisfiers.*

saturation: the phase of the product life cycle in which an item is no longer able to be sold because most consumers who are likely to be interested in it have already purchased it. See also *product life cycle.*

saturation campaign: intensive use of radio or television advertising to promote or sell a product in a market. There are usually special low rates for saturation-level advertising. See also *flight saturation.*

Saturday night special: (slang) a direct tender offer, made without any forewarning, that expires in one week. Such offerings were made possible by the Williams Act of 1968, which permits tender offers to run as short as seven days and does not require the bidder give advance notification.

saving: the amount of existing income that is not spent on consumption.

savings account: money that is deposited in a bank, usually in small amounts periodically over a long period, and is not subject to withdrawal by check. Savings accounts usually bear interest, and some banks levy a service charge for excess withdrawal activity on an account.

savings and investment theory: the concept developed by John Maynard Keynes and D. H. Robertson that business cycles occur because people save either more or less than the amounts invested in new capital. Cf. *veil of money theory.*

savings and loan association: a mutual, cooperative, quasi-public financial institution that is owned by its members (depositors) and chartered by a state or by the federal government. The association receives the savings of its members and uses these funds to finance long-term amortized mortgage loans to its members and to the general public. Such an association may also be organized as a corporation owned by stockholders. See also *Cincotta-Conklin Bill of 1976.*

savings bank: a banking association whose purpose is to promote thrift and savings habits in a community. It may be either a stock organization (a bank with a capital stock structure) or a mutual savings bank. Until passage of the Cincotta-Conklin Act in New York state and other similar bills, a savings bank had no power to perform commercial functions but specialized in interest-bearing savings accounts, investing these savings in long-term bonds, mortgage loans, and other investment opportunities for the benefit of all depositors. Now, in many states, a savings bank may offer checking account privileges to its customers.

Savings Bond: See *Bond, Savings (U.S.).*

savings rate: the ratio of income saved to income earned.

Say's law: a concept developed by Jean Baptiste Say in the late eighteenth century that the supply of all economic items must always equal the full demand for them. Therefore, any increase in output is an increase in demand, and overproduction is an impossibility. See also *underconsumption theory.*

SBA: See *Small Business Administration.*

SBUs: See *strategic business units.*

scab: (slang) a worker in a struck plant who continues on the job dur-

ing a strike; more specifically, one who fills the job of a striker. Synonymous with *boll weevil, rat.*

scalar chain principle: an organizational concept wherein the graded chain of authority is created through the delegation process.

scale order: an order to buy (or sell) a security that specifies the total amount to be bought (or sold) and the amount to be bought (or sold) at specified price variations.

scaling: trading in securities by placing orders for purchase or sale at intervals of price instead of giving the order in full at the market price or at a stated price.

scalper: a speculator who constantly sells his or her shares at fractional profit or at one or two points profit per share.

scamping: (slang) slowing down during a work period; goofing off; producing work of poor quality.

scan: the examination of stored information for a specific purpose, as for arrangement or content, in a computer.

Scanlon plan: a management incentive scheme designed by Joseph Scanlon of MIT to achieve increased productivity with improved efficiency by distributing accrued savings among the employees.

scanner: See *optical scanner.*

scarcity value: an increase in value caused by a demand for an item whose supply cannot be increased (e.g., works of art from the nineteenth century).

scare purchasing: purchasing to hoard; unusually heavy buying of items in short supply.

scattersite housing: federally sponsored public housing for low-income persons, usually in ghetto areas.

scavenger sale: property that is taken over by the state as the result of non-payment of taxes (e.g., failure of a state resident to pay state income taxes). After full notice, the state may hold a public sale of the property to recover monies to which it is entitled; the excess of the sale, beyond the taxes and penalties due the state, is returned to the resident.

schedule

(1) *insurance:* a type of individual risk rating that measures, based on physical characteristics of the risk, the extent to which a particular risk deviates from the average of its class. This deviation is reflected in the scheduled rate for the risk.

(2) *advertising:* a list of ads, by stated media, giving dates of appearance, space, time, and so on.

(3) *administration:* a systematic plan for future operations over a given period.

schedule bond: See *bond, schedule.*

scheduled maintenance: maintenance carried out in accordance with an established plan. It is often used as a preventive measure to assure efficiency in the operation of equipment (e.g., replacement of tubes, lubrication of moving parts).

scheduled production: the rate of activity assigned for the production of a given item in a specified period.

schedule of insurance: a list of individual items covered under one policy (e.g., various buildings, animals, and other property in farm insurance, rings and bracelets insured under a jewelry floater).

schedule of variance: the difference

between actual production and scheduled production.

scheduling: the organization and control of the time needed to carry out a sales effort.

schlock (shlock): (slang) cheap, inferior items or services.

scienter: awareness by a defrauding party of the falsity of a representation. See also *fraud.*

scientific management: a term popularized in the work of Frederick W. Taylor that includes approaches to increased efficiency, cost reductions, and maximum utilization of human and material resources. Cf. *prescientific management.*

scientific tariff: a duty to cover foreign and domestic manufacturing costs.

scintilla of evidence: a small amount of evidence that assists in the proof of an allegation.

scoop

(1) *general:* to beat out a rival.

(2) *slang:* a considerable profit following a transaction that is likely to involve advance notice over or exclusion of competitors.

scouting: a recruiting technique used to obtain the best-qualified persons in the nation. Scouting is carried out more actively in a tight labor market.

scrambled merchandising: an approach by retail outlets of maintaining types of goods not normally found in those stores (e.g., clothing and large appliances sold in a drugstore).

scrap value: the salvage value of an item that is going to be junked or destroyed.

scratch daily report: a copy of the daily report completed by the underwriter or rater, or both, for use by the policywriter in preparing the policy.

scratch endorsement: a copy of an endorsement completed by the underwriter or rater, or both, for use by the policywriter in incorporating the endorsement into the policy.

scrip: a temporary document that entitles the holder or bearer to receive stock or a fractional share of stock in a corporation, cash, or some other article of value on demand or at some specified future date. Some industries issue scrip to their employees, as a supplement to salary, for use in company-owned stores.

scrip dividend: a type of dividend issued by a corporation to its stockholders, entitling the holder or bearer to receive cash, stock, or a fractional share of stock, or one or more units of the product manufactured upon presentation or at a specified future date.

script: short for "manuscript"; a document; a form of writing.

scrivener's error: a typographical error introduced when reducing an oral agreement to writing or when an agreement is typed or printed in final form.

scruff: (slang) to earn sufficient monies for the basic necessities of life.

SCT: See *service counter terminal.*

scuffle: (slang) working on a dull, repetitive job.

scuttlebutt: rumors without support. Synonymous with *gossip.*

SD: See *standard deviation.*

SDR: See *special drawing rights.*

sealing

(1) *advertising:* reducing or enlarging an illustration or ad.

(2) *packaging:* holding a closed box or package adequately by cord, tape, glue, or other means.

(3) *securities:* concealed bids that are simultaneously revealed. The most attractive one is accepted on the spot, without further bidding.

search

(1) *computers:* to locate a desired word or record in a set of words or records. Cf. *dump.*

(2) *real estate:* in the consideration of property transfer, the examination of records for evidence of encumbrances against the property (unpaid taxes, mortgages, etc.). Synonymous with *title search.*

(3) *management:* the process of recruiting executive talent for a specific organization.

search cycle: normally, the location of an item and its comparison with others in the course of a computer search. The cycle must be repeated for each item.

search firms: private, for-profit organizations that exist to help employers locate hard-to-find applicants. Cf. *private placement agencies.*

seasonal appointment: a temporary appointment.

seasonal discount: a price reduction given for purchases made out of season (e.g., ski equipment can usually be bought at a discount in the spring). Cf. *static inventory problem.*

seasonal employee: a worker who is employed for limited periods of activity (e.g., for harvesting during the fall).

seasonal fluctuations: regular and predictable shifts in business activity created by changes in the season (e.g., housing construction increases during the spring).

seasonal forecast: changes in market demand that depend primarily on the time of year.

seasonal industry: an industry that has high peaks of employment at specified times of the year and down periods during other seasons.

seasonal unemployment: joblessness due to seasonality of the work. Teachers who do not work during the summer months are representative of the seasonally unemployed.

seasoned issues: securities from well-established corporations that have been favorably known to the investment population over time, including good and bad periods.

seasoned mortgage: periodic payments of a mortgage that are made over a long span, based on the borrower's payment structure.

seasoned security: a security possessing a fine performance record in the paying of dividends or interest; one that has been listed for a considerable period of time and sells at a relatively stable price.

seat on the exchange: a traditional figure of speech designating membership on an exchange. Price and admission requirements vary.

seaworthiness: the condition of a vessel at the commencement of its initial voyage. It must be suitably constructed and equipped, properly officered and manned, and sufficiently loaded with fuel and provisions to carry the specified cargo insured on the particular voyage described.

SEC: the Securities and Exchange Commission, established by Congress to protect investors. The SEC administers the Securities Act of 1933, the Securities Exchange Act of 1934, the Trust Indenture Act, the Investment Company Act, the Invest-ment Advisers Act, and the Public Utility Holding Company Act. The principal provisions of these acts are (1) that the Securities and Exchange Commission, created in 1934, administers the federal laws applying to securities; (2) that corporations issuing securities and investment bankers selling them must make full disclosure of the character of the securities (i.e., they must state all relevant facts in registration statements to the SEC and in prospectuses submitted to the public); see also *waiting period;* (3) that any omission of fact or insertion of false information makes all persons (bankers, lawyers, accountants, etc.) whose names appear on the prospectus and the registration statement liable to the purchasers of the securities for any losses suffered; (4) that organization of people (brokers, traders, etc.) to manipulate the prices of securities is forbidden; see *pool;* (5) that dealings by corporation officers in securities of their own corporations are restricted; and (6) that the Board of Governors of the Federal Reserve System is given power to fix margin requirements on loans secured by bonds and stocks. See also *National Association of Securities Dealers, pool, waiting period.*

secondary boycott: See *boycott.*

secondary console: in a system with multiple consoles, any console other than the master console.

secondary data: information not received by a user from its original source, but coming instead from references gathered earlier.

secondary distribution: the redistribution of a block of stock some time after it has been sold by the issuing company. The sale is handled off the exchange by a securities firm or group of firms, and the shares are usually offered at a fixed price that is related to the current market price of the stock.

secondary employment: Synonymous with *moonlighting.*

secondary offering: the selling by a large stockholder of a large block of shares. Such a sale is frequently made on an exchange, to minimize the impact on the general market. Synonymous with *secondary distribution.*

secondary picketing: See *picketing.*

secondary rental: a lease determined in part by the landlord's costs. As the landlord's costs (taxes, fuel, etc.) increase, proportionate rent increases are demanded.

secondary reserves: assets other than primary reserves retained by banks and capable of being rapidly converted into cash. Government bonds are a prime example.

secondary strike: a strike called against an employer doing business with another company whose workers are on strike.

secondary worker: a person who is part of a household that has a major earner and who can therefore choose whether or not to work, depending on wage and unemployment conditions. Secondary workers include children, retired persons, and spouses.

second-generation computer: a computer that uses solid-state components.

secondhand: not new; describing merchandise offered for sale that has already been used.

second-level outcome: the effect brought about by a first-level outcome, such as a promotion (second-level outcome) brought about by increased productivity (first-level outcome).

second lien: a lien that ranks after the first lien and is to be fulfilled next.

second-mortgage bond: See *bond, second-mortgage.*

seconds: goods bearing defects that have possible effects on wearability and appearance. See also *bargain store.*

second sale: a sale achieved by building on a customer's receptive mood following an initial purchase; an additional sale to the same person.

secret partner: an active partner in an organization whose capacity as a partner is not known to the public. Cf. *silent partner.*

secular inflation: the most serious economic problem of the late 1960s and the 1970s. In contrast to cyclical inflation, which moves in and out of the economic system roughly every two years, secular inflation is primarily a long-term social phenomenon. Cf. *cyclical inflation.*

secular stagnation: a low level of economic movement measured over an extended time period.

secular trend: a tendency of values in a time series to move upward or downward over a number of years.

secular unemployment: unemployment resulting from changes in the economic system whose long-run effect is a decline in employment. See also *technological unemployment.*

secured bond: See *bond, secured.*

secured creditor: a creditor whose

obligation is made safe or backed by a pledge or collateral. See also *collateral.*

secured debt: any debt for which some form of acceptable collateral has been pledged. See also *hypothecate.*

secured loan: a loan that is made safe, or backed, by marketable securities or other marketable values.

securities: documents that identify legal ownership of a physical commodity or legal claims to another's wealth.

Securities and Exchange Commission: See *SEC.*

Securities Exchange Act: See *SEC.*

securities firm: an organization that relies for its income on other firms' securities, which it retains for investment. It may also issue stocks and bonds of its own. Synonymous with *investment company;* see also *holding company.*

securities trading: selling or buying securities through recognized channels. The term also applies to the operations of brokers in the various exchanges.

security
(1) *general:* property pledged as collateral.
(2) *insurance:* protection against risk.
(3) *business law:* any evidence of debt or right to a property.
(4) *business law:* an individual who agrees to make good the failure of another to pay.
(5) *securities:* stocks and bonds placed by a debtor with a creditor, with authority to sell for the creditor's account if the debt is not paid.

security agreement: the agreement between a seller and a buyer that the seller shall have an interest in the goods. The security agreement must be signed by the buyer and must describe the goods.

security capital: low-risk capital (e.g., government bonds, mortgages).

security needs: Maslow's second set of human needs, which reflect the desire to keep free from physical harm. Cf. *hierarchy of needs.*

segment
(1) *computers:* to divide a computer program into parts such that parts of the program can be executed without the entire program being in internal storage at any one time.
(2) *communications:* a portion of a message that can be contained in a buffer.

segmentation research: a form of marketing research that uncovers new bases for market segmentation.

segregation: separating from an operating or holding firm one or more of its subsidiaries or operating divisions, effected by distributing stock of the subsidiary to the parent company's shareholders.

seignorage: a government's profit from issuing coins at a face value higher than the metal's intrinsic worth. It is the difference between the bullion price and the face value of the coins made from it. See also *brassage.*

seisin (seizin): taking legal possession of real estate. The rightful owner seizes the property. See also *right of possession;* cf. *disseisin, replevin.*

seizure: the act of taking possession of property. See also *condemnation.*

selection
(1) *personnel:* the process of deciding from a number of job appli-

cants the one individual to be offered a position and/or advancement.

(2) **computers:** addressing a terminal or a component on a selective calling circuit.

selection ratio: a ratio expressed as the number of individuals hired to fill a particular job divided by the number of applicants.

selective demand: demand for a particular brand.

selective distribution (selling): choosing retail outlets that will be permitted to receive one's merchandise for sale.

selector: a device for directing electrical input pulses onto one or two output lines, depending on the presence of a predetermined accompanying control pulse.

self-actualization: the desired result of a process of individual development of capacities and talents, and the evolution of self-realization. Cf. *hierarchy of needs.*

self-adapting: the ability of a system to change its performance characteristics in response to the environment.

self-appraisal: an appraisal method that allows employees to become actively involved in thinking about their work contributions and appraising themselves.

self-assessment: an evaluation that can help one gain a realistic understanding of oneself in terms of likes and dislikes and/or strengths and weaknesses. Cf. *self-audit.*

self-audit: an evaluation of organizational performance that is carried out by individuals working in the enterprise. Cf. *self-assessment.*

self-concept theory: the notion that two factors influencing an individual's purchasing behavior are how the person perceives himself or herself and how he or she wishes to be perceived by others. Cf. *motivation, unconscious.*

self-employed: describing the gainfully occupied part of the work force whose members work for themselves, as opposed to salaried or commissioned workers who are the employees of others.

self-insurance: a system whereby a firm or individual, by setting aside an amount of money, provides for the occurrence of any losses that could ordinarily be covered under an insurance program. The monies that would normally be used for premium payments are added to this special fund for payment of losses incurred. See also *service excess.*

self-liquidating: describing an asset that can be converted into cash or is subject to total recovery of invested money over a period of time.

self-liquidating loan: a short-term commercial loan, usually supported by a lien on a given product or on sale of the product or commodities.

self-mailer: a direct-mail piece that can be sent through the mail without using an envelope or wrap.

self-reducing clause: a life insurance statement that has the effect of lowering an obligation or mortgage. The amount of insurance automatically drops during the term of the policy, matching the lowering amount of the debt involved.

self-selection selling: a merchandising approach that allows customers to make their choices without the initial assistance of sales help.

self-service: describing a sales outlet or store in which the customer chooses the items to be purchased, removes them from the shelves, carries them to a checkout counter for completion of the transaction, and carries or sends them to the place of use.

self-serving activities: activities that satisfy individual needs at the expense of the group.

sell and leaseback agreement: an arrangement whereby a business that owns and occupies improved real estate sells it to an investor (e.g., an insurance company) and takes back a long-term lease on the property and usually an option to buy it at the termination of the lease. Cf. *repurchase agreement.*

seller's lien: the seller's privilege of holding onto certain items until the buyer has delivered payment. See also *general lien;* cf. *carrier's lien, vendor's lien.*

sellers' market: a market in which demand is greater than supply, resulting in sellers setting the prices and terms of sale. It is a market characterized by rising or high prices.

seller's option: a special transaction on an exchange whereby the seller holding the option can deliver the stocks or bonds at any time within a specified period, ranging from not less than 6 business days to not more than 60 days.

seller's seven sale: an agreed-upon delay of seven or more days for the delivery of a security. See also *settlement day.*

seller's surplus: the difference between the price a seller actually receives and the lowest price that he or she would accept.

selling: the process of assisting and/or persuading a potential customer to buy merchandise or services.

selling costs: marketing costs (e.g., advertising, sales promotion) necessary to attract a potential buyer to an item or service.

selling group: syndicated dealers of an underwriting company that operate in the public sale of an issue of securities.

selling price: the cash price that a customer must pay for purchased items.

selling short: a trading technique employed when a drop in the market price of a security is expected. A temporarily borrowed stock is sold to effect delivery. If the price drops, the trader can purchase the security for less than he or she sold it, pay the borrowing cost, and clear a profit. See also *bear position, loaned flat.*

sell out

(1) *general:* to betray a person, organization, or cause, usually for profit or special treatment.

(2) *securities:* to close out a customer's account by selling held securities or commodities.

(3) *business:* to dispose of an entire stock or set of products.

(4) *labor relations:* pertaining to a union leader, to conclude a negotiation that is unpopular with the membership. This may imply that the leader is believed to have received personal gain from the settlement.

semiskilled labor: a worker's level of performance between skilled and unskilled. It is often applied to workers who have had some training and perform routine tasks.

semivariable costs: Synonymous with *mixed costs.*

send money: funds set aside to commence an activity.

senior bond: See *bond, senior.*

seniority: an employee's length of service, used as a factor in determining salary, benefits, and promotion priorities. See also *bumping.*

sensitive market: a market characterized by fluctuations determined by the announcement of favorable or unfavorable news.

sensitivity analysis: a method of assessing the reasonableness of a decision that was based on estimates. It tests how far reality can differ from an estimate without invalidating the decision.

sensitivity training: a form of educational experience, conducted in small classes called T-groups, that stresses the emotional dynamics of self-development training. The training may be highly structured or highly unstructured, to permit the participants to learn more about their strengths and weaknesses. See also *critical incident, role playing, situational theory of leadership.*

sensor: a device that is capable of converting measurable information into meaningful data for a computer. See also *magnetic core.*

sentinel: a symbol or mark to indicate the occurrence of a unit of information (e.g., the end of an item, file, or tape). Synonymous with *flag.*

separate property: property that is owned individually and is not jointly held.

separation: permanent termination of employment, initiated by either the employee or the employer.

separation rate: the average number of persons dropped from a payroll per 100 employees. See also *turnover;* cf. *accession rate.*

sequence
(1) *computers:* an arrangement of items according to a specified set of rules.
(2) *statistics:* a group of records whose control fields are in ascending or descending order, according to the collating sequence.
(3) *systems:* an arbitrarily defined order of a set of symbols.

sequential access storage: a storage technique in which the information becomes available in a one-after-the-other sequence only. Cf. *random access.*

sequential computer: a computer in which events occur in time sequence, with little or no simultaneity or overlap of events. See also *asynchronous computer.*

sequential interdependence: the relationship between units of an organization such that the product of one is passed along to the next in order, after which the final product results.

sequestered account: an account that has been impounded under due process of law. Since disbursement of such an account is subject to court order, the account is usually set up in a separate control. See also *frozen account, receiver.*

sequestration: legal appropriation of property by a third party until there is a settlement of a stated dispute.

serial
(1) *general:* to be handled one after the other.
(2) *computers:* the sequential or consecutive occurrence of two or

more related activities in a single device or channel.

serial bond: See *bond, serial.*

serial computer: a computer that has a single unit that performs arithmetic and logic functions.

serial organization: a type of organization in which the entire process of accomplishing a job is assigned to one specific department, division, or unit.

serial transfer: a system of data transfer in which elements of information are transferred in succession over a single line.

serrated edge: a sawtooth edge, as around the mouth of a paper bag.

service charge: a payment by a financial institution against an individual or organization for services rendered.

service costs: the operating costs of service departments that are usually allocated to production departments.

service counter terminal (SCT): a device for handling information, located in retail stores and similar places, through which individuals can obtain access to funds and possibly credit at their disposal, for purposes of making deposits and withdrawals and potentially for making third-party payments. See also *electronic funds-transfer system, Hinky Dinky.*

service department: an organizational unit that does not directly produce goods but serves other departments.

service excess: a special program for large risks wherein claims within a large-deductible or self-insured retention are serviced by the insurer for a fee. Excess insurance is then written by the company to cover the losses above the insured's retention. Cf. *excess insurance.*

service life: the anticipated time of usefulness of an asset.

service salesperson: a person who sells intangibles, such as insurance and advertising.

servomechanism: an automatic control system incorporating feedback that governs the physical position of an element by adjusting either the values of the coordinates or the values of their time derivatives.

"set aside" farm plan: President Carter's voluntary program, created in 1978, for wheat and feedgrain farmers to leave 10 to 20 percent of their land unplanted. The objective was to boost farm prices by reducing the size of crop output. Farmers who ignore the plan are disqualified from federal price supports and paid "set aside" programs.

setback

(1) *real estate:* a common restriction in zoning ordinances that specifies the distance a new structure must be set away from a street or from the lot boundaries.

(2) *administration:* a reversal or partial loss in an activity.

settlement day: the deadline by which a purchaser of stock must pay for what has been bought and the seller must deliver the certificates for the securities that have been sold. The settlement day is usually the fifth business day following the execution of an order. Cf. *shave.*

settlement options: provisions in a life policy or annuity contract for alternative methods of settlement in place of lump-sum payments.

settlor: an individual who finalizes a

property settlement (e.g., the creator of a trust).

setup

(1) *computers:* in a computer that consists of an assembly of individual computing units, the arrangement of interconnections between the units and the adjustments needed for the computer to solve a particular problem. See also *simulation.*

(2) *production:* the time or costs needed before production of an item can commence. See also *lead time.*

severalty: property owned by one person only. See also *singular property title, sole owner.*

severance pay: Synonymous with *dismissal pay.*

severance taxes: taxes imposed on removal from land or water of natural products, such as minerals, timber, or fish.

severity rate: a formula used to compute the number of days lost because of accidents per million people-hours worked.

sex differential: differences in rates for work of comparable quality and quantity that are based on the worker's sex. It is now generally forbidden by federal law. See also *Civil Right Act of 1964, Equal Pay Act of 1963, equal pay for equal work.*

shading: giving a small reduction in a price or terms of a sale.

shakeout

(1) *securities:* shift in activity that forces speculators to sell their shares.

(2) *finance:* a trend or shift in an industry that forces weaker members toward bankruptcy.

shapeup: a lineup of men seeking work in the maritime industry, from which steamship or stevedoring companies select the workers they want. Cf. *hiring hall.*

share: a unit of stock that names the holder and indicates ownership in a corporation.

share draft: an order by a credit union member to pay to a third party against funds on deposit with the credit union and cleared through a commercial bank.

shared revenue: payments to the states and localities of a portion of the proceeds from the sale of certain federal property, products, and services, and payments to the territories of certain federal tax collections derived within their boundaries or from transactions affecting them. Synonymous with *intergovernmental revenue;* cf. *revenue sharing.*

shareholder: the possessor of shares or stocks in an organization (company, corporation, etc.).

share loan: a simple interest loan secured by funds on deposit at a credit union or a savings and loan institution. One purpose of a share loan is to preserve dividends due on deposits by not withdrawing the funds until the dividend payment date.

share of advertising method: a method of setting the advertising budget based on a share of the total advertising expenditures in a specific field.

share of audience: the percentage of radio or television sets in use or households watching a particular program. Cf. *Hooperating, Nielsen rating.*

share of the market: the ratio or pecentage of an advertiser's sales to the total industry sales, based on an actual or potential standard.

shares outstanding: the shares issued by a corporation, excluding treasury stock.

share-the-work: retention of jobs by shortening the work week for the entire employee group rather than laying off some of the workers. See also *work sharing.*

shark repellent: (slang) a state statute that demands strict notification and disclosure of tender offers for companies incorporated or transacting business within its boundaries.

shave

(1) *finance:* a charge higher than the accepted rate that is made for handling a note or other instrument of low quality or for which the seller will take a smaller amount for any reason.

(2) *securities:* the additional charge (premium) made for the right to extend the delivery time on a security.

shelf registration: a Securities and Exchange Commission ruling effective March 1983 permitting an issuer to register one big issue of bonds with the SEC. Instead of selling the bonds all at once, issuers will put at least some of them aside—on the shelf—to be sold piecemeal whenever they see a need for funds, find favorable market conditions, or receive a call from a trader or institution offering attractive terms.

shelf-sitters: (slang) upwardly immobile managers who block promotion channels.

shell firm: an organization that is incorporated but does not function or produce any goods or services.

sheriff: a public officer whose authority and responsibilities are created by legislation. His or her duties are to execute the law.

Sherman Antitrust Act of 1890: federal legislation aimed at preventing business monopoly. Some courts, however, applied the sanctions of the law against strikes, and unions were fined triple damages for acts that were considered to be in restraint of trade. New legislation was required to protect the unions against further misinterpretations, since, in the absence of legislative action, antiunion rulings would continue to be sustained under the principle of *res adjudicata.* See also *Clayton Antitrust Act of 1914.*

shift

(1) *administration:* the part of a 24-hour work day comprising a working schedule (e.g., the 8:00 A.M. to 4:00 P.M. shift).

(2) *computers:* to move information right or left in the arithmetic registers. See also *register, shift.*

shift differential: additional pay for working more than one shift.

shifting tax: a tax whose burden is transferred from the original taxpayer (individual or organization) to another.

shift premium: extra compensation given to a shift worker for the inconvenience of altering his or her daily working hours. See also *shift differential.*

shinplaster

(1) *general:* any money made worthless either by inflation or by inadequate security.

(2) *banking:* a pre-Civil War term used to deprecate the value of paper money.

(3) *finance:* paper money, usually

of less than one dollar face value, once used by some private banks.

shipment

(1) *general:* delivery and transport of items by a carrier.

(2) *transportation:* a collection of items that are transported as a unit.

(3) *marketing:* merchandise sent to a manufacturer to be processed, or items sent from the manufacturer to a wholesaler or retailer. See also *drop shipper, middleman.*

shock loss: a loss larger than expected.

shop chairman: the principal union spokesperson in a work place, usually a worker who is selected by his or her co-workers. Cf. *shop steward.*

shop committee: a group of union members named to speak for the whole union on grievances, negotiations, and other labor-management issues.

shoplifting: thievery of a store's items by a customer. See also *inventory shortage;* cf. *pilferage.*

shop merchandising: establishing certain locations in a store for serving buyers with special interests (e.g., tennis shop, teen-age corner).

shopping goods: consumer goods that are purchased only after the buyer compares the offerings of more than one store.

shop steward: a union official who represents a specific group of members and the union in grievance matters and other employment conditions. Sometimes called a committeeman. Stewards are usually part of the work force they represent. Cf. *business agent, shop chairman;* Synonymous with "committeeman."

shortage: an excess of quantity de-manded over quantity supplied, indicating that price is below equilibrium.

short bill: a bill of exchange that is payable upon request, at sight, or within a brief period, usually less than 10 days.

short covering: buying a stock to return stock previously borrowed to make delivery on a short sale.

shortcut foreclosure: a method of foreclosure in which a power of sale clause in the mortgage allows the lender to sell a property if it goes into default. The borrower must be informed, but the issuing of a public statement need not be carried out. Upon property foreclosure, the junior mortgage holders' positions are wiped out unless the sale yields more than the outstanding first mortgage.

shorter work week: today, any working schedule that is less than the equivalent of five working days. With the signing of the United Auto Workers' contract in 1976 and the end of a strike at the Ford Motor Company, the framework for a potential four-day work week was created. For the labor movement, this contract acted as a springboard for moving closer to a real four-day week.

shortfall: spending, usually in a governmental agency, that falls sharply below projections, thus contributing to economic sluggishness. Cf. *overage.*

short-form mortgage clause: a mortgage clause permitting the buyer to take over the mortgage, subject to and not assuming liability for its payment.

short interest: the sum of the short sales outstanding in a security or commodity or on an exchange stock.

short merchandise

(1) *general:* goods bought in small quantities, usually in extreme sizes, to complete an assortment.

(2) *merchandising:* purchased goods that were not included in a shipment. See also *over, short, and damaged.*

short of destination: prior to reaching the final port, warehouse, or destination.

short of exchange: the position of a foreign exchange trader who has sold more foreign bills than the quantity of bills he or she has in possession to cover the sales.

short position: stocks sold short and not covered as of a particular date. On an exchange, a tabulation is usually issued once a month, listing all issues on the exchange in which there was a short position of 5000 or more shares and issues in which the short position had changed by 2000 or more shares in the preceding month. The term is also used for the total amount of stock an individual has sold short and has covered as of a particular date.

short purchase: buying a stock to cover an earlier short sale of the same stock.

short rate: the higher rate an advertiser pays when he or she fails to use the space or time contracted for.

short-rate cancellation: the charge required for insurance or bonds taken for less than one year. In some cases, it denotes the earned premium for insurance or bonds canceled by the insured before the end of the policy period or term of bond. Cf. *pro rata cancellation.*

short run

(1) *general:* a one-time job.

(2) *finance:* the time during which a firm can alter the price or output of its goods but not change the size of its plant or close down operations.

short-run planning: the process of making decisions about current and future operations, including day-to-day decisions and nonroutine operating decisions.

short sale: a transaction made by a person who believes a stock will decline and places a sell order, although he or she does not own any of the shares. Stock exchange and federal regulations govern and limit the conditions under which a short sale may be made. Sometimes a person will sell short a stock already owned to protect a paper profit; this is known as "selling against the box."

short selling: selling a stock and purchasing it at a lower price to receive a profit.

short-staker: (slang) an individual who works only to earn sufficient money for the moment and then moves on.

short-tail: (slang) a nonunion worker.

short-term capital flows: investments, such as purchases of stock, deposits of funds in U.S. banks, and investments in Treasury bills and other money market securities, that are expected to remain in a foreign country for less than one year.

short-term capital movements: an item in the balance-of-payments accounts indicating financial obligations due or payable within a year.

short-term debt: an obligation that is usually due within the year.

short-term funds: money borrowed for from 30 days to one year.

short-term investment: an expenditure for nonoperating assets that a business enterprise intends to hold for only a short period of time, usually less than a year.

short ton: 2000 pounds. Cf. *long ton.*

shotgun approach: a disorganized approach to selling or advertising, aimed at reaching a large number of potential customers without expecting to making sales to all. Cf. *rifle technique.*

showing: See *one hundred showing.*

shrinkage: See *inventory shortage (shrinkage).*

shrink wrapping: a plastic coating applied over a package. When subjected to heat, the coating conforms to the shape of the package.

shuffler: (slang) an unemployed worker; a migratory worker.

shutdown: a stoppage of production due to installation or breakdown of equipment, shortage of work orders, lack of materials or skilled labor, and so on.

shyster: an unethical and unscrupulous person.

SIC: See *Standard Industrial Classification System.*

sick leave: contractually provided conditions under which employees are paid during illness. The individual retains all job rights, including seniority and other privileges.

sick pay: compensation given an employee because of illness, accident, or some other incapacity. The worker retains his or her job rights, including seniority, during the period of receiving sick pay.

sideline stores: stores whose primary interest is other than retailing (e.g., a wholesaler who also sells to the consumer as an accommodation).

sight bill of exchange: a bill of exchange that becomes due and payable when presented by the holder to the party on whom it is drawn. See also *short bill.*

sight draft: a draft payable upon delivery and presentation to the drawee, or upon sight.

signal: the output of a circuit, used for control and/or timing of various computer operations.

significance, statistical: statistical importance; the degree of probability that in an infinite series of measurements of the type in question, the value actually obtained will not occur with meaningful frequency by chance alone and hence can be attributed to something other than chance.

significance of task: the degree to which a job has an impact on the lives or work of other people.

sign off: the closing instruction to the computer, which terminates communication with the system.

sign on: the opening instruction to the computer, which begins communication with the system.

silent partner: an individual who gives funds for a business partnership but takes no part in the management of the firm. This is not to be confused with *secret partner.*

simple interest: interest calculated on a principal sum and not on any interest that has been earned by that sum. See (Appendixes E and F); cf. *compound interest.*

simulation

(1) *computers:* the technique of setting up a routine for one computer to make it operate as nearly as possi-

ble like some other computer.

(2) **systems:** the representation of certain features of the behavior of a physical or abstract system by means of the behavior of another system.

(3) **systems:** a method of reviewing an operation or problem that overcomes the difficulty of not being able to study it in real-life form. A model of the system or process is subjected to a series of assumptions and manipulations in an effort to find one or more acceptable solutions.

simulation, real-time: a simulation program operation such that the instants of occurrence of basic events occur at the same time as they would in the system being simulated.

simulation model: a model that replicates some aspect of a firm's operation. By performing step-by-step computations with the model, it is possible to duplicate the manner in which the actual system might perform.

simulator program: a program that represents certain features of the behavior of a physical or abstract system. See also *translator*.

simulcast: a program that is broadcast simultaneously over radio and television.

simultaneous inflation and unemployment (inflump): a situation calling for a value judgment of whether inflation or unemployment is the more serious problem and whether the economy is moving toward worse inflation or worse unemployment.

simultaneous processing: the performance of two or more data-processing tasks at the same time. See also *multiprocessing*.

sinecure: a position of limited or non-existent responsibility that demands little or no labor or service.

single address message: a message that is to be delivered to only one destination.

single entry: a bookkeeping approach in which each transaction is entered only once on the account books. The single-entry system is used primarily by small businesses. Cf. *double entry*.

single-line store: a store that carries a wide variety of one type of goods.

single-payment loan: a loan whose entire principal is due on one maturity date.

single propietorship: ownership of a business by one person.

single rate: a wage rate that is identical for all employees working in the same job or classification.

single step: pertaining to a method of operating a computer in which each operation is performed in response to a single manual act.

single strand: an informal communication chain in which information is passed from one person to another through a line of recipients.

single tax: the principal feature of Henry George's proposal that all income from the ownership of land be taxed for the total amount, thus eliminating the need to collect other taxes. See also *land value tax*.

single-use plans: plans that are used only once or a few times because they focus on organizational situations that do not occur repeatedly.

singular property title: property title granted to only one person. See also *severalty*.

sinking fund: a fund used to accumulate the cash needed to pay off a bond or other security. By accumulating cash in a sinking fund, the firm is in a better position to pay its securities when due, and the risk is therefore reduced to the security holder.

sinking fund bonds: See *bond, sinking fund.*

sinking fund depreciation: a system for calculating depreciation whereby the yearly amount is presumed to be deposited in a sinking fund that will also increase as a result of earnings from the fund investment.

sit-down strike: a work stoppage in which employees report for work but remain idle at the job. This form of strike is forbidden by law. Cf. *blacking.*

situational analysis: an assessment of the marketing environment; key part of the marketing plan, often referred to as the market review.

situational design theory: the concept that there is no single best way to design an organization. Cf. *universal design theory.*

situational theory of leadership: the concept that, before selecting a leadership style, leaders must understand their own behavior, that of their subordinates, and the demands of the tasks. Such understanding requires diagnostic skills in human behavior. See also *organic structure, process principles, sensitivity training.*

situs: a place or situation where a thing is located. An owner's home is the situs of his or her property.

situs picketing: picketing a subcontractor at a construction site. Under the Taft-Hartley Act, this is a secondary boycott and therefore an illegal practice.

six and seven nations of (economic)

Europe: See *European Economic Community, European Free Trade Association.*

skewness: the property of a distribution curve that is not symmetrical. See also *kurtosis.*

skill: an inherent or learned ability to apply one's knowledge and/or experience to one's job, vocation, or profession.

skills inventories: summaries of each workers' skills and abilities, usually used for nonmanagement workers. See also *management inventories.*

skill variety: the degree to which a person must perform several different activities to complete a job, involving the use of a number of skills and talents.

skimming prices: use of a high introductory price followed by a series of price reductions, designed to get all the trade the market will bear at one price level before lowering the price and also to appeal to the more price-conscious consumer.

skim-the-cream pricing: the pricing technique of establishing price at the upper limit of the range.

skip: a customer who moves from a known address without paying the bill of a business or utility.

skippy strike: (slang) an employee's way of showing annoyance with working conditions by disregarding some of the work assignment.

sky lease: a lease of a property's air rights. The lease is usually long term; upon termination, the changes and additions remain as a fixed part of the property. See also *air rights.*

slack

(1) *production:* the time in which a minor operation can be completed in

advance of the next major operation that depends on it.

(2) *business:* a dull or inactive business period (e.g., a slack season).

slander: an oral utterance that tends to harm the reputation of another.

slave computer: a backup system consisting of a second computer that performs the same steps of the same programs executed by the master computer. If the master computer fails or malfunctions, the slave computer takes over without interruption of operation. See also *system, failsafe; volatile memory;* cf. *rescue dump, satellite processor.*

slave market: (slang) an employment office or activity.

sleeper: an fast-selling item that has the potential to become a runner. Cf. *runner.*

slide: a posting error by which an amount is wrongly recorded by a bookkeeper who unintentionally places the decimal one or more digits to the right or left of the true decimal position.

sliding scale: a reason for increasing or decreasing charges to a customer in relation to the volume of activity or usage over a stated time (e.g., a gas company may charge for gas on a sliding scale, with lower rates for greater consumption).

slippage: lost time.

slow asset: an asset that can be converted into cash, near its book value, only after a lengthy passage of time.

slowdown: lessening of work effort, by concerted agreement among employees, to force, management concessins. A slowdown is sometimes used as an alternative to a strike. Cf. *blacking.*

slow loan: a loan on which payments have been delayed beyond the due dates specified in a mortgage.

slump: a short-lived decline in the activity of a business or economy.

Small Business Administration (SBA): a federal agency established in 1953 solely to advise and assist the nation's small businesses. The SBA provides loans, loan guarantees, and other financial assistance, and offers loans to victims of floods, riots, and other catastrophes and to those who have suffered economic harm as a result of federal programs. It also conducts economic research on conditions that affect small businesses.

smart money: experienced and professional security traders who exploit inside information to make profits at the expense of other investors.

Smith-Hughes Act of 1917: a federal law that provides for basic vocational education with federal grants to states to encourage the training of skills in agriculture, trade, and industry.

smoke damage insurance: insurance against damage caused by smoke from the sudden, unusual, and faulty operation of a heating or cooking unit, but only when such a unit is connected to a chimney by a smoke pipe and while it is on the premises described in the policy. Smoke damage from fireplaces and industrial operations is usually excluded. Cf. *fire insurance.*

smoothing style: the tendency to minimize or suppress open recognition of real or perceived differences while emphasizing common interests in conflict situations.

smuggling: removing from or putting in goods or persons without permission. Smuggling can be done across the borders of countries or other political entities (e.g., cigarette smuggling across state lines).

snake system: an international agreement between Belgium, the Netherlands, Luxembourg, Denmark, Sweden, Norway, and West Germany, linking the currencies of these countries in an exchange rate system. The signatories have agreed to limit fluctuations in exchange rates among their currencies to 2.25 percent above or below set median rates. The snake was designed to be the first stage in forming a uniform Common Market currency. Members maintain fairly even exchange rates among themselves by buying or selling their currencies when the rates threaten to drop or rise beyond the 2.25 percent limits. See also *European Economic Community, European Free Trade Association, swap.*

snap strike: a stoppage of work by employees without authorization of the union. See also *illegal strike.*

snowbird: (slang) a worker who seeks employment in the South to escape the cold of the North.

social audit: an identification and evaluation of organizational activities that are believed to have a positive social impact.

social benefit: the value to a society resulting from a specific act or action (e.g., the discovery of penicillin; the invention of the automobile).

social contract: a model conceptualizing the relationship between a firm and society as a whole, whereby the organization is granted freedom to exist and is obligated to function in the public interest.

social (opportunity) cost: the price paid by citizens for the side effects of economic performance (e.g., pollution, destruction of forests). See also *comparative advantage.*

social infrastructure expenditures: expenditures for public projects that are established for the good of the community (e.g., highway construction, health care programs).

socialism: a theory of economic organization in which all or most of the means of production is controlled or owned by a government or collective institution and planning is centralized.

socialization: a formal and informal process of training, guidance, indoctrination, influence, or even coercion, whereby a new or potential organization member is made to internalize the norms, values, attitudes or behavior patterns of the organization.

social marketing: the use of marketing philosophy and techniques in the dissemination of societally useful ideas. The concept was propounded by Phillip Kotler and Gerald Zaltman in the 1970s, and the first book on social marketing was written by Seymour H. Fine.

social responsibility: the expectation that companies should act in the public interest and contribute to the solution of social and ecological problems.

social responsiveness approach: an approach to meeting social obligations that considers business to have societal and economic goals as well as the obligation to anticipate upcoming social problems and work actively to prevent their appearance.

social security: the combination of social insurance plans sponsored by the federal government, including old age and survivors' insurance and unemployment insurance. Wage and payroll deductions are made to finance these programs. Federal employees are exempt from contributing to the costs of such coverage.

Social Security Act of 1935: legislation that resulted in a national social insurance program to provide old age and survivors' benefits, public assistance to the aged, the blind, and needy children, unemployment insurance, and disability benefits.

social security taxes (FICA): the Federal Insurance Contributions Act taxes imposed on employees and employers, used mainly to provide retirement benefits.

societal environment: forces external to an organization that influence what happens internally. Among these forces are political, regulatory, resource, economic, and technological factors.

sociogram: a means of describing the preferences people have in being with others. The sociogram is used in choosing teams, work partners, and so on. See also *sociometric testing.*

sociometric testing: a technique developed by J. L. Moreno in which a rater identifies those people in a group who possess specified qualifications that are useful in forming task-oriented teams. A visual analysis of sociometric testing is displayed in a sociogram. See also *sociometry.*

sociometry: a technique developed by J. L. Moreno for attempting to match individuals to tasks based on their preferences for co-workers. See also *sociogram.*

sociotechnical systems: an organizational development technique that seeks to obtain a good fit between the organization's technical system and its social system.

soft currency: the funds of a country that are controlled by exchange procedures, thereby having limited convertibility into gold and other currencies.

soft goods: ready-to-wear clothing, piece goods, linens, towels, and small fashion accessories.

soft loan: a loan whose terms of repayment are generous and sometimes have a low rate of interest.

soft money: paper currency, as contrasted with coinage (hard money).

soft sell: a selling technique that is convincing, subtle, and indirect. Cf. *hard sell.*

software

(1) *computers:* a set of programs and procedures concerned with the operation of a data-processing system.

(2) *computers:* a set of coded instructions prepared to simplify programming and computer operations.

(3) *computers:* a term applied to computer operations that includes compilers, assemblers, executive routines, and input and output libraries.

SOH: stock on hand.

soil bank: a farm program established by the government to pay farmers for removing land from cultivation. See also *acreage quota.*

soldiering: the act of loafing on the job or otherwise reducing productivity. See also *blacking.*

sold notice: Synonymous with *notice sale.*

sole owner: the only person holding the title to a specific property or business. See also *severalty.*

sole proprietorship: a proprietorship in which all equity lies with one individual.

solid state computer: a computer that uses solid state, or semiconductor, components; a second-generation computer.

solvency: the condition that exists when liabilities, other than those of ownership, amount to less than total assets; the ability to pay debts.

solvent: the condition of an individual who is able to pay his or her debts.

SOP: standard operating procedure.

sort

(1) *systems:* to segregate items into groups according to some definite rules.

(2) *computers:* a programmer routine that orders data. See also *tag sort.*

sorter: a person, device, or computer routine that sorts.

sound value: a term used to indicate the value of property for fire insurance purposes. See also *actual cash value.*

source document: a form containing data that are eventually processed by a computer. See also *raw data.*

sovereign: an individual who holds supreme power, usually in a nation.

space

(1) *computers:* a site intended for the storage of data.

(2) *computers:* a basic unit of area, usually the size of a single character.

(3) *computers:* to advance the reading or display position according to a prescribed format.

(4) *advertising:* the area or medium in which an advertisement is placed.

space buyer: an advertising agency executive who assists in the planning of printed media campaigns and chooses and purchases space in the media. Cf. *time buyer.*

span of control: the extent of a supervisor's responsibility, usually identified in the organizational chart by lines of authority. See also *Lockheed model.*

special assessment: the process, by an assessor, court, or board of review, of making formal and official estimation of the value of a property as a basis for levying taxes for raising revenue for special purposes.

special assessment bond: See *bond, special assessment.*

special audit: an audit that is selected to cover a particular phase of activity of a specified time period.

special bid: a method of filling an order to buy a large block of stock on the exchange floor. The bidder for the block of stock pays a special commission to the broker who represents him or her in making the purchase. The seller does not pay a commission. The special bid is made on the floor of the exchange at a fixed price, which may not be below the last sale of the security or the current bid in the regular market, whichever is higher. Member firms may sell this stock for customers directly to the buyer's broker during trading hours.

special districts: independent governmental units that are created to serve a single function or a limited function and that have the power to tax, impose service charges, or incur debt therefor.

special drawing rights (SDRs): the amount by which each country is permitted to have its international checking account with the International Monetary Fund go negative before the nation must ask for additional loans. SDRs were established at the Rio de Janeiro conference of 1967.

special events recruiting: an effort on the part of a single employer or group of employers to attract a large number of applicants for interviews by use of job fairs, open houses, and the like. See also *recruiting.*

special interest account: the term used by commercial banks to describe a savings account. Some states do not permit a commercial bank to accept savings accounts. In such cases, deposits may be accepted on which interest is paid under the same interest-bearing rates as a savings bank, but another name, such as "special interest accounts," must be used.

special issues: securities issued by the Treasury for investment of reserves of government trust funds and for certain payments to veterans.

specialist: a member of an exchange who has two functions: to maintain an orderly market, insofar as is reasonably practicable, in the stocks in which he is registered by an exchange as a specialist; and to act as a broker's broker.

specialization: reducing an operation or task into separate simplified, individual activities. See also *therbligs.*

special lien: Synonymous with *particular lien.*

special offering: a large block of stock that becomes available for sale but requires special handling because of its size and the market in that particular issue. A notice is printed on the ticker tape announcing that the stock will be offered for sale on the exchange floor at a fixed price. Member firms may buy this stock for customers directly from the seller's broker during trading hours. The price is usually based on the last transaction in the regular auction market. Only the seller pays a commission on a special offering. Special offerings must be approved by the SEC.

special order: an order that may be priced below the normal price in order to utilize excess capacity and thereby contribute to company profits.

special-purpose computer: a computer that is designed to handle a restricted class of problems.

special-purpose funds: mutual funds that invest exclusively in securities from one industry. See also *investment company.*

specialty merchandise: consumer goods that have special features for which buyers are willing to make a major purchasing effort (e.g., imported foods, hi-fi equipment, cameras).

specialty stores: retail outlets that maintain a large selection in a limited line of merchandise (e.g., men's apparel stores).

special warranty deed: a deed in which the grantor defends the property title against demands made by grantees, heirs, and other claimants. No other liability is assumed by the grantor. Trustees often use this deed when transferring title, and following a court decision, to convey tax titles.

specie: money in coin.

specification

(1) *general:* a written identification of the work to be done and materials to be used in the completion of a task.

(2) *computers:* a precise definition of the records and programs needed to carry out a particular processing function.

specific identification: a method of valuing inventory and determining cost of goods sold whereby the actual costs of specific inventory items are assigned to those items of inventory on hand and to those that have been sold.

specific insurance: coverage that applies to separate and specifically named objects or locations, as distinguished from blanket insurance.

specific subsidy: the per-unit subsidy on a commodity.

specific tariff: a tariff based on a fixed amount charged per unit of the goods imported.

specific tax: the per-unit tax on a commodity.

speculation: the employment of funds by a speculator. Safety of principal is a factor secondary to increasing capital. See also *letter stock;* cf. *defensive investment, digested securities.*

speculative demand for money: a demand for liquidity generated by the expectation that changes in interest rates and bond prices will make it profitable to temporarily hold cash rather than income-earning assets.

speculative purchasing: buying items when prices appear lowest, with the expectation that there will be a future price increase that will make possible a profit.

speculator: one who is willing to assume a relatively large risk in the hope of gain. The speculator's principal concern is to increase capital rather than dividend income. Speculators may buy and sell the same day or may invest in enterprises that they do not expect to be profitable for years.

speed-up: a management-directed attempt to increase production without any increase in pay. A worker slowdown may follow as a reaction against a speed-up. Cf. *incentive pay, stretch-out.*

spendable earnings: net earnings after deductions for taxes, or the amount available for spending. Synonymous with *take-home pay.*

spillovers: external benefits or costs of efforts for which there is no compensation. Synonymous with *externalities.*

spinoff: with respect to federal income taxes, a transfer by a firm of a portion of its assets to a newly formed organization in exchange for the latter's capital stock, which is thereupon distributed as a property dividend to the stockholders of the initial corporation.

split: the division of the outstanding shares of a corporation into a larger number of shares. A 3-for-1 split by a company with 1 million shares outstanding would result in 3 million shares outstanding. Each holder of 100 shares before the 3-for-1 split would have 300 shares. Of course, the shareholder's proportionate equity in the company would remain the same, since 100 parts of 1 million is the equivalent of 300 parts of 3 million. Ordinarily, a split must be voted by directors and approved by shareholders. Such action by a corporation does not alter the total contributed capital but merely increases the number of shares issued and outstanding and the par value per share. Cf. *stock split down.*

split investment company: a closed-end investment firm that issues two types of capital stock. The first (income shares) receives dividends from investments; the second (capital shares) receives dividends from the appreciation of investments. Synonymous with *dual-purpose fund.*

split load: cargo in a single shipping unit that has more than one terminal destination.

split-off point. See *joint production costs.*

split order: a large order that is separated into smaller units that are sold over a period of time. When purchasing or selling a security or commodity, a very large transaction could cause substantial price fluctuation, and the splitting is supposed to prevent this.

split run: two or more ads of equal size with the identical position in different copies of the same publication issue. This affords a means of determining the impact of differing versions of an advertisement, and it allows an advertiser to feature different products in regional printings of a national publication.

split shift: the daily working time of an employee that is divided into two or

more working periods, to meet peak needs (e.g., bus drivers who work in morning and afternoon transportation rush hours).

split up: the issuance of two or more stock shares to replace each outstanding share, used for financial and tax purposes. This increase, although lowering the value per share, does not alter the total liability of the issuing firm for the outstanding capital stock. See also *split.*

spokesperson role: a manager's role in speaking for the unit and representing it to others. A key concept of the spokesperson role is that of representation; the manager must act as an advocate for subordinates.

sponsor: a radio or television advertiser. Cf. *sustaining program.*

spooling: the reading and writing of input and output streams on auxiliary storage devices, concurrently with job execution, in a format convenient for later processing or output operations.

spot
(1) *finance:* describing the ready delivery of commodities and foreign exchange that are usually delivered less rapidly.
(2) *media:* a place or position in a listing or schedule (e.g., having a spot on television).

spot advertising: a campaign wherein advertisers choose specific stations to be used. This contrasts with network or local advertising. See also *flight saturation.*

spot announcement: a brief commercial, usually one minute long or less, inserted between portions of a radio or television program.

spot delivery: immediate delivery.

spot market: a market in which commodities are sold for cash and delivered quickly. See also *fixing the price.*

spot price: the selling price of a physical commodity.

spot punch: a device for punching one hole at a time on a computer card.

spout: a fitting on a container for the purpose of directing the pouring stream of liquid or granular contents.

spread

(1) *securities:* two different options, a put (price below the prevailing market) and a call (price above the prevailing market), with both options pertaining to the same stock and expiring on the same day. Thus the trader is guaranteed a sale at a price not lower than the put price if the market drops and a buy at a price not higher than the call price if the market increases. See also *butterfly spread, straddle.*

(2) *securities:* the differences between the bid and asked prices of securities.

(3) *securities:* two prices given instead of one.

(4) *finance:* the difference between two prices.

SRDS: Standard Rate and Data Service, Inc., an organization that releases up-to-date data on advertising rates, standards, and so on, of various media. SRDS is considered the prime source of advertising media information.

stability: the objective of creating a sense of predictability, control, and certainty in an organization.

stabilization policy: the efforts of government to use fiscal and monetary means to eliminate inflation, unemployment, or both. See also *wage stabilization.*

stable environment: an environment that is characterized by relatively small changes in technology and customers who have a minimal impact on the internal operations of the organization.

stable money: currency that remains constant in terms of the items and services it can purchase.

stacker: a freight handler who loads a vehicle.

staff: employees who advise and assist line managers and employees but are not directly engaged in the production of the final good or service.

staff authority: See *line and staff authority.*

staff department: a department that provides assistance and support to line departments in attaining basic objectives of the organization. In a manufacturing firm, purchasing and accounting would be staff departments.

staff function: service, advisory, or otherwise supportive activities performed by staff units in line and staff organizations.

staffing table: a list of anticipated employment openings for each type of job.

staff organization: an administrative concept by which planning, research, organizing, fact-finding, and advisory assistance is provided to the line (command) through departments, units, or individual officers who are specifically created and maintained for such purposes, usually with limited functional authority and control.

stag: an individual speculator who rapidly buys and then sells shares for profit, having had no intention of retaining the securities for any length of time. Cf. *digested securities.*

stagflation: inflation coexisting with economic stagnation. Prices for goods and services continue to increase during a period of minimal capital investment in equipment, research and development, and so on.

staggering of hours: a procedure for adjusting hours of employment in order to schedule work more evenly.

stagnation: conditions of minimal growth rate, or growth that is increasing at a lower rate than expected.

stakeholders: persons whom the organization is dedicated to serve.

stale check: any check dated 90 days prior to presentation for payment.

stamp tax: a government tax collected through the sale of stamps that are affixed to certain products (e.g., liquor, tobacco, stock certificates, title deeds). See also *transfer tax.*

Standard & Poor's 500 Stock Average: an index of stock prices composed of 425 industrials, 50 utilities, and 25 railroads. Cf. *Dow-Jones averages.*

Standard Container Acts of 1916 and 1928: federal legislation that fixed standard sizes for baskets and containers for fruits and vegetables.

standard costs: an estimate of what actual costs should be under projected conditions.

standard deviation (SD): See *deviation, standard.*

standard error: a measure or an estimate of the sampling errors affecting a statistic; a measure of the amount a statistic may be expected to differ by chance from the true value of the statistic.

standard hour plan: a method of incentive compensation that uses time allowances rather than piece rates.

Standard Industrial Classification System (SIC): a numerical system developed by the U.S. Bureau of the Budget to classify establishments by type of activity for purposes of facilitating the collection, tabulation, presentation, and analysis of data relating to such establishments and for promoting uniformity within U.S. agencies. Cf. *Dictionary of Occupational Titles.*

standardization

(1) *general:* the determination of basic limits or grade ranges in the form of specifications to which produced items should conform.

(2) *manufacturing:* establishing specific criteria levels (size, quality, weight, etc.).

standardized test: an examination administered under fixed conditions to a large group of persons who are representative of the individuals for whom the test was intended.

standard of living: the level of material affluence of a nation as measured by per capita output. See also *per capita output.*

standard program: a computer program that meets certain criteria, such as being written in a standard machine language (FORTRAN, COBOL, ALGOL, etc.) and bringing forth an approved solution to a problem.

standby blocking: ensuring that spare input/output blocks of information are always in memory, to make more efficient use of buffers.

standing committee: a committee, often advisory in nature, that exists for an indefinite period of time.

standing order: an authority given by a customer for the bank to regularly pay funds, usually a fixed dollar amount, from his or her demand deposit account.

standing plans: plans which are used again and again. They include policies, procedures, and rules.

standstill agreement: an arrangement between a debtor and a creditor under which new limits and conditions for the loan are established. Typically, a postponement of obligation payment is the result. Cf. *novation.*

staple stock: goods on hand that are in continuous demand.

starboard: the right side of a ship, barge, or airplane.

stars: individuals who are active, effective group members and exhibit a variety of behaviors.

start-stop time: Synonymous with *acceleration time.*

state bank: a bank that is organized according to the laws of a state and is chartered by the state in which it is located to operate as a banking business. The various states have different laws governing the operation of banks.

stated capital: the sum of capital amounts contributed by stockholders.

state disability plan: a plan of some states that involves short-term insurance to replace income lost by eligible persons employed in that state. Cf. *workers' compensation.*

stated value: a nominal value assigned to no-par stock by the board of directors of a corporation.

statement

(1) *computers:* an instruction to perform some sequence of operations.

(2) *banking:* a record prepared by a bank for a depositor, listing all checks drawn and deposits made together with the new balance after each posting.

(3) *accounting:* a summary of transactions between a creditor and his or her debts or a presentation of names and amounts of accounts to show a financial condition (e.g., an IRS statement).

states of nature: conditions beyond the control of decision makers that can influence the results of their decisions.

static analysis: the determination of an equilibrium at a single point in time without considering the impact of the passage of time.

static budgeting: financial planning that establishes absolute amounts of revenues, costs, and expenses for a specific activity level.

static dump: a dump that is performed at a particular point in time with respect to a machine run, frequently at the end of a run. See also *postmortem dump.*

static inventory problem: the tendency of items bought for a specific selling season to lose value, either partly or completely, because of changes in the market at the season's end.

static model: a concept for studying economic events without reference to time and without relation to preceding or succeeding events. Time is not permitted to alter analysis in any way to affect conclusions.

static payment loan: Synonymous with *level payment mortgage.*

station

(1) *computers:* one of the input or output points of a system that uses communication facilities.

(2) *securities:* the place where a specialist on an exchange transacts orders.

(3) *transportation:* a place at which trains stop to pick up or discharge passengers or freight.

(4) *administration:* a worker's assigned post or place of activity.

station break: giving the call letters or identification of a radio or television station.

station option time: time over which a network affiliate station has priority on first sales.

statism: any indication of increased government intervention in a nation's economic activity, with primary focus on movement toward greater control over major industries. See also *controlled economy.*

statistical accounting: the application of probability theory and statistical sampling approaches to the evolution of prime accounting information and/or verification, authentication, and audit of accounting data prepared by other means.

statistics: the mathematics of gathering data and the approaches used in describing and analyzing numerical information.

status: an individual's relative social or power position in a group; may also apply to the position of an organization in a broad social context.

status consensus: the agreement of group members about the relative status of members of the group. Synonymous with *status consequence.*

status consequence: Synonymous with *status consensus.*

status quo: the existing state of affairs.

status symbol: an item purchased in the hope that it will communicate one's desired or real status to others.

statute: a law passed by the legislative body of a state.

statute of limitations: See *limitations of actions.*

steering controls: controls in which results are predicted and corrective action is taken while the operation or task is being performed.

step: one operation in a computer routine. See also *job step.*

stepped costs: costs that climb by increments with increased volumes of activity.

step-up: an automatic wage increase based on length of service.

stereotypes: preconceived notions, often based on superficial characteristics, that often distort communication between people. See also *bias.*

sterling: the currency basis of Great Britain, the unit of which is the pound sterling. It may also represent bills of exchange that are drawn in terms of British currency. Sterling silver is silver of at least 222 parts pure silver out of 240 and no more than 18 parts of an alloy.

steward: See *shop steward.*

sticker: an employee who is unwilling to accept an offer for promotion.

stimulus-response: the basic unit of learning (habit) in both the classical and instrumental conditioning models.

stipend: Synonymous with *salary.*

stock

(1) *merchandising:* merchandise held for sale (e.g., inventory).

(2) *securities:* the legal capital of a corporation divided into shares. See also *assented securities, authorized stock, blue chip, callable, capital stock, common stock, convertibles, cumulative preferred, deferred stock, float, growth stock, guaranteed stock, inactive stock, issue, listed securities, nonassessable stock, noncumulative, no par value stock, ordinary stock, outstanding, over-the-counter securities, paid-up stock, participating preferred, par value, penny stocks, preferred stock, prior preferred, redeemable stock, treasury stock, unissued stock, unlisted, voting right, watered stock.*

stock ahead

(1) *merchandising:* to maintain sufficient quantities of goods in inventory to cover an anticipated surge in future demand for the items.

(2) *securities:* describing a situation when an investor who has entered an order to buy or sell a stock at a certain price sees transactions at that price reported on the ticker tape before his or her own order has been executed. This may have occurred because other buy and sell orders at the same price came in to a trading specialist earlier and had priority.

stock-appreciation rights (SARs): privileges that can be attached to a nonqualified option. With an SAR, an executive can ignore the option and take a bonus equal to the value of the stock's appreciation over a span of time. An SEC rule permits an SAR bonus to be paid in cash, rather than in company shares. The SAR can be acted on at any time during the 10-year term of the attached nonqualified stock option.

stock broker: an individual who acts as a middleman between buyers and sellers of stock. Cf. *specialist.*

stock certificate: written evidence of ownership of a company's shares, indicating the number of shares registered in the name of the owner, the corporation issuing the capital stock, and whether the stock is a par value or a no par-value stock.

Stock Clearing Corporation: the New York Stock Exchange's clearinghouse. Its major responsibilities include the clearing and settling of money balances between members, the clearing of purchases and sales transactions, and the delivery of stock.

stock dividend: a portion of the net earnings of a corporation, payable (in shares of fractional shares of designated stock of a given corporation) to the stockholders of record of corporation. It is paid in securities rather than cash, and it may be additional shares of the issuing company or shares of another company held by the corporation.

stock exchanges: organizations that provide a market for the trading of bonds and stocks. Regulations for the admission of securities for trading on the stock exchanges are very stringent.

stockholder of record: a stockholder whose name is registered on the books of the issuing corporation. See *voting right.*

stockholders' equity: Synonymous with *owners' equity.*

stocking allowance: a special allowance by a manufacturer to encourage distributor organizations to carry a particular product.

stock in trade

(1) *general:* the business activity that is usually carried on by a firm.

(2) *securities:* the quantity of securities held.

stock jobbing: irresponsible or dishonest manipulation of the price of securities.

stock levels: the inventory carried by a business firm.

stock market: the buying and selling of stock for the purpose of profit for both buyers and sellers of the security. See also *market.*

stock option: an arrangement for compensating top management, in addition to salary, with an opportunity to buy a certain amount of company stock, often at a price under the market price. See also *Tax Reform Act of 1976.*

stockout: a condition that occurs when all inventory has been used or sold. Stockouts are very costly, as other inputs must then be utilized.

stockpiling: government purchases of various agricultural commodities and raw materials for storage, to support the prices of these products. Cf. *hoarding, subsidy.*

stock power: a power of attorney permitting a person other than the owner of stock to legally transfer the title of ownership to a third party. Stock powers are usually given when stock is pledged as collateral to loans.

stock purchase plan: a company plan for the purchase of stock by employees, with or without a contribution from the employer, at terms usually below the market price.

stock-sales ratio: the inventory retail value at the beginning of a given month, divided by sales for that month. This relationship is used to control the sales and inventory balance.

stock shortage: a condition that occurs when the dollar value of the real inventory in stock is less than that which is shown on the inventory books.

stock split: See *split.*

stock split down: the reverse of a stock split, whereby the total number of shares outstanding is lowered, without reducing the total value of the issue, by issuing a new stock share to replace each of two or more shares presently in circulation. The motivation is to increase the market price of a stock. Synonymous with *reverse stock split.*

stock transfer: the act of canceling a stock certificate submitted for transfer, issuing a new certificate in the name of the designated transferee, and recording the change in ownership on the records of a corporation's stock transfer book. See also *stock transfer tax.*

stock transfer tax: a tax levied by some states on the transfer of securities from one owner to another, either when purchased or given as a gift. See also *stock transfer.*

stock turnover: See *turnover.*

stock watering: See *watered stock.*

STOL: short takeoff and landing. This capability allows an aircraft of considerable weight to take off and land within a relatively short horizontal distance.

stonewalling

(1) *general:* a term popularized by members of Richard Nixon's admin-

istration in their attempt to delay legal procedures against them by avoidance of the conflict or by distorting the available facts.

(2) *business law:* obstruction or delay of parliamentary proceedings by filibuster or lengthy debate.

stoolpigeon: a worker who is paid by an employer to report to management on union activities; a company spy. See also *hooking, roping.*

stoop labor: agricultural work that requires constant bending and kneeling.

stopgo: a British concept of fiscal policy, shifting between economic growth and slowdown. Synonymous with *go-stop.*

stop limit order: a stop order that becomes a limit order after the specified stop price has been reached.

stop loss: a guarantee from one company (the reinsurer) to another (the reinsured) that losses over and above an agreed-upon amount will be paid by the reinsuring company.

stop order: an order to buy at a price above or to sell at a price below the current market. Stop buy orders are generally used to limit loss or to protect unrealized profits on a short sale. Stop sell orders are generally used to protect unrealized profits or to limit loss on a holding. A stop order becomes a market order when the stock sells at or beyond the specified price and thus may not necessarily be executed at that price.

stoppage in transit (in transitu): under certain conditions, a shipper's right to halt delivery of a shipment that is already in transit, when payment has not been made. Cf. *carrier's lien.*

stop payment: the order given to a bank by a depositor who wishes to prevent payment on a check he or she has issued. The depositor requests in writing that the bank stop payment or telephones the instructions and confirms them in writing.

stop price: the price at which a customer's stop order to his broker becomes a market order.

storage

(1) *general:* the holding of goods for future use.

(2) *systems:* loosely, any device that can store data.

(3) *computers:* any device into which units of information can be transferred, which will hold information, and from which the information can be obtained. Synonymous with *memory.*

storage, external: See *external storage.*

storage, magnetic core: the main storage device, in which binary data are represented by the direction of magnetization in each unit of an array of magnetic material.

storage capacity: the amount of data that can be contained in a storage device.

storage drum: a random-access storage device that can hold 4 million alphanumeric characters or up to 8 million digits, which can be retrieved at a rate of 1.2 million characters per second.

store

(1) *computers:* to transfer information to a device (e.g., a drum) from which the unaltered information can be obtained at a later time.

(2) *merchandising:* any place where merchandise, goods, or ser-

vices can be purchased, or a place for storage.

store audit: a count of the merchandise carried and sold in a retail outlet.

store count distribution: a measure of distribution based on the number of stores. A product sold in 90 percent of all grocery stores would have 90 percent store count distribution.

stored program computer: a computer in which the instructions specifying the operations to be performed are stored in the form of coded information in main memory along with the data currently being operated on, making possible simple repetition of operations and modification by the computer of its own instructions.

stowage: cargo that is properly stored.

straddle: an option that allows the trader to buy or sell securities at an agreed-upon price within a given period. See also *butterfly spread, spread.*

straight bill of lading: a bill of lading that cannot be negotiated, identifying the individual who is to receive goods.

straight investment: a preferred stock or bond, limited in interest or dividend rate, that is bought because of its income return and not for expectation of any rise in value. See also *investment.*

straight lease: a lease that describes regular rental payments (e.g., monthly, quarterly). Synonymous with *flat lease.*

straight life: Synonymous with *ordinary life.*

straight-line depreciation: the simplest method of depreciation, where-

by capital cost is amortized in uniform periodic amounts over the anticipated life of the asset.

straight-line interest amortization: a method of systematically writing off a bond premium or discount in equal amounts each period until maturity. Cf. *effective-interest amortization.*

straight loan: a loan to an individual or other legal entity in which the basis for granting credit is the debtor's general ability to pay, unsupported by any form of collateral security.

straight piecework plan: a method of compensation whereby a predetermined amount of money is paid for each unit produced. It is an alternative to the hourly rate.

straight time: the wage rate paid for hours worked during the normal period prescribed by a union contract or by law.

strategic business units (SBUs): divisions composed of key businesses within multiproduct companies, with specific managers, resources, objectives, and competitors. SBUs may encompass a division, a product line, or a single product.

strategic groups: work groups whose jobs are mostly individual operations requiring high skill levels. They experience a high degree of internal unity and relatively good production records over the long run.

strategic planning: a basic type of planning by which a firm formulates its long-range goals and selects activities for achieving those goals.

strategic planning gap: the difference between the present position of a company and its desired future position.

strategic posture: the actual relationship between a firm and its environment.

strategic resource monopoly: an organization that has a monopoly by virtue of controlling a vital input to a production process (e.g., DeBeers of South Africa owns most of the world's diamond mines).

strategy: guidelines for making directional decisions that influence an organization's long-run performance.

straw: untrue, valueless, or financially irresponsible (e.g., a straw bid is one whose maker is unable to fulfill the requirements for acquisition).

straw boss: a group leader or assistant foreman, often one who has no formal title or permanent status.

straw-cat: (slang) a migratory harvest worker.

straw man: a person who purchases property for another without identifying the valid buyer. The result is that the straw man maintains a naked title on the property and is a dummy buyer.

Street: the New York financial community; the lower Manhattan (i.e., Wall Street) area.

street broker: an over-the-counter broker, as distinguished from a broker who is a member of an exchange.

street name: describing a stock certificate in the name of a broker who trades in securities and is a member of an exchange. This stock is never considered to be part of the broker's personal wealth.

stretch-out

(1) *administration:* a management term for malingering.

(2) *labor relations:* an increase in work without comparable pay increases. Cf. *speed-up.*

strictness bias: a condition that occurs when workers are rated lower than their performance justifies. See also *bias.*

strike: a concerted work stoppage designed to pressure management into agreeing on contract terms, to correct an unsettled grievance, or to recognize a union as a collective-bargaining agent. A *general strike* is an action by all or most organized workers (rare in this country). A *quickie strike* is a spontaneously organized strike, triggered by some incident on the job and occurring without authorization of the union. A *wildcat strike* is a nonspontaneous strike organized and carried out by the members without union authorization and in violation of the contract. A *sympathy strike* is a strike by workers who are not directly involved in the labor dispute but wish to display solidarity with the strikers. An *economic strike* is a strike because of wages, hours, or other conditions, usually resulting from a strike vote of the union membership taken when an existing labor agreement is about to expire. Cf. *boycott, downer, picketing;* see also *illegal strike, jurisdictional strike, secondary strike, work stoppages.*

strike authorization: a strike vote that invests a designated group with the right to call a strike on a given issue without further consultation with the union membership.

strike benefits: payments by the union to members who are on strike in the form of a flat sum or graduated according to family needs. See also *out-of-work benefits.*

strikebreaker: a person who accepts

employment in place of a striker or organizes a back-to-work movement. See also *scab*.

strike fund: funds taken from union dues and held by the union to cover the costs of approved programs (e.g., benefits, printing of union literature, picket signs). See also *strike pay*.

strike notice: a formal notice to an employer, to the Federal Mediation and Conciliation Service, or to a state labor-management relations agency that a union has rejected the company's latest offer and that a strike is impending.

strike pay: monies paid by the union to members of a union to compensate for income lost during a strike. See also *strike fund*.

striking price: Synonymous with *exercise price*.

string: a set of characters in ascending or descending sequence, according to a key contained in the records of the computer.

stringency: a money market condition of hard-to-obtain credit, accompanied by an increase in the rates of interest.

strong market: a market that has a greater demand for purchasing than for selling.

struck work: goods produced by strikebreakers, or goods produced by a firm that is not on strike for the use or relief of a struck company. Cf. *unfair goods*.

structural change approaches: changes that are brought about through new formal guidelines, procedures, policies, and organizational rearrangements.

structural inflation: increasing prices caused by an uneven upward demand or cost pressures in a key industry, even when total demand remains in balance with total supply for the economy as a whole.

structural intervention: changing the structure of an organization so that people can develop new approaches for dealing with others on the job. See also *group dynamics*.

structural principles: principles that assist a manager in designing the formal task and authority relationships in the organization. See also *classical design theory, task orientation*.

structural unemployment: unemployment resulting from a mismatch between the skills that available workers have to offer and the skills that potential employers are seeking.

stub shift: a work shift that has fewer hours than the regular shift. See also *shift*.

stuff: (slang) to sell goods that are not genuine or have been stolen.

stuffing: loading cargo or goods into a container or envelope.

SUB: See *supplemental unemployment benefits*.

Subchapter S corporation: a company that is legally organized as a corporation in which income or loss is passed through and taxed to individual stockholders.

subcontracting: work given out to another employer. If done to evade bargaining with a union, subcontracting is an unfair practice under the Taft-Hartley Act.

subenvironment: characteristics of people and their tasks that affect the performance of employees in their work and their relationships with each other. Cf. *certainty, differentiation*.

subject bid: a bid that is negotiable, rather than firm.

subjective method: a forecasting method based on the subjective opinions of people who are knowledgeable about the field for which the forecast is being made.

subject to sale: when property has been offered for sale, a stipulation that provides for the automatic withdrawal of the offer if the property is sold before the party to whom the stipulation was made has accepted the offer.

sublease: the letting of premises to a third party with the original tenant retaining an interest in the property. All or part of the leased property may be subleased. If the tenant gives up his or her entire interest, the sublease transaction becomes an assignment of lease. Synonymous with *underlease.*

subliminal advertising: the delivery of a message below a receiver's awareness level, to be registered subconsciously. The receivers do not realize that they have seen or heard these messages, by which advertisers attempt to promote sales of a product or service. Cf. *motivation, unconscious.*

submarginal: yielding less than enough to cover the cost of production.

submittal notice: a broker's notification to a property owner that the owner's property has been offered for sale. The offering price and prospect's name and address are included in the notice.

submortgage: the result of a pledge by a lender of a mortgage in his or her possession as collateral to obtain a loan.

suboptimization: operating at a less-than-optimal level in one segment of a firm in order to optimize the functioning of the organization as a whole. See also *optimization.*

subordinated interest: an interest in property that is inferior to another interest (e.g., a second mortgage that is inferior to the first mortgage). Cf. *equal dignity.*

subpoena: a process by a court to require the attendance of a witness, usually at a trial. Failure to comply can result in a penalty. A subpoena can also be used to compel a witness to appear at proceedings of a grand jury and at other investigations.

subprogram: a section of a large program that can be compiled independently.

subrogation

(1) *business law:* substitution of one person for another, either as a creditor or as the owner of any lawful right, so that the substituted individual succeeds to the rights, remedies, or proceeds of the claim.

(2) *insurance:* the legal process by which an insurance company seeks recovery of the amount paid to the policyholder from a third party who has caused the loss.

subroutine: a computer routine that can be part of another routine.

subscriber: one who agrees in writing to purchase a certain offering (e.g., a certain number of shares of designated stock of a given corporation, a certain number of bonds of a stipulated face value).

subscription: an agreement to purchase a security; a solicitation of subscribers.

subset: a group of items that is contained in a larger grouping of items.

subsidiary: an organization whose voting stock is more than 50 percent owned by another firm.

subsidy: federal payments to an individual or organization for which the government receives no products or services. The primary objective of a subsidy is to allow for production of the goods at prices that will attract buyers. Cf. *stockpiling.*

subsistence law of wages: See *iron law of wages.*

subsistence theory of wages: an economic theory of the late eighteenth and early nineteenth centuries claiming that wages per employee tend to equal what the worker needs to maintain himself and his family. See also *standard of living.*

substandard: describing conditions that make a risk less desirable than normal for its class. See also *referral risks.*

substandard health insurance: insurance policies for those who cannot meet normal health requirements of standard health policies (e.g., older people who may be in ill health). In most cases, such policies involve a greater premium.

substandard rate: a wage rate that is below established plant or occupational minimum, federal or state minimum laws, or prevailing levels.

substitute goods: items that can easily replace one another either in production or in consumption (e.g., natural and synthetic fibers, strawberries and raspberries). An increase in the price of one substitute good encourages purchase of the other(s).

substitution: See *subrogation.*

substitution law: the economic statement that if one product or service can be a replacement for another, the prices of the two must be very close to each other.

subsystem: a secondary or subordinate system that is usually capable of operating independently or asynchronously with a controlling system.

subtenant: a tenant who leases premises from another tenant; a sublessee. See also *sublease.*

subvention: a grant-in-aid from a government or other public agency for purposes of public benefit.

succession

(1) *business law:* the transfer of all the rights and obligations of a deceased person to those who are entitled to inherit.

(2) *administration:* following another in an office, an estate, and so on.

succession tax: a tax on the privilege of receiving property, either by descent or by will. It is not a burden on property.

suggestion box: a designated place in an organization where workers deposit suggestions concerning policies, procedures, activities, or methods.

suggestion programs: specific procedures designed to encourage workers to recommend improvements.

suggestive selling: the strategy of suggesting to a potential purchaser that he or she might have an additional need related to what has already been purchased (e.g., it might be suggested that a woman who has bought a dress also select appropriate shoes or a sweater). See also *complementary products;* cf. *derived demand.*

suit: a proceeding at law for the purpose of obtaining a legal decision.

suitable employment: a provision of unemployment compensation that recipients are not required to accept any available job but are required only to accept jobs for which they are suited by training, education, or experience.

summary of international transactions: a revised version of the balance-of-payments accounts, adopted in 1976, that purports to deemphasize the concept of balances and to encourage more detailed assessment of international transactions.

summary powers: powers possessed by executives to act promptly in certain matters that are considered to be of prime importance.

summons: a court writ directing the sheriff to notify the defendant that the plaintiff claims to have a cause of action against the defendant, who is expected to appear in court. A summons does not strictly compel the defendant to appear but merely gives notice that if he or she fails to appear, judgment is taken by default and the action will be decided against him or her.

sumptuary laws: laws that attempt to minimize the consumption of items that are believed to be harmful to individuals or to society in general. Cf. *public consumption monopoly.*

sunk cost: a cost that has already been incurred and is now irrelevant to the decision-making process.

sunset ruling: an approach for the phasing out of ineffective governmental programs. Once a program is found to be unproductive, it is not renewed (i.e., it "fades into the sunset").

Sunshine Act: federal legislation of August 1976 stating that the public must be allowed to sit in on all meetings of some 50 different federal agencies, ranging from the Indian Claims Commission to such regulatory institutions as the SEC and the Federal Trade Commission.

sunspot theory: a nineteenth-century British theory that cyclically recurring disturbances on the sun's surface (sunspots) are closely related to farming cycles over a number of years.

superior goods: commodities and services that are demanded in larger quantities as incomes rise (e.g., expensive cars, caviar, fur coats).

superordinate goals: goals for all subordinate persons or departments that can best be achieved through cooperation.

supervisor: any individual who has management responsibilities, usually including the right to hire and fire or to recommend such action.

supplemental air carriers: air carriers that hold Civil Aeronautics Board certificates permitting them to render passenger and freight charter services to supplement the scheduled service of other approved air carriers.

supplemental monthly budget: a budgetary approach in which a firm determines a minimum operational budget and, prior to the beginning of each month, provides the units with additional funds to supplement this minimum.

Supplementary Security Income (SSI):

a federal program of income assistance to the aged, blind, and disabled.

supplementary unemployment benefits (SUB): a company provision for benefits to laid-off workers, in addition to unemployment insurance. Funds may come from individual employee contributions made over the years or from contributions made to a pool of funds. See also *pool.*

supply: the quantity of items available for sale. See also *Say's law.*

supply curve: a graphic representation of the quantity of output supplied as a function of price. See also *excess supply curve.*

supply price: the lowest price needed to produce a specified output. It is the lowest price a seller will accept for the act of supplying a given quantity of a commodity.

supply schedule: a table of prices and corresponding quantities offered for sale in a given period.

supporting the market: placing purchasing orders at or somewhat below the prevailing market level in order to maintain and balance existing prices and to encourage a price rise.

supportive approach to supervision: an approach whereby employees are given opportunities for self-direction, participation in decision making, and some freedom in their work. Cf. *collegial approach to supervision, custodial approach to supervision.*

support level: the point at which demand for a product or service is reached. It is the moment when the resistance level is overcome.

supramarginal: yielding more than the cost of production.

supreme court of finance: Synonymous with *Federal Reserve Board.*

surcharge: an added charge to a tax or other cost or account.

surety
(1) *business law:* an individual who agrees, usually in writing, to be responsible for the performance of another person on a contract or for a certain debt or debts of the other individual.
(2) *insurance:* a bond, guaranty, or other security that protects a person, corporation, or other legal entity in cases of another's default in the payment of a given obligation, improper performance of a given contract, malfeasance of office, and so on.

surety bond: See *bond, surety.*

surface changes: shifts in consumer preferences and interests that direct spending patterns from one activity to another without signaling a basic change in fundamental cultural values.

sur mortgage: a document that demands that a person who has defaulted on mortgage payments show cause why the mortgagee should not foreclose.

surplus
(1) *general:* anything remaining or left over.
(2) *accounting:* an excess of assets over the total of liabilities and capital.

surplus value: in Marxian philosophy, the profit derived from the amount above labor costs.

surrender of lease: a mutual agreement between landlord and tenant to terminate all aspects of a lease before its normal expiration date.

surrender value: designating the amount of the total life insurance in force that will be paid to the policyholder, after a certain stipulated number of premiums have been paid, if the policyholder elects to surrender the policy and receive such proportionate part. The cash surrender value of a policy is also the amount used to determine how much will be loaned against the policy.

surtax: the extra tax applied to corporations when their net taxable income has exceeded a certain amount. For example, a surtax is demanded at the rate of 26 percent for all corporate income over $25,000. See also *Tax Reform Act of 1969*.

survey-feedback activities: activities that focus on collecting survey data and designing a plan of action based on the interpretation of the data.

suspended trading: a binding stock exchange decision to cease trading that results from an unusual occurrence, such as an unexpected jump in buy or sell orders on all or several securities. Sometimes suspended trading may be brought about by equipment failure or other unexpected emergencies.

suspense account: an account in the general ledger that is used to hold over unposted items so that the business day can be closed in a state of balance.

suspension
(1) *personnel:* a disciplinary layoff of a worker without pay.
(2) *administration:* termination of a business.
(3) *banking:* a temporary closing of a bank.
(4) *securities:* a decision made by a stock exchange board of directors prohibiting a securities firm or broker

from conducting business for a period. See also *under the rule*.
(5) *labor relations:* an employer's disciplinary action against an employee. It is less critical than a discharge. See also *trusteeship*.

sustaining program: an unsponsored broadcast program on radio or television.

swap
(1) *general:* to exchange or barter.
(2) *computers:* to write the main storage aspects of a job into auxiliary storage and read the image of another job into main storage.
(3) *banking:* an arrangement between the central banks of two countries for standby credit to facilitate the exchange of each other's currencies. See also *credit, swap network*.

swap fund: a fund into which many investors put their own investments and receive a share in the pooled investment portfolio. The purpose of this exchange of investments is to obtain a diversified portfolio without selling stock and paying capital gains taxes.

swap network: to finance U.S. interventions in the foreign exchange market, a series of short-term reciprocal credit lines between foreign banks under which the Federal Reserve System exchanges dollars for the currencies of other nations within the group, thereby allowing the Fed to buy dollars in the foreign exchange market. See also *swap*.

sweatshop: a place of work considered to be far below acceptable standards of working conditions.

sweet: (slang) describing an easy job or work assignment.

sweetheart agreement: a secret deal with management by a corrupt union agent for an inferior contract, made without the knowledge of the membership and without genuine collective bargaining. Sweetheart contracts are denounced by the AFL–CIO in its Code of Ethical Practices.

swindling: selling worthless shares through misrepresentation.

swing shift: in a factory under continuous production, a systematic rotation of crews among work shifts to provide for days off.

switch: a device or programmed technique for making a selection by opening, closing, or directing an electric circuit.

switching: selling one security and buying another. See also *switch (contingent) order.*

switching customers: bringing in a sales specialist when the salesperson who originally served a customer is unable to close a sale.

switch (contingent) order: an order for the purchase (sale) of one stock and the sale (purchase) of another stock at a stipulated price difference.

switch selling: an unethical practice of using high-pressure tactics to sell an item that is more expensive than one advertised at a lower price. See also *bait and switch.*

symbol

(1) *general:* a representation of characteristics or transformations of ideas or things.

(2) *computers:* a representation of something by reason of relationship, association, or convention.

(3) *business:* the single capital letter or combination of letters ac-quired by a corporation when it is to be listed on an exchange (e.g., International Business Machines is IBM, American Telephone and Telegraph is T).

(4) *securities:* the letters used to identify traded securities on a ticker tape, exchange board, or newspaper listing.

symbolic coding: any coding system in which symbols other than machine addresses are used.

symbolic pricing: using price to create an impression about a product or a brand in the minds of consumers.

symmetry problem: the problem of devising an international monetary system that will produce equal pressure on countries to revalue or devalue to correct balance-of-payments surpluses or deficits.

sympathy strike: See *strike.*

synchronous computer: a computer in which each event, or the performance of any basic operation, is constrained to start on, and usually to keep in step with, signals from a clock.

syndicalism: an economic concept whereby workers exert control over the industries that employ them.

syndicate

(1) *general:* the association of two or more individuals, established to carry out a business activity. Members share in all profits or losses in proportion to their contribution to the resources of the syndicate. Cf. *joint venture, partnership.*

(2) *publishing:* an organization that distributes material of writers, artists, and others to newspapers, magazines, periodicals, and so on, with the contributor receiving either a

stated fee or a royalty.

(3) *finance:* a group of investment bankers and securities dealers who, by agreement among themselves, have joined together for the purpose of distributing a new issue of securities for a corporation.

synergy: the feature of a system whereby, when the parts are properly interrelated and functioning, an output is achieved that is greater than or superior to the effects obtained when the parts function independently.

system

(1) *systems:* an assembly of methods, procedures, or techniques that are united by regulated interaction to form an organized whole. See also *systems theory.*

(2) *computers:* a collection of operations and procedures by which activity is carried on.

(3) *administration:* any purposeful organization of resources.

system, fail-safe: a real-time system that processes variables to be locked into present values and saves some vital information before termination of the operation in case of catastrophic breakdown. See also *slave computer;* cf. *volatile memory.*

system, hybrid: a system that uses the best characteristics of both analog and digital computers. In the hybrid configuration, an analog computer is used to obtain the continuous solution, and a digital computer is used for control purposes and to provide the program.

system, job-processing: a monitor system composed of a series of individual programs that work together to form a complete operating system.

system, multiprocessing: See *mul-*

tiprocessing.

system, request-repeat: a system designed to employ an error-detecting code so that a signal can be detected automatically as being in error and a request can be made, also automatically, for retransmission of the detected signal because it is in error.

systematic error: the result of a relatively predictable tendency toward error when making a judgment. Cf. *variable error.*

System Four: a form of organization development, designed by Rensis Likert, that emphasizes participative, employee-centered leadership, open communication, and group decision making and goal setting.

system input device: a device specified as a source of an input stream.

system output device: a device assigned to identify output data for a series of jobs.

system programmer: a programmer who plans, generates, maintains, extends, and controls the use of an operating system, with the aim of improving overall productivity.

systems analysis: the analysis of business activity to determine precisely what must be accomplished and how to accomplish it. See also *operations research.*

systems approach: the overall, macroscopic treatment of organizational systems.

systems design: the formulation and graphic outlining of the nature and content of input, files, procedures, and output in order to display the necessary connection processes and procedures.

systems flow chart: a visual representation of the system through which information provided by the source documents is changed into final documents.

systems management: designing and operating a business as a system, including consideration of the human element and the firm's goals.

systems research: the study of the daily operations of an organization, purporting to upgrade efficiency and lower costs.

systems selling: the merchandising of a group of items that have some functional relationship to one another as a package, rather than as single items (e.g., matching tie and handkerchief sets).

systems theory: an analysis that stresses the necessity for maintaining the basic elements of input-process-output and for adapting to the larger environment that sustains the organization.

systems-type leadership: a leadership style in which all corporate activities are directed toward the achievement of specified objectives.

table: a statement of factual information, usually assembled for reference purposes.

table look-up: the coding technique of locating a word (argument) in a table corresponding to a specified word and, usually, obtaining some other word (function) that corresponds to the word located.

tabulating equipment: machines and equipment that use punched cards. Synonymous with *electronic accounting machine.*

tacit: designating rules that are accepted as law by reason of custom, tradition, and mores.

tacking: a process of adding a junior claim to a senior one in order to create some gain. (e.g., when the holder of a third mortgage adds it to the first mortgage to assume a superior position over the second mortgage holder). Cf. *equal dignity.*

tactic: an approach used to attain certain goals that relate directly to the overall objectives of an organization.

Taft-Hartley Act: the Labor-Management Relations Act of 1947, amending the Wagner-Connery Act of 1935. Its major provisions are (1) that the closed shop is forbidden; (2) that the government is authorized to seek an injunction preventing any work stoppage for 80 days when a strike threatens the nation's welfare and health; (3) that unions cannot use union monies in connection with national elections (4) that officers of unions must swear that they are not members of the Communist party before the union can be certified (amended by the Landrum-Griffin Act); (5) that unions must file financial reports with the U.S. Department of Labor, along with a membership list; and (6) that the states are permitted to pass right-to-work laws. Certain unfair labor practices are also identified in the act. See also *COPE, Hatch Act, jurisdictional strike.*

tag

(1) *broadcasting:* an addition to a

commercial broadcast (e.g., a voice-over message following a transcribed statement, an announcement or insertion of music serving as a conclusion).

(2) *merchandising:* See *Kimball tags.*

(3) *computers:* Synonymous with *Flag.*

tag sort: a sort in which addresses of records (tags), not the records themselves, are moved during the comparison procedure.

tailor-made: made according to individual specifications; just right.

take

(1) *general:* (slang) any profit from a business activity, usually one of a suspicious nature.

(2) *business law:* to lay hold of, seize, or have in possession. See also *seisin.*

take a bath: (slang) to have a substantial financial loss.

take-back mortgage: a mortgage that is held by the seller of a property.

take-home pay: Synonymous with *spendable earnings.*

take-out loan: the permanent financing that replaces an interim or construction loan.

takeover: the acquisition of an on-going organization by another through purchase of the firm and/or exchange of capital stock. Cf. *consolidation, merger.*

takeover time: the time required in marketing for a superior new product to go from 10 to 90 percent displacement of an inferior older product.

take stock: to make an inventory of items on hand.

take-withs: See *carryouts.*

taking inventory: the procedure of counting all inventory on hand at a time set aside for this purpose. Cf. *unit control.*

tall organization structure: an organizational structure in which there is a narrow span of control within a large number of levels in the hierarchy. Cf. *flat organization.*

tall pyramid structure: an organizational structure that fosters narrow spans of control, a large number of management levels, and more centralized decision making.

talon

(1) *general:* a special coupon (e.g., a voucher stub).

(2) *finance:* the part of a debt instrument remaining on an unmatured bond after the interest coupons that were formerly attached have been presented.

tamperproof container: a container designed so that it cannot be opened and resealed without leaving evidence of tampering.

tandem increase: a pay increase given to certain groups in a factory (usually office workers) as the result of a raise negotiated by the production workers.

tangible assets: physical and material (perceptible to touch) assets, as distinguished from intangible assets, which are imperceptible to touch. (e.g., cash, land, buildings).

tangible, personal, depreciable business property: property used in a business that is not considered to be real estate.

tangible property: property in physical form that can be touched, such as a house or land.

tank car: a rail car used for transporting liquids in bulk.

tanktainer: a tank constructed into the standard container frame and used to ship liquids.

tape to card: describing equipment or methods that transmit data from either magnetic tape or punched tape to punched cards.

tare: an unproductive weight; an amount that is part of the gross weight of an article (e.g., the weight of a truck, a package, or any other container or vehicle). Net weight is gross weight less the tare.

target customers: the people who are the objects of a store's total efforts to attract business. Cf. *market target.*

target language: the machine language to which a statement or source document is translated.

target market: See *market target.*

target net income: a desired profit level that is predetermined by management.

target pricing: a technique of establishing prices to reach a profit objective.

target risk

(1) *insurance:* a policyholder or prospect for insurance whose business develops large premiums and who is considered to be a target for competing insurance producers.

(2) *insurance:* a risk of large value or limits; a severe hazard that is difficult to insure or have reinsured.

tariff

(1) *government:* a schedule of taxes on items imported or exported. In the United States, tariffs are imposed on imported goods only.

(2) *finance:* any list of prices, charges, duties, and so on.

tariff rate: the charge rate or schedule established by the rating organiza-tion that has jurisdiction over a given class and territory (e.g., a schedule of freight rates for transporting different items to various cities).

tariff war: a form of competition between nations as evidenced by tariff discrimination of various forms. See also *retaliatory duty.*

task: a unit of work assigned to an employee or a group of workers.

task accomplishment activities: activities aimed at helping a group accomplish its goals.

task and bonus system: a compensation approach that guarantees the employee a fixed daily wage for efforts to finish a given assignment and a bonus when the employee exceeds the task.

task behaviors: such actions as giving suggestions, providing information, analyzing problems, evaluating alternatives, and making decisions.

task dependency: the situation in which one group or individual must rely on another group or individual for services, information, or goods.

task environment: all the factors and forces external to the organization that are important to managerial decision making.

task force: a team of individuals, often representing various departments or interests, that has responsibility for coordinating a study or other efforts that involve a number of organizational units.

task group: a group of employees working as a unit to complete a project or task.

task identity: the opportunity to do an entire piece of work, which enables an employee to have a sense of responsibility and pride.

task interdependency: the extent to which two or more groups or individuals rely on each other for service, information, and goods to accomplish their own goals.

task management: the functions of the control program that regulate the use by tasks of the central processing unit and other resources, except input/output devices.

task-motivated leadership: a leadership style in which the manager tends to describe his or her least-preferred co-worker in an unfavorable light. Such a leader is primarily involved in task controlling and managing and is less concerned with the human relations aspects of the job.

task orientation: a dimension of leadership behavior that focuses on organizational structure, task assignments, specification of the ways in which tasks are to be completed, and clarification of schedules. See also *structural principles.*

task significance: the degree to which a job has a substantial impact on the lives or work of others in the company.

task structure: the extent to which a task is simple (routine) or complex (nonroutine).

task uncertainty: the extent to which internal or external events create a state of uncertainty with respect to job predictability.

tax: a charge levied by a government against the income of an individual, corporation, or other profit-making center of activity. In addition to federal income taxes, other types of taxes include state, city, sales, excise, etc.

tax abatement: a decrease or rebate of a tax or burden that was improperly levied. Sometimes a tax abatement may only reflect an acknowledgment of a changed situation.

taxable estate: as defined by a state, the gross estate of a citizen or resident less allowable administrative and funeral expenses, indebtedness, taxes, losses, transfer for public, charitable, and religious uses, transfer to a surviving spouse; and a specific exemption. See also *marital deduction.*

taxable income: the amount of income remaining after all permitted deductions and exemptions have been subtracted, thus the income that is subject to taxation.

taxable value: an assessed value utilized for taxing property, items, or income.

Tax Act of 1981: See *Economic Recovery Tax Act of 1981.*

Tax Adjustment Act of 1966: federal legislation that restored excise tax rates on transportation equipment and telephone service to the rates in effect prior to January 1966. It also introduced graduated withholding on personal tax collections.

tax-and-board: charges included in premiums (almost always percentages of the paid premium) for state or local taxes and for the support of the various rating offices, bureaus, and boards.

tax anticipation note: a short-term, interest-bearing obligation created to be bought by businesses with monies assembled as a reserve in order to pay taxes. These notes are sold by government agencies to increase revenue.

tax avoidance: taking advantage of deductions and other provisions of tax law to reduce one's taxes. See also *tax shelter;* cf. *tax dodge.*

tax base: the commodity, income, or service on which a tax is levied; the part of the value of an item that can be taxed.

tax-based income policy (TIP): a surcharge placed on the corporate income tax if the firm grants its employees wage increases in excess of some government-set standard. Likewise, by holding its average wage increases below the standards, a company becomes eligible for a government tax reduction.

tax credit: a direct reduction in tax liability, usually granted to encourage a particular action or to provide tax relief for certain classes of taxpayers.

tax deed: a deed issued to the buyer of property that is sold because of nonpayment of taxes.

tax-deferred annuity (tax-sheltered annuity): an annuity available to public school teachers and employees of certain nonprofit organizations that enables the employee to contribute monies toward retirement. Accumulations of these funds are not taxed at the time of contribution in that federal income taxes are not paid until monies are withdrawn from the plan. See also *exclusion allowance.*

tax dodge: an activity that constitutes an illegal attempt to avoid paying taxes (e.g., moving out of the country). See also *tax exile.*

Tax Equity and Fiscal Responsibility Act of 1982 (TEFRA): aside from the fundamental objective of increasing government revenues, TEFRA is intended to curtail perceived abuses and unintended benefits in the present tax system, assure better compliance with existing tax laws, and impose increased excise taxes on selected products and services.

tax evasion: unlawful attempts to avoid payment of a tax (e.g., not properly reporting all earned income).

tax-exempt bond: See *bond, tax-exempt.*

tax-exempt corporation: a legal entity that is chartered by a state for scientific, religious, educational, charitable, or similar purposes.

tax exemption: a right, secured by law, permitting freedom from a charge of taxes (e.g., on income that constitutes primary support of a child).

tax exile (expatriate): an individual who chooses to leave his or her country rather than pay taxes.

tax foreclosure: the taking of property because of unpaid taxes.

tax haven: a nation that offers low tax rates and other incentives for corporations of other countries. See also *flight of capital.*

tax incidence: the business and/or persons on whom a tax finally comes to rest. See also *nexus.*

tax lease: a long-term lease issued to the buyer of tax-delinquent property when the law prevents an outright sale.

tax lien: a lien by the government against real property for failure to pay taxes. Cf. *municipal lien.*

tax limit: a legislative decision that limits the tax ceiling that can be imposed by an appropriate authority.

taxpayer
(1) *general:* a small building or store.

(2) *real estate:* an owner of property who pays taxes.

(3) *government:* a person who pays taxes.

tax policy: the policy whereby a government structures its tax rates.

tax rate: the amount of tax applied per unit of tax base, expressed as a percentage (e.g., a tax of $5 on a base of $100 represents a tax rate of 5 percent).

Tax Reduction Act of 1975: federal legislation that provided for a 10 percent rebate on 1974 taxes up to a maximum of $200 for individuals and provided tax cuts retroactive to January 1975 for both individuals and corporations. For individuals, the reduction was in the form of increased standard deductions, a $30 exemption credit, and an earned income credit for low-income families. The act also reduced corporate income tax, and increased the investment surtax exemption, and increased the investment tax credit to 10 percent. See also *Revenue Adjustment Act of 1975.*

Tax Reduction and Simplification Act of 1977: legislation signed by President Carter for a $34 billion tax cut, giving credit to industry to create jobs and attempting to simplify tax filing procedures.

Tax Reform Act of 1969: federal legislation removing major benefits from controlled corporations. See also *Tax Reform Act of 1976.*

Tax Reform Act of 1976: federal legislation revising tax rates, exemptions, and deductions in various areas (e.g., capital gains and losses, tax shelters, estate and gift taxes).

tax roll: an official statement describing taxed property, including the names of the taxpayers and the amounts of their taxes.

tax sale: sale of property in default because of nonpayment of taxes. See also *scavenger sale.*

tax-saving retirement plan: See *Keogh Plan.*

tax search: a search of official records to determine whether there are any unpaid property taxes.

tax sharing: See *revenue sharing, shared revenue.*

tax shelter: a means of legal avoidance of paying a portion of one's income taxes by careful interpretation of tax regulations and adjustment of one's finances to take advantage of IRS rulings. The Tax Reform Act of 1976 placed new restrictions on tax shelters.

tax shield: the amount of depreciation charged against income, thus protecting that amount from tax (e.g., a depreciation deduction of $10,000 produces a tax shield of $3,600 when the tax rate is 36 percent).

tax title: title to property acquired by purchasing land that was sold as the result of unpaid taxes.

Taylorism: the work of Frederick W. Taylor (1856–1915), who outlined the concepts of scientific management and work efficiency.

team building: a conscious effort to develop effective work groups throughout an organization.

tear sheet: a page bearing advertising to appear in a publication that is sent to the advertiser for purposes of proofing.

teaser: an ad that purports to increase curiosity by holding back the name of the advertiser or the product but pledging additional data in future statements.

tech: (slang) a school of engineering or technology.

technical efficiency: the condition achieved when there is no way to use less of one input without using more of another input to yield the same level of output.

technical level: a low organizational level that is concerned primarily with the production and distribution of goods and services.

technical managers: low-level managers who are concerned with turning out goods and services as economically as possible. These managers tend to have an engineering point of view.

technical position: a term applied to the various internal factors affecting the market, as opposed to external forces such as earnings, dividends, and general economic conditions. Some internal factors are the size of the short-term interest, whether the market has had a sustained advance or decline without interruption, and the amount of credit in use in the market.

technical skill: the skill of working with the resources and knowledge in a specific area. Such skill is most important to first-level managers.

technical specialists: group members who show a great deal of concern with task-related problems and use their expertise to solve them.

technological assessment: a technique for evaluating the impact of technological change on society. Cf. *technological forecasting.*

technological forecasting: predicting changes in technology and their or-

ganizational and societal implications. See also *public policy;* cf. *technological assessment.*

technological unemployment: unemployment resulting from the introduction of new methods of production and/or operations. See also *labor-augmenting technical change, redeployment, secular unemployment.*

technology: industrial science, especially when applied to the replacement of skilled labor by advanced equipment; applied scientific knowledge utilized in the resolution of practical issues and problems, in the evolution of new products and new processes of manufacture, and in the introduction of major changes in techniques of physical distribution.

TEFRA: see *Tax Equity and Fiscal Responsibility Act of 1982.*

telemeter: to transmit digital or analog metering data by communication facilities (e.g., equipment used in sending information by electromagnetic waves over long distances).

telescope box: a paper box having the ends and sides of the lid cut to the same height as the ends and sides of the base. The lid of the box fits over the base.

Teller Act: See *Welfare and Pension Plans Disclosure Act of 1958.*

temporary bond: See bond, temporary.

temporary disability benefits: the weekly benefits payable (out of company pension plans) to employees for nonoccupational accidents and sickness.

temporary employees: nonpermanent members of an organization's work force, often hired to do clerical work.

temporary restraining order: See *injunction.*

temporary storage: an area of working storage that is not reserved for a single use but is used by numerous sections of a program at differing times.

temporary total disability benefits: the weekly benefit payable to an employee, as prescribed by a workers' compensation law, when he or she is temporarily unable to perform any job duties because of an accident or sickness sustained during and arising out of his or her employment.

tenancy: residence on property that belongs to someone else.

tenancy at sufferance: the situation that exists when a tenant continues to occupy the premises after the termination of his or her tenancy (i.e., without permission but prior to eviction); a holdover tenant. Cf. *tenancy at will.*

tenancy at will: the situation that exists when a tenant resides on property legally but has no lease. It is based on permission of the property owner. Synonymous with *periodic tenancy;* cf. *holdover tenant, tenancy at sufferance.*

tenancy by the entirety: an estate jointly owned by a husband and wife. The survivor receives the total estate. This agreement cannot be broken without the consent of both spouses. See also *right of survivorship.*

tenancy in common: ownership of property by two or more persons, each holding a separate interest. No right of survivorship exists. See also *undivided right.*

tenant: one who holds or has the use of real property that is owned by an-other; a lessee.

tenant in dower: a wife who has survived her husband and, in most states, receives one-third of his inherited estate for the remainder of her life.

tender

(1) *business law:* to offer money in satisfaction of a debt by producing the money and stating to the creditor a desire to pay.

(2) *securities:* a corporation's offer of securities by asking for bids for them, at prices above a minimum.

tenement

(1) *general:* popularly, an old, rundown apartment structure.

(2) *real estate:* originally, any property held by one person for another; things of a permanent nature.

ten-forty: a United States bond that is redeemable after 10 years and due and payable after 40 years.

tenor: the period between the formation of a debt and the date of expected payment.

tenure: assuming satisfactory performance, the period of time an employee may expect to serve under his or her current appointment without fear of arbitrary dismissal.

term: the prescribed time a person has to make installment or other payments as identified in a loan or credit contract.

term bond: See *bond, term.*

terminal

(1) *computers:* a device, usually equipped with a keyboard and some kind of display, that is capable of sending and receiving information over a communication channel. See also *media typewriter.*

(2) *transportation:* a location

and/or structure for the temporary storage of goods as they are transferred between carriers and/or await transportation.

terminal, remote: a device used to provide the capability of sending 80- or 90-column punch cards, paper tape, and keyboard information from a remote location to a central processor. It also has the capability of punching these column cards, punching paper tape, and printing information received from a central processor.

terminal market: a market (e.g., a commodity market) that deals in futures.

terminal positions: jobs in an organization that do not offer any possibilities for advancement. Cf. *upgrading.*

termination: voluntary or involuntary separation from employment.

termination pay: Synonymous with *dismissal pay.*

term life insurance: life insurance protection during a certain number of years, usually expiring without policy cash value if the insured survives the stated period. See also *extended term insurance, family income rider;* cf. *term policy.*

term loan: usually a long-term loan running up to 10 years. Such loans generally are made by the larger commercial banks and insurance companies to large, well-established business enterprises for capital expenditures such as plant improvements and purchases of equipment.

term mortgage: a mortgage with a fixed time period, usually less than five years, in which only interest is paid. Following termination of the mortgage, the total principal is de-

manded.

term policy: usually a fire or casualty policy written for more than one year; not to be confused with *term life insurance.*

terms: the details, specifications, and conditions of a loan.

terms of sale: identification of a vendor's given time to pay an invoice, any discounts offered, and other conditions of the sale.

terms of trade: the number of units of items that must be surrendered for one unit of goods obtained by a group or nation that is a party to a transaction.

territorial departmentalization: organization of a department according to geographic location (e.g., a company with four major divisions: eastern, midwestern, western, and foreign).

territory screening: examining a list of buyers or potential customers to determine the priorities of sales visits in terms of time, opportunity, and profitability. Synonymous with *canvass;* cf. *cold canvassing, preapproach.*

test, diagnostic

(1) *personnel:* an instrument designed to identify the particular source of a person's difficulties in learning a skill or a subject or in mastering some other educational concept. Cf. *aptitude test.*

(2) *computers:* the running of a machine routine for the purpose of discovering a possible failure and the location of the malfunction. See also *debug, postmortem;* cf. *volume test.*

testament: the declaration of an individual's intentions for the disposition of his or her property following death. Synonymous with *will.*

testamentary trust: a trust established through a will. The trustee (an individual or a bank) is named in the will to receive designated property from the executor of an estate and to hold it in trust for the benefit of named beneficiaries.

testate: having completed and left an acceptable will.

testator: a deceased male who left a will setting forth the disposition of his wealth (total assets).

testatrix: a deceased female who has died leaving a will.

testimonial: a statement by a satisfied customer praising a product or service that is used in advertising or sales promotion to influence others. Cf. *blurb*.

testimony: statements by a witness under oath in a legal proceeding.

testing: examining human resources for qualities that are relevant to performance of available jobs.

test marketing: trial distribution of a new product in a small market to determine its likely acceptance in the total market. Cf. *market fit*.

TF: See *till forbid*.

T-groups: See *sensitivity training*.

theme: the major idea of an advertising campaign.

theory of games: See *game theory*.

Theory X and Theory Y. concept presented by Douglas McGregor in *The Human Side of Enterprise*. Theory X describes a worker who is lazy and money oriented and produces only because of the presence of an authoritarian supervisor. Theory Y describes a worker who is eager to work, is motivated by various means, and requires a flexible, human relations style of leadership. See also *au-*

tocratic, mirror principle, organic structure.

therbligs: motions of the body, classified by Frank G. Gilbreth, that are needed to carry out any form of work. In all, there are 17 basic types of movement. "Therblig" is an anagram of Gilbreth. See also *motion study*.

thin corporation: a corporation that owes a large number of debts relative to its equity position.

think tank: an organization purporting to examine issues of society, science, technology, and business.

thin market: a market in which there are comparatively few bids to buy or offers to sell, or both. The term may apply to a single security or to the entire stock market. In a thin market, price fluctuations between transactions are usually larger than they are when the market is liquid. A thin market in a particular stock may reflect a lack of interest or a lack of demand for stock.

third-generation computer: a computer that uses tiny circuits and components instead of vacuum tubes to increase accuracy and speed up the processing of work.

third market: listed stocks that are not traded on a securities exchange; over-the-counter trading in listed securities.

third mortgage: a mortgage that is junior to both the first and second mortgages.

third-party insurance: generally, coverage that protects the insured against his or her liability arising out of bodily injury to others or damage to their property.

third-party transaction: a three-way

business activity involving a buyer, a seller, and a source of consumer credit.

thirds: goods of extremely poor quality, lower in grade than seconds.

third shift: Synonymous with *midnight shift.*

third wave of change: changes that are now occurring as a result of recent developments in such areas as technology, information handling, the world of work, organizational loyalty, organizational structures, redefinition of organizational purpose, and multinational corporations.

thirty-three: (slang) a potential customer who refuses to make a purchase from one salesman and is then turned over to another.

three-dimensional leadership model: a model developed by William J. Reddin that stresses the importance of three factors: task orientation, relationships orientation, and effectiveness.

three-ply company: an organization that has the primary managerial levels—top, middle, and lower.

three-sheet: (slang) an advertising circular, brochure, or handbill.

threshold companies: companies that are on the threshold of corporate maturity in that they are not yet managed by professionals but are run intuitively by a handful of entrepreneurs. The concept was developed by Donald Clifford, Jr.

thrift account: Synonymous with *savings account, special interest account.*

through bill of lading: a bill of lading covering items that are moving from the origin point to a final location, even if they are moved from one carrier to another.

throughput: the total volume of work performed by a computing system over a given period.

ticker: an instrument that prints prices and volume of security transactions in cities and towns throughout the United States and Canada within minutes of each trade on any listed exchange.

tickler file: a follow-up diary or folder containing memos, letters, and so on, ordered by future dates and pulled periodically for review and action. Cf. *deferred premium file.*

tied loan: a foreign loan that limits the borrower to spending the proceeds only in the nation making the loan. Cf. *counterpart monies.*

tie-in sales: sales that are limited so that a buyer cannot purchase one product or service without purchasing something else from the same manufacturer. The Clayton Antitrust Act of 1914 made this practice illegal in interstate commerce. See also *tying arrangement.*

tie it off: (slang) to stop the day's work.

tie it up: (slang) to complete a task.

tight credit: Synonymous with *tight money.*

tight money: high interest rates demanded in the borrowing of money. Synonymous with *tight credit.*

till forbid (TF): instructions to continue using an advertisement until told otherwise.

till money: funds kept at a front desk or register, as distinguished from monies held in a bank.

time, access: the interval of time between the instant at which information is called for from storage and the instant at which delivery is terminated.

time, read: the time needed to identify data or an instruction word in a storage section and transfer it to an arithmetic unit where the required computations are performed.

time, response: See *response time.*

time-adjusted rate of return: the rate of interest at which the existing value of anticipated cash inflows from a particular project equals the present value of expected cash outflow of the same activity.

time-and-a-half pay: compensation at the rate of one and one-half times the worker's regular pay. The Fair Labor Standards Act of 1938 made this rate mandatory for work performed beyond 40 hours a week by workers employed by firms engaged in interstate commerce. Cf. *straight time.*

time and motion study: an approach for studying the time used and the motions made by an employee to perform a specified task, or a portion thereof, so as to identify job standards. cf. *job analysis, micromotion study, motion study, predetermined motion times system, time study.*

time bargain: an agreement between a seller and a purchaser of securities to exchange a specific stock at a stated price at a stated future time.

time buyer: an executive in an advertising agency who assists in the planning of media campaigns and chooses and buys radio and television time. Cf. *space buyer.*

time deposit (open account): funds deposited under agreement that bear interest from the date of deposit, although the agreement usually requires that such funds remain on deposit for at least 30 days. The agreement stipulates a fixed maturity date or number of days after which payment will be made, or it is stipulated that payment will be made after a given period following notice by the depositor of intention to withdraw. See also *Regulation Q.*

time discount: a reduction in an advertising rate determined by the frequency of appearance of an ad. Cf. *transient rate.*

time-event analyses: control techniques that permit the manager to monitor and evaluate elapsed time and attained progress on an undertaking.

time loan: a loan made for a specified period. The maturity date generally is 30, 60, 90, or 120 days after the date of the loan. Interest is usually collected in advance, at the time the loan is made, in the form of a discount.

time log: a device for measuring how a person uses his or her time.

time order: an order that becomes a market or limited price order at a specified time.

time-series forecast: a method of forecasting in which historical trends are projected into the future.

time sharing: a method of using a computing system that allows a number of users to execute programs on the same hardware and to interact with the programs during execution. See also *interleave.*

time-sharing priority: a ranking within the group of tasks associated with a single user, used to determine their precedence for the allocation of system resources.

time standard: the period an average

employee needs to complete a task or job under normal conditions of work. Cf. *normal time.*

time study: a procedure by which the actual elapsed time for performing an operation or subdivisions or elements thereof is determined by use of a suitable timing device and recorded. The procedure usually includes adjustment of the actual time according to performance rating to derive the time that should be required to perform the task at a standard pace. Synonymous with *work measurement.*

time ticket: a record of each production employee's hour-by-hour activities, kept so that labor costs can be allocated to the proper jobs or products.

tinge: (slang) a salesman who specializes in the sale of undesirable merchandise that earn him bonus payments.

TIP: See *tax-based income policy.*

tips

(1) *general:* monies offered to encourage or ensure promptness; monies given for services rendered (e.g., 15 percent of a restaurant bill constitutes the waiter's tip).

(2) *securities:* supposedly inside information on corporation affairs; a subjective recommendation to buy or sell a particular stock.

tire kickers: (slang) inspectors or troubleshooters who are assigned to closely examine a project, item, or service for defects, flaws, or inadequacies.

title: proper and rightful ownership.

title defect: a fact or circumstance that challenges property ownership. See also *cloud on title.*

title flows: the path of the title to or ownership of products as they flow through channels of distribution.

title guaranty company: a business firm created to examine real estate files (i.e., to conduct title searches) to determine the legal status of the property and to find any evidence of encumbrances, faults, or other title defects. Once a search has been completed and the property has been found sound, the company receives a fee from the property purchaser who had needed to determine that his or her title was clear and good. The property purchaser receives an abstract of the prepared title, and the title is verified by an attorney of the company, who gives an opinion but does not guarantee the accuracy of the title. The company agrees to indemnify the owner against any loss that may be experienced resulting from a subsequent defect. A title guaranty policy is evidence of the title insurance, with costs based on the value of the property and the risk involved, as determined by the condition of the title. See also *title insurance.*

title insurance: an insurance contract from a title guaranty company presented to owners of property, indemnifying them against having a defective or unsalable title while they possess the property. This contract is considered to be a true indemnity for loss actually sustained by reason of the defects or encumbrances against which the insurer agrees to indemnify. Title insurance includes a thorough examination of the evidences of title by the insurer. See also *title guaranty company.*

title insurance company: See *title guaranty company.*

title search: See *search, title guaranty company, title insurance.*

Title VII: See *Civil Rights Act of 1964.*

titlewave: (slang) a shakeup in the hierarchy of an organization.

toggle: Synonymous with *flip-flop.*

tokenism: as applied to equal employment, the gesture of hiring a few minority group members in an attempt to satisfy government affirmative action requirements or the demands of pressure groups.

token money: an object, usually coins, whose value as money is greater than the market value of the materials of which it is composed.

tolerance: the standard or limit within which a measurement should fall.

toll: originally, a tax for permission to produce something; currently, a charge for permission to utilize a public facility or service (e.g., a bridge, highway, ferry, long-distance telephone system).

ton: a heavy weight. A long ton is 2240 pounds, a short ton is 2000 pounds, and a metric ton is 2204.6 pounds.

ton-mile: a measure equal to the transportation of one ton of cargo moved one mile. See *net ton-miles, unit of traffic.*

tonnage: the number of tons of cargo handled.

top credit: ready credit.

top-down approach: an approach to strategy whereby the major decisions are made at the top levels of the organization and transmitted to the bottom levels.

top management: the top level of an administrative hierarchy. Managers at this level coordinate the work of other managers but do not report to a manager.

top out: the peak period of demand for a product or service, after which demand decreases.

tort: a wrongful act committed by a person against another person or against his or her property.

tortfeasor: a person who commits a tort.

total cost: the sum of a firm's total fixed costs and total variable costs.

total debt: all long-term obligations of the government and its agencies and all interest-bearing short-term credit obligations. Long-term obligations are those that are repayable more than one year after issue.

total fixed costs: the costs that do not change with an organization's output (e.g., payments on rent, property taxes).

total loss: items that have been so badly damaged that they are not considered to be worth repairing (e.g., a car that has suffered a head-on collision with a truck, merchandise that is partly destroyed by fire). See also *incurably depreciated.*

total overhead variance: the extent to which actual overhead varies from the amount included in work-in-process inventory; the difference between actual and applied overhead.

total revenue: total receipts of a company. It is equal to the price per unit times the number of units sold.

total variable costs: costs that change directly with the firm's output, increasing as output rises over the total range of production (e.g., labor, fuel).

tour of duty: the hours an employee is

scheduled to work. Synonymous with *shift.*

Toxic Substances Control Act of 1976: federal legislation requiring chemical manufacturers to give the Environmental Protection Agency at least three months' notice before beginning commercial production of a new chemical or before marketing an existing chemical for a new use. If the EPA sees no risks, the firm may proceed.

trace

(1) *general:* the record of a series of events.

(2) *postal system:* to locate delayed or undelivered mail.

(3) *insurance:* to record a policy holder's record of premium payments.

traceable costs: costs that are directly associated with and assigned to specific responsibility centers.

tracer

(1) *transportation:* a request to trace a shipment in order to determine its location, alter instructions, or affect its status.

(2) *postal system:* an official form used in locating delayed or undelivered mail.

track: the portion of a moving storage medium (drum, tape, disk, etc.) that is accessible to a given reading head position.

tractor: a vehicle that is used primarily to pull other vehicles.

trade advertising: advertising directed at wholesalers or retailers.

trade association: a nonprofit organization that purports to serve the common interest of its membership. Usually, members of trade associations work in closely related indus-

tries.

trade deficit: a negative trade balance.

trade discount: a deduction from the agreed price, usually expressed as a percentage or a series of percentages, that is used in commerce to encourage prompt payment of bills. Trade discount should not be entered in the books of account, nor should it be considered to be a type of earnings.

Trade Expansion Act of 1962: federal legislation permitting the president to negotiate additional tariff reductions, eliminate or reduce tariffs on items of the European Common Market, reduce tariffs on the basis of reciprocal trade agreements, and grant technical and financial assistance to employers whose business is adversely affected by tariff reductions.

trade in: to surrender an old product for a new one, accompanied by additional payment to make up for depreciation of the item traded in.

trademark:

(1) *production:* a word or symbol affixed to goods or their package to identify the manufacturer or place or origin.

(2) *business law:* a distinctive identification of a manufactured product or of a service in the form of a name, logo, motto, and so on. A trademarked brand has legal protection, and only the owner can use the mark. Organizations that file an application at the U.S. Patent Office and use the brand for five years may be granted a trademark. A firm may lose a trademark that has become generic. Generic names are those that consumers use to identify the prod-

uct, rather than to specify a particular brand (e.g., escalator, aspirin, nylon).

trade name: the name under which an organization conducts business or by which the business or its goods and services are identified. It may or may not be registered as a trademark.

tradeoffs: the exchange of one benefit or value at the sacrifice of another (e.g., reducing air pollution at the price of increased costs for unleaded gasoline).

trader

(1) *general:* anyone who is engaged in trade or commerce.

(2) *securities:* one who buys and sells for his or her own account for short-term profit.

trade reference: a person or firm to which a seller is referred for credit data on a potential customer.

trade union: workers organized into a voluntary association to further their mutual interests with respect to wages, hours, and working conditions.

trading area: the area surrounding an economic institution from which it derives most of its business.

trading difference: a difference of a fraction of a point in the charged price for securities bought and sold in an odd-lot transaction that is in excess of the price at which the security would be traded in traditional round lots.

trading down: attempting to increase the market of a store or item with an established reputation by lowering price or quality or by changing promotional strategy to appeal to a larger potential market, which is frequently in a lower socioeconomic

level. By trading down, the image of the item is often sacrificed for gains in profit. See also *trading up, wheel of retailing.*

trading floor: See *floor.*

trading post: one of many trading locations on the floor of stock exchanges at which stocks assigned to that location are bought and sold. See also *floor, specialist.*

trading stamp: a promotional device; a stamp given to customers that is worth a small percentage of the total amount paid for purchases. When a large number of stamps have been accumulated, they can be redeemed at the store or at a warehouse for merchandise.

trading up: attempting to improve the image of a store or item by increasing prices or quality or by altering advertisement approaches, usually to appeal to a market in a higher socioeconomic level. See also *wheel of retailing;* cf. *trading down.*

traditio: delivery and transfer of possession of property by an owner.

traditional corporation: the corporation viewed as an instrumentality of a single group—the shareholders—and as having one clear-cut purpose—conducting business for maximal profit. This view recognizes no public responsibilities except legal ones and leaves the public interest to the care of the state. Cf. *metrocorporation, well-tempered corporation.*

traffic

(1) *merchandising:* the flow of people who are exposed to a store's goods. Measurement of traffic (i.e., counting the people) is usually done as customers enter and leave the store's premises.

(2) *transportation:* business done by a transportation or communications company.

traffic department: the department that schedules the work responsibilities of other units in an advertising agency and has primary responsibility for ensuring that deadlines are met.

trailer ship: a vessel equipped with ramps that permit trailers to be driven on and off for loading and unloading.

trainee: a worker who is assigned to a prescribed training program that is designed to prepare him to perform the normal operations of a specified task.

training: the methods for imparting job-related knowledge to employees.

training, blitz: rapid training, accomplished during a short period, that attempts to bring personnel to the highest skill level possible under such pressure conditions.

training, cold storage: a form of training that is offered to prepare employees for positions that they may fill at some future date. Synonymous with *training, reserve.*

training, reserve: Synonymous with *training, cold storage.*

training, vestibule: training provided in an area that is removed from the factory floor, where similar equipment is available and teachers can function without disturbing the other workers. Cf. *on-the-job training.*

training groups: See *sensitivity training.*

training laboratory: an organized and controlled social situation or setting that is used for the training and development of managers, executives, or officers in various related leadership positions. See also *sensitivity training.*

trait theory of leadership: identification of the physical, mental, and personality characteristics believed to be linked to successful leadership.

transaction: any agreement between two or more parties that establishes a legal obligation.

transaction analysis: the procedures for analyzing, recording, summarizing, and reporting the transactions of an entity.

transaction file: a file containing relatively transient data to be processed in combination with a master file.

transactions demand for money: the demand for cash to finance regular expenses. Transactions demand depends on the frequency with which income payments are received and expenses must be paid.

transactions motive: the holding, by consumers and businessmen, of some of their assets in liquid form to make possible participation in day-to-day spending activities.

transcriber: specific equipment associated with a computer for the purpose of transferring the input or output data from a record of information in a given language to the computer medium and language or from a computer to a record of information.

transfer

(1) *computers:* to move information from one storage device to another or from one part of memory to another.

(2) *personnel:* to shift an employee from one job to another within the same organization.

(3) *securities:* See *stock transfer.*

transfer agent: an agent who keeps a record of the name of each registered shareowner, his or her address, and the number of shares owned. It is the agent's responsibility to see that certificates presented to the office for transfer are properly canceled and that new certificates are issued in the name of the transferee.

transfer clause: a clause in a lease that terminates the agreement if and when the tenant changes employment, usually requiring 30 days notice along with proof of job transfer.

transfer costs: the costs that a department accepts for items supplied by other departments. See also *transfer price.*

transference: the applicability of training to actual job situations, as evaluated by how readily the trainee can transfer the learning to his or her job.

transfer of title: the change of property title from one person to another. Synonymous with *voluntary alienation.*

transfer payment: in government statistics, money transactions between people, government, and business for which no services are provided. There is no addition to the national product.

transfer price: the price charged by one segment of an organization for a product or service it supplies to another part of the same firm. See also *transfer costs.*

transfer tax: a tax imposed by the federal government and some state governments when a security is sold or transferred from one person to another. The tax is paid by the seller. There is no tax on transfers of bonds.

The transfer tax is usually collected as a stamp tax.

transformation process: See *black box concept.*

transient rate: the one-time rate for ads, without quantity or frequency reductions. Cf. *time discount.*

transition card: in the loading of a deck of program cards, the card that causes the termination of loading and then initiates execution of the program.

translator

(1) *computers:* a device that converts information from one system of representation into equivalent information in another system of representation.

(2) *systems:* a routine for changing information from one representation or language to another.

transmit

(1) *general:* to move or communicate.

(2) *computers:* to send data from one location and receive it at another location.

transportation: the movement of vehicular or marine traffic from one place to another.

transportation, linear programming: when there are a large number of warehouses of fixed capacities and a known number of distributors and their demands, procedures that enable preparation of a shipping schedule that minimizes total costs.

transshipping

(1) *transportation:* the transfer of items from one carrier to another.

(2) *sales:* the shipment of merchandise by a dealer or distributor to another dealer or distributor beyond the usual selling area.

trapping: a unique feature of some computers that enables an unscheduled jump (transfer) to be made to a predetermined location in response to a machine condition. See also *jump, transfer.*

travel and entertainment credit card (T & E card): a credit card issued for use primarily for the purchase of meals, lodging, and transportation. The major American T & E cards are American Express, Carte Blanche, and Diner's Club.

traveler's checks: a form of check designed especially for travelers, including persons on vacation and business trips. These checks, usually preprinted in denominations of $10, $20, $50, and $100, can be cashed and used to purchase goods and services in places of business that accept them.

traveler's letter of credit: a letter of credit issued by a bank to a customer who is preparing for an extended trip. The customer pays for the letter of credit, which is issued for a specified period of time in the amount purchased. The bank furnishes a list of correspondent banks at which drafts drawn against the letter of credit will be honored. See also *guaranteed letters of credit, letter of indication.*

traveling sales representative: a salesperson who travels considerably to obtain orders.

travel time: the period required to report from a designated point to the place of work, compensated at negotiated rates of pay. Synonymous with *portal-to-portal pay.*

treasureship: the functions of management that are responsible for the custody and investment of money, the granting of credit and collection of accounts, capital provision, maintenance of a market for the firm's securities, and so on.

Treasury bill: a U.S. government short-term security, sold to the public each week and maturing in 91 to 182 days.

Treasury bond: See *bond, Treasury.*

Treasury certificates: U.S. government short-term securities, sold to the public and maturing in one year.

Treasury deposits: federal government tax receipts that the U.S. Treasury keeps on deposit in Federal Reserve Banks.

Treasury note: a U.S. government long-term security, sold to the public and maturing in one to five years.

Treasury obligations: See *Treasury bill; bond, Treasury; Treasury certificates; Treasury note.*

treasury stock: the title to previously issued stock of a corporation that has been reacquired by that corporation by purchase, gift, donation, inheritance, or other means. The value of such stock should be considered to be a deduction from the value of outstanding stock of similar type, rather than as an asset of the issuing corporation.

treaty: a reinsurance contract between companies.

Trendex: a research firm that issues statements on the relative popularity of network television programs. Most of the Trendex data are gathered by using the coincidental-telephone approach.

trend extensions: a group of forecasting techniques that extrapolate historical records.

trend forecast: the long-term changes in market demand.

trespass: unlawful, unauthorized entry on the property of another.

trial

(1) *business law:* a proceeding by authorized officials to examine the evidence for the purpose of determining an issue presented according to proper rules of law.

(2) *marketing:* in the adoption process of a consumer, the period when a product is first used. This is a critical point in determining the continued acceptance of the item by consumers.

trial and error pricing: selling an item at varying prices in different locations and then assessing the response to each of the prices.

trial balance: a listing of all account balances that provides a means of testing whether debits equal credits for the total of all accounts.

trial close: an attempt, based on perpetual clues, to zero in on the close of a sale before the natural termination of the sales presentation.

trial period: See *probationary employee.*

triangular trade: trade among three countries in which an attempt is made to create a favorable balance for each.

trick: (slang) a working period (i.e., a shift).

trickle-down: the process by which federal funds flowing into the national economy stimulate growth by being distributed into organizations, as opposed to stimulating growth by direct payments (e.g., welfare).

trigger points: events that are designated to set a contingency plan in ac-

tion.

trigger-price system: a federal system for identifying cut-rate steel that is dumped in the United States. It sets minimum prices below which imported steel cannot be sold in this country without triggering an investigation by the Treasury Department. If the agency determines that the steel has been sold at unfairly low prices, bonds and, ultimately antidumping duties can be imposed on the products.

troubleshoot

(1) *computers:* Synonymous with *debug.*

(2) *administration:* the activity of an individual who is engaged in locating and eliminating the source of trouble in a task or operation.

trough: the lowest point of economic activity.

truck, center-control: an industrial truck in which the operating controls are placed between the load and the power unit.

truck, end-control: a truck in which the operating controls are located at the rear end of the vehicle.

truck, fork: a truck with vertical, elevating back plates and horizontal forks for raising and lowering goods, usually used for short-distance hauls in warehouses.

truck, fork-lift: a power-driven fork truck that is able to lift a load on large forks, carry it, and place it relatively high above the floor.

truck, straddle: a truck with a high frame, enabling it to be driven to a position over a load (pipes, lumber, etc.).

truck jobber: a middleman who delivers at the time of sale, (e.g., vendors of ice cream, lunch specialties, and other items that must be sold fresh).

true interest: Synonymous with *pure interest*.

truncate: to terminate a computational process in accordance with a given rule. See also *paper truncation*.

trunk show: the display of a vendor's total line of merchandise before an audience that is gathered for the purpose of inspecting the wares.

trust

(1) *general:* a feeling of confidence in an individual or group.

(2) *real estate:* a fiduciary relationship between persons whereby one holds property for the benefit and use of another.

(3) *securities:* a combination of corporations, usually in the same industry. Stockholders relinquish their stock to a board of trustees, which then issues certificates and dividends. The purposes of creating a trust include controlling costs of production, increasing profits, and reducing competition. See also *monopoly*.

trust, corporate: the division of a bank that handles the trust and agency business of corporations.

trust agreement (trust instrument): an agreement between an employer and a trustee that is used in connection with a pension plan. It defines the trustee's powers and duties and states how the funds of the pension plan shall be invested and how payments shall be made to those who benefit under the plan. A trust agreement is usually used in connection with self-administered pension plans and individual policy pension plans.

trust company: an institution, usually

state supervised, that engages in the trust business and, usually, in all commercial banking activities.

trustee

(1) *business law:* a person to whom the title to property has been conveyed for the benefit of another.

(2) *real estate:* an individual who assumes the obligations that are not connected with the direct holding of property.

trustee in bankruptcy: the individual appointed by a court or by creditors to carry out the responsibilities of trust in a bankruptcy proceeding.

trustee management: a management system whereby managers are responsible for and to the claims of stockholders, the broader community, employees, suppliers, and customers, in addition to being responsible for making a profit.

trusteeship: suspension by an international union of the officers of a local union, with the international taking over control and administration of the local. The Landrum-Griffin Act of 1959 established controls over the creation and administration of trusteeships.

trust estate: an estate held in trust by one individual for the welfare of another.

trust fund: the funds held by a trustee for the benefit of another person.

trust funds, federal: trust funds established to account for receipts that are held in trust by the government for use in carrying out specific purposes and programs in accordance with a trust agreement or a statute.

trust indenture: a written instrument that contains a description of all property originally placed in a trust, the agreement with respect to the duties of the trustee in administering the property, the rights of all beneficiaries named and their proportionate shares in the trust, the duration of the trusteeship, the distribution of income from the trust principal to the life tenants, and the distribution of the trust property to the remaindermen at the termination of the trust.

trustor: an individual who establishes a trust.

Truth in Lending Act of 1968: officially, the Consumer Credit Protection Act of 1968, which requires that most categories of lenders disclose the true annual interest rate on virtually all types of loans and credit sales as well as the total dollar cost and other terms of a loan. See also *Fair Credit Billing Act, right of rescission.*

truth table: a table that describes a logic function by listing all possible combinations of input values and indicating the true output values for each combination.

Turing machine: designed and built by Alan Turing of Great Britain, a device that changes its internal state and reads from, writes on, and moves a potentially infinite tape, all in accordance with its present state, thereby constituting a model for computerlike behavior. See also *Universal Turing machine.*

turn

(1) *general:* (slang) to earn money by performing a task.

(2) *securities:* a description of the full cycle in the buying and selling of a security or a commodity.

(3) *merchandising:* a turnover of merchandise in an inventory.

turnaround: movement by a freight carrier in which the driver returns to the point of origin following the unloading and reloading of cargo.

turnaround time: the elapsed time between submission of a job to a computing center and the return of results. Synonymous with *response time.*

turnkey: a contractual agreement between a customer and an organization to provide full services or a complete product.

turnover

(1) *administration:* the rate at which workers move into and out of employment, usually expressed as the number of accessions and separations during a fixed period for every 100 employees. The Bureau of Labor Statistics computes monthly turnover rates by industry.

(2) *retailing:* the frequency with which an inventory is sold and replaced over a stated period, usually determined by dividing the net sales for the period by the average retail value of the inventory during that period.

(3) *securities:* the volume of business in a security or in the entire market. If turnover on the exchange is reported at 15 million shares on a particular day, this means that 15 million shares changed hands. Odd-lot turnover is tabulated separately and ordinarily is not included in reported volume.

turnover ratio: a measure of capital activity or another factor of business (e.g., when the portfolio of securities is altered, or turned over, within one year). See also *operating profit ratio.*

turnover tax: a form of sales tax employed in the Soviet Union.

turn over the cover: to investigate both sides of a proposal, idea, proposition, and the like.

twelve edge: the uppermost edge of an 80-column Hollerith card. Computer interpreting devices require a 12-edge feed for the commencement of operations.

twisting: the practice of inducing a policyholder to lapse or cancel a policy for the purpose of replacing it with another, to the detriment of the policyholder. This practice is both unethical and illegal.

two-dimensional leadership model: a model that addresses the importance of two factors: task orientation and relationship orientation.

two-dollar brokers: members on the floor of the exchange who execute orders for other brokers who have more business at that time than they can handle themselves or for firms that do not have their exchange member on the floor. The term recalls the time when these independent brokers received $2 per hundred shares for executing such orders. See also *give-up.*

two faces of power: a concept of power in which the negative face involves personal domination of others and the positive face involves power that is exercised not for personal advancement or benefit but for the good of the organization or society.

two-factor theory: a concept developed by Frederick Herzberg that job motivation has two independent sources: hygiene factors and motivators. See also *dissatisfiers, satisfiers.*

two-name paper: a short-term negotiable instrument wherein two people

guarantee payment.

two-tier gold system: a system devised in 1968 to keep the world's monetary gold from being depleted by speculation and hoarding. International Monetary Fund member nations agreed to keep their present gold reserves for use in settlement of international trade balances only. All gold that was not part of this official tier supply and all newly minted gold would be traded in the open market. The open market gold no longer had any potential monetary value, since all IMF members had promised not to buy any of it for their reserves. See also *International Monetary Fund.*

two-way communication: transmission of information and ideas both up and down the hierarchy.

tycoon: an extremely wealthy and potentially influential business person.

tying arrangement: an agreement in which a purchaser agrees to buy one good from a supplier in order to obtain supplies of another good. Tying arrangements were outlawed by the Clayton Act. See also *tie-in sales.*

tying contract: See *tie-in sales.*

type A behavior: a behavior pattern in which the person has a sense of time urgency, attempts to achieve more in less time, has a high need for achievement, is insecure, and is generally hostile. Cf. *type B behavior.*

type B behavior: a behavior pattern in which the person is easygoing, confident, and generally pleasant and unaggressive. Cf. *type A behavior.*

typewriter, console: a typewriter that is attached to or part of the control unit or programmer desk of a computer and is available both to enter and to receive information. This typewriter controls the computer, corrects errors, and manually influ- ences the storage component.

ultimate consumer: the individual who actually uses the bought merchandise.

ultimo: the month prior to the present one.

ultra vires: "beyond power" (Latin); describing acts of a corporation when they exceed the power or capability of the corporation as granted by the state in its charter.

umbrella liability: a form of insurance protection against losses in excess of amounts covered by other liability insurance policies. It also protects the insured in many situations that are not covered by the usual liability policies. Such insurance is usually written for sums in the $1 million range for professionals, executives, and businessmen who may be liable to malpractice suits and other large liability claims.

umpire: an individual who is called in to decide a controversy. Synonymous with *arbitrator*.

unadjusted rate of return: an expression of the utility of a given project as the ratio of the increase in future average annual net income to the initial increase in needed investment.

unaffiliated union: a local or national union that is not affiliated with the parent labor organization, the AFL–CIO.

unamortized bond discount: the portion of the original bond discount that has not been charged off against earnings.

unappropriated profits: the portion of a firm's profit which has not been paid out in dividends or allocated for any special purpose.

unauthorized strike: a strike that does not have the authorization of the union. See also *illegal strike, snap strike, strike.*

unbalanced growth: capital investment that grows at different rates in different areas of an economy.

unbilled revenue: fees earned in a given period for which bills have not yet been sent to the customers.

uncalled capital: the portion of the issued share capital of a corporation that has not yet been called up.

uncertainty theory: the theory that profit arises from uncertainties due to innovations, changes in taste, price fluctuations, and the vagaries of competition.

unclaimed balances: the balances of the accounts for funds on deposit that have remained inactive for a period designated by the bank. Eventually these unclaimed balances are handed over to the U.S. Comptroller of the Currency.

uncollected funds: a portion of a deposit balance that has not yet been collected by the depository bank; that is, sufficient time has not elapsed to permit checks drawn on other banks to have been returned for nonpayment. See also *float.*

uncontrollable factors: factors beyond the direct control of the manager (e.g., competitors' activities, international developments, economic conditions).

underapplied overhead: the excess of factory overhead incurred over factory overhead applied. In practice, this means that the actual cost of overhead incurred was more than the amount charged to the manufacturing process during the year.

under bond: See *warehouse, U.S. Customs bonded.*

undercharge: to charge less than the legal amount.

underchosen: participants who are uncommitted to the group and tend to show interest only in their personal needs.

underclass: describing people on the lowest economic level.

underconsumption theory: a concept presented by the English economist J. A. Hobson that prosperity must always be brought to an end because consumption lags behind expanding output. Cf. *overproduction theory, Say's law.*

underdeveloped country: a nation in which per capita real income is proportionately low in comparison to the per capita real income of nations where industry flourishes. See also *less-developed country, vent for surplus;* cf. *mature economy.*

underemployed: describing an individual who is working on a job at a lower level than that for which he or she was trained or is experienced to handle. Total skills are untapped, and the employee is often frustrated and/or angry with the job situation.

underflow: the condition that arises when a machine computation yields a nonzero result smaller than the smallest nonzero quantity that the intended unit of storage is capable of storing.

underinsurance: a situation in which not enough insurance is being carried to cover the value of the property or to satisfy a coinsurance clause.

underlease: a tenant's lease of property to a third party. Synonymous with *sublease.*

underlying bond: See *bond, underlying.*

underlying company: Synonymous with *subsidiary.*

underlying mortgage: a mortgage that is senior to a larger one (e.g., a first mortgage of $100,000 that has a prior claim over a second one of $200,000). Cf. *equal dignity.*

underpackaging: the use of packaging methods that are inadequate for the level of protection needed.

underselling: selling at a price lower than that listed by a competitor. See also *rate war.*

under the rule: an action of selling or buying by stock exchange officers to complete a transaction entered into by a delinquent member of the exchange, who is charged with any difference in price that occurs.

underutilization: a situation in which a department or employer has a smaller proportion of members of a protected class than are found in the employer's labor market. See also *concentration in employment.*

under way: the condition of a vessel when the anchor has been lifted or the lines have been cast off from the wharf.

underwriter
(1) *general:* an individual or organization that assumes a risk for a fee.
(2) *insurance:* an individual in the insurance business who has the responsibility of accepting risks and determining the amount of insurance the company will write on each acceptable risk.
(3) *securities:* an individual or party that agrees to underwrite a securities issue. Cf. *letter stock.*

undigested securities: securities that are issued beyond the need or ability of the public to absorb them. See also *overissue;* cf. *float, oversubscribed.*

undistributed profits: the profits of a partnership, syndicate, or joint venture prior to division among the individuals concerned.

undivided right: a part owner's right

that cannot be excluded from the other owner's rights. This right exists in tenancy in common and in joint tenancy.

unearned discount: interest that is received but not yet earned.

unearned income: income that has been collected in advance of the performance of a contract; income derived from investment dividends, property rentals, and other sources that do not involve the individual's personal efforts. Cf. *earned income.*

unearned increment: the increase in the value of property that can be attributed to changing social or economic conditions beyond the control of the title holder, as distinguished from an increase in value that can be attributed to the improvements made or additions made by the labor or investment of the title holder.

unearned premium: the portion of the original premium that has not yet been earned by the company because the policy still has some time to run before expiration. A fire or casualty insurance company must carry all unearned premiums as a liability in its financial statement, for if the policy were canceled, the company would have to pay back part of the premium. See also *pro rata cancellation.*

unearned revenues: amounts that are received before they have been earned.

unemployable: describing a person who is unable to find work. The term usually refers to an individual who is too sick, too young, too old, or too badly impaired in mind or body, or to anyone who attempts to avoid work or is a criminal. Cf. *hard-core unem-*

ployed, working poor.

unemployment: a condition of not being employed; according to the U.S. government, the condition of a member of the labor force who seeks work but does not find it. Unemployment may be caused by numerous changes in business activity. See also *chronic unemployment, cyclical unemployment, frictional unemployment, technological unemployment.*

unemployment compensation: a system of insuring workers against hardship during periods of unemployment. The Unemployment Insurance Act of 1935, as part of the social security program, is administered by the states individually, allowing for variations in rates, duration of payments, and eligibility. Costs are borne by the employers, who get allowances in the form of tax credits. See also *supplementary unemployment benefits.*

unencumbered property: real estate that is free and clear of mortgages, liens, or debts of any type. See also *perfect title.*

unexpired cost: any asset.

unfair competition: practices employed by a seller to increase profit by means of misleading advertising, selling below cost or dumping, obtaining rebates from suppliers, or utilizing other devices that unfairly take advantage of a competing firm.

unfair goods: products or items that are not produced by members of a union. See also *hot cargo, hot cargo provisions;* cf. *struck work.*

unfair labor practices: illegal anti-union behavior or illegal union behavior as determined by the National Labor Relations Board, subject to court appeal. For unfair labor prac-

tices on the part of management, see *Wagner-Connery Act.* For unfair labor practices on the part of unions, see *Taft-Hartley Act.*

unfair labor practice strike: a strike that is provoked by the employer. This strategy is considered an unfair labor practice under federal and state labor laws.

unfair list: a list of firms that are considered to be unfair to labor, distributed by unions to reduce patronage or otherwise exert pressure.

unfair practices acts: state regulations establishing minimum resale prices. Such laws stipulate that goods must be sold for cost plus some nominal percentage. In practice, there is little enforcement of these rulings. Cf. *fair trade acts.*

unfunded: describing a pension fund for which there has been no advance funding and from which payments are made when actual needs arise to pay the pensioners. It is a pay-as-you-go plan.

uniform cash flows: cash flows that are the same for every year.

Uniform Commercial Code: a set of statutes purporting to provide some consistency among states' commercial laws. It includes uniform laws dealing with bills of lading, negotiable instruments, sales, stock transfers, trust receipts, and warehouse receipts.

uniform delivered price: a pricing method whereby all the products are sold at the same delivery price in a stated area, without regard for delivery costs.

uniformed services: public employees (e.g., police, fire, and sanitation workers).

Uniform Negotiable Instruments Act: See *negotiable instrument.*

unifunctionalism: a process of combining related organizational functions or activities under a few large departments or units. See also *centralization.*

unilateral strategy: an organizational development approach that precludes participation by employees. The management hierarchy exercises authority to determine the development program. See also *classical design theory;* cf. *human relations theory, multiple management.*

unilateral transfers: international transfers of resources that involve no exchange or return. They are gifts.

uninsurable title: property that a title insurance company will not insure.

uninsured motorist protection: a form of insurance that covers the policyholder and members of his or her family in the event of injury by a hit-and-run motorist or by a driver who carries no liability insurance, assuming that the other driver is at fault. Cf. *nonownership automobile insurance.*

union: a worker's organization whose major objective is representation of its members in bargaining with employers.

union label: See *label.*

union rate: the minimum hourly wage rate accepted by a union for a specific type of activity. It is employed in negotiations.

union recognition: acceptance by an employer of a union as the collective-bargaining representative of his or her workers.

union security clauses: negotiated contract clauses providing for a union shop, maintenance-of-membership, agency shop, or payroll deduction of union dues. These clauses protect the institutional life of the union.

union shop: a contract clause requiring that all members of a bargaining unit retain union membership as a condition of employment, and further requiring that new employees join the union after a stated period, usually 60 to 90 days after being hired. See also *union security clauses;* cf. *Rand formula.*

union steward: See *shop steward.*

unissued stock: part of the authorized capital stock of a corporation that is not issued or outstanding. It is not part of the corporation's capital stock and receives no dividends. It must be shown on the firm's balance sheet, even though it is neither an asset nor a liability. See also *when issued.*

unit

(1) *general:* a basic element; a standard of measurement; a single person or group.

(2) *systems:* a device that has a special function.

(3) *statistics:* the smallest whole number, one.

unitary elasticity: the concept that a change in price will be compensated by a corresponding change in demand, so that total income will remain the same.

unit billing: a list of all purchases by a customer, prepared on a single statement.

unit contribution margin: the excess of the sales price of one unit over its variable costs.

unit control: an approach for listing

the quantity of goods bought, sold, in stock, and on order, with additional breakdowns as needed. Cf. *taking inventory.*

unit cost: the cost of producing or distributing one unit of a processed item.

United States Employment Service (USES): a federal-state system for helping the jobless to find work or for giving advice on opportunities to workers who seek better jobs.

unitize: to combine a number of freight pieces into one large piece by banding, placing in a container, stacking, or any other means of assembling into a unit.

unitized load: a load in which all the containers are bound together in one or more units.

unit labor cost: the cost of an employee needed to produce one unit of output, determined by dividing compensation by output.

unit of traffic: the average tons of cargo hauled per mile.

unit pricing: the quotation of prices given in terms of a standard of measurement (by weight, length, count, etc.).

unit record: a punched card that contains one complete record.

unit–small batch technology: custom manufacturing of individual items.

unit technology: the approach of a company that spends a large amount of capital on labor relative to its investment in machinery.

unit trust: a British term for mutual investment; a mutual fund.

unity of command: the concept in classical management that a subordinate must be responsible to only one superior. Cf. *chain of command.*

unity of direction: Synonymous with *unity of management.*

unity of management: one of Henri Fayol's classic principles, calling for one manager and one plan for all operations that have the same objectives. Synonymous with *unity of direction.*

universal design theory: the concept that there is a single best way to design an organization. Cf. *situational design theory.*

universal Turing machine: a Turing machine that can simulate any other Turing machine.

unlawful: See *illegal.*

unlimited accounts: large or reputable businesses that are eligible for any amount of credit.

unlimited tax bond: See *bond, unlimited tax.*

unlisted: describing a security that is not listed on a stock exchange (i.e., an over-the-counter stock). See also *discontinuous market.*

unloading

(1) *merchandising:* selling merchandise at a relatively low price. Synonymous with *dumping.*

(2) *securities:* the sale of stocks and commodities to avoid a loss during a period of a falling market. Cf. *profit taking.*

unpaid balance: on a credit purchase, the difference between the purchase price and the down payment or the value of a trade-in; on a cash loan, the difference between the total loan and the amount that is still owed.

unpaid dividend: a dividend that is declared but not yet distributed.

unrealized profits: paper profits that are not made actual until the firm's securities have been sold.

unrecorded expenses and accrued liabilities: expenses that have not previously been recognized, and companion payable accounts that were incurred during a period but were not paid for by the end of that period.

unrecorded revenues and accrued assets: revenues that have not previously been recognized, and companion receivable accounts that were earned during a period but were not received by the end of that period.

unsecured bond: See *bond, debenture.*

unsecured debt: a debt for which no collateral has been pledged.

unsecured loan: a loan made by a bank based on credit information about the borrower and his or her ability to repay the obligation. The loan is not secured by collateral but is made on the signature of the borrower and sometimes his or her spouse. See also *comaker, debenture.*

unskilled worker: a person who can perform only simple manual operations that are easily learned and require no complex skill. Synonymous with *common laborer.*

unstable market: a market in which forces of disequilibrium are reinforced so that movements away from equilibrium are not reversible.

unstuffing: unloading cargo from a container.

update: to modify a master file with current information, according to a specified procedure.

upgrading
(1) *administration:* a well-defined approach for training and advancement of qualified workers in an or-

ganization. Cf. *terminal positions.*
(2) *retailing:* offering superior goods and a greater assortment to customers.

upkeep: the cost of maintaining property or machinery in sound, workable condition.

upper turning point: a short period during which an upswing ends and a downswing begins. Cf. *lower turning point.*

upscale: describing people and households of well above average income and education.

upset price: the minimal price at which a seller is willing to sell; the beginning price asked at an auction prior to public bidding. See also *marginal seller;* cf. *negotiated price, reservation price.*

up tick: a transaction made at a price higher than the preceding transaction. A stock may be sold short only on an up tick or on a "zero-plus" tick (i.e., a transaction at the same price as the preceding trade but higher than the preceding different price). Synonymous with *plus tick.*

uptime: the time during which a computer is available for productive work.

upward communication: the flow of communication from lower levels in an organization's hierarchy to employees on higher levels. This is the primary source of feedback in an organization. Cf. *downward communication.*

urbank: first proposed by Professor Charles Haar in 1968, an urban development bank, controlled by a federal agency, to assist communities in building needed facilities. The urbank would be a federally financed institution, making long-term loans at favorable interest rates to employers who are willing to return or upgrade plants in cities.

urban renewal: planned rehabilitation of run-down central areas of a city or community.

usance

(1) *economics:* employment.

(2) *finance:* interest or income.

(3) *finance:* the period allowed for payment of a foreign obligation.

useless quality: describing goods created with quality, dependability, and/or performance that is superior to that demanded by the public.

user: anyone who requires the services of a system or product or who employs a service.

user calls: callbacks made by a sales representative to a customer who has already made a purchase from him or her or from the organization.

user expectation: a sales forecast that is construed after a consumer survey or some other form of consumer research has been conducted.

use tax: a tax levied on the initial use of an item rather than on the merchandise when it is sold.

U.S. Savings Bond: see *Bond, Savings (U.S.)*.

usufructuary right: a right to appropriate use and pleasure from property owned by another.

usurious: describing a contract for a loan of money that is made at a rate of interest in excess of that authorized by the statute.

usury: a rate of interest paid for the use of another's money, or for credit extended, that exceeds the legal limit allowed for that type of transaction by the state whose laws govern the legality of the transaction. See also *legal interest.*

utility

(1) *general:* the capability or power of an item to satisfy a need, as determined by the satisfaction one receives from consuming something.

(2) *economics:* a publicly owned facility (e.g., an electric power plant).

utility expenditures: expenditures for construction or acquisition of publicly owned utility facilities or equipment, for production and distribution of utility commodities and services, and for interest on debt.

utility program: a computer program designed to perform an everyday task, such as transcribing data from one storage device to another.

utter: to put out or pass off (e.g., to utter a check is to give it to another in payment of an obligation).

vacancy factor: a calculation of unrented space over a fixed time period as a percentage, often determined by the gross income generated minus losses because of vacancies.

vacation: a period of time when an employee is away from his or her existing work environment. The employer gives the worker earned pay, and the length of the vacation is usually defined by contract or by company policy.

vacation pay: compensention received for a specified vacation period, which usually varies in time with the employee's length of service.

vacuumize: to remove air from a filled container before closing it.

vacuum packaging: packaging in containers from which almost all air has been removed before the container is sealed.

valence: a person's preference for a first-level outcome. See also *expectancy theory of motivation, first-level outcome.*

valid: describing that which is sufficient to satisfy the requirement of the law, a fact.

validation: proof or confirmation; an instrument or other evidence to confirm or give legal support to a claim or contract (e.g., factual data from an experiment).

validity: the quality of being truthful and/or factual. It presupposes that the antecedent reasoning process is formal and correct.

validity check: an appraisal to determine that a code group is actually a character of the particular code in use.

valorization: government action leading to the establishment of a price or value for an item or service.

valuation:
(1) *real estate:* Synonymous with *appraising.*
(2) *finance:* setting a value for anything.

valuation reserves
(1) *finance:* reserves established

to provide for a drop in the existing value of the assets to which they pertain. See also *appraisal.*

(2) *finance:* reserves established to provide for a reasonably probable failure to achieve full value.

value: the worth of property, goods, services, and so on; purchasing power. See also *book value.*

value added: the part of the value of produced goods that is developed in a company. It is determined by subtracting from sales the costs of materials and supplies, energy, contract work, and so on, and it includes labor expenses, administrative and sales costs, and other operating profits.

value-added tax (VAT): a government tax on the value added; a tax on the selling price of manufactured items less the cost of the materials and expenses used in their production.

value analysis: a purchasing strategy of asking the buyer's engineers to project the cost of goods in an attempt to keep the vendor's prices low.

value approach: including ethical and value judgments in the decision-making process to effect change in an organization.

value compensated: describing a purchase or sale of foreign exchange to be executed by cable. The purchaser reimburses the seller for the earlier value on the data of actual payment abroad of the foreign currency, theoretically resulting in no loss of interest to either party.

value date: the date on which a bank deposit becomes effective. The date fixed is based on the time required to collect a payment on the item deposited from another bank. See also *collection.*

valued policy: a policy providing for the payment of a stipulated amount in event of a total loss of the insured property. Most fine arts policies and some inland marine policies have this provision. Such provisions are illegal in fire insurance in most states.

value engineering: the systematic use of tools that identify the required function, establish a value for that function, and ultimately provide the function at the lowest overall cost.

value in use: the value of goods to the individual who uses them.

van container: a standard trailer used to carry general cargo.

vanning: loading a container.

van shipment: a padded van or railroad car shipment.

variable: a quantity that may assume any of a given set of values.

variable, dependent: a variable whose changes are treated as being consequent upon changes in one or more other variables, which are referred to as independent variables.

variable, independent: a variable whose changes are regarded as not dependent on any other variables. It is the variable that is manipulated experimentally to determine the effect of a change on the dependent variable that is being investigated.

variable annuity: an annuity contract providing lifetime retirement payments that vary in amount with the results of investment in a separate account portfolio. See also *annuity accumulation unit.*

variable budget: a budget that divides expenses into fixed costs and variable costs. The latter are allowed to vary on a predetermined basis with differing levels of output.

variable cost: a cost that is uniform per unit but changes in total in direct proportion to changes in the related total activity or volume.

variable error: an error of judgment that varies uniformly in either direction from the norm. Cf. *systematic error.*

variable expenses: expenses that vary with the level of factory output or plant capacity (e.g., the expenses of power, oils, and lubricants vary with the number of machines in operation; the expense of compensation insurance varies with the number of employees in the department). Generally, variable expenses are controllable.

variable inspection: a method of quality control in which measurements are used to determine the deviation from standards.

variable life insurance: a relatively new form of coverage, in which the death benefit is based on the performance of the stock market or, more specifically, on the performance of stocks in the insurer's portfolio. The better the market performs over the life of the policy (i.e., a lifetime), the more cash the benefit will receive. If the market should collapse, a specified minimum death benefit will be paid nonetheless. A variable life insurance policy costs a little less than a standard whole life policy that pays dividends on its investments, but somewhat more than one that pays no dividends.

variance

(1) *general:* a disagreement between two sets of figures or facts.

(2) *administration:* the difference between budgeted expectations and actual results; a means for reporting on management by exception. A variance may be positive or negative, depending on the relationship between budget and actual results.

(3) *real estate:* permission to vary from zoning regulations, a building code, and so on; any change from what currently exists.

(4) *statistics:* the measure of dispersion within a distribution of events.

(5) *accounting:* the difference between expected and actual production costs.

variety of skill: the degree to which a job calls for activities that involve different talents and skills.

variety store: a retail operation that carries limited quantities of apparel and accessories for the family as well as other goods, with prices set somewhat lower than in retail stores.

VAT: See *value-added tax.*

vault: a large room or rooms in a bank or financial institution where the cash on hand is stored and safe deposit boxes are located.

veep: (slang) a vice-president of an organization.

veil of money theory: the theory that money is neutral and does not reflect a nation's true economic condition but is merely a cosmetic for other social and financial forces and activity. Cf. *savings and investment theory.*

velocity of circulation: the rate at which money supply is spent for a stated time period, usually one year.

velvet: (slang) an unearned income or profit.

vend: to offer to sell something.

vendee: the party who purchases or

agrees to purchase property owned by another.

vendor: a manufacturer, wholesaler, or importer from whom goods are purchased.

vendor chargebacks: the return of goods to a vendor, accompanied by an adjusted invoice. Proof of delivery to the vendor is usually provided.

vendor reliability: the capability of the seller to meet the conditions of the contract.

vendor's lien: an unpaid seller's right to take possession of property until the purchase price has been recovered. See also *general lien*; cf. *seller's lien.*

vendue: a public auction.

vent for surplus: the hypothesis that economic progress spreads from developing industrial locations to less-developed geographic locations by means of the increasing demand for items in former areas.

venture: a business activity or undertaking that involves some or considerable risk.

venture capital
(1) *securities:* funds available from the issue of new stock.
(2) *finance:* reinvested monies from stockholders.
(3) *finance:* funds invested in enterprises that do not usually have access to conventional sources of capital (banks, stock market, etc.).

venture capital funds: mutual funds invested in securities of firms that are little known and often are not yet registered with the SEC.

venue: the location or geographical area over which a court presides.

verbal communication: the sharing of ideas through words.

verdict: a jury's decision.

verify
(1) *general:* to prove to be true by demonstration or presentation of fact.
(2) *computers:* to check the results of keypunching.
(3) *computers:* to determine whether a data transaction or other operation has been accomplished accurately. See also *redundancey check.*

vertical equity: the principle that those who are different should be treated in correspondingly different ways.

vertically combined (integrated): describing a business firm that performs all the various stages of production of a single finished item.

vertical merger: the joining of firms that are responsible for different production stages of a particular product so that more of the entire process, from raw material to retail sales, is under the control of a single management.

vertical mobility: See *labor mobility.*

vertical promotion: a form of advancement that increases employee opportunities, provides for additional training, increases responsibility, and in most cases is accompanied by additional pay.

vertical specialization: factors in the division of labor that involve degrees of power, influence, and decision making. Cf. *horizontal specialization.*

vertical strain: the competition that exists between different hierarchical levels in a company.

vertical union: Synonymous with *industrial union.*

vessel: any floating structure that carries passengers and/or cargo.

vested estate: an interest in property that holds present and future rights, but with the existing interest able to be transferred.

vested rights: provisions in a pension program ensuring that if a worker leaves the firm for any reason, he or she can retain the pension rights acquired while employed by the company offering the plan. See also *fully vested, instant vesting.*

vestibule school: See *training, vestibule.*

vesting: the right of an employee under a retirement plan to retain part or all of the annuities purchased by the employer's contributions on his or her behalf; or, in some plans, the right to receive a cash payment of equivalent value on termination of employment after certain qualifying conditions have been met. See also *contingent interest.*

viability: the ability of an individual, group, company, or nation to support itself.

vicarious liability: the principle that an employer is legally responsible for the actions of his or her employees while they are on the job. See also *liability.*

Videodex: a research firm that supplies indices of television program popularity, employing the diary technique to obtain information. See also *diary method.*

Vietnam Era Veteran's Readjustment Act of 1974: legislation that prohibits certain government contractors from discriminating in employment against Vietnam era veterans.

vignette: a display that simulates a product in actual use.

vintage capital: a measure of capital stock that assumes that newly produced capital goods are more productive than older ones.

virtual machine: a functional simulation of a computer and its associated devices.

Visa: the name for the Bank Americard as used around the world.

visible trade: the portion of commerce between nations that is shown by records of transactions involving the exchange of tangible items.

visionary objectives: objectives that cannot be stated in terms of a time dimension. They are too far in the future to establish a specific time for accomplishing them.

vis major: an act of God, occurrence of which excuses an individual or organization from liability.

vitalist theory: a concept that it is more important to plan in terms of the total economic system and then integrate the full system relative to its individual smaller parts.

vital statistics: data on individuals having to do with dates of birth and death, ownership of a house, marriages, divorces, and so on.

VLCC: very large crude carrier.

vocabulary: a list of operations or instructions that are available to a computer programmer to use in writing the program for a given problem on a specific computer. See also *character.*

vocation: a person's business, profession, or occupation.

Vocational Rehabilitation Act of 1973: a federal law prohibiting discrimination against physically or mentally handicapped workers who are employed by organizations with government contracts of $2500 or more.

void: describing that which has no legal effect.

voidable contract: an agreement that can be rescinded by either of the parties in the event of fraud, incompetence, or other sufficient cause.

volatile memory: a storage medium in which information is destroyed when power is removed from the system. Cf. *slave computer.*

volume

(1) *general:* a quantity, bulk, or amount.

(2) *computers:* a recording medium that is mounted and demounted as a unit.

(3) *computers:* the portion of a single unit of storage that is accessible to a single read/write mechanism.

volume test: the processing of a volume of actual data to check for program malfunctions. See also *debug;* cf. *redundancy check.*

voluntarism: Synonymous with *satisfaction.*

voluntary alienation: transfer of title when a property assumes a new owner.

voluntary bankruptcy: See *bankruptcy.*

voluntary chain: a wholesaling organization established by independent retailers or wholesalers to gather increased purchasing power.

voluntary conveyance (deed): the instrument of transfer of an owner's title to property to a lien holder. Usually such conveyance serves to bypass the legal situation of a court judgment showing insufficient security to satisfy a debt, and it occurs

without transfer of a valuable consideration. See also *particular lien.*

voluntary issue: an issue that may be raised in collective bargaining, although neither side may insist that it be bargained over.

voluntary trust: a trust established by a deed of transfer of certain property, made voluntarily by an individual or other legal entity to a trustee for a specified purpose.

vostro account: an account maintained with a depository bank by a bank in a foreign country. Cf. *nostro account.*

voting right: a stockholder's right to vote his or her stock in the affairs of the company. Most common shares have one vote each. Preferred stock usually carries the right to vote when preferred dividends are in default for a specified period. The right to vote is usually delegated by proxy of the stockholder to another person.

voting trust: an agreement whereby stockholders turn over their voting rights to a small group of people, who are called voting trustees.

voucher: a written statement that bears witness or vouches for something (e.g., a voucher showing that services have been rendered or goods bought).

voucher check: a form of check to which a voucher is attached. The voucher portion of the check is used to describe or otherwise designate the purpose for which the check is drawn. When a voucher check is received from a buyer by a seller, the seller detaches the voucher from the check before presenting the check for payment. The voucher is then used as the posting medium to credit the accounts receivable ledger, thereby showing payment received from the buyer. Many businesses use copies of voucher checks as their record of invoices paid.

Vroom-Yetton model: a contingency model of leadership that focuses on the degree of participation leaders should use in reaching a decision. The diagnosis of situational factors determines the degree of participation required.

wage: compensation of employees who receive a stated sum per piece, hour, day, or any other unit or period. The term usually refers to all compensation paid, including salaries. Cf. *earnings, payroll, rate variance.*

Wage and Hour Law: See *Fair Labor Standards Act of 1938.*

wage and salary administration: a well-defined approach for establishing wages and salaries according to an organization's rules and policies and in line with the practice of other companies in the same industry and/or area of work.

wage bracket (range): the range of salary payment for a specific occupation.

wage compression: the condition that occurs when the difference between wages for the top and lowest jobs is narrowed. This usually results from giving larger pay increases to lower-paid jobs than to higher-paid jobs.

wage control: centralized control and stabilization of wages, usually during national crises.

wage curve: a graphic representation of a smooth progression between pay grades.

wage determination: a finding by the Secretary of Labor, after hearings, on wage rates in industries covered by the Walsh-Healey or Davis-Bacon acts.

wage floor: a minimum wage, established by contract, below which an employee cannot be hired, or the legal minimum defined by the Fair Labor Standards Act or state labor laws.

wage freeze: a limit on salary increases, usually imposed by a government.

wage incentive plan: See *incentive pay.*

wage minimum: See *minimum wage.*

wage-price spiral: See *inflationary spiral.*

wage rate: the amount of pay for a given period (hour, day, week, etc.). See *rate variance, wage scale.*

wage scale: a wage rate structure

covering all employees in a department, division, plant, or office. In most cases, the scale is based on the employer's judgment of a task's value.

wages fund theory: a theory proposed by John Stuart Mill in 1848, stating that manufacturers should put aside a portion of their capital funds for the purpose of hiring workers needed for production.

wage stabilization: a governmental program to keep wages for a particular industry or location from rapidly increasing beyond existing levels. See also *inflationary spiral, stabilization policy*.

wage stop: a practice of not permitting an unemployed worker to receive more public monies than he or she would earn while working. See also *workfare*.

Wagner Act: the National Labor Relations Act of 1935. See also *Wagner-Connery Act*.

Wagner-Connery Act: federal legislation that guarantees the right of workers to organize and bargain collectively for a contract and declares specific employer actions to be unfair labor practices. The law created the National Labor Relations Board to administer its functions. See also *Baby Wagner Acts, bargaining unit, blacklist, discriminatory discharge, employer interference, subcontracting, unfair labor practices*.

waiting line theory: an approach to maximizing the efficient servicing of arrivals at a service facility by balancing the costs associated with waiting time and idle time; the application of queueing theory to practical problems.

waiting period
(1) *insurance:* the time specified in certain policies that insure against loss of use, or against disability, that must pass before payment will begin.
(2) *administration:* the time between filing a claim for unemployment benefits or workers' compensation and the beginning of such benefit payments.
(3) *securities:* the time, usually 20 days, that must pass between the application for listing a new security with the SEC and the date when the securities can be offered to the public.

wait order: a request to a medium to hold an advertisement and not release it until a date in the future is named.

wait state: the condition of a specific task that is dependent on one or more events before it can enter the ready condition.

waiver: the voluntary relinquishment of a right in a piece of property or to a claim against another's property that would be legally enforceable if the person waiving so elected.

waiver of premium: a life insurance clause providing that if the insured becomes totally and permanently disabled, his or her insurance policy will be continued in full force and the company will exempt the insured from paying further premiums during disability.

waiver of protest: a statement, signed by the endorser of a note, indicating that he or she will remain liable even if he or she is not notified that the note has not been paid when due.

waiver of restoration premium: a provision in many contracts whereby the company agrees not to charge an additional premium for reinstating the amount of the contract after loss has occurred.

walk: (slang) a customer who fails to purchase something and walks out of the store.

walking delegate: a local union's officer who is responsible for the union's financial, administrative, or labor relations activities. Synonymous with *business agent.*

walk-ins: job seekers who arrive at the personnel department in search of a position without any prior referrals and not in response to a specific ad or request.

walkout: Synonymous with *strike.*

Wall Street: popular name for the New York City business and financial district.

Walsh-Healey Public Contracts Act of 1936: a federal law setting basic labor standard for work on government contracts exceeding $10,000 in value. Employees must be paid at least the prevailing wage rates, and they must be paid time and one-half for work in excess of 8 hours a day or 40 hours a week, whichever is greater. The act is administered by the Department of Labor. See also *Davis-Bacon Act of 1931, wage floor.*

want ads: ads that describe an available job and its benefits, identify the employer, and tell those who are interested how to apply.

want slips: written statements submitted to buyers by salespersons indicating items not in stock that have been requested by customers.

warehouse: a structure where goods are stored prior to distribution.

warehouse, bonded: See *bonded.*

warehouse, bulk: a warehouse for the tank storage of liquids and open, dry products (e.g., coal, sand, stone).

warehouse, captive: Synonymous with *warehouse, private.*

warehouse, commodity: a warehouse that stores commodity goods (cotton, wool, tobacco, and other grown items). See also *godown.*

warehouse, company: Synonymous with *warehouse, private.*

warehouse, private: a warehouse operated by an owner, which holds his goods. Synonymous with *warehouse, captive; warehouse, company;* See also *locker stocks.*

warehouse, public: a warehouse that is rented out by the owner as a facility for storing goods.

warehouse, state bonded: a public warehouse, under government supervision, that has been licensed by a state prior to operation. Merchandise is stored there without payment of duties or taxes until it is withdrawn from the warehouse.

warehouse, U.S. Customs bonded: a federal warehouse where goods remain until duty has been collected from the importer. Goods under bond are also kept there.

warehouse, U.S. Internal Revenue: a public warehouse in which the owner of goods has posted a bond guaranteeing payment of internal revenue tax on U.S.-produced items.

warehouse customs bond: See *bond, warehouse customs.*

warehouse receipt: an instrument listing the goods or commodities deposited in a warehouse. It is a receipt for the commodities listed, for which the warehouse is the bailee. Warehouse receipts may be either nonnegotiable or negotiable.

warehouse stock: goods held in quantity in a warehouse for reasons of economy.

wares: items or commodities that are offered for sale.

warrant

(1) *securities:* a certificate giving the holder the right to purchase securities at a stipulated price within a specified time limit or at any time. Sometimes a warrant is offered with securities as an inducement to buy.

(2) *business law:* a written order, in the name of the state and signed by a magistrate, directing an officer to make an arrest.

warranty

(1) *business law:* a statement, either written, expressed, or implied, that a certain statement identified in a contract is true or will be true.

(2) *sales:* a promise by a seller that the product or property that is being sold is as he or she has represented it. Usually a warranty is presented with the sold goods. See also *caveat emptor, express warranty.*

(3) *insurance:* a statement in a policy of the existence of a fact or a condition of the subject of insurance that, if found to be untrue by misrepresentation, will void the policy.

warranty deed: a deed stating that a grantor is giving the grantee good title, free of debt. The most secure of deeds, it guarantees that the grantor will defend the title against any claims. It is a deed in full covenant. See also *perfect title.*

warranty price: the price established for a property that is deemed fair and just by both seller and buyer.

war theory: the concept that wars causing economic prosperity are followed by postwar depression.

wash sale: a spurious sale in which the seller becomes the purchaser of what he sells. The purpose is to create activity in the item or to establish a market price. A wash sale is prohibited by law.

wastage: wear of property or machinery; loss because of usage, deterioration, and so on.

waste circulation: advertising that is done in a location where there is no distribution for the advertised product.

wasting assets: assets whose value is depleted and will eventually be exhausted by the continued operations of an extractive business (e.g., oil wells, mining claims). See also *depletion allowance.*

wasting trust: a trust of property that is gradually being consumed.

watch filing: a procedure by which losses on small risks are referred to the underwriter for attention.

watered stock: corporate stock issued by a corporation for property at an overvaluation, or stock released for which the corporation receives nothing in payment.

Watergate: a new term used to describe corruption, deception, and/or coverup by individuals in power in their attempt to stay in power. The Watergate office building in Washington, D.C., was the scene in 1972 of a break-in to the Democratic Party National Headquarters.

waterlogged: a ship's condition of staying afloat only by the buoyancy of the cargo.

watermark: a distinctive mark or design produced in paper to identify the manufacturer.

wave wash: damage caused by severe wave action. A loss attributed to wave wash is not usually covered by insurance policies, except at a very high rate.

waybill: a statement identifying a shipment, showing the shipper, consignee, routing, rate, and weights. It is used by the carrier as an internal record.

way station: a stop along a route, especially in railroading.

weakest-link theory: the concept that the least durable component in a product will control its useful life. According to this theory, all components should be built so that their life span will be equal in all units of similar function and price. See also *functional obsolescence.*

weak market: a situation characterized by a greater demand for selling than for purchasing.

wealth: an economic term designating the value of a person's total possessions and rights in property. Cf. *national wealth.*

wealth effect: See *Pigou effect concept.*

wealth tax: an annual tax on a person's assets above a stated minimum, even if these assets which do not yield any income.

Webb-Pomerene Act of 1918: federal legislation exempting exporters' associations from antitrust regulations.

weekly compensation: See *average weekly benefit.*

weight, gross: the weight of a complete package that is ready for shipment, including the item, the inner and outer container, and any packaging materials. Cf. *tare.*

weight, net: the weight of an item alone, excluding packaging material or containers.

weight, tare: the weight of an item's container or packaging materials.

weight breaks: the levels at which the charges per 100 pounds decrease as the shipment increases in weight.

weighted application blank: a technique used to differentiate between successful and less successful employees through the use of application blank factors.

weighted average: a periodic inventory cost flow assumption whereby the cost of goods sold and the ending inventory are determined to be a weighted-average cost of all merchandise available for sale during the period.

weighted checklist: a method of appraisal in which the rater completes a form similar to the forced-choice performance, but the various responses have been assigned different weights.

Welfare and Pension Plans Disclosure Act of 1958: a federal law covering all nongovernmental welfare and pension plans that affect more than 25 employees. Administrators must file annual reports to the Secretary of Labor, describing annual financial statements. Synonymous with *Teller Act;* see also *Employee Retirement Income Security Act of 1974.*

welfare economics: a branch of economic theory that deals with the evolution of principles for maximizing social welfare.

welfare statism: a major characteristic of government whereby most social welfare activities are undertaken for its citizens.

wellhead tax: a government proposal to tax domestic oil as it leaves the well. The amount of the tax is the difference between its current controlled price and the world market price imposed by the OPEC cartel.

well rail car: a flat, open-platform freight car with a center opening.

well-tempered corporation: the corporation viewed as lying between the two extremes of the traditional corporation and the metrocorporation. This type of corporation takes public expectations into account, but with full regard for management's responsibilities to the stockholders. Its supporters hold that the claims of stockholders and creditors will more likely be met if a firm develops a position as a socially responsible company. Cf. *metrocorporation, traditional corporation.*

wetbacks: (slang) Mexican workers who enter this country without passports or visas to obtain employment, usually at substandard pay. The name derives from those who are said to swim or wade the Rio Grande to gain entry into Texas.

wet goods: liquids.

wet lease: a contractual aircraft leasing agreement whereby the lessor leases the craft and the personnel, fuel, and provisioning necessary to operate the plane.

WFTU: See *World Federation of Trade Unions.*

wharf: a structure that reaches out from the shoreline to a depth of water sufficient to hold ships. A wharf permits the loading or unloading of cargo or people.

wharfage: a charge levied against a vessel resting at a wharf. Synonymous with *dockage and moorage.*

Wheeler-Lea Act of 1938: federal legislation, amending the Federal Trade Commission Act of 1914, to protect the consumer against unfair trade practices in interestate commerce and against false or misleading advertising of foods, drugs, and cosmetics. See also *Consumer Product Safety Act.*

wheel of retailing: the theory that, when entering the market, new forms of retailing first emphasize lower prices but as time passes the prices rise, making the merchandise subject to competition from newer organizations, which commence operations with lower prices. See also *trading down, trading up.*

when issued: a short form of "when, as, and if issued," a term that indicates a conditional transaction in a security authorized for issuance but not yet actually issued. All "when-issued" transactions are on a conditional basis, to be settled if and when the actual security is issued and the exchange or the National Association of Securities Dealers rules that the transactions are to be settled.

whipsawed: to have experienced a substantial loss at both ends of a securities transaction.

white-collar: describing workers in offices and other nonproduction phases of industry. During the 1960s, white-collar personnel for the first time came to outnumber blue-collar workers.

white elephant: property that is so costly to maintain that it is virtually impossible to operate it at a profit; or property with respect to which a loss is certain.

white goods: appliances of substantial size and cost (e.g., refrigerators, freezers, washing machines, stoves).

white house: (slang) an employer's residence.

white knight: in order to encourage a successful company takeover by another firm, a friendly bidder who is brought in to put down another bidder. Cf. *gray knight.*

whole coverage: any type of insurance that provides for payment from all losses without any deductions.

whole life: Synonymous with *ordinary life.*

wholesale: to sell goods in gross to retailers, who then sell the merchandise to customers.

wholesale price: the price for a good that is paid by retailers to suppliers.

wholesale price index: a measure compiled by the U.S. Bureau of Labor Statistics, showing the average change in the price of approximately 2200 commodities at the primary market level (usually the level at which the commodity is first sold commercially in substantial volume) compared to the average level in selected base years.

wholesaler: an individual who buys and sells goods to retailers and other users but does not sell in significant amounts to the consumer. Cf. *merchant wholesaler;* see also *full-service wholesaler.*

wholesaling: selling merchandise to firms that purchase for reasons other than consumption, usually to resell the items for profit. See also *merchandise mart.*

wide opening: a securities situation characterized by a considerable difference in the bid and asked prices at the beginning of the market day.

wider environment: the aspects of an organization's environment that are outside the task environment.

wildcat bank: one of the unsound banks chartered by the states during the hectic banking years between 1816 and 1863. Most of these banks failed.

wildcat strike: See *strike.*

will: a document in which an individual (the testator or testatrix), having full mental faculties, sets forth his or her desires and bequests regarding the disposition of his or her total wealth after death. Cf. *nuncupative will.*

Williams Act of 1968: See *Saturday night special.*

windfall profit: an unexpected profit arising from causes that were not controlled by the recipient.

winding up: the process of liquidating a company.

window dressing: statements that appear to be more positive than warranted; statements that make something appear better than it is. See also *painting the bus.*

win (one's) spurs: (slang) to arrive at a level of acceptance by one's co-workers; to become a skilled worker or professional.

wired in: (slang) having knowledge or information that is not known to others in the organization.

wire house: a member firm of an exchange that maintains a communications network either linking its own branch offices to offices of correspondent firms or linking some combination of such offices.

with all faults: without a guarantee of the absence of imperfections, usually in real estate transactions; as is.

withholding tax: federal, state, or city taxes that are withheld by employers from the salaries of employees and paid directly to the taxing agency.

without dividend: Synonymous with *ex-dividend.*

without recourse

(1) *finance:* a term used in endorsing a negotiable instrument when the endorser of a note is no longer responsible, should the obligation not be paid. See also *qualified endorsement.*

(2) *sales:* an agreement that the purchaser accepts all risks in the transaction and gives up all rights of recourse. See also *caveat emptor.*

with recourse

(1) *finance:* a term used in endorsing a negotiable instrument when the endorser of a note continues to be responsible, should the obligation not be paid.

(2) *sales:* an agreement that if the seller is unable to meet his or her obligations, the purchaser has the right to endorse a claim against the seller for sustained damages.

wobblies: See *Industrial Workers of the World.*

wolf: an experienced and often crafty speculator.

word:

(1) *computers:* a character string or a bit string considered as an entity.

(2) *computers:* a unit of data or a set of characters of any length that occupies only one storage location.

word length: a measure of the size of a word, usually specified in units such as characters or binary digits.

word processing: the dissemination of all written material in an office. A word-processing center is a department equipped with media typewriters and staffed with trained operators who process large volumes of material to be typed, recorded, stored, and retrieved.

word time: in a storage device that provides serial access to storage locations, the time interval between the appearance of corresponding parts of successive words. See also *response time.*

workaholic: an individual who desires to work constantly.

work audit: Synonymous with *desk audit.*

workers' surplus: the excess of revenues over costs in a Soviet enterprise. The workers' surplus is used to purchase housing, recreational facilities, and the like, for the benefit of the employees of an enterprise.

work ethic: a belief in the inherent value of work in a society.

workfare: a recently introduced concept authorizing state and local officials to require that welfare recipients perform any kind of work assigned to them as a condition of getting welfare checks. See also *wage stop.*

work flow: the sequence of jobs in an organization needed to produce the firm's goods or services.

work force: See *labor force.*

work group: the group of employees formally assigned to perform a specific task or function.

working capital: the excess of current assets over current liabilities, representing the capital immediately available for the continued operation of a business.

working capital turnover: a measure of the amount of working capital used in sustaining the sales of a period, computed by dividing net sales by average working capital.

working control: theoretically, ownership of 51 percent of a company's voting stock—thus a controlling interest. In practice, however—and this is particularly true in the case of a large corporation—effective (i.e., working) control sometimes can be exerted through ownership, individually or by a group acting in concert, of less than 50 percent of the stock.

working poor: marginal employees whose skills and jobs do not provide them with an income above the poverty index.

working storage: a portion of a computer's internal storage that is reserved for specific functions such as input and output areas.

work-in-process inventory: all products that have begun the manufacturing process but have not been completed. Work-in-process inventory is the cost of partially completed production. Cf. *finished-goods inventory.*

workload: a quantitative measure of the amount of work performed, measured by the hour or by day.

workload analysis: Synonymous with *personnel demand analysis.*

work measurement: Synonymous with *time study.*

workmens' compensation: a system for compensating workers who are injured or disabled on the job. Workmens' compensation programs are established by state law and differ widely. Typically, benefits are paid under private insurance policies, but awards are determined by state boards. Cf. *state disability plan, temporary disability temporary total disability benefits;* see also *average benefits, weekly benefits.*

work overload: a situation in which someone has too much to do (quantitative overload) or someone does not have the necessary skills to perform the job (qualitative overload). Cf. *work underload.*

work place politics: organization members intentionally seeking selfish goals that conflict with those of others in the organization.

work rules: usually part of a union contract, rules that regulate on-the-job working conditions, to protect employees from arbitrary employer action, to ensure decent conditions and health standards, and often to prescribe a code of conduct for the workers.

work sampling: random observation of work activities, processes, or operations.

work sharing: distribution of work evenly among employees to prevent layoffs during slack periods. See also *share-the-work.*

work simplification: a reorganization of methods, equipment, resources, and working conditions to minimize worker fatigue and increase worker efficiency and output.

work stoppages: strikes or lockouts that involve six or more workers and extend to a full work shift or longer.

work title: a distinctive, designative, but usually unofficial name or title given to a work activity, process, or operation.

work underload: a situation in which someone has too little to do (quantitative underload) or someone has many more skills than are necessary to perform the job (qualitative underload). Cf. *work overload.*

work unit: the smallest subdivision of a job or operation.

workweek: the scheduled number of working hours for a week or for any seven-day period of work.

World Bank: See *International Bank for Reconstruction and Development.*

World Federation of Trade Unions (WF-TU): an international group of labor organizations dominated by the Communist trade unions. The CIO was a member of the WFTU but left in 1949 in opposition to its policies.

worldwide coverage: insurance coverage of all goods (e.g., jewelry, furs) throughout the world.

worldwide product division: a structure in which each product unit is given international responsibilities.

worth: the total value of something, including an investment in a business. See also *net worth.*

wrapper: the sheet of flexible material (paper, foil, etc.) or lamination used to cover a product for storage, sale, or shipment.

wrap-up: (slang) a customer who buys readily.

writ: a written instrument, under a state's seal and issued by a court, directing an officer of the court to do some act or enjoining an individual to do or refrain from doing some act.

write
(1) *computers:* to record data in a storage device or a data medium.
(2) *insurance:* to insure or to underwrite.
(3) *insurance:* sometimes, to sell insurance.

write-down: the book value to which an asset has been reduced to adjust for the capital that has been lost on a decline of the asset's value.

write-off: an asset that has been determined to be uncollectible and therefore has been charged off as a loss. Sometimes it is the debt itself. Cf. *written-down value.*

writer: the seller of an option contract.

write-up:
(1) *accounting:* an increase in an asset's book value that does not result from added costs, or an adjustment of an asset account to correspond to an appraisal value.
(2) *sales:* documentation of the making of a sale.

writ of entry: a legal action to regain possession of property once a party has been removed from the premises: See *ejectment, evicition, right of possession, seisin.*

written-down value: an accounting term for the valuation or cost of any asset minus the written-off depreciation.

XD: a symbol in a newspaper listing of stock prices indicating that a stock is ex dividend.

x-off: transmitter off.
x-on: transmitter on.

Yankee bond market: issues floated in the United States, in dollars, by foreign governments and corporations.

yard: a place where railway cars or locomotives are stored and made ready for use.

yard horse (mule): a tractor used for transporting trailers in a terminal yard.

yellow-dog contract: an individual agreement between an employer and an employee that, as a condition of employment, the latter, will not join a union. This form of unfair labor practice was declared unenforceable by the Norris–LaGuardia Act.

yes-man: (slang) an employee who constantly agrees with his superior.

yes-no controls: controls that allow for a screening process point at which specific approval is needed to permit the activity to continue.

yield

(1) *real estate:* the profit or income created through an investment in property.

(2) *finance:* to give up possession; to pay.

(3) *government:* the net return of a tax.

(4) *finance:* the rate of return received from an investment in a specific security or a specific piece of property, most commonly expressed in terms that designate the annual rate of return on the investment. Synonymous with return; See also *ROI.*

yield to maturity: the rate of return on an investment when it is retained until maturity, given as a percentage.

youth market: people under 25 years of age, who are often interested in goods and services that are different, unusual, or suggest values other than those held by older people.

yo-yo stocks: highly volatile securities. These stocks are high-priced specialty issues that fluctuate greatly in price.

Z

ZBB: See *zero-base budgeting.*

zero balance: See *balance of account.*

zero-balance account: a practice, currently illegal, involving the establishment by commercial banks of a demand deposit account and a savings account for the same customer, with the understanding that funds would not be allowed to remain idle in the demand deposit account. Deposits to the demand account would be transferred into the savings account, and funds would be transferred (for a service charge) automatically by the bank from the savings account to the demand account to cover checks written on the demand account.

zero-base budgeting (ZBB)

(1) *accounting and budgeting:* a financial management technique to redirect funds from lower-priority current programs to higher ones to pinpoint opportunities for improved efficiency and effectiveness, to reduce budgets while raising operating performance, and to improve profitability. See also *planning-programming-budgeting.*

(2) *government:* the approach of justifying the budget and its program for each year or two, instead of studying funding increases or decreases in the programs separately as the need arises.

zero-base media planning: a media selection process that involves (1) listing and ranking media objectives in order of importance; (2) examining and ranking possible media components in terms of their compatibility with the stated media objectives; (3) forming decision packages (i.e., plans consisting of one or more of these components); (4) comparing the decision packages with other packages that are retained and compatible with objectives; and (5) reviewing, making tradeoffs, and arriving at resolution of the plan.

zero defects: describing an approach to reward employees who make no mistakes and waste no resources while discharging their function over a given period.

zero floor limit: See *floor limit*.

zero-plus tick: See *up tick*.

zero proof: a mechanical method of posting records in a manner serving to prove that the previous balance on each line of posting was made correctly.

zero-sum situation: a competitive situation in which resources are fixed so that when one group succeeds, the other group must fail.

zero suppression: the elimination of nonsignificant zeros in a numeral.

ZIP code: in the Zoning Improvement Plan, a five-digit code that identifies every individual post office and metropolitan area delivery station in the United States. ZIP-coded mail can be processed more rapidly by postal service automated equipment than noncoded mail.

zipper clause: a standard clause in a negotiated contract that represents an attempt to preclude any discussion of contract conditions during the life of the agreement. The clause states that the agreement is the sole and complete instrument between the two parties. Cf. *reopener clause*.

zone of indifference: a category of subordinates' attitudes toward authority in which certain orders are accepted without question.

zoning ordinance: a municipal ordinance to regulate and prescribe the types of buildings, residences, or commercial structures that can be built and used in different sections of a city. See also *setback, variance*.

zoning price: the result of a policy of separating a total marketing area into areas (zones) for which different prices are established. All buyers in a zone pay the same price. See also *market segmentation*.

Appendix A.   A Table of Equivalents, Including Measures of Area (or Surface), Capacity, Length, Volume, and Weight

The order of information in each entry is the *unit* of measure, its *abbreviation,** the *kind* of measure, and the *equivalents.*

acre.—**; area; 10 square surveyor's chains, 160 square rods, 4840 square yards, 43,560 square feet, 0.40469 hectare, 40.4687 ares, 4,046.8726 square meters

angstrom. A; length; 0.0000001 millimeter (10^{-10}meter), 0.0001 micron, 0.1 millimicron, 0.000000004 inch

are. a.; area; 119.5989 square yards, 1076.387 square feet, 0.02471 acre, 1 square decameter, 100 square meters

barleycorn.—; length, 0.33 inch, 8.5 millimeter

barrel, dry, for most fruits, vegetables, and other dry commodities, except cranberries. dry bbl; capacity; 7056 cubic inches, 105 dry quarts, 3.281 bushels, 115.62 liters

barrel, dry, for cranberries. dry bbl; capacity; 5826 cubic inches, $86^{45}/_{64}$ dry quarts, 2.709 bushels, 95.47 liters

barrel, liquid. lq bbl; capacity; 31.5 gallons, 119.237 liters

barrel, petroleum. bbl; capacity; 42 gallons (U.S.), 34.97 gallons (imperial), 158.9 liters, 0.15899 cubic meters

barrel, U.S., beef, pork, fish. bbl; weight; 200 pounds, 90.72 kilograms

barrel, U.S., flour. bbl; weight; 196 pounds, 88.90 kilograms

barrel, U.S., cement. bbl; weight; 376 pounds, 170.55 kilograms

barrel, U.S. lime, small. bbl; weight; 180 pounds, 81.65 kilograms

barrel, U.S., lime, large. bbl; weight; 280 pounds, 127.01 kilograms

board foot. bd ft; volume; 144 cubic inches (12 in. × 12 in. × 1 in.)

bolt (cloth).—; length; 40 yards

bolt (wallpaper).—; length; 16 yards

bushel, British, struck measure. bu; capacity; 1.0320 U.S. bushels, struck measure, 33.026 U.S. dry quarts, 2,219.36 cubic inches

bushel, U.S., struck measure. bu; capacity; 32 dry quarts, 4 pecks, 2,150.42 cubic inches, 35.2383 liters

bushel, U.S., heaped. bu; capacity; 1.278 U.S. bushels, struck measure (also commonly regarded as 1¼ bushels, struck measure), 2/747.715 cubic inches

bushel. bu; weight; a wide variety of legal weights for different commodities in different states

butt.—; capacity; 2 hogsheads, 126 U.S. gallons

cable's length, U.S. Navy.—; nautical; 120 fathoms, 720 feet, 219.456 meters

cable's length, marine measure.—; nautical; 100–120 fathoms, 600–720 feet, 182.88–219.456 meters

carat. c; precious stones; 3.0865 grains troy, 200 milligrams

cental.—; weight; 100 pounds, 45.36 kilograms

centare or centiare. ca; area; 1.196 square yards, 10.764 square feet, 1 square meter, 0.01 are

centigram. cg; weight; 0.15432 grain, 0.01 gram

centiliter. cl; capacity; 0.3381 fluid ounce, 0.01 liter; volume, 0.6102 cubic inch

centimeter. cm; length; 0.39370 inch, 0.01 meter, 10 millimeters

centistere.—; volume; 0.353 cubic foot, 0.01 cubic meter

chain, engineer's. ch; length; 100 feet, 30.48 meters

chain, Gunter's or surveyor's. ch; length; 100 surveyor's links, 4 rods, 22 yards, 66 feet, 20.117 meters

cord. cd; volume; 128 cubic feet (usually arranged 8 ft long, 4 ft high, 4 wide), 8 cord feet, 3.625 cubic meters

cord foot. cd ft; volume; ⅛ cord, 16 cubic feet

cubic centimeter. cm³; capacity; 0.0610 cubic inch, 0.000001 cubic meter, 0.001 cubic decimeter, 1 millimeter (precisely, 1 millimeter = 1.000027 cubic centimeters)

cubic decameter. dkm³; volume; 1,307.942 cubic yards, 1000 cubic meters

cubic decimeter. dm³; volume; 61.023 cubic inches, 0.001 cubic meter, 1 liter (precisely, 1 liter = 1.000027 cubic decimeters)

cubic foot, ft³; volume; 1728 cubic inches, 0.037 cubic yards, 28.317 cubic decimeters, 0.0283 cubic meter; capacity; 7.481 gallons, 60 liquid pints, 28.316 liters

cubic hectometer. hm³; volume; 1,000,000 cubic meters

cubic inch. in.³; volume; 0.000579 cubic foot, or ¹⁄₁₇₂₈ cubic foot, 16.387 cubic centimeters. capacity; 0.0173 liquid quart, 0.554 fluid ounce, 4.433 fluid drams, 0.0164 liter

cubic kilometer. km³; volume; 1,000,000,000 cubic meters

cubic meter. m³; volume; 1.3079 cubic yards, 35.31445 cubic feet, 61,023.38 cubic inches, 1,000 cubic decimeters. capacity; 264.1776 gallons, 1000 liters

cubic millimeter. mm³; volume; 0.00006 cubic inch, 0.001 cubic centimeter

cubic yard. yd³; volume; 27 cubic feet, 46,656 cubic inches, 0.76456 cubic meter

cubit.—; length; 18 inches

decagram. dkg; weight; 0.35274 ounce, avoirdupois, 0.32151 ounce, apothecaries or troy, 10 grams

decaliter. dkl; capacity; 2.6418 gallons, 10.5671 liquid quarts, 10 liters. volume; 0.284 bushel, 1.1351 pecks, 9.081 dry quarts, 610.25 cubic inches

decameter. dkm; length; 10.9361 yards,

32.8083 feet, 393.7 inches, 10 meters

decare.—; area; 0.2471 acre, 10 ares

decastere. dks; volume; 13.08 cubic yards, 353.15 cubic feet, 10 cubic meters, 10 steres

deciare.—; area; 11.96 square yards, 0.1 are, 10 square meters

decigram. dg; weight; 0.003527, 1.5432 grains, 0.1 gram

deciliter. dl; capacity; 0.1816 dry pint, 0.211 liquid pint, 0.8454 gill, 3.38147 fluid ounces, 0.1 liter; volume; 6.1025 cubic inches

decimeter. dm; length; 0.328 foot, 3.937 inches, 0.1 meter, 10 centimeters

decistere, ds; volume; 3.5315 cubic feet, 0.1 cubic meter, 0.1 stere

digit.—; length, 0.75 inch

dozen. doz.; count; 12 items

dram, apothecaries'. dr ap; weight; 2.1943 dram, avoirdupois, 0.125 apothecaries' ounce, 2.5 pennyweights, 3 scruples, 60 grains, 3.888 grams

dram, avoirdupois. dr avdp; weight; 0.4558 dram, apothecaries, 0.0625 avoirdupois ounce, 1.1393 pennyweights, 1.3672 scruples, 27.344 grains, 1.7718 grams

dram, fluid or liquid, British. fl dr; capacity; 0.9607 fluid dram, U.S., 0.125 fluid ounce, British, 60 minims, British, 0.2167 cubic inch, 3.5514 milliliters

dram, fluid or liquid, U.S. fl dr; capacity; 0.03125 gill, 0.125 fluid ounce, U.S., 60 minims, U.S., 0.2256 cubic inch, 3.6966 milliliters

ell, English.—; cloth, length; $\frac{1}{32}$ bolt, 45 inches

em, pica.—; printing; $\frac{1}{6}$ inch by $\frac{1}{6}$ inch

fathom. fath.; depth; 6 feet, 8 spans, 1.829 meters

finger.—; length; 0.125 yard, 4.5 inches. width; 0.25 hand, 0.75 to 1 inch

foot. ft; length; 0.333 yard, 1.515 links 12 inches, 0.3048006 meter

furlong. fur; length; 0.125 statute mile, 10 chains, 40 rods, 220 yards, 660 feet, 201.168 meters

gallon, British or imperial. gal; capacity; 1.20094 U.S. gallons, 4 British quarts, 8 British pints, 160 British fluid ounces, 277.42 cubic inches, 4.5460 liters

gallon, U.S. gal; capacity; 0.83268 British gallons, 4 quarts, 8 pints, 32 gills, 128 fluid ounces, 231 cubic inches, 3.7853 liters

gill, British. gi; capacity; 1.20094 U.S. gills, $\frac{1}{8}$ British quart, $\frac{1}{4}$ British pint, 8.6694 cubic inches, 0.1421 liter

gill, U.S. gi; capacity; 0.83268 British gill, $\frac{1}{8}$ liquid quart, $\frac{1}{4}$ liquid pint, 4 fluid ounces, 32 fluid drams, 7.2188 cubic inches, 0.1183 liter

grain.—; weight; $\frac{1}{5760}$ troy pound, $\frac{1}{7000}$ avoirdupois pound, 0.01666 apothecaries dram, 0.03657 avoirdupois dram, 0.05 scruple, 0.0648 gram, 64.799 milligrams

gram. g; weight; 0.03215 apothecaries ounce, 0.03527 avoirdupois ounce, 0.2572 apothecaries' dram, 0.5644 avoirdupois dram, 15.432 grains

great gross, g gr; count; 12 gross

gross. gr; count; 12 dozen items

hairsbreadth.—; width; $\frac{1}{4}$ line, $\frac{1}{48}$ inch

hand.—; length or height; 4 inches, 10.16 centimeters

hectare. ha; area; 2.471 acres, 395.367 square rods, 1 square hectometer, 100 ares, 10,000 square meters

hectogram. hg; weight; 3.5274 ounces, 0.1 kilogram, 100 grams

hectoliter. hl; capacity; 2 bushels and 3.35 pecks, or 2.838 bushels, 26.418 gallons, 100 liters. volume; 6102.5 cubic inches, 0.1 cubic meter

hectometer. hm; length; 109.361 yards,

328 feet and 1 inch, or 328.083 feet, 10 decameters, 100 meters

hectostere.—; volume; 130.794 cubic yards, 3531.445 cubic feet, 100 cubic meters, 100 steres

hogshead, British. hhd; capacity; 52.4 British or imperial gallons, 238.476 liters

hogshead, U.S. hhd; capacity; $\frac{1}{2}$ butt, 63 U.S. gallons, 2 liquid barrels, 238.476 liters

hundredweight, gross or long. gross cwt or l. cwt; weight; 112 pounds, 50.802 kilograms

hundredweight, net or short. cwt, or sh. cwt; weight; 100 pounds, 45.359 kilograms

inch. in.; length; $\frac{1}{12}$ foot, 1000 mils, 2.540 centimeters, 25.40 millimeters

iron.—; shoe leather; $\frac{1}{48}$ inch

keg, nail.—; weight; 100 pounds, 45.359 kilograms

kilogram. kg; weight; 2.2046 avoirdupois pounds, 2.6792 apothecaries' pounds, 1000 grams

kiloliter. kl; capacity; 28.378 bushels, 264.18 gallons, 1000 liters. volume; 1.308 cubic yards, 35.315 cubic feet

kilometer. km; length; 0.621370 mile, 1093.611 yards, 3280 feet and 10 inches, or 3280.83 feet, 1000 meters

kilostere.—; volume; 1,308 cubic yards, 1000 cubic meters, 1000 steres

knot. k; speed; one nautical mile per hour (*see* mile, nautical)

league. l; length; 3 statute miles, 4.82805 kilometers

league, marine. l; length; 3 nautical miles, 3.45 statute miles, 5.56 kilometers

line. l; printing; $\frac{1}{12}$ inch (0.0833), 2.12 millimeters. button; $\frac{1}{40}$ inch

link, engineer's. li; length; $\frac{1}{100}$ chain, 12 inches, 0.3048 meter

link, Gunter's or surveyor's. li; length; $\frac{1}{100}$ chain, 0.66 ft, 7.92 inches, 0.2012 meter

liter. l; capacity; 1.0567 liquid quarts, 0.9081 dry quart, 61.0250 cubic inches, 1 cubic decimeter (precisely, 1.000027 cubic decimeters)

meter. m; length; 1.093611 yards, 3.280833 feet, 39.37 inches, 10 decimeters, 100 centimeters

metric ton. *see* **millier**

micron. μ; length; 0.00003937 inch, 0.03937 mil, 0.001 millimeter

mil.—; wire, length; 0.001 inch, 0.0254 millimeter

mile, nautical or admiralty, British.—; length; 6080 feet, 1.8532 kilometers

mile, nautical, geographical or sea, U.S.—; length; 1.0007 nautical miles, international, 1.1515 statute miles, 6080.20 feet, 1.853248 kilometers

mile, nautical, International Hydrographic Bureau.—; length; 0.999 U.S. nautical mile, 1.151 statute miles, 6076.10 feet, 1.852 kilometers

mile, statute or land.—; length; 0.868 U.S. nautical mile, 8 furlongs, 80 chains, 320 rods or poles, 1760 yards, 5280 feet, 1.6093 kilometers, 1609.3472 meters

millier. t; weight; 0.98421 long ton, 1.1023 short tons, 2204.622 pounds avoirdupois, 2679.23 pounds troy, 1,000 kilograms, 1 metric ton

milligram. mg; weight; 0.01543 grain, 0.001 gram

milliliter. ml; capacity; 0.27052 fluid dram, 16.231 minims, 0.001 liter. volume; 0.06102 cubic inch, 1 cubic centimeter (precisely, 1.000027 cubic centimeters)

millimeter. mm; length; 0.03937 inch, 0.001 meter

millimicron. mμ; length; 0.001 micron, 0.00003937 mil, 0.00000003937 inch

minim, British. min; capacity; 0.96073

U.S. minim, 0.05919 milliliter

minim, U.S. min; capacity; $\frac{1}{60}$ fluid dram, 0.00376 cubic inch, 0.06161 milliliter

myriagram.—; weight; 22.046 pounds, 10 kilograms, 10,000 grams

myriameter.—; length; 6.2137 miles, 10 kilometers

nail.—; cloth, length; $\frac{1}{16}$ yard, $\frac{1}{4}$ span, 2.25 inches, 5.715 centimeters

ounce, avoirdupois. oz advp; weight; 0.911 troy or apothecaries ounce, $\frac{1}{16}$ avoirdupois pound, 16 avoirdupois drams, 437.5 grains, 28.3495 grams

ounce, fluid, British. fl oz; capacity; 0.96073 U.S. fluid ounce, 1.734 cubic inches, 28.4130 cubic centimeters, 28.4122 milliliters

ounce, fluid, U.S. fl oz; capacity; 1.041 British fluid ounces, $\frac{1}{32}$ liquid quart, $\frac{1}{16}$ liquid pint, $\frac{1}{4}$ gill, 8 fluid drams, 480 minims, 29.5737 cubic centimeters, 29.5729 milliliters

ounce, troy or apothecaries'. oz t, or oz ap; weight; 1.0971 avoirdupois ounces, 0.0833 troy or apothecaries' pound, 8 apothecaries' drams, 20 pennyweights, 24 scruples, 480 grains, 31.1035 grams

pace, common.—; length; 2.5, 3, or 3.3 feet

pace, military, double time.—; length; 36 inches

pace, military, quick time.—; length; 30 inches

palm.—; length; 7–9 inches. width; 3 inches

peck, British. pk; capacity; 1.0320 U.S. pecks; 554.84 cubic inches, 9.0919 liters

peck, U.S. pk; capacity; $\frac{1}{4}$ bushel, 8 dry quarts, 16 dry pints, 537.605 cubic inches, 8.8096 liters

pennyweight. dwt; weight; 0.05 troy or apothecaries' ounce, 0.4 apotheca-

ries' dram, 1.2 scruples, 24 grains, 1.5552 grams

perch. *see* rod

pint, dry, U.S. dry pt; capacity; $\frac{1}{16}$ peck, $\frac{1}{2}$ dry quart, 33.60 cubic inches, 0.5506 liter

pint, liquid, British. liq pt; capacity; 1.0320 U.S. dry pints, 1.2009 U.S. liquid pints, 20 fluid ounces, 34.6775 cubic inches, 0.5682 liters

pint, liquid, U.S. liq pt; capacity; 0.5 liquid quart, 4 gills, 16 fluid ounces, 128 fluid drams, 28.875 cubic inches, 0.47317 liters

pipe.—; capacity; $\frac{1}{2}$ tun, 2 hogsheads, 126 gallons, 476.952 liters

point. pt; printing; $\frac{1}{6}$ line, 0.013837 inch (nearly $\frac{1}{72}$ inch), 0.351 millimeter

pole. p; *see* rod

pound, avoirdupois. lb advp; weight; 1.215 troy or apothecaries' pound, 16 avoirdupois ounces, 256 avoirdupois drams, 350 scruples, 7000 grains, 543.592 grams

pound, troy or apothecaries'. lb t, or lb ap; weight; 0.82286 avoirdupois pound, 12 apothecaries' or troy ounces, 96 apothecaries' or troy drams, 240 pennyweights, 288 scruples, 5760 grains, 373.242 grams

quart, British or imperial. qt or imp qt; capacity; 1.0320 U.S. dry quarts, 1.2009 U.S. liquid quarts, 2 British or imperial pints, 69.35 cubic inches, 1.1365 liters

quart, dry, U.S. dry qt; capacity; 0.969 British or imperial quart, $\frac{1}{8}$ peck, $\frac{1}{32}$ bushel, 2 U.S. dry pints, 67.201 cubic inches, 1.1012 liters

quart, liquid, U.S. liq qt; capacity; 0.833 British quart, $\frac{1}{4}$ gallon, 2 liquid pints, 8 gills, 57.75 cubic inches, 0.9463 liter

quarter. qtr; length; $\frac{1}{4}$ mile, 440 yards, 402.34 meters

quarter. qtr; cloth, length; $\frac{1}{4}$ yard, 1 span, 9 inches

quarter, dry, U.S.—; capacity; 8 bushels, 32 pecks

quarter, long ($\frac{1}{4}$ ton).—; weight; 560 pounds, 254.0 kilograms

quarter, long ($\frac{1}{2}$ hundredweight).—; weight; 28 pounds, 12.701 kilograms

quarter, short ($\frac{1}{4}$ ton).— weight; 500 pounds, 226.8 kilograms

quarter, short ($\frac{1}{4}$ hundredweight).—; weight; 25 pounds, 11.34 kilograms

quartern.—; volume; $\frac{1}{4}$ pint, 1 gill weight; $\frac{1}{4}$ stone, $3\frac{1}{2}$ pounds

quintal. q; weight; 1 hundredweight weight, metric; 220.46 pounds, 100 kilograms

rod.—; length; $\frac{1}{320}$ mile, $\frac{1}{40}$, chain, 5.5 yards, 16.5 feet, 25 links, 5.0292 meters

roll.—; wallpaper, length; 1 bolt (wallpaper), 16 yards

score.—; count; 20 items

scruple, apothecaries'. s ap; weight; 0.04166 apothecaries' ounce, 0.3333 apothecaries' dram, 20 grains, 1.2959 grams

section.—; area; $\frac{1}{36}$ township, 1 square mile, 640 acres, 2.59 square kilometers

span.—; length; $\frac{1}{8}$ fathom, 9 inches, 22.86 centimeters

square.—; building; 100 square feet, 9.29 square meters

square centimeter. cm²; area; 0.155 square inch, 0.0001 square meter, 100 square millimeters

square chain, surveyor's. ch²; area; 16 square rods, 484 square yards, 4,356 square feet, 10,000 square links, 404.687 square meters

square decameter. dkm²; area; 1 are, 155,000 square inches, 100 square meters, 1,000,000 square centimeters

square foot. ft²; area; $\frac{1}{9}$ square yard (0.1111 yd²), 144 square inches, 0.09290 square meter, 929.034 square centimeters

square furlong. fur²; area; 10 acres, 404.7 ares

square hectometer. hm²; area; 1 hectare

square inch. in².; area; $\frac{1}{1296}$ square yard, $\frac{1}{144}$ square foot, 6.4516 square centimeters

square kilometer. km²; area; 0.3861 square mile, 247.104 acres, 100 square hectometers, 10,000 ares, 1,000,000 square meters

square link. li², area; 0.0001 square chain, 0.0484 square yard, 0.4356 square foot, 62.7264 square inches, 0.04047 square meter

square meter. m²; area; 1.1960 square yards, 10.764 square feet, 0.01 are, 100 square decimeters

square mil. mil².; area; 0.000001 square inch, 0.000645 square millimeter

square mile. mi².; area; 640 acres, 6400 square chains, 102,400 square rods, 3,097,600 square yards, 27,878,400 square feet, 2.5899 square kilometers, 258.999 hectares

square millimeter. mm²; area; 0.00155 square inch, 0.01 sq. centimeter

square myriameter. myr²; area; 38.610 square miles, 100 square kilometers

square perch.—; area; *see* square rod

square pole. sq. p²; area; *see* square rod

square rod, pole, or perch. rd², area; acre, 30.25 square yards, 272.25 square feet, 625 square links, 25,293 square meters

square yard. yd².; area; 9 square feet, 1,296 square inches, 0.83613 square meter

stere. s; volume; 1.308 cubic yards, 35.314 cubic feet, 1 cubic meter

stone.—; weight; 14 pounds, 6.35 kilograms

tierce, liquid, U.S.—; capacity; $\frac{1}{3}$ pipe, 42 gallons, 159 liters

ton, gross or **long.** gross tn, 1. tn; weight; 1.016 metric tons or milliers, 1.12 short tons, 2,240 pounds, 1.016.05 kilograms

ton, metric.—; weight; 1 millier

ton, net or short. net tn, sh tn; weight; 0.89286 long ton, 0.90718 metric ton or millier, 2,000 pounds, 907.18 kilograms

tonneau.—; weight; 1 millier

township. twp; area; 36 square miles, 36 sections, 9324.0 ares

tun.—; capacity; 2 pipes, 4 hogsheads, 252 gallons, 953.9 liters

yard. yd; length; 3 feet, 36 inches, 0.9144 meter

Appendix B. Celsius and Fahrenheit Equivalents

Celsius	Fahrenheit	Celsius	Fahrenheit	Celsius	Fahrenheit	Celsius	Fahrenheit
0	32.0	25	77.0	50	122.0	75	167.0
1	33.8	26	78.8	51	123.8	76	168.8
2	35.6	27	80.6	52	125.6	77	170.6
3	37.4	28	82.4	53	127.4	78	172.4
4	39.2	29	84.2	54	129.2	79	174.2
5	41.0	30	86.0	55	131.0	80	176.0
6	42.8	31	87.8	56	132.8	81	177.8
7	44.6	32	89.6	57	134.6	82	179.6
8	46.4	33	91.4	58	136.4	83	181.4
9	48.2	34	93.2	59	138.2	84	183.2
10	50.0	35	95.0	60	140.0	85	185.0
11	51.8	36	96.8	61	141.8	86	186.8
12	53.6	37	98.6	62	143.6	87	188.6
13	55.4	38	100.4	63	145.4	88	190.4
14	57.2	39	102.2	64	147.2	89	192.2
15	59.0	40	104.0	65	149.0	90	194.0
16	60.8	41	105.8	66	150.8	91	195.8
17	62.6	42	107.6	67	152.6	92	197.6
18	64.4	43	109.4	68	154.4	93	199.4
19	66.2	44	111.2	69	156.2	94	201.2
20	68.0	45	113.0	70	158.0	95	203.0
21	69.8	46	114.8	71	159.8	96	204.8
22	71.6	47	116.6	72	161.6	97	206.6
23	73.4	48	118.4	73	163.4	98	208.4
24	75.2	49	120.2	74	165.2	99	210.2
						100	212.0

Appendix C.   Metric Conversion Tables

Basic Metric Units

Weight			Length		
1 kilogram	=	1000 grams	1 kilometer	=	1000 meters
1 hectogram	=	100 grams	1 hectometer	=	100 meters
1 decagram	=	10 grams	1 decameter	=	10 meters
1 gram	=	1 gram	1 meter	=	1 meter
1 decigram	=	0.1 gram	1 decimeter	=	0.1 meter
1 centigram	=	0.01 gram	1 centimeter	=	0.01 meter
1 milligram	=	0.001 gram	1 millimeter	=	0.001 meter

Volume

1 hectoliter	=	100 liters	1 deciliter	=	0.1 liter
1 decaliter	=	10 liters	1 centiliter	=	0.01 liter
1 liter	=	1 liter	1 millilitier	=	0.001 liter

Temperature[a]

0	°C	=	freezing point of water (32 °F)
10	°C	=	a warm winter day (50 °F)
20	°C	=	a mild spring day (68 °F)
30	°C	=	quite warm—almost hot (86 °F)
37	°C	=	normal body temperature (98.6 °F)
40	°C	=	heatwave conditions (104 °F)
100	°C	=	boiling point of water (212 °F)

[a]Prefixes are not commonly used with temperature measurements as they are with those for weight, length, and volume. Temperatures in degrees Celsius (often referred to as Centigrade), as in the familiar Fahrenheit system, can only be learned through experience. The points selected may help to orient you with regard to normally encountered temperatures.

Approximate Conversion Factors

To Metric Measures

Symbol	When You Know	Multiply by	To Find	Symbol
Length				
in.	inches	2.5	centimeters	cm
ft	feet	30	centimeters	cm
yd	yards	0.9	meters	m
mi	miles	1.6	kilometers	km
Area				
in.^{2}	square inches	6.5	square centimeters	cm^2
ft^2	square feet	0.09	square meters	m^2
yd^2	square yards	0.8	square meters	m^2
mi^2	square miles	2.6	square kilometers	km^2
	acres	0.4	hectares	ha

Approximate Conversion Factors (*Cont.*)

To Metric Measures

Symbol	When You Know	Multiply by	To Find	Symbol
Mass (Weight)				
oz	ounces	28	grams	g
lb	pounds	0.45	kilograms	kg
	short tons (2000 lb)	0.9	metric tons	t
Volume				
tsp	teaspoons	5	milliliters	ml
tbsp	tablespoons	15	milliliters	ml
fl oz	fluid ounces	30	milliliters	ml
c	cups	0.24	liters	l
pt	pints	0.47	liters	l
qt	quarts	0.95	liters	l
gal	gallons	3.8	liters	l
ft^3	cubic feet	0.03	cubic meters	m^3
yd^3	cubic yards	0.76	cubic meters	m^3
Temperature (exact)				
°F	Fahrenheit	5/9 (after subtracting 32)	Celsius temperature	°C

From Metric Measures

Symbol	When You Know	Multiply by	To Find	Symbol
Length				
mm	millimeters	0.04	inches	in.
cm	centimeters	0.4	inches	in.
m	meters	3.3	feet	ft
m	meters	1.1	yards	yd
km	kilometers	0.6	miles	mi
Area				
cm^2	square centimeters	0.16	square inches	$in.^2$
m^2	square meters	1.2	square yards	yd^2
km^2	square kilometers	0.4	square miles	mi^2
ha	hectares (10,000 m^2)	2.5	acres	
Mass (weight)				
g	grams	0.035	ounces	oz
kg	kilograms	2.2	pounds	lb
t	metric tons (1000 kg)	1.1	short tons	
Volume				
ml	milliliters	0.03	fluid ounces	fl oz
l	liters	2.1	pints	pt
l	liters	1.06	quarts	qt
l	liters	0.26	gallons	gal
m^3	cubic meters	35	cubic feet	ft^3
m^3	cubic meters	1.3	cubic yards	yd^3
Temperature (exact)				
°C	Celsius temperature	9/5 (then add 32)	Fahrenheit temperature	°F

Exact Conversion Factors

Linear Measures	Square Measures

1 inch
= 0.0245 meter
= 2.54 centimeters
1 foot
= 0.333 yard
= 12 inches
= 0.305 meter
1 yard
= 3 feet
= 36 inches
= 0.914 meter
1 meter
= 1.094 yards
= 3.281 feet
= 39.37 inches
= 0.001 kilometer
1 kilometer
= 1.000 meters
= 0.621 statute mile
·1 statute mile
= 1.760 yards
= 1.609 kilometers
1 nautical mile
= 6080 feet
= 1.15152 statute miles
= 1.853 kilometer

1 square inch
= 6.452 square centimeters
1 square foot
= 0.093 square meter
1 square yard
= 9 square feet
= 0.836 square meter
1 square meter
= 1.196 square yards
= 10.764 square feet
= 1550 square inches
1 acre
= 0.405 hectare
= 4.840 square yards
1 hectare
= 0.01 square kilometer
= 2.471 acres
1 square kilometer
= 0.386 square mile
= 100 hectares
1 square mile
= 2.590 square kilometers
= 640 acres
= 259 hectares

Cubic Measures

1 cubic inch
= 16.387 cubic centimeters
1 pint
= 0.5683 liter
1 liter
= 1.000 cubic centimeters
= 61.024 cubic inches
= 1.7597 pints
= 0.26417 U.S. gallon
= 0.21997 Imperial gallon
= 0.035314 cubic foot
1 hectoliter
= 100 liters
1 U.S. gallon
= 231 cubic inches
= 3.7854 liters
= 0.83268 Imperial gallon
= 0.133681 cubic foot
= 0.0238095 U.S. barrel
= 0.0037854 cubic meter

1 U.S. barrel
= 9702 cubic inches
= 158.99 liters
= 42 U.S. gallons
= 34.9726 Imperial gallons
= 5.6146 cubic feet
= 0.15899 cubic meter
1 Imperial gallon
= 277.42 cubic inches
= 4.5461 liters
= 0.160544 cubic foot
= 1.20094 U.S. gallons
= 0.02894 U.S. barrel
= 0.0045461 cubic meter
1 cubic foot
= 28.317 liters
= 7.4805 U.S. gallons
= 6.2288 Imperial gallons
= 0.17811 U.S. barrel
= 0.028317 cubic meter

Exact Conversion Factors (*Cont.*)

Cubic Measures

1 cubic meter
 = 35.315 cubic feet
 = 1000 liters
 = 264.17 U.S. gallons
 = 219.97 Imperial gallons
 = 6.2898 U.S. barrels
1 kiloliter
 = 1.000 liters
 = 6.2898 U.S. barrels

1 gross ton (shipping)
 = 100 cubic feet or 2.83 cubic meters
 of permanently enclosed space.
1 ton of liquefield methane
 = approximately 16 barrels
 = approximately 50,000 cubic feet
 (1400 cubic meters of natural gas,
 depending on methane content.)

Weights

Power and Heat Units

1 ounce
 = 28.35 grams
1 pound
 = 0.453592 kilogram
 = 0.009 hundredweight
1 kilogram
 = 2.20462 pounds
 = 0.01 quintal
1 hundredweight
 = 112 pounds
 = 50.802 kilograms
1 metric ton
 = 0.98421 long ton[a]
 = 1.10231 short tons[a]
 = 2204.6 pounds
1 English or long ton
 = 1.01605 metric tons[a]
 = 1.12 short tons[a]
 = 2240 pounds
1 short ton
 = 0.892857 long ton[a]
 = 0.907185 metric ton[a]
 = 2000 pounds

1 horsepower
 = 550 foot-pounds per second
 = 0.746 kilowatt
 = 1.014 PS (or *cheval vapeur*)
1 *Pferdestaerke* (PS) or *Cheval Vapeur* (CV)
 = 542 foot-pounds per second
 = 0.986 horsepower
 = 0.736 kilowatt
1 kilowatt
 = 1000 watts
 = 1.340 horsepower
 = 1.359 PS or CV
 = 737 foot-pounds per second
1 foot-pound per second
 = 0.00136 kilowatt
 = 0.00182 horsepower
 = 0.00184 PS or CV
1 therm
 = 100.000 Btu (British thermal units)
 = 25.200 kilocalories
 = 25.2 thermies
 = 29.3 kilowatt-hours
1.000 kilocalories (large calories)
 = 3968 Btu
 = 1.163 kilowatt-hours
 = 1 thermie
1 kilowatt-hour
 = 3411 Btu
 = 1.340 horsepower-hours
 = 859.6 kilocalories

[a]These conversions are based on the assumption that all weights are weights in air, which is the correct basis for computing bulk commercial quantities.

Appendix D. Roman Numerals

I = 1	X = 10	C = 100	M = 1000
II = 2	XX = 20	CC = 200	MD = 1500
III = 3	XXX = 30	CCC = 300	MM = 2000
IV = 4	XL = 40	CD = 400	MMM = 3000
V = 5	L = 50	D = 500	MMMM = 4000
			or
			$\overline{\text{MV}}$
VI = 6	LX = 60	DC = 600	
VII = 7	LXX = 70	DCC = 700	$\overline{\text{V}}$ = 5000
VIII = 8	LXXX = 80	DCCC = 800	$\overline{\text{M}}$ = 1,000,000
IX = 9	XC = 90	CM = 900	

When a letter is repeated, the value is repeated; thus XX = 20, III = 3, CCC = 300.

When a letter is followed by the same letter or a letter of less value, the values of the two letters are added; thus XI = 10 + 1 = 11.

When a letter is followed by a letter of greater value, the value of the lesser is subtracted from that of the greater; thus IX = 10 − 1 = 9.

A dash over a letter multiplies the value by 1000; thus $\overline{\text{X}}$ = 10,000; $\overline{\text{L}}$ = 50,000; $\overline{\text{C}}$ = 100,000; $\overline{\text{D}}$ = 500,000; $\overline{\text{M}}$ = 1,000,000; $\overline{\text{DCXIV}}$ = 614,000.

Appendix E.   Simple Interest Table

Showing at different rates the interest on $1 from 1 month to 1 year, and on $100 from 1 day to 1 year.

		3%	4%	5%	6%	7%	8%
$1.00	1 month	$.002	$.003	$.004	$.005	$.005	$.006
"	2 "	.005	.007	.008	.010	.011	.013
"	3 "	.008	.011	.013	.015	.017	.020
"	6 "	.015	.020	.025	.030	.035	.040
"	12 "	.030	.040	.050	.060	.070	.080
$100.00	1 day	.008	.011	.013	.016	.019	.022
"	2 "	.016	.022	.027	.032	.038	.044
"	3 "	.025	.034	.041	.050	.058	.067
"	4 "	.033	.045	.053	.066	.077	.089
"	5 "	.041	.056	.069	.082	.097	.111
"	6 "	.049	.067	.083	.110	.116	.133
"	1 month	.250	.334	.416	.500	.583	.667
"	2 "	.500	.667	.832	1.000	1.166	1.333
"	3 "	.750	1.000	1.250	1.500	1.750	2.000
"	6 "	1.500	2.000	2.500	3.000	3.500	4.000
"	12 "	3.000	4.000	5.000	6.000	7.000	8.000

Appendix F. Years in Which Given Amount Will Double at Several Rates of Interest

Rate	At Simple Interest	Compounded Yearly	Compounded Semi-annually	Compounded Quarterly
		At Compound Interest		
1	100 years	69.660	69.487	69.237
1½	66.66	46.556	46.382	46.297
2	50.00	35.003	34.830	34.743
2½	40.00	28.071	27.889	27.748
3	33.33	23.450	23.278	23.191
3½	28.57	20.149	19.977	19.890
4	25.00	17.673	17.501	17.415
4½	22.22	15.747	15.576	15.490
5	20.00	14.207	14.035	13.949
5½	18.18	12.942	12.775	12.689
6	16.67	11.896	11.725	11.639
6½	15.38	11.007	10.836	10.750
7	14.29	10.245	10.074	9.966
7½	13.38	9.584	9.414	9.328
8	12.50	9.006	8.837	8.751
8½	11.76	8.497	8.327	8.241
9	11.11	8.043	7.874	7.788
9½	10.52	7.638	7.468	7.383
10	10.00	7.273	7.103	7.018
12	8.34	6.116	5.948	5.862

Appendix G.   Compound Interest Table: Interest Compounded Seminannually

Years	1%	2%	3%	4%	4½%	5%	6%	7%	8%	10%
1	$1.0100	$1.0201	$1.0302	$1.0404	$1.0455	$1.0506	$1.0609	$1.0712	$1.0816	$1.1025
2	1.0201	1.0406	1.0613	1.0824	1.0930	1.1028	1.1255	1.1475	1.1692	1.2155
3	1.0303	1.0615	1.0934	1.1261	1.1438	1.1596	1.1940	1.2292	1.2646	1.3400
4	1.0407	1.0828	1.1264	1.1715	1.1948	1.2184	1.2667	1.3168	1.3678	1.4773
5	1.0511	1.1045	1.1605	1.2188	1.2481	1.2800	1.3439	1.4105	1.4794	1.6287
6	1.0616	1.1267	1.1956	1.2681	1.3004	1.3448	1.4257	1.5110	1.6002	1.7957
7	1.0723	1.1494	1.2317	1.3193	1.3643	1.4129	1.5125	1.6186	1.7307	1.9747
8	1.0830	1.1725	1.2689	1.3726	1.4264	1.4845	1.6047	1.7339	1.8720	2.1827
9	1.0949	1.1961	1.3073	1.4281	1.4913	1.5596	1.7024	1.8574	2.0247	2.4064
10	1.1059	1.2201	1.3463	1.4858	1.5592	1.6385	1.8061	1.9897	2.1899	2.6530
11	1.1170	1.2446	1.3875	1.5458	1.6301	1.7234	1.9161	2.1315	2.3687	2.9250
12	1.1281	1.2696	1.4295	1.6082	1.7044	1.8086	2.0326	2.2833	2.5619	3.2248
13	1.1394	1.2952	1.4727	1.6732	1.7820	1.9001	2.1564	2.4459	2.7710	3.5553
14	1.1508	1.3212	1.5172	1.7408	1.8631	1.9963	2.2878	2.6201	2.9971	3.9198
15	1.1623	1.3478	1.5630	1.8111	1.9479	2.0933	2.4271	2.8068	3.2417	4.3216
16	1.1740	1.3748	1.6103	1.8843	2.0365	2.2027	2.5749	3.0067	3.5062	4.7645
17	1.1857	1.4025	1.6589	1.9604	2.1272	2.3142	2.7317	3.2208	3.7923	5.2529
18	1.1976	1.4307	1.7091	2.0396	2.2240	2.4313	2.8981	3.4502	4.1018	5.7883
19	1.2096	1.4594	1.7607	2.1220	2.3252	2.5544	3.0746	3.6960	4.4365	6.3816
20	1.2218	1.4888	1.8140	2.2078	2.4310	2.6837	3.2618	3.9592	4.7985	7.0362
21	1.2341	1.5187	1.8686	2.2970	2.5415	2.8196	3.4605	4.2412	5.1900	7.7574
22	1.2465	1.5492	1.9253	2.3898	2.6572	2.9624	3.6712	4.5433	5.6136	8.5525
23	1.2590	1.5804	1.9835	2.4863	2.7781	3.1123	3.8948	4.8669	6.0716	9.4292
24	1.2716	1.6121	2.0434	2.5868	2.9045	3.2699	4.1320	5.2136	6.5670	10.3957
25	1.2843	1.6445	2.1052	2.6913	3.0367	3.4354	4.3836	5.5849	7.1030	11.4612
26	1.2973	1.6776	2.1688	2.8006	3.1749	3.6094	4.6506	5.9827	7.6826	12.6359
27	1.3103	1.7113	2.2344	2.9131	3.3193	3.7921	4.9338	6.4088	8.3094	13.9311
28	1.3235	1.7457	2.3019	3.0318	3.4703	3.9841	5.2343	6.8653	8.9875	15.3591
29	1.3367	1.7808	2.3715	3.1543	3.6282	4.1858	5.5531	7.3543	9.7208	16.9334
30	1.3501	1.8166	2.4432	3.2818	3.7933	4.3977	5.8913	7.8781	10.5143	18.6691
31	1.3637	1.8430	2.5170	3.4144	3.9660	4.6203	6.2500	8.4391	11.3742	20.5827
32	1.3773	1.8800	2.5931	3.5523	4.1465	4.8542	6.6307	9.0402	12.3024	22.6924
33	1.3911	1.9176	2.6715	3.6958	4.3351	5.0990	7.0345	9.6841	13.3062	25.0184
34	1.4051	1.9562	2.7522	3.8451	4.5324	5.3581	7.4629	10.3738	14.3920	27.5828
35	1.4192	1.9955	2.8354	4.0005	4.7387	5.6294	7.9174	11.1126	15.5664	30.4081
36	1.4334	2.0356	2.9211	4.1621	4.9543	5.9144	8.3996	11.9041	16.8367	33.5249
37	1.4478	2.0765	3.0094	4.3302	5.1798	6.2138	8.9111	12.7620	18.2105	36.9612
38	1.4623	2.1183	3.1004	4.5052	5.4146	6.5284	9.4538	13.6709	19.6965	40.7497
39	1.4770	2.1608	3.1941	4.6872	5.6610	6.8589	10.0295	14.6446	21.3038	44.9266
40	1.4918	2.2043	3.2907	4.8766	5.9288	7.2061	10.6403	15.6877	23.0422	49.5316
41	1.5067	2.2486	3.3901	5.0736	6.1986	7.5709	11.2883	16.8050	24.9224	54.6086
42	1.5218	2.2938	3.4926	5.2785	6.4807	7.9542	11.9758	18.0020	26.9561	60.2059
43	1.5371	2.3399	3.5982	5.4928	6.7756	8.3569	12.7051	19.2842	29.1857	66.3771
44	1.5545	2.3869	3.7070	5.7147	7.0840	8.7800	13.8832	20.6577	31.5348	73.1807
45	1.5701	2.4349	3.8191	5.9456	7.4062	9.2245	14.7287	22.1290	34.1080	80.6817
46	1.5858	2.4838	3.9345	6.1858	7.7430	9.6915	15.6257	23.7052	36.8813	88.9516
47	1.6017	2.5338	4.0432	6.4357	8.0954	10.1822	16.5773	25.3936	39.8908	98.0692
48	1.6178	2.5847	4.1655	6.6957	8.4638	10.6967	17.5868	27.2022	43.1459	107.1213
49	1.6330	2.6367	4.2914	6.9662	8.8490	11.2383	18.6597	29.1397	46.6666	118.1012
50	1.6494	2.6897	4.4211	7.2477	9.2516	11.8072	19.7941	31.2141	50.4746	130.2066

Appendix H. Bond Interest Table: Interest on $1000 from 1 Day to 6 Months

Exclude day of delivery and add to the interest for the full month or months the interest for the remaining days. Calculate 30 days to the month and 360 days to the year.

Days	3½%	3¾%	4%	4¼%	4½%	4¾%	5%	6%	7%
1	$0.0972	$0.1041	$0.1111	$0.1180	$0.125	$0.1319	$0.1389	$0.1667	$0.1944
2	0.1944	0.2083	0.2222	0.2361	0.250	0.2638	0.2778	0.3333	0.3889
3	0.2916	0.3125	0.3333	0.3541	0.375	0.3958	0.4167	0.5000	0.5833
4	0.3889	0.4166	0.4444	0.4722	0.500	0.5277	0.5556	0.6667	0.7778
5	0.4861	0.5208	0.5555	0.5903	0.625	0.6597	0.6944	0.8333	0.9722
6	0.5833	0.6250	0.6667	0.7083	0.750	0.7916	0.8333	1.0000	1.1667
7	0.6805	0.7291	0.7778	0.8264	0.875	0.9236	0.9722	1.1667	1.3611
8	0.7778	0.8333	0.8889	0.9444	1.000	1.0555	1.1111	1.3333	1.5556
9	0.8750	0.9375	1.0000	1.0625	1.125	1.1875	1.2500	1.5000	1.7500
10	0.9722	1.0416	1.1111	1.1805	1.250	1.3194	1.3889	1.6667	1.9444
11	1.0694	1.1458	1.2222	1.2986	1.375	1.4513	1.5278	1.8333	2.1389
12	1.1667	1.2500	1.3333	1.4166	1.500	1.5833	1.6667	2.0000	2.3333
13	1.2639	1.3541	1.4444	1.5347	1.625	1.7152	1.8055	2.1667	2.5278
14	1.3611	1.4583	1.5555	1.6527	1.750	1.8472	1.9444	2.3333	2.7222
15	1.4583	1.5625	1.6667	1.7708	1.875	1.9791	2.0833	2.5000	2.9167
16	1.5555	1.6666	1.7778	1.8888	2.000	2.1111	2.2222	2.6667	3.1111
17	1.6528	1.7708	1.8889	2.0069	2.125	2.2430	2.3611	2.8333	3.3056
18	1.7500	1.8750	2.0000	2.1250	2.250	2.3750	2.5000	3.0000	3.5000
19	1.8472	1.9791	2.1111	2.2430	2.375	2.5069	2.6389	3.1667	3.6944
20	1.9444	2.0833	2.2222	2.3610	2.500	2.6388	2.7778	3.3333	3.8889
21	2.0417	2.1875	2.3333	2.4791	2.625	2.7708	2.9167	3.5000	4.0833
22	2.1389	2.2916	2.4444	2.5972	2.750	2.9027	3.0555	2.6667	4.2778
23	2.2361	2.3958	2.5555	2.7153	2.875	3.0347	3.1944	3.8333	4.4722
24	2.3333	2.5000	2.6667	2.8333	3.000	3.1666	3.3333	4.0000	4.6667
25	2.4305	2.6041	2.7778	2.9514	3.125	3.2986	3.4722	4.1667	4.8611
26	2.5278	2.7083	2.8889	3.0694	3.250	3.4305	3.6111	4.3333	5.0556
27	2.6250	2.8125	3.0000	3.1875	3.375	3.5625	3.7500	4.5000	5.2500
28	2.7222	2.9166	3.1111	3.3055	3.500	3.6944	3.8889	4.6667	5.4444
29	2.8194	3.0208	3.2222	3.4236	3.625	3.8263	4.0278	4.8333	5.6389
30	2.9167	3.1250	3.3333	3.5416	3.750	3.9583	4.1667	5.0000	5.8333
Months									
1	2.9167	3.1250	3.3333	3.5416	3.750	3.9583	4.1667	5.0000	5.8333
2	5.8333	6.2500	6.6667	7.0833	7.500	7.9166	8.3333	10.0000	11.6667
3	8.7500	9.3750	10.0000	10.6250	11.250	11.8749	12.5000	15.0000	17.5000
4	11.6667	12.5000	13.3333	14.1666	15.000	15.8332	16.6667	20.0000	23.3333
5	14.5833	15.6250	16.6667	17.7083	18.750	19.7915	20.8333	25.0000	29.1667

Appendix I.   Income Table

Purchase Price	1%	1½%	2%	2½%	3%	3½%	4%	4½%
10	10	15	20	25	30	35	40	45
15	6.66	10	13.33	16.66	20	23.33	26.66	30
20	5	7.50	10	12.50	15	17.50	20	22.50
22	4.54	6.81	9.09	11.36	13.63	15.90	18.18	20.45
24	4.16	6.25	8.33	10.41	12.50	14.58	16.66	18.75
26	3.84	5.76	7.69	9.61	11.53	13.46	15.38	17.30
28	3.57	5.35	7.14	8.92	10.71	12.50	14.28	16.07
30	3.33	5	6.66	8.33	10	11.66	13.33	15
32	3.12	4.68	6.25	7.81	9.37	10.93	12.50	14.06
34	2.94	4.41	5.88	7.35	8.82	10.29	11.76	13.23
36	2.77	4.16	5.55	6.94	8.33	9.72	11.11	12.50
38	2.63	3.94	5.26	6.57	7.89	9.21	10.52	11.84
40	2.50	3.75	5	6.25	7.50	8.75	10	11.25
42	2.38	3.57	4.76	5.95	7.14	8.33	9.52	10.71
44	2.27	3.40	4.54	5.68	6.81	7.95	9.09	10.22
46	2.17	3.26	4.34	5.43	6.52	7.60	8.69	9.78
48	2.08	3.12	4.16	5.20	6.25	7.29	8.33	9.37
50	2	3	4	5	6	7	8	9
51	1.96	2.94	3.92	4.90	5.88	6.86	7.84	8.82
52	1.92	2.88	3.84	4.80	5.76	6.73	7.60	8.65
53	1.88	2.83	3.77	4.71	5.66	6.60	7.54	8.49
54	1.85	2.77	3.70	4.62	5.55	6.48	7.40	8.33
55	1.81	2.72	3.63	4.54	5.45	6.36	7.27	8.18
56	1.78	2.67	3.57	4.46	5.35	6.23	7.14	8.03
57	1.75	2.63	3.50	4.38	5.26	6.14	7.01	7.89
58	1.72	2.58	3.44	4.31	5.17	6.03	6.89	7.75
59	1.69	2.54	3.38	4.23	5.08	5.93	6.77	7.62
60	1.66	2.50	3.33	4.16	5	5.83	6.66	7.50
61	1.63	2.45	3.27	4.09	4.91	5.73	6.55	7.37
62	1.61	2.41	3.22	4.03	4.83	5.64	6.45	7.25
63	1.58	2.38	3.17	3.96	4.76	5.55	6.34	7.14
64	1.56	2.34	3.12	3.90	4.68	5.46	6.25	7.03
65	1.53	2.30	3.07	3.84	4.61	5.38	6.15	6.92
66	1.51	2.27	3.03	3.78	4.54	5.30	6.06	6.81
67	1.49	2.23	2.98	3.73	4.47	5.22	5.97	6.71
68	1.47	2.20	2.94	3.67	4.41	5.14	5.88	6.61
69	1.44	2.17	2.89	3.62	4.34	5.07	5.79	6.52
70	1.42	2.14	2.85	3.57	4.28	5	5.71	6.42
71	1.40	2.11	2.81	3.52	4.22	4.92	5.63	6.33
72	1.38	2.08	2.77	3.47	4.16	4.86	5.55	6.25
73	1.36	2.05	2.73	3.42	4.10	4.79	5.47	6.16
74	1.35	2.02	2.70	3.37	4.05	4.72	5.40	6.08
75	1.33	2	2.66	3.33	4	4.66	5.33	6
76	1.31	1.97	2.63	3.28	3.94	4.60	5.26	5.92
77	1.29	1.94	2.59	3.24	3.89	4.54	5.19	5.84
78	1.28	1.92	2.56	3.20	3.84	4.48	5.12	5.76
79	1.26	1.89	2.53	3.16	3.79	4.43	5.06	5.69
80	1.25	1.87	2.50	3.12	3.75	4.37	5	5.62
81	1.23	1.85	2.46	3.08	3.70	4.32	4.93	5.55
82	1.21	1.83	2.43	3.04	3.65	4.26	4.87	5.48
83	1.20	1.80	2.40	3.01	3.61	4.21	4.81	5.42
84	1.19	1.78	2.38	2.97	3.57	4.16	4.76	5.35
85	1.17	1.76	2.35	2.94	3.52	4.11	4.70	5.29
86	1.16	1.74	2.32	2.90	3.48	4.06	4.65	5.23
87	1.14	1.72	2.29	2.87	3.44	4.02	4.59	5.17
88	1.13	1.70	2.27	2.84	3.40	3.97	4.54	5.11
89	1.12	1.68	2.24	2.80	3.37	3.93	4.49	5.05
90	1.11	1.66	2.22	2.77	3.33	3.88	4.44	5

Appendix I (*Cont.*)

Purchase Price	1%	1½%	2%	2½%	3%	3½%	4%	4½%
91	1.09	1.64	2.19	2.74	3.29	3.84	4.39	4.94
92	1.08	1.63	2.17	2.71	3.26	3.80	4.34	4.89
93	1.07	1.61	2.15	2.68	3.22	3.76	4.30	4.83
94	1.06	1.59	2.12	2.65	3.19	3.72	4.25	4.78
95	1.05	1.57	2.10	2.63	3.15	3.68	4.21	4.73
96	1.04	1.56	2.08	2.60	3.10	3.64	4.16	4.68
97	1.03	1.54	2.06	2.57	3.09	3.60	4.12	4.63
98	1.02	1.53	2.04	2.55	3.06	3.57	4.08	4.59
99	1.01	1.51	2.02	2.52	3.03	3.53	4.04	4.54
100	1	1.50	2	2.50	3	3.50	4	4.50
101	.99	1.48	1.98	2.47	2.97	3.46	3.96	4.45
102	.98	1.47	1.96	2.45	2.94	3.43	3.92	4.41
103	.97	1.45	1.94	2.42	2.91	3.39	3.88	4.36
104	.96	1.44	1.92	2.40	2.88	3.36	3.84	4.32
105	.95	1.42	1.90	2.38	2.85	3.33	3.80	4.28
106	.94	1.41	1.88	2.35	2.83	3.30	3.77	4.24
107	.93	1.40	1.86	2.33	2.80	3.27	3.73	4.20
108	.92	1.38	1.845	2.31	2.77	3.24	3.70	4.16
109	.91	1.37	1.83	2.29	2.75	3.21	3.66	4.12
110	.90	1.36	1.81	2.27	2.72	3.18	3.63	4.09
111	.90	1.35	1.80	2.25	2.70	3.15	3.60	4.05
112	.89	1.33	1.78	2.23	2.67	3.12	3.57	4.01
113	.88	1.32	1.77	2.21	2.65	3.09	3.54	3.98
114	.87	1.31	1.75	2.19	2.63	3.07	3.50	3.94
115	.86	1.30	1.73	2.17	2.60	3.04	3.47	3.91
116	.86	1.29	1.72	2.15	2.58	3.01	3.44	3.87
117	.85	1.28	1.70	2.13	2.56	2.99	3.41	3.84
118	.84	1.27	1.69	2.11	2.54	2.96	3.38	3.81
119	.84	1.26	1.68	2.10	2.52	2.94	3.36	3.78
120	.83	1.25	1.66	2.08	2.50	2.91	3.33	3.75
121	.82	1.23	1.65	2.06	2.47	2.89	3.30	3.71
122	.81	1.22	1.63	2.04	2.45	2.86	3.27	3.68
123	.81	1.21	1.62	2.03	2.43	2.84	3.25	3.65
124	.80	1.20	1.60	2.01	2.41	2.82	3.22	3.62
125	.80	1.20	1.60	2	2.40	2.80	3.20	3.60
130	.76	1.15	1.53	1.92	2.30	2.69	3.08	3.46
135	.74	1.11	1.48	1.85	2.22	2.59	2.96	3.33
140	.71	1.07	1.42	1.78	2.14	2.50	2.85	3.21
145	.68	1.03	1.37	1.72	2.06	2.41	2.75	3.10
150	.66	1	1.33	1.66	2	2.33	2.66	3
155	.64	.96	1.29	1.61	1.93	2.25	2.58	2.90
160	.62	.93	1.25	1.56	1.87	2.18	2.50	2.81
165	.60	.90	1.21	1.51	1.81	2.12	2.42	2.72
170	.58	.88	1.17	1.47	1.76	2.05	2.35	2.64
175	.57	.85	1.14	1.42	1.71	2	2.28	2.57
180	.55	.83	1.11	1.38	1.66	1.94	2.22	2.50
185	.54	.81	1.08	1.35	1.62	1.89	2.16	2.43
190	.52	.78	1.05	1.31	1.57	1.84	2.10	2.36
195	.51	.76	1.02	1.28	1.53	1.79	2.05	2.30
200	.50	.75	1	1.25	1.50	1.75	2	2.25
210	.47	.71	.95	1.19	1.42	1.66	1.90	2.14
220	.45	.68	.90	1.13	1.36	1.59	1.81	2.04
225	.44	.66	.88	1.11	1.33	1.55	1.77	2
230	.43	.65	.86	1.08	1.30	1.52	1.73	1.97
240	.41	.62	.83	1.04	1.25	1.45	1.66	1.87
250	.40	.60	.80	1	1.20	1.40	1.60	1.80
275	.36	.54	.72	.90	1.09	1.27	1.45	1.63
300	.33	.50	.66	.83	1	1.16	1.33	1.50

Appendix I (*Cont.*)

Purchase Price	5%	5½%	6%	6½%	7%	7⅗₀%	7½%	8%
10	50	55	60	65	70	73	75	80
15	33.33	36.66	40	43.33	46.66	48.66	50	53.33
20	25	27.50	30	32.50	35	36.50	37.50	40
22	22.72	25	27.27	29.54	31.81	33.18	34.09	36.36
24	20.83	22.91	25	27.08	29.16	30.41	31.25	33.33
26	19.23	21.15	23.07	25	26.92	28.07	28.84	30.76
28	17.85	19.64	21.42	23.21	25	26.07	26.78	28.57
30	16.66	18.33	20	21.66	23.33	24.33	25	26.66
32	15.62	17.18	18.75	20.31	21.87	22.81	23.43	25
34	14.70	16.17	17.64	19.11	20.58	21.47	22.05	23.52
36	13.88	15.27	16.66	18.05	19.44	20.27	20.83	22.22
38	13.15	14.47	15.78	17.10	18.42	19.21	19.73	21.05
40	12.50	13.75	15	16.25	17.50	18.25	18.75	20
42	11.90	13.09	14.28	15.47	16.66	17.38	17.85	19.04
44	11.36	12.50	13.63	14.77	15.90	16.59	17.04	18.18
46	10.86	11.95	13.04	14.13	15.21	15.86	16.30	17.39
48	10.41	11.45	12.50	13.54	14.58	15.20	15.62	16.66
50	10	11	12	13	14	14.60	15	16
51	9.80	10.78	11.76	12.74	13.72	14.31	14.70	15.68
52	9.61	10.57	11.53	12.50	13.46	14.03	14.42	15.38
53	9.43	10.37	11.32	12.26	13.20	13.77	14.15	15.09
54	9.25	10.18	11.11	12.03	12.96	13.51	13.88	14.81
55	9.09	10	10.90	11.81	12.72	13.27	13.63	14.54
56	8.92	9.82	10.70	11.60	12.50	13.03	13.39	14.28
57	8.77	9.64	10.52	11.40	12.27	12.80	13.15	14.03
58	8.62	9.48	10.34	11.20	12.06	12.58	12.93	13.79
59	8.47	9.32	10.16	11.01	11.86	12.37	12.71	13.55
60	8.33	9.16	10	10.83	11.66	12.16	12.50	13.33
61	8.19	9.01	9.83	10.65	11.47	11.95	12.39	13.11
62	8.06	8.87	9.67	10.48	11.29	11.77	12.09	12.90
63	7.93	8.73	9.52	10.31	11.11	11.58	11.90	12.69
64	7.81	8.59	9.37	10.15	10.93	11.40	11.68	12.50
65	7.69	8.46	9.23	10	10.76	11.23	11.53	12.30
66	7.57	8.33	9.09	9.84	10.60	11.06	11.36	12.12
67	7.46	8.20	8.95	9.70	10.44	10.89	11.19	11.94
68	7.35	8.08	8.82	9.55	10.29	10.73	11.02	11.76
69	7.24	7.97	8.69	9.42	10.14	10.57	10.86	11.59
70	7.14	7.85	8.57	9.28	10	10.42	10.71	11.43
71	7.04	7.74	8.45	9.15	9.85	10.28	10.56	11.26
72	6.94	7.63	8.33	9.02	9.72	10.13	10.41	11.11
73	6.84	7.53	8.21	8.90	9.58	10	10.27	10.95
74	6.75	7.43	8.10	8.78	9.45	9.86	10.13	10.80
75	6.66	7.33	8	8.66	9.33	9.73	10	10.66
76	6.57	7.23	7.89	8.55	9.21	9.60	9.86	10.52
77	6.49	7.14	7.79	8.44	9.09	9.48	9.74	10.38
78	6.41	7.05	7.69	8.33	8.97	9.35	9.61	10.25
79	6.32	6.96	7.59	8.22	8.86	9.24	9.49	10.12
80	6.25	6.87	7.50	8.12	8.75	9.12	9.37	10
81	6.17	6.79	7.40	8.02	8.64	9.01	9.25	9.87
82	6.09	6.70	7.31	7.92	8.53	8.90	9.14	9.75
83	6.02	6.62	7.22	7.83	8.43	8.79	9.03	9.63
84	5.95	6.54	7.14	7.73	8.33	8.69	8.92	9.52
85	5.88	6.47	7.05	7.64	8.23	8.58	8.82	9.41
86	5.81	6.39	6.97	7.55	8.13	8.48	8.72	9.30
87	5.74	6.32	6.89	7.47	8.04	8.39	8.62	9.19
88	5.68	6.25	6.81	7.38	7.94	8.29	8.52	9.09
89	5.61	6.17	6.74	7.30	7.86	8.20	8.42	8.98
90	5.55	6.11	6.66	7.22	7.77	8.11	8.33	8.88

Appendix I (*Cont.*)

Purchase Price	5%	5½%	6%	6½%	7%	7³/₁₀%	7½%	8%
91	5.49	6.04	6.59	7.14	7.69	8.02	8.24	8.79
92	5.43	5.97	6.52	7.06	7.60	7.93	8.15	8.69
93	5.37	5.91	6.45	6.98	7.52	7.84	8.06	8.60
94	5.31	5.85	6.38	6.91	7.44	7.76	7.97	8.51
95	5.26	5.78	6.31	6.84	7.36	7.68	7.89	8.42
96	5.20	5.72	6.25	6.77	7.29	7.60	7.81	8.33
97	5.15	5.67	6.18	6.69	7.21	7.52	7.73	8.24
98	5.10	5.61	6.12	6.63	7.14	7.45	7.65	8.16
99	5.05	5.55	6.06	6.56	7.07	7.37	7.57	8.08
100	5	5.50	6	6.50	7	7.30	7.50	8
101	4.95	5.44	5.94	6.43	6.93	7.22	7.42	7.92
102	4.90	5.39	5.88	6.37	6.86	7.15	7.35	7.84
103	4.85	5.33	5.82	6.31	6.79	7.08	7.28	7.76
104	4.80	5.28	5.76	6.25	6.72	7.01	7.21	7.69
105	4.76	5.23	5.71	6.19	6.66	6.95	7.14	7.61
106	4.71	5.18	5.66	6.13	6.60	6.88	7.07	7.54
107	4.67	5.14	5.60	6.07	6.54	6.82	7	7.47
108	4.62	5.09	5.55	6.01	6.48	6.75	6.94	7.40
109	4.58	5.04	5.50	5.96	6.42	6.69	6.88	7.33
110	4.54	5	5.45	5.90	6.36	6.63	6.81	7.27
111	4.50	4.95	5.40	5.85	6.30	6.57	6.75	7.20
112	4.46	4.90	5.35	5.80	6.25	6.51	6.69	7.14
113	4.42	4.86	5.30	5.75	6.19	6.46	6.63	7.07
114	4.38	4.82	5.26	5.70	6.14	6.40	6.57	7.01
115	4.35	4.78	5.21	5.65	6.08	6.34	6.52	6.95
116	4.31	4.74	5.17	5.60	6.03	6.29	6.46	6.89
117	4.27	4.70	5.12	5.55	5.98	6.23	6.41	6.83
118	4.23	4.66	5.08	5.50	5.93	6.18	6.35	6.77
119	4.20	4.62	5.04	5.46	5.88	6.13	6.30	6.72
120	4.16	4.58	5	5.41	5.83	6.08	6.25	6.66
121	4.13	4.54	4.95	5.37	5.78	6.03	6.19	6.61
122	4.09	4.50	4.91	5.32	5.73	5.98	6.14	6.55
123	4.06	4.47	4.87	5.28	5.69	5.93	6.09	6.50
124	4.03	4.43	4.83	5.24	5.65	5.88	6.04	6.45
125	4	4.40	4.80	5.20	5.60	5.80	6	6.40
130	3.84	4.23	4.61	5	5.38	5.61	5.76	6.15
135	3.70	4.07	4.44	4.81	5.18	5.33	5.55	5.92
140	3.57	3.92	4.28	4.64	5	5.21	5.35	5.71
145	3.44	3.79	4.13	4.48	4.82	5.03	5.17	5.51
150	3.33	3.66	4	4.33	4.66	4.86	5	5.33
155	3.22	3.54	3.87	4.19	4.51	4.70	4.83	5.16
160	3.12	3.43	3.75	4.06	4.37	4.56	4.68	5
165	3.03	3.33	3.63	3.93	4.24	4.42	4.54	4.84
170	2.94	3.23	3.52	3.82	4.11	4.29	4.41	4.70
175	2.85	3.14	3.42	3.71	4	4.17	4.23	4.57
180	2.77	3.05	3.33	3.61	3.88	4.05	4.16	4.44
185	2.70	2.97	3.24	3.51	3.78	3.94	4.05	4.32
190	2.63	2.89	3.15	3.42	3.68	3.84	3.94	4.21
195	2.56	2.82	3.07	3.33	3.58	3.79	3.84	4.10
200	2.50	2.75	3	3.25	3.50	3.65	3.75	4
210	2.38	2.61	2.85	3.09	3.33	3.47	3.57	3.80
220	2.27	2.50	2.72	2.95	3.18	3.31	3.40	3.63
225	2.22	2.44	2.66	2.88	3.11	3.24	3.33	3.55
230	2.17	2.39	2.60	2.82	3.04	3.17	3.26	3.47
240	2.08	2.29	2.50	2.70	2.91	3.04	3.12	3.33
250	2	2.20	2.40	2.60	2.80	2.92	3	3.20
275	1.81	2	2.18	2.36	2.54	2.65	2.72	2.90
300	1.66	1.83	2	2.16	2.33	2.40	2.50	2.66

Appendix I (*Cont.*)

Purchase Price	8½%	9%	9½%	10%	11%	12%	15%	20%
10	85	90	100	110	120	150	200	
15	56.66	60	63.33	66.66	73.13	80	100	133.33
20	42.50	45	47.50	50	55	60	75	100
22	38.63	40.90	43.18	45.45	50	54.54	68.18	90.90
24	35.41	37.50	39.58	41.66	45.83	50	62.50	83.33
26	32.69	34.61	36.53	38.46	42.30	46.15	57.69	76.92
28	30.35	32.14	33.92	35.71	39.28	42.85	53.57	71.42
30	28.33	30	31.66	33.33	36.66	40	50	66.66
32	26.56	28.12	29.68	31.25	34.37	37.50	46.87	62.50
34	25	26.47	27.94	29.41	32.35	35.29	44.11	58.82
36	23.61	25	26.38	27.77	30.55	33.33	41.66	55.55
38	22.36	23.68	25	26.31	28.94	31.57	39.47	52.63
40	21.25	22.50	23.75	25	27.50	30	37.50	50
42	20.23	21.42	22.61	23.80	26.19	28.57	35.71	47.61
44	19.31	20.45	21.59	22.72	25	27.27	34.09	45.45
46	18.47	19.56	20.65	21.73	23.91	26.08	32.60	43.47
48	17.70	18.75	19.79	20.83	22.91	25	31.25	41.66
50	17	18	19	20	22	24	30	40
51	16.66	17.64	18.62	19.60	21.56	23.52	29.41	39.21
52	16.34	17.30	18.26	19.23	21.15	23.07	28.84	38.46
53	16.03	16.98	17.92	18.86	20.75	22.64	28.30	37.73
54	15.74	16.66	17.59	18.51	20.37	22.22	27.77	37.03
55	15.45	16.36	17.27	18.18	20	21.81	27.27	36.36
56	15.17	16.07	16.96	17.85	19.64	21.42	26.78	35.71
57	14.91	15.78	16.66	17.54	19.29	21.05	26.31	35.08
58	14.65	15.51	16.37	17.24	18.96	20.68	25.86	34.48
59	14.40	15.25	16.10	16.94	18.64	20.33	25.42	33.80
60	14.16	15	15.83	16.66	18.33	20	25	33.33
61	13.93	14.75	15.57	16.39	18.03	19.67	24.59	32.78
62	13.70	14.51	15.32	16.12	17.73	19.35	24.19	32.25
63	13.49	14.28	15.07	15.87	17.46	19.04	23.80	31.74
64	13.28	14.06	14.84	15.62	17.18	18.75	23.43	31.28
65	13.07	13.84	14.61	15.38	16.92	18.46	23.07	30.76
66	12.87	13.63	14.39	15.15	16.66	18.18	22.72	30.30
67	12.68	13.43	14.17	14.92	16.41	17.91	22.38	29.85
68	12.50	13.23	13.97	14.70	16.17	17.64	22.05	29.41
69	12.31	13.04	13.76	14.49	15.94	17.39	21.73	28.98
70	12.14	12.85	13.57	14.28	15.71	17.14	21.42	28.57
71	11.97	12.67	13.38	14.08	15.49	16.90	21.12	28.16
72	11.80	12.50	13.19	13.89	15.28	16.66	20.83	27.77
73	11.63	12.32	13.01	13.69	15.06	16.43	20.54	27.39
74	11.49	12.16	12.83	13.51	14.86	16.21	20.27	27.02
75	11.33	12	12.66	13.33	14.66	16	20	26.66
76	11.18	11.84	12.50	13.15	14.47	15.78	19.73	26.31
77	11.03	11.68	12.33	12.98	14.27	15.58	19.48	25.97
78	10.89	11.53	12.17	12.82	14.10	15.38	19.23	25.64
79	10.75	11.39	12.02	12.65	13.92	15.18	18.98	25.31
80	10.62	11.25	11.87	12.50	13.75	15	18.75	25
81	10.49	11.11	11.72	12.34	13.58	14.81	18.51	24.69
82	10.36	10.97	11.58	12.19	13.41	14.63	18.29	24.39
83	10.24	10.84	11.45	12.04	13.25	14.45	18.04	24.09
84	10.11	10.71	11.30	11.90	13.09	14.28	17.85	23.80
85	10	10.58	11.17	11.76	12.94	14.11	17.64	23.52
86	9.98	10.46	11.04	11.62	12.79	13.95	17.44	23.25
87	9.77	10.34	10.91	11.49	12.64	13.79	17.24	22.98
88	9.65	10.22	10.79	11.36	12.50	13.63	17.04	22.72
89	9.55	10.11	10.67	11.23	12.35	13.48	16.85	22.47
90	9.44	10	10.55	11.11	12.22	13.33	16.66	22.22

Appendix I (*Cont.*)

Purchase Price	8½%	9%	9½%	10%	11%	12%	15%	20%
91	9.34	9.89	10.44	10.98	12.08	13.18	16.48	21.97
92	9.23	9.78	10.32	10.86	11.95	13.04	16.30	21.73
93	9.13	9.67	10.21	10.75	11.82	12.90	16.12	21.50
94	9.04	9.57	10.10	10.63	11.70	12.76	15.95	21.27
95	8.94	9.47	10	10.52	11.57	12.63	15.78	21.05
96	8.85	9.37	9.89	10.41	11.46	12.50	15.72	20.83
97	8.76	9.27	9.79	10.30	11.34	12.37	15.46	20.61
98	8.67	9.18	9.69	10.20	11.22	12.24	15.30	20.40
99	8.58	9.09	9.59	10.10	11.11	12.12	15.15	20.20
100	8.50	9	9.50	10	11	12	15	20
101	8.41	8.91	9.40	9.90	10.89	11.88	14.85	19.80
102	8.33	8.82	9.31	9.80	10.78	11.76	14.709	19.60
103	8.25	8.73	9.22	9.70	10.67	11.65	14.56	19.41
104	8.17	8.65	9.13	9.61	10.57	11.53	14.42	19.23
105	8.09	8.57	9.04	9.52	10.47	11.42	14.28	19.04
106	8.01	8.49	8.96	9.43	10.37	11.32	14.15	18.86
107	7.94	8.41	8.87	9.34	10.28	11.21	14.01	18.69
108	7.87	8.33	8.79	9.25	10.18	11.11	13.88	18.51
109	7.79	8.25	8.71	9.17	10.09	11	13.76	18.34
110	7.72	8.18	8.63	9.09	10	10.90	13.63	18.18
111	7.65	8.10	8.55	9	9.90	10.81	13.51	18.01
112	7.58	8.03	8.48	8.92	9.81	10.71	13.39	17.85
113	7.52	7.96	8.40	8.84	9.73	10.61	13.27	17.69
114	7.45	7.89	8.33	8.77	9.64	10.52	13.15	17.54
115	7.39	7.82	8.26	8.69	9.56	10.43	13.04	17.39
116	7.32	7.75	8.18	8.61	9.48	10.34	12.93	17.24
117	7.26	7.69	8.11	8.54	9.40	10.25	12.83	17.09
118	7.20	7.62	8.05	8.47	9.32	10.16	12.71	16.94
119	7.14	7.56	7.98	8.40	9.24	10.08	12.60	16.80
120	7.08	7.50	7.91	8.33	9.16	10	12.50	16.66
121	7.02	7.43	7.85	8.26	9.09	9.91	12.39	16.52
122	6.96	7.37	7.78	8.19	9.01	9.83	12.29	16.39
123	6.91	7.31	7.72	8.13	8.94	9.76	12.19	16.26
124	6.85	7.66	7.85	8.06	8.87	9.67	12.09	16.12
125	6.80	7.20	7.60	8	8.80	9.60	12	16
130	6.53	6.92	7.30	7.69	8.46	9.23	11.53	15.38
135	6.29	6.66	7.03	7.40	8.14	8.88	11.11	14.81
140	6.07	6.42	6.78	7.14	7.85	8.57	10.71	14.28
145	5.86	6.20	6.55	6.89	7.58	8.27	10.34	13.79
150	5.66	6	6.33	6.66	7.33	8	10	13.33
155	5.48	5.80	6.12	6.45	7.09	7.74	9.67	12.90
160	5.31	5.62	5.93	6.25	6.87	7.50	9.37	12.50
165	5.15	5.45	5.75	6.06	6.66	7.27	9.09	12.12
170	5	5.29	5.58	5.88	6.47	7.05	8.82	11.76
175	4.85	5.14	5.42	5.71	6.28	6.85	8.57	11.42
180	4.72	5	5.27	5.55	6.11	6.66	8.33	11.11
185	4.59	4.86	5.13	5.40	5.94	6.48	8.10	10.81
190	4.47	4.73	5	5.26	5.78	6.31	7.89	10.52
195	4.35	4.61	4.87	5.13	5.64	6.15	7.69	10.25
200	4.25	4.50	4.75	5	5.50	6	7.50	10
210	4.04	4.28	4.52	4.76	5.23	5.71	7.14	9.52
220	3.86	4.09	4.31	4.54	5	5.45	6.81	9.09
225	3.77	4	4.22	4.44	4.88	5.33	6.66	8.88
230	3.69	3.91	3.90	4.34	4.78	5.21	6.52	8.69
240	3.54	3.75	3.90	4.16	4.58	5	6.25	8.33
250	3.40	3.60	3.80	4	4.40	4.80	6	8
275	3.09	3.27	3.45	3.63	4	4.36	5.45	7.27
300	2.83	3	3.16	3.33	3.66	4	5	6.66

Appendix J.   Foreign Exchange

Country	Currency	Consisting of:
Abu Dhabi	Dinar	1,000 fils
Aden	Dinar	1,000 fils
Afghanistan	Afghani	100 puls
Albania	Lek	100 qintar
Algeria	Dinar	100 centimes
Andorra	Peseta	100 centimos
Angola	Kwanza	100 centavos
Antigua	Dollar	100 cents
Argentina	Peso	100 centavos
Australia	Dollar	100 cents
Austria	Schilling	100 groschen
Azores	Escudo	100 cents
Bahamas	Dollar	100 cents
Bahrain	Dinar	1,000 fils
Balearic Island	Peseta	100 centimos
Bangladesh	Taka	100 paise
Barbados	Dollar	100 cents
Belgium	Franc	100 centimes
Belize	Pound	100 pence
Benin	Franc	100 centimes
Bermuda	Pound	100 pence
Bhutan	Ngultrum	100 chetrum
Bolivia	Peso	100 centavos
Botswana	Pula	100 cents
Brazil	Cruzeiro	100 centavos
British Honduras	Dollar	100 cents
Brunei	Dollar	100 cents
Bulgaria	Lev	100 stotinki
Burma	Kyat	100 pyas
Burundi	Franc	100 centimes
Cambodia	Riel	100 sen
Cameroons	Franc	100 centimes
Canada	Dollar	100 cents
Canary Islands	Peseta	100 centimos
Cape Verde Islands	Escudo	100 centavos
Central African Empire	Franc	100 centimes
Chad	Franc	100 centimes
Chile	Peso	100 centavos
China	Yuan	10,000 jen min piao
Columbia	Peso	100 centavos
Comoros	Franc	100 centimes
Congo (Kinshasa)	Zaire	100 makutu
Congo (Brazzaville)	Franc	100 centimes
Costa Rica	Colon	100 centimos
Cuba	Peso	100 centavos
Cyprus	Pound	1,000 mils
Czechoslovakia	Koruna	100 hellers

Country	Currency	Consisting of:
Dahomey	Franc	100 centimes
Denmark	Krona	100 ore
Djibouti	Franc	100 centimes
Dominica	Dollar	100 cents
Dominican Republic	Peso	100 centavos
Dubai	Gulf Riyal	100 dirhams
Ecuador	Sucre	100 centavos
Egypt	Pound	100 piasters = 1,000 milliemes
El Salvador	Colon	100 centavos
Equatorial Guinea	Ekuwele	100 centimos
Ethiopia	Dollar	100 cents
Fiji Islands	Pound	100 pence
Finland	Markka	100 pennis
France	Franc	100 centimes
French Somaliland	Franc	100 centimes
Gabon	Franc	100 centimes
Gambia	Dalasi	100 bututs
Germany	Deutsche mark	100 pfennig
Ghana	Cedi	100 pesewas
Gibraltar	Pound	100 pence
Grand Cayman Island	Pound	100 pence
Greece	Drachma	100 lepta
Grenada	Dollar	100 cents
Guadeloupe	Franc	100 centimes
Guam	U.S. dollar	100 cents
Guatemala	Quetzal	100 centavos
Guiana, French	Franc	100 centimes
Guinea	Syli	100 centimes
Guinea-Bissau	Escudo	100 centavos
Guyana	Dollar	100 cents
Haiti	Gourde	100 centimes
Honduras (Republic)	Lempira	100 centavos
Hong Kong	Dollar	100 cents
Hungary	Forint	100 fillers
Iceland	Krona	100 aurar
India	Rupee	100 paise
Indonesia	Rupiah	100 sen
Iran	Rial	100 dinars
Iraq	Dinar	1,000 fils
Ireland (Republic)	Pound	100 pence
Israel	Shekel	100 new agorot
Italy	Lira	100 centesimi
Ivory Coast	Franc	100 centimes
Jamaica	Dollar	100 cents
Japan	Yen	100 sen
Jordan	Dinar	1,000 fils
Kampuchea	Riel	100 sen
Kenya	Shilling	100 cents

Country	Currency	Consisting of:
Kiribati	Dollar	100 cents
Korea (North)	Won	100 chon
Korea (South)	Won	100 chon
Kuwait	Dinar	1,000 fils
Laos	Kip	100 at
Lebanon	Pound	100 piasters
Lesotho	Rand	100 cents
Liberia	U.S. dollar	100 cents
Libya	Dinar	1,000 fils
Liechtenstein	Franc, franken	100 centimes
Luxembourg	Franc	100 centimes
Macao	Pataca	100 avos
Madagascar	Franc	100 centimes
Madeira	Escudo	100 centavos
Malagasy	Franc	100 centimes
Malawi	Kwacha	100 tambala
Malaysia	Finggit	100 sen
Maldives	Rupee	100 cents
Mali	Franc	100 centimes
Malta	Pound	100 pence
Marshall Islands	U.S. dollar	100 cents
Martinique	Franc	100 centimes
Mauritania	Ouguiya	5 khoums
Mauritius	Rupee	100 cents
Mexico	Peso	100 centavos
Monaco	Franc	100 centimes
Mongolia	Tughrik	100 mongos
Montserrat	Dollar	100 cents
Morocco	Dirham	100 Moroccan francs
Mozambique	Escudo	100 centavos
Nauru	Dollar	100 cents
Nepal	Rupee	100 pice
Netherland Antilles	Guilder	100 cents
Netherlands	Guilder	100 cents
Nevis	Dollar	100 cents
New Caledonia	Franc	100 centimes
New Guinea	Dollar	100 cents
New Hebrides Islands	Franc	100 centimes
New Zealand	Dollar	100 cents
Nicaragua	Cordoba	100 centavos
Niger	Franc	100 centimes
Nigeria	Naira	100 kobo
Norway	Krone	100 ore
Oceania (French)	Franc	100 centimes
Oman	Rial	100 dinars
Pakistan	Rupee	100 paisa
Panama	Balboa	100 centesimos
Papua	Kina	100 cents

Country	Currency	Consisting of:
Paraguay	Guarani	100 centimos
Peru	Sol	100 centavos
Philippines	Peso	100 centavos
Poland	Zloty	100 grosze
Portugal	Escudo	100 centavos
Portuguese East Africa	Escudo	100 centavos
Portuguese Guinea	Escudo	100 centavos
Puerto Rico	U.S. dollar	100 cents
Qatar	Gulf Riyal	100 dirhams
Réunion Island	Franc	100 centimes
Romania	Leu	100 bani
Rwanda	Franc	100 centimes
Ryukyu Islands	U.S. dollar	100 cents
St. Kitts	Dollar	100 cents
St. Lucia	Dollar	100 cents
St. Vincent	Dollar	100 cents
Samoa	Tala	100 sene
San Marino	Lira	100 centesimi
San Tome and Principe	Dobra	100 cents
Saudi Arabia	Riyal	20 gurshes = 100 halalah
Senegal	Franc	100 centimes
Seychelles	Rupee	100 cents
Sierra Leone	Leone	100 cents
Singapore	Dollar	100 cents
Solomon Islands	Dollar	100 cents
Somalia	So. Schilling	100 centesimi
South Africa (Republic)	Rand	100 cents
South West Africa (Namibia)	Rand	100 cents
South Yemen	Dinar	1,000 fils
Spain	Peseta	100 centimos
Sri Lanka	Rupee	100 paise
Sudan	Pound	100 piasters = 1,000 milliemes
Suriname	Guilder	100 cents
Swaziland	Lilangeni	100 cents
Sweden	Krona	100 ore
Switzerland	Franc	100 centimes
Syria	Pound	100 piasters
Tahiti	Franc	100 centimes
Taiwan	Dollar	100 cents
Tanzania	Shilling	100 cents
Thailand	Baht	100 satang
Timor	Escudo	100 centavos
Togo	Franc	100 centimes
Tonga Islands	Pa'anga	100 cents
Trinidad and Tobago	Dollar	100 cents
Tunisia	Dinar	1,000 milliemes
Turkey	Lira	100 centesimi
Tuvalu	Dollar	100 cents

Country	Currency	Consisting of:
Uganda	Shilling	100 cents
United Arab Emirates	Dirham	100 francs
United Kingdom	Pound	100 pence
Upper Volta	Franc	100 centimes
Uruguay	Peso	100 centesimos
USA	Dollar	100 cents
USSR	Ruble	100 kopecks
Vatican City	Lira	100 centesimi
Venezuela	Bolivar	100 centimos
Viet-Nam	Dong	100 cents
Virgin Islands (U.S.)	U.S. dollar	100 cents
Yemen	Rial	100 dinars
Yugoslavia	Dinar	100 paras
Zaire	Zaire	100 makutu
Zambia	Kwacha	100 newee
Zimbabwe	Dollar	100 cents

Appendix K.   Programs of Graduate Study in Business and Management

Abilene Christian University
School of Business Administration
Abilene, Texas, 79601

Adelphi University
School of Business Administration
Garden City, New York 11530

Advanced Management Institute
Graduate School of Business
Management
Lake Forest, Illinois 60045

Air Force Institute of Technology
School of Systems and Logistics
Wright-Patterson Air Force Base,
Ohio 45433

Alabama Agricultural and Mechanical University
School of Business
Normal, Alabama 35762

American Graduate School of International Management
Glendale, Arizona 85306

American International College
School of Business Administration
Springfield, Massachusetts 01109

American School of Management
Kenosha, Wisconsin 53140

American University
School of Business Administration
Washington, D.C. 20016

Andrews University
Department of Business,
Graduate School
Berrien Springs, Michigan 49104

Angelo State University
Department of Business Administration
San Angelo, Texas 76901

Antioch College
Washington-Baltimore Center
Baltimore, Maryland 21202

Appalachian State University
Department of Business Administration
Boone, North Carolina 28608

Arizona State University
College of Business Administration
Tempe, Arizona 85281

Arkansas State University
School of Business
State University, Arkansas 72467

Armstrong College
Department of Business Administration
Berkeley, California 94704

Armstrong State College
Department of Business Administration
Savannah, Georgia 31406

Ashland College
Graduate Studies in Business
Administration
Ashland, Ohio 44805

Atlanta University
School of Business Administration
Atlanta, Georgia 30314

Auburn University
School of Business
Auburn, Alabama 36830

Augusta College
Department of Business Administration
Augusta, Georgia 30904

Austin Peay State University
Department of Business Administration
Clarksville, Tennessee 37040

Avila College
Department of Business and Economics
Kansas City, Missouri 64145

Azusa Pacific College
Division of Business Administration
Azusa, California 91702

Babson College
Graduate Programs
Babson Park, Massachusetts 02157

Baldwin-Wallace College
Department of Business
Administration
Berea, Ohio 44017

Ball State University
College of Business
Muncie, Indiana 47306

Barry College
Department of Business
Miami, Florida 33161

Bath University
School of Management
Bristol, England

Baylor University
Department of Business
Waco, Texas 76706

Bellarmine College
Department of Business
Administration
Louisville, Kentucky 40205

Bentley College
Graduate School
Waltham, Massachusetts 02154

Berry College
Graduate Studies in Business
Mount Berry, Georgia 30149

Bloomsburg State College
School of Business
Bloomsburg, Pennsylvania 17815

Boise State University
Graduate School of Business
Boise, Idaho 83725

Boston University
School of Management
Boston, Massachusetts 02215

Boston University—Brussels
Overseas MBA Program
1150 Brussels, Belgium

Bowling Green State University
College of Graduate Studies
Bowling Green, Ohio 43403

Bradley University
College of Business
Peoria, Illinois 61625

Brigham Young University
Graduate School of Management
Provo, Utah 84602

Bryant College
Graduate School
Smithfield, Rhode Island 02917

Bucknell University
Department of Management
Lewisburg, Pennsylvania 17837

Butler University
Department of Business
Administration
Indianapolis, Indiana 46208

California Lutheran College
Department of Economics
and Management
Thousand Oaks, California 91360

California Polytechnic State University
Department of Business
Administration
San Luis Obispo, California 93407

California State College
School of Business and
Public Administration
Bakersfield, California 93309

California State College
School of Management
Dominguez Hills, California 90747

California State College
School of Administration
San Bernardino, California 92407

California State Polytechnic University
School of Business Administration
Pomona, California 91768

California State University
School of Administration
Chico, California 95926

California State University
School of Business and
Administrative Sciences
Fresno, California 93740

California State University
School of Business Administration
and Economics
Fullerton, California 92634

California State University
School of Business
Hayward, California 94542

California State University
School of Business Administration
Long Beach, California 90840

California State University
School of Business and Economics
Los Angeles, California 90032

California State University
School of Business and Economics
Northridge, California 91324

California State University
School of Business and Public
Administration
Sacramento, California 95819

Campbell University
Department of Business Administration
Buies Creek, North Carolina 27506

Canisius College
School of Business Administration
Buffalo, New York 14208

Capital University
Graduate School of Administration
Columbus, Ohio 43209

Carnegie-Mellon University
Graduate School of Industrial
Administration
Pittsburgh, Pennsylvania 15213

Case Western Reserve University
School of Management
Cleveland, Ohio 44106

Catholic University of America
School of Business
Washington, D.C. 20064

Catholic University of Puerto Rico
Department of Business
Administration
Ponce, Puerto Rico 00731
(instruction in English and Spanish)

Centenary College of Louisiana
Department of Business
Administration
Shreveport, Louisiana 71104

Central Michigan University
School of Business Administration
Mount Pleasant, Michigan 48858

Central Missouri State University
Department of Business
Administration
Warrenburg, Missouri 64093

Central State University
School of Business
Edmond, Oklahoma 73034

Chaminade University of Honolulu
MBA Program
Honolulu, Hawaii 96816

Chapman College
Department of Economics and
Business Administration
Orange, California 92666

Chinese University of Hong Kong
Graduate Studies in Business
Administration
Shatin, NT, Hong Kong

Citadel
Department of Business
Administration
Charleston, South Carolina 29409

City University
School of Business Administration
Los Angeles, California 90044

City University of New York
Baruch College
New York, New York 10010

Claremont Graduate School
Claremont, California 91711

Clarion State College
School of Business Administration
Clarion, Pennsylvania 16214

Clarkson College of Technology
School of Management
Potsdam, New York 13676

Clark University
Department of Management
Worcester, Massachusetts 01610

Clemson University
Department of Industrial
Management
Clemson, South Carolina 29631

Cleveland State University
School of Business Administration
Cleveland, Ohio 44115

College of Insurance
Graduate Program for the M.B.A.
Degree
New York, New York 10038

College of Notre Dame
Department of Business
Administration
Belmont, California 94002

College of Saint Rose
Program in Management
Albany, New York 12203

College of St. Thomas
Graduate Program in Management
St. Paul, Minnesota 55105

College of Steubenville
MBA Program
Steubenville, Ohio 43952

College of William and Mary
School of Business Administration
Williamsburg, Virginia 23185

Colorado State University
College of Business
Fort Collins, Colorado 80523

Columbia University
Graduate School of Business
New York, New York 10027

Columbus College
University System of Georgia
School of Business
Columbus, Georgia 31907

Concordia University
Faculty of Commerce and Administration
Montreal, Quebec H3G1M8, Canada

Cornell University
Graduate School of Business
and Public Administration
Ithaca, New York 14853

Cranfield Institute of Technology
School of Management
Bedford, England

Creighton University
Eugene C. Eppley College of
Business Administration
Omaha, Nebraska 68178

**C. W. Post Center of Long Island
University**
School of Business Administration
Greenvale, New York 11548

Dalhousie University
Department of Business
Administration
Halifax, Nova Scotia, Canada

Dartmouth College
Amos Tuck School of Business
Administration
Hanover, New Hampshire 03755

Deakin University
School of Management
Victoria 3217, Australia

Delta State University
School of Business
Cleveland, Mississippi 38732

De Paul University
School of Business
Chicago, Illinois 60604

De Pauw University
Department of Business
Administration
Greencastle, Indiana 46135

Dowling College
MBA Program
Oakdale, New York 11769

Drake University
Graduate School
Des Moines, Iowa 50311

Drexel University
College of Business Administration
Philadelphia, Pennsylvania 19104

Drury College
Breech School of Business
Administration
Springfield, Missouri 65802

Duke University
Graduate School of Business
Administration
Durham, North Carolina 27710

Duquesne University
Graduate School of Business
Administration
Pittsburgh, Pennsylvania 15219

Durham University
Business School
Durham, England

East Carolina University
School of Business
Greenville, North Carolina 27834

Eastern Illinois University
School of Business
Charleston, Illinois 61920

Eastern Kentucky University
College of Business
Richmond, Kentucky 40475

Eastern Michigan University
College of Business
Ypsilanti, Michigan 48197

Eastern New Mexico University
Department of Business
Administration
Portales, New Mexico 88130

Eastern Washington State College
Department of Business
Administration
Cheney, Washington 99004

East Tennessee State University
College of Business Administration
Johnson City, Tennessee 37601

East Texas State University
School of Business
Commerce, Texas 75428

Emory University
School of Business Administration
Atlanta, Georgia 30322

Emporia Kansas State College
Department of Business
Administration
Emporia, Kansas 66801

Fairleigh Dickinson University
College of Business Administration
Madison, New Jersey 07940

Federal City College
School of Business and Public
Management
Washington, D.C. 20004

Florida Atlantic University
Department of Business
Administration
Boca Raton, Florida 33432

Florida Institute of Technology
Department of Management Science
Melbourne, Florida 32901

Florida International University
School of Business and
Organizational Sciences
Miami, Florida 33199

Florida State University
College of Business
Tallahassee, Florida 32306

Florida Technological University
College of Business Administration
Orlando, Florida 32816

Fordham University
School of Business Administration
Bronx, New York 10458

Fordham University
Martino Graduate School of Business
Administration
Lincoln Center
New York, New York 10023

Fort Hays Kansas State College
Department of Business
Hays, Kansas 67601

Furman University
College of Business Administration
Greenville, South Carolina 29613

Gannon College
Graduate Program in Business
Administration
Erie, Pennsylvania 16501

George Mason University
Department of Business
Administration
Fairfax, Virginia 22030

Georgetown University
School of Business Administration
Washington, D.C. 20057

George Washington University
School of Business Administration
Washington, D.C. 20052

George Williams College
Department of Administration and
Organizational Behavior
Downers Grove, Illinois 60515

Georgia College
Department of Business
Administration
Milledgeville, Georgia 31061

Georgia Institute of Technology
College of Industrial Management
Atlanta, Georgia 30332

Georgia Southern College
School of Business
Statesboro, Georgia 30458

Georgia State University
School of Business Administration
Atlanta, Georgia 30303

Golden Gate University
School of Business
San Francisco, California 94105

Gonzaga University
School of Business
Spokane, Washington 99258

Governors State University
College of Business and
Public Service
Park Forest South, Illinois 60466

Grand Valley State
F.E. Seidman Graduate College of
Business
Allendale, Michigan 49401

Hardin-Simmons University
Division of Business and Economics
Abilene, Texas 79601

Hartford Graduate Center
Hartford, Connecticut 06120

Harvard University
Graduate School of Business
Administration
Cambridge, Massachusetts 02163

Hofstra University
School of Business
Hempstead, New York 11550

Howard University
School of Business Administration
Washington, D.C. 20001

Humboldt State University
School of Business
Arcata, California 95521

Idaho State University
College of Business
Pocatello, Idaho 83201

Illinois Benedictine College
MBA Program
Lisle, Illinois 60532

Illinois Institute of Technology
Department of Management
Chicago, Illinois 60616

Illinois State University
School of Business
Normal, Illinois 61761

IMEDE (Management Development Institute)
Lausanne, Switzerland
(instruction in French and English)

Imperial College of Science and Technology
University of London
Department of Management Science
London SW72AZ, England

Indiana Central University
Department of Business and Economics
Indianapolis, Indiana 46227

Indiana State University
School of Business
Terre Haute, Indiana 47809

Indiana University
Department of Business and Economics
Kokomo, Indiana 46901

Indiana University
Division of Business
Gary, Indiana 46408

Indiana University of Pennsylvania
Department of Business
Indiana, Pennsylvania 15701

Indiana University—Purdue University
School of Business
Fort Wayne, Indiana 46805

INSEAD (The European Institutue of Business Administration)
Fontainebleau, France
(instruction in French and English)

Inter-American University of Puerto Rico
Department of Business
Hato Rey, Puerto Rico 00919
(instruction in Spanish and English)

Inter-American University of Puerto Rico
Department of Business Administration
San German, Puerto Rico 00753
(instruction in Spanish and English

Iona College
School of Business Administration
New Rochelle, New York 10801

Iran Center for Management Studies
M.B.A. Program
Tehran, Iran
(instruction in Arabic and English)

Jackson State University
School of Business
Jackson, Mississippi 39217

Jacksonville State University
School of Business
Jacksonville, Alabama, 36265

James Madison University
School of Business
Harrisonburg, Virginia 22807

John Carroll University
The Graduate School
University Heights, Ohio 44118

John F. Kennedy University
School of Management
Martinez, California 94553

Johns Hopkins University
Department of Business Administration
Baltimore, Maryland 21218

Kansas State College
Kelce Center for Business and Economic Development
Pittsburg, Kansas 66762

Kansas State University
College of Business Administration
Manhattan, Kansas 66502

Keller Graduate School of Management
Chicago, Illinois 60606

Kent State University
Graduate School of Business Administration
Kent, Ohio 44242

Lake Forest School of Management
Graduate School of Management
Lake Forest, Illinois 60045

Lamar University
School of Business
Beaumont, Texas 77710

LaSalle College
School of Business Administration
Philadelphia, Pennsylvania 19141

Laurentian University
School of Business
Sudbury, Ontario, Canada

LaVal University
School of Business
Quebec, Canada
(instruction primarily in French)

La Verne College
Department of Economics and
Business
La Verne, California 91750

Lehigh University
College of Business and Economics
Bethlehem, Pennsylvania 18015

Lewis University
College of Business
Romeoville, Illinois 60441

The Lindenwood Colleges
MBA Program
St. Charles, Missouri 63301

London Business School
Graduate School of Business Studies
London, England

Long Island University
School of Business Administration
Brooklyn, New York 11201

Long Island University
C. W. Post Center
Greenvale, New York 11548

Louisiana State University
College of Business Administration
Baton Rouge, Louisiana 70803

Lousiana Technological University
College of Administration and
Business
Ruston, Louisiana 71270

Lowell Technological Institute
College of Management Science
Lowell, Massachusetts 01854

Loyola College
Graduate Division of Business
Administration
Baltimore, Maryland 21210

Loyola Marymount University
School of Business Administration
Los Angeles, California 90045

Loyola University
College of Business Administration
New Orleans, Louisiana 70118

Loyola University
Graduate School of Business
Chicago, Illinois 60611

Lynchburg College
Department of Business
Administration
Lynchburg, Virginia 24504

MacQuarie University
Graduate Studies in Business
Administration
Sydney, New South Wales, Australia

Madison College
Department of Business
Harrisonburg, Virginia 22801

Manhattan College
Graduate Division
Bronx, New York 10471

Mankato State University
College of Business
Mankato, Minnesota 56001

Marist College
Department of Business and
Economics
Poughkeepsie, New York 12601

Marquette University
School of Business
Milwaukee, Wisconsin 53233

Marshall University
College of Business and Applied
Science
Huntington, West Virginia 25701

Marywood College
Department of Business/Managerial
Science
Scranton, Pennsylvania 18509

**Massachusetts Institute of
Technology**
Alfred P. Sloan School of
Management
Cambridge, Massachusetts 02139

McGill University
Faculty of Management
Montreal, Quebec, Canada
(instruction primarily in French)

McMaster University
Faculty of Business
Hamilton, Ontario, Canada

McNeese State University
School of Business
Lake Charles, Louisiana 70601

Memorial University of Newfoundland
School of Business Administration and
Commerce
St. John's, Newfoundland CA1B3X5,
Canada

Memphis State University
College of Business Administration
Memphis, Tennessee 38152

Mercer University
Division of Business and Economics
Atlanta, Georgia 30341

Miami University
School of Business Administration
Oxford, Ohio 45056

Michigan State University
Graduate School of Business
Administration
East Lansing, Michigan 48824

Michigan Technological University
School of Business and Engineering
Administration
Houghton, Michigan 49931

Middle Tennessee State University
School of Business and Economics
Murfreesboro, Tennessee 37130

Midwestern State University
Business School
Wichita Falls, Texas 76308

Mississippi College
Department of Business
Clinton, Mississippi 39058

Mississippi State University
School of Business and Industry
State College, Mississippi 38762

Monmouth College
Department of Business
Administration
West Long Branch, New Jersey 07764

Moorhead State University
School of Business
Moorhead, Minnesota 56560

Morehead State University
Department of Business
Administration
Morehead, Kentucky 40351

Morgan State University
Department of Business
Administration
Baltimore, Maryland 21239

Mount Saint Mary's College
Graduate School of Business
Emmitsburg, Maryland 21727

Murray State University
School of Business and
Public Affairs
Murray, Kentucky 42071

Naval Postgraduate School
Monterey, California 93940

New Hampshire College
Department of Business
Administration
Manchester, New Hampshire 03104

New Jersey Institute of Technology
Department of Organization and Social
Sciences
Newark, New Jersey 07102

New Mexico Highlands University
Department of Business
Administration
Las Vegas, New Mexico 87701

New Mexico State University
College of Business Administration
and Economics
Las Cruces, New Mexico 88003

New York Institute of Technology
Division of Business and
Management
New York, New York 10023
Old Westbury, New York 11568

New York University
Graduate School of Business
Administration
New York, New York 10006

Nicholls State University
Graduate School of Business
Administration
Thibodaux, Louisiana 70301

North Carolina Central University
School of Business
Durham, North Carolina 27707

North Carolina State University
School of Business
Raleigh, North Carolina 27607

Northeastern University
Graduate School of Business
Administration
Boston, Massachusetts 02115

Northeast Louisiana University
College of Business Administration
Monroe, Louisiana 71201

Northern Arizona University
College of Business Administration
Flagstaff, Arizona 86011

Northern Illinois University
College of Business
Dekalb, Illinois 60115

Northern Kentucky University
Graduate Studies
Highland Heights, Kentucky 41076

Northern Michigan University
School of Business
Marquette, Michigan 49855

Northrop University
School of Business
Inglewood, California 90306

North Texas State University
School of Business
Denton, Texas 76203

Northwestern State University
College of Business
Natchitoches, Louisiana 71457

Northwestern University
Graduate School of Management
Evanston, Illinois 60201

Northwest Missouri State University
Department of Business and
Economics
Maryville, Missouri 64468

Nova University
Graduate Management Programs
Ft. Lauderdale, Florida 33314

Oakland University
School of Economics and
Management
Rochester, Michigan 48063

Ohio State University
College of Administrative Science
Columbus, Ohio 43210

Ohio University
College of Business Administration
Athens, Ohio 45701

Oklahoma City University
School of Business
Oklahoma City, Oklahoma 73106

Oklahoma State University
College of Business Administration
Stillwater, Oklahoma 74074

Old Dominion University
School of Business
Norfolk, Virginia 23508

Oral Roberts University
Department of Business
Administration
Tulsa, Oklahoma 74105

Oregon State University
School of Business and Technology
Corvallis, Oregon 97331

Pace University
Graduate School
White Plains, New York 10603
New York, New York 10038
Pleasantville, New York 10570

Pacific Lutheran University
School of Business Administration
Tacoma, Washington 98447

Pacific States University
College of Business
Los Angeles, California 90006

Pan American University
School of Business Administration
Edinburg, Texas 78539

Pan American University at Brownsville
Department of Business Administration
Brownsville, Texas 78520

Pennsylvania State University
College of Business Administration
Middletown, Pennsylvania 17057

Pennsylvania State University
School of Business Administration
University Park, Pennsylvania 16802

Pepperdine University
School of Business and Management
Los Angeles, California 90044

Philadelphia College of Textiles and Science
MBA Program
Philadelphia, Pennsylvania 19144

Pittsburg State University
Gladys A. Kelce School of Business and
Economics
Pittsburg, Kansas 66762

Plymouth State College
Graduate Studies
Plymouth, New Hampshire 03264

Polytechnic Institute of New York
Division of Management
Brooklyn, New York 11201

Portland State University
School of Business Administration
Portland, Oregon 97207

Prairie View Agricultural and
Mechanical University
Department of Business Administration
Prairie View, Texas 77445

Providence College
Department of Business Administration
Providence, Rhode Island 02918

Purdue University
Krannert Graduate School of Management
Lafayette, Indiana 47907

Purdue University
Graduate School of Industrial Management
Hammond, Indiana 46323

Queens College
The Graduate School
Charlotte, North Carolina 28274

Queen's University
School of Business
Kingston, Ontario, Canada

Quinnipiac College
School of Business
Hamden, Connecticut 06518

Radford College
Department of Business and Economics
Radford, Virginia 24141

Regis College
MBA Program
Denver, Colorado 80221

Rensselaer Polytechnic Institute
School of Management
Troy, New York 12181

Rice University
Jesse H. Jones Graduate School of
Administration
Houston, Texas 77001

Rider College
School of Business Administration
Lawrenceville, New Jersey 08648

Rivier College
Department of Business
Nashua, New Hampshire 03060

Robert Morris College
Graduate School
Coraopolis, Pennsylvania 15108

Rochester Institute of Technology
College of Business
Rochester, New York 14623

Rockhurst College
Graduate Business Division
Kansas City, Missouri 64110

Rollins College
Department of Economics and Business
Administration
Winter Park, Florida 32789

Roosevelt University
Walter E. Heller College of Business
Administration
Chicago, Illinois 60605

Rosary College
MBA Program
River Forest, Illinois 60305

Rutgers University
Department of Business and Economics
Camden, New Jersey 08102

Rutgers University
Graduate School of Management
Newark, New Jersey 07102
New Brunswick, New Jersey 08903

Sacred Heart College
MBA Program
Bridgeport, Connecticut 06606

Saginaw Valley State College
SVSC School of Business and
Management
University Center, Michigan 48710

St. Ambrose College
Graduate Programs in Business
Administration
Davenport, Iowa 52803

St. Bonaventure University
Department of Business Administration
St. Bonaventure, New York 14778

St. Cloud State University
School of Business
St. Cloud, Minnesota 56301

Saint Edward's University
Center of Business Administration
Austin, Texas 78704

Saint Francis College
Department of Business
Fort Wayne, Indiana 46808

St. Francis College
Department of Business Administration
Loretto, Pennsylvania 15940

St. John's University
College of Business Administration
Jamaica, New York 11439

St. Joseph's University
MBA Program
Philadelphia, Pennsylvania 19131

Saint Louis University
School of Business and Administration
St. Louis, Missouri 63103

Saint Mary's University
Department of Business Administration
Halifax, Nova Scotia, Canada

St. Mary's University
School of Business Administration
San Antonio, Texas 78284

Salve Regina College
Graduate School
Newport, Rhode Island 02840

Samford University
School of Business
Birmingham, Alabama 35209

Sam Houston State University
College of Business Administration
Huntsville, Texas 77340

San Diego State University
School of Business Administration
San Diego, California 92182

San Francisco State University
School of Business
San Francisco, California 94132

Sangamon State University
Department of Business Administration
Springfield, Illinois 62708

San Jose State University
School of Business
San Jose, California 95192

Savannah State College
School of Business
Savannah, Georgia 31404

Seattle University
School of Business
Seattle, Washington 98122

Seton Hall University
W. Paul Stillman School of Business
South Orange, New Jersey 07079

Shippensburg State College
School of Business
Shippensburg, Pennsylvania 17257

Simmons College
Graduate Program in Management
Boston, Massachusetts 02215

Simon Fraser University
School of Business
Burnaby, British Columbia, Canada

Sir George Williams University
Faculty of Commerce and Administration
Montreal, Quebec, Canada
(instruction primarily in French)

Sonoma State University
Department of Management Science
Rohnert Park, California 94928

Southeastern Louisiana University
School of Business
Hammond, Louisiana 70401

Southeastern Massachussetts University
MBA Program
North Dartmouth, Massachusetts 02747

Southeastern Oklahoma State University
School of Business and Industry
Durant, Oklahoma 74701

Southeastern University
Graduate School of Business
and Public Administration
Washington, D.C. 20024

Southern Illinois University
School of Business
Carbondale, Illinois 62901
Edwardsville, Illinois 62026

Southern Methodist University
School of Business Administration
Dallas, Texas 75275

Southern Oregon State College
School of Business
Ashland, Oregon 97520

Southwest Missouri State University
School of Business
Springfield, Missouri 65802

Southwest Texas State University
School of Business
San Marcos, Texas 78666

Stanford University
Graduate School of Business
Stanford, California 94305

State University of New York
School of Business
Albany, New York 12222

State University of New York
School of Management
Binghamton, New York 13901
Buffalo, New York 14214

State University of New York Maritime College
Department of Marine Transportation
Fort Schuyler, Bronx, New York 10465

Stephen F. Austin State University
Graduate School
Nacogdoches, Texas 75961

Stetson University
School of Business Administration
Deland, Florida 32720

Stevens Institute of Technology
Management Science Department
Hoboken, New Jersey 07030

Suffolk University
Graduate School of Administration
Boston, Massachusetts 02114

Sul Ross State University
Department of Business Administration
Alpine, Texas 79830

Syracuse University
School of Management
Syracuse, New York 13210

Tel-Aviv University
Leon Recanati Graduate School of
Business Administration
Tel-Aviv, Israel
(instruction in Hebrew and English)

Temple University
School of Business Administration
Philadelphia, Pennsylvania 19122

Tennessee State University
School of Business
Nashville, Tennessee 37203

Tennessee Technological University
School of Business
Cookeville, Tennessee 38501

Texas Agricultural and Mechanical University
College of Business Administration
College Station, Texas 77843

Texas Arts and Industries University
Department of Business Administration
Corpus Christi, Texas 78411
Kingsville, Texas 78363

Texas Christian University
M. J. Neeley School of Business
Fort Worth, Texas 76129

Texas Eastern University
School of Business Administration
Tyler, Texas 75701

Texas Southern University
School of Business
Houston, Texas 77004

Texas Technological University
School of Business Administration
Lubbock, Texas 79409

Texas Woman's University
Department of Business and Economics
Denton, Texas 76204

Thomas College
Graduate School of Management
Waterville, Maine 04901

Trenton State College
Division of Business Administration and
Economics
Trenton, New Jersey 08625

Trinity University
School of Business
San Antonio, Texas 78284

Troy State University
School of Business and Commerce
Dothan, Alabama 36301
Troy, Alabama 36081

Tulane University
Graduate School of Business
Administration
New Orleans, Louisiana 70118

Union College and University
Institute of Administration and
Management
Schenectady, New York 12308

United States International University
School of Business Administration
San Diego, California 92131

Université de Sherbrooke
Faculte d' administration
Sherbrooke, Quebec, Canada

University of Akron
College of Business Administration
Akron, Ohio 44325

University of Alabama
Department of Administration Science
Birmingham, Alabama 35294
Huntsville, Alabama 35807

University of Alabama
School of Business
Birmingham, Alabama 35294
University, Alabama 35486

University of Alaska
Department of Business
Anchorage, Alaska 99504

University of Alaska
Department of Business Administration
Fairbanks, Alaska 99701

University of Alberta
Faculty of Business Administration and
Commerce
Edmonton, Alberta, Canada

University of Arizona
College of Business and Public
Administration
Tucson, Arizona 85721

University of Arkansas
College of Business Administration
Fayetteville, Arkansas 72701

University of Baltimore
School of Business
Baltimore, Maryland 21201

University of Bath
School of Management
Bath BA 27A4m, England

University Of Bridgeport
School of Business Administration
Bridgeport, Connecticut 06602

University of British Columbia
Faculty of Commerce and Business
Administration
Vancouver, British Columbia, Canada

University of Calgary
Faculty of Management
Calgary, Alberta T2N1N4, Canada

University of California
School of Management
Berkeley, California 94720

University of California
School of Administration
Irvine, California 92664

University of California
School of Management
Los Angeles, California 90024

University of California
Graduate School of Administration
Riverside, California 92502

University of Cape Town
School of Business
Rondebosch, Cape Province, South Africa

University of Central Arkansas
College of Business
Conway, Arkansas 72032

University of Central Florida
College of Business Administration
Orlando, Florida 32816

University of Chicago
Graduate School of Business
Chicago, Illinois 60637

University of Cincinnati
School of Business Administration
Cincinnati, Ohio 45221

University of Colorado
Graduate School of Business
Boulder, Colorado 80309

University of Connecticut
School of Business Administration
Storrs, Connecticut 06268

University of Dallas
Graduate School of Management
Irving, Texas 75061

University of Dayton
School of Business Administration
Dayton, Ohio 45469

University of Delaware
School of Business and Economics
Newark, Delaware 19711

University of Denver
College of Business Administration
Denver, Colorado 80210

University of Detroit
College of Business and Administration
Detroit, Michigan 48221

University of Evansville
School of Business Administration
Evansville, Indiana 47702

University of Florida
School of Business Administration
Gainesville, Florida 32611

University of Georgia
School of Business Administration
Athens, Georgia 30602

University of Glasgow
Glasgow Division of the Scottish Business
School
Glasgow, Scotland

University of Guam
College of Business and Public
Administration
Agana, Guam 96910

University of Guelph
School of Business
Guelph, Ontario, Canada

University of Hartford
School of Business and Public
Administration
West Hartford, Connecticut 06117

University of Hawaii
College of Business Administration
Honolulu, Hawaii 96822

University of Hong Kong
Management Studies
Hong Kong

University of Houston
College of Business
Houston, Texas 77004

University of Idaho
College of Business and Economics
Moscow, Idaho 83843

University of Illinois
College of Business Administration
Chicago, Illinois 60680

University of Illinois
College of Commerce and Business
Administration
Urban, Illinois 61801

University of Iowa
College of Business Administration
Iowa City, Iowa 52242

University of Kansas
School of Business
Lawrence, Kansas 66045

University of Kentucky
School of Business and Economics
Lexington, Kentucky 40506

University of Liverpool
School of Business Studies
Liverpool, England

University of Louisville
School of Business
Louisville, Kentucky 40208

University of Lowell
School of Management Science
Lowell, Massachusetts 01854

University of Maine
School of Business Administration
Orono, Maine 04473
Portland, Maine 04103

University of Manchester
Manchester Business School
Manchester, England

University of Manitoba
Faculty of Administrative Studies
Winnipeg, Manitoba, Canada

University of Maryland
Department of Business and Management
College Park, Maryland 20742

University of Massachusetts
School of Business Administration
Amherst, Massachusetts 01002

University of Miami
School of Business Administration
Coral Gables, Florida 33124

University of Michigan
School of Business Administration
Ann Arbor, Michigan 48109

University of Michigan–Dearborn
School of Management
Dearborn, Michigan 48128

University of Minnesota
School of Business Administration
Duluth, Minnesota 55812
Minneapolis, Minnesota 55455

University of Mississippi
School of Business Administration
University, Mississippi 38677

University of Missouri
School of Business Administration
Columbia, Missouri 65201
Kansas City, Missouri 64110
St. Louis, Missouri 63121

University of Moncton
Faculty of Administration
Moncton, New Brunswick, Canada

University of Montana
School of Business Administration
Missoula, Montana 59801

University of Montreal
School of Business Administration
Montreal, Quebec, Canada
(instruction primarily in French)

University of Nairobi
Faculty of Commerce
Nairobi, Kenya

University of Nebraska
College of Business Administration
Lincoln, Nebraska 68508
Omaha, Nebraska 68101

University of Nevada
College of Business Administration
Las Vegas, Nevada 89154
Reno, Nevada 89557

University of Newcastle
Faculty of Economics and Commerce
New South Wales 2308, Australia

University of New Hampshire
Whittemore School of Business and
Ecomonics
Durham, New Hampshire 03824

University of New Haven
School of Business Administration
West Haven, Connecticut 06516

University of New Mexico
School of Business and Administrative
Sciences
Albuquerque, New Mexico 87131

University of New Orleans
College of Business Administration
New Orleans, Louisiana 70122

University of New South Wales
School of Business
Sydney, New South Wales, Australia

University of North Alabama
School of Business
Florence, Alabama 35630

University of North Carolina
College of Business Administration
Chapel Hill, North Carolina 27514
Charlotte, North Carolina 28223
Greensboro, North Carolina 27412

University of North Dakota
College of Business and Public
Administration
Grand Forks, North Dakota 58201

University of Northern Colorado
School of Business
Greeley, Colorado 80639

University of Northern Iowa
School of Business
Cedar Falls, Iowa 50613

University of Notre Dame
College of Business Administration
Notre Dame, Indiana 46556

University of Oklahoma
College of Business Administration
Norman, Oklahoma 73069

University of Oregon
School of Business
Eugene, Oregon 97403

University of Otago
Advanced Business Program
Dunedin, New Zealand

University of Ottawa
Faculty of Management Sciences
Ottawa, Ontario, Canada

University of Pennsylvania
Wharton School of Business
Philadelphia, Pennsylvania 19174

University of Petroleum and Minerals
College of Industrial Management
Dhahran, Saudi Arabia

University of Pittsburgh
School of Business
Pittsburgh, Pennsylvania 15260

University of Portland
School of Business Administration
Portland, Oregon 97207

University of Puerto Rico
School of Business Administration
Rio Piedras, Puerto Rico 00931
(instruction in Spanish and English)

University of Puget Sound
School of Business and Public
Administration
Tacoma, Washington 98416

University of Reading
Department of Construction Management
Reading, Berkshire, England

University of Rhode Island
School of Business
Kingston, Rhode Island 02881

University of Richmond
School of Business
Richmond, Virginia 23173

University of Rochester
Graduate School of Management
Rochester, New York 14627

University of San Diego
School of Business Administration ·
San Diego, California 92110

University of San Francisco
College of Business Administration
San Francisco, California 94117

University of Santa Clara
School of Business
Santa Clara, California 95053

University of Saskatchewan
College of Commerce
Saskatoon, Saskatchewan, Canada

University of Scranton
Department of Business Administration
Scranton, Pennsylvania 18510

University of Sheffield
Postgraduate Business Programme
Sheffield, York, England

University of South Alabama
College of Business and Management
Studies
Mobile, Alabama 36688

University of South Carolina
College of Business Administration
Columbia, South Carolina 29208

University of South Dakota
School of Business
Vermillion, South Dakota 57069

University of Southern California
Graduate School of Business
Administration
Los Angeles, California 90007

University of Southern Mississippi
School of Business Administration
Hattiesburg, Mississippi 39401

University of South Florida
School of Business Administration
Tampa, Florida 33620

University of Southwestern Louisiana
Department of Business Administration
Lafayette, Louisiana 70504

University of Strathclyde
Strathclyde Division of the Scottish
Business School
Glasgow, Scotland

University of Sydney
Faculty of Economics
New South Wales 2006, Australia

University of Tampa
Division of Business and Economics
Tampa, Florida 33606

University of Tennessee
School of Business Administration
Chattanooga, Tennessee 37403
Knoxville, Tennessee 37916

University of Texas
School of Business
Arlington, Texas 76019
Austin, Texas 78712
Dallas, Texas 75230
El Paso, Texas 79968
Odessa, Texas 79762
San Antonio, Texas 78275

University of the District of Columbia
College of Business and Public
Management
Washington, D.C. 20005

University of the Witwatersrand
Graduate School of Business
Administration
Johannesburg, Transvaal, Republic of
South Africa

University of Toledo
College of Business Administration
Toledo, Ohio 43606

University of Toronto
Faculty of Management Studies
Toronto, Ontario, Canada

University of Tulsa
College of Business Administration
Tulsa, Oklahoma 74104

University of Utah
College of Business
Salt Lake City, Utah 84112

University of Vermont
Department of Business Administration
Burlington, Vermont 05401

University of Virginia
Colgate Darden Graduate School of
Business Administration
Charlottesville, Virginia 22903

University of Washington
Graduate School of Business
Administration
Seattle, Washington 98195

University of Western Australia
School of Commerce
Nedlands, Western Australia 6009,
Australia

University of Western Ontario
School of Business Administration
London, Ontario, Canada

University of West Florida
Department of Management
Pensacola, Florida 32504

University of Windsor
Faculty of Business Administration
Windsor, Ontario, Canada

University of Wisconsin
School of Business
Eau Claire, Wisconsin 54701
Madison, Wisconsin 53706
Milwaukee, Wisconsin 53201
Oshkosh, Wisconsin 54901
Platteville, Wisconsin 53818
Whitewater, Wisconsin 53190

University of Wyoming
Department of Business Administration
Laramie, Wyoming 82071

Utah State University
School of Business
Logan, Utah 84322

Valdosta State College
School of Business Administration
Valdosta, Georgia 31601

Vanderbilt University
Graduate School of Management
Nashville, Tennessee 37240

Virginia Commonwealth University
School of Business
Richmond, Virginia 23284

Virginia Polytechnic Institute and State University
College of Business
Blacksburg, Virginia 24061

Virginia State College
Department of Business Administration
Petersburg, Virginia 23803

Wagner College
Department of Business Administration
Staten Island, New York 10301

Wake Forest University
Babcock Graduate School of Management
Winston-Salem, North Carolina 27109

Walsh College of Accounting and Business Administration
Troy, Michigan 48084

Washington State University
College of Economics and Business
Pullman, Washington 99163

Washington University
Administration Graduate School of Business
St. Louis, Missouri 63130

Wayne State University
School of Business Administration
Detroit, Michigan 48202

Western Carolina University
School of Business
Cullowhee, North Carolina 28723

Western Connecticut State College
School of Business and Public Administration
Danbury, Connecticut 06810

Western Illinois University
School of Business
Macomb, Illinois 61455

Western Kentucky University
College of Business and Public Affairs
Bowling Green, Kentucky 42101

Western Michigan University
College of Business
Kalamazoo, Michigan 49001

Western New England College
Department of Business Administration
Springfield, Massachusetts 01119

Western New Mexico University
College of Business
Silver City, New Mexico 88061

Western State College of Colorado
Department of Business
Gunnison, Colorado 81230

Western Washington State College
Department of Business Administration
Bellingham, Washington 98225

West Georgia College
School of Business
Carrollton, Georgia 30117

West Texas State University
School of Business
Canyon, Texas 79016

West Virginia College of Graduate Studies
Division of Business and Management
Institute, West Virginia 25112

West Virginia University
College of Business and Economics
Morgantown, West Virginia 26506

Whittier College
MBA Program
Whittier, California 90608

Wichita State University
School of Business Administration
Wichita, Kansas 67208

Widener College
Center of Management and Applied Economics
Chester, Pennsylvania 19013

Wilfrid Laurier University
School of Business
Waterloo, Ontario, Canada

Wilkes College
Department of Commerce and Finance
Wilkes-Barre, Pennsylvania 18703

Willamette University
George H. Atkinson Graduate School of Administration
Salem, Oregon 97301

Winthrop College
School of Business Administration
Rock Hill, South Carolina 29730

Woodbury College
Department of Business Management
Los Angeles, California 90017

Worcester Polytechnic Institute
Program in Management Science and
Engineering
Worcester, Massachusetts 01609

World University
Graduate School of Business, Accounting
and Management Science
Hato Rey, Puerto Rico 00917

Wright State University
College of Business and Administration
Dayton, Ohio 45431

Xavier University
Graduate School of Business
Cincinnati, Ohio 45207

Yale University
School of Organization and Management
New Haven, Connecticut 06520

York College of Pennsylvania
MBA Program
York, Pennsylvania 17405

York University
Department of Business Administration
Downsview, Ontario, Canada

Youngstown State University
School of Business Administration
Youngstown, Ohio 44555

Appendix L. Relevant Quotations

587

Work

1, 40, 41, 77, 85, 87, 88, 105, 132, 135, 141, 148, 149, 175, 187, 202, 203, 212, 213, 226, 232, 235, 251, 254, 258, 282, 283, 284, 287, 291, 342, 347, 348, 355, 361, 373, 388, 407, 411, 420, 421, 437, 445

Relevant Quotations

MARK ABRAMS   1906–

We continue to overlook the fact that work has become a leisure activity. (*Observer,* June 3, 1962) [1]

JOHN EMERICH EDWARD DALBERG, LORD ACTON   1834–1902

Power tends to corrupt; absolute power corrupts absolutely. (Letter to Bishop Creighton, 1887) [2]

FRANKLIN PIERCE ADAMS   1881–1960

Christmas is over and Business is Business (for the other 364 days). [3]

The rich man has his motor car.
His country and his town estate.
He smokes a fifty-cent cigar
and Jeers at Fate.
(*The Rich Man*) [4]

GEORGE ADE   1866–1944

Draw your salary before spending it. (*The People's Choice*) [5]

AESOP   floruit 550 B.C.

Never trust the advice of a man in difficulties. (The Fox and the Goat) [6]

ANONYMOUS

When business is good it pays to advertise; when business is bad you've got to advertise. [7]

A banker is a man who lends you an umbrella when the weather is fair, and takes it away from you when it rains. [8]

In God we trust; all others must pay cash. [9]

An army of stags led by a lion would be better than an army of lions led by a stag. [10]

JEAN ANOUILH   1910–

What fun it would be to be poor, as long as one was excessively poor! Anything in excess is most exhilarating. (*Ring Round the Moon,* Act 11) [11]

SUSAN B. ANTHONY   1820–1906

Modern invention has banished the spinning-wheel, and the same law of progress makes the woman of today a different woman from her grandmother. [12]

LAWRENCE APPLEY   1904–
(president, American Management Association)

Management is now where the medical profession was when it decided that working in a drug store was not sufficient training to become a doctor. (*Elliott's Men at the Top*) [13]

ARISTODEMUS   c.750 B.C.

Money makes the man. [14]

ARISTOTLE   384–322 B.C.

Poverty is the parent of revolution and crime. (*Politics,* Book II) [15]

JOHN JACOB ASTOR III   1864–1912

A man who has a million dollars is as well off as if he were rich. (Attr.) [16]

JANE AUSTEN   1775–1817

Business, you know, may bring money, but friendship hardly ever does. (*John Knightley*) [17]

MALTBIE BABCOCK   1858–1901

Business is religion, and religion is business. The man who does not make a business of his religion has a religious life of no force, and the man who does not make a religion of his business has a business life of no character. [18]

FRANCIS BACON   1561–1626

We are much beholden to Machiavelli and others, that write what men do, and not what they ought to do. (*The Advancement of Learning*) [19]

Fortunes . . . come tumbling into some men's laps. (*The Advancement of Learning*) [20]

Riches are a good handmaiden, but the worst mistress. (*De dignitate et augmentis scientiarium*) [21]

Prosperity is not without many fears and distastes; and adversity is not without comforts and hopes. (*Of Adversity*) [22]

Fortune is like the market, where many times, if you can stay a little, the price will fall. *(Of Delays)* [23]

MIKHAIL BAKUNIN   1814–1876

Property is at once the consequence and the basis of the state. [24]

JAMES BALDWIN   1924–

Consider the history of labor in a country (USA) in which, spirtually speaking, there are no workers, only candidates for the hand of the boss's daughter. (*The Fire Next Time*) [25]

HONORE DE BALZAC   1799–1850

Manufacturing industry depends solely on itself, competition is its life. Protect it, and it goes to sleep; it dies from monopoly as well as from the tariff. The nation that succeeds in making all other nations its vassals will be the one which first proclaims commerical liberty; it will have enough manufacturing power to supply its productions at a cheaper price than those of its rivals. (*The Country Doctor*) [26]

H. GRANVILLE BARKER   1899–1946

And what we men of business should remember is that art, philosophy and religion can and should, in the widest sense of the term, be made to pay. And it's pay or perish; in this world. (*The Madras House*) [27]

BRUCE BARTON   1886–1967

The faults of advertising are only those common to all human institutions. If advertising speaks to a thousand in order to influence one, so does the church. And if it encourages people to live beyond their means, so does matrimony. Good times, bad times, there will always be advertising. In good times, people want to advertise; in bad times, they have to. *(Town and Country,* February 1955) [28]

BERNARD BARUCH   1870–1965

I will never be an old man. To me, old age is always fifteen years older than I am. (*Observer,* August 21, 1955) [29]

J. L. BASFORD   c.1897

It requires a strong constitution to withstand repeated attacks of prosperity. [30]

THOMAS HAYNES BAYLY   1797–1839

Those who have wealth must be watchful and wary. Power. Alas! naught but misery brings. (*I'd Be a Butterfly*) [31]

AUGUST BEBEL   1840–1913

The nature of business is swindling. [32]

HENRY WARD BEECHER   1813–1887

It takes a man to make a devil; and the fittest man for such a purpose is a snarling, waspish, red-hot, fiery creditor. [33]

A tool is but the extension of a man's hand, and a machine is but a complex tool. And he that invents a machine augments the power of a man and the well-being of mankind. [34]

APHRA BEHN   1640–1689

Money speaks sense in a language all nations understand. (*The Rover*) [35]

ARNOLD BENNETT   1867–1931

A man accustomed to think in millions—other people's millions. (*Journal,* June 1929) [36]

WILLIAM BERNBACH   1911–1982
(advertising executive)

The most powerful element in advertising is the truth. (*New York Times,* May 25, 1976) [37]

HUGH M. BEVILLE   1908–
(former director of Research and Planning, NBC)

In advertising there is a saying that if you can keep your head while all those around you are losing theirs—then you just don't understand the problem. (NBC corporate brochure, November 18, 1954) [38]

AMBROSE BIERCE   1842–1914

The gambling known as business looks with austere disfavor upon the business known as gambling. (Mencken, *A New Dictionary of Quotations*) [39]

WILLIAM BLAKE   1757–1827

I must create a system, or be enslaved by another man's;
will not reason and compare; my business is to create. (*Jerusalem*) [40]
Tools were made and born were hands,
Every farmer understands. (Proverbs) [41]
I have mental jobs and mental health,
Mental friends and mental wealth,
I've a wife that I love and that loves me;
I've all but riches bodily. (Mammon) [42]

STEUART HENDERSON BRITT   1907–1979

Doing business without advertising is like winking at a girl in the dark. You know

what you are doing, but nobody else does. (*New York Herald Tribune,* October 30, 1956) [43]

CHARLES BROWER   1901–
(president, Batten, Barton, Durstine & Osborn)

There is no such thing as "soft sell" and "hard sell." There is only "smart sell" and "stupid sell." (National Sales Executives Convention, May 20, 1958) [44]

WILLIAM J. BRYAN   1860–1925

You shall not press down upon the brow of labor this crown of thorns, you shall not crucify mankind upon a cross of gold. (Speech at the National Democratic Convention, 1896) [45]

GEORGE BUCHANAN   1506–1582

A fool and his money are soon parted. [46]

GEORGE-LOUIS DE BUFFON   1707–1788

Genius is nothing but a great aptitude for patience. (Attr.) [47]

EDMUND BURKE   1729–1797

People will not look forward to posterity who never look backward to their ancestors. (*Reflections on the Revolution in France*) [48]

Good order is the foundation of all things. (*Reflections on the Revolution in France*) [49]

If we command our wealth, we shall be rich and free; if our wealth commands us, we are poor indeed. (*Letters on a Regicide Peace*) [50]

H. S. M. BURNS   1900–1971
(president, Shell Oil Co.)

A good manager is a man who isn't worried about his own career but rather the careers of those who work for him. My advice: Don't worry about yourself. Take care of those who work for you and you'll float to greatness on their achievements. (*Elliott's Men at the Top*) [51]

ROBERT BURNS   1759–1797

We labor soon, we labor late,
To feed the titled knave, man;
And a' the comfort we're to get
Is that ayont the grave, man. (*The Tree of Liberty*) [52]

ROBERT BURTON   1577–1640

The rich are indeed rather possessed by their money than possessors. (*Anatomy of Melancholy*) [53]

Machiavel says virtue and riches seldom settle on one man. (*Anatomy of Melancholy*) [54]

NICHOLAS MURRAY BUTLER   1862–1947

An expert is one who knows more and more about less and less. (Commencement address, Columbia University) [55]

SAMUEL BUTLER   1835–1902

It has been said that the love of money is the root of all evil. The want of money is so quite as truly. (*Erewhon* [56]

GEORGE BYRON   1788–1824

When we think we lead we most are led. (*The Two Foscari*) [57]

HENRY J. BYRON   1834–1884

Life's too short for chess. (*Our Boys*) [58]

He's up to these grand games, but one of these days, I'll loose him on to skittles— and astonish him. (*Our Boys*) [59]

JAMES BRANCH CABELL   1879–1958

The optimist proclaims that we live in the best of all possible worlds; and the pessimist fears this is so. (*The Silver Stallion*) [60]

ALBERT CAMUS   1913–1960

Every fulfillment is slavery. It drives us to a higher fulfillment. (*The Notebooks*) [61]

THOMAS CARLYLE   1795–1881

Debt is a bottomless sea. [62]

A fair day's wages for a fair day's work: it is as just a demand as governed men ever made of governing. (*Past and Present*) [63]

ANDREW CARNEGIE   1837–1919

Surplus wealth is a sacred trust which its possessor is bound to administer in his lifetime for the good of the community. (*Gospel of Wealth*) [64]

DALE CARNEGIE   1888–1955

The ideas I stand for are not mine. I borrowed them from Socrates. I swiped them from Chesterfield. I stole them from Jesus. And I put them in a book. If you don't like their rules, whose would you use? (*How To Win Friends and Influence People*) [65]

MARCUS CATO   234–149 B.C.

Buy not what you want, but what you have need of; what you do not want is dear at a farthing. (*The Censor*) [66]

SUSANNA CENTLIVRE   1667–1723

Want, the mistress of invention. (*The Busy Body*) [67]

OLIVER LYTTLETON, 1st VISCOUNT, LORD CHANDOS   1920–
(banking executive)

I have heard speakers . . . use the phrase, "I can say without fear of contradiction. . . ." Anyone who says this in a modern democracy, or to the shareholders of a modern company, should see the doctor. (*Memoirs of Lord Chandos,*1963) [68]

PHILIP DORMER STANHOPE, EARL OF CHES-
TERFIELD   1694–1773

Whatever is worth doing at all, is worth doing well. (*Letters*, March 10, 1746) [69]

Without some dissimulation no business
can be carried on at all. (*Letters,* May 22,
1749) [70]

G. K. CHESTERTON   1874–1936

To be clever enough to get all that money,
one must be stupid enough to want it.
(*The Innocence of Father Brown*) [71]

SIR WINSTON CHURCHILL   1874–1965

It is a fine thing to be honest but it is also
very important to be right. (*Of Mr. Baldwin*) [72]

The destiny of mankind is not decided by
material computation. When great causes
are on the move in the world . . . we learn
that we are spirits, not animals, and that
something is going on in space and time,
and beyond space and time, which
whether we like it or not, spells duty. (University of Rochester, New York, June 16,
1941) [73]

CICERO   106–43 B.C.

Borrowing from Peter to pay Paul. [74]

It is fortune, not wisdom, that rules man's
life.[75]

GROVER CLEVELAND   1837–1908

When more of the people's sustenance is
exacted through the form of taxation that
is necessary to meet the just obligations
of Government and expenses of its economical administration, such exaction
becomes ruthless extortion and a violation of the fundamental principles of a
free Government. (Annual presidential
message. December 1886) [76]

A truly American sentiment recognizes the
dignity of labor and the fact that honor lies

in honest toil. [77]

SIR EDWARD COKE   1552–1634

They [corporations] cannot commit trea-
son, nor be outlawed nor excommunicat-
ed, for they have no souls. (*Case of
Sutton's Hospital*) [78]

J. B. COLBERT   1619–1683

The art of taxation consists in so plucking
the goose as to obtain the largest amount
of feathers with the least possible amount
of hissing. [79]

FAIRFAX CONE   1903–
(advertising executive)

Advertising is what you do when you can't
go see somebody. That's all it is. (*Christian Science Monitor*, March 20, 1963)
[80]

CONFUCIUS   551–478 B.C.

He who will not economize will have to ago-
nize. [81]

CALVIN COOLIDGE   1872–1933

The business of America is business.
(Speech in Washington, D.C., January 17,
1925) [82]

After order and liberty, economy is one of
the highest essentials of a free government. . . . Economy is always a guarantee
of peace. (Speech, 1923) [83]

L. L. CORLBERT

When I've had a rough day, before I go to
sleep I ask myself if there's anything more
I can do right now. If there isn't, I sleep
sound. (*Newsweek*, August 22, 1955) [84]

BISHOP CUMBERLAND   1631–1718

Better to wear out than to rust out. [85]

LEONARDO DA VINCI   1452–1519

As a well-spent day brings happy sleep, so life well used brings happy death. (From his notebooks) [86]

EUGENE V. DEBS   1855–1926

The workers are the saviors of society, the redeemers of the race. (Speech, 1905) [87]

THOMAS DEKKER   1572–1632

Honest Labor bears a lovely face. (*Patient Grissill*) [88]

VALERY GISCARD D'ESTAING   1926–

How do the French see America? As an attractive, animated drawing that tends to be simplistic, just like any image that one people conjures up about another. Pell-mell you would doubtless see the landing of the G.I.s in Normandy, Roosevelt, Ike and Kennedy, Wall Street, cavalcades of Indians in the Far West, Al Capone, Marilyn Monroe, Marlon Brando, Muhammad Ali, pretty majorettes, West Side Story, bourbon and Coca-Cola, man's first steps on the moon—with a musical background of Louis Armstrong and Duke Ellington. (on the U.S. Bicentennial, *Time,* May 24, 1976) [89]

CHARLES DICKENS   1812–1870

Here are all kinds of employers wanting all sorts of servants, and all sorts of servants wanting all kinds of employers, and they never seem to come together. (*Martin Chuzzlewit*) [90]

Here's the rule for bargains: "Do other men, for they would do you." That's the true business precept. (*Martin Chuzzlewit*) [91]

Buy an annuity cheap, and make your life interesting to yourself and everybody else that watches the speculation. (*Martin Chuzzlewit*) [92]

BENJAMIN DISRAELI   1804–1881

The secret of success is constancy to pur-

pose. (Speech, June 24, 1870) [93]

Increased means and increased leisure are the two civilizers of man. (Speech, April 3, 1872) [94]

(GEORGE) NORMAN DOUGLAS   1868–1952

You can tell the ideals of a nation by its advertisements. (*South Wind*) [95]

. . . impoverished them to such an extent that for three consecutive months they could barely afford the most unnecessary luxuries of life. (*South Wind*) [96]

SIR ALEC DOUGLAS-HOME   1903–

There are two problems in my life. The political ones are insoluble and the economic ones are imcomprehensible. (Speech, January 1964) [97]

PETER DRUCKER   1909–

The great majority of executives tend to focus downward. They are occupied with efforts rather than with results. They worry over what the organization and their superiors "owe" them and should do for them. And they are conscious above all of the authority they "should have." As a result, they render themselves ineffectual. [98]

THOMAS DRUMMOND   1797–1840

Property has its duties as well as its rights. (Letter, May 22, 1838) [99]

ALEXANDER DUMAS   1824–1895

Business? It's quite simple. It's other people's money. (*La Question d'Argent*) [100]

FINLEY PETER DUNNE   1867–1936

I don't know what a chamber of commerce is unless 'tis a place where business men go to sleep. (*Mr. Dooley on the Amateur Ambassadors*) [101]

WILL DURANT   1885–1981

The health of nations is more important than the wealth of nations. (*What Is Civilization?*) [102]

MARIA EDGEWORTH   1767–1849

Business was his pleasure; pleasure was his business. (*The Contrast*) [103]

THOMAS ALVA EDISON   1847–1931

Genius is one percent inspiration and ninety-nine percent perspiration. (Interview) [104]

I never did anything worth doing by accident, nor did any of my inventions come by accident; they came by work. [105]

HAVELOCK ELLIS   1859–1939

To be a leader of men one must turn one's back on men. (Introduction to *Against the Grain*) [106]

The greatest task before civilization at present is to make machines what they ought to be, the slaves, instead of the masters of men. (*Little Essays of Love and Virtue*) [107]

RALPH WALDO EMERSON   1803–1882

Money, which represents the prose of life, and which is hardly spoken of in parlors without an apology, is, in its effects and laws, as beautiful as roses. (*Nominalist and Realist*) [108]

Can anybody remember when the times were not hard and money not scarce? (*Works and Days*) [109]

Ah, if the rich were rich as the poor fancy riches! [110]

FRIEDRICH ENGELS   1820–1895

By bourgeoisie is meant the class of modern capitalists, owners of the means of social production and employers of wage-labor. By proletariat, the class of modern wage-laborers who, having no means of production of their own, are reduced to sell-ing their labor-power in order to live. (Footnote to *Manifesto of the Communist Party*) [111]

EURIPIDES   480–406 B.C.

Fortune truly helps those who are of good judgment. [112]

GEORGE FARQUHAR   1678–1707

There's no scandal like rags, nor any crime so shameful as poverty. (*The Beaux' Strategem*) [113]

WILLIAM FAULKNER   1897–1962

The Swiss . . . are not a people so much as a neat clean solvent business. (*Intruder in the Dust*) [114]

FRANÇOIS DE SALIGNAC DE LA MOTHE FENELON 1651–1715

Commerce is a kind of spring, which, diverted from its natural channel, ceases to flow. (*Telemachus*) [115]

HENRY FORD   1863–1947

History is bunk. (On the witness stand, when suing the *Chicago Tribune,* July 1919) [116]

I did not say it [history] was bunk. It was bunk to me. . . . I did not need it very bad. (Quoted in A. Nevins, *Ford: Expansion and Challenge*) [117]

ANATOLE FRANCE   1844–1924

In every well-governed state wealth is a sacred thing; in democracies it is the only sacred thing. (*Penguin Island*) [118]

BENJAMIN FRANKLIN   1706–1790

He that goes a borrowing goes a sorrowing. (*Poor Richard's Almanac*) [119]

Remember that time is money. (*Advice to Young Tradesmen*) [120]

In this world nothing can be said to be certain, except death and taxes. (Letter to Jean-Baptiste Le Roy, November 13, 1789) [121]

Creditors have been memories than debtors. [122]

Beware of little expenses; a small leak will sink a great ship. [123]

A life of leisure and a life of laziness are two things. (*Poor Richard's Almanac*) [124]

If you would be wealthy, think of saving as well as of getting. [125]

SIGMUND FREUD   1856–1939

A woman who is very anxious to get children always reads storks instead of stocks. (*Psychopathology of Everyday Life*) [126]

MAX FRISCH   1911–

Technology ... the knack of so arranging the world that we don't have to experience it. (Quoted in D. J. Boorstin, *The Image*) [127]

ROBERT FROST   1874–1963

A diplomat is a man who always remembers a woman's birthday but never remembers her age. (Quoted in *Treasury of Humorous Quotations*) [128]

Nobody was ever meant to remember or invent what he did with every cent. (*The Hardship of Accounting*) [129]

JOHN K. GALBRAITH   1908–

Wealth is not without its advantages, and the case to the contrary, although it has often been made, has never proved widely persuasive. (*The Affluent Society*) [130]

Wealth has never been a sufficient source of honor in itself. It must be advertised, and the normal medium is obtrusively expensive goods. (*The Affluent Society*)

[131]

The greater the wealth the thicker will be the dirt. This indubitably describes a tendency of our time. (*The Affluent Society*) [132]

The test will be less the effectiveness of our material investment than the effectiveness of our investment in men. (*The Affluent Society*) [133]

JAMES A. GARFIELD   1831–1881

Commerce links all mankind in one common brotherhood of mutual dependence and interests. [134]

HENRY GEORGE   1839–1897

Capital is a result of labor, and is used by labor to assist in further production. Labor is the active and initial force, and labor is therefore the employer of capital. (*Progress and Poverty*) [135]

For as labor cannot produce without the use of land, the denial of the equal right to use of land is necessarily the denial of the right of labor to its own produce. (*Progress and Poverty*) [136]

The tax upon land values (Single Tax) is the most just and equal of all taxes. It is the taking by the community, for the use of the community, of that value which is the creation of the community. (*Progress and Poverty*) [137]

JOHN PAUL GETTY   1892–1976

I have often maintained that I possess a rare talent and strong inclination to be a beachcomber.... If it were not for the demands made upon me by my business, I would provide living proof that a man can live quite happily for decades without even doing any work. (*My Life and Fortunes*) [138]

... remember, a billion dollars isn't worth what it used to be (*Fortune*, 1957) [139]

EDWARD GIBBON   1737–1794

... vicissitudes of fortune, which spares neither man nor the proudest of his works, which buries empires and cities in a common grave. (*Decline and Fall of the Roman Empire*) [140]

KAHLIL GIBRAN   1883–1931

Work is love made visible. And if you cannot work with love but only with distaste, it is better that you should leave your work and sit at the gate of the temple and take alms of those who work with joy. (*The Prophet*) [141]

HENRY GILES   1809–1882

If the poor man cannot always get meat, the rich man cannot always digest it. [142]

MME de GIRARDIN   1804–1855

Business is other people's money. (*Marguerites*) [143]

WILLIAM GLADSTONE   1809–1898

Commerce is the equalizer of the wealth of nations. [144]

LOUIS GLICKMAN

The best investment on earth is earth. (*New York Post*, September 3, 1957) [145]

SAMUEL GOLDWYN   1882–1974

A verbal contract isn't worth the paper it's written on. (Attr.) [146]

JAMES GRAHAME   1765–1811

Business is like oil. It won't mix with anything but business. [147]

ULYSSES S. GRANT   1822–1885

Labor disgraces no man; unfortunately you occasionally find men disgrace labor. (Speech at Midland International Arbitration Union, Birmingham, England, 1877)

[148]

ROBERT GRAVES   1895–1977

Among the working classes one of the unforgivable words of abuse is "bastard"—because they take bastardy seriously. (*Occupation: Writer*) [149]

HORACE GREELEY   1811–1872

The illusion that times that were are better than those that are, has probably pervaded all ages. (*The American Conflict*) [150]

The best business you can go into you will find on your father's farm or in his workshop. If you have no family or friends to aid you, and no prospect opened to you there, turn your face to the great West, and there build up a home and fortune. (*To Aspiring Young Men*) [151]

WALTER KNOWLETON GUTMAN

There is nothing like the ticker tape except a woman—nothing that promises, hour after hour, day after day, such sudden developments; nothing that disappoints so often or occasionally fulfills with such unbelievable, passionate magnificence. (*Coronet*, March 1960) [152]

T. C. HALIBURTON   1796–1865

No man is rich whose expenditure exceeds his means; and no one is poor whose incomings exceed his outgoings. [153]

Death and taxes are inevitable. [154]

ALEXANDER HAMILTON   1757–1804

A national debt, if it is not excessive, will be to us a national blessing. [155]

GILBERT HARDING

I've never consciously striven for worldly success. But once I was aware I had it I must say that I'm terrified of losing it. (*Gilbert Harding and His Friends*) [156]

ALAN HARRINGTON

A corporation prefers to offer a job to a man who already has one, or doesn't immediately need one. The company accepts you if you are already accepted. To obtain entry into paradise, in terms of employment, you should be in a full state of grace. (*Life in the Crystal Palace*, 1959) [157]

I have found it to be the craft of arranging truths so that people will like you. Public-relations specialists make flower arrangements of the facts, placing them so that the wilted and less attractive petals are hidden by sturdy blooms. (*Life in the Crystal Palace,* 1959) [158]

SIR JOHN HARRINGTON   1561–1612

Fortune, men say doth give too much to many, But yet she never gave enough to any. (*Epigrams*) [159]

JOSEPH HELLER   1923–

He was a self-made man who owed his lack of success to nobody. (*Catch-22*)[160]

Frankly, I'd like to see the government get out of war altogether and leave the whole field to private industry. (*Catch-22*) [161]

WALTER HELLER   1915–

In the old days we used to say that when the United States economy sneezed, the rest of the world went to bed with pneumonia. Now when the United States economy sneezes the other countries say "Gesundheit." (*New York Times,* May 8, 1961) [162]

O. HENRY (WILLIAM S. PORTER)   1862–1910

Whenever he saw a dollar in another man's hands he took it as a personal grudge, if he couldn't take it any other way. (*The Octopus Marooned*) [163]

When a poor man finds a long-hidden quarter-dollar that has slipped through a rip in his vest lining, he sounds the pleasure of life with a deeper plummet than any millionaire can hope to case. (*The Voice of the City*) [164]

GEORGE HERBERT   1593–1632

Poverty is no sin. (*Jacula Prudentum*) [165]

The buyer needs a hundred eyes, the seller not one. (*Jacula Prudentum*) [166]

JOHN HEYWOOD   1497–1580

The loss of wealth is loss of dirt, as sages in all times assert; The happy man's without a shirt. (*Be Merry Friends*) [167]

CLAIRE GIANNINI HOFFMAN   1903–
(first woman director of the Bank of America)

The woman who climbs to a high post and then wants everybody to know how important she is, is the worst enemy of her own sex. (July 7, 1954) [168]

HOMER   c. 1000 B.C.

The bitter dregs of fortune's cup to drain. [169]

HERBERT C. HOOVER   1874–1964

. . . the American system of rugged individualism. (Campaign speech, New York, October 22, 1928) [170]

ANTHONY HOPE   1863–1933

Economy is going without something you do want in case you should, some day, want something you probably won't want. (*The Dolly Dialogues*) [171]

HORACE   65–8 B.C.

Riches either serve or govern the possessor. [172]

RICHARD HOVEY   1864–1900

The wealth of nations is men, not silk and

cotton and gold. (*Peace*) [173]

E. W. HOWE   1853–1937

No man's credit is as good as his money. (*Sinner Sermons*) [174]

ELBERT HUBBARD   1856–1915

One machine can do the work of fifty ordinary men. No machine can do the work of one extraordinary man. (*Roycroft Dictionary and Book of Epigrams*) [175]

VICTOR HUGO   1802–1885

A creditor is worse than a master; for a master owns only your person, a creditor owns your dignity, and can belabor that. (*Les Misérables*) [176]

DAVID HUME   1711–1776

Avarice, the spur of industry. (*Essays, Of Civil Liberty*) [177]

SIR JULIAN HUXLEY   1887–1975

We all know how the size of sums of money appears to vary in a remarkable way according as they are being paid in or paid out. (*Essays of a Biologist*) [178]

THOMAS H. HUXLEY   1825–1895

Every great advance in natural knowledge has involved the absolute rejection of authority. (*Lay Sermons*) [179]

ROGER GREEN INGERSOLL   1833–1899

Few rich men own their own property. The property owns them. (Address to the McKinley League, New York, October 29, 1896) [180]

WASHINGTON IRVING   1783–1859

The almighty dollar, that great object of universal devotion throughout our land, seems to have no genuine devotees in these peculiar villages. (*Wolfert's Roost*, ''The Creole Village'') [181]

WILLIAM JAMES   1842–1910

The instinct of ownership is fundamental in man's nature. [182]

RICHARD JEFFERIES   1848–1887

The most extraordinary spectacle is the vast expenditure of labor and time wasted in obtaining mere subsistance. (*The Story of My Heart*) [183]

THOMAS JEFFERSON   1743–1826

Advertisements contain the only truths to be relied on in a newspaper. (Letter to Nathaniel Macon) [184]

Banking establishments are more dangerous than standing armies. (Letter to Gerry) [185]

Whenever there is, in any country, uncultivated land and unemployed poor, it is clear that the laws of property have been so far extended as to violate natural right. (Letter, 1785) [186]

JEROME K. JEROME   1859–1927

I like work; it fascinates me. I can sit and look at it for hours. I love to keep it by me; the idea of getting rid of it nearly breaks my heart. (*Three Men in a Boat*) [187]

LYNDON B. JOHNSON   1908–1973

Every man has a right to a Saturday night bath. (*Observer*, March 13, 1960) [188]

SAMUEL JOHNSON   1709–1784

Whatever you have, spend less. (Boswell's *Life of Dr. Johnson*) [189]

Life is short. The sooner that a man begins to enjoy his wealth the better. [190]

ERIC JOHNSTON

The dinosaur's eloquent lesson is that if some bigness is good, an overabundance of bigness is not necessarily better. (U.S.

Chamber of Commerce, February 23, 1958) [191]

JOHN ALEXANDER JOYCE   1842–1915

You must leave your many millions
And the gay and festive crowd;
Though you roll in royal billions,
There's no pocket in a shroud.
(*There's No Pocket in a Shroud*) [192]

FREDERICK KAPPEL   1902–
(former chairman, American Telephone &
    Telegraph Co.)

The Bell system is like a damn big dragon.
    You kick it in the tail, and two years later, it
    feels it in its head. (*Look,* August 28, 1962)
    [193]

ALPHONSE KARR   1808–1890

The more things change, the more they are
    the same. (*Les Guepes,* January 1849)
    [194]

JOHN KETAS

If Detroit is right . . . there is little wrong with
    the American car that is not wrong with
    the American public. (*The Insolent Chari-
    ots*) [195]

JOHN MAYNARD KEYNES (Lord Keynes)
                                                    1883–1946

It is ideas, not vested interests, which are
    dangerous for good or evil. (*The Power of
    Ideas*) [196]

"Sound" finance may be right psychologi-
    cally; but economically it is a depressing
    influence. (*Observer,* May 31, 1933) [197]

The recent gyrations of the dollars have
    looked to me more like a gold standard on
    the booze than the ideal managed curren-
    cy which I hope for. (*Observer,* 1933)
    [198]

It is Enterprise which builds and improves
    the world's possessions. . . . If Enterprise
    is afoot, wealth accumulates whatever

may be happening to Thrift; and if Enterprise is asleep, Wealth decays, whatever
Thrift may be doing. (*Treatise on Money*)
[199]

OMAR KHAYYAM   d.1123

Ah, take the cash, and let the credit go. (*Ru-
baiyat*) [200]

JAMES MICHAEL KIERAN   1863–1936

The Brain Trust (Description of the professional advisors selected by President F.
D. Roosevelt) [201]

RUDYARD KIPLING   1865–1936

Each in his place, by right, not grace,
Shall rule his heritage—
The men who simply do the work
For which they draw the wage. (*The Wage-
Slaves*) [202]

And no one shall work for money, and no
one shall work for fame,
But each for the joy of working. (*When
Earth's Last Picture Is Painted*) [203]

ANDREW LANG   1844–1912

He uses statistics as a drunken man uses
lamp-posts—for support rather than illu-
mination. (Quoted in *Treasury of Humorous Quotations*) [204]

HAROLD JOSEPH LASKI   1893–1950

It would be madness to let the purposes or
the methods of private enterprise set the
habits of the age of atomic energy. (*Plan
or Perish*) [205]

LE   CORBUSIER   (EDUOARD   JEANNERET)
                                                    1887–1965

A house is a machine for living in. (*Vers une
architecture*) [206]

GERALD STANLEY LEE   1862–1944

A man's success in business today turns
upon his power of getting people to be-

lieve he has something that they want. (*Crowds*) [207]

V. I. LENIN   1870–1924

Under capitalism we have a state in the proper sense of the word, that is, a special machine for the suppression of one class by another. (*The State and Revolution*) [208]

Political institutions are a superstructure resting on an economic foundation. (*The Three Sources and Three Constituent Parts of Marxism*) [209]

POPE LEO XIII (JOACHIM PECCI)   1810–1903

Every man has by nature the right to possess property as his own. (Encyclical letter, May 15, 1891) [210]

It is one thing to have a right to the possession of money, and another to have a right to use money as one pleases. (Encyclical letter, May 15, 1891) [211]

Among the purposes of a society should be to try to arrange for a continuous supply of work at all times and seasons (Encyclical letter, May 15, 1891 [212]

A workman ought to have leisure in proportion to the wear and tear of his strength. [213]

Each needs the other: capital cannot do without labor, nor labor without capital. [214]

MAX LERNER   1902–

American capitalism has been both overpraised and overindicted . . . it is neither the Plumed Knight nor the monstrous Robber Baron. (*America as a Civilization*, 1958) [215]

JOHN L. LEWIS   1880–1967

All forms of government fail when it comes up to the question of bread—bread for the family, something to eat. Bread to a man

with a hungry family comes first—before his union, before his citizenship, before his church affiliation. Bread! (*Saturday Evening Post*, October 12, 1963) [216]

SINCLAIR LEWIS   1885–1951

He was nimble in the calling of selling houses for more than people could afford to pay. (*Babbitt*) [217]

M. G. LICHTWER   1719–1783

Debt is the worst poverty. [218]

ABRAHAM LINCOLN   1809–1865

Labor is prior to, and independent of, capital. Capital is only the fruit of labor, and could never have existed if labor had not first existed. (First annual message to Congress, December 3, 1861) [219]

Property is desirable, is a positive good in the world. Let not him who is houseless pull down the house of another, but let him work diligently and build one for himself, thus by example assuring that his own shall be safe from violence when built. [220]

WALTER LIPPMANN   1889–1974

The final test of a leader is that he leaves behind him in other men the conviction and the will to carry on. . . . The genius of a good leader is to leave behind him a situation which common sense, without the grace of genius, can deal with successfully. (*Roosevelt Has Gone*) [221]

DAVID, EARL LLOYD GEORGE   1863–1945

You cannot feed the hungry on statistics. (Speech, 1904) [222]

JOHN LOCKE   1632–1704

The reason why men enter into society is the preservation of their property. (*Treatise on Government*) [223]

LONGUS   FIFTH CENTURY

He is so poor that he could not keep a dog. (*Daphnis and Chloe*) [224]

WILLIAM LOWNDES   1652–1724

Take care of the pence, and the pounds will take care of themselves. [225]

SIR JOHN LUBBOCK   1834–1913

The idle man does not know what it is to enjoy rest. Hard work, moreover, not only tends to give us rest for the body, but, what is even more important, peace to the mind. (*The Pleasures of Life*) [226]

HENRY LUCE   1898–1967

Business more than any other occupation is a continual dealing with the future; it is a continual calculation an instinctive exercise in foresight. (*Fortune*, October 1960) [227]

CHARLES LUCKMAN   1909–
(architect and executive)

Success is that old ABC—ability, breaks, and courage. (*New York Mirror*, September 19, 1955) [228]

THOMAS BABINGTON, LORD MACAULAY
                       1800–1859

Free trade, one of the greatest blessings which a government can confer on a people, is in almost every country unpopular. (*Knight's Quarterly*, November 1824) [229]

NICCOLO MACHIAVELLI   1469–1527

When neither their property nor their honor is touched, the majority of men live content. (*The Prince*) [230]

MOSES BEN MAIMON (MAIMONIDES)1135–1204

Anticipate charity by preventing poverty; assist the reduced fellowman, either by a considerable gift, or a sum of money, or by teaching him a trade, or by putting him in the way of business, so that he may earn an honest livelihood, and not be forced to the dreadful alternative of holding out his hand for charity. This is the highest step and the summit of charity's golden ladder. (*Charity's Eight Degrees*) [231]

EDWIN MARKHAM   1852–1940

Bowed by the weight of centuries he leans
Upon his hoe and gazes on the ground,
The emptiness of ages in his face,
And on his back the burden of the world.
(*The Man with the Hoe*) [232]

ALFRED MARSHALL   1842–1924

Capital is that part of wealth which is devoted to obtaining further wealth. [233]

THOMAS RILEY MARSHALL   1854–1925

What this country needs is a good five-cent cigar. (Remark to John Crockett, chief clerk of the U.S. Senate) [234]

"ABE MARTIN"   1868–1930

It's no disgrace to be poor, but it might as well be. (*The Sayings of Abe Martin*) [235]

GROUCHO MARX   1890–1977

I've worked myself up from nothing to a state of extreme poverty. (film, *Monkey Business*) [236]

KARL MARX   1818–1883

The capitalist himself is a practical man, who, it is true, does not always reflect on what he says outside his office, but who always knows what he does inside the latter. (*Capital*) [237]

Constant labor of one uniform kind destroys the intensity and flow of a man's animal spirits, which find recreation and delight in mere change of activity. (*Capital*) [238]

... the intellectual desolation, artificially produced by converting immature human beings into mere machines. (*Capital*)

[239]

The proletarians have nothing to lose but their chains. They have a world to win. Workers of the world, unite! (*Manifesto of the Communist Party*) [240]

Capital is dead labor that, vampire-like, lives only by sucking living labor, and lives the more, the more labor it sucks. (*Capital*) [241]

All our inventions have endowed material forces with intellectual life, and degraded human life into a material force. (Speech, 1856) [242]

WILLIAM SOMERSET MAUGHAM   1874–1965

There is nothing so degrading as the constant anxiety about one's means of livelihood.... Money is like a sixth sense without which you cannot make a complete use of the other five. (*Of Human Bondage*) [243]

If a nation values anything more than freedom, it will lose its freedom; and the irony of it is that if it is comfort of money that it values more, it will lose that too. (*Strictly Personal*) [244]

STEVE MAYHAM
(Toilet Goods Association executive)

This is an industry of ideas and imagination, and what we are selling is hope. (Speech before the Toilet Goods Association, *Time*, June 16, 1958) [245]

GEORGE MEANY   1894–1980

Anybody who has any doubt about the ingenuity or the resourcefulness of a plumber never got a bill from one. (CBS-TV, January 8, 1954) [246]

The American people would rather give away some of their rice, wheat, butter, textiles and medicines to the needy people in Communist China, Cuba and elsewhere behind the Iron Curtain than to sell these goods for gold mined by slave la-

bor. (*New York Times*, April 1, 1962) [247]

ANDREW MELLON   1855–1937

A nation is not in danger of financial disaster merely because it owes itself money. (1933) [248]

H. L. MENCKEN   1880–1956

Poverty is a soft pedal upon all branches of human activity, not excepting the spiritual. (*A Book of Prefaces*) [249]

All successful newspapers are ceaselessly querulous and bellicose. They never defend anyone or anything if they can help it; if the job is forced upon them, they tackle it by denouncing someone or something else. (*Prejudices, First Series*) [250]

The average male gets his living by such depressing devices that boredom becomes a sort of natural state to him. (*In Defence of Women*) [251]

He [the businessman] is the only man who is forever apologizing for his occupation. (*Prejudices, Types of Men*) [252]

GEORGE MIKES   1912–

The Swiss managed to build a lovely country around their hotels. (*Down with Everybody*) [253]

JOHN STUART MILL   1806–1873

What capital does for production is to afford the shelter, protection, tools, and materials which the work requires, and to feed and so otherwise maintain the laborers during the process. Whatever things are destined for this use—destined to supply productive labor with these various prerequisites—are Capital. (*The Principles of Political Economy*) [254]

ARTHUR MILLER   1915–

All organization is and must be grounded on the idea of exclusion and prohibition just as two objects cannot occupy the same space. (*The Crucible*) [255]

He's a man way out there in the blue, riding on a smile and a shoeshine. And when they start not smiling back—that's an earthquake.... A salesman is got to dream, boy. It comes with the territory. (*Death of a Salesman*) [256]

SPIKE MILLIGAN   1918–

Money can't buy friends, but you can get a better class of enemy. (*Puckoon*) [257]

C. WRIGHT MILLS   1916–1962

When white-collar people get jobs, they sell not only their time and energy, but their personalities as well. They sell by the week, or month, their smiles and their kindly gestures, and they must practice that prompt repression of resentment and aggression. (*White Collar*) [258]

CHARLES MINER   1780–1865

When I see a merchant over-polite to his customers, begging them to taste a little brandy and throwing half his goods on the counter—thinks I, that man has an axe to grind. (*Who'll Turn Grindstones?*) [259]

EDWARD MOORE   1712–1757

I am rich beyond the dream of avarice. (*The Gamester*) [260]

CHRISTOPHER MORLEY   1890–1957

There are three ingredients in the good life: learning, earning and yearning. (*Parnassus on Wheels*) [261]

JAMES MORRIS   1926–

The language of economics is seldom limpid, but in H Street they usually manage to remove from it the very last flickering colophon of charm. (*The Road to Huddersfield: A Journey to Five Continents*) [262]

CHARLES MORTIMER   1900–

The phenomenon I refer to ... is the tidal wave of craving for convenience that is sweeping over America. Today convenience is the success factor of just about every type of produce and service that is showing steady growth. (*New York Herald Tribune*, May 14, 1959) [263]

... the creeping notion that additives are badditives. (*Wall Street Journal*, December 29, 1960) [264]

J. L. MOTLEY   1818–1877

Give us the luxuries of life, and we will dispense with its necessities. (O. W. Holmes, Sr., *Autocrat of the Breakfast Table*) [265]

CLINT MURCHISON, JR.
(Texas financier)

Money is like manure. If you spread it around, it does a lot of good. But if you pile it up in one place, it stinks like hell. (quoting his father's advice, *Time*, June 16, 1961) [266]

LEWIS MUMFORD   1895–1979

However far modern science and technics have fallen short of their inherent possibilities, they have taught mankind at least one lesson: Nothing is impossible. (*Technics and Civilization*) [267]

NAPOLEON I   1769–1821

Ability is of little account without opportunity. [268]

OGDEN NASH   1902–1971

I think that I shall never see
a billboard lovely as a tree.
Perhaps unless the billboards fall,
I'll never see a tree at all. (*Song of the Open Road*) [269]

Someone invented the telephone,
and interrupted a nation's slumbers,
Ringing wrong but similar numbers. (*Look What You Did, Christopher*) [270]

O money, money, money, I am not necessarily one of those who think thee holy,
But I often stop to wonder how thou canst go out so fast when thou comest in so slowly. (*Hymn to the Thing That Makes the Wolf Go*) [271]

EARL NEWSOM
(public relations consultant)

Today's public opinion, though it may appear as light as air, may become tomorrow's legislation—for better or for worse. (American Petroleum Institute, Winter, 1963) [272]

SIR ISAAC NEWTON   1642–1727

In the architectural structure, man's pride, man's triumph over gravitation, man's will to power, assume a visible form. Architecture is a sort of oratory of power by means of forms. (*The Twilight of the Idols*) [273]

A. J. NOCK   1873–1945

It is an economic axiom as old as the hills that goods and services can be paid for only with goods and services. (*Memories of a Superfluous Man*) [274]

DAVID OGILVY   1911–

The consumer is not a moron. She is your wife. (*New York Herald Tribune*, August 19, 1956) [275]
It has taken more than a hundred scientists two years to find out how to make the product. . . . I have been given thirty days to create its personality and plan its launching. If I do my job well, I shall contribute as much as the hundred scientists to the success of this product. (*Confessions of an Advertising Man*) [276]

ONASANDER   floruit A.D. 49

Envy is a pain of mind that successful men cause their neighbors. (*The General*) [277]

JAMES OTIS   1725–1783

Taxation without representation is tyranny. (Watchword of the American Revolution) [278]

OVID   43 B.C.–18 A.D.

Fortune and love befriend the bold. [279]

THOMAS PAINE   1737–1809

I care not how affluent some may be, provided that none be miserable in consequence of it (1976) [280]

Whatever has a tendency to promote the civil intercourse of nations by an exchange of benefits is a subject as worthy of philosophy as of politics. [281]

C. NORTHCOTE PARKINSON   1909–

Work expands so as to fill the time available for its completion. General recognition of this fact is shown in the proverbial phrase "It is the busiest man who has time to spare." (*Parkinson's Law*) [282]

Perfection of planning is a symptom of decay. During a period of exciting discovery or progress, there is not time to plan the perfect headquarters. The time for that comes later, when all the important work has been done. (*Parkinson's Second Law*) [283]

WILLIAM PATTEN   c. 1548–1580

Many hands make light work. [284]

SAMUEL PEPYS   1633–1703

But it is pretty to see what money will do. (*Diary*, September 20, 1665) [285]

THOMAS PERCY   1728–1811

For without money, George,
A man is but a beast;
But bringing money, thou shalt be
Always my welcome guest. (*Religues of Ancient English Poetry*) [286]

LAURENCE J. PETER and RAYMOND HULL

Work is accomplished by those employees who have not yet reached their level incompetence. (*The Peter Principle*) [287]

Competence, like truth, beauty and contact lenses, is in the eye of the beholder. (*The Peter Principle*) [288]

POPE PIUS XI 1857–1939

If a business be unprofitable on account of bad management, want of enterprise, or out-worn methods, that is not a just reason for reducing the wages of its workers. [289]

PLATO 427–347 B.C.

Necessity, who is the mother of invention. (*The Republic*) [290]

Under the influence either of poverty or of wealth, workmen and their work are equally liable to degenerate. (*The Republic*) [291]

PIERRE B. PROUDHON 1809–1865

Property is theft. [292]

MARCEL PROUST 1871–1922

A powerful idea communicates some of its strength to him who challenges it. (*Remembrance of Things Past*) [293]

FRANÇOIS RABELAIS 1495–1553

. . . subject to a kind of disease, which at that time they called lack of money. (*Works. To The Readers*) [294]

GOTTFRIED REINHARDT

Money is good for bribing yourself through the inconveniences of life. (L. Ross, *Picture*) [295]

CHARLES REVSON 1906–1975

I don't meet competition. I crush it. (*Time,* June 16, 1958) [296]

We have got to understand women, the way they do each other. We must learn to use a woman's inconsistency as the key to approaching her. (*Sales Management*, March 3, 1961) [297]

SIR JOSHUA REYNOLDS 1723–1792

If you have great talents, industry will improve them; if you have but moderate abilities, industry will supply their deficiency. (*Discourses*) [298]

DAVID RICARDO 1772–1823

Capital is that part of the wealth of a country which is employed in production, and consists of food, clothing, tools, raw materials, machinery, etc., necessary to give effect to labor. (*Principles of Political Economy and Taxation*) [299]

PAUL RICHARD 1874–1968

The vagabond, when rich is called a tourist. (*The Scourge of Christ*) [300]

When the rich assemble to concern themselves with the business of the poor, it is called charity. When the poor assemble to concern themselves with the business of the rich, it is called anarchy. (*The Scourge of Christ*) [301]

GEORGE ROBEY 1869–1954

Complaints should be made to the management in writing and placed in the receptacle installed for that purpose at the Entrance, which is cleared twice weekly by the Dustman. (*George Robey's Advertiser*) [302]

JOHN D. ROCKEFELLER, JR. 1874–1960

Well, yes, you could say we have independent means. (News summary of October 24, 1955) [303]

LAURENCE ROCKEFELLER 1910–

Father taught us that opportunity and resonsibility go hand in hand. I think we all act on that principle; on the basic human impulse that makes a men want to make the best of what's in him and what's been given him. (*U.S. News and World Report,* February 1, 1960) [304]

ROBERT EMMONS ROGERS 1888–1935

Marry the boss's daughter. (Advice to the class of 1929, Massachusetts Institute of Technology) [303]

WILL ROGERS 1879–1941

Politics has got so expensive that it takes lots of money to even get beat with. (June 28, 1931) [306]

It [income tax] has made more liars out of the American people than Golf. (*Saturday Review,* August 25, 1962) [307]

Our country has plenty of good five-cent cigars, but the trouble is they charge fifteen cents for them. (Quoted in *Treasury of Humorous Quotations*) [308]

FRANKLIN DELANO ROOSEVELT 1882–1945

. . . the forgotten man at the bottom of the economic pyramid. (Radio address, April 7, 1932) [309]

We have always known that heedless self-interest was bad morals; we know now that it is bad economics. (Second Inaugural Address, Januray 20, 1937) [310]

The test of our progress is not whether we add more to the abundance of those who have much; it is whether we provide enough for those who have too little. (Second Inaugural Address, January 20, 1937) [311]

THEODORE ROOSEVELT 1858–1919

We demand that big business give people a square deal; in return we must insist that when anyone engaged in big business honestly endeavors to do right, he shall himself be given a square deal. [312]

JERRY M. ROSENBERG 1935–

Removing the right to privacy can lead to a conforming society fearful of experimenting with the challenges of the day. (*The Death of Privacy*) [313]

If man loses his right to be wrong, will he react by withdrawing from society? Will his curiosity to experiment with life falter? If this happens, man truly becomes nothing more than a machine. (*The Death of Privacy*) [314]

When man decided that his ten fingers were insufficient for computing large quantities of data, he was motivated to invent various tools, to assist him in his endeavors. Thus began a love affair between man and the magic of the number which continues today. (*The Computer Prophets*) [315]

Automation, if properly channeled and understood, can give us abundance and freedom and a means for achieving self-realization and fulfillment. (*Automation, Manpower and Education*) [316]

JEAN-JACQUES ROUSSEAU 1712–1778

Happiness: a good bank account, a good cook, and a good digestion. (quoted in *Treasury of Humorous Quotations*) [317]

Money is the seed of money, and the first quinea is sometimes more difficult to acquire than the second million. (*A Discourse on Political Economy*) [318]

Temperance and industry are man's true remedies; work sharpens his appetite and temperance teaches him to control it. (*Emile, or Education*) [319]

HELENA RUBENSTEIN 1882–1965

I can't help from making money, that is all. (*New York Journal-American,* March 12, 1958) [320]

RAYMOND RUBICAM 1892–1978
(advertising executive)

American advertisers and American free enterprise will increase respect for them [selves] with the American public if they will modify sensational hard-sell commercials about trivialities on news broadcasts at this time of world crisis. They will also increase respect for America from foreigners who listen to such broadcasts. And they might even sell more goods. (*Advertising Age,* July 21, 1958) [321]

DAMON RUNYON   1884–1946

My boy . . . always try to rub up against money, for if you rub up against money long enough, some of it may rub off on you. (*Furthermore*) [322]

JOHN RUSKIN   1819–1900

Borrowers are nearly always ill-spenders, and it is with lent money that all evil is mainly done, and all unjust war protracted. (*The Crown of Wild Olive*) [323]

Life without industry is guilt, industry without art is brutality. (*Lectures on Art,* III, *The Relation of Art to Morals*) [324]

There is no wealth but life. (*Unto This Last*) [325]

BERTRAND RUSSELL   1872–1970

It is preoccupation with possession, more than anything else, that prevents men from living freely and nobly. (*Principles of Social Reconstruction*) [326]

Suspicion of one's own motives is especially necessary for the philanthropist and the executive. (*The Conquest of Happiness*) [327]

J. D. SALINGER   1919–

Take most people, they're crazy about cars . . . and if they get a brand-new car already they start thinking about trading it in for one that's even newer. I don't even like old cars. I mean they don't even interest me. I'd rather have a god-damn horse. A horse is at least human, for God's sake.

(*The Catcher in the Rye*) [328]

SALLUST   86–34 B.C.

Coveting other men's property, and squandering his own. (*Catiline*) [329]

Every man is the architect of his own fortune. [330]

PAUL SALZBERG
(director of research, E.I. du Pont de Nemours)

There is no magic formula for achieving creativity—it is simply a way of life in a laboratory dedicated to discovering and invention. (*Think,* November-December 1962) [331]

LEON SAMSON

Money is the power of impotence. (*The New Humanism*) [332]

Property is the pivot of civilization (*The New Humanism*) [333]

GEORGE SANTAYANA   1863–1952

I like to walk about amidst the beautiful things that adorn the world; but private wealth I should decline, or any sort of personal possessions, because they would take away my liberty. (*Soliloquies in England*) [334]

DAVID SARNOFF   1891–1971

Atoms for peace. Man is still the greatest miracle and the greatest problem on this earth. (*New York Post,* January 27, 1954) [335]

America, supremely the land of liberty, is also supremely the land of science. Freedom is the oxygen without which science cannot breathe. (*Profile of America*) [336]

JOSEPHINE SCHAEFER
(real estate broker)

He called me during the depression . . . and

said he wanted to buy a large building. I asked him if the Empire State would do. (*New York Times*, May 8, 1963, on selling the Hotel Pierre to John Paul Getty) [337]

ALBERT SCHWABACHER, JR.

Most women would be better off it they paid less atention to their investments, not more. . . . And the women could continue to do what they do best—be women. (*Vogue*, April 1, 1963) [338]

STUART LUMAN SEATON
(engineering consultant)

The human brain is a most unusual instrument of elegance and as yet unknown capacity. (*Time,* February 17, 1958) [339]

SENECA   8 B.C.–65 A.D.

It is not the man who has too little, but the man who craves more, that is poor. (*Epistles*) [340]

A good fortune is a great slavery. (*Moral Essays*) [341]

WILLIAM SHAKESPEARE   1564–1616

I am a true labourer: I earn that I eat, get that I wear, owe no man hate, envy no man's happiness, am glad of other men's good. (*As You Like It*) [342]

My pride fell with my fortunes. (*As You Like It*) [343]

He that wants money, means, and content is without three good things. (*As You Like It*) [344]

Some are born great, some achieve greatness, and some have greatness thrust upon them. (*Twelfth-Night*) [345]

You may buy land now as cheap as stinking mackeral. (*King Henry IV*) [346]

'Tis my vocation, Hal; 'tis sin for a man to labour in his vocation. (*King Henry IV*) [347]

If all the year were playing holidays, To sport would be as tedious as to work. (*King Henry IV*) [348]

Words pay no debts. (King Richard III) [349]

The Gods sent not Corn for the rich men only. (*Coriolanus*) [350]

When Fortune means to men most good, She looks upon them with a threatening eye. (*King John*) [351]

He is well paid that is well satisfied. (*The Merchant of Venice*) [352]

Neither a borrower, nor a lender be; For loan oft loses both itself and friend. (*Hamlet*) [353]

Has this fellow no feeling of his business? (*Hamlet*) [354]

The hand of little employment hath the daintier sense. (*Hamlet*) [355]

Fortune brings in some boats that are not steer'd (*Cymbeline*) [356]

GEORGE BERNARD SHAW   1856–1950

We have no more right to consume happiness without producing it than to consume wealth without producing it. (*Candida*) [357]

I am a gentleman: I live by robbing the poor. (*Man and Superman*) [358]

My needs is as great as the most deserving widow's that ever got money out of six different charities in one week for the death of the same husband. (*Pygmalion*) [359]

If all economists were laid end to end, they would not reach a conclusion. (Attr.) [360]

A day's work is a day's work, neither more nor less, and the man who does it needs a day's sustenance, a night's repose, and due leisure, whether he be a painter of ploughman. (*Unsocial Socialist*) [361]

ARTHUR FREDERICK SHELDON   1868–1935

He profits most who serves best. (Motto for Rotary International) [362]

PERCY BYSSHE SHELLEY   1792–1822

Power, like a desolating pestilence,
Pollutes whate'er it touches; and obedience,
Bane of all genius, virtue, freedom, truth,
Makes slaves of men, and, of the human fame,
A Mechanized automaton. (*Queen Mab, III*) [363]

CHARLES P. SHIRAS   1824–1854

Oh, the debtor is but a shamefaced dog With the creditor's name on his collar; While I am king and you are queen, For we own no man a dollar! (*I Owe No Man a Dollar*) [364]

SIME SILVERMAN   1873–1933

Wall Street Lays an Egg (Headline in *Variety,* announcing collapse of stock market, October 1929) [365]

N. F. SIMPSON   1919–

And suppose we solve all the problems it presents? What happens? We end up with more problems than we started with. Because that's the way problems propagate their species. A problem left to itself dries up or goes rotten. But fertilize a problem with a solution—you'll hatch out dozens. (*A Resounding Tinkle*) [366]

ALFRED P. SLOAN, JR.   1875–1966

He banged the door on the way out, and out of that bang came eventually the Chrysler Corporation. (on Walter Chrysler's departure from General Motors, *My Years with General Motors,* in *Fortune*, September 1963) [367]

ADAM SMITH   1723–1790

As every individual . . . by directing [his] industry in such a manner as its produce may be of greatest value, intends only his own gain, he is in this as in many cases led by an invisible hand to promote an end which was no part of his intention. . . . By pursuing his own interest he frequently promotes that of society more effectively than when he really intends to promote it. (*An Inquiry into the Nature and Causes of the Wealth of Nations*) [368]

People of the same trade seldom meet together, even for merriment and diversion, but the conversation ends in a comspiracy against the public, or in some contrivance to raise prices. (*Wealth of Nations*) [369]

Consumption is the sole end and purpose of all production; and the interest of the producer ought to be attended to, only so far as it may be necessary for promoting that of the consumer. (*Wealth of Nations*) [370]

The man whose whole life is spent in performing a few simple operations . . . has no occasion to exert his understanding, or to exercise his invention. . . . He naturally loses, therefore, the habit of such exertion, and generally becomes as stupid and ignorant as it is possible for a human creature to become. (*Wealth of Nations*) [371]

Labor was the first price, the original purchase money that was paid for all things. (*Wealth of Nations*) [372]

ALEXANDER SMITH   1830–1867

If you do your fair day's work, you are certain to get your fair day's wage—in praise or pudding, whichever happens to suit your taste. (*Dreamthorp*) [373]

LOGAN PEARSALL SMITH   1865–1946

It is the wretchedness of being rich that you have to live with rich people. [374]

RICHARD AUSTIN SMITH   1911–

Even for the neurotic executive—as for everyone else—work has great therapeutic value; it is generally his last refuge, and deterioration there marks the final collapse of the man; his marriage, his social life, and the outside interests—all have suffered beforehand. (*Fortune,*) [375]

REV. SYDNEY SMITH   1771–1845

Poverty is no disgrace to a man, but it is confoundedly inconvenient. (*His Wit and Wisdom*) [376]

SIR. RICHARD STEELE   1672–1729

Every rich man has usually some sly way of jesting, which would make no great figure were he not a rich man. (*The Spectator*) [377]

ROGER STEVENS   1906–

Whenever I think, I make a mistake. (*Fortune*, August 1955) [378]

ROBERT LOUIS STEVENSON   1850–1894

Everyone lives by selling something. (*Across the Plains*) [379]

Perpetual devotion to what a man calls his business, is only to be sustained by perpetual neglect of many other things. (*Virginibus Puerisque*) [380]

Science carries us into zones of speculation, where there is no habitable city for the mind of man. (*Pulvis et Umbra*) [381]

MAX STIRNER   1806–1856

Property exists by grace of the law. It is not a fact, but a legal fiction. (*The Ego and His Own*) [382]

NORMAN STROUSE   1906–

Today's mousetraps must go to market. (*New York Times*, May 26, 1976) [383]

SIMEON STRUNSKY   1879–1948

The milkman alone is enough to redeem the night from its undeserved evil reputation. A carload of pasteurized milk for nurslings at four o'clock in the morning represents more service to civilization than a cartful of bullion on its way from the Subtreasury to the vaults of national bank five hours later. (*Belshazzar Court*) [384]

People who want to understand democracy should spend less time in the library with Aristotle and more time on the buses and in the subway. (*No Mean City*) [385]

JONATHAN SWIFT   1667–1745

I have heard of a man who had a mind to sell his house, and therefore carried a piece of brick in his pocket, which he showed as a pattern to encourage purchasers. (*The Drapier's Letters*) [386]

Nothing is so hard for those who abound in riches as to conceive how others can be in want. [387]

LEO SZILARD   1898–1964

Devote six years to your work but in the seventh go into solitude or among strangers so that your friends, by remembering what you were, do not prevent you from being what you have become. (*Harper's* July 1960) [388]

TACITUS   54–119

He had talents equal to business, and aspired no higher. (*Annals*) [389]

Reason and Judgment are the qualities of a leader. [390]

LEO TALLEY   1900–1976
(president of Coca-Cola Co.)

There is nothing as universal in this world as human thirst. . . . Our market is as big as the world and the people in it. (on being elected president of Coca-Cola, *Newsweek*, May 19, 1958) [391]

C. M. TAN

The Chinese laundry doesn't have to compete; it's competed against. (*New York Herald Tribune,* October 23, 1960) [392]

TERENCE   195–159 B.C.

Fortune favours the brave. (*Phormio*) [393]

THEOGNIS   570?–490? B.C.

No one goes to Hades with all his immense wealth. (*Maxims*) [394]

R. B. THOMAS   1766–1846

If you want the time to pass quickly, just give your note for 90 days. (*Farmer's Almanac*) [395]

HENRY DAVID THOREAU   1817–1862

Men have become the tools of their tools (*Walden*) [396]

Money is not required to buy one necessity of the soul. [397]

The highest law gives a thing to him who can use it. [398]

That man is the richest whose pleasures are the cheapest. [399]

JAMES THURBER   1894–1961

In those days all the heads of business firms adopted a guarded kind of double talk, commonly expressed in low, muffled tones, because nobody knew what was going to happen and nobody understood what had. (*The Secret Life of James Thurber*) [400]

EDWARD, FIRST BARON THURLOW   1731–1806

Did you ever expect a corporation to have a conscience, when it has no soul to be damned, and no body to be kicked? (Attr.) [401]

LON TINKLE
(book editor)

Air-conditioning has bequeathed America a new—some say even better—reading season. People with brains spend the summer in their nonsweat, air-conditioned cars, offices, and homes, reaching for a good book instead of a hot beer, leaving the delights of ant-ridden picnics ... to those who would rather burn their skins than illuminate their minds. (*Saturday Review,* April 12, 1958) [402]

LEO TOLSTOY   1818–1910

Money is a new form of slavery, and distinguishable from the old simply by the fact that it is impersonal—that there is no human relation between master and slave. (*What Shall We Do?*) [403]

SIR HERBERT BEERBOHM TREE   1853–1917

Sirs, I have tested your machine. It adds a new terror to life and makes a death a long-felt want. (Quoted in H. Pearson, *Beerbohm Tree*) [404]

HARRY S TRUMAN   1884–1972

The buck stops here. (notice on his presidential desk) [405]

It's a recession when your neighbor loses his job; it's a depression when you lose your own. (*Observer,* April 6, 1958) [406]

Any man who has had the job I've had and didn't have a sense of humor wouldn't still be here. (April 19, 1955) [407]

DALTON TRUMBO   1905–1980
(screenwriter)

Never steal more than you actually need, for the possession of surplus money leads to extravagance, foppish attire, frivolous thought. (*Time,* January 2, 1961) [408]

A. R. J. TURGOT   1727–1781

The iron law of wages. [409]

MARK TWAIN (Samuel Langhorne Clemens)
                                          1835–1910

He is now fast rising from affluence to poverty. (*Henry Ward Beecher's Farm*) [410]

Work consists of whatever a body is obliged to do, and play consists of whatever a body is not obliged to do (*The Adventures of Tom Sawyer*) [411]

There are two times in a man's life when he should not speculate: when he can't afford it, and when he can. [412]

W. H. VANDERBILT   1821–1885

The public be damned! (*New York Times,* August 25, 1918) [413]

LUC DE CLAPIERS, MARQUIS DE
    VAUVENARGUES   1715–1747

In order to carry out great enterprises, one must live as if one will never have to die. (*Reflexions et maximes*) [414]

THORSTEIN VEBLEN   1857–1929

The walking-stick serves the purpose of an advertisement that the bearer's hands are employed otherwise than in useful effort, and it therefore has utility as an evidence of leisure. (*The Theory of the Leisure Class*) [415]

All business sagacity reduces itself in the last analysis to a judicious use of sabotage. (*The Nature of Peace*) [416]

FRANÇOIS VILLON   1430–1484

If you have money, it doth not stay, But this way and that it wastes amain: What does it profit you anyway? Ill-gotten good is nobody's gain. (*The Greater Testament*) [417]

VIRGIL   70–19 B.C.

The way down to hell is easy. The gates of black Dis stand open night and day. But to retrace one's steps and escape to the upper air—that is toil, that is labor. (*Aeneid*) [418]

They are able because they think they are able. (*Aeneid*) [419]

Persistent work triumphed, and the stress of need in a hard life. (*Georgics*) [420]

VOLTAIRE (FRANÇOIS-MARIE AROUET)
                    1694–1778

Work banishes those three great evils, boredom, vice, and poverty. (*Candide*) [421]

IZAAK WALTON   1593–1683

I have laid aside business, and gone a-fishing. (*The Compleat Angler*) [422]

Health is the second blessing that we mortals are capable of—a blessing that money cannot buy. (*The Compleat Angler*) [423]

That which is everybody's business, is nobody's business. (*The Compleat Angler*) [424]

ARTEMUS WARD (CHARLES FARRAR BROWN)
                    1834–1867

Let us be happy and live within our means, even if we have to borrow the money to do it with. (*Science and Natural History*) [425]

DANIEL WEBSTER   1782–1852

Labor in this country is independent and proud. It has not to ask the patronage of capital, but capital solicits the aid of labor. (Speech, April 2, 1824) [426]

ARTHUR WELLINGTON (DUKE)   1769–1852

Call on a business man at business times only, and on business, transact your business and go about your business, in order to give him time to finish his business. [427]

H. G. WELLS   1866–1946

You can't have money like that and not swell out. (*Kipps*) [428]

Rich men amenable to use are hard to find and often very intractable when found. (*The Autocracy of Mr. Parham*) [429]

JOHN WESLEY 1703–1791

Make all you can, save all you can, give all you can. [430]

WILLIAM H. WHYTE 1927–

This book is about the organization man. . . . I can think of no other way to describe the people I am talking about. They are not the workers, nor are they the white-collar people in the usual, clerk sense of the word. These people only work for the Organization. The ones I am talking about belong to it as well. (*The Organization Man*) [431]

OSCAR WILDE 1854–1900

Experience is the name every one gives to their mistakes. (*Definitions of a Cynic*) [432]

As for the virtuous poor, one can pity them, of course, but one cannot possibly admire them. (*The Soul of Man Under Socialism*) [433]

THORNTON WILDER 1875–1975

The future is the most expensive luxury in the world. (*The Matchmaker*) [434]

Money should circulate like rainwater. (*The Matchmaker*) [435]

JOHN H. WILLIAMS
(Harvard University Professor)

The instability of the economy is equaled only by the instability of economists. (*New York Times,* June 2, 1956) [436]

FRANCES WILLIS
(U.S. Ambassador to Switzerland)

Have the mental equipment to do your job, then take the job seriously, yourself not too seriously. (*Look*, November 17, 1953) [437]

CHARLES E. WILSON 1886–1972

What is good for the country is good for General Motors, and what's good for General Motors is good for the country. (to a Congressional committee, 1952) [438]

Back in Detroit we had a saying that an expert is a mechanic away from home. (January 11, 1954 [439]

THOMAS WOODROW WILSON 1856–1924

Business underlies everything in our national life, including our spiritual life. Witness the fact that in the Lord's Prayer the first petition is for daily bread. No one can worship God or love his neighbor on an empty stomach. (Speech, 1912) [440]

The way to stop financial "joy-riding" is to arrest the chauffeur, not the automobile. [441]

JON WYNNE-TYSON

The wrong sort of people are always in power because they would not be in power if they were not the wrong sort of people. (*Times Literary Supplement*) [442]

JOHN ORR YOUNG 1886–1976
(advertising executive)

Their dedication is to competitive creativity—a deep desire within the consciousness of each man to create something better today than yesterday's best. (*New York Times,* September 29, 1960) [443]

OWEN D. YOUNG 1874–1962

I really believe that more harm is done by old men who cling to their influence than by young men who anticipate it. (*New York Herald Tribune,* July 12, 1962) [444]

ROBERT R. YOUNG 1897–1958

Beware of inherited wealth. The job of getting is better than spending. I have often marveled at the fact that so many large

Eastern businesses are headed by Western boys. Is it because the son of the well-to-do Eastern family is exposed to social temptations which sap his energies and dull his perceptions, thus causing him to be outrun in life's race despite his heritage of accomplishment and family connections? (*Newsweek*, June 20, 1955) [445]

WILLIAM ZECKENDORF SR. 1905–1976
(president, Webb & Knapp)

They come from all over the country to New York. The executive's wife decides they will move to New York. She says, "John, you're the boss now. I've been doing the laundry and raising the kids all my life. It's time we enjoyed opening nights in New York." So the company packs up and moves to New York. (*Life*, August 10, 1959) [446]

Appendix M. Summary of Major Business and Economic Events in the United States, 1776–1983

1776 Declaration of independence adopted by delegates of the thirteen colonies in the year that saw the publication of *Wealth of Nations* by Adam Smith. This book would have major influence on economic thought in the United States.

1778 United States concluded an alliance with France and established a treaty of commerce (February 6).

The Continental Congress ratified Articles of Confederation. One weakness of the Articles was its failure to give the legislature the authority to collect taxes (June 26).

1781 Robert Morris appointed first superintendent of finance (February 20). He established first private commercial bank—the Bank of North America (December 31).

1784 Major economic depression was created when France annulled its decrees giving the United States special economic privileges. England and Spain also barred the importation of numerous U.S. products. Captain John Greene, sailing from New York to Canton, China, purchased tea and silks to compensate for the loss of European income. A new market was uncovered (February 22).

1785 Oliver Evans invented the automatic flour mill and reduced labor needs by 50 percent.

Congress established the money decimal system (July 6).

1786 Shays's Rebellion in Massachusetts: an armed insurrection by farmers to bring attention to their economic conditions (November).

John Fitch invented first American steamboat, which sailed on New Jersey waters.

1789 Articles of Confederation superseded by U.S. Constitution.

The first Revenue Bill enacted by Congress (July 4).

Alexander Hamilton chosen as first Secretary of the Treasury (September 2).

1790 House of Representatives received Report on Public Credit, urging the federal government to take on the responsibility for national debts (January 14).

Congress passed Hamilton's Assumption Bill that permitted funds of many states debts, which were taken over by the federal government (July).

Hamilton, over Jefferson's objections, won approval for the establishment of a national bank, The Bank of the United States (December 14).

Samuel Slater spun cotton for the first time, utilizing water power in Pawtucket, Rhode Island December 21).

Samuel Hopkins obtained first U.S. patent, for a process used in producing potash and pearl ash for the making of glass.

1791 Congress created the first U.S. bank, with a capital of $10 million (February 8).

Charter of the Bank of the United States signed by President Washington (February 25).

First eight branches of the national bank established in Philadelphia (December 12).

Securities exchange established in Philadelphia.

1792 Securities exchange established in New York.

Passage of Mint Act established the decimal system of coinage (April 2).

1793 Eli Whitney invented the cotton gin.

1800 Robert Morris released from prison under terms of the first federal bankruptcy law to protect merchants and traders (April 4).

1803 France sold Louisiana Territory to the United States for $12 million (April 30).

1806 Prosecution of striking Philadelphia Cordwainers was the first legal action against a trade union for common-law conspiracy. The union was dissolved.

1807 Robert Fulton's *Clermont* became the first operational steamboat, sailing from New York to Albany in 32 hours (August 17).

President Jefferson received Congressional support for the notion that the federal government is empowered to place embargoes to restrict commerce with any foreign country (December 18).

Eli Terry and Seth Thomas manufactured mass-produced clocks with interchangeable components.

1808 John Jacob Astor, the wealthiest American in his day, incorporated the American Fur Company.

1809 Congress passed the Non-Intercourse Act, permitting trade with all nations except Great Britain and France (March 1).

1810 Macon's Bill No. 2 enacted, repealing all restrictions on foreign trade (May 12).

1811 First steamboat used on the Mississippi River.

Charter of Bank of the United States terminated and not renewed. Led to financial crisis during War of 1812 (February 20).

New York became the first state to replace general incorporation regulations with special charters from the state, thus encouraging business ventures.

1812 War declared against England, in part over seizure of U.S. ships and British restrictions on American trade.

The Pennsylvania Company for Insurance on Lives and Granting Annuities, the first life insurance company in the United States, incorporated in Philadelphia.

1813 First textile plant that could perform all cloth-making tasks by power established in Waltham, Massachusetts.

1814 President Madison won repeal of the Embargo and Non-Importation Acts (April 14).

1816 Second Bank of the United States chartered by Congress for

20 years (August 10).

First incorporated savings bank established in Boston.

1817 Production of iron by the process of puddling; practice spreads throughout Pennsylvania.

Thomas Gilpin produced the first machine-made paper in United States.

1818 Trans-Atlantic Packet lines, with sails, commenced runs between Liverpool, England, and New York, taking an average of 39 days each way.

1819 Spain ceded Florida to United States for $5 million (February 22).

The *Savannah*, the first steamboat to cross the Atlantic ocean, set sail from Georgia (June 20).

Jethrow Wood produced the three-piece plow with interchangeable parts.

John Hall invented the breech-loading flintlock rifle.

1822 Water-powered equipment used to operate cotton mills in Massachusetts.

C.M. Graham received first patent for false teeth.

1823 Nicholas Biddle chosen as third president of the second Bank of the United States.

1824 Congress passed a tariff bill to protect manufacturers.

First strike by women in United States took place in Pawtucket, Rhode Island.

1825 Erie Canal opened by New York Governor De Witt Clinton, making available new commercial markets (October 26).

1826 First experiments in electricity by

Joseph Henry. He invented insulated wire, multiple-coil magnet.

First railroads constructed to be powered by horses, sail, and cable.

1827 First city central trade council established in Philadelphia—the Mechanics' Union of Trade Associations.

1828 Congress passed the Tariff of Abominations and manufacturers obtained additional increases of duties (May 19).

Completion of the first passenger railroad in Baltimore (July 4).

1830 First steam locomotive built in the United States *Tom Thumb*, constructed in Baltimore by Peter Cooper for the Baltimore and Ohio Railroad.

1832 Congress passed a new Tariff Act that removed many of the "abominations" of the 1828 act (July 14).

Samuel F. B. Morse outlined the principles of the electromagnetic recording telegraph.

1833 Henry Clay's Compromise tariff Bill provided for a reduction of duties during coming years (March 2).

President Jackson signed the Force Act, authorizing the collection of duties by armed force (March 16).

New York General Trades' Union formed: first national union federation (August).

1834 Federal soldiers used for the first time to quell a labor dispute, at the Chesapeake and Ohio Canal construction site (January 29).

Cyrus H. McCormick received a

patent for his reaper.

Thomas Davenport invented first electric motor with spinning armature.

1835 Samuel Colt built pistol with revolving cartridge cylinder.

1836 President Jackson refused to renew the charter of the second Bank of the United States. The surplus above $5 million was to be distributed among the states in quarterly installments, as decreed by Congress (June 23).

1837 Panic of 1837, in part caused by the surplus distributions that upset the money market following the closing of the national bank. Supreme Court ruled that a state could charter a bank and issue notes (September 5).

John Deere invented plow with steel moldboard.

1838 First steamship crossed from England to New York (April 8–23).

1839 Charles Goodyear discovered vulcanizing process to give rubber added strength.

1841 The *New York Tribune* founded by Horace Greeley (April 10).

Lewis Tappan established the first commercial credit-rating agency—the Mercantile Agency.

1842 Massachusetts Supreme Court decided that trade unions were legal organizations (*Commonwealth* v. *Hunt*).

A Tariff Bill was passed that restored most of the duties in force in 1832.

1843 The first telegraph line established.

1844 Samuel F. B. Morse's electric tel-

egraph system used for the first time. The message "What Hath God Wrought!" was transmitted from Washington, D.C., to Baltimore (May 29).

1845 The Postal Act approved the subsidizing of steamers carrying mail across the Atlantic.

1846 Congress reestablished an independent Treasury system.

Elias Howe invented the sewing machine.

Richard M. Hoe invented the rotary press, enabling 8000 newspapers to be printed in one hour.

1848 Gold discovered in Sutter's property in the Sacramento Valley, California (January 24).

Under the Treaty of Guadalupe Hidalgo, Mexico ceded New Mexico and California to the United States for $15 million (February 2).

1849 Pacific Railroad Company chartered.

Walter Hunt, to satisfy a $15 debt, designed the modern safety pin and sold the rights to J. R. Chapin for $400.

1851 Henry J. Raymond founded the *New York Daily Times*, which became the *New York Times* in 1857.

1852 Elisha G. Otis invented the elevator.

1853 Commodore Matthew C. Perry arrived in Tokyo Bay and opened trade relations with Japan (July).

1854 Limited trade with Japan under the Treaty of Kanawaya began (May 31).

1856 Gail Borden received patent for the process for making condensed milk.

1857 The failure of the Ohio Life Insurance and Trust Company created the Panic of 1857.

1858 Macy's department store established in New York City.

"Pikes Peak or Bust!" was the slogan for gold seekers on their way to Colorado.

1859 Edwin L. Drake discovered oil near Titusville, Pennsylvania (August 27).

1860 Pony Express commenced ten-day mail service from Missouri to California (April 3).

1861 First federal income tax of 3 percent on incomes over $800 was enacted to help defray Civil War costs (August 5).

First transcontinental telegraph began service (October 24).

Pony Express discontinued with completion of telegraph (October 24). Goods in addition to letters carried for the first time by the U.S. mails.

1862 Enactment of the Legal Tender Act, which declared Treasury notes to be legal tender (February 25).

Department of Agriculture created (May 15).

Homestead Act passed, which offered 160 acres of government land to any bona fide settler; 15,000 homesteads, totaling 2.5 million acres, were given away during the Civil War (May 20).

Morrill Land Grant Act approved the sales of public land for the endowment of state institutions for agricultural education (July 2).

Richard Jordan Gatling's machine gun invented; able to fire 350 rounds per minute. It was not used until after the Civil War.

1863 The first national bank in Philadelphia started by Jay Cooke (June 20).

Congress authorized free mail delivery in selected cities for the first time.

1864 Immigration Act passed, authorizing importation of workers.

First Bessemer-process steel plant began operations in Wyandotte, Michigan.

George Pullman built first practical railroad sleeping car.

1865 Union Stockyards opened in Chicago; became largest in the country.

1866 Ira Steward and George McNeil formed the National Labor Union in Baltimore (August 20).

In Pennsylvania, first oil pipeline (5 miles long) opened.

1867 Purchase of Alaska Territory from Russia for $7.2 million by Secretary of State W. H. Seward (March 30).

Bill passed by Congress limiting the working day for federal employees to eight hours.

Open-hearth steel process first used in Trenton, New Jersey.

First efficient typewriter constructed.

1869 Jay Gould and James Fisk attempted to corner the gold in the money market, holding it until prices rose and then selling it; created "Black Friday" (September 24).

Knights of Labor established as a secret workers' association.

First electric voting machine patented by Thomas A. Edison.

1870 John D. Rockefeller formed the Standard Oil Company of Ohio with $1 million.

Pennsylvania Railroad Company formed.

First commercial production of celluloid, invented by J. W. and I. S. Hyatt, commencing the synthetic materials era.

Montgomery Ward and Company commenced operation in Pittsburgh.

1874 Stephen Dudley Field's electric streetcar operated in New York City.

1876 Alexander Graham Bell's telephone first shown at the International Centennial Exhibition in Philadelphia.

1877 Federal troops and state militia broke the first major U.S. railroad strike (July 17).

Edison patented first useful phonograph. "Mary had a little lamb" were first words recorded on tinfoil around a cylinder.

1879 Cable communication established with France.

Frank W. Woolworth and W. H. Moore opened "five-cent" store in Utica, New York.

Edison demonstrated his incandescent lamp for home lighting (December 31).

1881 The Wharton School of Finance and Commerce at the University of Pennsylvania opened and became the first university business school.

1882 Pearl Street electric power station began operation in New York City; built by Edison, it supplied power for 59 buildings (September 4).

First Labor Day celebration in New York City (September).

John D. Rockefeller, with a virtual monopoly over the oil market, established the Standard Oil Trust, whose nine directors held the entire stock of all Standard Oil Companies.

1883 John A. Roebling's Brooklyn Bridge, the longest suspension bridge to date, completed.

1884 Linotype machine patented by Ottmar Mergenthaler.

First functional fountain pen made by Lewis Waterman.

1885 Home Life Insurance Building in Chicago, an all-iron frame structure, became the first U.S. skyscraper.

1886 American Federation of Labor, under the leadership of Samuel Gompers, founded in Columbus, Ohio (December 8).

Elihu Thomson patented an electric welding machine.

1887 Interstate Commerce Act passed by Congress (February 4).

1888 Congress established the Department of Labor (June 13).

The Kodak camera developed by George Eastman.

1890 The Sherman Anti-Trust Law, in opposition to monopolies, passed; any trust in restraint of trade declared illegal and the trustees punishable (July 2).

McKinley Tariff Law provided for "reduction in revenue but increases in protection" and limited reciprocal treaties (October

1).

1891 Passage of the International Copyright Act (March 4).

Edison patented a kinetoscopic camera, permitting a strip of film to take moving pictures (July 31).

The zipper patented by Whitcomb L. Judson.

1892 Ten people killed by strikers at Carnegie steel plant in Homestead, Pennsylvania (July 6).

Frank and Charles Duryea constructed first gasoline-powered automobile in United States (September).

1893 U.S. gold reserves dropped below $100 million, leading to the Panic of 1893 (April 21).

Bell Telephone Company's patent expired, thus ending Bell's monopoly on telephone services across the country.

Henry Ford sold his first automobile.

1894 American Railway Union Strike occurred; the most violent labor revolt to date (June 26).

Wilson-Gorman Tariff Act passed; became the first graduated income tax in the United States (August 28).

1895 National Association of Manufacturers held first meeting, in Ohio (January 22).

First generators able to yield hydroelectric power for a wide area built by George Westinghouse in Niagara Falls, New York.

Sears, Roebuck Company established mail-order business.

Woodville Latham introduced his moving-picture projector.

1897 First U.S. subway finished in Boston.

Dingley Tariff Act passed to increase revenue and protection.

1898 Erdman Arbitration Act passed, authorizing federal mediation in conflicts with interstate carriers and employees (June 1).

In the Paris Peace Treaty, Spain ceded Puerto Rico, Guam, and the Philippines (for $20 million) to the United States.

Adolphus Busch constructed first diesel engine in the United States.

1899 Louis Sullivan designed the Schlesinger and Mayer department store in Chicago. Now Carson, Pirie Scott and Company, it was the first U.S. commercial modern-style building.

1900 Gold became the only currency standard in the United States under the Gold Standard Act (March 14).

Orville and Wilbur Wright flew their glider at Kitty Hawk, North Carolina (September).

International Ladies' Garment Workers' Union founded in New York City.

Olds Company in Detroit began operations; first mass-produced cars in the United States. Olds made 400 automobiles in their first year.

1901 U.S. Steel Corporation founded by Elbert Gary and J. P. Morgan with a capital of $1,319,000,000, becoming the first billion-dollar company (February 25).

Reginald A. Fessenden patented radio transmitter in the United States.

King C. Gillette produced the safety razor, with disposable blades.

1902 Spooner Act approved by Congress for the construction of the Panama Canal (June 28).

Arthur D. Little patented processes for making rayon and artificial silk.

1903 Theodore Roosevelt sent an around-the-world message in 12 minutes on the Pacific cable (July 4).

First car traversed United States in 52 days. The Packard car left from San Francisco, arriving in New York on August 1.

Orville Wright the first to fly a powered heavier-than-air machine, for 12 seconds (December 17).

1904 Morton Street Tunnel under the Hudson River in New York City was opened (March 11).

First subway opened in New York City (October 27).

1905 New York Central's "Twentieth Century Limited" and Pennsylvania Railroad's "fastest long-distance train in the world" completed 18-hour ride between New York and Chicago (June).

1906 Laws passed aimed at reforming the insurance industry (February 21).

Interstate Commerce Commission given additional strength by the Hepburn Rate Bill to determine railroad rates and to supervise in the accounting of the lines (June 29).

Broadcasting by radio first demonstrated by Reginald A. Fessenden (December 24).

1907 Passage of the Pure Food and Drugs Act and the Meat Inspection Law (January 1).

1908 The Model T automobile, costing $850, introduced by Henry Ford (October 1).

1909 The first movie house, called a nickelodeon, in McKeesport, Pennsylvania, built by John P. Harris and Harry Davis.

An income tax proposal introduced to Congress; finally ratified as Sixteenth Amendment to the U.S. Constitution in 1913 (July 12).

Leo H. Baekeland received a patent for his thermosetting plastic, called Bakelite.

1910 Mann-Elkins Railroad Act passed, strengthening the powers of the Interstate Commerce Commission (June 18).

1911 Clyde J. Coleman's electric self-starter, perfected by Charles F. Kettering, introduced to General Motors. The need to crank the car engine manually would soon vanish (February).

Supreme Court found the Standard Oil Company and the American Tobacco Company guilty of violations of the Sherman Anti-Trust Act (May).

Elmer Sperry patented the gyro-compass and later the automatic pilot.

1912 Congress authorized a domestic parcel post system (August 24).

1913 Sixteenth Amendment to the U.S. Constitution gave Congress the right to tax private incomes (February 3).

The U.S. Department of Commerce and Labor split, forming two separate departments (March 4).

Federal Reserve Banking Act enacted, creating 12 Reserve Banks guided by a Board (December 23).

1914 The Panama Canal opened (August 15).

Creation of the Federal Trade Commission to supervise big corporations and investigate alleged violations of the antitrust law (October 15).

Clayton Antitrust Act signed by President Wilson to protect unions (October 15).

1915 Alexander Graham Bell, in New York, spoke to Dr. Thomas A. Watson, in San Francisco, in the first transcontinental telephone call.

The taxi industry was born. The fare is a ''jitney'' (a nickel) for a short car ride.

1917 United States declared war against Germany (April 6).

Two-way communication by radio telephone from the ground to an airplane done for the first time (August).

1918 As part of the war effort, U.S. government took over administrative control of the railroads (March 21).

First scheduled airmail service from New York City to Washington, D.C., began (May 15).

As part of the war effort, U.S. government took over administrative control of telegraph, telephone, and cables (July 23).

1919 Four-month strike at U.S. Steel Corporation (September 22).

1920 Federal Power Commission authorized by Congress (June 10).

Detroit station WWJ became first licensed radio broadcaster (August 20).

1922 Fordney-McCumber Tariff Bill enacted, containing highest tariff rates in history and establishing a Tariff Commission to impose flexible rates (September 19).

Albert H. Taylor and Leo C. Young developed the forerunner to radar.

1923 Teapot Dome scandal: it was revealed that Secretary of the Interior Albert Fall had accepted bribes from oil companies.

Lee De Forest developed a sound system to be used on movie films. It was used for the first time in full-length movie, *The Jazz Singer*, starring Al Jolson, in 1927.

Du Pont Company acquired rights to produce cellophane from a company in France.

1924 Wireless telegraph transmission of photographs demonstrated by Radio Corporation of America (November 30).

1925 C. Francis Jenkins gave a demonstration of the results of his research on television signals.

1926 American Telephone and Telegraph Company, Radio Corporation of America, and the British General Post Office conducted the first successful trans-Atlantic radiotelephone exchange between New York City and London

(March 7).

Revenue Act reduced the normal income tax to 5 percent maximum.

First nationwide radio broadcasting system—National Broadcasting Company—organized.

1927 First underwater tunnel for cars built under the Hudson River; Holland Tunnel opened.

1928 First color motion pictures shown by George Eastman in Rochester, New York (July 30).

1929 Stock market collapsed, leading to the greatest depression in U.S. history (October 24).

Losses in stock paper value of shares were approximately $26 billion (November).

1930 Bank of the United States in New York City closed (December 11). Within the year more than 1300 banks were forced to close.

First cyclotron, needed to develop atomic fission, constructed by Ernest O. Lawrence.

1931 The 102-story Empire State Building opened in New York City (May 1).

In 41 hours, traveling from Japan to Washington State, Clyde Pangborn and Hugh Herndon concluded the first nonstop trans-Pacific flight (October 5).

1932 Reconstruction Finance Corporation created to lend money to railroads, insurance companies, and banks (January 22).

Norris-LaGuardia Anti-Injunction Act passed by Congress (March 23).

1933 Civilian Conservation Corps (CCC) created to employ young men in public projects (March 31).

Agricultural Adjustment Administration passed; offered compensation to farmers if they agreed to reduce the acreage of certain surplus crops (May 12).

Laws passed enabling the Federal Emergency Relief Administration (FERA) to contribute $500 million of federal monies to state relief agencies (May 12).

Tennessee Valley Authority created (May 18).

Federal Securities Act passed, relative to the regulation of the securities industry (May 27).

National Industrial Recovery Act (NIRA) passed (June 13).

Home Owner's Refinancing Act passed to permit refinancing of small mortgages on privately owned homes (June 13).

Farm Credit Act passed to assist in refinancing farm mortgages and crops (June 16).

Glass-Steagall Banking Act created the Federal Deposit Insurance corporation (FDIC) to protect bank deposits up to $5000 against bank failures (June 16).

1934 The Export-Import Bank created to encourage foreign investment (February 2).

Dr. Wallace H. Carothers, while working at Du Pont laboratories, produced polymer 66, patented as Nylon (May 23).

Securities and Exchange Commission (SEC) created (June 6).

Reciprocal Trade Agreements Act gave President Roosevelt

authority to enter into tariff agreements with other countries, given Senate approval (June 12).

Federal Communications Commission replaced Federal Radio Commission.

1935 With the passage of the Emergency Relief Appropriation Act, the Works Progress Administration (WPA) was created (April 8).

The National Industrial Recovery Act declared unconstitutional by the Supreme Court A. L. Schechter v. United States) (May 27).

Wagner-Connery Labor Relations Act enacted, creating the National Labor Relations Board (July 5).

Social Security Act passed (August 14).

Committee for Industrial Organization (CIO) formed under the leadership of John L. Lewis (November 9).

1936 Passage of the Robinson-Patman Act, prohibiting lowering prices to curtail competition (June 19).

1937 First sit-down strike in U.S. history took place at General Motors Fisher Body Plant in Flint, Michigan (January).

U.S. Steel Corporation agreed to first union contract with United Steel Workers—CIO (March 1).

1938 Second Agricultural Adjustment Act enacted; ensured continuance of subsidies to producers of basic crops (February 16).

Civil Aeronautics Authority formed (June 23).

Wages and Hours Act estab-lished minimum wages and maximum working hours for industries engaged in interstate commerce (June 25).

Congress of Industrial Organizations (CIO) expelled from the American Federation of Labor (AFL) (November).

1939 Supreme Court declared the sit-down strike an illegal practice (February 27).

Albert Einstein and other prominent scientists informed President Roosevelt that atomic fission could be used to make enormously powerful bombs (August 2).

1940 Ford Motor Company accused of encouraging brutality in their Texas plant by the National Labor Relations Board (April 19).

First electron microscope displayed by Radio Corporation of America (April 20).

1941 With only one dissenting vote, Congress declared war on Japan (December 8).

Department of Justice filed suit against NBC and CBS for alleged monopoly in broadcasting (December 31).

1942 Bell Aircraft Corporation pilot flew first American jet plane in California (October 1).

Revenue Act signed, to raise nearly $10 billion in addition to revenue accruing from existing taxes (October 21).

Enrico Fermi and colleagues at the University of Chicago set off the first controlled nuclear chain reaction (December 2).

1943 World's longest oil pipelines

(1300 miles) dedicated. The "Big Inch" ran from Texas to Pennsylvania (July 19).

1944 War Production Board approved plans for the gradual conversion of war industries to domestic output (August 14).

1945 First atomic bomb exploded at Alamogordo, New Mexico (July 16).

Atomic bomb dropped on Hiroshima, Japan; 450,000 people (60 percent of the population) were killed and 90 percent of the city's housing was destroyed (August 6).

Second atomic bomb dropped on Nagasaki, Japan (August 9).

1946 400,000 members on the United Mine Workers struck (April 1).

President Truman seized railroads to prevent a strike by railroad workers (May 15).

U.S. Atomic Energy Commission created (August 1).

1947 House of Representatives passed Taft-Hartley Labor Bill (May 9).

Taft-Hartley Act passed over President Truman's veto (June 23); went into effect on August 22.

The transistor invented by three scientists at the Bell Telephone Laboratories.

1948 United Automobile Workers and General Motors Corporation agreed to the first sliding wage scale contract (May 25).

1951 Federal Communications Commission authorized color television broadcasting.

First U.S. microwave radio-relay system operated (August 17).

Atomic energy used to produce electric power for the first time at Arco, Idaho (December 21).

1952 President Truman seized Youngstown Sheet and Tube steel plants to prevent a strike by 600,000 steelworkers (April 8).

Supreme Court ruled that President Truman's action of April 8th was unconstitutional (*Youngstown Sheet and Tube* v. *Sawyer*) (June 2).

First-generation electronic computers introduced for commercial purposes.

1953 Tidelands Oil Bills signed by President Eisenhower, giving coastal states offshore oil lands within a limit of 3 miles (10-1/2-mile limit for Texas and Florida) (May 22).

1954 Atomic Energy Act permitted the development of projects for the peaceful use of atomic energy (August 30).

U.S.S. Nautilus, the first atomic-powered submarine, commissioned at Groton, Connecticut (September 30).

1955 Ford Motor Company and General Motors Corporation agreed to a union contract with the United Automobile Workers, providing for pay during periods of layoff (June).

American Federation of Labor and Congress of Industrial Organizations merged (December 5).

1956 Agricultural Act (Soil Bank) passed; monies were given to farmers for removing cropland from production (May 28).

Federal Aid Highway Act passed, providing for a 13-year highway construction program (June 29).

First trans-Atlantic telephone cable made operational; covered 2250 miles from Newfoundland to Scotland (September 25).

1958 Following *Sputnik*, the first rocket-powered artificial earth satellite, sent into orbit by the USSR on October 4, 1957, the U.S. Navy launched a 3-pound satellite *Vanguard I* (March 17).

1958 National Aeronautics and Space Administration established to coordinate space research (July 29).

President Eisenhower signed the Welfare and Pension Plans Disclosure Act (August 29).

Trans-Atlantic jet flights introduced by Pan American World Airways (October 26).

For the first time, airlines carried more passengers across the Atlantic Ocean than did ships.

1959 Nation's longest steel strike (116 days) ended (November 7).

To meet slumping sales and competition of foreign cars, the Big Three of the automobile industry introduced compact economy cars. American Motors already had its compact Rambler American.

Results of laser beam research and potential applications made public.

1961 Federal Communications Commission authorized the first communications satellite to be built with a solar-powered receiver and transmitter (January 19).

Twenty-nine electronics companies found guilty of conspiring to fix prices (January).

President Kennedy approved legislation fixing minimum wages at $1.15 per hour for two years, to be raised in 1963 to $1.25 per hour (May 5).

First major plant for desalination of seawater began operations at Freeport, Texas, with a daily capacity of 1 million gallons (June 21).

1962 President Kennedy persuaded six major steel companies to refrain, in the public interest, from raising their prices (April 13).

Trade Expansion Act increased the president's authority to reduce tariffs (October 4).

1963 Third and longest trans-Atlantic telephone cable completed. American Telephone and Telegraph Company announced that all future expansion would be via satellites (October 16).

1964 President Johnson's Economic Opportunity Act passed by Congress (August 11).

1965 Medicare Bill signed by President Johnson (July 30).

Department of Housing and Urban Affairs created (August 31).

1966 Largest merger in U.S. history took place: the New York Central Railroad and the Pennsylvania Railroad joined (April 27).

Department of Transportation created (October 13).

1967 Population of the United States reached 200 million (November 20).

1968 Supreme Court approved merger of the New York Central and Pennsylvania Railroads (January 15).

Truth-in-Lending Bill signed by President Johnson (May 29).

1969 Large oil spills found near Santa Barbara, California, from offshore oil-drilling installations (January).

Department of Agriculture announced plans to reduce the use of DDT by 1971 to a level of not more than 10 percent (November 20).

S.S. Manhattan, an oil tanker, became first commercial ship to complete the Northwest Passage from Alaska (September 14).

1971 National Railroad Passenger Corporation (Amtrak) formed (May 1).

President Nixon declared a 90-day freeze on wages and prices (August 15).

1972 Five men arrested for breaking into the offices of the Democratic National Committee in Washington, D.C.; beginning of Watergate scandal (June 17).

The first U.S. space station, Skylab, placed into orbit (May 14).

1974 Gerald Ford became president of the United States, following the resignation of Richard Nixon (August 9).

Collapse of a New York financial institution, the Franklin National Bank, the largest bank failure in U.S. history (October 8).

1975 Chrysler Corporation offered a system of rebates on purchases of certain cars. Ford and General Motors follow (January 7).

Labor Department reported national unemployment at a 33-year high (February 7).

President Ford imposed a $1 per barrel increase in fees on imported oil (May 27).

Eight employees and officials of the Franklin National Bank on Long Island indicted on 76 counts in the loss of more than $30 million through unauthorized speculation in foreign currencies (August 11).

1976 Social security taxes increased 8.5 percent for workers earning $15,300 a year or more (January 1).

Wall Street finished month with the largest point advance on record: 122 (January 30).

W. T. Grant Company ordered by a federal judge to be liquidated, making the largest retail bankruptcy in history (February 13).

Internal Revenue Service revokes tax-exempt status of Teamsters' Union's pension fund, citing mismanagement and questionable loan activities (June 29).

Jimmy Carter edged out Gerald Ford for the presidency of the United States (November).

Worst oil spill off U.S. coast recorded. The 640 foot *Argo Merchant* grounded off Nantucket and broke in half, with a total spill of about 7.5 million gallons of oil (December 22).

1977 Food and Drug Administration proposed a ban on the use of saccharin in food and beverages (March 9).

President Carter signed legislation creating the Department of Energy (August 4).

U.S. Supreme court lifted a temporary ban on supersonic *Concorde* airliner flights to John F. Kennedy Airport in New York City (October 17).

Employment at a new high, 92.6 million workers (December).

Unemployment dropped to 6.4 percent of labor force (December).

American Telephone and Telegraph Company earned $4.54 billion in 1977, a record for any U.S. corporation.

1978 At 2:36 P.M. the country's gross national product crossed the $2 trillion mark (January 27).

The U.S. had a 1977 trade deficit of $26.7 billion, the largest in the nation's history, more than four times the 1976 trade deficit of $5.9 billion (January 31).

The Age Discrimination in Employment Act was amended, raising the legal mandatory retirement age from 65 to 70 for most employees (April 6).

The heaviest trading in New York Stock Exchange history occurred when turnover of securities soared to 63.5 million shares, with a record of 17.48 million shares traded during the first hour (April 17).

Humphrey-Hawkins "full-employment" bill passed. It contained goal of reducing unemployment to 4 percent by 1983 (October 15).

Worst week in Wall Street his-

tory, as Dow Jones Industrial average dropped 59.08 (October 20).

City of Cleveland defaulted on $14 million in debts (December 16).

1979 Western Union Corporation's 36-year monopoly over domestic telegram service ended by Federal Commerce Commission (January 29).

First major nuclear disaster occurred at Three Mile Island Power Plant on the Susquehanna River, near Middletown, Pennsylvania (March 28).

President Carter ordered the gradual phasing out of controls on domestic oil prices (April 5).

United States and China signed a trade agreement that gave China most-favored-nation tariff treatment (July 7).

Chrysler Corporation reported a $207.1 million loss in second quarter, its biggest three-month deficit ever and greater than its loss for all of 1978 (August 1).

The Carter administration proposed a $1.5 billion federal loan guarantee plan for Chrysler Corporation (November 1).

1980 Exxon became the nation's biggest seller of gasoline, passing Shell Oil and Indiana Standard (January 10).

Gold prices hit $875 an ounce in New York; the following day it plunged $143.50 (January 22).

The price of silver plummeted to $10.80 an ounce, down $5 during the day. The Hunt brothers failed to meet $100 million on margin calls on their silver accounts, which caused panic in the silver market (March 27).

President Carter signed the Crude Oil Windfall Profit Tax Act of 1980, the largest single tax ever imposed on industry (April 2).

After 17 years of feuding, the J. P. Stevens Company and the Amalgamated Clothing and Textile Workers Union announced a collective-bargaining agreement for ten plants (October 17).

1981 Antitrust suit against AT&T goes to trial (January 15).

IBM and the government rested their cases in their 12-year-old antitrust battle (June 2).

Prudential merged with Bache, Halsey Stuart (June 11).

American Express merged with Shearson Loeb Rhoades, the nation's second-largest securities firm (June 25).

Du Pont acquired Conoco, the nation's ninth-largest oil company, by outbidding Seagram, the world's biggest liquor distiller, and Mobil Oil, the second-largest American petroleum firm; became the costliest takeover in history (August 5).

President Reagan signed into law both tax- and budget-cut bills. The measures were called the most far-reaching domestic economic legislation since the New Deal (August 14).

The country's gross national product crossed the $3 trillion mark (December 11).

Sears, Roebuck, the nation's biggest retail store chain, bought Dean Witter Reynolds, Inc., the fifth-largest brokerage house (December 31).

1982 United States terms IBM antitrust case, filed 13 years earlier, without merit. Justice Department drops case to dismember the computer company (January 8).

AT & T settled the Justice Department's antitrust lawsuit by agreeing to give up the 22 Bell System companies, worth $80 billion (January 8).

The American Telephone & Telegraph Company announced its entry into the data processing business with a subsidiary— American Bell (July 1).

The 97th Congress passed the "Tax Equity and Fiscal Responsibility Act of 1982" (TEFRA) (August 15).

Xerox Corporation announced its intention to acquire Crum & Foster, an insurance holding company, for about $1.65 billion in cash and securities (September 21).

President Reagan signs legislation providing substantial aid to the nations savings institutions, allowing them for the first time to make loans similar to those offered by commercial banks. Also permitted commercial and savings banks to offer a federally insured account nearly identical to high-yielding money market funds (October 15).

The New York Stock Exchange fined Bache Halsey Stuart Shields, Inc. $400,000 for permitting the Hunt brothers of Texas to speculate so heavily in silver. The fine was the largest ever levied by the exchange (October 20).

1983 American Bell, a separate subsidiary of AT&T begins offering new communications equipment (January 1).